MASTERPIECES

of

CHRISTIAN LITERATURE

in Summary Form

Edited by
FRANK N. MAGILL

Associate Editor
IAN P. McGREAL

VOLUME TWO—FROM 1695

SALEM PRESS
INCORPORATED
NEW YORK

FIRST EDITION

PRINTED IN THE UNITED STATES OF AMERICA

THE REASONABLENESS OF CHRISTIANITY

Author: John Locke (1632-1704)
Type of work: Philosophical theology
First published: 1695

PRINCIPAL IDEAS ADVANCED

Although theological systems are often unreasonable, there is nothing unreasonable in Christianity as taught in Scripture.

Adam's sin deprived all men of eternal life, but this was restored to all men through Christ.

Through the covenant of grace, God has offered to forgive any man's sins on condition that he believe in Christ.

The universal failure of mankind to profit from natural reason and natural religion in matters of correct belief and conduct, and the comparative improvement which Christianity brings in this respect, suggest that Christianity is indeed a divine revelation.

In his *An Essay Concerning Human Understanding* (1690), John Locke distinguishes between what we can know, and what we merely judge, believe, or opine. In the strict sense, we can know only that which is intuitively evident, or that which is logically demonstrable from evident truths. All else is belief, no matter how high the probability in its favor. Our knowledge of any event in the external world is never more than a highly probable belief. Such beliefs are called *reasonable,* not in the sense of being logically demonstrable, but in the sense that they are not logically contradictory, and that probable reasons can be adduced which persuade us to give them our assent. The same principle, according to Locke, applies to the claims of revealed religion. In *The Reasonableness of Christianity* Locke does not attempt to demonstrate that the claims of Christianity are evident to reason, but that there is nothing incredible or improbable in them, and

that they can be supported by good arguments.

Theologians have done their cause more harm than good, says Locke, by refusing to let the words of Scripture speak in a plain sense. The story that the Bible tells is simple, intelligible, and quite in harmony with reason. Consider, to begin with, the account of Adam's disobedience and Fall. The Scriptures say quite plainly that what befell Adam and his posterity was the loss of immortality and blessedness. This account is reasonable. Adam had no claim on eternal life, nor did his descendants, nor does the Bible say that death, which is natural to all finite creatures, is the punishment for sin; nothing at all is said about eternal damnation, which the theologians read into the word "death," but only that Adam and his posterity should cease to enjoy the benefits of life. One may reasonably complain about the justice of the doctrine, alleged by the theologians, that God punishes Adam's posterity for a fault that was Adam's alone, but there is no reason to complain about what Scripture teaches. Furthermore, Scripture teaches that just as in Adam all die, so in Christ shall all be made alive. Thus, through Christ, God freely bestows on all men that immortality which Adam lost for us, which is another way of saying that Christ nullifies the effects of Adam's indiscretion; Christ acts for all men, believers and unbelievers alike, and places every man that comes into the world in the same independent position in which Adam stood, with the difference that, if a man sins, he cannot lose his immortality, but must endure the consequences of his sin throughout eternity.

Locke borrows, with some modification, the Puritan concepts of the alternative covenants of works and of grace. By the covenant of works, a covenant which God made with mankind, every man has the option of undertaking to fulfill the righteousness of the eternal moral law, to be rewarded if he succeeds, but to be punished if he fails. But because God knew that few could expect to enter the Kingdom of glory on such terms, He devised a covenant of grace, according to which a man need only assent to the proposition that Jesus is the divinely appointed Messiah and undertake to live the best life of which he is capable, in order to enjoy the full benefits of divine favor.

Such, according to Locke, is the beautiful clarity of the Scriptural teaching. Numerous passages from the words of Christ and of the Apostles show the necessity of believing that Jesus is the Messiah. His miracles and the manner in which He fulfills the Old Testament prophecies, together with the holiness of His life and the purity of His doctrine, combine to bring to men's hearts the conviction that this one was indeed the Son of God. But the Scriptures are equally forceful on the other point; namely, that no one shall be numbered among the blessed with Christ who has not also repented of his wickedness and made an effort to live a good life. He need not be perfect, as the covenant of works requires, but he must have made a sincere attempt. For, according to Locke, nothing could be more unreasonable than that God, being just, should receive men into His favor without requiring that they amend their lives.

The question arises, what judgment awaits those who, through no fault of their own, have never learned of the covenant of grace? Locke points out that we do not know what God's wisdom affords to these persons. To men of Israel, before Christ's time, the way of grace was opened in terms of the Promise, which they were asked to believe, and the Mosaic law. Why not suppose that to every nation and clime God has proved Himself equally gracious, and opened conditions well within every man's capacity, which, if he conforms to them, will open to him a blessed eternity? Part of God's eternal law is that a man should forgive not merely his friends but his enemies if they repent and show amendment. Would not God, therefore, as the Author of this law, and as One who is merciful, "forgive his frail offspring, if they acknowledged their faults, disapproved the iniquity of their transgressions, begged his pardon, and resolved in earnest for the future to conform their action to this rule, which they owned to be just and right?" The hope of reconciliation and atonement is, Locke believed, part of "the light of nature," the "candle of the Lord," the "spark of the divine nature and knowledge in man," and is certainly not excluded by anything in the Gospel.

But if God's mercy is thus widely extended, what reason is there to believe that God sent His Son into the world, and that He made it a requirement of salvation that men believe in Him? Locke attempts to show that Christianity has proved its worth in practical terms, thus vindicating those who claim that Christianity is the work of God. Generally speaking, Locke's argument is that, outside the pale of Christianity, natural religion and natural reason have failed. Locke, it will be remembered, maintained (in *An Essay Concerning Human Understanding*) that the existence of God, as the Author and Legislator of our world, is demonstrable to reason in the strict sense. So, he maintained, are the principles of morals. These have a certainty of the highest order for those persons who are capable of following a rational demonstration. But nowhere has philosophy succeeded in impressing these truths effectively on the lives of men in the way that the preaching of Christ has done.

The power of the Gospel, Locke maintains, stems almost exclusively from the impression which Jesus' holy and miraculous person makes upon those who hear the Gospel story; for the masses of mankind, this is as it must be. "The greatest part cannot know, and therefore they must believe. And I ask, whether one coming from heaven in the power of God, in full and clear evidence and demonstration of miracles, giving plain and direct rules of morality and obedience, be not likelier to enlighten the bulk of mankind, and set them right in their duties, and bring them to do them, than by reasoning with them from general notions and principles of human reason?" Nor is this way of teaching suited only to the humbler sort. "The most elevated understandings cannot but submit to the authority of this doctrine as divine; which coming from the mouths of a company of illiterate men, hath not only the attestation of miracles, but reason to confirm it, since they delivered no precepts, but such, as though reason of itself had not clearly made out, yet it could not but assent to when thus discovered, and think itself indebted for the discovery." Locke warns us against the kind of arrogance which might lead educated persons to overlook their own debt to Christianity and suppose that by their reasons alone they could have arrived at the rational systems of belief that they now entertain. They are, he says, like one traveling along a highway who applauds the strength of his legs for the rapid progress which he is able to make, little thinking how much he owes to those who drained the swamps, bridged the streams, and cleared the woods, in order to build the road which he walks on.

As we have seen, Locke does not deny the idea of the miracle. In fact, he accepts, as part of the story of Christ, His birth of a virgin, and His resurrection from the grave. He does, however, give little time to the systems of the theologians, paying no respect at all to their theories of the Trinity, the Incarnation, and the atonement. By limiting his account of Christianity to simple belief in and obedience to Christ, he is able to maintain a link between faith and rea- son, not merely for the vulgar, but for the learned as well.

CHRISTIANITY NOT MYSTERIOUS

Author: John Toland (1670-1722)
Type of work: Deistic theology
First published: 1696

Principal Ideas Advanced

There is nothing mysterious or incomprehensible in Christianity.
True religion must be reasonable and intelligible.
Reason is the judge of what is regarded as revelation.
No event can be called miraculous which is contrary to reason.
Though the clergy may seek to hide the message of Christianity behind the veil of revelation, man can penetrate to the inherently reasonable nature of the New Testament.

John Toland's *Christianity Not Mysterious: or, A Treatise Shewing that there is nothing in the Gospel Contrary to Reason, Nor Above it: And that no Christian Doctrine can be properly call'd a Mystery,* first published in 1696, marked the beginning of the deistic controversy. Though the essay was condemned by many within the Church and was ordered to be burned by the parliament of Ireland, it is not noted for the strength of its message, its style, or the reputation of its author.

The context in which the book appeared accounts in large part for the furor caused by its publication. A decade earlier the Act of Toleration (1689) had been issued by William and Mary; this Act, which offered toleration to the dissenters within the Church of England, enlarged the bounds of permissible theological discussion. The deist movement began at this time, though many of its major ideas were anticipated by the earlier Cambridge Platonists and Latitudinarians. The deists were concerned with a reasoned and reasonable Christianity, stripped of doctrinal accretions, devoid of reliance on miracles and supernatural intervention in natural events, and freed of the weight of institutional and clerical control. Though it was not as extreme as subsequent expressions of deistic thought, *Christianity Not Mysterious* served as an opening wedge for later deistic writings. The major intent of Toland's essay, an intent which, in turn, reflected the dominant interest of eighteenth century English deism, was to examine the relation of the content of Christian faith to the form in which it is expressed.

Toland had three main aims in view: to show (1) that true religion "must necessarily be reasonable and intelligible", (2) "that these requisite Conditions are found in Christianity . . ." and, (3) "that the Christian Religion . . . was divinely revealed from Heaven."

Behind the work of Toland and his successors stood the commanding figure of John Locke (1632-1704). Though Toland did not make any direct reference to this British philosopher, the relation between them was clear. Locke's *The Reasonableness of Christianity* (1695) touched on the interests of the later deistic movement; namely, the simplicity of Christianity, the stress upon the ethical assertions of the Gospels, the nondogmatic character of Christian faith, and its inherently reasonable nature. Locke's *Essay Concerning Human Understanding* (1690) proved to be more influential on deism than did his excursion into theology. Locke defined reason as natural revelation; we can call nothing revelation which is in conflict with reason. Knowledge involves a relation, agreement or disagreement, between ideas. That which is "mysterious" or incomprehensible is by definition beyond all understanding and, therefore, is as foreign to faith as to knowledge.

It was a reasonable, nonmysterious Christianity which Toland sought to promulgate. He wrote that since *"Reason* is the only Foundation of all Certitude," reason is to be used as a judge of revelation. "Again, since nothing reveal'd, whether as to its *Manner* or *Existence,* is more exempted from its [reason's] Disquisitions, than the ordinary Phenomena of Nature, . . . we . . . maintain . . . that *there is nothing in the Gospel contrary to Reason, nor above it; and that no Christian Doctrine can be properly call'd a Mystery."* God does not demand that man believe what is improbable; probability is not knowledge and, Toland wrote, ". . . I banish all *Hypotheses* from my *Philosophy. . . ."* Toland and other deist writers viewed reason as a separate and, if properly used, infallible faculty of the human mind. This insistence on reason as the sole judge of truth was characteristic of English religious thought in the first half of the eighteenth century.

The role of revelation was thus circumscribed by this view of reason. Revelation served as a "means of information," though what is revealed must not conflict with reason and possibility. God could not disclose that which was unintelligible or impossible. Toland's intent was not to disparage revelation, as did later deist writers, but to recast the significance of revelation and to provide the ground for the transfer of the function of revelation to that of reason. Reason is, therefore, of more importance than revelation in the same way in which "a *Greek Grammar* is superior to the *New Testament. . . ."*

A prime cause of his thorough attack on traditional methodology stemmed from his notable distrust of the organized Church and its clergy. Throughout history, he wrote, the clergy has been unwilling to unravel the doctrines of Christianity; instead, they have made "the most trifling things in the World *mysterious,* that we might constantly depend upon them for the Explication." The result has been obscurantism. Those who held to the dictum of Tertullian (c.160-c.220), "I believe because it is absurd," were scathingly attacked by Toland. He wrote that "many affirm, that tho the Doctrines of the latter [Gospel] cannot in themselves be contradictory to the Principles of the former [Reason], as proceeding both from God; yet, that according to our Conceptions of them, *they may seem directly to clash:* And that tho we cannot reconcile them by reason of our corrupt and limited Understandings; yet that from the Authority of *Divine Revelation,* we are bound to believe and acquiesce in them; or, as the *Fathers* taught 'em to speak, *to adore what we cannot comprehend.*" In Toland's judgment, this "refuge" protected the mysteries but caused such confusion that it was no longer possible to determine what is essential to the Gospel. If, Toland claims, we affirm that the Christian believes on the ground of revelation and not of reason, then "I know not what we can deny that is told us in the Name of the Lord." There is no reason to hide behind the cloak of revelation when examination would show that there is nothing in the New Testament that is contrary to or above reason. The fact is, Toland insisted, *"no Christian Doctrine can be properly call'd a Mystery."*

The accompanying change in attitude toward the authority of Scripture became explicit in *Christianity Not Mysterious.* Though Toland assumed the centrality of the New Testament writings for Christianity, he insisted that evidence of its "divine" character depended on reason. There is no "different Rule to be follow'd in the Interpretation of *Scripture* from what is common to all other Books." He continually appealed to the meaning behind the New Testament words, though his statement of the intent of the New Testament writers reflects all too frequently the perspective of the eighteenth century English enlight-

ened man. The validity of the miracles recorded in Scripture received his attention and, here again, he insisted that a miracle must be inherently intelligible and possible; no event can be called miraculous which is contrary to reason. "The *miraculous* Action therefore must be some thing in itself intelligible and possible, tho the manner of doing it be extraordinary."

Thus, there is nothing in Christianity which is fundamentally mysterious or unknowable. In those New Testament passages which refer to the "mystery" of the Gospel, the term mystery is used to mean *"things naturally very intelligible, but so cover'd by figurative Words or Rites, that Reason could not discover them without special Revelation. . . ."* But what is unclear to the Jews and the pagans has now been made clear; the "Vail is actually taken away . . ." and "the Doctrines so reveal'd cannot now be properly call'd *Mysteries.*" There is nothing inconceivable in the New Testament. All ideas must exist in our consciousness; that which is inconceivable could not be. When Christ spoke in parable what He said was not incomprehensible, but it appeared mysterious only for those for whom the truth was not unfolded. Faith does not imply assent to that which is above reason.

Toland could not subscribe to the thesis that because of sin man's reasoning power was corrupted. This position is essential to the theology of John Calvin, who argued that though man was originally able to determine the nature, will, and providential concern of God by means of his insight into the created world and by use of his God-given capacities, this endowment had been lost in the Fall. This view Toland could not accept. *"For,* not willing to own their Ignorance and Miscarriages (which proceed from Passion, Sloth, or Inconsideration) they would remove all the Blame from their Will, and charge it upon a natural Impotency not in their Power to cure." According to this view, Toland argued, man has become no more than an animal or machine, or at best, one who seeks to escape the responsibilities of using his reason. In contrast, the center of man's potential lies in his capacity to fathom the nature and will of God and in his freedom to exercise this ability. "But 'tis the Perfection of our Reason and Liberty that makes us deserve Rewards and Punishments. We are persuaded that *all our thoughts* are entirely free, we can expend the Force of Words, compare Ideas, distinguish clear from obscure Conceptions, suspend our Judgments about Uncertainties, and yield only to Evidence."

The deist movement had little lasting effect, though it did serve to open the questions of the authority of the Scriptures and the relation of natural and revealed theology. It is striking how little interest Toland and other deists had in the person of Jesus of Nazareth. Their interest was primarily in an intellectual defense of Christianity, though the product they defended had little relevance for the man in the pew. The amazing lack of historical perspective shared by most of the deists meant that their interpretation of Christianity reflected much more the concerns and interests of eighteenth century England than it did the intent of the New Testament writers themselves. Their critique of traditional theological affirmations, however, served to shape a new Christian perspective which has had significant consequences.

MAGNALIA CHRISTI AMERICANA

Author: Cotton Mather (1663-1728)
Type of work: Ecclesiastical history
First published: 1702

PRINCIPAL IDEAS ADVANCED

The rising generation of New England is in danger of neglecting its heritage and needs to be brought back to the principles and practices of its founders.

New England owes its foundation to divine favor, but Satan has manifestly worked for its destruction.

The memory of New England's great men should be held up for imitation; the doctrines and regulations of her synods should be taught and defended; supernatural influences, both divine and Satanic, should not be ignored.

Cotton Mather's *Magnalia Christi Americana*, subtitled "The Ecclesiastical History of New England from its first Planting, in the year 1620, unto the year of our Lord 1698," is not a consecutive narrative, but a collection of essays, memorials, and addresses intended to call a wayward generation back to the principles and practices upon which the colony was founded. In the opinion of this third-generation New Englander, whose forebearers on both sides were prominent Puritan ministers, God's eye had selected the location and His hand had prospered the building of this wilderness Jerusalem. Quite predictably, God's great enemy, Satan, had used every means within his power to overthrow it. The title, which may be translated "The Wonders of Christ in America," attests to the divine favors which the Plantation had enjoyed from its beginning; but in the course of the book the author also gives many examples of the "cunning and malice of Satan" as he endeavored to undo God's work.

Apparently Cotton Mather was not the only person who was concerned for the future of the colony. As early as 1679 a series of divine chastisements in the form of fires, crop failures, shipwrecks, epidemics, and Indian wars prompted the General Court of Massachusetts to call a synod of churchmen to discuss two questions: "What are the provoking evils of New England?" and "What is to be done, that so those evils may be reformed?" The synod found that the Ten Commandments were being disobeyed to an alarming degree, and it called for a renewal of the covenant throughout the churches. Pastors preached on the subject, and a special catechism was drawn up so that the people "might echo back, upon fit questions, those things which were needful to be known and to be done, relating to the reformation of the land." But these efforts to "recover the dying 'power of godliness'" failed, and apostasies increased. "The old spirit of New-England," says Mather, "hath been sensibly going out of the world, as the old saints in which it was have gone; and instead thereof the spirit of the world, with a lamentable neglect of strict piety, has crept in upon the rising generation." Not merely apostasies increased, but troubles also, so that, in 1689, the General Council again took notice of the situation, and solemnly declared that the colony was "in eminent danger of perishing, if a speedy reformation of our provoking evils prevent it not."

Cotton Mather and, even more importantly, his father, Increase Mather (1639-1723), exerted great influence upon public events of the time. Cotton Mather shows no false modesty in his work, but sometimes he neglects to mention a detail, such as the fact that it was on petition of his father and other ministers that the General Court was prompted to call the reforming synod of 1679. Moreover, it is only by reading between the lines that one can detect the emergence of a new, liberal sentiment, which contested the conservatism of the Mathers. For example, no mention is made of so prominent a figure as Solomon Stoddard (1634-1729), the grandfather of Jonathan Edwards and his predecessor in the pulpit at Northampton, who, in opposition to the Mathers, favored admitting to communion persons not members of the Congregational churches if they exhibited "a good conversation and a competent knowledge."

One of the things which the reforming synod felt that it could do was to reaffirm its adherence to the doctrinal standards which had been adopted by the New England Churches in 1649. Mather devotes the fifth book of the *Magnalia* to reprinting and commenting upon the Savoy Declaration, which is the Congregationalist version of the Westminster Confession of 1647; the New England Platform of Church Discipline, of 1649; and other "acts and monuments" by which successive synods attempted to reinforce the principles of the "scriptural reformation" to which Puritanism was dedicated. The seriousness and competence with which Mather's generation set themselves to the task of reviving their churches by certifying the orthodoxy of their teachings and the legitimacy of their government gives food for reflection, especially in view of the subsequent history of Christianity in New England.

Book Five is a hub around which the rest of the *Magnalia* turns. The four preceding books are given over to praising New England's great men; the two following, to reporting instances of God's goodness and of Satan's malice toward the colonies.

The books devoted by Mather to the founding of New England and to the lives of her magistrates, her ministers, and the graduates of Harvard College are a disappointment to the modern reader. Mather, who had a prodigious knowledge of ancient language and literature, affects to find parallels between the New England worthies and the heroes of Israel, Greece, and Rome. Thus, introducing John Winthrop, Governor of Massachusetts, Mather writes: "Let Greece boast her patient Lycurgus, the lawgiver, by whom diligence, temperance, fortitude and wit were made the fashions of a therefore long-lasting and renowned commonwealth; let Rome tell of her devout Numa, the lawgiver, by whom the most famous commonwealth saw

peace triumphing over extinguished war and cruel plunders; and murders giving place to the more mollifying exercises of his religion. Our New-England shall tell and boast of her *Winthrop,* a lawgiver as patient as Lycurgus, but not admitting any of his criminal disorders; as devout as Numa, but not liable to any of *his* heathenish madnesses; a governour in whom the excellencies of Christianity made a most improving addition unto the virtues, wherein even without *those* he would have made a *parallel* for the great men of Greece, or of Rome, which the pen of a Plutarch has eternized."

Most of Mather's biographical notices are brief, rarely exceeding six or seven pages, except for those devoted to Boston's four greatest divines. His biography of Sir William Phips (1651-1695) is, however, sixty-five pages in length and contains hints, at least, of the vigor and romance that surrounded this colonial patriot. Indeed, the *Magnalia* is an important source for the life of Sir William, whom Mather knew personally and served briefly as secretary. Mather's account tells of Phips's remarkable rise from shepherd lad to shipbuilder, and of Phips's adventures in connection with recovering Spanish gold and laying siege to Quebec. But, perhaps because the matter was sufficiently well-known to his readers, Mather becomes almost unintelligible when he recounts the civil upheaval which resulted in the overthrow of Governor Andros and the appointment of Phips, in 1691, to take his place. Here Cotton Mather was in a unique position to record an important historical development, since his father was the colonial representative in London who won the concessions from the new monarch. But his account, though full of charges and vindications, is so short on facts as not even to mention Governor Andros by name. Phips was a highly controversial personage, with the deportment of a typical seventeenth century sea captain. But by Mather's report he was a model of discretion, "a person of so sweet a temper, that they who were most intimately acquainted with him, would commonly pronounce him, 'The best conditioned gentleman in the world!' "

Because it was during Phip's brief administration that the witch-mania arose in Salem, Mather discusses that issue in his biography of Phips as well as in the later section devoted to supernatural manifestations. Mather believed in demon-possession and witchcraft, and had no doubts respecting its occurrence in New England. His writings and sermons on the subject were in great part responsible for exciting the persecutions. It is true that he and his father urged caution when a commission was appointed to bring the witches to trial, and they argued that demons could impersonate innocent people and so deceive honest witnesses; but these warnings were little heeded until the affair reached such dimensions that common sense demanded that a halt be called. "The last courts," Mather says, "that sate upon this *thorny business,* finding that it was impossible to penetrate into the whole meaning of the things that had happened, and that so many *unsearchable cheats* were interwoven into the *conclusion* of a mysterious business, which perhaps had not crept thereinto at the *beginning* of it, they *cleared* the accused as fast as they *tried* them; and within a little while the afflicted were

most of them delivered out of their troubles also; and the land had peace restored unto it, by the 'God of peace, treading Satan under foot.' "

Mather commends the judges for consulting precedents and learned writers on the subject of witches, and he testifies to their "conscientious endeavor to do the thing that was right." But he also defends the governor for reversing the former accusations when it became clear that "there was a going too far in this affair." Among the reasons that Mather gives for halting the trials and acquitting those already condemned was that when the numbers kept growing and many of blameless life were included, it began to appear that Satan was using the trials as a means of dividing the colony against itself. It also struck Mather that, of the nineteen that were executed, all denied the crime to their deaths, in spite of the fact that some were intelligent and pious persons; this was in marked contrast to the usual behavior of Puritans convicted of crime, who, as Mather reveals in other parts of his work, were zealous in confessing their sins as they went to the scaffold. In the end, he concluded that the affair at Salem "proceeded from some mistaken principles." But he continued to affirm the existence of witchcraft and demonic possession, and he gathered from the trials new material for refuting those modern Sadducees who deny the existence of supernatural beings. Anyone who wishes to read how Goody F. and her daughter rode their broomsticks to witch meetings can find it all in the chapter entitled "Thaumatographia Pneumatica, Relating the Wonders of the Invisible World in Preternatural Occurrences."

Probably the most interesting part

of the *Magnalia* is Book Six, devoted to "Illustrious Discoveries and Demonstrations of the Divine Providence in Remarkable Mercies and Judgments of Many Particular Persons." It is to the alertness of the President and Fellows of Harvard College that we owe this record, for they sent a proposal to the clergy of New England recommending that the churches collect for the benefit of posterity instances of "all *unusual accidents,* in the heaven, or earth, or water; all wonderful *deliverances* of the distressed; *mercies* to the godly; *judgments* on the wicked; and more glorious fulfillment of either the *promises* or the *threatenings* in the Scriptures of truth; with *apparitions, possessions, inchantments,* and all extraordinary things wherein the existence and agency of the *invisible world* is more sensibly demonstrated." Because Increase Mather was the President of Harvard, and Cotton Mather the most energetic of its fellows, the various narrations that were in this way collected have found their repository in the *Magnalia*. In this book the author lays aside his declamatory manner, and he proves himself a master of description and narration. His circumstantial stories of shipwrecks and pirates, of Indian raids, adulteries, and murders must have contributed greatly to the popularity of the *Magnalia* in his own day.

Mather concludes his *Magnalia* with an account of "disturbances given to the Churches of New-England," an account otherwise entitled "A Book of the Wars of the Lord." Here, after speaking briefly of the difficulties ministers had in collecting their salaries, and of scandals occasioned by "high professors of religion" falling into open sin, he chiefly deals with heretical teachings. Particular notice is given of Roger Williams (c.1603-1683), as advocating rigid separatism; of Anne Hutchinson (c.1600-1643) as a leader of antinomianism; and of Quaker and Anabaptist groups which tried to get a foothold. It is amusing to hear Cotton Mather call Williams *quixotic,* and embarrassing to hear him charge Anne Hutchinson with lying and tale-bearing, while he himself passes on the report that she, when great with child, gave birth not to anything human but to thirty monsters. He has no patience with Quakers, whom he calls lunatics, and he argues that the colonies have good cause to guard against these "dangerous villains"; still, he seems to be of the opinion that a minor punishment might be sufficient for discouraging them—perhaps shaving their heads. Toward the Anabaptists he is less severe. He can understand their scruples concerning infant baptism, but he considers that their separate societies are dangerous because they permit uneducated persons to preach; and he finds them intolerant when they deny that the Congregational churches, since they baptize infants, are truly churches.

Mather was aware that the temper of the times had changed. People had become critical of the persecution of religion and had come to accept the necessity for a degree of forbearance. Nor did Mather wish to fall behind enlightened opinion in these matters. Quoting from one of his own sermons, he writes: "A man has a *right* unto his life, his estate, his liberty, and his family, although he should not come up unto these and those blessed institutions of our Lord. When a man sins in his political capacity, let *political* societies animadvert upon him; but when he sins only in a religious capacity, societies more purely *religious* are fittest then to deal with him." Taken in context, this is no ringing declaration for religious freedom. Magistrates are told that it is their duty to "punish all the vices which disturb the good order and repose of human society," and that "to live without any *worship* of God, or to *blaspheme* and *revile* his blessed name, is to be chastised as abominably criminal." But at least those who are recognizably Christians ought to be tolerated, even though they dissent from the New England way. "Nor," declaims Mather, "would I desire myself to suffer persecution upon a clearer cause than that of testifying against our persecution of other Christians that are not of my own opinion."

The general assent with which these remarks were received by representative leaders in the province encouraged Mather to prophesy that, as long as this temper prevailed in the people of New England, "sectaries will never be able to make any great impressions upon them." He concludes: "Well, the enemy of the New-English churches is hitherto disappointed: *hac non successit, alia aggrediatur via*—he has not been successful in this region; let him try another."

THE SCRIPTURE-DOCTRINE OF THE TRINITY

Author: Samuel Clarke (1675-1729)
Type of work: Theology
First published: 1712

PRINCIPAL IDEAS ADVANCED

The New Testament is the sole source for theological statements concerning the person of Christ and His relation to God the Father.

Traditional dogmatic definitions of the doctrine of the Trinity lead in the direction of Sabellianism or Tritheism.

In the New Testament the Son is regarded as subordinate to the Father.

The Word of God is derived from the Father, though the precise relation of the Word of God (the Son) to the Father cannot be explained by human reason.

Samuel Clarke's *The Scripture-Doctrine of the Trinity*, published in 1712, marked the beginning of the Arian controversy in English religious thought. Though the essay has not been regarded as an unusually perceptive or imaginative theological treatise, it is noted as one of the major works of eighteenth century English liberalism.

The term "Arianism" stems from the controversy of the fourth century when the Christian Church was in the process of defining its position on the relation of Jesus Christ to God the Father. Arius, a presbyter in the Church of Alexandria, was accused of heresy by his bishop for asserting that the Son of God was brought into being by the Father, that He was not co-eternal with the Father, and that "there was a time when he was not." Under the Emperor Constantine, a council was called to deal with the Arian position, and at Nicaea in 325 Arius and his followers were declared heretical and the first Nicene Creed was formulated.

Eighteenth century Arianism had different interests from those of its fourth century progenitors, but the label continued to be used. Whereas the earlier controversy revolved more centrally around metaphysical questions, Clarke and his fellow critics of the traditional trinitarian formula centered their attention on an examination of Scripture with the aim in view to show that nowhere can one find Biblical justification for the doctrine. For this reason, English Arianism had closer ties to the Socinian movement than to fourth century Arianism.

The seventeenth century English Socinians, related to the sixteenth century Polish group, adopted an essentially unitarian position. They viewed Christ as a creature, and they interpreted His entire mission as that of a prophet calling men to live the righteous and ethical life. Though they discarded the traditional affirmations of original sin and predestination, together with the satisfaction theory of the atonement, and centered their attention on the ethical commands of Christ, they accepted in a most orthodox fashion the Biblical accounts of the miracles and other narratives relating to Jesus of Nazareth. The dogmatic definitions of the Church concerning the person of Christ were viewed as perversions of the simple New Testament gospel. In the 1690's a number of Socinian tracts appeared in England. These were immediately attacked by the more orthodox theologians, though with no great success. By the beginning of the eighteenth century the orthodox churchmen equated the Socinian and the developing Arian positions. Many felt that Arianism would become Socinianism and thus that it must be rooted out; the doctrine of the Trinity had become one of the most debated theological issues of the church.

The Scripture-Doctrine of the Trinity was published in the midst of this discussion. It sought to focus the issue on one central question: What does the Bible say? Clarke's contribution to the entire debate involved an analysis of Biblical texts, rather than, as had been the case in fourth century Arianism, a critique of philosophical ambiguities. He sought to dissociate his own view from that of the Socinians. Though the orthodox defenders of the trinitarian formula took up the charge of the Socinians, that the doctrine was irrational, and sought to defend it on rational grounds, Clarke focused the issue on an analysis of the New Testament. In his other works, however, Clarke did not shun the task of indicating the rational basis of Christianity, of formulating rational grounds for the existence of God, and of arguing that no article of the Christian religion is contrary to reason; but this effort was not the central task in his essay on the Trinity.

Thus Clarke's work had two major objectives: (1) to dissociate his position from that of the Socinians and (2) to show that the traditional doctrine of the Trinity led to the greater heresies of Sabellianism and tritheism. It is indicative of Clarke's effort that he himself disclaimed the label Arian, though not with conspicuous success. Consistent with the dominant concern of this period in English religious thought, he sought a return to primitive Christianity and a re-evaluation of the use of the traditional Nicene and Athanasian creeds.

His method of approach is stated in the first words of his book: "As, in Matters of *Speculation and Philosophical Inquiry*, the only Judge of what is right or wrong, is *Reason and Experience*; so in Matters either of *humane Testimony* or *divine Revelation*, the only certain Rule of Truth is the *Testimony* or *the Revelation itself*." In clearing up disputed theological points, the tradition of the Church serves as a helpful guide, but it can by no means be the only authority; Scripture alone is the true guide. In addition, and not unlike John Toland (1670-1722), the deist of the previous century, Clarke argued that Scripture must not conflict with reason; the disciple of Christ is not obliged to believe that which is contrary to his reason. But his central point was that ". . . the *Books of Scripture* are to Us Now not only *the Rule*, but the *Whole* and *the Only Rule of Truth* in matters of Religion." His task, therefore, was clear, and the three parts of his essay deal with the following topics: (1) an examination of Biblical texts which make direct or indirect reference to the doctrine of the Trinity, (2) a statement of the theological propositions concerning the trinitarian doctrine which the Scriptures allow, (3) an attempt to reconcile the liturgies of the Church of England with his understanding of the Biblical text. There can be no doubt that throughout Clarke's treatise his effort is to remain a loyal churchman and to rescue from obscurity the Biblical doctrines

concerning Jesus Christ. The foundation of the Christian religion, he wrote, is "The *Supremacy of God the Father* over all, and our *Reconciliation and Subjection* to him as such our *Supreme Governour*; the *Redemption* purchased by *the Son*; and the *Sanctification* worked in us by the *Holy Spirit*. . . ." The confusion of this simple truth has resulted in "*Tritheism, Sabellianism, Arianism,* and *Socinianism*" which have ". . . to the great disparagement of Christianity, puzzled the plain and practical Doctrine of Scripture, with endless speculative Disputes. . . ."

In Part I of the essay, Clarke examined every New Testament text, 1,251 in all, which related to the question. He did not attempt an elaborate analysis of the passages he cited, but sought only to list them under relevant categories. The following are samples of the headings he used: "*The Passages of the New Testament, wherein He is stiled the One or Only God*," with seventeen Scriptural references; "*The Passages wherein He is stiled God absolutely, by way of Eminence and Supremacy*," with 319 Scriptural references; *The Passages wherein it is declared, that All* Prayers and Praises *ought* primarily *to be offered* to Him, and that every thing *ought to be directed* ultimately to His Honour and Glory," with ninety Scriptural references. In this manner Clarke dealt with all passages refering to God the Father, the Son of God, and the Holy Spirit. His comments on the passage in the Gospel of John, "In the beginning was the Word, and the Word was with God, and the Word was God," reveal his own position. For Clarke, the phrase, "and the Word was God," had three possible interpretations: "The *first is*; that the Word was *That same*

Person, whom he was *with. . . ."* But this interpretation, Clarke argued, leads to the heresy of Sabellianism. A second possible interpretation is that *". . .* the Word was Another *Self-existent, Underived, Independent Person, co-ordinate to Him with whom he was. . . ."* This view, however, is a polytheistic denial of the unity of God. The only possible interpretation of the passage, therefore, is that *". . .* the Word is a Person, *deriving* from the Father (with whom he existed before the World was), both his Being itself, and incomprehensible Power and Knowledge, and other *divine* Attributes and Authority, in a Manner not revealed, and which humane Wisdom ought not to presume to be able to explain: And This is the Interpretation of the Learnedest and most Antient Writers in the Primitive Church." This analysis, however, avoided the theological problem; it actually served to cloud rather than clear the issue. There are striking resemblances between Clarke's position and that held by the men who dominated Christological discussion after the Council of Nicaea; they also feared that the phrase, "of the same substance," which the Nicene Creed used when dealing with the relation of the Son to the Father, led to Sabellianism, and yet they did not want to commend the Arian position. This was also Clarke's dilemma, but he solved it by an ambiguous statement; his interpretation of the passage, "and the Word was God," could itself be interpreted in an Arian fashion, though its lack of theological precision could allow for an interpretation which was not dissimilar from that made by the later defenders of the Nicene decision.

The second part of his essay re-flected much more clearly a position in accord with Arianism, though again, theological clarity is frequently lacking. He sought to maintain the supremacy of God the Father, while avoiding a clearly Arian position. For example, he wrote: "The Scripture, in declaring the *Sons Derivation* from the Father, never makes mention of any Limitation of *Time;* but always supposes and affirms him to have existed with the Father *from the Beginning,* and *before All Worlds."* The statement has an Arian ring to it, but it is not a precise statement. It is this consistent ambiguity in Clarke's thought which made it so easy to characterize him as an Arian, especially when he did not accept with ease the traditional doctrinal statements and when any criticism of the doctrine of the Trinity called immediately to mind the recent Socinian debates. Seldom did he make a statement so clearly Arian as this: "The *Son,* whatever his metaphysical Essence or Substance be, and whatever divine Greatness and Dignity is ascribed to him in Scripture; yet in This He is evidently *Subordinate to the Father,* that He *derives* his *Being* and Attributes from the *Father,* the *Father* nothing from *Him."*

In the concluding section of the volume Clarke sought to show how his interpretation of the doctrine of the Trinity could be compatible with Anglican liturgical forms. To be sure, Clarke did not consider himself at variance with the true understanding of the formularies of the Church.

In summary, *The Scripture-Doctrine of the Trinity* was an effort of a theologian in the period of developing English rationalism to defend the doctrine of the Trinity on Biblical grounds, while avoiding the extremes of Sabellianism (as exemplified to Clarke in the Athanasian Creed) and Socinianism. The work, however, served more to illustrate the dominant interests of the period—namely, the reliance on Scripture and the avoidance of philosophical terminology in theological formulation, and the accompanying dependence on reasonableness—than it did to offer a consistent or original interpretation of the doctrine of the Trinity.

A SERIOUS CALL TO A DEVOUT AND HOLY LIFE

Author: William Law (1686-1761)
Type of work: Devotional philosophy; devotional guide
First published: 1728

PRINCIPAL IDEAS ADVANCED

Devotion consists not merely in prayers but in a life devoted to God.

Religion and philosophy agree that a devout life is the only prudent life both now and hereafter.

The rules of religion apply to all the actions of one's life.

Our active life should be devoted to useful occupations and to works of charity and mercy.

Our contemplative life should be disciplined by a daily regimen of prayer and meditation.

William Law, a clergyman of the Church of England and (until he refused to take the oath abjuring the Stuarts) a fellow of Cambridge University, believed that although the official religion was continuing to call men to a devout and holy life, its call was neither seriously meant nor seriously taken. The forms of prayer poured contempt upon life in this world and avowed affection only for things of Heaven, but neither people nor priests really attempted to govern their lives according to these professions. A growing number favored abandoning the prayers in favor of a frank secularism. Law favored keeping the prayers and bringing men's lives back under the rule of devotion.

Devotion, according to Law, does not consist merely in prayers. Prayer is an important part of devotion, but devotion is nothing less than "a life given, or devoted, to God." In his view, Christianity prescribes rules governing all the ordinary actions of life; and if one does not make it his daily study to govern his conduct by these rules, he may as well give up saying his prayers. The Christian is called upon to lay everything upon the altar; his time, his wealth, his abilities are no longer his; and whatever he does (what he eats, how he dresses, where he spends his leisure, how much he charges for his wares) must be governed by the rules of religion.

But William Law was living in the

"age of reason" and of "enlightenment." In his opinion the demands of religion are no different from those of reason. He was not interested in the doctrinal controversies which had rocked the Church for nearly two centuries. In his opinion, Christian orthodoxy agrees in essential points with true philosophy, as represented by Socrates, Epictetus, and Marcus Aurelius. It is a kind of ethical eudaemonism, a higher prudence, which rightly estimates the vanity and bitterness of earthly striving and knows the peace and fruition that comes with ordering one's life according to righteousness. Law never doubts that our earthly life is merely a preparation for an eternal life to follow, so that those who neglect to improve their opportunities stand convicted as fools. But he does not rest his case on an afterlife; even here and now, he maintains, a life regulated by the rules of religion is sweeter and more joyous than a life which is governed by the spirit of the age. Piety, according to Law, should be based on the eternal laws of nature.

Law regards every individual as called to devote his life to God. There is, he maintains, no other way of salvation. He sets aside the view that Christ's death is a substitutionary atonement for the sins of men; he argues instead that Christ is our representative, whose death makes our sacrifices acceptable to God. "And we are to suffer, to be crucified, to die and rise with Christ; or else His Crucifixion, Death, and Resurrection will profit us nothing." Law accepts the Catholic distinction between "two orders" of obedience. Some, he admits, are called to serve God in the married state while carrying on the common business of the world, and others are called to retire from the world and to live in virginity and poverty in order to carry out more fully the requirements of God's love. But he finds in this distinction no excuse for laxity. It is, according to Law, quite possible to serve God perfectly whatever our circumstances. If our lives lack the luster which adorned the piety of the early confessors, there is no need to look for the cause in differences of circumstances or of ability. The only cause for anyone's failure to live Christianly is that he "never thoroughly intended it."

A Serious Call consists of two main parts. The first half is an attempt to set a pattern for serving God in the external affairs of life. The second half is a guide to prayer and to the interior life.

Whether because his own experience was limited, or because he had in view the circumstances of his likely reader, the author addressed his practical suggestions almost entirely to middle class people of comfortable station. His remarks to tradesmen are limited to the brief suggestion that it is agreeable to the will of God for them to sell such things as are useful in life at a "reasonable" profit and that it is wrong to make it the end of commerce to enrich themselves. He has much more to say about how the men, and particularly their wives, should spend the wealth and leisure which comes to them. Their great temptation, Law says, lies in "the indiscreet use of such things as are lawful to be used." There is nothing unlawful in eating and drinking, in buying houses and lands, in taking one's ease with pleasant company, but there is great danger in the "vain and imprudent use" of these things, which, although not so immediately destructive as gross sins, are none the less inimical to piety and fatal to man's true end. Holy living is an art which consists in "the right and prudent management" of things lawful in themselves. Mastery in the art is gained through following the strict rules laid down by religion.

In Law's opinion, persons of leisure and of some estate are the ones referred to in the Gospel parable as having received five talents. They are not permitted to squander their time, their health, and their fortune, but must employ these in improving their own souls and in assisting others to improve themselves. In Law's opinion we do this, as far as our active life is concerned, when we impose upon ourselves a voluntary poverty and employ our time and our goods for the relief of the poor and the unfortunate. In brief, charitable activity should be the main employment of those who do not have to earn their own bread. As God bestows His largesse upon the deserving and the undeserving without discriminating between them, so His servants should give to any who appear to be in need, without inquiring too minutely into their circumstances. Law, however, does value the principle of helping others to help themselves, and he praises the discretion of a godly woman who helped set up tradesmen in business, paid the rent of working men while they were sick, made good the loss of a horse or a cow to a poor family, and reared three children whom she took from the home of profligate parents. He especially enjoins tenderness and friendliness toward old people and toward the sick and the maimed.

Law's directions for the nurture of the inner life take the form of a daily order for prayer. One should set apart a place to which he may retire six times a day in order to recover his spiritual presence and to present himself before God. He should begin by chanting a psalm. Law is very particular about this. Singing, he says, is a generic talent. Its value in devotions is that it awakens the soul, calls it to its proper duty, and addresses it toward Heaven. Following this exercise, Law recommends the use of formal prayers, chiefly for the power which their exalted language has to make us sensible of the Divine Nature. But when our hearts are stirred sufficiently to frame their own praises and petitions, traditional forms should be laid aside.

According to Law, we best employ these devotional hours when we form the habit of taking up the same subject every day at the same time. He suggests the following plan. On rising (and it will be early, for religion is no friend of sleep or of sloth), our first acts should be to praise and thank God and to offer up body and soul to His service and glory. At nine o'clock, we should pray for humility. At noon, our theme should be love, and we should take upon ourselves the burden of intercession for all God's creatures. At three o'clock we should seek resignation and conformity to God's will. At six o'clock, we should confess our sins, reviewing all our actions for the day and acknowledging our shortcomings. There remains only the preparation of the soul for sleep, when the most proper subject is death. Approximately half of *A Serious Call* is taken up with this schedule of prayer and with the author's meditations upon the themes suggested.

A remarkable feature of the book is

the series of character sketches, seemingly drawn from life. Cognatus is a clergyman, orthodox and meticulous with the liturgy, but also a diligent observer of the markets, a man esteemed by his parishioners most of all for his advice on the time for selling wheat. Calidus is a great merchant who does business from dawn till late at night, when he dines heartily at the tavern; his prayers are short ejaculations, but he never misses saying them in stormy weather because he always has something or other at sea. Flavia is a maiden woman with a small income, which she expends mostly on dress, and by judicious management outdoes many ladies of greater fortune; she thinks that those who play cards on Sunday are atheists, but as soon as she comes from church she will tell you all the cards she held at the last night's party. Miranda, her sister, on the other hand, is the pious woman whose exemplary works of charity were mentioned above. These are but samples from an impressive gallery of eighteenth century types; these character sketches help to make *A Serious Call* something of a literary as well as a religious classic. Samuel Johnson said that it was the finest work of its kind in any language, and he testified to the influence it had exerted on his own life. "I took up Law's *Serious Call to A Devout and Holy Life*," he said, "expecting to find it a dull book (as such books generally are) and perhaps to laugh at it. But I found Law quite an overmatch for me."

CHRISTIANITY AS OLD AS THE CREATION

Author: Matthew Tindal (1655-1733)
Type of work: Deistic theology
First published: 1730

PRINCIPAL IDEAS ADVANCED

Because the nature of God is unchangeable, it can be inferred that God will treat all men at all times in the same way by supplying them all with the same sufficient means of recognizing and discharging their duties.

The religion of nature is the standard of judgment of what is acceptable in revelation, for the latter can add nothing to the perfection of the former.

Whether externally or internally revealed, true religion is constant in both doctrine and precept.

The Gospel is a republication of the religion of nature.

Christianity as Old as the Creation is the best known work of Matthew Tindal, Fellow of All Soul's College, Oxford. First published in 1730, it marks the culmination of deism. The work is a skillful collection of the arguments upon which the deists relied. Its express purpose is to distinguish between religion and superstition. Like such predecessors as John Toland (1670-1722) and Anthony Collins (1676-1729), Matthew Tindal espoused a religion which, it was claimed, any man at any time was capable of discovering by reason.

God has provided men with the means of knowing what He requires of them, writes Tindal. Natural religion, the religion man can discover, differs from revealed religion only in the manner of its being communicated. Natural religion is the *internal* revelation of God, whereas revealed religion is the *external* revelation of the same God. Since God is Himself unchangeable, infinitely wise and infinitely good, natural and revealed religion can differ in nothing as far as their content is concerned.

From the very beginning God has given men a rule or law for their conduct, the observance of which renders them acceptable to Himself. What originates with a perfect, all-wise God must itself be perfect. An absolutely perfect religion cannot be altered, nor increased nor decreased. Man's original religion is as immutable as God, its author. Revelation, therefore, can add nothing to a religion that is absolutely perfect, universal, and immutable.

Not only has God given mankind a law, Tindal continues, but also He has given sufficient means for making men capable of knowing what His infinite goodness would have them know. God was always willing that every man should come to the knowledge of true religion, and since the Christian religion is the only true and absolutely perfect religion, it was designed for all mankind from the beginning. The name "Christianity" is of more recent origin, but the Christian religion itself has existed from the beginning; it is

as old and extensive as human nature; it is in fact the law of creation, implanted in us by God Himself. God from the beginning has given all men sufficient means to know, believe, profess, and practice Christianity.

The means by which the whole race of mankind is able to discover what God would have them know are those faculties which distinguish man from the animals. Reason enables man to discover whether there is a God who is concerned with human affairs and who has given certain laws for human conduct.

God will judge men because they are rational, writes Tindal; the judgment will be exactly proportional to the use that men make of their reason. If the proper use of reason could not justify man before God, it would be vain to use reason at all. Our human condition would indeed be miserable if men were held to be criminal whether they used reason or not. If God would have everyone know His will at all times and has given no means other than reason, then the use of reason must be the means by which God would have us know what to profess and to practice. God has made us rational creatures. It is our reason that tells us that it is the will of God that we act up to the dignity of our natures and it is also reason that tells us when we do so. What God requires us to believe and practice must itself be a reasonable service, and whether what is offered to us as such is really reasonable must itself be judged by reason. Reason is the judge of what is reasonable. Nothing should be admitted into Christianity except what our reason tells us is worthy of having God for its author.

God requires nothing of men but

what is founded on the nature of things and on the immutable relations which things have to one another. Whenever men sincerely try to discover the will of God, they become aware of a law of nature, or reason, a law which is common or natural to all rational creatures. This law, like God Himself, is absolutely perfect, eternal, and unchangeable. The Gospel never intended to add or to detract from it. The purpose of the Gospel was to free men from their own superstition. True Christianity is, therefore, not a religion of yesterday, but it is the religion which God dictated at the beginning, and which He continues to dictate to all men.

The Gospel has been disclosed by Jesus, the person who was sent by God. By living what He taught, Jesus has set us a noble example, and just as He was highly exalted for so doing, we too may expect a suitable reward if we do our best to follow the divine precepts, which are the same whether revealed in the Gospel or discovered by reason.

Mankind was always under a law, even before the external revelation of the Scriptures was given, Tindal asserts. God has given the animals sufficient means to act in their own preservation. He certainly does not have less kindness for the immortal souls created in His image. God has given to men the light of understanding by which they can discover what makes for the good of their souls. Man is capable of perceiving eternal truths and of knowing what will contribute to his temporal and eternal happiness.

The Gospel is not a new religion but a "republication" of the religion of nature, Tindal claims. Natural religion is able to demonstrate with certainty that there is an absolutely perfect Being, the source of all other beings and of their perfections. That such a being exists is as certain as our own existence. It is, moreover, equally demonstrable that no creature can add to or detract from the happiness of a being who is infinitely happy in Himself. God did not create His creatures for His own good, but He created them for their own good. To imagine otherwise is to suppose that God was not perfectly happy before the Creation, and that His creatures could add or detract from His happiness by the observance or nonobservance of certain rules.

Since God is infinitely happy, all wise, and all good, nothing can be included in the divine law unless it promotes the common interest and happiness of His rational creatures; and, conversely, whatever does benefit His rational creatures must be included in the divine law.

God cannot require anything of us unless it contributes to our happiness, and He can forbid only that which leads to our suffering. His laws can lead only to our good, and His infinite power can bring to pass only what he designs for our good. Thus, concludes Tindal, to sin against such a being is to act against ourselves, against our reasonable natures.

Our reason is not limited to a demonstration of the existence of God and of the nature of the divine perfections. We can also demonstrate the nature of the duties God requires of us, both in relation to Himself and in relation to ourselves and to one another.

By recognizing that God has endowed us with such a nature that we desire our own good, and by realizing that God could not require anything that would do us harm, we know that we should act in relation to ourselves in such a way that our natural appetites will become regulated so as to achieve the exercise of reason, the health of the body, and the pleasure of the senses.

Our duty with respect to our fellow man is readily ascertainable if it be remembered that God is the common parent of all mankind, and that the whole human species is under the divine protection, so that God will punish anyone who injures anyone else. It is a person's duty to deal with others as he would have them deal with him in like circumstances. God has so constituted men that they are able to assist one another in the concerns of life. Infinite goodness has sown the seeds of pity in the human heart; God Himself has implanted in man, His image bearer, a love for His species, a desire to perform acts of benevolence.

Man's duty is always the same, since inconstancy cannot belong to the infinitely wise and powerful being. God is free of all partiality. His laws extend to all times and places. Since religion consists in the practice of those duties that result from man's relation to God, religion is as constant as God.

From the beginning of the world until the end, our duty to God and man is unalterable, Tindal emphasizes. Duty is always plain and clear; it is never changed in whole, or in part; hence, no person, if he comes from God, can teach any religion other than natural religion, or give us any precepts other than those which natural religion suggests. True religion is thus a constant disposition of our minds to do all the good we can; and by so doing we render ourselves acceptable

to God in answering the end of His creation.

Human actions are guided by man's innate desire for happiness, a desire that is fulfilled by the perfection of man's nature, by living up to the dictates of right reason.

The religion of nature is absolutely perfect Tindal asserts; revelation can neither add to nor take from its perfection. In fact, the truth of revelation itself is to be judged by revelation's agreement with natural religion. All particular precepts that fail to contribute to the honor of God or to the good of man fail to carry any obligation.

The failure to make reason the judge concerning the nature of God and the duties He requires of us has given rise to all sorts of superstitions, bigotry, and intolerance. The abandonment of reason has debased God by clothing Him in our own infirmities; it has resulted in the practice of placing man's individual conscience in the hands of corrupt men, in the hands of priests and clerics. True religion, Tindal insists, consists in imitating the perfections of God; nothing arbitrary is contained in a religion that comes from God. To insist upon obeying human ordinances as necessary to pleasing God is to suppose that some men who obey the law of nature may yet suffer eternal punishment for not obeying certain other laws. It is erroneous to hold that God requires in the Gospels what the law of nature does not. It is superstitious to represent God as a most cruel being who damns men to eternity for mistaken opinions and who condemns men for sins which reason cannot oppose.

To magnify revelation is to weaken the force of reason and nature, Tindal claims; to venerate revelation is to strike at all natural order, for there cannot be two conflicting standards of divine government. Fortunately, most men are, by reason, able to distinguish between religion and superstition and thus to extricate themselves from a reliance upon revelation.

The thesis defended by Tindal and other deists, namely, that a man can at any time discover his duties by exercising reason, and that there is a natural religion as old as the creation, was later to collapse under the criticism of philosophers such as David Hume (1711-1776), who argued that the religion of primitive man consists of a medley of crude superstitions.

The optimism of deism with respect to the rationality implicit in human nature and the subjection of revelation to the tests of reason exerted and continues to exert its influence upon liberal forms of Protestantism.

THE ANALOGY OF RELIGION

Author: Joseph Butler (1692-1752)
Type of work: Apologetics
First published: 1736

PRINCIPAL IDEAS ADVANCED

By analogy the course and constitution of nature can be shown to support the religious doctrines that man is to live in a future state, rewarded or punished for his present virtuous or vicious acts; that our present life is a probation; and that because of human apostasy a new dispensation is necessary.

The new dispensation of providence has been revealed by God, proven by miracles, and carried on by the Mediator, Jesus Christ.

Objections to religion can equally be alleged against the course of nature itself; they are inconclusive, and the weight of the evidence is on the side of religion.

The *Analogy of Religion, Natural and Revealed, to the Course and Constitution of Nature* is a masterpiece of Christian argument by Joseph Butler, who at the time of his death in 1752 was the Bishop of Durham in the Church of England. Butler's *Analogy* attempts to dispose of objections against Christianity and to reveal the evidence for it. The existence of God as an intelligent author of nature and a natural governor of the world was not at issue in the eighteenth century.

There was, however, an ever-increasing conviction that Christianity was a fit subject for ridicule. The *Analogy* seeks to prove that there is strong evidence for the truth of Christianity, and that Christianity cannot be shown to be false.

The work is divided into two parts; the first deals with natural religion; the second, with revealed religion. The argument of the entire work is an application of analogical reasoning to religion. The teachings of religion are observed to correspond to the known constitution and course of nature, so that objections to the former amount to an attack on the latter.

Degrees of likeness between things or events yield probable evidence, which, in contrast to demonstrative evidence, admits of degrees, and produces a presumption, an opinion, or a full conviction. To an infinite intelligence, Butler claims, no possible object of knowledge is merely probable, but for finite creatures "probability is the very guide of life."

If we presuppose the existence of an author of nature, Butler argues, the analogy between the system of revelation and the known course of nature makes it probable that they have the same author, and to the extent that the teachings of religion are shown to be like the course of nature, such analogies will either amount to a practical proof of their truth or will serve to answer objections against them.

The objection to the doctrine that mankind has been appointed to live in a future state is answered by showing that there is no reason to hold that death destroys living agents, or even suspends their powers of reflection. It is probably true that we shall live on in a future state in which every one will be rewarded and punished. In our present life we are governed in such a manner that one course of action is followed by the reward of pleasure, and another by the punishment of pain. There is nothing incredible in supposing that the future will be like the past, and that an infinite being is a righteous governor, who will punish and reward men in exact proportion to their virtues or vices.

The principles and beginnings of a moral government are discernible in nature, so that the final judgment of man in terms of distributive justice differs only in degree, not in kind, from what we now experience. There is a strong presumption that our present life is a probation for a future state.

We are under God's moral government, Butler insists, and we must give an account of our actions, both in our natural and our moral capacity. That we are now in a state of trial is attributable to our own nature, our inordinately excited passions, and the circumstances of our environment. The state of trial taught by religion is rendered credible because of its likeness to our present danger of losing temporal happiness. No more is required of men than they are able to do. Their success and happiness or their failure and misery depends upon their own diligence or negligence.

Butler contends that the general analogy of providence enables us to apprehend the danger of yielding to temptations and of losing a future good to satisfy an inferior interest. It may not be possible for us to understand the reasons why we have been placed on trial, but the end is our improvement in virtue and piety, so that we may enjoy a future state of happiness. The state of trial is analogous to our childhood education as preparation for our mature years. The present world is a state of moral discipline for another; it is a state of discipline for moral improvement, for what we become is the effect of what we do.

Butler grants that a fatalist might allege that a moral plan is impossible, but if the principle of universal necessity is reconcilable with the order of nature, it is also compatible with religion.

The teachings of religion are sufficiently credible to encourage men to live a life of virtue and piety. Butler concedes that God's scheme for the moral government of the world is not perfectly comprehended, but we are in no way competent to pass judgment concerning the course of providence. If we were not ignorant, if we could comprehend the whole plan of God, Butler argues, then what appear to be irregularities would be found to be consistent with and a part of justice and goodness.

The light of nature in nowise minimizes the importance of Christianity and the necessity of revelation, Butler insists. That revelation is not useless is shown by the condition of men in the heathen world, by man's skepticism in matters of importance, and by the general ignorance and inattention of men. Even if it were possible for man to reason out the whole system of natural religion, there is no probability that he would, and he would still need to be reminded of it. The very best of men are in need of supernatural instruction.

To minimize the importance of the Christian revelation is to forget that it has been given by God and that in addition to restating the truths of natural religion with increased light, attested to by the authority of miracles and prophecy, revelation also contains a record of what is not discoverable by reason; namely, a disclosure of the particular dispensation of God's providence in achieving man's salvation through the Son and the Holy Spirit.

The disclosure of God's special dealings with men places us under the moral obligation to render worship to the Son, our Mediator, and to the Holy Spirit, our Sanctifier. Such duties cannot be neglected with impunity.

Christianity is credible, Butler claims. There is no presumption against revelation in general on the ground that it is not discovered by reason or experience, since many things in the natural and moral system of the world are also beyond our natural faculties. There is, moreover, no reason to hold that everything that is unknown must be like what is known, although the scheme of Christianity is not unlike the scheme of nature. Nor is there a presumption against the miraculous character of revelation. The power exercised to make a world at the beginning, before there was a course of nature, could be further extended to make a revelation, and even after nature received its appointed course, there is no presumption against the occasional occurrence of miraculous interpositions.

There are, as a matter of fact, Butler insists, no valid objections against the Christian revelation. Objections raised against Christianity are based on the false supposition that we already possess knowledge as to what God's revealed dispensation ought to be, a knowledge that we do not possess even with respect to the natural governance of the world.

The situation with regard to revelation is analogous to that of natural information. We have no *a priori* knowledge of what God will permit us to know, or of the means to be used, or of the degree of evidence we can achieve.

The real issue is not whether the Christian revelation is what we might have expected God to reveal, but whether or not it truly is revelation. Moreover, Butler argues, it is invalid to object to the Scriptures because of their alleged obscurity and ambiguity, unless the Scriptures themselves promise that they are free of such faults. The authority of Scripture can be overturned, if, and only if, it can be shown that there is absolutely no proof of the miracles originally wrought to attest its authority, that there is nothing miraculous in its success, and that it contains no prophecy of events that human wisdom could not foresee.

Serious objections to Christianity are not forthcoming, Butler writes. If objections are to be made they must be made against the evidence for Christianity. For the analogy of nature makes it highly credible that if a revelation is to be made, it must contain many things different from what might be expected. Christianity is a scheme that is beyond our comprehension; it is not to be judged by reason. We do not have sufficient knowledge to protest against its wisdom, goodness, or justice.

The presence of a divine Mediator between God and man is, moreover, in accordance with the analogy of nature, Butler argues. Our life and its blessings are due to others. Prior to revelation, however, we have no means of knowing whether a mediator was necessary, or how the work of redemption was to be accomplished.

That the evidence of religion is considered doubtful is in no way inconsistent with the analogy of nature, Butler claims, for there is also much uncertainty concerning our temporal interests. Nor is the fact that Christianity is not universally revealed either an argument against its justice or inconsistent with its wisdom and goodness.

There is positive evidence for Christianity, Butler argues. The two most direct and fundamental proofs of Christianity are the miracles and the prophecies recorded in the Scriptures.

With respect to miracles it is to be observed that they are recorded in books which, until proved to the contrary, are to be regarded as genuine history. From its inception, Christianity was accepted upon the basis of miracles, and thus it differs from all other religions. Its success constitutes evidence of the actuality of the miracles recorded, for unless they were fully convinced of the truth of miracles, the Apostles and their contemporaries would not have undergone the suffering and martyrdom provoked by their belief in miracles.

Human testimony is a natural ground of assent, and even when marked by enthusiasm, such testimony is not overthrown unless there is either incredibility in the things attested or conflicting testimony. The evidence of testimony can be destroyed either by a proof or a probability that the witnesses are incompetent to judge the facts to which they bear witness, or that they are under some indirect pressure in giving evidence. Neither case is likely in Christianity. Because of the importance of their Christian beliefs, Christians would not want to be deceived themselves, nor would they wish to deceive others.

With respect to prophecy, Butler observes that the obscurity of a part of a prophecy in nowise destroys the proof of foreknowledge of the parts that are understood. The fact that a long series of prophecies is applicable to certain events constitutes proof that the events were intended to be known.

Collateral evidence may also be adduced from the character of the Christian revelation, from its content, and from facts relating to it. It is, however, easier to attack Christianity than to defend it, Butler concedes, for it is easier to assault a single point than to accumulate the whole mass of evidence in its defense. However, when the positive evidence for Christianity is considered in mass, and the objections against it are carefully considered, as well as the practical consequences of its denial, then if complete satisfaction as to its truth is not given, the most extreme skepticism cannot reach further than a middle position between complete satisfaction of the truth of Christianity and complete satisfaction of its falsity. If the proper evidence for Christianity is presented and considered, the skeptic cannot avoid the serious apprehension that Christianity might be true, although he may still doubt whether it be so. "If this be a just account of things," Butler writes, "and yet men go on to vilify or disregard Christianity, which is to talk and act as if they had a demonstration of its falsehood; there is no reason to think they would alter their behavior to any purpose, though there were a demonstration of its truth."

Butler's *Analogy of Religion* is significant as an attempt to stem the tide of deism and skepticism with respect to the reasonableness of the Christian faith. Its argument exerted considerable influence upon orthodox Christians, and the work commanded and continues to command the respect and attention of both its defenders and its opponents.

THE JOURNALS OF GEORGE WHITEFIELD

Author: George Whitefield (1714-1770)
Type of work: Spiritual autobiography
First published: 1738, 1740, 1747

PRINCIPAL IDEAS ADVANCED

Jesus Christ is the one Mediator between God and man; each man must achieve a new birth through Christ.

Success in converting men to the love of God is the effect of God's free grace.

God bestows His saving grace on only a certain number of men; the rest of mankind will suffer eternal death, the wages of sin.

The *Journals* of George Whitefield originally appeared as individual publications. They constitute the spiritual autobiography of a man who has been called the prince of preachers. Whitefield was born in 1714 in Gloucester, England. He confesses that as a child he hated instruction and was much given to lying, filthy talking, foolish jesting, and Sabbath breaking. Such actions later served to convince him that he was conceived and born in sin, that by nature nothing good dwelt within him, and that had he had not been restrained by the free grace of God, he would have been banished from His divine presence forever.

Whitefield attributed his early sense

of calling to the free grace of God, for although corruption worked strongly in his soul and produced early and bitter fruits, the very early influence of the blessed Spirit upon his heart satisfied him that God's love for him was everlasting, and that he had been separated from his mother's womb to be a preacher of the Gospel.

With considerable financial difficulty he managed, at seventeen years of age, to enter Pembroke College of Oxford University, where he resisted the worldly temptations of student life, and he began the practice of praying and singing psalms several times each day.

At Oxford he came into contact with the despised Methodists, and under the influence of his never-to-be-forgotten friend, Charles Wesley (1707-1788), Whitefield came to know that true religion was union of the soul with God and Christ. He now knew for the first time that to be a Christian he had to become a new creature, and that God had begun a good work in his soul, for he had experienced the new birth.

Whitefield now began to receive instruction in the faith from Charles Wesley. From the Methodists he learned to live like a good soldier of Jesus Christ and to live by rule so that not a single moment of his time would be wasted. Everything that he now did was done to the glory of God. No means were left unused which Whitefield thought would lead him nearer to Jesus Christ. Acts of charity were performed each day. Whitefield visited the sick and prisoners, and he read to the poor. The course of his studies was entirely changed. Whereas before he had been occupied in studying soulless sciences and superficial books,

he now resolved to read only such as entered into the heart of religion and which led him directly into an experimental knowledge of Jesus Christ.

Whitefield now passed through a period of trials and temptations, during which he incurred the contempt of his fellow students, provoked the displeasure of the Master of the College, and suffered periods of illness. It was during a period of absence from the University that Whitefield's soul was enlightened by God in the knowledge of his free grace, and in the necessity of being justified in his sight by faith only. After extensive soul-searching Whitefield was ordained at Gloucester in 1736, and his formal ministry began. He finished his degree of Bachelor of Arts at Oxford, and then he continued his work of distributing money and books among the poor prisoners. His early attempts at preaching were marked by increasing popularity. The congregations were very large, and the doctrine of the new birth and justification by faith in Jesus Christ which he preached made its way like lightning into the hearers' consciences.

The publication of his sermon *On the Nature and Necessity of our Regeneration or New Birth in Christ Jesus* marked the beginning of a spiritual revival or awakening at London, Bristol, Gloucester, and Gloucestershire. Whitefield's preaching began to attract considerable attention. He generally preached nine times a week to thousands. On Sunday mornings, long before day, the streets were filled with people going to church. The people gave liberally, but Whitefield preached gratis, and the money collected went to charity.

As Whitefield's popularity increased,

opposition also increased. Many of the clergy grew angry, and complaints were made that the churches were so crowded that there was no room for the parishioners. Whitefield was accused of being a spiritual pickpocket who used charm to get the people's money. A few clergymen would not let him preach in their pulpits. His practices of keeping company with the dissenters was criticized, but his sermons were called for everywhere. He was offered large sums of money if he would stay in England, but he was determined to go to Georgia, for which he set sail in December of 1737, at the age of twenty-three.

The account of his voyage to America at the end of 1737 was sent back to England in the early summer of 1738. Although it was designed for the edification of his personal friends, it was published without the author's consent and became known as Whitefield's *First Journal*. A slightly revised edition was then published and went through four editions in 1738. The *First Journal* enjoyed such a marked success that Whitefield published six more journals detailing his life down to March, 1741.

During his second voyage to America in 1739, Whitefield wrote the story of his early life prior to his ordination in 1735, which he published in 1740 with the title *A Short Account*. It was on his third voyage to America in 1744 that he wrote *A Further Account* (published in 1747), which covered the period following his ordination until the time of his *First Journal*. His works were republished in a revised form in 1756. *An Unpublished Journal* covering Whitefield's second tour in New England between August 1744 and the spring of 1745 was recently discovered in the

Library of Princeton Theological Seminary and was first published in the December, 1938, number of *Church History*.

Whitefield lost no opportunity to care for the souls of men. Even aboard ship on his voyages to and from America he continued to preach, to read prayers, and to visit the sick. Whenever he could he held private conversations concerning our fall in Adam, and the necessity of our new birth in Christ Jesus. He catechised whoever would listen.

Whitefield continued his evangelical ministry in the New World. He continued to preach that Jesus Christ is the one Mediator between God and man, and he proclaimed unhesitatingly the judgment to come.

Upon his return to England after his first stay in America, Whitefield was warmly received. Crowds continued to flock by the thousands to hear his message that we are justified by an act of faith in Jesus Christ, without any regard to past, present, or future works. He reports that God enabled him to speak upon the doctrine of the new birth.

In all his success Whitefield remained humble, filled with love, peace, and joy in the Holy Spirit, attributing all success to the free grace in Christ Jesus, which Whitefield freely offered to all sinners who would lay hold of Christ by faith. Many who heard were touched to the quick and felt what was spoken, uttering hearty and loud amens. Many conversions were wrought. In February of 1739, because he was refused the use of a church, Whitefield began to preach outdoors to tens of thousands, in spite of official opposition on the part of the officials of the Church of England. In spite of slanderous remarks to the effect that he was mad and that he had said he was the Holy Ghost, Whitefield found his way into the hearts of the people; he preached with a passionate power that brought souls home to Christ. At no time did he desire separation from the Established Church. He saw no reason to leave the Established Church, no matter how badly he was treated by corrupt members and ministers. He judged the state of the Church, not from the practice of its members, but by its primitive and public constitutions; and as long as the articles of the Church of England were agreeable to Scripture, Whitefield purposed to preach them without bigotry or party zeal.

Thus, in spite of all opposition and threats, Whitefield continued to preach throughout the length and breadth of England, as well as throughout the colonies of the New World. In Georgia he established an orphanage for children, and he utilized the funds he raised from his ever-growing audiences to maintain it.

His dependence upon the Spirit of God for his message, and the effect that he had upon his audience can be seen from an entry made in his *Seventh Journal*, on November 2, 1740, concerning his preaching in New York: "Preached in the morning with some freedom, but was dejected before the evening sermon, and when I came into the pulpit, I could have chosen to be silent rather than speak. After I had begun, however, the Spirit of the Lord gave me freedom, and at length came down like a mighty rushing wind, and carried all before it. Immediately, the whole congregation was alarmed. Crying, weeping, and wailing were to be heard in every corner;

men's hearts failing them for fear, and many were to be seen falling into the arms of their friends. My soul was carried out till I could scarce speak anywhere. A sense of God's goodness overwhelmed me. A little boy was much concerned, on the pulpit stairs. One of my friends asked him why he cried. 'Who can help it?' he said, 'Mr. Whitefield's words cut me to the heart.' After I came home, I threw myself upon the bed and in awful silence admired the infinite freeness, sovereignty, and condescension of the love of God."

Whitefield was interested in theological issues. He regarded his converts as remarkable proofs of the doctrine of God's eternal election and everlasting love. For if believers are to do God justice, they will acknowledge that God first chose them. If God has chosen the believer, it must be from all eternity, without regard to anything foreseen in them. It is God's electing grace that assures that Christ did not die in vain and that sinners will in fact be saved.

Although Whitefield's preaching emphasized faith and repentance, he was motivated by the Calvinistic doctrine of election and predestination. His theology included the doctrine of a free and electing grace. Whitefield did not hesitate to disagree strongly in a letter to John Wesley in answer to the latter's sermon entitled *Free Grace*. Whitefield rebuked Wesley's doctrine of universal redemption and his attack on the doctrine of predestination. Against Wesley, Whitefield firmly held that God intends to bestow His saving grace, through Jesus Christ, only to a certain number, and that the rest of mankind will suffer eternal death, which is the proper wages of sin.

The doctrine of election in no way

dampened Whitefield's enthusiasm for evangelistic preaching; he believed that the God who appointed salvation for a certain number also appointed the preaching of the Word to bring them to it. The Gospel was designed by God to be the power of God unto the eternal salvation of the elect, but since no one knows who are the elect and who are the reprobate, the ministers of the Word must preach to everyone. The doctrine of election in no way tended to destroy Whitefield's desire for the salvation of sinners, for as a true lover of the Lord Jesus Christ, he continued to preach until the day before his death in 1770.

THE JOURNAL OF JOHN WESLEY

Author: John Wesley (1703-1791)
Type of work: Spiritual autobiography
First published: 1739 and following, seriatim

PRINCIPAL IDEAS ADVANCED

The command to live holy lives needs to be accompanied by a free proclamation of Christ's atoning work and of the witness of the Holy Spirit in the hearts of believers.

The work of God in the lives of men is often accompanied by emotional upheavals, but the evidence that it is God's work lies only in the moral changes it produces in men's lives.

Christians ought to gather in small societies for their mutual improvement, and these societies ought to be organized in a common undertaking.

The educational, economic, and social needs of men are a worthy concern of these societies.

John Wesley began keeping a diary during his student days at Oxford upon reading in Jeremy Taylor's *The Rule and Exercise of Holy Living and Holy Dying* (1650-1651) that a Christian ought to keep systematic account of how he employs every hour of his time. About 1739, when Methodism was beginning to be a controversial issue, Wesley published the parts of the diary which he considered most material to his cause, together with "such little reflections" as came to his mind. Throughout his life he continued this practice, recording his thoughts daily, and later publishing excerpts. Over his long life, twenty-one installments were made available to an eager and growing body of followers. Wesley kept his diaries in a private cipher, transcribing only the parts he thought would enhance the cause of evangelical revival. In 1909, Nehemiah Curnock unraveled Wesley's code and, drawing upon previously unpublished materials, produced the standard modern edition of the *Journal.*

John Wesley came from a remarkable family. In an age when piety was greatly in decline, his father, Samuel

Wesley (1662-1735), and his mother, Susannah, daughter of a famous nonconformist clergyman, kept alive the best traditions of the English Church. At John's request, his mother set down in writing the rules which she used in bringing up her family. The letter in which she recounts these principles is one of the most interesting parts of the *Journal*. Strict by modern standards, Susannah was nevertheless sympathetic and, above all, understanding. Her principle was to conquer the child's will early. "As self-will is the root of all sin and misery," she wrote, "so whatever cherishes this in children insures their after-wretchedness and irreligion; whatever checks and mortifies it promotes their future happiness and piety." She taught her children their prayers and catechism as soon as they could speak, and she taught them to read at the age of five, using the Bible as a textbook. For six hours a day for a quarter of the year, her house was turned into a school. In addition, she set aside a regular time every night of the week to talk to one of her children in private. Observing that children sometimes lie in order to avoid being punished, she made it a rule that whoever, when charged with a fault of which he was guilty, confessed and promised to amend, would be spared punishment; and consequently she commended and frequently rewarded children when they were obedient, especially in matters which went against their inclinations. Distinguishing between intention and performance, she argued that when a child did something wrong, if the intention were to obey, the will to do well should be accepted with kind words and the child tenderly directed how to do better in the future.

But if, in this way, Samuel and Susannah Wesley laid the foundation for Methodism, it must not be supposed that when the young John Wesley went out into the world he was already a saint. He had devout qualities, but, as a fellow at Oxford, he was an enthusiastic sportsman and far from immune to the charms of young women. After his ordination, in 1726, John acted for more than a year as his father's curate, at Epworth, finding time to attend village fairs and dances with his sisters, to shoot plover, and to read plays. Twice he was in love, but he was too poor to think of marriage.

It was one of his young lady acquaintances who directed Wesley's attention to the writings of Thomas à Kempis and of Jeremy Taylor, which, together with William Law's *A Treatise of Christian Perfection* (1726) and *A Serious Call to a Devout and Holy Life* (1728), intensified his interest in religion. His younger brother, Charles (1707-1788), who had come up to Oxford while John was away, had begun to meet with two friends; they met to help one another with their studies and with their spiritual life. John, on his return, was welcomed into the group and soon became its leader. Besides meeting three or four times a week, the members made it a practice to visit the prison regularly and to distribute alms to needy families. Such a display of piety seemed excessive, not merely to students but also to university officials, and there was some talk that "the censors were going to blow up The Godly Club," or, as they were sometimes called, "The Methodists."

Wesley's understanding of Christianity at this period of his life centered on the ideal of Christian perfection. In a sermon before the University, January, 1733, entitled "The Circumcision of the Heart," he stressed the need for "that habitual disposition of the soul, which in the sacred writings is termed holiness, and which directly implies the being cleansed from sin; from all filthiness both of flesh and spirit; and, by consequence, the being endued with those virtues which were in Christ Jesus." This concern for perfection and holiness, which was so characteristic of high church Anglican theology in the previous century, was the main motive in Wesley's life when he visited America in 1735, where he ministered for two years, chiefly in Savannah, Georgia. His purpose in going to America had been to convert the Indians; but his high-church practices were too rigorous even for the colonists; and he fled from Georgia in order to avoid prosecution at the hands of influential persons whom he had offended.

The story of Wesley's acquaintance with the Moravian Brethren during the crossing of the Atlantic is well known. The joyful confidence which these simple people possessed in time of storm convinced Wesley that his was but "a fair summer religion." "I went to America," he says, "to convert the Indians; but O! who shall convert me? who, what is he that will deliver me from this evil heart of unbelief?" (January, 1738.) Commenting later on his experience, he says that he had trusted too much to his own works and his own righteousness and not enough in the free mercy of God. The Moravian Brethren tried to show him "a more excellent way," but he was "too learned and too wise to understand." (May, 1738.) This was his condition when, a few months after his re-

turn to England, he attended a religious meeting on Aldersgate Street, where he heard one of the Moravian Brethren reading Luther's preface to the Epistle to the Romans. "About a quarter before nine," he writes, "while he was describing the change which God works in the heart through faith in Christ, I felt myself strangely warmed. I felt I did trust in Christ, Christ alone, for salvation; and an assurance was given me that He had taken away my sins, even mine, and saved me from the law of sin and death." (May, 1738). Wesley confesses that, when he returned home, he was still buffeted by temptation and doubt, but, he says, there was this difference that, whereas before, the temptations often got the better of him, now help came from Heaven and he was always conqueror.

The witness within his heart to the forgiveness of his sins greatly strengthened Wesley's preaching. After a visit to the Moravian churches in Germany, he entered upon a busy but undistinguished ministry in London and vicinity. A society which he had formed the previous year now numbered thirty-two persons. Besides meeting with them, he visited jails and workhouses and preached in different churches to growing congregations. That the churches, one after another, refused him their pulpits did not prevent his keeping a busy round of appointments. Still, it was only when, on the urging of George Whitefield (1714-1770), whose ministry closely paralleled his own, Wesley so far broke with formality as to consent to preach in the open, that great numbers were enrolled in his following. From then on, Wesley could well say,

"I look upon all the world as my parish."

Although not the dramatic orator that Whitefield was, Wesley nevertheless proved an impressive speaker. Because of the force of his argument and his burning conviction, many hearers carried away the impression that Wesley was speaking to them personally. Frequently, various individuals shed tears, fell into fits, and cried out hysterically. Such emotional displays, which his rivals deplored under the name of "enthusiasm," Wesley defended. He explained that it was not the external signs that he rejoiced in but in the changed lives which resulted. He said to his critics, "You deny that God does now work these effects; at least, that He works them in this manner. I affirm both, because I have . . . seen (as far as a thing of this kind can be seen) very many persons changed in a moment from the spirit of fear, horror, despair, to the spirit of love, joy, and peace; and from sinful desire, till then reigning over them, to a pure desire of doing the will of God." (May, 1739.)

But it was Wesley's mastery of organization, rather than his effectiveness as a preacher, that contributed most to the success of his revival. Preaching in the open was unorthodox, but forming religious societies was very much in the approved Anglican tradition. Wherever Wesley preached, he organized groups. Classes of twelve were formed, each under a leader who was responsible for assembling the others for weekly class meetings, for taking their offerings (typically a penny a week), and for reporting to Wesley which ones were in good standing. Wesley visited each class once a quarter and on each visit gave a ticket "under his own hand" to each member whose "seriousness and good conversation" was reported to him. The class leaders became a kind of lay ministry who were assembled in district conferences once a year.

It was Wesley's intention that, so far as feasible, the members of his "connexion" would continue to be members of their respective parishes and receive sacraments from the local clergy. The arrangement worked hardships in many instances, and because there were only a handful of priests in his organization, Wesley was pressed to have some of his lay preachers ordained. At first he availed himself of the services of an accommodating bishop of the Greek Orthodox Church to lay hands on his candidates for ordination. Afterwards, however, arguing that he was as much a bishop as any man in England, he performed the ordination himself—so far had he moved from his early High-Church principles. Nevertheless, to the end of his days he resisted those in his societies who wanted to separate from the Anglican Church. To one group he said (January, 1787), "If you are resolved, you may have your service in church-hours; but remember, from that time, you will see my face no more." This altered their purpose, and "from that hour I have heard no more of separating from the Church."

From the time he began to preach the gospel of free forgiveness, Wesley ran into opposition from within the Church. When he took to field-preaching, he incited the fury of all sorts. Magistrates tried to arrest him and his preachers and impress them into the militia, on the grounds of vagrancy. Landowners threatened to drive him from their towns. Mobs of ordinary people sought to break up the meetings, not infrequently under the impression that Wesley was a Roman Catholic and that he was working in the interests of the Pretender to the Crown. Wesley showed great courage and adroitness in dealing with these mobs, and he often succeeded in winning the leaders to his side.

It was given to Wesley to outlive most of his enemies and to see his work everywhere bearing fruit. Even those who did not approve of his gospel could scarcely object to the changes which they saw in the lives of men. Wesley records a letter which he wrote to *The Chronicle* (January, 1761) on the changes he had lately found in Newgate prison. The place was clean. Men were provided with tools and materials so that they might work. "By the blessing of God on these regulations the prison now has a new face: nothing offends either the eye or ear; and the whole has the appearance of a quiet, serious family." Similar changes were found in textile factories. In Epworth, Wesley reports, there were four of these, employing large numbers of workers. Some of the workers attended prayer meeting, and finding themselves dissatisfied with the immoral conditions that prevailed at their work, they urged their fellows to make the factories models of propriety. In May, 1782, Wesley visited three of these factories and "found religion had taken deep root in them. No trifling word was heard among [the workers], and they watch over each other in love."

The social products of Methodism were by no means accidental. Far ahead of his time, Wesley took a direct interest in the education and economic condition of his converts. He established schools, opened dispensaries, and organized loan funds. One of his most effective innovations was the publication of a wide range of books and pamphlets at low cost, partly for children in the schools, but also for the general public. It has been remarked that no man in the eighteenth century did so much to create in the English people a taste for good reading.

Another innovation was less effective. Convinced that electricity has healing properties, he procured apparatus which he made available to any who desired treatment. The patients became so numerous that he had to set up three different centers. "Hundreds, and perhaps thousands," he says, "received unspeakable good, . . . so that when I hear any talk of the danger of being electrified (especially if they are medical men who talk so), I cannot but impute it to great want either of sense or honesty." (November, 1757.)

As a student, Wesley had exhibited a strong classical taste, and throughout his life he read widely in both ancient and modern authors. He personally composed Latin and French grammars, wrote short histories of Rome and of England, and made selections from Milton and Isaac Watts for use in Methodist schools. Of Handel's *Messiah,* he writes: "In many parts, especially several of the choruses, it exceeded my expectation." (August, 1759.) He was, of course, inclined to judge the products of human culture from the standpoint of eternity; if he was willing to commend the play "Adelphi" by Terence as "an entertainment not unworthy of a Christian," (December, 1768), he was equally ready to censure the misanthropy of Rousseau and "his brother-infidel, Voltaire." (February, 1770.) Taken by friends to visit the British Museum when he was seventy-seven, Wesley remarked on the wide range such a place afforded one's curiosity, but added that he could not resist reckoning what account man would have to give to the Judge of the quick and dead for the time and money expended in collecting all these things. (December, 1780.)

The work which Wesley originated made great demands upon him. He was constantly moving, preaching fifteen sermons a week and traveling from five to eight thousand miles a year, over all parts of the British Isles. When he married he said, "I cannot understand how a Methodist preacher can answer it to God to preach one sermon or travel one day less in a married than in a single state." (March, 1751.)

Because of Wesley's itinerate life, the *Journal* is an excellent travelogue. Wesley was a keen observer of nature and places, and the excitement which his presence everywhere caused was a source of countless anecdotes. Occasionally, a comment suggests that Wesley might have liked to settle down, as, when in his seventy-ninth year, he admired the pleasant garden and shady walk of a certain Miss Harvey. "How gladly could I repose awhile here!" he writes. "But repose is not for me in this world." (July, 1782.) The next summer he did take a little vacation—a trip to the Netherlands, where he was welcomed as a dignitary and saw many things of interest.

"I am now an old man," he writes near the close of his *Journal*, "decayed from head to foot. My eyes are dim; my right hand shakes much; my mouth is hot and dry every morning; I have a lingering fever almost every day; my motion is weak and slow. However, blessed be God, I do not slack my labour: I can preach and write still." (January, 1790.)

That Wesley could write, and that he kept his powers to the end, his *Journal* is witness. The man "whose eloquence and logical acuteness," Macaulay said, "might have made him eminent in literature, whose genius for government was not inferior to that of Richelieu," left, in his *Journal*, a monument which is, in its own way, a world classic.

SEASONABLE THOUGHTS ON THE STATE OF RELIGION IN NEW ENGLAND

Author: Charles Chauncy (1705-1787)
Type of work: Criticism of revival movements
First published: 1743

PRINCIPAL IDEAS ADVANCED

The Great Awakening has caused disruption in the order of the churches of New England.

Antinomianism and revivalism tend to develop similar theological concerns.

The itinerant clergy intrude upon settled congregations; by their unwarranted accusations against the pastors of churches they have denied the true fruits of the new birth of regenerated Christians.

True conversion involves a transformation of the mind as well as the heart, though primary attention in the "awakenings" has been given to the affections.

In the fourth and fifth decades of the eighteenth century the churches along the Atlantic coastline were in the midst of the First Great Awakening, the revival of religion which affected practically all American church life. Two names stand out as contemporary interpreters of that period: Jonathan Edwards (1703-1758) and Charles Chauncy (1705-1787). Edwards, the famed pastor of the church in Northampton, Massachusetts, and renowned Calvinistic theologian, had been a prime figure in promoting the revivals. Assisted by George Whitefield (1714-1770), Gilbert Tennent (1703-1764), and others, Edwards, through vivid theological imagery and tireless labor, sought to awaken sinners to their true condition. In 1736 he published an essay entitled *A Faithful Narrative of the Surprising Work of God in the Conversion of Many Hundred Souls in Northampton,* which received wide attention in the New England churches. Only seven years earlier Edwards had received the mantle of leadership for a large segment of Congregationalism from his grandfather, Solomon Stoddard (1643-1729). A mere five years earlier Edwards had visited Boston to deliver his first lecture before the clergy of that area. An unassuming member of his audience was Charles Chauncy, then assistant to Thomas Foxcroft (1696-1769) in the Congregational Church of Boston.

Charles Chauncy, a graduate of Harvard in 1721 and great grandson of his namesake and second President of Harvard, was to serve the Boston Church for sixty years. His name was brought to the attention of the New England churches when he published his own interpretation of the revivals under the title *Seasonable Thoughts on the State of Religion in New England.*

The immediate effect of the revivals was divisive, in both political and theological matters. In the coastal and inland regions, churches divided over the issues raised by the "awakening." Edwards and Chauncy represented two developing parties in New England church life. Edwards, a graduate of Yale, spoke for an increasingly larger group within western Massachusetts and Connecticut Congregationalism; from him stems the New Divinity or consistent Calvinist theological tradition which was carried on by such men as Samuel Hopkins (1721-1803) and Joseph Bellamy (1719-1790). Chauncy, reflecting the more liberal interests of the eastern Massachusetts churches, gradually made more evident his dissent from the more severe aspects of Calvinism. Though his sympathy for the developing Arminian theology was not clear by the early 1740's, he later became one of the key spokesmen for the movement. When the revival began neither Edwards nor Chauncy was conscious of being anything other than a loyal defender of the Calvinistic tradition, but it was not long until the dispute over the revivals had turned into protracted theological warfare.

After the second wave of the revival (1741-1742), Chauncy became publicly concerned about its excesses. A main cause for his developing disenchantment were the visits of itinerant clergy to the Boston area. George Whitefield, Gilbert Tennent, and James Davenport had stopped to preach in the vicinity. At the same time, Edwards, in Northampton, was concerned lest the churches of New England fail to give the revivals their full support, and in 1741 he published *The Distinguishing Marks of a Work of the Spirit of God*. This essay, while critical of some of the excesses of the revivals, sought to encourage the clergy of New England to promote the revival movement. Chauncy felt that the essay needed an answer; the conflict had now been brought to the printed page.

The publication of Chauncy's *Seasonable Thoughts* made clear his dissent from the practices and underlying theology of the revivals. By drawing out the more severe aspects of seventeenth century New England antinomianism, he attempted to make the implications of the awakenings evident to all his readers. The threat, posed by the revivals, to the order of the New England churches had become evident to him in conversations with other pastors. "Few, perhaps, have taken more Pains to inform themselves than I have done. I have been a Circle of more than three hundred Miles, and had, by this Means, an Opportunity of going thro' a great Number of Towns in this, and the neighbouring Government of Connecticut, and of having personal Conversation with most of the Ministers, and many

other Gentlemen, in the Country, and of setting a Correspondence with several of them, with a particular View to know, as nearly as might be, the Truth of Things, upon better Evidence than that of meer Hear-Say." He was now convinced: "There never was a Time, in this Land, wherein there was such flocking after some *particular Ministers*, and *glorying* in them, as though they were Gods rather than *Men*; never a Time, wherein *Men's Professions* and *Affections* rose higher; never a Time, wherein *Conversions, numerous* Conversions were so much boasted of: Would to God, there was no Reason to suspect the Truth of any one of them!" He observed that ". . . there may be a very *specious Shew* where there is not the Substance of Religion. . . ."

Edwards and the other supporters of the Awakening had declared the new vigor in the churches to be evidence of God's work in this land of "steady habits." It was this claim that Chauncy wanted to examine. Unlike the revivalists, Chauncy insisted that man could not ordinarily be converted without considerable preparation; the mind as well as the heart needed transformation for a true conversion. The public evidences of a "new birth" are no sure sign of an inward change; it is too easy, Chauncy argued, for a man to deceive himself and to be mistaken about his true state. Though it is not possible for one man to peer into the heart and mind of another to discover if the "change" has been a work of God, there are certain evidences which, if they continue, give strong support for the claim of regeneration. These signs are: love to God and love to neighbor, joy, peace, long-suffering, gentleness, goodness, meekness, and temperance. But, unfortunately, it is frequently the case that these new gifts are lacking in those who have been converted by the revivalists. In their place appear physical disturbances, untempered criticism, and unjustified accusations. "Moreover," Chauncy writes, "the Way in which these Terrors spread themselves is a Circumstance, that does not much favour their *divine Origin*. They seem to be suddenly propagated, from one to another, as in a great Fright Consternation they often begin with a single Person, a *Child*, or *Woman*, or *Lad*, whose *Shrieks* set others a *Shrieking*. . . . And where this has been the Case, there is no great Difficulty in finding out the Cause: Tis far more reasonable to look for it in Nature, than in Grace."

Chauncy attributed much of the excess of the revivals to the itinerant preachers; he describes the preachers as "the true Cause of most of the Disorders." Whitefield, Tennent, and Davenport were not successful diplomats; they entered the "Lord's vineyard" with enthusiasm, not with trepidation. As a result they did not shun attacks on settled clergy or refrain from accusing them of being unconverted and, therefore, unworthy pastors. The Boston area had received visits from these traveling parsons and the eastern Massachusetts churches did not relish their outspoken ways. Chauncy's concern was clear. "I complain not of People's hearing Ministers that are not their own, as they may occasionally happen among them; Nay, I object not against *one* Minister's coming among the People of *another*, on Purpose, that they might have the Benefit of his Gifts and Labours; provided there be a mutual Agreement between *All* the Parties concern'd, and the Case such as may properly call for such an Expedient: But for Ministers to make a Business of going out of their own, into other *Men's* Parishes, unask'd; or, at the Desire of only some disaffected People; And this, in known Opposition to the *settled* Pastors: it's contrary to all *Reason,* as well as *Scripture,* and subversive of all Order in the *Churches;* Especially, when they carry the Matter so far as to *creep into private Houses,* when they can't any longer force themselves into the *Pulpits.* . . ." "Scripture," "reason," and "order": these words recur throughout Chauncy's essay. The New Testament does not encourage the kind of preaching the revivalists offer; reason demands a critical attitude, not merely an emotional response; and the order of the churches must be preserved, or chaos will result. Itineracy can lead only to the disruption of the Church and its Gospel.

Chauncy's *Seasonable Thoughts* was not a theological essay, but it was the first full-length critique of the Great Awakening. Unlike Edwards, Chauncy could analyze the revivals without becoming involved in theological speculation; Edwards could never extricate himself from theological reflection. In addition, Edwards could excuse the excesses of the revivals by arguing that these were but accompanying and secondary features of a "work of God," but Chauncy saw the repeated displays of emotionalism and extravagance as inevitable and undesirable components of the "awakenings." This, in short, was Chauncy's point: "There is the Religion of the Understanding and Judgment, and Will, as well as of the Affections; and if little Account is made of the former, while great Stress is laid upon the latter, it can't be but People should run into Disorders." This advocate of stability, order, and reasonableness was to become one of the leaders of more liberal Arminian theology later in the century and he continued to be a thorn in the side of the consistent Calvinism of Edwards and his successors.

A TREATISE CONCERNING RELIGIOUS AFFECTIONS

Author: Jonathan Edwards (1703-1758)
Type of work: Christian ethics
First published: 1746

PRINCIPAL IDEAS ADVANCED

True religion consists in great part of holy affections.

The affections are vigorous inclinations toward something, or away from something; love, desire, hope, and gratitude are of the former sort; while hatred, fear, anger, and grief are of the latter.

The true religious affections differ from the false affections in the following twelve respects: they are spiritual; they are grounded in the excellence of divine things considered in themselves; they are founded on the moral excellency of divine things; they arise from the mind's enlightenment by divine things; they are attended with a spiritual conviction of the certainty of divine things; they are attended with evangelical humiliation; they are attended with a change of nature in the soul; they promote the spirit of love which was in Christ; they are attended with a Christian tenderness of spirit; they exhibit a beautiful symmetry and proportion; they increase the appetite for spiritual attainments; and they lead to the practice of a Christian life.

Jonathan Edwards' *Treatise Concerning Religious Affections* is a careful attempt to resolve a question of critical pertinence during the Great Awakening of 1740-1743: How is the genuine piety of the true believer to be distinguished from the spurious piety of the emotionally affected convert? How is true religion to be distinguished from false? Edwards put the question in the following manner: "What is the nature of true religion? and wherein do lie the distinguishing notes of that virtue and holiness, that is acceptable in the sight of God."

The thesis is presented almost immediately: "True religion, in great part, consists in holy affections." Edwards claims that this idea is supported by a passage from I Peter 1:8: "Whom having not seen, ye love: in whom, though now ye see him not, yet believing, ye rejoice with joy unspeakable, and full of glory." The words of the Apostle suggest that Christians under persecution were sustained by "a supernatural principle of love to something *unseen;* they loved Jesus Christ. . . ." Furthermore, although the persecuted Christians experienced great suffering, they knew a great spiritual joy. Love and joy— these are holy affections by which true faith can be known. But the problem was to discover signs by which the true religious affections could be distinguished from the false. Not all love and joy are of the gracious and spiritual sort; if it is by reference to the affections that true religion is to be understood, there must be ways of distinguishing the true, holy affections from the false.

But before Edwards could undertake the task of distinguishing the signs of true religious affections, he had to clarify the notion of the affections. He defines the affections as "the more vigorous and sensible exercises of the inclination and will of the soul." The faculty of the soul by which it perceives and speculates, a faculty which Edwards calls the understanding, must be distinguished, he argues, from that other faculty by which the soul is inclined or disinclined, by which it likes or dislikes, is pleased or displeased. The latter faculty, he writes, "is sometimes called the *inclination:* and, as it has respect to the actions that are determined and governed by it, is called the *will:* and the *mind,* with regard to the exercises of this faculty, is often called the *heart.*"

Edwards is careful to point out that what are ordinarily called the affections do not differ essentially from the will; the will is the soul's faculty of inclination, and the affections—such as love and hatred—are distinguishable from the inclinations of the soul which we would call acts of will, only by the greater vigor and liveliness of the affections.

If true religion consists in "vigorous and lively actings of the inclination and will of the soul, or the fervent exercises of the heart," and if by the affections one means precisely the more vigorous and lively of the soul's inclinations, then it follows—so Edwards insists—that true religion consists, in great part, of the affections.

One would be misreading Edwards if one supposed that what Edwards here proposes is that true religion be distinguished from false religion by reference to sentiments, feelings, or emotions. Edwards' criterion is not subjective, for he has defined the affections as inclinations; his definition is pragmatic. It is by the quality of the whole response of the human being to the divine—by the vigorous inclination toward the divine—that the true believer is to be distinguished.

Among the affections which are signs of true religion are the following: godly fear; hope in God; love of God, Christ, and mankind; the hatred of sin, holy joy; religious sorrow, mourning, and "brokenness of heart"; gratitude, compassion, mercy, and zeal. Edwards cites passages from Scripture which lend support to his claims in regard to the particular religious affections.

Of all the affections, Edwards writes, love is the chief religious affection, the "fountain of all other affections." Christ, "the perfect example of true religion and virtue," was the greatest instance of the exercise of the holy affections; and love received its most transforming expression through Him.

Having at some length argued in support of his thesis, Edwards draws some inferences from the proposition that true religion consists in great part of the holy affections. He asserts that those are in error who would abandon the affections as being insubstantial. If true religion lies in the holy affections, then the effort must be made to move those affections; that is, to affect the hearts of men.

Having devoted Part One of his book to the nature of the religious affections and to their importance, Edwards in Part Two reviews twelve presumed signs of the true affections, and the author argues that the presumed signs are not signs at all. One cannot conclude, for example, from the height of affections—that is, from their pitch and intensity—that they are true religious affections; nor can one suppose that when affections are raised to a high degree, they are not true religious affections. Nor can the fact that some affections have a great effect on the body be taken as a sign one way or the other, that those affections are holy. Nor can the tendency of some affections to make men "fervent and abundant" in talking about religious matters be taken as a sign of the spirituality of the affections (nor can it be taken as a sign that the affections are not holy). Nor is the fact that sometimes the affections arise through no effort on the part of the persons who have them, a sign of their being, or not being, true religious affections. Other features of affections which are not significant one way or the other are the following: their being occasioned by Scriptural passages, their giving the appearance of love, their being of great number and of many kinds, their following awakenings of conscience, their disposing persons to spend a great deal of time in external religious duties, their leading persons to praise and glorify God with their mouths, their giving the conviction that the divine is being experienced, and their enabling a per-

son to be affecting and pleasing to the truly godly.

Before going on to present the distinguishing signs of truly holy affections, Edwards warns the reader that there are no rules by which one man can with *certainty* distinguish the true followers of religion from the false; nor can any saint know of his saintly condition with certainty, particularly if he has fallen into "a dead, carnal and unchristian frame." Nor can it be hoped that knowledge of the signs of true religion will lead hypocrites to reform themselves. The rules are nevertheless useful, especially for those who are themselves truly holy, provided that the rules, or signs, are not taken as sufficient in themselves, but as matters to be considered in the context of the Christian experience.

Edwards devotes the remainder of his book to a careful and detailed exposition of twelve signs of true religious affections. He regards extended discussion of the signs as necessary because language is not flexible enough to permit him to make himself clear unless he makes the effort to explore the depth of meaning involved in each summary remark about the signs. Early in the book Edwards remarks: "It must be confessed, that language is here somewhat imperfect, and the meaning of words in a considerable measure loose and unfixed, and not precisely limited by custom, which governs the use of language." To appreciate the true character of Edwards' ideas, then, one must go to the book itself.

The true religious affections "arise from those influences and operations on the heart, which are *spiritual, supernatural* and *divine*." The first sign, then, is *spirituality,* by which Edwards means, not an aspect of the soul as distinguished from the body, but the state of one in whom the Spirit of God dwells; such a one is directly under the influence of the divine supernatural.

The second sign of true religious affections is that they are directed toward the *excellence* of divine things, not out of self-love, but as moved by the glory of the divine considered for its own sake.

The true religious affections are founded, in particular, on the *moral* excellence of divine things. In presenting this third sign of true affections, Edwards emphasizes the power of *holiness*. Although true religious affections are aroused by the excellence of the divine, it is worthy of special mention that they are provoked by the holiness, the moral virtue, of the divine.

The fourth sign of true affections is that they arise from the mind's *understanding* of divine things; enlightenment stirs the affections.

The spiritual *conviction* of those who enjoy truly gracious affections can be taken as a fifth sign of the true affections; those who are truly religious have no doubts about the truth of the Gospel.

Evangelical humiliation is the sixth sign of the gracious affections. By evangelical humiliation Edwards means the sense of insufficiency that a Christian has when he considers how ineffective he would be without God's help, and how unlikely it is that he will be worthy of that help.

The seventh sign of the true religious affections is that they lead to a *change of nature*; the truly religious person is so affected by the divine that he is transformed.

The truly gracious affections *promote the spirit of love*, meekness, mercy, and forgiveness, which Christ possessed. The presence of such a spirit is the eighth sign of the true affections.

The ninth sign is *softness of heart*, the Christian tenderness of spirit. Unlike those who have false affections, true believers do not seek the exaltation of themselves; those with a true love of the divine are not bold or forward.

Those who possess truly gracious affections exhibit *symmetry and proportion* in their affections; the saints "have the whole image of Christ upon them. . . ."

The eleventh sign discussed by Edwards is the *increase of spiritual appetite* which accompanies the true religious affections.

Finally, Edwards presents, as a twelfth sign, the tendency of the true affections to promote *Christian practice*. Since by the affections Edwards meant the inclinations of the soul, and since the inclinations can be understood only by reference to practice, it is inevitable that the true affections "have their exercise and fruit in Christian practice."

Most writers on religious subjects are aware of the difference between the mere profession of belief and the true practice of it, but few writers have, like Edwards, made that difference clear. Edwards' final sign is, in effect, a general sign of the true religious affections. If one wishes to distinguish between the true and the false believer, one has only to see the difference that is made in the lives of those whose inclinations are toward the divine. For Edwards, as for William James, a true religious belief is neither an idle idea nor a passing sentiment; it is an active commitment to the ideal and the divine, and it shows itself in practice. The *Treatise Concerning Religious Affections* is a sensitive appraisal of the difference that true religious affections make in the life of the Christian.

THE DIARY OF DAVID BRAINERD

Author: David Brainerd (1718-1747)
Type of work: Spiritual autobiography
First published: 1749

PRINCIPAL IDEAS ADVANCED

Men must live in such a way that God alone is exalted.

Salvation is through faith in the righteousness of Christ; but before anyone can believe, he must be emptied of all pride and self-righteousness.

Christians ought to pray and work for the conversion of all nations, and to hope for the reign of Christ throughout the world.

David Brainerd is usually remembered in Church history as one of the early Colonial missionaries to the Indians. His enduring importance, however, is rather owing to his *Diary*, which was widely read in evangelical circles both in England and in America during the century following his death. This essentially private record of a soul struggling to be at one with God was partially edited by Brainerd in the closing weeks of his life and was published with additional materials by Jonathan Edwards (1703-1758) as *The Life and Diary of David Brainerd*. Neither Brainerd nor Edwards believed in perfectionism, and there is no attempt in the published any more than in the private work to represent the author as without faults. "But," says Edwards in the Preface, "notwithstanding all these imperfections, I am persuaded, every pious and judicious reader will acknowledge that what is here set before him is indeed a remarkable instance of true and eminent Christian piety in heart and practice, tending greatly to confirm the reality of vital religion, and the power of godliness, that it is most worthy of imitation, and in many ways calculated to promote the spiritual benefit of the careful observer."

David Brainerd was born in Connecticut and reached manhood during the New England Awakening, the religious revival of 1740-1743. A serious youth from a Christian home, he accepted without question the Calvinistic doctrine of God's sovereignty and of the efficacy of Christ's death for the salvation of the elect. His difficulty came when, in line with the new revivalist emphasis, he tried to achieve a personal experience of salvation. Examination of his life merely convinced him that he was among the damned; and the demand of evangelical preaching that he trust only in Christ in order to be saved seemed an impossibility. Frequently, he says, he rebelled against God: "I could not bear that it should be wholly at God's pleasure, to save or damn me, just as He would." But, reflecting on his rebellion, he was more than ever convinced that he belonged to those who deserve to be condemned.

For over a year he spent much of his time in prayer and fasting, spending whole days "in almost incessant cries to God for mercy, that He would open my eyes to see the evil of sin and the way of life by Jesus Christ." Gradually he came to understand that all his religious strivings were centered in himself and that he had no profound regard for God. These thoughts oppressed him, until, one Sabbath evening while "walking in a dark, thick grove," he seemed to have a sense of "unspeakable glory" in his soul. There was, he says, no vision or image, "but it was a new inward apprehension or view that I had of God, such as I had never had before. . . . I never had seen before anything comparable to it for excellency and beauty; it was widely different from all the conceptions that ever I had of God, or things divine. . . . My soul was so captivated and delighted with the excellency, loveliness, greatness, and other perfections of God, that I was even swallowed up in Him. At least to that degree that I had no thought at first, about my own salvation, and scarce reflected there was such a creature as I." In this way, he was brought to exalt God alone, and to subordinate his own life "to aim at His honor and glory, as King of the universe." In addition to perceiving the sovereignty of God, he had a new sense of the wisdom and grandeur of "the way of salvation" which God had ordained, and he became amazed that "all the world did not see and comply with this way of salvation, entirely by the righteousness of Christ."

The sense of God's presence, which remained with Brainerd unbroken for several days, was to return to him frequently through the remainder of his life, in spite of grievous periods of distress and darkness. If Brainerd had been a Roman Catholic, he would no doubt have withdrawn from the world, which, from this time forward, appeared to him always as a distraction, tending to draw his thoughts away from God. But, being a Puritan, he decided to attend Yale College and to prepare himself for the ministry, in spite of his premonitions that his studies and associations would prevent him from leading a life of strict devotion.

The faculty at Yale was unsympathetic with the Great Awakening; and when, during Brainerd's second year, a spirit of revival was felt among Yale students, occasion was found for expelling Brainerd from the College. Two books, parts of the *Diary*, which were written immediately following this trying experience, were destroyed by the author shortly before his death; but the matter is rehearsed at two times subsequently, when evangelical ministers tried to get the college to reverse its decision. With wonderful humility, Brainerd used the event to teach himself meekness and love toward men, and to wean himself away from attachment to worldly honor and approbation.

After his expulsion, Brainerd read theology with various ministers, an experience which may well have been more satisfying than attending Yale would have been. In the course of his devotions, he began to intercede "for poor souls and for the enlargement of Christ's kingdom in the world," and he felt that he ought himself to undertake something for the salvation of "the heathen."

In 1743, he was engaged by the Scottish Society for the Propagation of Christian Knowledge to carry on missionary work, first among the Stockbridge Indians in New England, and later among the Delaware Indians in Pennsylvania and New Jersey. The work at first gave little encouragement, at least for one who sought to bring the experience of vital religion to others. Remarkably, however, Brainerd's preaching produced among the Indians, who had never heard the Gospel before, all the manifestations which characterized the revival of religion in the churches. In the course of a few months, Brainerd brought his new converts to an understanding of Christian doctrine and to an acceptance of Christian obedience which, he testifies, equaled that of awakened Christians anywhere.

The *Diary* tells very little about Brainerd's missionary achievements, being almost entirely a record of his own spiritual pilgrimage; but, at the request of the Scottish Society which employed him, he also kept a *Journal*, in which he related the circumstances of his labors at greater length. Brainerd did not write in order to entertain, and the *Journal*, strictly a report of the progress of Christ's mission, is unadorned with geographical or ethnographical details. An exception is a detailed account of a sacrifice and dance which he came upon at the Indian town of Juneauta, on the Susquehanna: "I sat at a small distance, not more than thirty feet from them

(though undiscovered), with my Bible in my hand, resolving, if possible, to spoil their sport, and prevent their receiving any answers from the infernal world, and there viewed the whole scene." Another is his report of a meeting with an Indian priest, who was something of a reformer among his own people. The priest received him with great courtesy, and told him his own experience. "It was manifest," writes Brainerd, "he had a set of religious notions that he had looked into for himself, and not taken for granted upon bare tradition; and he relished or disrelished whatever was spoken of a religious nature, according as it either agreed or disagreed with his standard." Indians looked upon the Indian priest as a fanatic, but Brainerd remarks, "there was something in his temper and disposition that looked more like true religion than anything I ever observed amongst other heathens."

For the most part, the *Journal* is an account of Brainerd's work at Crossweeksung, in New Jersey, and of the difficulties and discouragements he met with at other points where he regularly preached. The encouraging work at Crossweeksung began with a handful of women and children, who "like the woman of Samaria," traveled several miles to bring their friends together to hear him. In two weeks' time, some fifty persons were brought together; they listened twice a day as Brainerd taught them. When he had to leave, they urged him to come again. One woman said "she wished God would change her heart"; another that "she wanted to find Christ"; a chieftain "wept bitterly with concern for his soul." A month later, when Brainerd returned, "a surprising concern soon became apparent among them." All their conversation seemed to turn on religious matters. In the evening, they would not eat their food until they sent for him to ask a blessing on it. When he preached, there was scarcely one in ten that did not weep and cry out for his sins.

Brainerd made it a point to present to them only "the love and compassion of God in sending His Son to suffer for the sins of men," and thus he said nothing of the wrath of God upon unbelievers. But many of his hearers had the same kind of scruples as he had experienced, and, though invited to come and partake of God's love, were distressed "because they felt themselves unable to come." About a week after his return to Crossweeksung, while he was preaching, "the power of God seemed to descend upon the assembly 'like a mighty rushing wind.'" There was a universal crying out for mercy, those who had previously obtained relief were greatly comforted, and were able to help distressed friends. Many remained for hours, insensible of the time, praying for salvation. "This was indeed a surprising day," writes Brainerd, "and seemed enough to convince an atheist of the truth, importance and power of God's Word."

Like Jonathan Edwards and John Wesley, when they were faced with emotional upheavals caused by their preaching, Brainerd was careful to distinguish between experiences which "appeared solid, rational, and scriptural," and "visionary scenes, imaginary terrors, and all manner of mental disorders and delusions." He relates the story of an Indian woman who went into a trance, and cried out for Christ to take her. "I am very sensible," he says, "there may be great joys arising even to an ecstacy where there is still

no substantial evidence of their being well grounded. But in the present case there seemed to be no evidence wanting in order to prove this joy to be divine, either in regard of its *preparatives, attendants,* or *consequents.*"

Brainerd first entered upon his Indian work in the spring of 1743. He was forced to leave it in the fall of 1746 because of tuberculosis, which had plagued him since his student days. When he left Crossweeksung, it was clear that death was not far off. He was advised to travel when he was able, as a means of prolonging life; but much of the next twelve months he spent in bed, attended by loving friends. He died in Northampton, Mass., at the home of Jonathan Edwards in October, 1747, at the age of twenty-nine.

In the closing months of his life, Brainerd had the opportunity, long denied him, of fellowship with other ministers. He expressed himself at this time much concerned about the counterfeits of true religion, particularly the rise of a kind of sectarian piety which offered salvation by faith without stressing the necessity for godly living. Against these "antinomians," he maintained that "humiliation, self-emptiness, or full conviction of a person's being utterly undone in himself" is essential to a "saving faith," and "that persons being never effectually to die in themselves are never truly united to Christ, and so perish." Another concern which he emphasized was the "future prosperity of Zion," and the necessity for ministers to devote themselves steadfastly to the task of advancing the Kingdom of Christ throughout the world. It seemed to him that the people of Scotland, who sponsored his mission, were more zealous in this matter than those in New England.

The violence of Brainerd's illness sometimes disturbed his reason toward the end, but between attacks of fever he enjoyed great serenity. "I think my mind never penetrated with so much ease and freedom into divine things," he writes after one spell of sickness; "I never felt so capable of demonstrating the truth of many important doctrines of the gospel as now. And as I saw clearly the truth of those great doc-trines, which are justly styled the doctrines of grace; so I saw with no less clearness, that the *essence of religion* consisted in the soul's *conformity to God*, and acting above all selfish views, for *His glory*, longing to be *for Him*, to live to *Him*, and please and honor Him in all things. And this from a clear view of His infinite excellency and worthiness in Himself to be loved, adored, worshiped, and served by all intelligent creatures."

FREEDOM OF THE WILL

Author: Jonathan Edwards (1703-1758)
Type of work: Philosophical theology
First published: 1754

PRINCIPAL IDEAS ADVANCED

The act of volition is determined by the strongest motive which comes to the mind.

Man, being totally depraved, is under a moral necessity of sinning, though he has the natural ability not to sin; that is, there is no physical impediment or external force preventing him from willing the good.

The Arminian notion of liberty as involving self-determination, indifference, and contingency is neither logically defensible nor theologically accurate; the freedom of self determination is inconsistent with moral responsibility.

Man's salvation does not depend on any action of man but is entirely within the control of divine initiative and determination.

In 1754, Jonathan Edwards published *A Careful and strict Enquiry into the modern prevailing Notions of the Freedom of Will, Which is supposed to be essential to Moral Agency, Vertue and Vice, Reward and Punishment, Praise and Blame.* This essay has served to establish Edwards as America's greatest philosopher-theologian and one of the most incisive minds in Christian history. In the two hundred years since its publication over twenty editions have appeared in America and England.

The *Freedom of the Will,* or the *Inquiry,* as Edwards called it, was written during the winter months of 1753 while Edwards was pastor of the small Indian mission church in Stockbridge, Massachusetts. In 1750 he had been dismissed from the pastorate of the Congregational Church in Northampton, Massachusetts, where he had served since 1727. Though the cause for his separation from that church cannot be traced to one source, his strong and persistent defense of Calvinism was a primary factor. In the seven-year period, 1751-1757, during which he served the Stockbridge mission, he was able to complete several of his major treatises: *A Dissertation on the Nature of True Virtue, The Great Christian Doctrine of Original Sin Defended,* and the *Inquiry into the Freedom of Will.* His departure from Stockbridge in 1758 to assume the Presidency of the College of New Jersey (Princeton) and his illness and death in March of that year put an end to a distinguished theological career.

During Edwards' lifetime, the Arminian movement gained support in England and America. Jacob Arminius (1560-1609), a Dutch Reformed theologian, had sought to overcome the harsher aspects of seventeenth century scholastic Calvinism. The issues he raised were dealt with by the Synod of Dort (1619) which reasserted stringent Calvinism: total depravity, unconditional election, limited atonement, irresistible grace, and perseverance of the saints. The Arminians, who were condemned by the Synod, were in conflict with the doctrine of irresistible grace and stressed the view that the decrees of God are conditional upon man's acceptance. In the eighteenth and nineteenth centuries, the Arminians placed more emphasis on human responsibility and agency; less attention was given to divine initiative and decree. The center of Arminian thought in Edwards' time was England, and his treatise was prompted by the writings

of men such as Daniel Whitby (1638-1726), John Taylor (1694-1761), and Isaac Watts (1674-1748).

The theological issue with which the *Inquiry* dealt is simple to state but difficult to solve. If God foreknows human volition, is man's will free? If man's will is self-determined, is God sovereign? Are freedom and necessity exclusive terms? In dealing with this general problem, Edwards divided his essay into two major divisions: 1) the definition and clarification of terms; 2) an analysis of the Arminian position.

The will is determined by the "strongest motive." By motive Edwards meant "the whole of that which moves, excites or invites the mind to volition, whether that be one thing singly, or many things conjunctly. . . . And when I speak of the *strongest motive,* I have respect to the strength of the whole that operates to induce to a particular act of volition, whether that be the strength of one thing alone, or of many together." Every effect has a cause; every act of volition will be the result of the choice of the "greatest apparent good" or "strongest motive." There is a necessary relation between an act of the will and its cause. But this "necessity" may be of two kinds. "Moral necessity" is the "necessity of connection and consequence" which arises from moral causes; "natural necessity" is the "necessity of connection and consequence" which arises from natural causes. Moral necessity is as absolute as natural necessity. For there to be freedom of will, man must have natural ability to will; that is, there must not be any physical impediment or natural defect or extrinsic factor which prevents him from doing as he wills. But man may be morally unable to will other than he does and yet his will is free. Edwards defined "moral inability" as a "want of inclination" or "want of sufficient motives in view" to produce the act of volition. Thus, freedom and liberty meant the "power, opportunity or advantage, that any one has, to do as he pleases." When this discussion is tied to the doctrine of total depravity, the implications of this view become clear. Man, because of original sin, is morally unable to will the good; yet he has no physical impediment standing in the way. Man is free, but free only to sin. To put it in another way, man is free to do what he wills, but not to do what he does not will. Because man is inherently depraved, he does not will to do the good.

In Part II of the essay, Edwards turned to the problem of whether there can be any freedom of the will as the Arminians spoke of it. According to Edwards, the Arminian idea of liberty involved three points: 1) self-determination of the will; that is, the will is not dependent on any cause outside itself; 2) indifference; that is, previous to the act of volition the mind is in a state of equilibrium; 3) contingency; that is, the will is governed by no necessity. Edwards dealt with each of these assertions.

If the will is self-determined, which means that it has its actions under its control, every volition must arise from a previous volition. As the train of choices is carried back, Edwards argued, we must come to the first volition in the whole series. If that first volition be self-determined, then it is not really the first volition, for a previous volition must have determined it. Yet, if that first volition is not determined by a preceding act of the will, the will is not self-determined. If the first act of the will is not free, in the Arminian

sense of freedom, then none of the following acts are free. Thus, it follows that the will cannot be self-determined.

The argument that the act of volition is the result of the mind's state of indifference was equally inconsistent to Edwards, for this view implies that the mind prefers a choice, but has no preference. The "grand argument . . . that among several things the Will actually chooses one before another, at the same time that it is perfectly indifferent . . . is the very same thing as to say, the mind has a preference, at the same time that it has no preference." Edwards' assumption that every effect has a cause, that every act of volition is the result of the "strongest motive," would not allow this Arminian position. In a similar vein he dealt with the idea of liberty as consisting in contingency. Either an act of the will has a cause or it does not. If it does, it is not contingent, but necessary; that is, dependent on its cause. If it does not have a cause, which Edwards would allow only for the argument, then the will operates contingently without any determining cause. Under such circumstances, however, the will would not be active but passive; it would will by accident. Such willing would be mere capriciousness, not liberty or freedom, and consequently the freedom of indifference cannot allow for moral responsibility.

Underlying the Arminians' position was their difficulty with Calvinistic theology in relation to human responsibility. If man's will is not self-determined, they argued, then man is not deserving of praise or blame for his actions. Edwards agreed that if the "necessity" under which man wills is a *natural* necessity, then an act of volition cannot be described as praiseworthy or blameworthy. But if the act is done under "moral necessity," then the agent is subject to judgment. Man cannot will except as causally determined; hence, the only question is one concerning the nature of the cause. Since man is unable without the saving grace of Christ to do anything good and acceptable in God's sight, he is under a *moral* necessity to sin, the conditions of which have been determined and foreknown by God. "Providence infers some kind of necessity of all events, such a necessity as implies an infallible, previous fixedness of the futurity of the event. . . ."

Edwards did not intend to suggest that God commits sin, but that He is the "disposer of events" in such a way that sin will inevitably follow, though for holy ends. God's foreknowledge of events does not limit man's freedom. Critics then charged Edwards with making God into the cause of sin and, therefore, denying human responsibility. But, as Edwards argued, since all free actions are necessary actions, since no free act is undetermined, God's determination of events does not preclude human freedom. Man is free, even though he sins, because the "strongest motive" which determines his mind is a sinful motive; nevertheless, it is man's will that is responsible, not God's will. Man is responsible for his actions even though they are committed under a moral necessity of sinning. Freedom consists in the absence of any external compulsion, not in the absence of all causes whatsoever. Thus, in attempting to reconcile God's sovereignty with human freedom, Edwards calls attention to the fact that man chooses in accordance with his inclination; that is, as determined by the "strongest motive." Man is free, even though his nature

puts him under a moral necessity to sin; that is, man is free, and in the exercise of his freedom he wills to sin.

Edwards' position illustrates the dilemma of a Calvinist who was both a revivalist and a predestinarian. God has determined that some will be damned, others saved. How is it possible to call men to repentance and also to assert God's predetermined election of some and damnation of others? The only solution that Edwards offered was to insist that although the "means of grace," that is, Church communion, participation in the sacraments, hearing and reading the Word, do not determine a man's ultimate destiny, unless one attends to the "means of grace," evidence is given of a lost condition. Edwards always presupposed that God's choice of some and damnation of others was in no way affected by man's action, except that those who participated in the Church gave stronger evidence of their saved state. The work of redemption is entirely God's action. True faith does not depend on man's "free" will, but on the sovereign Will of God; conversion is not the result of man's self-determination, but of God's impressing the soul with holy affections; the perseverance of the saints is due not to human action, but to God's saving and sustaining grace. Man's salvation is not dependent on his contingent, self-determined will, but is "absolutely fixed in God's decree. . . ." Reason and Scripture attest to this fact, Edwards claims.

The *Inquiry* prompted immediate discussion, though few who challenged Edwards were his equals. By far the best reply was that of James Dana, *An Examination of the Late Reverend President Edwards's 'Enquiry on Freedom of Will'*, published in 1770.

Throughout the remainder of the eighteenth century the essay of Edwards received attention from its defenders and opponents. The *Inquiry into the* *Freedom of Will* is a key document in the total theological work of Jonathan Edwards.

THE GREAT CHRISTIAN DOCTRINE OF ORIGINAL SIN DEFENDED

Author: Jonathan Edwards (1703-1758)
Type of work: Theology
First published: 1758

PRINCIPAL IDEAS ADVANCED

The doctrine of original sin is a cornerstone of the Christian Gospel.

Unless man were totally depraved, there would be no need for the redemptive work of Christ or the Scriptural requirement for a change of heart for entrance into the Kingdom of God.

To explain sin by asserting that it is the result of bad example or the misuse of freedom is to neglect its basic cause.

The universality of sin is evidence for the inherent depravity of human nature.

Any transgression of God's law deserves eternal punishment, and no good act can remove the damage to God's moral government.

Jonathan Edwards' *The Great Christian Doctrine of Original Sin Defended; Evidences of Its Truth Produced, and Arguments to the Contrary Answered* was published shortly after his death in 1758. Though the subject had long been a primary concern of Edwards, he had to wait until the later years of his life, during the time of his missionary work at Stockbridge, Massachusetts, to complete the treatise. The essay was directed against Arminian theology and was specifically prompted by the work of the English theologian, John Taylor, who published *The Scripture-Doctrine of Original Sin* in 1740.

The Arminian movement began in reaction to the severe and legalistic flavor of scholastic Calvinism and its stringent assertions of total depravity, unconditional election, and irresistible grace. Jacob Arminius (1560-1609) and his followers regarded themselves as Calvinists, but were concerned to uphold the moral responsibility of man for his actions and the necessary response of man to God's redeeming work. In the eighteenth century Arminian theologians openly attacked such key Calvinistic assertions as the doctrine of the total depravity of man and the imputation of Adam's sin. They emphasized man's ability to comply with the demands of the Gospel. By the third decade of the eighteenth century Arminianism in England had become orthodoxy, not heresy.

In his essay, John Taylor argued that Scripture does not teach the imputation of Adam's sin to his descendants. Our nature is not to blame for our sin. Sin is the choice to do wrong, though nothing within man's nature compels such action. The denial of original sin, the emphasis on moral responsibility as in itself incompatible with a doctrine of total depravity, the denial of the doctrine of election, the stress on moral living, the rejection of creed or confession as being determinative of theological formulation—these were the interests of Taylor and the Arminian movement of the eighteenth century. Jonathan Edwards was the only theologian of the time to give Taylor's essay a thoroughgoing critique; others tried, but most, like Isaac Watts, found themselves embarrassed by the answers a strict Calvinist should give.

Edwards' *Doctrine of Original Sin Defended* is a different kind of work from his *Inquiry into the Freedom of Will,* though these two are complementary and integrally related. In the *Inquiry* Edwards argued from certain given premises and proceeded through logical analysis and semantic clarification to reduce the Arminian position to confusion. The later work, *Doctrine of Original Sin Defended,* attempted to refute the Arminians on the basis of common evidence. Edwards insisted that his opponents were simply not facing up to the hard facts of life and that their explanations for the existence of human wrongdoing were highly superficial and grossly misleading. No Arminian would deny that man is sinner, but the Arminians differed with the Calvinists concerning the nature and extent of sin.

In his analysis, Edwards' first appeal was to the "evidences of original sin from facts and events, as founded by observation and experience. . . ." The very fact that there is an acknowledged tendency to sin in man, as is witnessed to in history and present experience, displays the "propensity" of man's nature. It is irrelevant to speak of "the innocent and kind actions, even of criminals themselves . . . and of the prevailing innocence, good nature, industry, felicity, and cheerfulness of the greater part of mankind." To argue that men are able to do some good is the same as "to pronounce that road a good road to go to such a place, the greater part of which is plain and safe, though some parts of it are dangerous, and certainly fatal to them that travel in it. . . ." Good cannot balance out evil. Any transgression of God's law, of whatever degree, deserves eternal punishment; no good act can erase sin.

Taylor and other Arminians attempted to explain the existence of sin. One of these arguments was similar to that expressed by the fifth century monk, Pelagius (c. 360-c.420); namely, that man sins because of bad examples of his predecessors. This argument, to Edwards, "is accounting for the thing by the thing itself." It does not explain the "bad example." That "bad examples" are general all over the world and "have been so from the beginning, is only an instance, or rather a description of that corruption of the world which is to be accounted for." Some argued that sin is a misuse of freedom. The Arminians had continually insisted that if men are to be morally responsible for their action, the sins they commit must be the result of free choices. In reply Edwards asks the question: "If their wills are in the first place as free to good as evil, what is it to be ascribed to, that the world of mankind, consisting of so many millions, in so many successive generations, without consultation, all agree to exercise their freedom in favor of evil?" His own answer was that the general and continuing disobedience of man is evidence for the fact that the cause of sin is "fixed, and that the fixed cause is *internal,* in man's nature. . . ."

There were three main arguments used by Arminian theologians against the doctrine of total depravity. Taylor, for example, insisted that if man is totally depraved, then he is under a necessity of sinning; a necessary sin is not a sin. Edwards dealt with this charge in his *Inquiry into the Freedom of Will,* in which he made the celebrated distinction between moral and natural necessity, insisting that moral necessity in no way cancels accountability, though natural necessity does.

The Arminians also argued that if men come into existence in a state of corruption, God must be the author of sin. Edwards offered another explanation. In creating man, God implanted within him two kinds of principles. One was of an inferior nature, the natural principle, which the "Scriptures sometimes call *flesh.*" In addition, the superior principle, that is, the image of God, was also present. As long as these two principles operated within Adam's nature, he lived in communion with God. When he sinned, however, the superior principle left him and Adam was "in a state of darkness, woeful corruption and ruin; nothing but flesh without spirit." Adam's sin, therefore, was due to the violation of his own inferior nature and not to any creating act of God.

A third Arminian challenge to the doctrine of total depravity rested on a rejection of the imputation of Adam's sin to his descendants. Taylor regarded this imputation as unjust, because no man should be held responsible for another man's wrongdoing. There are two traditional interpretations of the doctrine of imputation. One, traducianism, asserted that Adam's sin was transmitted through human genes; parents pass on guilt to their children. Another interpretation, the federal theory, spoke of Adam as the representative of mankind; when he sinned, his guilt was imputed to his descendants because Adam was chosen to stand in their place. Jonathan Edwards offered another interpretation. He answered Taylor by saying that God has always treated Adam as being one with his posterity. "The *first existing* of a corrupt disposition in their hearts is not to be looked upon as sin belonging to them, *distinct* from their participation of Adam's first sin: it is as it were the *extended pollution* of that sin, through the whole tree, by virtue of the constituted *union* of the branches with the root. . . ." Man's involvement in Adam's first sin is the result of a personal identity between Adam and his descendants. "And therefore the sin of the apostasy is not theirs [Adam's descendants'], merely because God *imputes* it to them; but it is *truly* and *properly* theirs, and on that ground, God *imputes* it to them." Edwards was denying the traditional ways of defending the imputation of Adam's sin to mankind and asserting that men sin because of their "constituted oneness" with Adam, a oneness which is dependent upon God's continual creation of each individual through time as one with Adam.

In discussing the centrality of the doctrine of original sin in the scheme of the Christian Gospel, Edwards also considered corollary issues. He devoted an entire section of his treatise to the relation of this doctrine to the work of Christ. "The representations of the redemption by Christ, everywhere in Scripture, lead us to suppose, that *all* whom he came to redeem, are *sinners;* that his salvation, as to the term *from which* (or the evil to be redeemed from) in *all* is *sin,* and the deserved *punishment* of sin." If men were not totally and inherently sinners, the work of Christ would be unnecessary and meaningless. Scripture also insists that a "change of heart" is necessary for entrance into the Kingdom of God. If

men were not totally and inherently sinful, there would be no need to undergo such a "change of heart." The whole scheme of the Christian Gospel rests upon the doctrine of original sin.

Edwards' essay provoked lengthy and involved debate. Some Calvinists were unhappy with Edwards' metaphysical excursions, especially in relation to his discussion of imputation. The Arminians were not convinced by his argument, for they were still bothered by the problem of moral responsibility; neither the *Inquiry into the Freedom of Will* nor the *Doctrine of Original Sin Defended* solved this issue for them. Edwards' treatise, however, served to keep the doctrine of original sin in the forefront of New England theological debate for the remainder of the eighteenth century.

THE CREED OF A SAVOYARD PRIEST

Author: Jean Jacques Rousseau (1712-1778)
Type of work: Philosophy of natural religion
First published: 1762

Principal Ideas Advanced

Although man's intellect cannot fathom these matters, his heart witnesses to the existence of God, to the freedom of the will, and to a life beyond the grave.

Positive religions are inferior to the natural religion of the heart; men ought, however, to worship God according to the usage of the country of their birth.

The Christian Gospel, in spite of many absurdities, speaks faithfully to men's hearts.

When, in *Émile,* Rousseau comes to the question how his young man is to be taught religion, he tells of the encouragement which he himself received as a youth from a kindly but unorthodox priest whom he chanced to

meet during his wanderings in northern Italy. *The Creed of a Savoyard Priest* is Rousseau's reconstruction of remarks privately made to him when the priest judged that his pupil was ready to consider fundamental religious ideas. The ideas expressed are those of Rousseau's own maturity. How far the anonymous Savoyard is responsible for introducing them to Rousseau is difficult to determine.

Writing in France at the height of the Enlightenment, Rousseau takes the ground of natural theology. Reason and the testimony of the heart are pitted against revelation and authority. Rousseau objects that alleged revelations are always remote in time and place, so that their claim to be authentic is properly an object of historical scholarship, not a requirement for holy living. The testimony of the heart, on the other hand, is immediate and universal. Montaigne to the contrary notwithstanding, man's heart everywhere inclines him to revere the Author of Nature, and to obey the law which is inscribed in conscience.

Rousseau protested against the extreme forms which rationalism had taken in his time. Like contemporary pietists, who found more reality in the "religion of the heart" than in the dogmas of the churches, he found feeling to be a surer guide than the arguments of the philosophers. "In vain," he makes his priest declare, "do you argue this point with me; I feel it, and it is this feeling which speaks to me more forcibly than the reason which disputes it." And again, "If all the philosophers in the world should prove that I am wrong, and you feel that I am right, that is all I ask." We must note, however, that the feeling (*sensibilité*) of which Rousseau speaks is less an emotion than a kind of moral insight comparable to what English philosophers such as Lord Shaftesbury (1671-1713) referred to as "moral sense." Rousseau's complaint is directed against strict materialists like

Julien Offray de La Mettrie (1709-1751), who tried to reason out the nature of the world and man on the basis of certain axioms concerning matter and motion. It is against their "absurdities" that the native witness of the heart speaks out.

The vicar's beliefs may fairly be described as a variety of deism. Beginning with reflections upon his own nature, he arrives at three fundamental principles of belief. The first is that, just as in man there is an active principle or will which is the origin of our spontaneous motions, so in the world at large we may reason back from one cause to another until we come to a spontaneous, voluntary action. "I believe, therefore, that there is a will which sets the universe in motion and gives life to nature," says the vicar. The second article of his creed arises out of the uniformity and harmony of nature, which is so far from the chaos which would have resulted if the world were simply the result of chance. These considerations point him to an intelligent, thinking being. "If matter in motion points me to a will, matter in motion according to fixed laws points me to an intelligence; that is the second article of my creed," claims the vicar. The third principle has to do not with God but with man's place in the order of things. Reflecting upon the disparity within man's breast between the part of him which raises him to truth, justice, and benevolence, and that part which draws him downward and enslaves him to matter, the vicar concludes that man's soul belongs to another realm than the body: "Man is therefore free to act, and as such he is animated by an immaterial substance; that is the third article of my creed."

From these three principles, says the vicar, the remainder of his system can be deduced. He is particularly concerned to deal with the problem of evil, which, as in Rousseau's earlier *Essay on Inequality* (1754), is explained as arising out of human progress. Essentially, the solution offered by the vicar is the Stoic solution: "There is no evil but the evil you do or the evil you suffer, and both come from yourself." Evil arises only out of disorder, but there can be no disorder in the physical world. Hence, evil "exists only in the minds of those who experience it; and this feeling is not the gift of nature, but the work of man himself." He admits that God has an obligation to His creatures; namely, to perform all that His act of creating them implied. But man can have no complaint on this score, because "God's justice consists in demanding from each of us an account of that which he has given us." To question whether God was wise and benevolent in not preventing us from doing wrong is to murmur against Him "because he has made man of so excellent a nature, that he has endowed his actions with that morality by which they are ennobled, that he has made virtue man's birthright." Happiness, according to the vicar, does not reside in the absence of pain or struggle, but in the sense of achievement which comes from being a co-creator with God. God has limited man's power, the vicar points out, so that man's misuse of freedom cannot upset the general order; thus limited, man's capacity for choosing his own way is his greatest dignity.

God's providence is further vindicated in the assurance of a life beyond the grave. "Had I no other proof of the immaterial nature of the soul," says the vicar, "the triumph of the wicked and the oppression of the righteous in this world would be enough to convince me." But, as we have seen, there are other evidences that the soul does not die, and these arguments suggest not only that the righteous will be happy, but that the wicked too will repent once they have been freed from the deceit and grossness of their bodily senses. God has no need for vengeance, says the priest. Such Hell as there is "is here in the breast of the wicked." When men have ceased to be bad, they can never be miserable. If, contrary to these speculations, there is eternal punishment, we must submit our feeble reason to divine justice, but if the remorse of the wicked comes to an end, so that the same peace shall be the lot of all mankind, then we shall be grateful. "Is not the wicked my brother?" asks the vicar; "How often have I been tempted to be like him? Let him be delivered from his misery and freed from the spirit of hatred that accompanied it; let him be as happy as I myself; his happiness, far from arousing my jealousy, will only increase my own."

In eighteenth century Europe, as the priest points out, there are three major faiths: the Jews have one revelation, the Christians two, the Turks three. Because it is impossible to decide between them, each man is wise to follow the faith in which he was brought up. He can do this without subscribing to all its dogmas and without hating or persecuting adherents of other faiths. Moreover, he should do it, both for his own and for his neighbor's well-being, for, according to Rousseau, "irreligion, and the argumentative philosophic spirit generally . . . assaults life and enfeebles it, degrades the soul, concentrates all the passions in the basest self-interest, in the meanness of the human self; thus it saps unnoticed the very foundations of all society."

In line with these principles, the Savoyard priest advised the youthful Rousseau to return to the Church of Geneva, which is commended by the vicar for its purity of life. As for himself, brought up in the Roman Church, he could imagine no higher privilege than serving as a priest in a humble mountain parish, mixing works of charity with reverent worship, and teaching men the sublime truths of the Gospel.

The vicar testifies that the Gospel speaks with the voice of the heart itself, so simply and convincingly that one might well ask whether it is not of divine, rather than human, origin. He finds the portrait of Christ quite without parallel in human history, and, contrary to the vogue of eighteenth century deism, he refuses to place Soc-

rates on the same level with Christ. However, the Gospel contains inconsistencies and other features repugnant to reason, which make one wary of accepting it as divine. Let a man, therefore, suspend judgment "in the sight of the Divine Being who alone knows the truth," and respect in silence what he can neither leave aside nor comprehend. Such "skepticism," continues the vicar, need not be painful, because it does not extend to matters of practice. It is not to be confused with the destructive skepticism of the dogmatic philosophers who, claiming that they alone are enlightened, overthrow all that men revere, rob the afflicted of their consolation, remove the bridle from men's passions, and abolish the very distinction between virtue and vice. "Truth, they say, can never do a man harm. I think so too," says the vicar; "and to my mind that is strong evidence that what they teach is not true."

A PLAIN ACCOUNT OF CHRISTIAN PERFECTION

Author: John Wesley (1703-1791)
Type of work: Theology of holiness
First published: 1766

PRINCIPAL IDEAS ADVANCED

Christian perfection is attained when perfect love of God and neighbor rules a person's heart and words and actions.

Christian perfection is a gift of God's grace that may be experienced in earthly life, occurring sometime after justification and before death and being wrought by faith.

Christian perfection is both instantaneous and gradual; the process of sanctification (cleansing from sin) that begins with justification (forgiveness of sin) may culminate in an instant in entire sanctification (perfect holiness).

Christian perfection is not necessarily permanent, for it may be lost and recovered; it may also be improved, and growth in grace is expected after entire sanctification and, indeed, throughout eternity.

Christian perfection is not absolute, for God alone is absolutely perfect; nor should it be called sinless, unless the term "sin" is limited to denote a voluntary transgression of a known divine law.

John Wesley, a priest of the Church of England from 1728 until his death in 1791, was the leading spirit of the Evangelical Revival in Great Britain during the eighteenth century. Together with his brother Charles (1707-1788) and George Whitefield (1714-1770), a forceful preacher who leaned toward a Calvinist theological position, Wesley organized the "societies" and "bands" within the Anglican communion that subsequently were called "Methodist," a term initially meant to be derisive. One of the cardinal emphases of the Methodist movement was personal holiness, and Wesley explicated and defended this doctrine in his *A Plain Account of Christian Perfection.*

Theological emphases are rarely understood apart from their historical context, and this is true of John Wesley's call for Christians to lead a holy life. In a time when deism offered an absentee God and rationalism a shallow moralism, there arose an alarming lack of spiritual vitality and discipline in the Church of England, which seemed more intent upon political affiliation than the regeneration of the individual and social life of the people. The laboring classes were becoming more and more estranged from the established Church, and public morality and responsibility had reached a low ebb. Religious figures sensitive to the problems of the age began to express concern, but it was the Wesleys and their co-workers who both focused and

fanned the protesting spirit and kindled a revival that swept through the British Isles and then to America. The heart of the message proclaimed and sung by these eighteenth century evangelists was "salvation through Jesus Christ," and the response demanded was "faith working through love."

In *A Plain Account of Christian Perfection,* which he published in 1766 at the age of 63, John Wesley looks back upon forty years of teaching this most controversial of all Methodist doctrines. His purpose, he declares, is "to give a plain and distinct account of the steps by which I was led, during a course of many years, to embrace the doctrine of Christian perfection." He believes he owes this to "the serious part of mankind"; namely, those who desire to know all the truth as it is in Jesus. For Wesley, "all the truth" included not only justification by faith, but also the holy life of love.

Already in 1725, when only 23 years old, Wesley had resolved to dedicate his whole life to God, since he was convinced that there was no middle way between serving God and serving the Devil. At that time he was greatly impressed by the emphasis on purity of intention in *Rules and Exercises of Holy Living and Holy Dying,* devotional writings by Anglican Bishop Jeremy Taylor (1613-1667). During the following two years he was further affected by the stress on the inward religion of the heart in *Imitation of*

Christ, the medieval ascetical writing attributed to Thomas à Kempis (c.1380-1471), and by the spiritual writings of William Law (1686-1761), whose *On Christian Perfection* and *A Serious Call to a Devout and Holy Life* convinced Wesley that it was impossible to be "half a Christian."

Wesley asserts that in 1729 he began not merely to read but also to study the Bible as the one and only standard of truth and model of pure religion, which he defined as "a uniform following of Christ, an entire inward and outward conformity to our Master." In his renowned sermon on "The Circumcision of the Heart," which he preached in St. Mary's Church at Oxford University on January 1, 1733, Wesley struck the note that characterized his understanding of perfection; namely, that *love* is the perfect good, the sum of the perfect law. He exhorted his hearers with these words: "Let the spirit return to God that gave it, with the whole train of its affections. Other sacrifices from us He would not: but the living sacrifice of the heart hath He chosen. Let it be continually offered up to God, through Christ, in flames of holy love."

This understanding of Christian perfection as perfect love, and of perfect holiness as the habitual disposition of soul that implies being cleansed from sin and from all filthiness of flesh and spirit and being endued with those virtues that were in Christ Jesus, remained unchanged throughout Wesley's missionary service in Georgia, his inspiring encounter with the German Moravians, and his famous heart-warming experience during the reading of Luther's *Introduction to Romans* at Aldersgate Street Chapel on May 24, 1738. These experiences undoubtedly deepened his understanding of faith and the need for individual conversion, but the essence of Christian perfection remained the same throughout the remainder of his life. A perfect Christian is one who loves the Lord with all his heart and soul and mind and strength, and Wesley intended that a Methodist be no less than this.

The Methodist doctrine of perfection, celebrated especially in the various volumes of hymns and sacred poems published by John and Charles Wesley, drew sharp criticism from opponents who argued that there is no perfection on earth and that the mere notion of perfection not only attacked the Reformation principle of justification by faith, but also dishonored Christ by implying that some Christians could reach a stage in life in which they no longer needed a Savior. Wesley expresses surprise that the doctrine should be so misunderstood, since he and his brother had always held to justification by faith and had ascribed the whole of salvation to the mere grace of God. The point the Wesleys wanted to emphasize is that Christ not only justifies the sinner, but also renews him in the image of God, in righteousness and true holiness. The gift of salvation entails both the forgiveness of sin and the cleansing from sin, the latter being the work of the Holy Spirit, who dwells in the heart of the man of faith and sets him free.

Wesley takes care to specify the nature of Christian freedom. Perfection does not imply freedom from ignorance or mistake or temptation or any of the numerous infirmities connected with flesh and blood. Nor does perfection imply freedom from doing good or from attending all the ordinances of

God, such as participating in the Lord's Supper, searching the Scriptures, fasting, and praying. The freedom of "perfect Christian" is a freedom not to commit sin (knowingly) and a freedom from evil thought and evil tempers. The perfect Christian is both outwardly and inwardly devoted to God, and he has the mind of Christ, so that all his thoughts, words, and actions are governed by pure love. Wesley conceded that one filled with pure love might make a mistake that would occasion a transgression of God's perfect law and thus require Christ's atonement, but it was his opinion that such an error is not properly called a "sin."

Every Christian, including those who live without sin, needs Christ as Mediator. All are dependent upon Christ, just as branches are dependent upon their root. The free gift of grace is not simply from Christ, but also *in* Him, and all blessings depend on His continual intercession. Furthermore, even the best of men need Christ to atone for their involuntary transgressions of the divine law, those omissions, shortcomings, mistakes, and defects of various kinds that are inseparable from mortal existence. Since Wesley defines sin as "a voluntary transgression of a known law," he does not consider involuntary transgressions to be sins in the proper sense. Because of the ambiguity of the phrase, however, he prefers never to speak of "sinless perfection." He also makes it clear that Christian perfection is not absolute, since absolute perfection belongs to God alone; Christian perfection is capable of being lost and recovered and improved, since one never stops "growing in grace."

In regard to the question when perfection is attained in life, Wesley contends that it happens instantaneously, being wrought by faith in a moment, and this generally just before death. Nevertheless, it should be striven after and expected *every moment*, and it often occurs years before death. The Christian life begins with justification, when man's sin is forgiven, and continues from this point of new birth with a process of sanctification which involves the gradual removal of all inward sin. Perfection is reached in the instant that all sin is removed and man is entirely sanctified. For this reason it can be conceived as both gradual and instantaneous.

Wesley was convinced that few attain perfection in this life, because there are few who really seek it. Although he emphasized that it was a gift received by faith, he also stressed that faith is not given by God unless it is diligently sought in the way He has ordained; namely, through vigorous obedience, vigilant watchfulness, daily self-denial and cross-bearing, regular prayer and fasting, and close attendance upon all the ordinances of God. Wesley saw little use of speaking about perfection to anyone who was not striving after it, for the doctrine would inevitably be misunderstood.

To the question how one can know that he has attained perfect love, Wesley answered that there is no infallible proof. No one is in a position to judge another, although "reasonable proof" would certainly include clear evidence of exemplary behavior for some time before the supposed change, the rendering of a distinct account of the time and manner wherein the change was wrought, and an indication that all subsequent words and actions were holy and blameless. An individual might judge himself to have attained perfection if he has experienced the gradual mortification of sin and the renewal to a full life of love, but to this must be added an indispensable element: the inner testimony of the Holy Spirit.

Although Wesley was deeply impressed by the witness of personal experience and by the visible fruits of the Spirit, he was opposed to "enthusiasts" who made a vain show of perfection, and who fancied that they could no longer be tempted or feel pain, or that they had special gifts of prophecy and of discerning the spirits. Such enthusiasm, asserted Wesley, is the daughter of pride, and it leads quite naturally to antinomianism. Rather than having purity of intention, the mind that was

in Christ, and the love of God and neighbor, enthusiasts distort Scripture, disesteem reason, expect the end without the means, misunderstand growing in grace, and fail to consider that love is the highest gift of all.

In spite of its terminological and theological difficulties, the doctrine of Christian perfection was filled with profound meaning by John Wesley, who believed in the promise and power of the Spirit to effect a "real, inward change" in the believer, and who took seriously the injunction of Christ: "Therefore ye shall be perfect, as your Father who is in heaven is perfect." (Matthew 5:48.)

THE JOURNAL OF JOHN WOOLMAN

Author: John Woolman (1720-1772)
Type of work: Religious autobiography
First published: 1774

PRINCIPAL IDEAS ADVANCED

The person who truly loves God loves Him in all His manifestations in the visible world; that is, in all living beings, animals as well as men.

All men, if they patiently listen for the inner divine voice, will hear it clearly and certainly.

The individual should live according to the light of his conscience no matter what his neighbors or the world in general may think of his actions.

John Woolman was born in 1720 into a large Quaker family in Northampton, Burlington County, in West Jersey, about twenty miles east of Philadelphia. His first twenty-one years were spent on his father's farm, after which he became an assistant in a general store in nearby Mount Holly. He learned the trade of tailoring from his master and later established his own

business. He married in 1749 and was the father of one child. He was a schoolmaster for a period of time and published a primer. Active among the Friends, he often undertook extensive journeys—often uncomfortable and sometimes dangerous—to visit Friends' meetings in the American colonies. He died while in England.

These are the externals of the life of

Woolman but they tell us little of the power and lasting influence of the man. It is the inner development of John Woolman, as revealed in his *Journal*, that indicates the profound relevance for our time of this simple, unpretentious man. Woolman began his *Journal* when he was thirty-six. Due to the fact that he was well-read from early childhood, the *Journal*, as well as his other works, is written in a felicitous and often moving style.

Although Woolman is careful to note details of his life and especially of his travels, these act merely as a framework for the development of his spiritual life. The *Journal* more than anything else is a diary of the development of an amazingly sensitive conscience. But Woolman could not rest with the cultivation of the inner life. Like Friends before and since, he was impelled by conscience to witness publicly to his convictions. At times this attitude marked him as curiously individualistic and eccentric.

Woolman begins the *Journal* with an account of his religious growth. From early childhood he was intensely serious. "Before I was seven Years old I began to be acquainted with the Operations of divine Love. Through the Care of my Parents, I was taught to read nearly as soon as I was capable of it; and, as I went from School one seventh Day, I remember, while my Companions went to play by the Way, I went forward out of Sight, and, sitting down, I read the 22d Chapter of the *Revelations:* 'He shewed me a pure River of Water of Life, clear as Chrystal, proceeding out of the Throne of God and of the Lamb, *etc.*' and, in reading it, my Mind was drawn to seek after that pure Habitation, which, I then believed, God had prepared for his Serv-

ants. The Place where I sat, and the Sweetness that attended my Mind, remain fresh in my Memory."

It is to be expected that a child who so early became aware of the demands of the religious life was to suffer many temptations and backslidings. Looking back, Woolman makes much of his involvement with "wanton" company, but, like Augustine, he was writing many years after the event and from a puritanical viewpoint and thus no doubt exaggerates the seriousness of his offenses. In time he put such "snares" behind him and by attending regularly the Friends' Meetings and by reading the Scriptures "and other good Books" so developed in piety and devotion that he was recognized by his fellow Friends as worthy of recognition as a minister. (Among the Friends, of course, ministerial status did not involve clerical duties.)

Woolman's developing sensitivity was not restricted to his fellow man; he "was early convinced in Mind" that the person who truly learns to love God and to "exercise true Justice and Goodness" loves Him "in all his Manifestations in the visible World." For a person to say he loves God and at the same time to act cruelly toward "the least Creature, is a Contradiction in itself." Throughout his *Journal* Woolman expresses the most poignant concern for the sufferings of animals.

Woolman chose to learn the trade of tailoring because he was convinced that it was the kind of occupation that would leave his mind free to ponder religious problems. He admitted, however, that there were times when he found it difficult to repress the feeling that he should aspire to a more exalted station in life. But Woolman's tailoring did not shelter him from problems of conscience. Indeed, so successful did his business become that he found it necessary to discontinue these profitable sources of income in order to preserve his peace of mind.

It was his literacy, relatively rare then, that caused Woolman's greatest problems and, it can be said, made it possible for him to struggle with the greatest evil of his day. Because of his facility with the pen he was often called upon to write bills of sale, wills, and other legal documents. This inevitably put him in the position of being the instrument by which human beings were exchanged as chattel. The problem of slavery, from the day he was first called upon to write a bill of sale to the day of his death, was to be Woolman's major concern. His first bill of sale of a Negro was his last; he wrote it only because the sale was to an elderly member of the Society of Friends. Woolman, uneasy in conscience, executed the instrument although protesting that he believed ownership of slaves inconsistent with Christianity. "This in some Degree abated my Uneasiness; yet, as often as I reflected seriously upon it, I thought I should have been clearer, if I had desired to have been excused from it, as a Thing against my Conscience. . . ." Woolman never hesitated again. From that day forth, whenever the occasion arose, he spoke his conscience to those making the request of him and, so earnest was his concern that many consciences were quickened thereby. Woolman, instead of being the instrument of evil, became an instrument of manumission.

John Woolman's campaign against slavery was not limited to his business life, however. Increasingly he agitated within Friends' circles against the evil.

He spoke in countless meetings throughout the colonies and published several tracts. He is often given credit for the major effort against slavery among the Friends, an effort which resulted in abolition of slaveholding in that body by the eve of the Revolution.

If Woolman's effort in behalf of abolition was his most dramatic accomplishment, it was by no means his only concern. His *Journal* is the record of the development of a multitude of religious and social concerns. Woolman had to witness against snares to the soul wherever he found them and no matter how much personal discomfort resulted. For example, he found it necessary for conscience's sake to give up the use of sugar because it was the product of slave labor. His self-consciousness must have been intense when he gave up the use of dye in his clothing because dye, too, was produced by slave labor and was responsible for the concealment of all manner of uncleanliness. Probably his most poignant protest was his refusal to accept space in the cabin of the ship that took him to England toward the close of his life. Such ornate comfort was more than his conscience would allow. So he holed up in the steerage where in cramped, stifling conditions his heart went out to the mariners who lived such a terrible life and who, as Woolman lamented, were subject to all manner of strong temptation.

His compulsion to witness inevitably clashed with practices sanctified by society. When he was requested to billet a soldier in his home in 1758 during the French and Indian War, Woolman was hard-pressed. He could not condone violence. But because he could not refuse hospitality to a fellow being, he chose the course of passive obedience and allowed the billeting. But when after the man was gone his military superior attempted to recompense Woolman for his room and board, Woolman refused to accept the money. Later, fearing that his motive had been misunderstood and that he was considered a benefactor of the army, he sought out the officer to make it clear to him that he had acted from conscience.

A humorous example of his didactic ways is seen in an incident involving a juggler who was to appear at a local "Publick-house" in Mount Holly. The showman created such a favorable impression the first evening he presented his act that his show was held over for another performance. Hearing of it, Woolman "felt an Exercise on that Account: So I went to the Publick-house in the Evening, and told the Man of the House that I had an Inclination to spend a Part of the Evening there; with which he signified that he was content. Then, sitting down by the Door, I spake to the People as they came together, concerning this Shew; and, more coming and sitting down with us, the Seats of the Door were mostly filled; and I had Conversation with them in the Fear of the Lord, and laboured to convince them that, thus assembling to see those Tricks of Slights of Hand, and bestowing their Money to support Men, who, in that Capacity, were of no Use in the World, was contrary to the Nature of the *Christian* Religion.

"There was one of the Company, who, for a Time, endeavoured, by Arguments, to shew the Reasonableness of their Proceedings herein; but, after considering some Texts of Scripture, and calmly debating the Matter, he gave up the Point. So, having spent about an Hour amongst them, and feeling my Mind easy, I departed."

It is part of the greatness of Woolman that so few of his concerns put him in the class of the moral zealot. This is due to the fact that he never allowed the demands of his conscience to blind him to the inevitableness of differences of opinion among men. His convictions did not transform him into a fanatic. Woolman believed that all men, if they tried, could "get down to the Rock, the sure Foundation, and there hearken to that divine Voice which gives a clear and certain Sound . . . ," but he knew that all life involves effort and that not all men can be expected to hear the voice at the same time. Woolman in following his conscience could condemn sin, but his gentle heart always went out to the sinner. Because John Woolman never forgot our common humanity his *Journal* remains a living testament to a great man and a continuing challenge to mankind.

DIALOGUES CONCERNING NATURAL RELIGION

Author: David Hume (1711-1776)
Type of work: Philosophical theology
First published: 1779

Principal Ideas Advanced

The arguments of natural theology which seek to establish the nature or existence of God by a priori arguments or by analogies drawn from sense experience are invalid.

Inferences based upon observed characteristics of the world do not justify the claim that there is a spiritual world beyond the material world, for the latter may contain within itself its own principle of order.

A priori arguments are equally futile, for whatever is a matter of fact can be conceived as not existing; existence is never demonstrable as necessary.

The sole conclusion that can be reached by natural theology is that the cause of the world probably bears some remote resemblance to human intelligence.

Theologians and philosophers have sought to reach conclusions concerning the existence and nature of God without appealing to revelation. David Hume's *Dialogues Concerning Natural Religion* subjects all such efforts to a critical analysis. The existence of God is not called into question. Any effort, however, to discover God's nature, either by rational argument or by inferences drawn from sense experience, is subjected to severe criticism.

The choice of the dialogue form makes it difficult to ascertain David Hume's own position with certainty. The three principal characters in the dialogue, Demea, Cleanthes, and Philo, respectively represent the orthodox rationalist, the theist, and the skeptic.

That Philo's principles are closer to the truth than those of Demea, and that those of Cleanthes are even nearer to the truth than those of Philo, is the conclusion of Pamphillus, the narrator of the dialogue. Whether David Hume chose Philo or Cleanthes to be the winner of the argument is of historical interest; the subsequent importance and significance of the dialogue largely rests upon the fact that

many have since declared Philo to be the victor.

The Dialogues Concerning Natural Religion, together with Immanuel Kant's *Critique of Pure Reason* (1781), led some to abandon natural theology altogether and others to seek to reformulate their arguments. Among those who abandon natural theology, some seek to get rid of God entirely, while others regard Humean skepticism as an ally which enables them to appeal unabashedly to revelation. No matter which course is followed, it is in any case evident that no serious student of philosophical theology can neglect David Hume's *Dialogues*.

Demea and Philo agree verbally in their opposition to Cleanthes' attempts to draw inferences about the nature of God from the nature of the world. Philo and Cleanthes agree in their opposition to Demea's *a priori* argument to establish the infinity and unity of the Deity. The main debate takes place between Philo and Cleanthes. It reaches its culmination in Part XI when Philo abandons his cavils against arguments from design and draws attention to the presence of natural and moral evil within the world.

Demea, the representative of orthodox rationalism, is opposed by Cleanthes and supported by Philo in his insistence upon the incomprehensibility of the divine nature. Demea's distrust of arguments based upon experience and probability does not stem from skepticism but from the conviction that it is impious to pry into the nature and essence of God. To reach conclusions which represent the Deity as similar to the human mind and understanding is to make ourselves the model of the whole universe. We cannot legitimately make inferences from ourselves to God. Human modes of thinking, ideas, and sentiments do not resemble anything true of the Deity. By reading a human author, a reader enters into the author's mind, but the order of the world, the book of nature, contains an inexplicable riddle. God's ways are not man's ways. Human reason is changing, whereas the incomprehensible nature of God is immutable and simple. There is no acquisition, diminution, change, or succession in God. To argue *a posteriori* from the world to God is to forget that a finite effect can never prove an infinite cause.

The infinity of the divine attributes and the unity of the Supreme Being can be demonstrated with absolute certainty, Demea insists, by the following *a priori* argument. Granted that everything has a cause and that nothing can be the cause of itself, either there is an infinite succession of causes and effects or there is an ultimate cause that is necessarily existent. The first disjunct is false. Therefore, there is an ultimate and necessarily existent cause.

Why, Demea asks, is it false to suppose that there can be an infinite succession of causes and effects? Because each effect within the infinite chain

of cause and effects exists by reason of the immediately preceding cause. The chain, itself, however, requires a cause or reason as much as does any individual member of the series. For why did this particular succession of causes exist from eternity, and not some other series, or no series at all? Why is there something and not nothing? Why did this particular possibility become actual and not some other? If there is no necessarily existent being, every supposition is equally possible. The consequent of this conditional is, however, false, for there is just this particular possibility that has been actualized. To deny the consequent of a conditional is to deny the antecedent. There is, therefore, a necessarily existent Being who carries the reason of His existence in Himself, and who cannot without contradiction be supposed not to exist.

Cleanthes attacks Demea's *a priori* argument as ill-grounded and of little consequence to piety and religion. A cause implies a priority in time and a beginning of existence. What exists from eternity has no beginning and, therefore, cannot have a cause. The material universe could have some unknown qualities which make it a noncontingent and necessarily existent being, except that the expression "necessary existence" has no meaning. For, if God is thought of as an existent being, that is, if His existence is taken to be a matter of fact, then His existence is not demonstrable. For, if "God exists," is demonstrable, "God does not exist" implies a contradiction, since nothing is demonstrable unless a contradiction is implied by its contrary. However, if we can clearly conceive of God as existing, we can also conceive of Him as not existing, since whatever we can conceive of as existent can also be thought of as nonexistent. Consequently, since God can, without contradiction, be conceived of as not existing, the proposition that God exists is not demonstrable. No matter of fact is ever logically demonstrable or necessary.

Cleanthes' attack on Demea is not prompted by skepticism. Complete skepticism makes survival impossible and is belied by the skeptic's reliance upon the maxims of science, ethics, and prudence in his daily conduct. Cleanthes admits that God possesses many powers and attributes which are incomprehensible, but unless our ideas are true as far as they go, then the name "God" lacks meaning. Demea's pious utterances are in fact more dangerous than Philo's skepticism. For, Philo's skepticism, like Descartes', is methodological, as he himself admits in Part XII when he states: "A purpose, an intention, a design strikes everywhere the most careless, the most stupid thinker; and no man can be so hardened in absurd systems as at all times to reject it. . . ." Demea's insistence that there is no analogy between the human mind and the divine mind, between the nature of the world and the nature of God, is virtually identical with an atheism which asserts that a first cause is unknown and unintelligible. A totally simple and immutable mind is no mind at all. It makes no sense to use the word "God" unless something is known about His nature. Such knowledge is attainable. The nature of God can be inferred from the nature of the world. The similarity of the world to a giant machine composed of an infinite number of little machines indicates the adaptation of means to ends through-

out nature, and such adaptation, analogous to human design, permits the ascription of intelligence, thought, and wisdom to the Deity. A rational cause is needed to account for the works of nature.

Philo's attack on Cleanthes originates in a methodological skepticism which presupposes the insufficiency of human reason to attain theoretical certainty with regard to the first principles of any system. His doubts do not arise on the practical level, for in the final section of the *Dialogue*, Part XII, Philo acknowledges that he is deeply religious and, in spite of his argument against design, he concedes that "no man can be so hardened in absurd systems as at all times to reject it. . . ." He permits natural theology to conclude that "the cause or causes of order in the universe probably bear some remote analogy to human intelligence . . . ," although such a conclusion does not provide the basis for any inferences that affect human life.

Philo does not object to Cleanthes' appeal to experience, but he insists that our ideas cannot go beyond experience. We may call the original cause of the universe God, but the attributes of the divine being are incomprehensible, since there is no reason to hold that the perfections of the Deity bear any analogy to the perfections of human creatures. We have no experience of the whole of the world, nor do we experience the origin of worlds. To suppose that the material world requires a mental cause is to forget that the mental world would itself require a cause. If the material world is dependent upon an ideal world, why not trace that ideal world to another, and so on *ad infinitum?* If it is possible to stop at all, why not stop at the very beginning, with the material world? "By supposing it to contain the principle of its order within itself, we really assert it to be God. . . ."

Moreover, even if we ascribe the material world to a mind like the human mind, Philo continues, there is still no reason to ascribe perfection or unity to the deity. The world may be the product of trial and error, or the work of many finite gods who came into being and are themselves corporeal.

Since there is an absence of data for the formulation of any system of cosmology, and there are no rules to follow, the world can be regarded as an animal with a deity for its soul. The world may contain its own eternal principle of order, attended by continual upheavals and changes. Philo then suggests that the origin of the world may be attributed to vegetation or to generation, rather than to reason and design; its resemblance to a plant or animal is greater than its likeness to a machine.

The present order of the world need not be explained in terms of design. For by supposing a finite number of particles, capable of finite transpositions, and given an infinite duration, every possible order or position must be tried an infinite number of times.

At the end of Part X, Philo admits that such objections to intelligence and design are forced, based upon dodges, subterfuges, cavils and sophisms. His more serious arguments seek to show that the existence of a cause, bearing some similarity to human intelligence, does not warrant the ascription of moral attributes to the Deity. The is-

sue is not whether misery is fleeting and momentary, nor whether it is outweighed by happiness, but why there is misery at all.

The present situation in which man finds himself might be compatible with the antecedent conviction that the world is the effect of a finite deity, but the world provides no basis for the inference that there is a supreme, benevolent, powerful intelligence.

Philo argues that the presence of pain, the uniform course of events, the frugality with which creatures are endowed with powers and faculties, and the inaccurate workmanship of the machine of nature preclude the inference that the Deity has moral attributes, although if we already had *a priori* knowledge of the moral qualities of the Deity, the circumstances of the world could be harmonized with them. From the phenomena of the world, it appears that the original source of all things is morally indifferent.

It is absurd to think that the Deity has human passions and is concerned with our vices and follies, Philo continues. A rational religion can be beneficial to a society, but the religion of the masses often ends in superstition and is detrimental. Remote promises and threats of future rewards and punishments are not as effective in promoting a stable social order as is man's natural inclination to honesty and benevolence.

David Hume's *Dialogues* is important to Christian thought, for many Christians have since heeded Philo's concluding words and have made philosophical skepticism "the first and most essential step towards being a sound, believing Christian. . . ."

THE JOURNALS OF HENRY MELCHIOR MÜHLENBERG

Author: Henry Melchior Mühlenberg (1711-1787)
Type of work: Diaries of a clergyman
First published: 1942-1958 (written: 1742-1787)

PRINCIPAL IDEAS ADVANCED

The German-speaking colonists of the Lutheran faith shared with many of their English-speaking neighbors of other persuasions a common understanding and practice of Christianity which was derived from similar roots in European Pietism.

It was a common practice in the eighteenth century for religiously inclined persons to keep diaries. Whatever other purposes may have moved them to do so, it was usually one of their aims to practice the kind of self-scrutiny which was a characteristic spiritual discipline of the time. Another aim was to preserve for the edification of others a record of a religious pilgrimage through life. Some journals of this sort which have come down to us have become religious classics. Among them, to mention only a few by way of illustration, are the journals of John Wesley (1703-1791) and George Whitefield (1714-1770), leaders respectively in the Methodist movement in England and the Great Awakening in America; David Brainerd (1718-1747), missionary to the American Indians; and John Woolman (1720-1772), Quaker opponent of slavery, war, and intemperance.

A contemporary of all these was Henry Melchior Mühlenberg. In response to repeated pleas from Lutheran colonists in southeastern Pennsylvania, he was sent to America from his native Germany in 1742. On his arrival in Philadelphia he revitalized existing congregations there and in nearby settlements. When he became aware of Lutheran colonists elsewhere, he made missionary tours into other parts of Pennsylvania, into New Jersey, New York, Delaware, Maryland, South Carolina, and Georgia. He entered into correspondence with still others, notably in Virginia and Nova Scotia, whom he was not able to visit. Wherever he went he revived the religious interest of German settlers and helped them to strengthen existing congregations or establish new ones. He secured additional ministers from Germany and contributed to the training of a native Lutheran ministry in America. He drafted congregational constitutions and was the leader in the formation in 1748 of the "Ministerium of North America," the first permanent Lutheran synodical organization on the Western continent. For forty-five years, until the time of his death, he was the recognized leader of his church and became known as "the patriarch of the Lutheran Church in America."

Like many of his contemporaries, Mühlenberg regularly jotted down entries in a diary. He did so not only as a spiritual exercise and for the sake of supplying others with edifying reading, but also in order to keep a record of his activities and make it easier to report on these to his ecclesiastical superiors in Europe. When he had leisure he expanded his original jottings into fuller accounts of his experiences, often pointing a moral, analysing situations and personalities, and adding bits of wry humor. Laboriously made copies of such journals were often sent to Germany to supplement more formal reports. A few excerpts from these were published in the so-called Halle Reports (Hallesche Nachrichten), a series of seventeen pamphlets printed in Halle, Saxony, between 1750 and 1787 under the general title "Reports of the United German Evangelical [Lutheran] Congregations in North America, Especially in Pennsylvania" and intended as missionary propaganda to awaken interest in and solicit funds for the expanding Church enterprise on the other side of the Atlantic ocean.

Very few portions of the journals were published in this way during Mühlenberg's life. Manuscript copies of the unpublished diaries were preserved in European archives and by his descendants in America (one of his sons was Peter, 1746-1807, a general during the American Revolution, and another was Frederick, 1750-1801, first speaker in the Congress of the United States). So they remained until, in connection with the 200th anniversary of the arrival in America of Henry Melchior Mühlenberg, the extant manuscripts were collated, edited, translated into English, furnished with notes, and published in three stout volumes between 1942 and 1958. Prefaced by a later account of his early life, the journals proper begin with January, 1742, when Mühlenberg was making preparations for his voyage to America, and conclude with

a brief entry made on September 29, 1787, when he baptized a child. Eight days later he died. There are few gaps to interrupt the daily record of forty-five years of intensive activity in what Mühlenberg often called "the wilderness" of colonial America.

As one would expect, the Journals constitutes the major source for our knowledge of the man who wrote them. Mühlenberg emerges as a sharp-eyed observer of men and events, although he tended to interpret things through the rather jaundiced eyes of a Pietist. He was a man of action, with a gift for administration. The situation in which he found himself demanded that a multitude of things be done, that divergent opinions and personalities be reconciled, that methods of the Old World be adapted to the needs of the New World. For the most part he measured up to the requirements of the task imposed on him. Yet he was a man of sensitive mold who often shrank before the necessity of making hard decisions.

Of even greater importance is the light which his journals throw on the life and manners of the people among whom Mühlenberg moved. He showed great interest in the illnesses which afflicted them and the medicines which were available. He recorded the changing prices of food, clothing, and other necessities of life. He observed the work of men and women in town and country, and with rather less sympathy noted their recreation and play. He discussed the slavery of Negroes, the servitude of white redemptioners, and the condition of American Indians. He commented on schools and courts, marriage and family life, modes of travel and the movements of people.

The relation of Church and state was of immediate concern to Mühlenberg, and since he lived through the years of the American Revolution it was inevitable that he should often reflect on it. In fact, he lived in an area which became one of the major theaters of military operations. At the beginning of hostilities he moved from Philadelphia into the country, but he soon found himself between the American encampment at Valley Forge and the British troops who were occupying Philadelphia. He witnessed the movements of soldiers, heard the rumble of cannons, ministered to the wants of fleeing refugees, and deplored the destruction caused by what he called "an unnatural war." His sympathies were especially engaged because his son Peter substituted a military uniform for a clerical gown and his son Frederick abandoned the ministry to enter politics, but the father steered a precarious course of political neutrality between the contending parties.

Useful as are all these contributions to our knowledge of the war, colonial life and manners, and Mühlenberg himself, the chief value of the *Journals* lies in its contributions to Church history. The German and Dutch Reformed, Presbyterians, Anglicans, Quakers, Moravians, Methodists, Mennonites, and others appear again and again on the pages of the *Journals,* but most of the attention is naturally devoted to Lutherans, whether of Dutch, Swedish, Finnish, or German provenance. Here we have firsthand accounts of how Lutherans built their churches, secured their ministers, conducted public worship, established schools, developed social concerns, and grew in numbers and strength.

The journals show to what an extent colonial Lutherans shared in the spirit which was characteristic of the Great Awakening of the eighteenth century. Not only do George Whitefield, Gilbert Tennent (1703-1764), and other representatives of the Awakening move in and out of the diary entries, but similar emphases on conversion experiences and on legalistic patterns of Christian conduct are seen to have informed the life of Lutheran colonists. This is not surprising when it is remembered that most of the Lutherans carried over with them from Europe an understanding and a practice of the Christian faith which had been shaped by Pietism. Moreover, most of the ministers were men who, like Mühlenberg himself, had been nurtured in Pietism and had been sent to America and continued to be supported through those institutions which the leader of German Pietism, August Hermann Francke (1663-1727), had founded in Halle, Saxony.

Although the *Journals* of Henry Melchoir Mühlenberg remained relatively unknown until the middle of the twentieth century, when they were for the first time published in their entirety, they deserve a place alongside the journals of such other religious leaders of the eighteenth century as Wesley and Whitefield, Brainerd and Woolman.

SONGS OF INNOCENCE AND OF EXPERIENCE

Author: William Blake (1757-1827)
Type of work: Religious poetry
First published: 1789 (*Innocence*); 1794 (*Experience*)

PRINCIPAL IDEAS ADVANCED

The child looks upon God as a loving father; nature is benign although it is challenging.

To the child, Jesus is the Lamb, which the child loves.

But experience shows the world to be corrupted; death, jealousy, fear, and ugliness destroy the child's naïve image of reality.

Behind the horror of man's acts there is a constant Mystery.

William Blake's two small collections of poems of childhood, collected into a single book, *The Songs of Innocence and of Experience,* contain some of the most haunting expressions in literature of the reality innocence cannot anticipate and of the Mystery experience cannot know. Who has read "The Lamb" ("Little Lamb, who made thee?/ Dost thou know who made thee?/") without thereby learning forever the forgotten experience of sensing the divine presence with the open eyes of innocence? And who has read "The Tiger" ("Tiger! Tiger! burning bright/ In the forests of the night. . . .") without learning through fear the awful power of the divine Creator? Blake's genius combined the images of Lamb and Tiger into a paradoxical pair, innocence and experience united by Mystery. Neither innocence nor experience provides a full view of reality, Blake appears to claim; neither is complete without the other; he who loves the Lamb has yet to know the Tiger; he who trembles before the Tiger is in fearful danger of forgetting the Lamb.

The songs of innocence are happy songs, as Blake explains in an intro-ductory verse. What musicians and singers have celebrated through music, the poet now celebrates through poetry. And to bring the mind to a clear perception of the nature which is the smiling face of God, Blake adopts the pastoral convention: "And I made a rural pen,/ And I stain'd the water clear,/ And I wrote my happy songs/ Every child may joy to hear."

"The Echoing Green" tells of the carefree play of children and of the rising of the sun. The old folk watch and remember the days when they, too, played on the green. Finally, the sun descends; the children return to the laps of their mothers, and it is the end of play on the echoing green.

Such a poem, which in its direct-ness and simplicity expresses the joy-ful quality of the child's existence, suggests the dimension beyond the child's understanding; old age and death are witnesses as the children play; the joy of the children finds its echo in the sober recollections of the old folk as the sun descends.

"The Shepherd" is a song which, without any direct allusion to the divine presence, sketches in eight effort-less lines the image of divine care;

while the shepherd watches, the lamb and the ewe are "in peace,/ For they know when their shepherd is nigh."

The poem "Infant Joy" tells us that the name of an infant should be Joy, for the infant's life is one of smiles and songs. But what is the song of innocence when the child is black? Sadly, it is a song of experience and of trust in God. In "The Little Black Boy" Blake achieves his most poignant image. The black child knows that he is different: "White as an angel is the English child,/But I am black, as if bereav'd of light. . . ." But there is no bitterness in the child's mind, for his mother explains that man must learn to bear the beams of God's love; black bodies are evidence of the power and all-pervasive presence of that love. The promise is that when God calls, the black boy will move out from the cloud and rejoice, like a lamb, around the golden tent of God. And then the black boy speaks, out of innocence and love, and declares that when he and the English boy are free from their clouds, "I'll shade him from the heat, till he can bear/ To lean in joy upon our Father's knee;/ And then I'll stand and stroke his silver hair,/ And be like him, and he will then love me."

"Laughing Song" is an expression of unconditional joy. The woods, the stream, the air, the hills, the meadows, the grasshopper, and all the girls with their "sweet round mouths" sing, "Ha, Ha, He!" The song of "Spring," which follows, is a song of welcome to the year, and once again the joy of childhood makes itself felt in all its delightful innocence.

As one continues to read of laughing and playing children, and as one contemplates their dreaming innocence (as in "Cradle Song"), one realizes that the wonder and novelty of childhood is in its distance from the adult world. The mother sings, the nurse calls to the children that the sun is descending. We all see the smile of the Maker on the face of the dreaming child, but we know that He wept for man, and we know, too, that the mother weeps while she prays that her child's dreams be happy dreams. Moments of experience intrude upon innocence, for innocence cannot be innocence except through the eyes of the mother, the nurse, and Old John, who sits beside the green and laughs at the children.

The promise of suffering, a doleful promise which puts into sharp relief the joy of the children, is a promise fulfilled in the lives of the children who are chimney sweepers. The poem "The Chimney Sweeper" begins with the lines, "When my mother died I was very young, /And my father sold me while yet my tongue/ Could scarcely cry ''weep! 'weep! 'weep! 'weep!' /So your chimneys I sweep, and in soot I sleep." In a dream of death the child joins with thousands of sweepers freed from their coffins by an angel with a bright key, and the sweeps are told that God will be their Father and that they will know joy. Tom, the sweep, rises in the dark of morning and goes forth with his brushes; he is warmed by the hope for a better life than the one he knows.

With the changing note introduced by the poem "The Chimney Sweeper," the songs begin to warn of suffering and of the coming of the night, but the promise of God's compassion still brightens the songs of innocence. Though the little boy is lost, God will find him; though man sorrows, God feels his sorrow and weeps for him.

The poems in the *Songs of Experience,* however, give unqualified expression to human despair and cynicism. Delightful as the songs of innocence are, they cannot be convincing except as expressions of innocence, for the child is ignorant of life, and he plays and laughs without knowledge of the onset of darkness. With such knowledge comes bitterness; in these poems the earth is pictured as filled with stony dread and as covered with locks of gray despair. Jealousy, selfishness, and fear spoil the quality of existence. The nurse's song is now one of depression, and she calls to the children to come home, for their time is wasted in play. Man is like a fly who at any moment can be brushed away by some blind hand. Nor does the Church provide an answer: the Chapel is locked, and "Thou shalt not" is written over the door. Priests with black gowns bind "with briars my joys and desires." A little vagabond cries out that the Church is cold but that were it an ale-house, he could be "healthy and pleasant and warm. . . ." The "invisible worm" with "dark secret love" destroys the rose. Now children are seen in poverty and tears; when the child sinks on its mother's breast, it is out of profound weariness after long struggle.

In the poem "London," Blake shows the dreadful limit of man's disillusionment. Every face shows marks of weakness and of woe; cries of men and infants reveal "mind-forg'd manacles"; the cries of the chimney sweep appall the "black'ning church" and the sigh of the soldier "Runs in blood down palace walls." Finally, the curse of the youthful harlot "Blasts the new-born infant's tear,/ And blights with plagues the marriage hearse."

Nothing in the *Songs of Experience* suggests an escape from the knowledge of man's corrupting power. In his innocence the child knows God as Father; if sorrow comes, the shepherd will shelter the lamb. But experience shows that man corrupts everything, including the joys of childhood; man destroys the Church, the state, the city, and the quality of his own existence, through his fears and vices. Man corrupts even Mystery so that the tree of mystery casts a "dismal shade" and "bears the fruit of Deceit."

How, then, can Blake have hoped for a positive statement? The *Songs of Experience* are songs of unconditional despair and cynicism. God is pictured as making a Heaven out of man's misery, and priests are shown as destroying everything joyful and lovely in the life of man.

But if one supposes that the *Songs of Innocence* presents the spirit of God's love, as that spirit is confirmed in a state of innocence, although the child's view of life is false, one may also suppose that the *Songs of Experience* shows the spirit of God's love as that spirit is corrupted through experience, although the mature view of life is true. Experience corrupts the natural and divine world the child knows. Since even the conception of God becomes a human abstraction, it is not surprising that the adult is often resentful and blasphemous toward God. The way out of paradox, then, cannot be through pure innocence or through pure experience, for innocence is naïve and experience is corrupt; paradox is resolved only when the spirit of innocence throws a divine light on the corrupting power of man. Through reading these contrasting books one understands the profound sense in which the child, for all his innocence, is right in his sentiment, while the man, for all his experience, is mistaken in his.

RELIGION WITHIN THE LIMITS OF REASON ALONE

Author: Immanuel Kant (1724-1804)
Type of work: Moral theology
First published: 1793

PRINCIPAL IDEAS ADVANCED

Religion is founded on moral concepts, particularly upon that of man as a free agent.

The central problem of religion is the opposition of good and evil; since an essentially good moral disposition can yet perform evil acts, explanation of man's possibility for self-restoration is required.

God is the moral Lawgiver and Judge, Jesus is the divinely given moral example of a perfect moral will, and natural religion is a moral ideal founded entirely on pure practical reason.

Morality, Kant tells us in *Religion Within the Limits of Reason Alone,* is based upon the idea of man as a free agent, and religion at its core is founded upon moral concepts. As a free agent man binds himself to unconditioned laws through the use of his reason, and without this moral activity religion would not be possible. Although guilt and reward depend upon the idea of man as free, it is not necessary to add to morality the idea of a Being over man, in order that man might be provided with a ground for duty other than the moral law. Morality itself does not require religious sanction. When it is a question of duty, morality is perfectly capable of ignoring all ends.

By virtue of practical reason, then, morality is self-sufficient. Yet it is still quite possible that morality is related to such an end as religion proposes, al-though that end does not arise out of morality itself. If we take the idea of a highest good in the world, then we must postulate a most holy and om-nipotent Being who alone could unite the two elements of this highest good; namely, duty and happiness. Thus, the idea of a highest Being arises out of morality although morality is not its basis. Morality ineluctably leads to religion, to the idea of a pow-erful moral Lawgiver whose will can and ought to be man's final end. In religion the holiness of moral law becomes the ultimate cause.

Human power is not sufficient to bring about happiness in the world proportionate to man's worthiness to be happy. Thus, an omnipotent moral being must be postulated as ruler of the world, under whose care this bal-ance will finally occur. However, de-spite the fact that religion surpasses morality, it cannot or ought not to declare war on reason, since religion will not be able to hold out against reason in the long run. The philosopher as a teacher of pure reason must confine himself to its narrower sphere. Revelation and Biblical theology remain unavailable to him, although he can examine revelation in the light of moral concepts. Mysteries concerning the divine nature must first be transformed into moral concepts if they are to become comprehensible to everyone.

The central problem of religion for Kant, since he approaches it from the perspective of morality, is that of the opposition of good and evil. How shall we account for the principle of radical evil in human nature, and how can the fact of evil be reconciled with the good and with morality? Kant works within the Biblical framework in claiming that the world began in a good state and that evil was introduced into it. We live, then, not in an original state but in a later and altered condition. By nature man's soul should be born healthy and free from evil. But could it be that man as a species is born neither good nor bad? We call a man evil only because the actions he performs are contrary to law. The "nature of man," then, is only the subjective ground of the exercise of his freedom.

The source of evil can only be in a rule made by the will for the use of its freedom. There is in man an ultimate ground for the adoption of either good or evil maxims, and the ultimate ground for the adoption of either maxim must itself lie in free choice, although such a fact cannot be revealed in experience. Good or evil is innate in man only in this sense, that the ground for the use of freedom is present in man at birth. However, man must decide; he must exercise this freedom. His disposition with respect to the moral law can never be indifferent, never neither good nor evil. In fact the will must always be something specific, always either good or evil.

"Propensity" means the subjective ground of the possibility of an inclination. A propensity towards evil must then consist in the subjective ground of the possibility of the deviation of maxims from the moral law. In this capacity for evil, Kant distinguishes three distinct degrees: frailty of human nature, impurity of the human heart, and wickedness or corruption of the human heart. This latter is a propensity of the will to accept maxims which neglect the incentives springing from the moral law and to favor other incentives which are not moral. Wickedness reverses the ethical order of priority among the incentives of a free will. On the other hand, the spirit of the moral law is that the law is sufficient in itself as an incentive; although it is still true that propensity to evil can inhere only in the moral capacity of the will, without such a capacity neither the moral law nor evil would be possible.

"Man is evil" means that he is conscious of the moral law but has nevertheless provided by his maxims for occasional deviations therefrom. Yet the ground of evil cannot be placed either in man's sensuous nature or in a corruption of his morally legislative reason. Because it concerns a relation to the will which is free, it must be apprehended *a priori* through the concept of evil, so far as evil is possible under the laws of freedom. Even the most wicked man does not repudiate the moral law in the manner of a rebel.

The distinction between the good man and the one who is evil is not due to a difference in the incentives for their maxims. The distinction depends, rather, upon subordination; that is, upon whether it is the moral law or self-love that is given priority. Evil is a matter of priority of incentive, not the absence of any incentive that is present in the good man. Man is evil only when he reverses the moral order of the incentive (the moral law first, self-love second). Evil is radical only in the sense that it tends to corrupt the ground of all maxims.

In order to make evil morally intelligible, it must always be connected with a continued state of free will. No matter how evil a man has been up to the moment of an impending free act, it is still his duty to better himself, and such a situation is intelligible only if it always remains within his power to do so. However, the rational origin of the perversion of our will, its making lower incentives supreme among its maxims, always remains inscrutable to us. There is then no conceivable ground from which the propensity to moral evil could originally have come. Its factual presence is undeniable but its origin is a mystery. Nevertheless, rationality is not thwarted, since there always remains hope for a return to the good from which man has strayed. Despite a corrupted heart the evil man still possesses a good will.

Man is created for good, Kant is convinced, and the original predisposition in man is good. Consequently, man himself must have made himself into whatever he has become morally, whether good or evil. An injunction to become better men resounds continually in our souls, and hence it must be within our power. We have never lost our greatest incentive, respect for the moral law. Hence the restoration of man to a good state requires nothing but the establishment of the purity of the moral law as the supreme ground of all our maxims. Original goodness is merely the holiness of maxims, doing one's duty for duty's sake. Man's moral growth, then, begins in transforming his cast of mind and in the grounding of a character, not in the improvement of his actual practice. When the moral law commands that we *ought* to be better men, Kant is convinced that it follows inevitably that we must *be able* to be better men.

There is present in us an active cause of evil to be combated, although natural inclinations considered in themselves are good. The cause of evil cannot be sought in the inclinations but only in that which determines the will as a free will, and it is our duty to oppose evil, to elevate ourselves to the ideal of moral perfection. Kant declares that Jesus is to be regarded as the divinely given moral example. Through His teachings, His conduct, and His sufferings we have as perfect an example of what it means to be a man well-pleasing to God as one can expect to find in external experience, since the archetype is really to be found in our own reason and not outside it.

Was Jesus divine? Kant answers this continually crucial theological problem by saying that He may be regarded as superhuman to the degree that His unchanging purity of will was innate and not achieved. Since all transgression on His part was utterly impossible, He must be set radically apart from mortal men. Divinity consists of the unalterableness of a holy moral will, rendering such a being immune to temptations. This is the ideal of the Son of God which is set up before us as our model. Thus, the good in us, when it appears in the guise of an action, is always inadequate to a holy law. Action itself is always defective in man, since motives other than pure will are always and necessarily involved.

Having once seen such a good and pure disposition, we acquire confidence in its permanence and stability. Yet the judge within a man, when he considers his own past and his future destiny, pronounces a severe verdict upon himself. He sees the model of the holy will, but he also sees his necessary distance from it. There exists no salvation for man except the sincerest adoption of genuinely moral principles into his disposition, yet how shall this be accomplished? Moral religion consists, then, in the heart's disposition to fulfill all human duties as divine commands. For this purpose miracles are superfluous. True religion, which once may have used miracles as expedients, can now maintain itself on purely rational grounds.

Nothing is more certain to Kant than that, if anything flatly contradicts morality, it cannot be of God. Anything holy must be moral and an object of reason. The idea of a moral Governor of the world is something presented by our practical reason.

Thus, the universally true religious belief conformable to this requirement of practical reason is belief in God as holy Legislator, benevolent Ruler, and righteous Judge. The highest goal of moral perfection in finite creatures is love of the law; the equivalent in religion of this idea would be an article of faith, "God is love." Religion is the recognition of all duties as divine commands.

Natural religion, as morality, is a pure practical idea of reason. Here then is a complete religion, one which can be presented to all men comprehensively and convincingly through their own reason. The one true religion is nothing but laws, those principles whose unconditioned necessity we become aware of, and which we recognize as revealed not empirically but through pure reason. True enlightenment involves conceiving the service of God as being, first and foremost, a free and hence a moral service. Whatever good man is able to do through his own efforts (under freedom, without supernatural assistance) can be related to *nature* as distinct from *grace*. At least we know the laws of freedom, the moral laws, whereas we cannot know anything at all about supernatural aid. Thus, natural religion was for Kant religion within the limits of reason alone.

SYSTEM OF DOCTRINES

Author: Samuel Hopkins (1721-1803)
Type of work: Systematic theology
First published: 1793

Principal Ideas Advanced

God as the Sovereign Creator and Ruler of the world has determined all things that come to pass, including physical and moral evil as necessary means to the greatest good of the whole.

Sin is selfishness or self-love, while virtue is identified with disinterested benevolence or love of being in general, entailing a willingness to give up one's private interest and happiness for the greater good of the whole.

Original sin, consisting in exercises or acts and therefore indistinguishable from actual sin, involves man in no inability to obey the law of God except his inclination to disobey, thus leaving him without excuse for his sin or for his opposition to the Gospel.

Samuel Hopkins's *System of Doctrines* is the first comprehensive treatise of New England or New School Theology developed on the foundation of the speculative views propounded by Jonathan Edwards (1703-1758) in his treatises on the will, on virtue, and on God's design in creation. As a student, Hopkins had spent over eight months in the Edwards home, and in later life he maintained a close relation to his teacher as well as to Joseph Bellamy (1719-1790) and Stephen West (1736-1819). His life as a pastor in Great Barrington, Massachusetts, and later in Newport, Rhode Island, exemplified the principles of self-sacrificing love he inculcated. His emphasis on the role of reason in theology aroused the admiration of William Ellery Channing (1780-1842). Hopkins's progressive outlook is expressed in his Preface to the *System:* "And there is no reason to doubt, that light will so increase in the church, and men will be raised up, who will make such advances in opening the Scripture . . . that what is now done and written will be so far superseded, as to appear imperfect and inconsiderable, compared

with that superior light with which the church will then be blessed."

Many of the theological loci are handled in the style of traditional Calvinist dogmatics. The innovations of Hopkinsianism are largely developments of themes derived from the work of Jonathan Edwards, principally the identification of virtue with disinterested benevolence. While Channing's impression "that President Edwards was a great deal indebted to Dr. Hopkins for his later views of religion" (Letter of February 14, 1840) is not supported by evidence, Hopkins himself claimed to have improved upon Edwards in more definitively stating the opposition of holiness to self-love.

The entire moral character of God is viewed by Hopkins as comprehended in love or benevolence. This benevolence has the highest good of being in general for its object. Benevolent love involves love of complacence, or delight in goodness. Divine love is perfectly disinterested, in opposition to all self-love or selfishness. Impartial benevolence requires God to be the chief and supreme object of His love and to make Himself the chief end of creation. To regard God as an al-

mighty tool existing only for His creatures is to inculcate a wholly selfish
religion. Infinite benevolence seeks
and promotes the greatest good of the
whole and is consequently the enemy
of all who oppose this good. Thus the
wrath of God against sin proceeds
from love, and infinite benevolence requires the due punishment of the
offender. The absolute, uncontrollable
sovereignty of God may also be identified with omnipotent love, doing whatever it pleases, infinitely above any control or obligation to any other being.
The sovereignty of God is not arbitrary
but is exercised in infinite wisdom
according to the dictates of moral perfection.

The distinctive Hopkinsian doctrine
of the decrees of God is a rigorous
deduction from the above conception of divine sovereignty. Hopkins
quotes the Westminster Shorter Catechism: "The decrees of God are his
eternal purpose, according to the counsel of his own will, whereby for his
own glory he hath foreordained whatsoever comes to pass." The glory of
God is understood as involving the
greatest possible good or happiness of
creatures as an expression of the greatest possible exercise and exhibition of
His goodness. Only in our imperfect
and partial conceptions are the glory
of God and the good of the creature
two distinct things. Every detail of the
universe has been predetermined for
the attainment of this end.

The foreordination of all events is
held to be consistent with the liberty
and moral agency of creatures. Flight
from foreordination to foreknowledge
does not make the assertion of freedom
easier, for foreknowledge supposes the
future to be fixed, and if not by God's
decree, then by blind fate. Even if

foreordination and freedom cannot be
reconciled by us, we ought to accept
both on the testimony of Scripture as
well as of reason. Hopkins does not
stop here with many theologians, but
in the Edwardian tradition proposes a
rational solution of the antinomy. The
only internal liberty of which we are
conscious consists in our voluntary
exercises, in choosing and willing.
Freedom of will therefore consists in
the exercise of volition and not in the
absence of determining events. No
other freedom is conceivable, and this
freedom is established by the divine
decree making the determinate choice
of the will certain.

The crucial problem in relation to
the divine decrees is the problem of
evil. Here the clarity and consistency
of the Hopkinsian solution is un-
equaled in the torturous history of
this thorny problem. Hopkins boldly
asserts that God is the cause of both
natural and moral evil. After dismiss-
ing inconsistent positions, Hopkins observes that "it is abundantly evident
and demonstrably certain from reason
assisted by divine revelation, that all
the sin and sufferings which have
taken place or ever will, are necessary
for the greatest good of the universe,
and to answer the wisest and best
ends, and therefore must be included
in the best, most wise and perfect
plan." There are things that appear evil
when considered as being in isolation, but there is no absolute evil in
the universe. The argument follows a
Leibnizian pattern to the extent of
claiming that no two possible worlds
can be indifferent in the divine mind,
since there must be a sufficient reason
for the choice of the one rather
than the other. Scripture also plainly
teaches that all moral evil is designed

by God to answer a good end and to contribute to the greatest good.

Moral evil cannot be the origin or cause of itself. Consequently to assert that God is the cause of moral evil is not to deny His infinite holiness. To hold that the origin or cause of sin must be sinful is to render the problem of the origin of moral evil insoluble. To ascribe sin to a negative cause is unsatisfactory, for a negative cause is really no cause. To say that sin is merely a negative thing is an evasion. If sin has no positive existence, then there is no sin. That people find the divine causality of sin shocking is no indication of its falsity. Common sense and emotion are not to be followed when their dictates are contrary to those of sound reason and the plain declarations of divine revelation.

The immediate exertion of divine power is the proper efficient cause of every event. The preservation of creatures in existence is really continued creation, and the fixed law and course of nature is nothing but the divine will operating in a certain steady fixed manner. Events contrary to this order are called miracles.

Some points related to the doctrine of original sin represent innovations destined to exercise a far-reaching influence in New England theology. Although Hopkins teaches that Adam as the natural and confederating head of the human race involved his posterity in his disobedience and the resulting curse, he explains that he does not mean that sin takes place in the posterity of Adam in consequence of his sin or that they are constituted sinners by his disobedience. The offense of Adam is not imputed to the innocent, but by a divine constitution there is a certain connection between Adam's first sin and his posterity's sinfulness. The distinction between original and actual sin is denied. All sin is actual, and original sin or total moral depravity consists in exercise or act as much as any sin can do. This view appears to be a consequence of the Hopkinsian theory of the will, and it was further developed in the "exercise theory" of Dr. Nathanael Emmons (1745-1840). Human responsibility for sin is stressed by the distinction between natural and moral inability. Man's inability to obey the law of God is entirely a function of his inclination to disobey. Man's natural ability is intact, but his moral disability is total and criminal.

Sin consists in exercises directly opposed to disinterested benevolence. Sin is self-love, the exclusive regard for one's own interest. Every degree of self-love is intrinsically evil. Where there is no selfishness there is no sin. Disinterested benevolence does imply a proper regard for self, but the benevolent person seeks his happiness not as his own, but as included in the interest of the whole.

The redemption of man by Jesus Christ is the greatest instance of the exercise of the benevolence of God. The atonement provided by God the Son through His suffering the punishment of sin in place of sinners is sufficient atonement for the sins of the whole world and provides the basis for a universal offer of salvation to sinners. But since mankind is totally depraved, none to whom the offer of salvation is made would comply with it, were it not for a special work of the Holy Spirit renewing the hearts of men.

Regeneration as the work of the divine Spirit is distinguished from conversion, its effect consisting in the exercises of the regenerate. Regeneration is instantaneous, and man is wholly passive in it. The subject of regeneration is the heart or will, not the intellect. Enlightenment of the mind is no part of regeneration, nor is the word of God a means to the change of heart. Light and truth belong to active conversion, not to regeneration.

All truly Christian exercises consist in disinterested affection, the willingness to give up any lesser good for the greater. The benevolent person is disposed to relinquish his own interest and happiness for the greatest good of the whole. The *System* does not explicitly teach that a man should be willing to be damned for the glory of God but in *A Dialogue between a Calvinist and a Semi-Calvinist,* the doctrine of disinterested submission to the will of God is expounded and defended.

In the preaching of the Gospel, Hopkins insisted on the duty of immediate repentance. All activities of the unregenerate could only be expressions of total depravity and therefore could not be the performance of any duty. Sincere striving is therefore an effect of regeneration, while unregenerate striving only adds to the sinner's guilt.

Appended to the *System* is a *Treatise on the Millennium.* The dedication to the people who shall live in the days of the millennium expresses the author's enthusiasm for this favorite theme. Hopkins cherished the hope that the number of the saved during the millennium would be so great that the total number of the redeemed would far exceed that of the damned. The harsh features of his system are thus softened if not absorbed by the spirit of benevolence that suffuses the whole.

EARLY THEOLOGICAL WRITINGS

Author: Georg Wilhelm Friedrich Hegel (1770-1831)
Type of work: Theology
First published: 1907

Principal Ideas Advanced

The positive elements of Jesus' teaching were made the basis of historical Christianity to the exclusion of the rational elements.

Catholicism and State Protestantism have made Christianity an enemy of free rationality by appealing to force and by the dogmatic character of their teaching.

The religion of Jesus overcomes the alienation which abstract thought produces.

Christ's teaching, that God is love, reconciles nature and morality.

Faith, not reason, is the highest stage of man's development.

Hegel's essays on Christianity, which antedate their author's emergence as a philosophical luminary, were never prepared by him for publication. Presumably Hegel came to regard them, as historians in our time are likely to do, as merely preliminary studies, in which he had not yet found the system which made him famous. Particularly interesting is the movement of Hegel's thought in the interval between *The Positivity of the Christian Religion* (1795-6) and *The Spirit of Christianity* (1798-9), during which interval he passed from the atmosphere of the Enlightenment to that of Romanticism. The work entitled *Early Theological Writings* is not a unified book, but a collection of essays and fragments.

Hegel's interest in theological problems was deeply personal. While he was a student at the theological seminary in Tübingen, he was torn between loyalty to Christianity and to the philosophical ideals of the Age. In many respects, Greek classicism was more appealing to him than the Hebraism of the gospels, and both seemed superior to the ecclesiasticism of Catholicism and State Protestantism. In *The Positivity of the Christian Religion,* Hegel reviews the history of Christianity in an effort to distinguish between what belongs to the teachings of Jesus and what was added by his successors.

By a "positive" religion, Hegel means one which is based upon authority, attested by miracles, and accepted on faith. It is at the opposite pole from philosophy, which is based on truths of nature and reason. The Hebrews, according to Hegel, had no conception of reason and no interest in truth; their religion was purely of the positive variety. Jesus, because He was a Jew ministering to Jews, was forced to clothe His teaching in a positive garb. On this account, He spoke much of His own credentials as a divine teacher, and He catered to his hearer's demand for miracles. But the truth which He sought to impart was that which is given to every man by his moral sense; thus, Jesus used positive religion merely as a means for bringing His teaching home to the hearts of men.

The effect of Jesus' method was to broaden the minds of His disciples. The narrow, nationalistic outlook of Judaism was broken down and replaced by one as comprehensive as reason itself, and a legalistic concern with the externals of conduct gave place to an appreciation of virtuous motives. Thus far, reason received its due. But because Jesus rested His teachings on an appeal to historical faith, His disciples never learned the independent use of reason, and they conceived that their task was simply to preserve and to transmit the teaching which they had heard.

Hegel contrasts the pupils of Socrates and those of Christ, to the disadvantage of the latter. The friends of Socrates, says Hegel, were attracted to him because of his virtue and his philosophy, instead of accepting the latter on the authority of his person. Thus, when they founded schools of their own, they did so in their own right, considering that they were at liberty to teach the truth as they understood it. Because they were concerned mainly with the spread of virtue and truth, they bore no hostility toward members of other schools, or toward devotees of popular religions, except insofar as others strayed from the path of righteousness. It was, indeed, their deepest conviction that every man has a right to his own convictions and his own will.

By contrast, the disciples of Jesus were imbued with a spirit of partisanship and sect which required them to contest any departure by members of their group from the supposed teachings of the Master and to regard as enemies members of the popular religions and of philosophical schools. Because they accepted their doctrine on the authority of God, the disciples could not but regard any defection from it as sinful and disobedient, and therefore as deserving of punishment. Thus, in the hands of Jesus' first disciples, Christianity abandoned the rational element of His teaching and became purely and simply a positive religion, which it has continued to be to this day.

Hegel recounts bitterly the conquest of Christianity over the State, as a result of which, in Protestant as well as in Catholic countries, infidelity or heresy became a civil offense. He further complains against the injustice done to men's minds when as children they are trained in a dogmatic tradition. By filling their minds with imaginary fears and hopes, instead of teaching them to use their understanding, the Church enslaves them as truly as when it resorts to civil measures. The morality that follows from such a faith, even when formally correct, can never be motivated by that love of goodness which Jesus intended, but will always be calculated toward self-interest.

Except for echoes of Kant's categorical imperative, *The Positivity of the Christian Religion* hardly goes beyond Rousseau's *Creed of the Savoyard Priest* (1762), or, for that matter, Herbert of Cherbury's *De religione laici* (1645). Hegel's subsequent essay, *The Spirit of Christianity*, belongs instead to the age of Schelling and Schleiermacher. Hegel seems to have gone through a period of self-estrangement, in the course of which he came under the influence of the Romantic revolt and emerged as a Christian mystic. Such, at least, is the interpretation of Richard Kroner, the biographer of these years. In his latter phase, instead of viewing Christianity in terms of Kant's ethical teachings, Hegel argues that reason and morality are transcended in what Kroner calls "the Pantheism of Love." The unity of nature now appears to him violated by the demands of the moral law, and he turns to religion to find the means of bringing them together in a higher unity. (The essentials of Hegel's later dialectic appear here.)

In *The Spirit of Christianity*, as in the earlier work, Hegel shows his bias toward the Greeks, who, as he represents them, lived in sympathetic unity with nature, loving life, and calling the world their own. The Hebrews, on the contrary, are described as having been dominated by abstract reason, somewhat in the manner of Immanuel Kant. Unable to love the world, the Hebrews sought salvation by condemning it and by pledging their allegiance to the idea of unity, to an object of thought. In this way, says Hegel, the Jews introduced into history that radical alienation which sets righteousness against beauty, duty against inclination, and the universal against the individual. Viewed against their Jewish background, the significance of the Gospels lies in their proclamation of the reconciling power of divine love.

Hegel maintains that the ethical teaching of Jesus was not based on reason, as he earlier supposed. On the contrary, Jesus shows that the law must serve man; He has no hesitancy in overstepping it on the slightest provocation; and He is more hopeful for spontaneous sinners than He is for legalistic moralists. In the Sermon on the Mount, He shows the insufficiency of law by pointing to the love which transcends it; not in the universality of laws such as those opposing murder, but in the spirit which reconciles a man with his brother, does man find deliverance. In the Parables of the Kingdom, Jesus shows the beauty and freedom that is possible for man once he puts away the bondage of law and lives in loving confidence toward the world and toward his fellowman.

But Hegel is now less interested in Jesus' exhortations than in what He has to say about reconciliation and forgiveness. Any law brings condemnation to men's hearts, which even punishment cannot remove. Only a love which is higher than law is able to bring wholeness to the guilty soul. Such is the love which Jesus proclaims, the universal love of God, no longer merely an object of thought, but the true Author of all life and being. Jesus' own consciousness of divine sonship, combined with His sense of oneness with man, is the perfect expression of Unity. He sought to impart this communion to His disciples through the symbolism of the Last Supper; but the effect was only to set Himself between His followers and the divine love; moreover, the fellowship and love which His disciples were able to find with each other through Him was an exclusive one, which left them unreconciled with the rest of the world. The true religion of Jesus, therefore, is not the religion of the churches. In His God "all beings are united; in him there are no members, as members, of a community."

In The Spirit of Christianity Hegel makes religion the final goal of human development, in opposition to the stand which he took later, for example in The Phenomenology of Spirit (1807), in which he places philosophy higher than religion. In this connection, the Fragment of a System (1800) is interesting, supporting, as it does, the stand taken in The Spirit of Christianity. In the Fragment, Hegel develops a philosophy of organism, finding in "life" the reconciliation of unity and diversity. "Reflection," on the other hand, is radically divisive, since whatever proposition is propounded, another must be excluded by it. In order, therefore, for man to find unity, he must transcend reflection and take his stand in "a reality beyond all reflection." This movement Hegel calls religion; by its means, "finite life rises to infinite life," and, thus, "The culmination of faith, the return to the Godhead whence man is born, closes the circle of man's development."

ON RELIGION: SPEECHES TO ITS CULTURED DESPISERS

Author: Friedrich Schleiermacher (1768-1834)
Type of work: Philosophy of religion; apologetics
First published: 1799

Principal Ideas Advanced

Modern culture's alienation from religion stems from failure to see beyond the latter's corrupt outer form, whereas the inner essence of religion is actually the center of all that is humanly normal and highest.

Independently given in man's nature and experience, and essentially different from knowing and doing, religion can be neither established nor supplanted by science, philosophy, morality, or art; nor does it threaten their autonomous activity.

Within the life of the spirit, religion's locus is the union of feeling and intuition; its "object"—which cannot literally be conceived as an object—is the Universe, the Ground and Unity of all that is.

As essentially concrete and historical, religion mediates between the Ultimate and the finite in its universal corruption; thus Christianity, centering upon this mediation, or redemption, embodies in the purest and highest way the principle of religion itself.

As Schleiermacher is the "father of modern theology," so *On Religion* is in many ways its primary manifesto. Nurtured in Moravian piety, the author had also entered avidly into the mind and spirit of the time. With Immanuel Kant (1724-1804), of whom he was critical, Baruch Spinoza (1632-1677), and J. G. Herder (1744-1803), as main philosophical sources, Schleiermacher wrote under the immediate stimulus of the Romantic circle in Berlin, where he had come as a hospital chaplain in 1796. *On Religion,* which appeared anonymously, was his first work, but it caught the attention of German intellectual leaders and quickly established Schleiermacher's significance. While the impress of Romanticism is deep, the import of the book far transcends that particular movement, the more so through Schleiermacher's repeated revisions (1806, 1811, 1821) and ap-

pended explanations, following the discontinuation of his Romantic associations. As professor of theology at Berlin, as original contributor to philosophy, pedagogy, and philology, as moving preacher and ecclesiastical statesman, Schleiermacher became one of the shaping forces of his age. Yet no later work, not even his monumental *The Christian Faith,* has eclipsed the inspiration and thrust with which *On Religion* launches a program of mediation between thoroughgoing openness to modernity and steadfast loyalty to the Christian substance.

Though not oral deliverances, the five parts of the book are appropriately called "speeches" because of their rhetorical, declarative style. Upon a groundplan of solid argumentation, Schleiermacher seeks to persuade and to encourage empathy and identification. The first speech, the "defense," establishes the apologetic premise that the author understands and shares the values of his audience. He too is committed to that free and higher life of the spirit for which modern culture stands. But also partaking by special affinity in the reality of religion, he is fitted for the necessary task of mediation. The complaints of the "cultured despisers" of religion are largely justified—indeed they have a prophetic function—as directed against the outward representations of religion in the present day. Thus, in fact, the "despisers" are allies of what religion truly is, just as it, in turn, is the ultimate stay of all that is enduring in their vision of beauty, truth, and good. But to grasp this, the "despisers" must go beyond the distortions to the incorruptible inner essence of religion.

Hence, the second speech, longest and with the fifth the most important, is devoted to the "nature of religion." Schleiermacher attempts to vindicate his subject by appeal to its foundational origins. He seeks the origins not in history but in human nature itself. Contrary to common opinion, religion is neither a knowing nor a doing, nor is it a combination of the two. It is an abuse of religion to defend it as a prop for some other spiritual or cultural function. Science, metaphysics, art, and morality have their autonomous scope, in which religion, rightly understood, has neither the right nor the need to interfere. For religion has its own distinct domain in man's being. "True science is complete vision; true practice is culture and art self-produced; true religion is sense and taste for the Infinite." As the awareness of the Infinite in the finite and of the Eternal in the temporal, religion can neither be based upon nor threatened by knowledge or action.

"If man is not one with the Eternal in the unity of intuition and feeling which is immediate, he remains, in the unity of consciousness which is derived, forever apart."

The first edition gave more prominence to intuition (*Anschauung*), the later ones to feeling (*Gefühl*). But the view is consistently maintained that religion's locus is that primary, nonobjectifiable moment or dimension of consciousness wherein feeling and intuition are as yet undifferentiated. "It fills no time and fashions nothing palpable. It is the holy wedlock of the Universe with the incarnated Reason. . . . It is immediate, raised above all error and misunderstanding. You lie directly on the bosom of the infinite world." But since religion is the consciousness of our immediate relationship to the Ultimate (the Universe, the All), it does not simply stand apart from knowing and doing. Without obtruding into cultural functions, it nevertheless comprises their integrating fulcrum, the ground from which they spontaneously arise and in which they cohere.

Schleiermacher goes on to explain that the traditional doctrinal content of religion need not be the stumbling block that rigid, rationalistic interpretation can make of it. Doctrines are not to be estimated as science or metaphysics, but as expressions of religious intuition and feeling. Some venerable notions have been accused of opposing natural law. But miracle, for instance, "is simply the religious name for event" when the event is seen as the operation of the Eternal. And revelation, another belabored idea, should be regarded as any truly original insight into man's relation to the Infinite. Nor can the essential interests of religion be identified with the theistic concept of God as a being distinct from the world, or with the theory of life after death. Religious feeling may employ such concepts, but in immediate certitude it precedes them and does not rest upon their correctness.

With this statement of its general nature, Schleiermacher turns in the third speech to the "cultivation of religion." He stresses the spontaneous and intuitive character of religious receptivity. "Instruction in religion, meaning that piety itself is teachable, is absurd and unmeaning." Merely imitative religion is a contradiction in terms. There is discipleship, but never by coercion. Everything depends upon awakening the seed that lies in each soul, for an individual's religion must be his own most sincere possession. Schleiermacher finds the contemporary state of religious cultivation deplorable, a condition which he traces to utilitarian preoccupation with the finite. There prevails a moralistic rationalism which no longer envisages the Infinite, and this is reinforced by the antithetical supernaturalism which puts the Infinite outside and apart from the finite. Against both, Schleiermacher welcomes as a sign of hope those tendencies of his audience which drive beyond self-sufficiency to the ground and limits of life. The strengthening of religious consciousness is greatly expedited by the free play of the imagination and the creative art embodied in the advance elements of modern culture.

The fourth speech takes up "association in religion, or church and priesthood." Schleiermacher proceeds from a distinction between the true Church, which is the natural and wholesome fellowship of the really pious, and the ecclesiastical institution, which "is very far from being a society of religious men." In the true Church there is no distinction of priest and layman, no intolerant separatism, and no demand for conformity to external authority. Individuality and free association are equally encouraged. Institutionalism does not exist, and no competing concerns detract from the all-pervading centrality of religion itself. However, if this were the entire Church, none but saints could belong. The actual ecclesiastical institution, for all its faults, mediates between the ideal Church and the world. Its educative purpose makes compromises unavoidable, although these should be held constantly under the corrective of the ideal. Schleiermacher takes particularly to task confessional exclusivism, religious professionalism, and the intermingling of Church and state. He calls for increasing openness and communion among the ecclesiastical bodies, for the overcoming of clericalism, and for the liberation of the purely religious from debilitating alliances with other interests.

The subject of the fifth speech is "the religions." The interpretation of *On Religion* as a whole turns upon the relation which this last part bears to the foregoing, especially to the second speech. For if the latter were taken as a full exposition of its essence, religion would appear as only an ideal generality, without decisive connection with any historical religion. But in the concluding speech Schleiermacher makes emphatically clear that he conceives the essence of religion to embrace the concrete historicity and particularity of the religions. Their plurality is not to be compared with the plurality of churches. For each authentically individual religion consists in a unique intuition of the Ultimate. Instead of being segregated behind ecclesiastical walls, differences of intuition should be allowed to work upon, enrich, and define each other. Lack of appreciation for other religions has no basis in religion itself. For the more adequately one apprehends the Infinite, the more humility and openness one will have for the unlimited range of its manifestations. Schleiermacher sharply repudiates the project of "natural religion," partly because it would reduce the living variety of religion to a series of abstractions, and partly because it proposes to remove religion from its historical bases to a supposedly more secure footing in reason. But "resistance to the positive and arbitrary is resistance to the definite and real. If a definite religion may not begin with an original fact, it cannot begin at all. There must be a common ground for selecting some one religious element and placing it at the centre, and this ground can only be a fact."

Thus the reality of religion is given in the concrete variety of the positive religions. But since these religions arise in time, they are subject to decay and death. Schleiermacher describes Judaism, which concentrates on the idea of divine reward and punishment, as "long since dead." How, then, does it stand with Christianity, which finally emerges as the real burden of Schleiermacher's apology? Is Christianity simply one among the other historical religions, each mediating in its limited and transient way between the Infinite and the finite? No, for it is "just the intuition of the universal resistance of finite things to the Whole, and of the way the Deity treats this resistance. Christianity sees how He reconciles the hostility to Himself, and sets bounds to the ever increasing alienation by scattering points here and there over the whole that are at once finite and infinite, human and divine." Christianity is the principle of religion itself. "It manipulates religion as matter for religion." Because of the corruption infecting all actual religiousness, including its own churchly existence, Christianity wages perpetual warfare in behalf of the ideal. Under the weight of the world's selfishness and the attendant evil, the dominant Christian tone is holy sadness. But the Christian spirit never comes to rest in simply an emotional state. On the basis of the life of Christ, it is always seeking the reconciliation and reunion of the finite with the Infinite, of every creature with God. Jesus never claimed to be the only mediator; indeed, He calls his disciples to be sharers and instruments of his purpose. And "nothing is more unchristian than to seek uniformity in religion." Nevertheless, as the Bible's authority is established not through dogma but through experienced power, so Christ proves Himself to all who are grasped by His "whole efficacy" as the One "who has become historically the center of all mediation."

Thus Schleiermacher, through a critical analysis of religion's integral role in human existence, reaches his climax and conclusion in the presentation of the redemption centered in Jesus Christ as the criterion and fulfillment of religion. Religion's ideal essence, considered in the second speech, is balanced by the concrete, historical specifics of the fifth speech. The tension between these two components—the general nature and need of religion, and the particularity of historically given revelation—has been a principal dynamic of modern theological development. The greatness of Schleiermacher's youthful masterpiece consists in the way in which it both determines and anticipates so much of that development.

NATURAL THEOLOGY

Author: William Paley (1743-1805)
Type of work: Apologetics; philosophy of religion
First published: 1802

PRINCIPAL IDEAS ADVANCED

The existence of a cosmic Designer can be demonstrated to be highly probable on the basis of empirical evidence drawn from nature.

Empirical evidence, further, can support the conclusion that this Designer possesses the characteristics of the Christian God.

Natural Theology was the crowning achievement of William Paley, Archdeacon of Carlisle, England, but while it remains the work for which this eighteenth century thinker is principally remembered, Paley's interests and achievements ranged widely within the fields of philosophy and theology. Son of the headmaster at Giggleswick School, Paley showed excellence in his early studies and later at Cambridge, where soon after his graduation in 1763 he gained a considerable reputation for his brilliant lectures on moral philosophy. Together with the English philosopher Jeremy Bentham (1748-1832), Paley is credited with laying the foundations of the ethics of utilitarianism.

After leaving Cambridge for an ecclesiastical "living" at the time of his marriage in 1776, Paley engaged himself in writing and in supporting various liberal movements for reform. His highly successful book in ethical theory, *The Principles of Moral and Political Philosophy* (1785), was adopted as a standard text at Cambridge, exerting an inevitable influence on developments in British moral philosophy. Translating his ethical theories into practice, Paley was active in the movement to abolish slavery in Britain; because of his abolitionist efforts (and his liberal political sympathies) his ecclesiastical advancement was blocked by more conservative persons in positions of authority. Far from conservative, Paley threw himself into an unsuccessful campaign for the reform and simplification of the Thirty-Nine Articles of the Anglican Church and thus dashed any lingering hope for advancement beyond his position of Archdeacon.

Other books followed, now in the field of theological apologetics to which Paley turned with energy and lucidity. *Horae Paulinae* (1790) and his *View of the Evidences of Christianity* (1794) led up to his master work in apologetics, *Natural Theology*, published only three years before his death.

The significance of *Natural Theology* was not in its originality—others had been saying similar things for years before Paley's book appeared—but, rather, in the consistency of its method and the thoroughness of its argument. Thanks to these qualities, *Natural Theology* remains the definitive statement of the classical teleological argument. His theistic proof is essentially an empirical argument, and in Paley is found a consistent empiricist whose approach and method were perfectly suited to his subject matter.

The senses, for Paley, are our sole trustworthy avenues to knowledge of the reality surrounding us; the inferences of natural knowledge should always be grounded in experience; finally, all beliefs so established—including those of theology—are to be judged as more or less probable hypotheses rather than as necessary truths or indubitable demonstrations. By amassing empirical evidence in support of a given hypothesis, however, a belief may be shown to be overwhelmingly probable; under such circumstances, disbelief must be condemned as arbitrary and irrational.

Paley provided his readers with a vast store of the best scientific data available to him, the overwhelming effect of which was to show—as conclusively as empirical methodology allows or requires—the irrational absurdity of atheism. Never before or since *Natural Theology* has empirical fact been served up in such indefatigable abundance and variety to support belief in God.

Paley's argument divides naturally into two parts; the first part is devoted to proving the existence of a Designer of the experienced world, while the second part is dedicated to deriving empirically the theistic characteristics of this Designer.

The proof for the existence of a cosmic Designer begins with an analysis of the criteria used in everyday experience to determine whether or not something is the product of design. Paley contrasts, in what is probably his best known single example, the characteristics of a stone with those of a watch. The watch, unlike the stone, requires explanation in terms of purpose or design because the former is found to be composed (1) of parts (springs, cogs, and so on) nicely fashioned to work together in the joint accomplishment, (2) of an end result (steady movement of a pointer around a visible face) which the parts alone or in different combination would have been incapable of bringing about, and (3) of some identifiable useful product (marking the hours of the day). Experience teaches us that when these characteristics are present they are due to intelligent design; that is, to the action of a designer.

Such design-implying characteristics are abundantly present in nature as well as in human artifacts. No one would doubt that the telescope, composed of parts fitted together to accomplish a valuable effect beyond the powers of any of the parts taken separately, must be explained in terms of design; no more, then, can one doubt that the eye, which manifests even more ingenious utilization of individually impotent parts for the sake of a valuable total result—vision—than does the finest telescope, must have been designed. The empirical criteria justifying one's inference that the existence of the eye is best accounted for as the product of an intelligent Designer are abundantly present. Only stubborn prejudice could lead one to refuse to draw the sole conclusion sanctioned by repeated experience.

Philosophic objections aimed at justifying such prejudice, Paley contends, are all without weight. Shall we appeal to mere chance as accounting for the complex facts of natural design? Such an appeal is no more than the willful clutching of an ungrounded and vastly improbable hypothesis in irrational preference to the one hypothesis for which widespread experiential precedent has been established. Shall we look to "natural law" or to some "principle of order" as an alternative explanation of the facts? Such an attempted escape is literally unintelligible, Paley maintains, since "natural laws" and "principles" are only *descriptions* of nature's working; to suppose them to be *agents* is to make a serious logical blunder leading to conceptual confusion and to the fallacy of treating an abstraction as though it were a concrete thing. Can the hypothesis of a Designer be evaded by postulating an infinite regress of undesigned causes to account for the present facts? Such a route, Paley insists, is indeed an evasion, since no question is adequately answered by appeal to the intrinsic absurdity of a literally infinite sequence of causes. Somewhere the sequence as a whole must be rooted in a sufficient cause, and the marks of design, as we have seen, require this sufficient cause to be no less than an intelligent Designer. No more impressive to Paley are objections arising from our own incapacity as finite designers to produce— or to observe directly the cosmic Designer at work in producing—the natural objects which have the marks of design. One need not himself be able

to produce every contrivance that is recognized (and admired) as the product of intelligence; nor need one actually observe the production of every artifact or type of artifact in order to be justifiably confident of its status as falling within the class of intelligent contrivances.

Although Paley goes on to present other examples of natural contrivances, each serving to support the same conclusion, he acknowledges that each piece of evidence taken alone is sufficient to prove his point. But the weight of his argument, he holds, is cumulative; its total effect should be to sweep away completely any hesitation in acknowledging the existence of a Designer.

A contrivance need not, indeed, work perfectly—or even very well—to be recognized as a contrivance. Unless its status as a product of design were first granted, it would be logically inappropriate to accuse it of "working well" or "working badly" at all. Natural contrivances, therefore, Paley points out, would not even need to be so skillfully wrought as is the eye, to support conclusively the hypothesis that a cosmic Designer exists.

The eye, like other products of the cosmic Designer, is, however, clearly a masterpiece of organization. From such considerations we may learn not only of the existence of the Designer (with whom we have until now been exclusively concerned) but also of His characteristics. We recognize, on reflection, that personal pronouns are fully appropriate with respect to Him, since the characteristics of any designer must be those—intelligence, consciousness of purpose, volitional powers—which constitute the very meaning of "personal" within our experience.

What kind of person is this Designer? He is beyond all finite measure *powerful*, it is clear, since the forces of the natural order that He has designed exceed our comprehension; thus, He is *omnipotent*. He is beyond all finite measure *knowing*, since His intelligence manifested in the observable universe passes beyond our limits of conception; thus, He is *omniscient*. He is *everywhere active*, as is indicated by the uniformity of nature as far as our farthest observations can extend; thus, He is *omnipresent*. He has *been from "the beginning"* of created time, since the contriver must precede His contrivance; thus, He is *eternal*. As the producer of the world, He is *not dependent* on His product for His own existence; thus, we can empirically understand Him to be *self-existent*. The Designer is found, therefore, on empirical grounds, to be powerful, omnipotent, omniscient, omnipresent, eternal, and self-existent; who is such a Designer if not God?

God's existence has thus been proved, Paley concludes, but unless the world's apparent evil due to suffering can be explained on this hypothesis, such a proof is no more than a mockery. But the presence of evil is explainable. Pain is itself useful to living organisms which, without sharp warning to deter them, might easily destroy themselves in countless ways. Suffering is never inflicted for its own sake; if God had desired pointless suffering, how much more effectively He could have made us miserable! Teeth are for eating, not for aching. What is more, pleasure is added to the world to an extent entirely beyond that necessary for the mere maintenance of biological functions. Benevolence, not its opposite, can best account for the facts. Despite the sufferings of the world, God's goodness is secure; into His everlasting arms we may put our trust for help with difficulties yet unsolved.

Unsolved difficulties in Paley's position there may indeed be, but these seem to have had little effect in discouraging the immediate and widespread popularity of *Natural Theology*, whose influence in Britain and America for the half-century after its publication was immense. Required reading in many colleges, universities, and schools of theology in the early decades of the nineteenth century, *Natural Theology* helped to mold popular theological thinking to a marked extent. Even today sermons, and occasional articles in mass circulation media, may be found to reflect the arguments presented in this classic source. Gradually, however, Paley's argument lost favor in the latter half of the nineteenth century and in the twentieth century, largely because of the growing philosophical influence of David Hume (1711-1776) and Immanuel Kant (1724-1804), whose criticisms of Paley's line of reasoning actually antedated the publication of *Natural Theology*, but also because of the triumph of the evolutionary concept of natural selection, a nonpurposive explanation of the facts on which Paley based his case.

The teleological argument itself, nevertheless, has not so easily been disposed of. Even Immanuel Kant, one of the argument's most effective critics, expressed his respect for the motives which led Paley to appeal to the hypothesis of cosmic intelligence, and numerous modern, post-evolutionary versions of the classical argument from design have continued to appear.

Opposed to the whole enterprise, of course, are those theological movements, prominent in the present century, which have neither place nor patience for the argument from design or for rational apologetics in general. From such a theological perspective Paley and his modern counterparts are engaged in an illegitimate quest after knowledge in the place of faith, understanding in the place of mystery, and investigation in the place of revelation. Paley might well have understood this objection, since he clearly recognized the difference between nat-

ural and revealed theology, accepted both, and firmly rejected any attempt to substitute one for the other, but he would have been unhappy to have been forced to choose between his head and his heart, as though they were somehow ultimately incompatible. Paley's attempt was to show that reason and faith can co-operate, neither violating the other but, rather, each offering support to the other. That attempt has fallen into considerable— though not universal—disfavor in the mid-twentieth century; it remains for the future to determine whether theologians generally will once again find merit in Paley's ideal.

THE PHENOMENOLOGY OF SPIRIT

Author: Georg Wilhelm Friedrich Hegel (1770-1831)
Type of work: Philosophy of religion
First published: 1807

PRINCIPAL IDEAS ADVANCED

Phenomenology as a philosophical method involves the presentation of successive forms of consciousness in their claim to truth, the criticism of the internal incoherence of each shape, the transition to new configurations which presuppose the previous experience of consciousness, and the objective of a self-contained, coherent, and comprehensive synthesis.

Religion appears in a preliminary way within the phenomenological dialectic as the state of the unhappy consciousness at the level of the individual self-consciousness and as the struggle of enlightenment with superstition at the level of the self-alienation of spirit in culture.

Religion as a phenomenological moment proper appears toward the end of the phenomenological process as the conscious manifestation of Absolute Spirit in various forms.

Religion as the form of Absolute Spirit in its totality culminates in revealed religion, in Absolute Spirit aware of its identity with Absolute Being.

Even though Hegel's early intellectual development was theological rather than philosophical, his posture toward the Christian religion was ever that of critic rather than that of apologist. His passion for the naturalness of pagan Greek religion forced into relief the repressive aspects of Christian religion. Hence the question: How was the teaching of Jesus transformed into the positivity of the Christian religion? In this formulation Hegel pictured the teaching of Jesus as essentially autonomous, its claim to authority resting solely upon its intrinsic moral rationality. Through the work of the early believers, Christianity was transformed into a positive religion, a heteronomous religion, depending for its authority upon the arbitrary concept of divine will and upon the repressive functions of the Church conceived as a state.

Further probing of this problem led Hegel to an expansion and revision of the terms of his problem. The idea of a heteronomous religion was projected as the spirit of Judaism. The teaching of Jesus was regarded as emphasizing the transcendence of love, whereby the individual might be reconciled to his fate. The teaching of Jesus was constrasted with the Kantian idea of an autonomous moral law, a hopeless ideal because it reflected the tension between "ought" and "is" and thereby rendered impossible any genuine reconciliation with fate. The ideal of love as a religious self-consciousness found its ultimate expression in reconciliation with death and in the consequent outpouring of the Spirit. Thereby the Christian community was stamped as a universal religion of love. Yet within the life of the Church tensions remained between the ethics of obligation and the ethics of virtue, between acceptance and hatred of the natural world, between the concept of the Church as community and as state. The existence of these tensions meant

that religious reconciliation in principle had not become reconciliation in fact and that the Christian religion has not been reconciled with its destiny in the world.

Hegel abandoned theology when he became convinced that the self-contradictions within Christianity could not be surmounted within the theological context. Yet Hegel abandoned theology for philosophy only when he was able to formulate a philosophical method which transcended the abstractness and lifelessness of the philosophy he found current. Hegel's thought became explicitly philosophical when he was able to give philosophical expression to his theological experience, when he found a philosophical method thoroughly imbued with religious insight.

In the *Phänomenologie des Geistes* Hegel presents this method. Phenomenology for Hegel means the logic of the experience of consciousness. The subject of phenomenology, consciousness, is neither the natural consciousness of unreflective experience nor the pure rational ego of universal science, but the tension between the two. Various forms of the natural consciousness each in turn present themselves as claims to absolute truth, yet in the process of presentation, each experiences its own onesidedness and hence its death as a claim to absolute truth. The experience of consciousness is at once the experience of the negation of every form of the natural consciousness and the subsuming of each annihilated form in the depth of succeeding forms of consciousness. Each moment of the natural consciousness is crucified in its claim to truth, yet through this death finds its resurrection in the new context of the developed scientific consciousness.

The intelligibility of the phenomenological process also depends upon the object of the development. The dialectical presentation of the various forms of consciousness is also the logical unfolding of the self-manifestation of spirit. Only because the Absolute is already secretly at work in the development of consciousness is consciousness enabled to sustain the burden of its complex experience. Seen from this perspective, phenomenology is the *parousia* of the Absolute. Each moment of the experience of consciousness is not simply an experience of an object but is also a particular form of relation between subject and object. Hence, the lack of coincidence between subject and object which immediately appears as a lack of correspondence is really a lack of coherence. This lack of coherence, which the full manifestation of spirit demands, drives consciousness to the next necessary attempt to formulate a relation between subject and object in which the lack of coherence in the previous moment is overcome. The object in the succeeding moment is not the object as it appeared in the previous moment, but rather the totality of the previous experience of the object. In this sense, the phenomenological process may be said to be a dialectical series of transfigurations of consciousness.

Phenomenology presupposes that consciousness is capable of experiencing an object in its essence, though in an alienated form. An object has an essence in itself apart from its relation to consciousness; at the same time it has an essence for itself and for others. The effective realization of the object takes place when these aspects of its essence can be reconciled and the object can appear in and for itself. Phenomenology also presupposes that consciousness is in principle capable of experiencing all essences. Consciousness is potentially infinite and universal and thereby that mode in which Absolute Spirit can fully manifest itself. The correlation of the essential experiences of consciousness within consciousness means that the necessary process of phenomenology aims at the full manifestation of Absolute Spirit as concrete universal. The process is toward universality inasmuch as the moments of natural consciousness are negated in favor of broadening contexts. The process is toward concreteness because each new form of manifestation of spirit presupposes the results of what has already transpired. The end of phenomenology comes when consciousness is no longer compelled to go beyond itself, when the Absolute realizes itself fully in consciousness.

A profoundly critical moment in the phenomenological dialectic is the state of the unhappy consciousness. This moment arises in connection with the struggle of the individual self-consciousness to attain certainty of itself. Prior to this moment is the duality of master and slave, forms of self-consciousness which exhibit the character of independence and dependence apart from awareness of the implicit dependence of both upon the objective mediation of labor. From this, stoic and skeptical forms of self-consciousness emerge as shapes in which the self, conscious of the implicit dependence upon objective reality in the self-understanding of master and slave, seeks to establish an independence of self-consciousness from the world. Stoicism is the abstract form of self-consciousness which thinks itself universal and free, while skepticism is aware of itself as a particular self-consciousness indifferent to the being of the world. Yet stoicism cannot overcome the fact that it is a particular self-consciousness, and skepticism cannot overcome its positive existence in the world.

The unhappy consciousness is constituted by the unification of the stoic and skeptical forms of consciousness within a single consciousness. The unhappy consciousness recognizes both changeless and changeable elements in itself without being able to reconcile them. These elements are internally present in a way such that the triumph of one over the other means the annihilation of the self. The first, immediate, level of the unhappy consciousness is devotion toward the changeless as transcendent. In this form the changeless is inapproachable; it is transcendent and unrealizable because it remains a mere hope. A second form of the unhappy consciousness is the attempt to reconcile the changeless and the changeable through sacrifice and good works. This is a reconciliation which fails genuinely to reconcile, for the individual consciousness is not resigned in its work, but is conscious of its work as the particular effect of its own will; thereby the changeless appears in the work only in a correspondingly arbitrary way. Only in the third form of the unhappy consciousness, when the consciousness despairs ever of achieving reconciliation with itself and abandons its claim to self-certainty, does reconciliation occur. Mediation appears, but not as the act of the self-consciousness seeking its own certainty. Mediation is understood to come from beyond the self. The self experiences a sense of being lifted up out of its irreconcilable contrition and

established at one with the kingdom of reason.

Another moment in the phenomenological process bearing upon religion is the struggle of enlightenment and belief. This moment arises in relation to the appearance of spirit, self-alienated in culture. Spirit here appears as a form of culture, as "belief," as thought in its universal unreflective immediacy. Belief is a cultural reflection which looks upon a supersensible Absolute as the object of devotion.

Antithetical to belief is "pure insight," spirit in its universal negativity. Pure insight is a spiritual shape characterized by the idealization of pure reason, understood to be self-justifying by its very rationality. These two manifestations of spirit as cultural forms exhibit different relations to the world. Belief is devoted to a supersensible reality, in terms of which this world is valued as vain and empty. Yet this world is necessary for belief because it is the place where belief is found and where service of the Absolute is practiced. Pure insight is present in the world, but it is not present in complete actuality. Pure insight exists as the pure intention to rationality, as the call to resolve the contradictions of the actual world by rational judgment.

Self-alienation of spirit in culture appears in its most radical form in the struggle between these two spiritual configurations. This struggle begins as a contest between the content of belief and the method of insight. In the course of this struggle belief, as naïve unreflective consciousness, is transformed into superstition because it is defended by deception and despotism and because its claims are falsified by enlightenment. Enlightenment is a kind of infection too widespread by the time of discovery to be overcome.

This struggle between belief and insight seems to issue in the victory of enlightenment, for enlightenment ends the possibility of unreflective consciousness. Enlightenment attacks in belief what it finds to be superstitious, and it questions the historical evidences of religious faith. Ironically, what enlightenment attacks is not what belief intends, and the historical evidences are not the grounds of religious faith. Enlightenment is victorious insofar as belief proceeds to defend itself by appealing to rational proof and historical evidences. By such action belief loses its immediacy and its genuine unreflective rationality.

The victory of enlightenment, however, does not overcome the self-alienation of spirit in culture. Enlightenment in vindicating its claim has failed to acknowledge its own abstractness. It has not recognized its own essential nature as a universal negativity depending for its rationality upon the superstition it discovers in its opponent. This essentially negative character of enlightenment manifests itself in the course of establishing pure insight in culture. The pure intention of rationality is transformed into the terror of absolute freedom.

Religion as a phenomenological moment proper occurs only when the spirit is fully conscious of itself as Absolute. Thus, religion is not merely a form of the individual self-consciousness or a form of culture. Religion is the self-consciousness of Absolute Spirit lending its form to individual and to culture alike. Religion as a phenomenological moment presupposes the entire preceding dialectic and is constituted by the grasping of this process according to the special nuances of the forms of religion and the penetration of these configurations into the totality of experience.

Natural religion is religion in which Absolute Spirit presents itself in the form of an immediate awareness of itself as an alienated other. The diversity of shapes in natural religion gives rise to a religious self-consciousness whereby Absolute Spirit appears as the embodiment of the spirit of the free community. This is religion in the form of art, a religion in which Absolute Spirit is conscious of itself as self-creating and free. Religion in the form of art finds its highest expression not in visual or plastic form, but in the medium of language, in which the divine expresses its self-consciousness. From the cultic language of hymn and oracle, religion as art develops forms of embodiment in the epic, tragedy, and comedy. In these latter forms religion expresses itself as spiritual action, mediated to the community through drama. In the epic, the world of the gods is connected with the world of men through the hero. In tragedy the world of the gods becomes a context of fate, and the connection of the world of the gods with the world of men is tragically divided between the powerless wisdom of the chorus and the ironic action of the hero. The world of tragedy, sundered by the fateful self-contradictions of conscious action, is a world from which the religious consciousness recoils in pity and terror. Yet the tragic moment has done its work, so that the self-understanding of religion in the form of art passes into the shape of comedy. The figures within the comic drama are consciously identified with the fate to which they are bound. It is their individuality, not their destiny, which constitutes their mask. In comedy, religion as the embodiment of the free ethical consciousness abandons itself as a mere vanity of individuality disguising the conscious identity of self with universal fate.

Only then can revealed religion become manifest. Revealed religion presupposes the abandonment of religion in the form of certainty of self and discovery of self in reconciliation with fate. The former process now appears as a yearning after revealed religion, wherein the Absolute Being manifests itself as Absolute Spirit in its self-consciousness. In this incarnation, the self-consciousness of Absolute Spirit is discovered and known to be identical with Absolute Being. In revealed religion, self-consciousness as spirit is disclosed to be at home with its object, Absolute Being.

Nevertheless, revealed religion is Absolute Spirit in the immediate universality of its self-certainty. The present moment of revelation is transformed into a past whereby the Absolute Spirit is known as a continuously resurrected Spirit. This shows that the mediating process is incomplete even though revealed religion has found expression. Revealed religion in its immediacy knows Absolute Spirit in the mode of imaginative idea or as pictorial thought. For Absolute Being to realize itself fully and for Absolute Spirit to manifest itself fully, revealed religion must be converted into conceptual thought and translated into absolute knowledge. Only then is the form of knowledge coincident with the truth known. Only then does Absolute Spirit know itself in its phenomenological fullness, as the "intellectually comprehended organization . . . of the ways in which knowledge appears." This moment of the self-knowledge of Absolute Spirit, Hegel writes, is the conclusion of phenomenology and the beginning of the systematic articulation of philosophical truth.

UNITARIAN CHRISTIANITY

Author: William Ellery Channing (1780-1842)
Type of work: Theology
First published: 1819

Principal Ideas Advanced

The Bible must be interpreted in the light of its cultural setting, the laws of nature, reason, and critical analysis.

The unity of God cannot be reconciled with the doctrine of the Trinity.

The unity of Christ cannot be reconciled with the doctrine of two natures in one person.

The moral perfection of God is incompatible with the doctrines of election, the innate moral depravity of man, and eternal damnation.

The work of Christ (atonement) was to prompt in man a love for God and Christ and benevolence to one's fellow men.

William Ellery Channing's essay *Unitarian Christianity* was published in 1819, the same year it was delivered as a sermon at the ordination of Jared Sparks in Baltimore, Maryland. It is a concise credo of early American Unitarianism.

Channing was born in Newport, Rhode Island, on April 7, 1780. In American theology, the age was dominated by conflicting interests. On the one hand, Calvinism, reinvigorated and reinterpreted by Jonathan Edwards (1703-1758), reigned supreme, though challenges to its structure were then being heard. Jonathan Edwards had restated traditional Calvinistic theology in clear and unmistakable language. The topics of divine election, predestination, and original sin received new definition from his incisive mind, and these issues were brought once again to the forefront of New England theological debate. His successors, Samuel Hopkins (1721-1803), Joseph Bellamy (1719-1790), and Jonathan Edwards the Younger (1745-1801), developed the school of thought which became known as the New Divinity theology. A second group, commonly called the Old Calvinist party, sought to soften the logically coherent and severe Calvinism of Jonathan Edwards and his followers, and continued the liberalizing of Calvinistic theology which had begun with the Half Way Covenant (1662) and which found expression in the work of Solomon Stoddard (1643-1729), pastor of the Congregational Church in Northampton, Massachusetts. The Arminian theologians, led by Charles Chauncy (1705-1787) and Jonathan Mayhew (1720-1766), were openly critical of Edwardsean thought; they emphasized the benevolence of God, His parental character, and the role of reason in theology. Out of the Arminian tradition and in opposition to the New Divinity and Old Calvinist parties grew Unitarianism.

William Ellery Channing received his early religious education under Samuel Hopkins, the New Divinity minister of the Congregational Church in Newport, Rhode Island. His formal education was received at Harvard, where he graduated in 1798. After serving for two years as a tutor to a family in Richmond, Virginia, he returned, in 1800, to Newport to study with Hopkins. In 1801 he entered Harvard Divinity School and in 1803 was ordained as a Congregational minister at the Federal Street Church in Boston, Massachusetts.

During these early years of his life, Enlightenment thought came to have its impact on American theology. Deism achieved vocal and prominent supporters; rational theology found open and avid proponents. The Boston area became the center of Arminianism in America and the seedbed for "liberal" theology. In 1805 the Unitarians won control of Harvard when Henry Ware (1764-1845) was elected to the Hollis Professorship of Divinity.

When, in 1819, William Ellery Channing was asked to deliver the ordination sermon for Jared Sparks at Baltimore, Maryland, he prepared the sermon, "Unitarian Christianity," which became the first clear statement of American Unitarianism. The essay prompted a protracted and involved debate in New England circles and engaged the attention of churchmen in the other parts of the country. Within a month after its delivery, the sermon was printed in Baltimore, with a second edition following shortly; within a year further editions were published in Boston.

Channing's essay was concerned with two general problems. First, he sought to establish the principles by which Scripture should be interpreted. Second, he sketched the doctrines which Scripture, properly interpreted, enunciates.

While displaying the interests of Enlightenment thought, the essay was not as deviationist as is often thought. Channing's position rested on firm Biblical grounds: "Whatever doctrines seem to us to be clearly taught in the Scriptures, we receive without reserve or exception." Channing did insist, however, that reason must be used in the interpretation of the Bible, for, like other liberal spokesmen, he was certain that no Scriptural doctrines could be in conflict with reason. A comparison of Channing's work with that of the English Arian, Samuel Clarke (1675-1729), who published *The Scripture-Doctrine of the Trinity* in 1712, shows clear similarities at this point. Clarke, a leading figure in the Arian movement of the eighteenth century, was widely read by the American Unitarians. The insistence that Biblical faith teaches nothing contrary to reason was a characteristic affirmation of Channing and his followers.

Unlike Samuel Clarke, who analyzed some 1,250 verses of Scripture to ascertain the meaning of obscure phrases and who assumed that the Biblical record was its own interpreter, Channing insisted that since the Bible is a product of a particular culture, it needs interpretation and historical criticism. "We reason about the Bible precisely as civilians do about the constitution under which we live. . . ." Channing was among the first in America to appreciate the work of the German Biblical critics. Language, cultural setting, Jewish history, and philology are indispensable tools for an understanding of Scripture.

On this basis, then, Channing laid out the doctrines derived from the study of the Bible. The largest bulk of the second part of the sermon dealt with the doctrine of the Trinity and the nature of Christ. "The proposition, that there is one God, seems to us exceedingly plain." In Channing's opinion, this simple truth has been obscured by discussions of the distinctions between being and person. The trinitarian formula presented three divine beings, having "different consciousness, different wills, and different perceptions, performing different acts, and sustaining different relations. . . ." To Channing this was "irrational and unscriptural," for the Bible is very clear in distinguishing Jesus from God the Father. "We challenge our opponents to adduce one passage in the New Testament, where the word God means three persons, where it is not limited to one person, and where, unless turned from its usual sense by the connexion, it does not mean the Father." His overriding concern was to uphold the unity of God; for him there were no reasonable or Scriptural grounds for asserting that there are three persons in the Godhead. Channing was clearly separating himself from the trinitarian position formulated at the Council of Nicaea in 325.

On the same grounds he rejected the Formula of Chalcedon (451), which declared as orthodox dogma the doctrine that in Christ there are "two natures, without confusion, without change, without division, without separation. . . ." Here again, Channing asked for "some plain, direct passage, where Christ is said to be composed of two minds infinitely different, yet constituting one person." He could find none.

The argument of the "trinitarians" that unless Christ were God, of the very nature of God, no atonement could occur, Channing found intolerable. Anselm of Canterbury, the medieval theologian, in his treatise, *Cur Deus homo* (*Why God Became Man*), had developed the theme that man's rebellion or sin against an infinite God deserves infinite satisfaction which man is incapable of offering. Therefore, only one who is of the very nature of God could offer this recompense; namely, Jesus Christ. This "satisfaction theory of the atonement" received further statement from John Calvin. Channing rejected this view as an "imposition on common minds, and very derogatory to God's justice. . . ." Instead he spoke of Jesus as having been sent by the Father "to effect a moral, or spiritual deliverance of mankind; that is, to rescue men from sin and its consequences, and to bring them to a state of everlasting purity and happiness."

This affirmation of the unity of God, the subordination of Christ to God the Father, and the moral rather than substitutionary work of Christ reflected a view of the nature of God which Channing held. God is like a parent, a benevolent father, who seeks to restore his children to a life of obedience, knowledge, and love of the Creator. "We believe that God is infinitely good, kind, benevolent, in the proper sense of these words; good in disposition, as well as in act; good, not to a few, but to all; good to every individual, as well as to the general system."

Because he knew personally of the results of theological disputation and was aware of its painful expressions in Christian history, Channing made a plea for tolerance and charity. "We can hardly conceive of a plainer obligation on beings of our frail and fallible nature . . . than to abstain from condemning men of apparent conscientiousness and sincerity, who are chargeable with no crime but that of differing from us in the interpretation of the Scriptures, and differing, too, on topics of great and acknowledged obscurity." His admonition to the ordinand Jared Sparks summed up his view of the ministry and his understanding of the nature of the Gospel: "Be careful, lest the desire of defending what you seem truth, and of repelling reproach and misrepresentation, turn you aside from your great business, which is to fix in men's minds a living conviction of the obligation, sublimity, and happiness of Christian virtue."

In later writings Channing developed the topics which were only lightly touched on in his essay on Unitarian Christianity. The central issue of debate between the growing Unitarian movement and its opponents was over the nature of man. In the essays entitled, "The Moral Argument Against Calvinism," "Likeness to God," and "Honor Due All Men," Channing contributed to the discussion. His "Unitarian Christianity" stands out not as an *Institutes of the Christian Religion* but as a clear statement of the Unitarian position in contrast to the heritage of Calvinism and as a catalyst for later debates.

THE JOURNAL OF FRANCIS ASBURY

Author: Francis Asbury (1745-1816)
Type of work: Spiritual autobiography
First published: 1821

Principal Ideas Advanced

The Christian must not rest content with the grace by which God forgives sin; he must strive also for the grace by which he may live a holy life.

Method and discipline are necessary not merely for the achievement of personal holiness, but also for the public communication of the Christian life.

The presence of God's Spirit in the preacher and in the hearer is essential to to the saving and sanctifying of souls.

The apostolic bishop, by traveling throughout the Church, helps give unity to the Body of Christ.

Sent to the American Colonies in 1771 by the conference of Methodist societies of Great Britain, Francis Asbury kept a *Journal*, as did most of his confreres. As the years went by and American Methodism passed through the inevitable strains of rapid growth, Asbury, who meanwhile had become the mainstay of the movement, began to publish his *Journal*. Extracts were printed in *The Arminian Magazine*, a Methodist periodical which he helped found in 1788. The complete *Journal* was published in three volumes in 1821 and, together with his *Letters*, has been republished (1958) in a carefully edited and annotated edition.

Asbury reflected on the requirements of a good journal. On reading the first volume of John Wesley's *Journal*, in the year 1795, he wrote: "I am now convinced of the great difficulty of journalizing. Mr. Wesley was, doubtless, a man of very general knowledge, learning, and reading, to which we may add a lively wit and humour; yet, I think I see too much credulity, long, flat narrations, and coarse letters taken from others, in his Journal: but when

I come to his own thoughts, they are lively, sentimental, interesting, and instructing. The Journal of a minister of the Gospel should be theological: only it will be well to wink at many things we see and hear, since men's feelings grow more and more refined." Although much of the work of editing his own *Journal* was left to others, Asbury reviewed the transcribed material, and noted: "I have buried in shades all that will be proper to forget, in which I personally am concerned; if truth and I have been wronged, we have both witnessed one day of triumph."

From this record, Asbury emerges as a truly apostolic figure in whom love of God and concern for men's souls are constantly pushing upon the limits of human endurance. The Gospel which Asbury labored to proclaim had a dreadful urgency about it, demanding that men renounce this world and hope for consolation in the world to come. The Christian ought not merely to trust in the grace by which God, through Christ, pardons men's sins; he ought also, by all means, to claim the second grace, that of sanctification, by means of which the power of sin in a man's life is overthrown and he is enabled to live from hour to hour and moment to moment in the knowledge of God's will and the joy of God's presence. It may be that persons who do not have the grace of sanctification will not be saved—one can only hope to meet them in Heaven; but those who persevere in sanctification need have no fear of death, but may even desire it, knowing that it releases them from the sorrows and pains of this life and gives them entrance to the unclouded joys of God's presence.

Methodism, as is well-known, originated in the effort to systematize the life of holiness. John Wesley followed William Law, who, in *A Serious Call to a Devout and Holy Life* (1728), showed the higher prudence involved in applying to private prayer and philanthropy the method of keeping accounts and observing schedules, but Wesley took the further step of applying the new techniques of organization and management to the task of communicating the godly life to others. At the age of eighteen, Francis Asbury became a preacher in the Wesleyan movement; he was twenty-six when he answered the call from colonial America. The remainder of his life he spent in "methodizing" frontiersmen; that is to say, in not merely preaching to them and praying for them, but also organizing them so that the work of God's grace might not be lost through worldliness or sloth.

Asbury's own life is an example of strenuous discipline, worthy of a place in the accounts of the great saints and missionaries of Christendom. Under the most harassing conditions, since he lived on the road (as far as there were roads) and slept wherever he could spread his blanket, Asbury observed a careful regimen of prayer and study. Schooled only through his thirteenth year, he made himself a learned man by spending every available hour in reading and writing. Chronically ill, he rode five or six thousand miles a year, accepting only his expenses and a trifling salary, which he dispensed in charity. That his life was burdensome, he never conceals, but his eminently sound mind never lost its sense of proportion or gave way to despair. "My soul at times is in heaviness through manifold temptations," he wrote in South Carolina in January, 1796; "I felt an impression on my mind when at prayer that I felt too much, and might fret myself because of evil doers; I resolve, through grace, to be more resigned to the Lord, and less distressed, lest I should lightly sin against God or myself in unnecessarily injuring my health." A few days later he wrote: "Friday, 5, I spent in reading and writing, and observed it as a day of fasting and prayer. I felt myself under dejection of spirit. Ah! what a dreary world is this! my mind is under solemn impressions—the result of my reflections on God and souls. I will endeavour not to distress myself above measure. If sinners are lost, I cannot save them, neither shall I be damned for them. I was happy last evening with the poor slaves in brother Wells's kitchen, whilst our white brother held a sacramental love feast in the front parlour upstairs. I must be poor: this is the will of God concerning me."

The spiritual foes which Asbury felt he had chiefly to contend with were formalism and antinomianism. Formalism had, in his opinion, destroyed the usefulness of the Episcopal and Puritan churches, especially in the older centers, such as Philadelphia and Boston. No good, he maintained, could come from "reading prophets" and "systematical preachers." By contrast, the Methodist preacher depended upon God to grant a certain "warmth" to his speech, and "melt" the hearts of his hearers. Frequent meetings of small, local societies and annual camp meetings attended by thousands helped keep the spirit aflame. The other danger lay in antinomianism, which was the term Asbury used for the teaching that man is saved by Christ's death alone. Asbury claimed that the overemphasis upon justification by faith, together with the Calvinistic doctrine of the perseverance of the elect, led to neglect of evangelical obedience. Methodist preachers, on the contrary, did not hesitate to proclaim that following Christ requires giving up worldliness, sin, and folly, and living in accordance with one's heavenly calling.

Asbury himself lived under extreme austerity, quite as if he had taken monastic vows. (In addition to the hardships incidental to his labors, he regularly kept Friday as a day of fasting.) But he made no attempt to impose any formal regimen on his followers, or even on preachers. The concept of worldly, as over against godly, behavior was, however, clear both to him and to his hearers. Methodists were expected to shun alike the vain, frivolous life of fashionable urbanity, and the boisterous freedom of the frontier tavern. The Methodist social-consciousness showed itself early in Asbury's uncompromising stand against slavery. Because of his insistence, Negroes regularly attended services together with white people. On one occasion, when the

Negroes were forced to stand outside a half-filled chapel, Asbury declared his intention never to preach in that place again.

It was Asbury, more than any other, who introduced the episcopal form of government into Methodism. When, after the War of Independence, Wesley recommended that the American societies separate from the Protestant Episcopal Church, he appointed Francis Asbury and Thomas Coke (1747-1814) to be superintendents, but Asbury and Coke, appealing to the New Testament use of the word "episcopos," decided to adopt the title "bishop." Asbury made it a point to study the government of the early Church. He concluded that the essential characteristic of apostolic bishops was that they traveled and by this means welded the separate churches together into the unity of the Body of Christ. This describes quite accurately the work of Paul and Barnabas, and equally describes the function performed by Wesley in England and Asbury in America. Asbury maintained that a sedentary bishop, no matter whose hands have been laid on his head, is no bishop at all, since the Church of Christ is not an organization ruled over by officials but a living body which draws its life from Christ's presence in it. The so-called Episcopal and Presbyterian churches, Asbury said, are really so many separate congregations, since neither Presbytery nor Episcopacy does anything to provide effective communication between isolated churches.

For all his zeal and singleness of purpose, Asbury was not a narrow denominationalist. Before the Methodist societies withdrew from the Anglican communion, he was faithful in attending its ordinances, and he stood on friendly terms with many of its clergymen. At all times he was cordial with ministers and laymen of other churches insofar as a common love of Christ and obedience to the Gospel provided a basis for spiritual fellowship. Sensitive to the dangers of sectarianism, he was, however, convinced that it is necessary for those responsible for governing the Church to take a firm stand against heresy and hypocrisy, and he maintained that such action is not schismatic. "Schism," he said, "is the dividing real Christians from each other, and breaking the unity of the Spirit." For Christians to separate themselves from nominal believers or to exclude these from their fellowship is not schism.

Asbury's *Journal* is an important document, not merely for Church historians, but for anyone interested in American history. Few men can have possessed a wider and more intimate knowledge of the early American terrain and its people than this man, who, for forty of the most interesting years in the nation's history, moved each year from New England to Georgia, and as far west as there were settlements. As an Englishman who refused to bear arms against the Motherland, Asbury was suspect during the early years of the Revolution, but his refusal to abandon his societies gradually earned him the respect of the young nation. Asbury admired Washington, whom he once had the honor to meet, and he was frequently a guest in the homes of governors and other important citizens. But he seems to have had little interest in political developments. At one place he writes, "I visit, dine, and ride out every day; but it is very hard work for me to eat, drink, talk, and do nothing. As I am not a man of the world, the most of the conversation about it is irksome to me." This does not mean that Asbury was an impractical man; rather, it reflects the fact that he was fully occupied with the task of running a kingdom within a kingdom; his time was spent in thinking of the needs of hundreds of societies, stationing preachers, meeting annual conferences, raising money, founding colleges, and organizing publication societies. The testimony of his practicality is that when Asbury came to America there were perhaps a thousand Methodists. When he died, there were two hundred thousand.

THE CHRISTIAN FAITH

Author: Friedrich Schleiermacher (1768-1834)
Type of work: Systematic theology
First published: 1821-1822

PRINCIPAL IDEAS ADVANCED

Systematic theology is a description of the religious self-consciousness, characterized by a feeling of absolute dependence, which presupposes the existence of God.

In the Christian faith this self-consciousness is determined by the antithesis of sin and grace, with redemption being achieved through the perfect God-consciousness of Jesus Christ.

Just as the divine was in Jesus Christ, so a common divine Spirit animates the Church, through which God-consciousness is constantly increasing its influence in the world.

Friedrich Schleiermacher's *The Christian Faith*, it is generally agreed, has a significance for Protestant systematic theology or dogmatics comparable to John Calvin's *The Institutes of the Christian Religion*, and marks the beginning of the modern era in systematic theology. The book was written in 1821 while Schleiermacher, already well known for his *On Religion: Speeches to Its Cultured Despisers* (1799), was professor of theology at the University of Berlin. While Schleiermacher's system has never won general acceptance, Protestant theologians throughout the nineteenth century, and thus far in this century, have felt it necessary to understand the approach to theology set forth in *The Christian Faith*.

According to Schleiermacher, dogmatics as a theological discipline is based on our understanding of the Christian Church. The religious self-consciousness, which Schleiermacher defines as a feeling of absolute dependence, necessarily leads to the formation of a fellowship or communion. There are several possible forms of such communions (fetishism, polytheism, monotheism), which represent different stages of human development. Monotheistic religions, which represent the highest level of development, may be either active and ethical in nature (Judaism and Christianity), or passive and resigned (Islam). Christianity as a type of ethical monotheism is distinguished from other types in that

everything in Christianity is related to the redemption accomplished by Jesus of Nazareth. Christian doctrines are accordingly descriptions of the Christian religious affections, and it is the task of dogmatic theology to systematize the doctrine prevalent in the Church at a given time.

In the selection of dogmatic material care must be taken to guard against a number of natural Christian heresies. Jesus Christ must not be interpreted as having been so much different from man that He is unable to redeem man, but also He must not be understood as having been so much like man that He Himself needs redemption. Man, on the other hand, must not be regarded as being so bad that he cannot be redeemed, nor must he be considered to be able to redeem himself and to need no redeemer. Schleiermacher furthermore feels that it is necessary to distinguish between Roman Catholic and Protestant understandings of the Christian faith. Both Roman Catholicism and Protestantism agree that Christian piety arises only in the Christian fellowship, but Roman Catholicism, according to Schleiermacher, makes our relationship to Jesus Christ depend on our relationship to the Church, whereas Protestantism makes our relationship to the Church depend on our relationship to Jesus Christ.

In the formation of Schleiermacher's dogmatic system, its Protestant character is assured by appealing to the Protestant confessions, which in turn appeal to the New Testament Scriptures. (Schleiermacher did not feel that the Old Testament is determinative for an understanding of the Christian faith.) Though the content of the Scriptures must be expressed, Biblical vocabulary need not be used. Rather the dialectical character of the language used and the systematic arrangement of the material presented give dogmatics its essential scientific form. Central to the system is the antithesis between man's inability to inform all moments of life with the feeling of absolute dependence, and the increasing ability to do this communicated to man by Jesus Christ. It is necessary therefore to set forth the doctrines which this antithesis presupposes, as well as those doctrines which this antithesis determines. The basic form of dogmatic proposition is a description of the human self-consciousness as characterized by the feeling of absolute dependence. From this basic form, however, other forms may be derived, propositions which describe the constitution of the world and propositions which describe divine attributes, since the world and God are the correlates to which the Christian self-consciousness points. These three forms of propositions, accordingly, appear throughout the system.

In the first part of the system Schleiermacher discusses the religious self-consciousness which is always both presupposed by and contained in every Christian religious affection. God is known through the feeling of absolute dependence (which for Christian faith is also a relationship to Jesus Christ). Recognition of this feeling of absolute dependence, which must be intuited, takes the place of proofs for the existence of God. In the feeling of absolute dependence, however, we are also aware that we are involved in the natural order, that we are parts of the world. The relationship in the religious self-consciousness between God and the world must therefore be examined.

Traditionally a distinction has been made between the creation and the preservation of the world; but, according to Schleiermacher, as far as the feeling of absolute dependence is concerned, creation and preservation are indistinguishable. Nothing can be excluded from origination by God. The divine creative activity, which conditions all change, must itself be conceived nontemporally, and thus as being fundamentally different from all human activity. Divine preservation coincides with the interdependence of nature. Thus the concept of miracle, as implying events which do not represent natural causation, is not required. Divine activity is recognized in both good and evil, though in evil only as it is related to good as one of its conditions. No distinction need be made between influences that issue from the mechanisms of nature and those which issue from free causality; both are equally ordained by God.

Schleiermacher, in discussing the divine attributes which may be derived from this understanding of the relationship between God and the world, points out that these attributes must be closely related to the feeling of absolute dependence, and that they are to be understood primarily in terms of causality. The absolute divine causality must, however, be distinguished from the causality of the natural order, at the same time that it is equated with this causality in its comprehensiveness.

The four attributes which Schleiermacher discusses in this connection are the eternity, the omnipresence, the omnipotence, and the omniscience of God. The eternity of God suggests not unlimited time, but something fundamentally different from time. Eternity implies changelessness, but since there is eternal omnipotence, God is also active. God's omnipresence affirms his spaceless causality, whereby space itself is conditioned. God is omnipotent in the sense that all nature is dependent upon divine causality, which as eternal and omnipresent differs from finite causality at the same time that the divine causality is completely presented in the totality of finite being. Since God's knowledge is identical with His almighty will, the possible as distinct from the real cannot be an object of the divine knowledge. Hence, God's omniscience means that God knows all that is; and all that God knows, is. Schleiermacher argues that divine foreknowledge does not exclude freedom, since we can have foreknowledge of what is at the same time our own free activity.

The universality of the feeling of absolute dependence presupposes an original nontemporal perfection of both man and the world. The world, which has not changed in any fundamental sense since its creation, can be known (the ideal aspect of its original perfection) and used (the real aspect of its original perfection). Man's original perfection consists in the fact that, in fellowship with other men, both in knowing and doing, he is capable of God-consciousness. No attempt is made, however, to define the condition of the first man. The original perfection of man is to be seen in Christ rather than in Adam.

The second part of Schleiermacher's system explicates the religious self-consciousness as it is determined by the antithesis of sin and grace, and it is divided into two sections dealing with our consciousness of sin and our consciousness of grace.

Sin, according to Schleiermacher, is a hindrance of the power of the spirit by man's sensuous nature. Given man's original perfection, sin arises as there is unequal development of will and insight. Though man is incapable of the good apart from redemption, he is capable of responding in some sense to grace, and he can thereby achieve civil righteousness. Original sin is individual and corporate. There is original sinfulness as well as original perfection. The actual sin of each generation is the originating original sin for the next generation, and original sin issues in actual sin. The sins of the redeemed, however, according to Schleiermacher, are always diminishing, nor do they obstruct the spiritual life, whereas the sins of the unredeemed are habitual and contagious, and they vitiate the God-consciousness. Yet even among the unredeemed there is a faint shadow of the good.

Without sin nothing in the world could properly be regarded as evil, but sin being given, there is both natural and social evil. Social evil and sin are directly related, though natural evil and sin are related only indirectly. Sin and evil are equally related only when one views the total community, although this equivalence may not be evident in the case of the individual.

Since sin is related to redemption, in that the merely gradual and imperfect unfolding of the power of God-consciousness is one of the necessary conditions of the human stage of existence, God may in this sense be said to be the author of sin. God's holiness, however, is that divine causality through which conscience in all corporate life is conjoined with the need for redemption. God's justice means that evil and sin are connected, but only so as to deter sin.

Schleiermacher next discusses the second aspect of the antithesis of sin and grace, as he describes the consciousness of grace. Man approaches blessedness through the influence of a divinely effected corporate life working in opposition to the corporate life of sin. In the Christian fellowship redemption is effected through the communication of the supernatural sinless perfection of Christ, but human receptivity is such that this perfection can also become natural. In the fellowship with God achieved through Jesus Christ His perfection is active while the believer is passive. The divine in Christ was the perfection of His God-consciousness, which developed gradually, but in such a way that there were no conflicts with His sense nature. In the union of the divine and the human in Christ the divine was active and the human passive, but in the state of union the activity was common to both.

Christ's redemptive activity consists of the fact that He brings believers into the power of His God-consciousness, and He may thus be understood in terms of the three offices of prophet, priest, and king. Christ as a prophet taught the original revelation of God in Himself, explaining both His calling of communicating eternal life in the Kingdom of God, and His unique relationship with the Father. With this teaching prophecy came to an end, since no more perfect understanding of man's relation to God is possible than that which is found in the teaching of Christ. Christ's priestly

office includes His perfect fulfillment of the law and His atoning death, by which we are animated to fulfill the divine will. Through His suffering punishment is abolished, for in fellowship with Him evil is no longer felt as punishment. His death occurred as He persisted in His redemptive activity, and we are also called to share His suffering and so to persist in our vocation. Christ now represents us before the Father to establish our fellowship with the Father and to support our prayers. Christ's kingly office consists in the fact that everything that the Christian fellowship needs for its well-being continually proceeds from Him. Since this is a Kingdom of grace, Christianity is not a political religion or a theocracy. Christ exerts a purely spiritual lordship, and therefore separation of Church and state is entirely appropriate.

Those assumed into living fellowship with Jesus Christ are regenerated and sanctified. Regeneration involves conversion, whereby man repents and believes, and justification, whereby man is forgiven and adopted by God. In sanctification the natural powers of the regenerate are put at the disposal of Christ, producing a life akin to His in perfection and blessedness. Since the sins of the regenerate are always being combated, they carry forgiveness with them and have no power to annul the grace of regeneration. No new sin enters and the truly regenerate cannot fall away from grace. Good works are the natural effects of faith, though the regenerate do not trust in them.

In discussing the constitution of the world in relation to redemption, Schleiermacher sets forth his doctrine of the Church and the means of grace. The Church originates as regenerate individuals come together to form a system of mutual interaction and co-operation. It appears that God has not willed that all those living at any one time should be uniformly taken into the Kingdom of Christ. Schleier-macher believes, however, that all are ultimately foreordained to blessedness. Predestination occurs through the divine government of the world. The elect are chosen, as Christ was chosen, to further the work of redemption; this explains why some are chosen prior to others.

The common spirit which animates the believers in the Church to co-operation and reciprocal influence is in the Christian fellowship what the divine was in Christ. It differs in that the union that is formed between the divine and the human in the Church is not a person-forming union.

The Church in its relation to the world retains its self-identity through the essential and invariable features of the Holy Scriptures and the ministry of the Word, which is the witness of Christ, and through the ordinances of baptism and the Lord's Supper, which form and maintain the fellowship.

The authority of the Scriptures is based on faith in Christ. The Scriptures are the first in a series of presentations of the Christian faith, and the norm for all succeeding generations. While originality continues in the Church, everything must be in harmony with the original Scriptures. The ministry of the Word is performed by the spontaneously active members of the Church for those primarily receptive, and there is to be both a public ministry as well as a more informal and occasional ministry of the Word. Through baptism the individual is received into the Church, and due to

the promise of Christ baptism is a channel of justifying activity. Ordinarily the Word should be known to the baptized person so that baptism and regeneration can coincide. Yet parents may prefer infant baptism with the understanding that it be supplemented with confirmation. In the Lord's Supper the spiritual life of Christians is strengthened as, according to the institution of Christ, His body and blood are administered to them. Schleier-macher claims that a new statement interpreting the connection between the body and blood of Christ and the elements of bread and wine is needed, a statement which will avoid both the extreme of affirming such a connection independent of the act of participation, as well as the extreme of denying any connection whatever between the elements and spiritual participation in Christ. The power of the keys is the power of the Church to decide what belongs to the Christian life and to deal with individuals in accord with such decisions. This power resides in the whole congregation. Its legislation must remain subject to constant review. Excommunication is allowed, but it must be only temporary. Prayer in the name of Christ has no other object than the divine good pleasure. Thus Christian prayers either express resignation or thankfulness. The inward state giving rise to such prayer is one of the conditions for the emergence of the result.

Since the world exercises influence on the Church, there is an antithesis between the visible and the invisible Church. The visible Church is divided and fallible, while the invisible Church, which is the active element in the visible Church, is undivided and infallible. Schleiermacher believes that the impulse leading to division will gradually weaken, though he grants that some divisions are effected by the Holy Spirit. There should not, however, be complete suspension of fellowship between different parts of the visible Church, since the visible Church thus separates itself from the unity of the invisible Church. The visible Church is fallible in that no definition of doctrine can be regarded as eternally valid. Error, however, is removed in the Church by the corrective power of truth (the Scriptures are the freest from error), which never ceases to work in it.

The consummation of the Church, which implies that no other religion remains as an organized fellowship, due to the continuing power of sin in succeeding generations, will not be reached in time. Yet it remains as an ideal to be achieved ultimately through the kingly power of Christ. The Christian conception of life after death is derived from faith in Christ. Since Christ was capable of survival, all of the human race must be capable of it too, though we are unable to imagine the form this future life will take. Schleiermacher does recognize some tension between attempts to affirm the consummation of the Church and to maintain at the same time continu-

ity in the personal survival of the individual. He attaches greater certainty to the concept of the consummation of the Church, though he prefers to affirm also the universal restoration of all souls.

The divine attributes which relate to redemption are love and wisdom. Love is the only attribute which is simply equated with God. We sense divine love directly in redemption, from which the God-consciousness grows. Hence it represents to us the essence of God. Where almighty love is, there also absolute wisdom must be. Through the divine wisdom the world, as the scene of redemption, is also the absolute revelation of God, and the world is therefore good.

Schleiermacher concludes his system with a discussion of the doctrine of the Trinity, a doctrine he regards not as an immediate utterance of the Christian self-consciousness, but as a combination of several such utterances. The doctrine of the Trinity attempts to assert a union of the divine essence with human nature in Christ and in the Church. There are difficulties, however, in simultaneously affirming unity and distinctions in the Trinity. Schleiermacher observes that no fresh treatment was given this doctrine at the Reformation, and he suggests that further doctrinal development at this point is needed.

AIDS TO REFLECTION

Author: Samuel Taylor Coleridge (1772-1834)
Type of work: Moral and spiritual aphorisms
First published: 1825

Principal Ideas Advanced

Reflection or self-knowledge is the means by which man realizes his spiritual end.

Religious prudence, morality, and spiritual religion are stages of man's spiritual development.

Because of sin, man needs divine grace in order to realize his highest potentialities.

Christian theology may be purged of speculative error by using the moral sense as a touchstone for what is true.

Confirmation of the truth of Christianity is found in the way it answers to the deepest needs of man's spirit.

Aids to Reflection, Coleridge tells us, is a didactic work, written especially for "the studious Young" as they complete their formal education, but also for "as many in all classes as wish for aid in disciplining their minds to habits of reflection." Coleridge was convinced that in order to realize his potentialities as a spiritual being, a man must cultivate the habit of self-examination or reflection. The book consists of a series of aphorisms taken from leading English churchmen; to the aphorisms Coleridge adds his criticisms and comments. In this way he hoped not merely to develop in the purposeful reader a skill in and habit of reading critically, but, more fundamentally, to awaken the innate faculties of the reader's spirit so that he would learn to appropriate inwardly and by natural affinity truths which for others are matters of rote.

Coleridge's interest in religion and in metaphysics dates from his early years. While he was a student at Cambridge, he became an enthusiastic disciple of the mechanistic psychologist, David Hartley (1705-1757), and preached in Unitarian chapels. Later, he embraced a more Platonic type of philosophy and became an apprecia-tive member of the Church of England. *Aids to Reflection* is a mature work, in which the author affirms the inadequacy of morality without religion and maintains that those who rightly understand the exigencies of their own inner development will perceive that the central affirmations of Christianity are true. Revelation is, thus, something beyond reason, but not unreasonable.

Against the materialistic philosophy which his age inherited from the eighteenth century, Coleridge raised anew the protest that man is not merely an object of nature. As a creature of flesh and blood, he is intelligible in physical categories; but as will, spirit, personality, he is incommensurate with material things, and, in a perfectly intelligible sense, "supernatural." According to Coleridge, this view of man is the meaning of the Scriptures when they say that man is made in God's image and that man's most important undertaking is to seek to recover that image. In this undertaking, man is a responsible agent. He must make it his business to achieve salvation; nevertheless, anyone who tries to attain salvation and makes any progress in the endeavor must admit that man does not labor alone; indeed, he can achieve nothing unless God is also actively involved in the same undertaking.

According to Coleridge, three kinds of undertaking are necessary if man is to achieve his end. The first is religious prudence, by means of which a man removes himself from temptation's path and generally endeavors to take advantage of all circumstances which will further his design. The second is morality, which, according to Coleridge, is not to be confused with prudence, because morality is concerned not with means and ends, but with obedience to law. Obedience comes much nearer than prudence to man's proper goal; namely, conforming his will to the perfect will of God. The man who undertakes to be moral cannot rest content with his current achievements but must constantly be pressing on; therefore, morality, in its higher reaches, becomes religious. On this plane, however, man is forced to recognize the limitations of his own efforts and his need for a Divine Redeemer. Thus, for its perfection, morality requires spiritual religion, Christianity, through which the soul of sinful man is born anew and enabled to overcome its hindrances.

These three aspects of man's moral quest—prudence, morality, and religion—provide the three divisions of Coleridge's book and the basis on which he selected his aphorisms. Since some of the aphorisms are immediately helpful, they are left by the editor to speak for themselves. Others are of the sort that are apt to raise questions in men's minds and may even turn them away from Christianity. These call forth Coleridge's criticisms, not always sympathetic, although, on the whole,

Coleridge has excerpted only from writers with whom he can agree: Jeremy Taylor (1613-1667), Henry More (1614-1687), and, more often than either of these, the Scottish archbishop, Robert Leighton (1611-1684).

Coleridge's eminently moral approach to Christianity finds expression in a certain impatience with purely speculative theology. The God of the philosophers, he says, answers to a purely intellectual need. Reason requires us to think in terms of unity, substance, attributes, and causes; and theologians who have a philosophical bias tend to mistake these ideas (*entia rationalia*) for real objects (*entia realia*), and to confuse them with the Living God who is the "supreme Object of our Faith, Love, Fear and Adoration." Many of the difficulties which people find in the doctrines of the theologians stem from this source; for example, the teaching that God's sovereign power leaves no freedom to the creature. But, says Coleridge, whenever a doctrine runs counter to conscience or to the interests of morality, it is to be rejected. He even raises the question whether it is legitimate to proceed by rational inference from one genuinely religious notion to another. Thus, the experience of redemption is firm ground for the notion that Christ is divine, but no basis for inferences concerning the internal life of the Godhead, of which we have no comparable revelation. "Grant, that in thus *realizing* the Notion I am warranted by Revelation, the Law of Conscience, and the interests and necessities of my Moral Being! Yet by what authority, by what inducement, am I entitled to attach the same reality to a second Notion, a Notion drawn from a Notion? It is evident, that if I have the same

Right, it must be on the same grounds. Revelation must have assured it, my Conscience required it—or in some way or other I must have an *interest* in this belief. It must *concern* me, as a moral and responsible Being."

Coleridge limits himself, therefore, to discussing those doctrines of the Church which are directly related to man's moral and spiritual endeavor, and mainly to three: the doctrine of election and reprobation, the doctrine of original sin, and the doctrine of vicarious atonement.

In discussing election, Coleridge stresses the difference between persons and things. The extreme Calvinists, such as Jonathan Edwards (1703-1758), err, he says, through failing to recognize the distinction between nature and spirit. Their notions of predestination all rest on the fallacy of supposing that the same kind of necessity governs spirits as governs physical objects. Still, there is no reason to go over to the opposite position and deny altogether the efficacy of God's will in the lives of men, and Coleridge favors the moderate Calvinism of Archbishop Leighton over the Arminianism which generally characterized post-Restoration Anglican thought.

Coleridge agrees with Jeremy Taylor that original sin is an indubitable fact in human experience, but he takes issue with Taylor's contention that Adam's descendants have their sinful natures as a punishment for their first father's offense. Man sins, according to Coleridge, when he acts on some private maxim which is opposed to the universal law of right reason in the conscience. The sin originates in each man; otherwise, it would be no act of the will and no sin. But, since sin is common to all, it must have a common

ground. "And this evil Ground we call Original Sin. It is a *Mystery*, that is, a Fact, which we see, but we cannot explain." Moral feeling, on the other hand, is adamant against the view that the descendants of Adam are guilty because of some supposed participation in Adam's act.

The mystery of redemption or atonement, says Coleridge, is central to Christianity, as the doctrines of election and original sin (which are known to most high religions) are not. But he holds that traditional theology has often interpreted the role of Christ's death in ways that give offense to reason and the moral sense, especially in teaching that Christ made satisfaction for our sins. This view, Coleridge says, is unscriptural, resting on a misunderstanding of the metaphorical nature of Paul's writings. If, instead, we follow the words of Christ Himself, as recorded by John, we see that the redemptive act is a regeneration or rebirth, which accords entirely with our moral need and with our spiritual experience of redemption in Christ.

For Coleridge, the moral faculties in man not merely provide the best guide for understanding Christianity, but in addition constitute the only adequate certification of its truth. Instead of arguing about the moral sense, the only practical course is to try it. In the posthumous work called *Confessions of an Inquiring Spirit* (1840), Coleridge says, "The truth revealed through Christ has its evidence in itself, and the proof of its divine authority in its fitness to our nature and needs;—the clearness and cogency of this proof being proportioned to the degree of self-knowledge in each individual hearer." Those who maintain the necessity of founding Christian faith on a belief in the infallibility of Scriptures are, he says, setting an obstacle in the way of many a person. Told that everything in the Bible is God's word, they will reject the entirety, but encouraged to read it in a free manner, bringing to it the same degree of reverence that they willingly accord to the writings of any wise man, they will find much in it "coincident with [their] pre-established convictions," and they will henceforth recognize what they have read as "the recorded workings of the Word and the Spirit in the minds, lives, and hearts of spiritual men."

Coleridge is aware that this appeal to inward conviction is likely to be confused with the kind of popular religious teaching known as "enthusiasm," and he insists on observing a distinction. Those who trust in visionary experiences and who talk confidently about "feeling" the presence of God's Spirit make the mistake of confusing the natural with the supernatural. The properties of things and the affections of our bodies belong to a different order from Spirit, which is commensurate rather with conscience and reason. Coleridge quotes the pagan philosopher Seneca (c. 3 B.C.-A.D. 65) to show that there is long-standing authority for identifying Spirit with reason. "A Holy Spirit abides within us," says Seneca, "the observer of our evil, the guardian of our good. Just as He has been drawn by us, so He himself draws us. No one is a good man without God."

The distinction between the realms of nature and Spirit corresponds closely to Kant's distinction between *phenomena* and *noumena,* as Coleridge readily acknowledges. Phenomenal knowledge, which the English Platonists called "discursive reason," and which Kant called "understanding," has sense experience as its basis and reason as its organizing principle. Here necessity manifests itself according to the law of causality, and human freedom in terms of the hypothetical imperative, or prudence. Our knowledge of the noumenal world, properly called reason, transcends the realm of sense, and lays hold directly on eternal truth. Speculative reason discloses the necessities of logic, and practical reason the categorical imperatives of conscience and the moral law. These distinctions are, according to Coleridge, among the most important aids to reflection, particularly as they enable us to avoid dealing with religious matters in sensible terms. They also help us toward an understanding of the nature of salvation. Speaking of *practical* reason, Coleridge says, "Whenever by self-subjection to this universal Light, the Will of the Individual, the *particular* Will, has become a Will of Reason, the man is regenerate: and Reason is then the *Spirit* of the regenerated man, whereby the Person is capable of a quickening intercommunion with the Divine Spirit. And herein consists the mystery of Redemption, that this has been rendered possible for us."

Aids to Reflection was the most popular of Coleridge's prose works, enjoying a wide public in both Great Britain and the United States. Its appearance in an American version greatly influenced the transcendentalist movement in New England.

ON THE ADAPTATION OF EXTERNAL NATURE TO THE MORAL AND INTELLECTUAL CONSTITUTION OF MAN

Author: Thomas Chalmers (1780-1847)
Type of work: Natural theology
First published: 1833

PRINCIPAL IDEAS ADVANCED

If by external nature the whole order of human society, as well as the physical world, is understood, the adaptations of external nature to the mind of man are prolific of evidence for the wisdom and moral attributes of a deity.

General considerations as to the supremacy of conscience, the pleasure of virtue and the pain of vice, and the law of habit lead to particular conclusions concerning adaptations, including those found in the civil, political, and economic structure of human society.

Evidence for the immortality of the human soul as well as for the attributes of God can be derived from a study of nature and society.

Thomas Chalmers, Professor of Divinity in the University of Edinburgh, destined to play a leading role in the disruption of the Church of Scotland and the foundation of the Free Church, was the author of the first of the Bridgewater Treatises *On the Power, Wisdom and Goodness of God as Manifested in the Creation.* Subsequent treatises in this series included John Kidd's *On the Adaptation of External Nature to the Physical Condition of Man,* William Whewell's *On Astronomy and General Physics,* Charles Bell's *The Hand: Its Mechanism and Vital Endowments as Evincing Design,* Peter Mark Roget's *On Animal and Vegetable Physiology,* William Buckland's *On Geology and Mineralogy,* William Kirby's *On the History, Habits and Instincts of Animals,* and William Prout's *On Chemistry, Meteorology, and the Function of Digestion.*

Chalmers devotes an introductory chapter to general and preliminary observations. The concept of external nature is to be understood in a wide sense as comprehending "not merely all that is external to mind, but all that is external to the individual possessor of a human mind." Relations between mind and mind, as well as between mind and matter, are to be viewed as attesting a wise and beneficent contrivance.

The argument for the wisdom and goodness of God is drawn chiefly from "the obvious adaptation wherewith creation teems, throughout all its borders, of means to a beneficial end." The evidence for design increases with the number of independent circumstances that concur for the production of a useful result. Anatomy thus provides more intense evidence for a God than does astronomy.

The laws of matter are to be distinguished from the dispositions of matter. Atheists tend to reason exclusively on the laws, and to overlook the dispositions of matter, Chalmers claims. The argument for theism rests on the dispositions of matter more than on its laws. Matter is "distributed into such parts as to ensure a right direction and a beneficial application for its powers," he writes. In performances of human art, matter does not receive laws or properties, but is arranged into parts by the workmanship of the designer. Without involving ourselves in the metaphysical obscurity surrounding the origination of matter, says Chalmers, we can "discern, in the mere arrangements of matter, the most obvious and decisive signatures of the artist hand which has been employed on it."

Mental phenomena lack the complexity possessed by bodily organs. In consciousness we are aware only of simple antecedents followed by simple consequents. Whether the mind is regarded as a complex of faculties or as a simple substance passing into different states, there is the same strength of evidence for a God. Although the argument derived from these materials is not as strong as that from the collocations of matter, mind does "furnish a peculiar argument of its own, which, though not grounded on mathematical data, and not derived from a lengthened and logical process of reasoning, is of a highly effective and practical character notwithstanding." The phenomena of mind present immediate evidence that they are the effect not of blind, unconscious matter but of an intelligence. The phenomena of mind inform us distinctly of the attributes of God, Chalmers states, while the phenomena of matter tell us more decisively of the existence of God.

The study not of the mind itself, but of the adaptation of external nature to its constitution, allows ample room for the evidence of collocation. The great object of philosophy, in which Chalmers obviously includes the natural sciences, is to ascertain the ultimate principles into which all natural phenomena may be resolved. Secondary laws may be shown by further analysis to be derived from primitive or elementary laws. Evidence of divine goodness based on such a secondary law as that of the tides is independent of the discovery of the primary law, gravitation, into which it is resolvable. Secondary laws "attest the multitude of useful parts in nature; and the skill, guided by benevolence which has been put forth in the distribution of them." This principle applies to mental as well as to material phenomena.

Part One of Chalmer's book considers the adaptation of external nature to man's moral constitution and opens with a chapter on the supremacy of conscience. The subject discussed is not ethical principles as such but man's moral nature, the fact that man has a conscience which tells him that moral law is binding. Conscience is sovereign *de jure,* though not *de facto.* It has the right to command, even though inferior principles of our nature rebel. The distinctive function of conscience is the regulation of all the other powers and passions of humanity. Chalmers acknowledges his agreement with Bishop Butler (1692-1752), whose sermons he speaks of as "the most precious repository of sound ethical principles extant in any language."

In the phenomena of conscience, Chalmers writes, nature offers her strongest argument for the moral character of God. In spite of aberrations in man's present constitution, the voice of conscience bears undying testimony to the supremacy of rectitude and provides the strongest argument that "in spite of all partial and temporary derangements, Supreme Power and Supreme Goodness are at one." The theology of conscience is both more widely diffused and of more practical influence than the theology of academic demonstration. The rapid inference from the law of the heart to the lawgiver appears like intuition. Yet it is an inference rather than an innate idea or instinctive sense of the divine. Though often greatly obscured, this testimony has never been wholly obliterated in any country or at any period of human history.

Conscience follows up her mandates with an obvious discipline of rewards and punishments, Chalmers claims; present satisfaction and remorse are tokens of future judgment.

The laws of conscience comprise all the virtues inscribed by God on the human heart and provide an argument for the moral character of God, in that they must have been transcribed from the prior tablet of His own nature.

The diversity of moral judgments among men does not nullify this argument, continues Chalmers, for diversity can be accounted for by the distorting effect of passion and interest. Disagreement in moral judgments is compatible with basic agreement as to moral principles. Differences in understanding account for differences in moral judgment. When conscience is rightly informed, she speaks the same lessons in all countries. Chalmers concludes: "In proportion as the understandings of men become more enlightened, do their consciences become more accordant with each other."

The theological inference is drawn not from the physical origin of conscience, but from the fact of its uniformity. Scientific discussion of the derivation of conscience from simpler or anterior principles in the human constitution does not affect the validity of the argument. Nor is the inference destroyed by the actual prevalence of vice in the world. Wherever there is vice there is occasion for the most impressive exercise of conscience in the remorse, terror, and bitter dissatisfaction experienced in the hearts of the wicked.

A second general argument from the moral constitution of man is based on the inherent pleasure of the virtuous affections and the misery of the vicious affections. Distinct from the pleasure attendant on the sense of the rightness of an act, there is a pleasure in the very sensation of virtue, and likewise a pain in moral evil itself, distinct from the pain inflicted by conscience. It is a proof both of a benevolent and righteous God that He should so have framed our mental economy that right and wholesome morality is palatable to the taste of the inner man and moral evil is essentially and inherently bitter.

Chalmers calls attention to Bishop Butler's distinction between pleasure taken as the final object of our desire and that pleasure which is inseparable from gratification of any desire whatsoever. This distinction strikes at the root of the selfish system of morals. The disinterested exercise of an affection brings satisfaction to the extent that the object of the affection and not the pleasure is in view.

While there is a certain pleasure in the indulgence even of evil affections, the pleasure of an affection such as anger consists largely in the removal of a pain, the emotion itself being an exceedingly painful one. A good affection has also a peculiar tendency to immortalize its objects, while an evil one destroys them. This tendency suggests the final triumph of virtue, at least in the sense that virtue alone is capable of a blissful immortality. The union of virtue and happiness is a contingent appointment of the Deity, at once the evidence and the effect of the goodness that is in His own nature.

The power and operation of habit provides material for a third general argument. Chalmers rejects the associationist theory of habit propounded by Thomas Brown (1778-1820), but points out that the argument from the power of habit is independent on any philosophical theory. It is a fact that the man who enters on a career of vice enters on a career of headlong degeneracy. The law of habit, enlisted on the side of righteousness, strengthens our resistance to vice and facilitates the most arduous performances of virtue. The acts of virtue ripen into habits, resulting in the formation of virtuous character. Death intercepts the view of the ultimate result of this process, from which it remains possible to draw a strong argument for immortality. On the side of the outcome of vice, the forebodings of guilty fear as to future punishment are even more striking than expectations of reward by the virtuous.

External nature may be viewed as adapted to the moral constitution of man with reference to the supremacy of conscience, the inherent pleasures and pains of virtue and vice, and the law and operation of habit. The exercise of conscience is capable of resuscitation even in the most abandoned criminals. Reciprocal influences between mind and mind in society multiply the pleasures of virtue and the sufferings of vice. Finally, the law of habit provides a ground for moral education and thus encourages the expectation

of a permanent as well as a universal reign of virtue in the world.

Special and subordinate adaptations of external nature to man's moral constitution are found in the mechanism of the mind by which affections such as resentment and shame serve for the maintenance of peace and decency in the life of society. Detailed attention is given to affections toward family and property that conduce to the civil and political well-being of society as well as to those conducing to the economic well-being of society. The advantages of the natural order are stressed by Chalmers, particularly in connection with the origin and rights of property, and he also delineates the disadvantages of deviations from this order by human legislation. Even the Malthusian doctrine of population is found to exhibit a pure case of adaptation to the external nature of the world by the moral nature of man.

The prevalence of truth in the world subserves the general good. The sustenance of the virtue of honesty on the soil of selfishness speaks emphatically for the wisdom and goodness of God. Man is not a utilitarian either in his propensities or his principles, but his inclinations have been so adapted to the external world that great utility results from God-given constitution. "Virtue is not right because it is useful," writes Chalmers, "but God hath made it useful because it is right."

From the capacities of the world for making a virtuous species happy, conclusions are derived which bear on the character of God and the immortality of man. The problem of evil cannot be adequately resolved by a sentimentalist theism that conceives of God as exclusively determined by benevolence. The connection of suffering with sin manifests the righteousness of God. The original design of the Creator can be read in the normal tendency of things, as distinguished from the tendencies exhibited by a deranged system. Not only the inequalities of the present system, but also the adaptation of desires to corresponding objects in nature may provide intimations of immortality.

The adaptation of external nature to the intellectual constitution of man is discussed briefly in the concluding part of the work, which ends with an illuminating analysis of the defects and uses of natural theology.

THE CHRISTIAN SYSTEM

Author: Alexander Campbell (1788-1866)
Type of work: Biblical doctrine and practice
First published: 1839

PRINCIPAL IDEAS ADVANCED

The unity of the Christian Church should be promoted on the foundation of those beliefs and practices contained in the Bible only.

A Christian is to be defined not by creeds, but by personal faith in Jesus as the true Messiah, and by obedience to Him as lawgiver and King.

Christian baptism is the means of regeneration to those who so believe and is not to be administered to any others.

Dissatisfaction with the divided state of Christendom has been a matter of great concern to many thoughtful Christians, and the name of Alexander Campbell is prominent among them. Campbell's *The Christian System in reference to the Union of Christians and Restoration of Primitive Christianity as plead by the Current Reformation* had as its inspiration the hope that it would contribute to harmony among Christian communions. The Christian Church, Disciples of Christ, or Campbellite movement, as it was variously called, was the product of a movement of reform in the interest of unity with which Thomas Campbell (1763-1854) and his son, Alexander, were closely identified. The theme in

Alexander Campbell's words was, "How may schisms cease and all Christians unite, harmonize and cooperate in one great community, as at the beginning?"

There was no hope of harmony, Campbell argued, in debating controversial points of systematic theology. By the title, *The Christian System,* Alexander Campbell did not mean to suggest that he was offering another system of theology. In his opinion theology had done great mischief in the Church, and he wanted no more of it. There was to be no highway to unity through syncretism.

Since the only book held in common by all Christians was the Bible, on it alone, Campbell asserted, could unity be advocated with any hope of success.

It was this article of faith which the author believed to be the distinguishing feature of his work. "Not until within the present generation," he wrote, "did any sect or party in Christendom unite and build upon the Bible alone." What he was advocating was a restoration movement with the primitive Church as the ideal and the Bible as the only textbook.

Campbell, of course, realized that other Christian groups accepted the Bible as a foundation for their faith. Indeed, in his opinion, the mystery was why the Bible should be accepted as central and yet "should work no happier results than the strifes, divisions and retaliatory excommunications of of rival Protestant sects." It could not be supposed that the Bible itself could be part of the cause of diversity. The fault, then, must lie in the churches, and in particular, in their failure to act upon the Scriptures. Lip service to the Bible was substituted for obedience. Campbell confesses in the Preface that it had taken him over twenty years' labor to discard his own misreadings of Scripture, and he identifies *The Christian System* as the result of his rigorous re-examination. He reduces the "capital principles" of Christianity to the form, *"Faith in Jesus as the true Messiah and obedience to him as Lawgiver and King, the ONLY TEST of Christian character, and the ONLY BOND of Christian union, communion and cooperation, irrespective of all creeds, opinions, commandments and traditions of men."*

From this vantage point the author proceeds to discuss the multiphasic interests, both theoretical and practical, of a Christian institution. He is careful to deny that what he had written is authoritative for the churches; "We speak for ourselves only," he writes, and he claims truth for his views only as they agree with *"the Bible, the whole Bible, and nothing but the Bible."*

In the first chapter the systematic nature of the universe is asserted; the second chapter is given to the Bible. Large claims are made for the Bible's contents; "There is not a spiriual idea in the whole human race that is not drawn from the Bible." To ascertain the true significance of these spiritual facts all the tools of exegesis should be employed, Campbell writes; the student must approach the Bible in humility, for without a teachable spirit even the interpreter's skill may prove faulty.

Other facets of belief are then reviewed by Campbell in a plain style of writing so as to avoid the technical language of the creeds. The result is a disputatious section on the spirit of God, a section which critics from classic trinitarian traditions found unsatisfactory. The Chalcedonian definition of the Godhead, together with Christology, is dismissed as theology that is unbiblical. Also, in Campbell's doctrine of man, contrary to some theology, ample room is given to the conditional nature of salvation. Man makes his own election or choice, Campbell claims; his view is a change from the ideas of Augustine and Calvin, ideas which influenced popular Christian beliefs during the period when Campbell wrote.

In his discussion of the facts of the atonement, Campbell reveals a point of some interest in his support of the explanation of the Dutch scholar, Hugo Grotius (1583-1645), as against that of the medieval theologian, Anselm (c.1033-1109), by refusing to think of sin in terms of a debt which has to be paid, and preferring to describe it as a crime which may be pardoned by the Moral Governor. According to Campbell, the divine pardon or forgiveness is accompanied by reconciliation and deliverance, and the whole wonderful act of grace was arranged before the foundation of the world. The literal way in which Campbell accepts Scripture is illustrated when Campbell claims "that Jesus, himself, intimates that the whole affair of man's redemption, even to the preparation of the eternal abodes of righteous, was arranged ere time was born."

Over against this literalism, there is a great deal of discussion of the relative significance of other Scriptural allusions. Campbell writes: "Thus the *death of Christ* is forced on our attention by the law, by the prophets and by the necessity of the case, enlightened Reason being in the chair, as the only real, true and proper sin-atoning offering." Enlightened reason functions as an evaluating agency in the clarification of truth and would thus appear to qualify the claim that doctrine can be determined by the Bible only. And, again, on the same issue Campbell is insistent on the personal presence of Christ with His people, and it is this personal identification that is the core of the idea of salvation. Faith is not simply belief in "any doctrine, testimony or truth, abstractly, but belief *in* Christ; trust or confidence in him as a person, not a thing." This conception of faith is, no doubt, true; but it is a different and additional factor in the position which emphasizes the Bible. In a similar manner, it might be said that Campbell's strong objections to the traditional statements of Christian doctrine lose some of their

force when he proceeds to write a large book of orderly doctrinal exposition. The principle of attending to the Bible only, if taken at its face value, would seem to make a volume of interpretation superfluous. It may well be that the author was forced to operate on a broader base than his initial principle permits, although his practice is not inconsistent with the thesis that the Bible is an indispensable and authentic measure for the determination of doctrine.

For Alexander Campbell the principal effect of his emphasis on the Bible alone was his rejection of the traditional doctrine and practice of infant baptism. It can best be stated in his own words: "Infant baptism and infant sprinkling, with all infantile imbecility, immediately expired in our minds, as soon as the *Bible alone* was made the only measure and standard of faith and duty. This foundation of the Pedobaptist temple being instantly destroyed, the whole edifice leaning upon it became a heap of ruins . . . the piles of rubbish that remained was immense." What replaced the former key concept was a doctrine of baptism which also separated Campbell from the Baptists. At first he was received among them, but separation came when he insisted that baptism to the repentant believer was the means of receiving absolution from sin. Campbell often expounded his views at length, for the point was one of great importance for anyone passionately interested in Christian unity. The significance of baptism had been a cardinal matter in disunity. Therefore, Campbell carefully guards himself from any notion that he believed immersion as such brought about the experience of regeneration. The physical action had to be associated with repentance, faith, restitution and all the personal and spiritual conditions stated in the New Testament as necessary to salvation. Nor was he willing to commit himself to the position that without baptism no one could be saved. His contention was that the New Testament connected baptism with all the blessings of salvation so openly and explicitly that he was compelled on the basis of his Bible principle to preach it in that form.

The "Breaking of the Loaf," as the author called the Lord's Supper, commemorates the crucifixion of Jesus Christ and ought to be a weekly institution because the Apostolic Church observed it every time they met for a stated worship service. If the Resurrection is marked each week by the observance of the first day, then it is incongruous not to mark the death of Jesus just as frequently. This breaking of the loaf was, in fact, the primary purpose of Apostolic gatherings on the first day of the week. Presiding officers in the churches should normally be in charge of this service in the interest of good order. Every Christian as a messenger of the Gospel has a right to preach, baptize, and officiate at the breaking of bread, but this right should not be asserted when the ordained officers are present.

In matters of discipline, Campbell contended a congregation should act through its elders to examine the charges and proceed appropriately. If repentance is not apparent, then the offender may, with justification, be excluded from the community. Wherever possible, investigation and all handling of the unfortunate situation should be done privately.

Campbell suggests that where the Bible does not offer an explicit guide on matters related to the ordering of congregational life, expediency should be followed in the interest of good order. On these concessions and forbearance will be expected, and the minority will acquiesce in the decision of the majority, with the law of love the guide of both.

This is the kind of Christian institution that Alexander Campbell believed could be justified by the Bible principle, and on the basis of it he believed that all Christians could find truth, unity, and love.

LECTURES ON REVIVALS OF RELIGION

Author: Charles Grandison Finney (1792-1875)
Type of work: Practical theology
First published: 1835

PRINCIPAL IDEAS ADVANCED

Revivals are necessary to keep Christians awake and to provide the proper conditions for bringing sinners to repentance.

Revivals can be promoted by man's efforts, through prayer and through the art of persuading men; revivals are hindered by the worldliness of Christians.

Insofar as men can be brought to obey God, economic and social difficulties will disappear.

Compelled by ill-health to pause in his career as a revival-preacher, Charles G. Finney delivered his celebrated *Lectures on Revivals in Religion* from the pulpit of the Chatham Street Presbyterian Church, New York City, on Friday evenings during the winter of 1834-5. The lectures were given extemporaneously, but were taken down and published in the *New York Evangelist*, a weekly periodical which Finney had been instrumental in founding. They appeared as a book in May, 1835.

Finney had been a schoolteacher and lawyer's clerk before he was converted at the age of twenty-nine. After studying theology privately with a Presbyterian minister in Western New York State, he was ordained under the Plan of Union worked out in 1801 between the Presbyterian and Congregational Churches. Revivals, of course, were not unknown in Calvinist denominations, but the meetings conducted by Jonathan Edwards (1703-1758) and George Whitefield (1714-1770) differed in important respects from revivals conducted by Methodist and Baptist frontier preachers. With Finney, many of those differences disappeared. Finney modified the Calvinistic theology until it was scarcely distinguishable from Arminianism, in order to make room for human agency in the salvation of souls. He also permitted and encouraged certain emotional responses, such as "groaning in the Spirit," which were familiar to frontier revivals but were not approved by the more conservative preachers. These innovations, together with the steady success of his meetings, first in

frontier towns, but later in the cities as well, brought Finney under censure from leading Congregational and Presbyterian churchmen. His *Lectures on Revivals in Religion* is his reply to his detractors. The lectures present a more or less systematic exposition of his own grassroots theology and a vigorous criticism of the staid, tradition-bound religion of the older churches.

Finney maintains that saving souls is the most important work in the world, and that it is a work in which every Christian must be actively engaged. Although he interprets religion broadly as including all the ordinary duties of life, and warns against supposing that piety is limited to private devotions and church work, he nevertheless insists that the only reason God leaves men and women in the world after they have been converted is to help in the work of converting others. It is all very simple and logical. The world is in a state of sin and rebellion against God. Every one who dies in his sin is destined to eternal punishment. God does not want any to perish. He sent Christ to make atonement for all men, and He is willing to give them new hearts by His Spirit. But the task of converting sinners to Christ remains with the Church. Since, for every opportunity missed, a soul is plunged into Hell, the lives of Christians ought to be lived at fever pitch, like those of a rescue party during a disaster. But the temptations of the flesh cause Christians to relax their efforts and to lose their sense of urgency. That is the reason revivals are necessary—to keep Christians awake to their own mission, and also to arouse sinners to their danger.

Calvinists, according to Finney, are used to excusing themselves from responsibility for the salvation of their fellow men, on the ground that nothing but the grace of God can convert the hearts of sinners. Thus, they customarily wait for revivals as a farmer waits for rain. Finney openly rejects this teaching. While not denying that God's Spirit is essential for a man's conversion, he maintains that human agents are also necessary. His teaching is that revivals are "to be *prompted*, by the use of means designed and adapted specially to that object." He cites the example of a minister who believed that since revivals come at five-year intervals, there is nothing man can do to hurry them. It happened that, about a year after a revival, this minister began to grieve in his soul at the number in his congregation who were still unconverted, and he set his pencil to work calculating the probabilities as to how many would die and go to Hell before another revival was due. The following Sunday he took the figures with him to his pulpit, not expecting any revival but merely to share his grief with his people. The effect, however, was to awaken more than forty adult heads of families to the peril of their souls, and a great revival took place. Another time, a young convert was responsible for showing her Calvinist minister his error. She came to him with her Bible, pointing to the passage in which God promises to send his Spirit when men ask him in faith. The minister tried to show her that such promises are always qualified by an "if it be thy will." She went away uncomprehending, but left such an impression on the minister's

mind that he searched the Scriptures and saw that no such condition is attached. He told his church what he had found, and a revival ensued.

Among the means of promoting revivals, first in importance is prayer. By prayer, Finney does not mean simply the offering up of desires to God, but rather a persistent wrestling with God until He is moved to act. Speaking from the text, "What things soever ye desire when ye pray, believe that ye receive them, and ye shall have them," Finney points out that the Scriptures are filled with promises which bind God to do the things which believers desire of him. It is up to Christians to claim these promises, but they can do this only by pouring out their souls in an agony of desire and resolution. Finney gives the example of a Christian who was daily oppressed with the burden of souls, until his body weakened of his great effort, and he died, "a prevailing prince in prayer." The dedicated man had prayed systematically, keeping a map of the world before him. Finney says, "I have known him pray as if he would do violence to heaven, and then seen the blessing come as plainly in answer to his prayer, as if it was revealed, so that no person would doubt it, any more than if God had spoken from heaven."

Finney explains that prayer does not change God's mind, but that it produces changes in men which render it consistent for God to do what he could not consistently do otherwise. In any case, men must prevail with God in order to obtain his blessing. This is so certainly true that, when a revival occurs, one can be sure that somewhere someone has been praying for that particular church to be revived.

The other means of promoting revivals have to do with influencing the minds of men. This requires knowledge and skill. Finney remarks that men are at great pains to learn what is necessary for them to know in order to conduct their wordly business; how much more should they study how to promote the conversion of sinners, seeing this is the main business of every Christian! In two addresses on the text, "He that winneth souls is wise," Finney points out that wisdom consists in "the selection of the most appropriate means for the accomplishment of an end." He then undertakes to set forth the means for accomplishing the "infinitely desirable end, the salvation of souls." In particular, he calls attention to the need for ministers to understand "the philosophy of the human mind." Truth, according to Finney, does not automatically turn men to righteousness. It must be used cunningly, with a view to the emotions that it can be made to arouse. "Truth, when brought to bear upon the mind, is in itself calculated to produce corresponding feelings. The minister must know what feelings he wishes to produce, and how to bring such truth to bear as is calculated to produce these feelings." He must know how to use the truth in order to stir believers to a revival pitch, and he must know how to confront sinners with the truth in such a manner that they will be convicted of their sin and converted to righteousness. "A wise minister will be successful," Finney maintains. Learning does not guaranty a minister success, neither does piety. The work of winning souls is like any other craft. If a man "understands his Bible, and understands human nature, and knows how to bring the truth to bear, and how to guide and manage minds, and to lead them

away from sin and lead them to God," there is no reason for him to fail.

If piety itself is not sufficient to produce a revival, the lack of piety is nevertheless enough to prevent one. Finney compiles a long list of sins of omission and commission. In order to promote a revival, Christians must go over their lives in a systematic fashion, enumerating their shortcomings. The fact of recalling them will generate an agony of remorse and lead to prayer and renewed effort. Among the sins to which Finney calls attention are such general ones as ingratitude, pride, want of love for God, and unconcern for one's neighbor. But he is also specific. "Resistance to the Temperance Reformation," he says, "will put a stop to revivals in a church." Similarly, "revivals are hindered when ministers and churches take wrong ground in regard to any question involving human rights," notably slaveholding.

Finney further maintains that Christians must resist all forms of worldliness, especially parties and dances, extravagance in dress and in style of living, and the use of such luxuries as coffee, tea, and tobacco. Such practices, he says, are sinful chiefly in diverting the Christian from his main enterprise; they constitute a misappropriation of divine gifts, as well as being a temptation toward more grievous sins.

Finney views the Christian life in simple terms. He maintains that there is no such thing as a conflict in a man's duties toward God, and he concludes that Christians ought to strive for nothing short of complete perfection. He argues that honest business practices are more profitable than dishonest ones and will gradually prevail over dishonest ones, especially in a Christian country such as the United States. He reasons in the same way concerning politics, maintaining that Christians ought to vote for honest men, and not to pay attention to party issues. We have observed that Finney opposed a Christian's holding slaves, but he was not an ardent abolitionist, urging rather that "the only hope of the country, the church, the oppressor, and the slave was in *wide spread* revivals." In opposition to millenarian groups, he maintained that the Kingdom of God will be established in the world by evangelical means before the return of Christ.

The influence of Finney upon American Protestantism is apparent, at least in a general way. His disregard for the older theological traditions, his contempt for clerical pretensions, his Biblical fundamentalism, his confidence in the power of religion to solve all the world's problems, and his dogmatic notions concerning what constitutes a godly life were widely reflected in the piety of middle-class Christians in the new churches which sprang up across the nation. No doubt many of these characteristics would have appeared without Finney, as frontier democracy became a molding force in the churches, but the personal influence of Finney, which was equalled in the nineteenth century only by that of his younger contemporary, Dwight L. Moody (1837-1899), was no doubt a decisive factor. The influence of Finney's intense activism is especially interesting to contemplate. After Finney's time, partly under the influence of Horace Bushnell (1802-1876), many churches reacted against revivalism and turned their energies in the direction of social reform. Those, on the other hand, which continued to emphasize revivals became increasingly indifferent to the wider applications of Christian teaching. Both parties, however, liberals and fundamentalists as we call them today, retained Finney's dynamism, together with something of his penchant for simplistic solutions.

THE LIFE OF JESUS CRITICALLY EXAMINED

Author: David Friedrich Strauss (1808-1874)
Type of work: New Testament criticism and theology
First published: 1835-1836 (in two volumes)

PRINCIPAL IDEAS ADVANCED

Rigorous critical understanding of the Bible requires that supernaturalism and rationalism give way to the mythical approach, which views the Biblical stories not as the efforts of eyewitnesses to record facts, but as fictitious representations of religious ideas; here for the first time the mythical approach is to be applied comprehensively to the accounts of Jesus in the four Gospels.

That an account is mythical and not factual is determinable in two principal ways: negatively, through conflict with the modern conception of the world, as in the representation of divine and demonic beings intruding miraculously in the causal process; positively, through agreement with pre-existing ideas or tendencies at work in the religious community which has produced the account in question.

The mythical representations of the life of Jesus in the Gospels are derived mainly from Jewish Messianic expectations; the precise influence of Jesus' actual personality and history, which undeniably worked upon these expectations in some measure, is now irrecoverable.

However, radical historical criticism does not threaten faith, since the latter's immediate security lies not in past facts but in ideal truths, which truths, are, in fact, better upheld by the mythical than by the orthodox or any alternative approach.

In the relationship between Christianity and modern knowledge, no factor has been more critical than the higher criticism of the Bible; and in the development of criticism no single work has played a larger role than *The Life of Jesus Critically Examined*. Educated at Tübingen and Berlin, David Friedrich Strauss, the twenty-seven-year-old author, had been deeply influenced by the historical theologian Ferdinand Christian Baur (1792-1860) and the philosopher Georg Wilhelm Friedrich Hegel (1770-1831). He had studied closely the development of recent theological thought, including both technical Biblical research and such new systematic construction as that of Friedrich Schleiermacher (1768-1834). From this preparation came a work which combined brilliant historical competency with incisive discussion of theological issues. The book's radical conclusions brought furious reaction, which ruined Strauss's academic career. As a celebrated man of letters, he moved in later life further and further from orthodoxy, until, finally, in *The Old Faith and the New* (1872), his abandonment of the Christian perspective became explicit. The English translation, by the novelist George Eliot (1819-1880), of *The Life of Jesus Critically*

Examined is from the fourth German edition of 1840, in which Strauss restored and elaborated the positions advanced originally, after having temporarily modified them under the storm of his critics.

At the beginning of the nineteenth century, Biblical interpretation was dominated by an antithesis between two main approaches. According to *orthodox supernaturalism*, the Scriptures contained a literal history correct in details, including the accounts of the miracles. For *rationalism*, on the other hand, the face value of stories out of keeping with natural law was used as a point of departure for the interpreter to offer his own plausible explanation of the original happening. For instance, the story of Adam's fall in Genesis might rest upon the actual eating of a poisonous fruit, or the descent of the dove at Jesus' baptism upon a tame bird fluttering about fortuitously. In this way the Biblical history was drastically revised, but it was still conceived as literal history. Meanwhile, another approach had been gaining currency. During the eighteenth century the *mythical theory* had been employed by some to discredit Christianity. But by the time Strauss wrote, there was a considerable volume of positive Christian interpretation using the concept of myth in the treatment of such elements of the Bible as the creation narratives and even, among advanced scholars, the stories of Jesus' miraculous birth. Eclecticism was becoming the rule, in which some matters were regarded mythically, some explained rationalistically, and others—especially where Jesus Himself was concerned—accepted as truly supernatural history.

In Strauss's judgment such eclectic procedure is an unacceptable compromise, with dogmatic presuppositions covertly circumscribing scientific rigor. The new undertaking he proposes is a thoroughly objective and consistent testing of the Gospels by the mythical theory. Without denying an underlying factual component, he "applies the notion of mythus to the entire history of the life of Jesus; recognizes mythi or mythical embellishments in every portion, and ranges under the category of mythus not merely the miraculous occurrences during the infancy of Jesus, but those also of his public life; not merely miracles operated on Jesus, but those wrought by him."

Myth is the creation, from and for a believing community, "of a fact out of an idea," the use of a "historical semblance merely as the shell . . . a religious conception." Strauss distinguishes *pure* from *historical* myth, the latter having a groundwork of individual fact—which has, however, been sublimated into interpretive representation. From both types of myth he further differentiates *legend*, also factually based but so garbled by long oral transmission as to defy precise assessment of the historical kernel. These, along with *editorial redaction*, are the categories of analysis used by Strauss in his minute dissection of the Gospels. His scheme requires the hypothesis of a considerable period of preliminary transmission, prior to the crystallization of the documents in their present form. Thus it collided with the still prevailing tradition of the eyewitness authenticity of the Gospels, which, were the mythical theory valid, must apparently be understood as forgeries. Apart from the intolerable offense that faith would feel in this thought, it seemed also historically incredible that such forgeries could have been accepted by the primitive Church. Strauss neutralizes these obstacles by arguing that the eyewitness character of the Gospels is in fact indemonstrable, the evidence pointing to a relatively late traditionary origin. On the other hand, knowledge of how the myth-forming process works in the developing self-portrayal of a religious community, together with knowledge of ancient notions of literary authenticity, precludes imputation of deliberate fraud to the Scriptural authors and editors. There were, moreover, the two primary factors of the Jewish Messianic expectations and the actuality of Jesus. Hence the Gospel myths, as such, did not have to evolve *after* Jesus' appearance. They already existed ready-made and had only to be transferred and adapted to Him. The Gospel stories were shaped by evangelists who hoped to show the fulfillment of the Messianic prophecies in the Old Testament.

How identify myth? Strauss proposes to use both negative and positive criteria. In the first place, we are sure that nothing can truly have happened which "is irreconcilable with the known and universal laws which govern the course of events." This categorically eliminates the miraculous, for philosophy and science teach us that the "absolute cause never disturbs the chain of secondary causes by single, arbitrary acts of interposition." Similarly, whatever is contrary to general and habitual human behavior, as remembering the long speeches presumably quoted in the Fourth Gospel, or whatever is psychologically or morally implausible, as the Sanhedrin bribing the watchmen at the tomb—all such matter is decidedly suspect. Furthermore, a historical account must be consistent with itself and with other accounts. Positively, myth is indicated by a poetical form, but more especially by a congruency in substance with ideas prevailing within the circle from which a narrative proceeds. For example, the tendency of the Jews to represent their great men as the children of parents who had long been childless renders doubtful such a story as that of John the Baptist's birth. However, all such considerations grow stronger *in concurrence.* Strauss is cautious of putting too much weight upon any one strand of evidence. In any event, he argues, the boundary between the mythical and the historical, in records such as our Gospels, "will ever remain fluctuating and insusceptible of precise attainment." One could hardly expect better than this of the first comprehensive application of the mythical theory to the life of Jesus.

In his actual handling of the Gospel materials, Strauss is ruthlessly critical but not undiscriminating. He painstakingly adduces and ponders the evidence. His criteria indicate that myth-forming faith has been at work everywhere. But even if there are no remaining islands of pure, untouched fact, Strauss often detects an influence of the original Jesus in and through the myth. The problem, for instance,

of Jesus' formal education is conditioned by the undoubted fact of His unique genius. That there is likewise an historical core underneath the mythicized narratives of the baptism by John, the teachings, and the ministry in general, Strauss is far from denying. In treating the details, he often feels the trace of history most strongly in the Synoptics.

Nearly three hundred pages are devoted to the climactic narratives of passion and the Resurrection. On his presuppositions Strauss must acquiesce in the dilemma of the modern "cultivated intellect . . . : either Jesus was not really dead, or he did not really rise again." Despite mythical embellishments, of the death there is a "precise and internally consistent attestation" —something altogether lacking with respect to the Resurrection. Whence, then, the Easter faith, with its power to revivify the shattered band of disciples? Strauss conjectures that it arose first in Galilee, where Peter and the others had fled to avoid persecution. Over weeks and months the mythical imagination found the means of resolving the apparent contradiction of Messianic hope. According to the Scriptures, it was necessary that the Messiah should die; and just as certain that He should rise again. Visionary enthusiasm, which proved transferable to Paul and others, did the rest. By the time the Resurrection claim got back to Jerusalem, it was too late to test it by the facts.

So much, then, for the question of the Gospel history as such. Strauss acknowledges that he may appear to have annihilated the heart of Christian belief; but, he insists, this is not in fact the case. Hence he sets out, in a concluding dissertation, "to reestablish dogmatically what has been destroyed critically." He reviews the orthodox Christological dogma, which the modern mind can no longer literally accept. Against it arose rationalism's picture of Jesus as a distinguished man, intellectually inoffensive but religiously empty. Schleiermacher's Christology was a noble effort, but its eclecticism could fully satisfy neither faith nor science. More promising had been the symbolical interpretation of Christ suggested by the philosopher Immanuel Kant (1724-1804). Yet Kant's symbol had remained merely ideal—representing the moral law rather than the reality of redemption. A really adequate standpoint at last emerges, however, in the speculative Christology inspired by the philosophy of G. W. F. Hegel. According to Hegel, religious ideas are symbolic expressions of philosophical truth—not merely of the ideal, as with Kant, but of the real. This insight supplies the basis for affirming the supreme truth of the whole complex of Christian symbols and dogmas; thus faith can be satisfied. But so also is the critical intellect appeased; for the symbols are true mythically, poetically, pictorially—and not literally.

In the symbol of the Incarnation, the speculative Christology perceives the truth that Absolute Spirit becomes finite and concrete over against itself. Strauss writes that the "man of Divine essence . . . is the power that subdues nature, a worker of miracles; but as God in a human manifestation, he is dependent on nature, subject to its necessities and sufferings. . . ." The abasement of God extends even to death, to the "lowest depths of the finite." But the Resurrection symbolizes the eternal return of God to God; and as the divine has come down to man, so man's spirit shares in the divine eternity. Thus the estrangement of the finite from the infinite is overcome in reconciliation and reunion. There is, however, a disagreement among those who profess to follow Hegel, as to how, or rather as to where, the idea of reconciliation has been realized and manifested. Some would maintain that the realization has occurred in the individual man Jesus. Strauss rejects this as an abortive effort, still at odds with science. For him, the proper subject of the Christ myth is not an individual but the human race as a whole. "Humanity is the union of the two natures . . . ," Strauss writes; "By faith in this Christ, especially in his death and resurrection, man is justified before God; that is, by the kindling within him of the idea of Humanity, the individual man participates in the divinely human life of the species."

Thus would Strauss retrieve, for the philosophically minded, the religious substance which his criticism had seemed to destroy. His book revealed unmistakably to the Christian world how formidable and relentless a challenge lay in objective historical research. It also stated, clearly and concisely, one of the alternatives according to which Christian faith might attempt to reconceive and thus honestly to understand itself in a scientific world. Strauss has been much attacked, but as a catalyst of modern Christian reflection he has had few equals.

THE DIVINITY SCHOOL ADDRESS

Author: Ralph Waldo Emerson (1803-1882)
Type of work: Religious epistemology
First published: 1838

PRINCIPAL IDEAS ADVANCED

The natural world exhibits a rational order, and man's ability to understand, use, and enjoy the world indicates a fundamental kinship between the human mind and the natural world.

There is a rational, fixed cosmic order of moral law which man recognizes intuitively.

The rational structure of the natural world and of moral experience indicates that the world is the product of a single benevolent cosmic mind and will.

Religion is the apprehension of the reign of divine law in the world of nature and in human experience.

The Christian Church has attempted to make a demigod of Jesus Christ, whereas His own intention was not to call attention to Himself but to stimulate men to discover God within their own souls.

Emerson's *An Address,* commonly referred to as the "divinity school address," is to be understood against the background of the emergence in America of Unitarianism and of the radical outgrowth of Unitarianism known as transcendentalism.

By the middle of the eighteenth century the hold of Calvinistic theology on New England Congregationalism was loosening. To prosperous business and professional men as well as to some clergymen such doctrines as double predestination and total depravity did not seem compatible with human dignity or divine justice. Gradually there developed—particularly in eastern Massachusetts—a faction of liberal clergymen who emphasized human freedom and moral responsibility, and who raised questions about the trinitarian conception of God. The friction between liberal and orthodox clergymen became intense in 1805 with the elec-

tion of a liberal, Henry Ware, to the Hollis professorship of divinity at Harvard University.

The evolution of the liberal faction into a denomination separate from Congregationalism was greatly accelerated in 1819 as the result of a sermon preached by William Ellery Channing (1780-1842), minister of the Federal Street Church in Boston. Entitled "Unitarian Christianity," the sermon was preached in Baltimore at the ordination of a Unitarian minister, Jared Sparks. In the sermon Channing exalted reason as the final religious authority. Employing the test of reason, he rejected the Trinity, Christ's twofold nature, and the sacrificial atonement. Channing's sermon became the platform of the Unitarian movement, and by 1825 over a hundred churches had organized themselves into a new denomination, the American Unitarian Fellowship.

Transcendentalism was a protest on the part of a few highly articulate and productive writers against the excessive and essentially negative rationalism of the more orthodox form of Unitarianism. The transcendentalists were romantics who believed that religious experience consists not so much of rational belief in propositions as of a direct, intuitive apprehension of God which engages the emotions and moral sensibilities as well as the intellect.

The transcendentalists, who constituted a small school of thinkers rather than a denominational movement, borrowed freely from Platonic philosophy and Oriental religions and philosophies. They also acknowledged indebtedness to the eminent German philosopher Immanuel Kant (1724-1804), who taught that knowledge contains elements contributed by the structure of the mind, as well as elements from sense experience. Kant confined knowledge to mathematics and the natural sciences, contending that religious and moral truths belong to a different category of experience from that of knowledge.

The transcendentalists became interested in Kant and other German philosophers through the British writers Thomas Carlyle (1795-1881) and Samuel Taylor Coleridge (1772-1834). Both these men had great influence upon the transcendentalists. Coleridge was a chief source of the distinction between reason and understanding, so important in Emerson's thought. Reason is man's intuitive faculty; it simply perceives; it does not deduce or prove. The understanding, on the other hand, compares, struggles, and argues. Man's moral, religious, and esthetic experiences are based upon reason, whereas understanding is involved in man's more mundane practical activities. The reason apprehends those realities which transcend the sense: God, the soul, duty, and beauty.

Emerson's intellectual odyssey into transcendentalism began with his experiences as a Congregational minister. Ordained in 1829, he became pastor of the Second Church in Boston. He resigned from the pastorate after three years because of his inability to accept the Lord's Supper as an obligatory and regular part of Christian worship. His departure from the pastorate was amiable, and he continued to supply pulpits for several years after his resignation in 1832. Increasingly, however, he grew weary and impatient with the trivial and joyless quality of church services. Journal entries in 1837 and 1838 reveal a growing desire on his part to deliver a public manifesto to the American clergy in which he would point out the disparity between their pathetic performance and their magnificent calling. His opportunity came in the spring of 1838 in the form of an invitation from the senior class of the Divinity School at Harvard. On Sunday evening, July 15, 1838, he delivered his address to the Harvard theological students and an audience containing many clergymen of the Boston area. The address was published later in the same year.

The *Address* begins with a rhapsodic celebration of the glories of nature in midsummer. Turning from vivid descriptions of the beauties of the world, Emerson comments upon the significance of man's capacity to subdue the powers and enjoy the beauties of nature. There is a rational order in nature as evidenced by the kinship between the human mind and the natural world.

Just as there is a rational order in the behavior of the universe, so, too, he argued, there is a rational, fixed cosmic order of moral law to which man conforms in his virtue. Man intuitively recognizes the divine laws of morality. Even when he violates moral principles he does so with the remorseful recognition that he was made for virtue and that vice is a violation of his nature. Virtuous behavior is always ennobling, whereas mean deeds immediately diminish one's moral stature.

The rational structure of the natural world and of moral experience indicates, Emerson claimed, that the world is not the product of blind forces, but of a single cosmic mind and will. Every event is the product of that mind. God is not only the source of rational order; He is also benevolent and just. God is the positive, dynamic force of goodness in the world. Evil is nothing positive, but is the absence of good, just as cold is the absence of heat.

Emerson goes on to describe religion as essentially the apprehension of the reign of divine law in the world of nature and human experience. Religion is man's apprehension of the world as the expression of divine rationality and benevolence. To the religious man all reality becomes resplendent in its exhibition of benevolence and rational order. Religious sentiment is deifying to man, because it leads him to seek his own fulfillment in virtue. Worship makes man illimitable by lifting him out of his self-centeredness and by making him aware of the "deeps of Reason."

Religious and moral insight can come only through the intuitions of one's own reason. The intuitions of reason cannot be taught, Emerson insisted; they can only be experienced. The truth which another person announces can be accepted only if one finds the same truth in oneself. When a nation or society neglects its own primary experience of reality and depends upon the experience of other peoples or other ages, cultural degradation sets in and there is a loss of vitality in the Church, the state, art, letters, and life generally.

Upon the basis of the conception of religion enunciated above, Emerson proceeds next to a criticism of Christianity in its historical development. He pays tribute to Jesus Christ as a religious genius who was acutely aware of the divine dimension in all reality and experience. "Alone in all history he estimated the greatness of man. One man was true to what is in you and me. He saw that God incarnates himself in man, and evermore goes forth anew to take possession of his World." Jesus was divine because he became the medium of God's activity. But Jesus' intention was to point to himself only by way of indicating the possibilities open to all men, not in order to claim special status for himself. The Church, however, has misinterpreted the significance of Jesus by trying to convert his intuitions of reason into conclusions of the understanding. The Church has surrounded Jesus with titles and claims which kill sympathy for him. The Church has made of Jesus a demigod who demands our submission rather than a friend who desires our joyous fulfillment. Whereas the Church has been preoccupied with the unique qualities of Jesus, it was Jesus' own intention to stimulate men to discover about themselves what he discovered about himself; namely, that God dwells within the soul.

Not only has the Church misinterpreted Jesus. It has also misrepresented revelation as over and done with, a thing of the past, as though God once lived but is now dead. Turning more directly to the young prospective preachers before him, Emerson challenges them to preach their own souls. The impotence of organized religion is due to the failure of preachers to proclaim the truths which grasp them personally. A sermon is inevitably dead when the preacher abandons the intuitions of his own reason for books which tell about the faith of other people of other ages.

It is the function of the preacher, Emerson proceeds, to "convert life into truth." In his sermons the true preacher "deals out to the people his life—life passed through the fire of thought." The preacher must make his hearers aware that God *is*, not *was*, and that God speaks still. The wisdom which one finds in his own immediate experience is to be preferred to all the second-hand wisdom which the world has to offer. The preacher who models his thought upon that of St. Paul, or George Fox, or Swedenborg, or any other man—no matter how saintly or wise—is doomed to mediocrity. Emerson admonishes his clerical hearers to bards of the Holy Ghost so that they may "acquaint men at first hand with Deity." When you encounter your parishioners, he advises them, let them see in you a divine man; let your presence elicit their "timid aspirations" and their "trampled instincts."

The magnitude of the controversy which followed Emerson's address to the divinity students may be indicated by the fact that he was not invited to speak again at Harvard until 1865, twenty-seven years later. Some denounced him as an atheist, and from some quarters there came the sugges-

tion that he deserved no better than Abner Kneeland, who was currently serving a jail sentence for blasphemy. Emerson himself had no taste for argument, but he quietly went ahead with plans to publish the address. The most determined attack against him came from the eminent Harvard Unitarian theologian, Andrews Norton. An address which Norton gave to Harvard divinity alumni was published under the title *A Discourse on the Latest Form of Infidelity*. Norton's reaction to Emerson's address was typical of the shock and anger of the more orthodox Unitarians. The orthodox Unitarians defended themselves as genuine Christians, and they were acutely aware that if they did not denounce Emerson, then they would be extremely vulnerable to the Congregational charge that the abandonment of the trinitarian conception of God leads to a dissolution of the whole structure of orthodox Christian belief.

It is not difficult to understand why the *Address* shocked Congregationalists and Unitarians alike. It humanizes Jesus and deifies man. It pictures God as a benevolent force, immanent in the processes of nature and history, and it omits any mention of God as a transcendent judge of man's sinfulness. Evil is defined simply as absence of good rather than as a dynamic force such as Satan. There is no suggestion of the retention of the concept of original sin. Christ is essentially the revealer of man's possibilities rather than a special manifestation of God. The Bible is a secondhand source of religious truth and thus is secondary in authority to the intuitions of reason.

Despite all of the clerical opposition which the *Address* aroused, it is now clear in retrospect that its theological ebullience and optimism constituted a special expression of the heady confidence characteristic of America in the era in which Emerson wrote. The romanticism and optimism were closely akin to that of the various forms of Protestant Evangelicalism which provided the primary religious expression on the American frontiers in the pre-Civil War decades of the nineteenth century. Both the transcendentalists and the evangelicals insisted upon a warm, firsthand experience of God, an experience which engaged the emotions as well as the mind. Both movements emphasized virtue and philanthropy. Both movements looked hopefully to the redemptive possibilities of the future. Apart from the more sophisticated thought forms of transcendentalism, the main difference between the two movements was the absence from transcendentalism of any emphasis upon tragedy, suffering, or sacrifice as necessary to religious fulfillment.

THE KINGDOM OF CHRIST

Author: Frederick Denison Maurice (1805-1872)
Type of work: Theological ethics
First published: 1838

PRINCIPAL IDEAS ADVANCED

Jesus Christ has actually established a universal, spiritual society, His Kingdom, of which every man is a member, whether he recognizes Christ as his head or not, and of which the ordinances of the Church are signs.

Men in every society have longed in different ways for the head or representative of all mankind; the Bible identifies this head as Jesus Christ, promised by the Old Testament and manifested in the New.

Even when religious principles outlive the particular religious bodies through which they have been expressed, those principles are of enduring value to the Catholic or Universal Church.

Since the nation and the Church are mutually correcting and supporting in their divinely appointed functions, nationality does not hinder, but furthers, the Church's universality.

It is nothing extraordinary for a theologian to stress the sovereignty of Christ. Frederick D. Maurice, however, was remarkable for the consistency with which he allowed the actuality of Christ's Kingdom to dominate other elements in his thought and for the robust way in which he was prepared to act on the basis of this central conviction. *The Kingdom of Christ* is one of the earliest and most important statements of Maurice's steadfast insistence that God's love for all mankind be announced to men and take shape in their economic, social, political, and religious life.

Maurice was born into the household of a Unitarian minister. He attended Oxford, where his attention was drawn especially to Plato, who was greatly to influence Maurice's thought. He had an intellectual affinity and a warm personal admiration for the English poet-philosopher, Samuel Taylor Coleridge (1772-1834), although he never met or personally heard him. Rebaptized in 1831, Maurice was ordained in the Anglican communion in 1834. He was appointed (1840) Professor of English Literature and History at Kings College, and later (1846) he gained the chair of Divinity there. Following the publication of his *Theological Essays* (1853), he was dismissed. Maurice and the social reformer Charles Kingsley (1819-1875) issued *Politics for the People* (1848) and fostered Christian Socialism to meet the challenge of Chartism. As an educator he was of great importance, founding Queen's College (1847), the first of its kind for women, and serving as Principal at the Working Man's College (1854). From 1866 to his death he was Professor of Moral Philosophy at Cambridge.

When a controversy arose among the English Quakers, Maurice wrote to urge an acquaintance not to abandon Friends' principles but to consider whether Quakerism as a system based on those principles could possibly be an adequate witness to the Gospel. *The Kingdom of Christ* (1838, with a new, expanded edition appearing in 1842) is the refashioning of a series of twelve such letters to a Quaker. Happily, the finished work preserves much of the tone of friendly concern, discussion, and admonition of its original form. Its generally unsystematic character is compensated for by the quality of its dialogue.

The several positions discussed are more than foils for the author's own argument: each party occupies, according to Maurice, a position necessary to the health and integrity of the Catholic Church (universal, not Roman). Throughout the book, Maurice is conversing with the Friends, "pure Protestantism," Unitarianism, contemporary philosophical thought, and the Roman Catholic Church. The first part of the book is devoted to a historical and critical examination of the "principles" of each of the first four of these groups and the "systems" fathered by those principles; the Roman Catholics receive special attention in the second part. Maurice seeks to demonstrate that each religious body as a system has proved to be inadequate, not because it has followed mistaken principles but because it has not been sufficiently true to its principles.

Maurice examines the "traces of a spiritual constitution" in the early ages of the world and finds that the clearest indications of such a moral constitution for mankind is that men exist in families and in nations. With help from Scripture to interpret the signs of this spiritual constitution, he finds that the faith of Abraham, "the beginner of the church on earth," was "that there is a God *related* to men and made known to men through their human relations." This truth was exhibited in the covenant with the family and then in the covenant with the nation. The family and nation depended, however, on a third relationship, a universal one. There are two possible forms for a universal society: one which destroys the family and national principles, the other which expands them. The first is what is called the World in Scripture; the second, what is called the Church. The principles of the world are the natural tendencies and inclinations of men; such tendencies exist in the heart of every family and nation and threaten to become predominant. "When they become predominant," Maurice writes, "there ceases to be any recognition of men as related to a Being above them, any recognition of them as possessing a common humanity." The Church, as the special witness to these facts which men tend to deny, must never lose its distinctness and universality.

The subject of the New Testament is the Son of David and Son of Abraham who comes preaching the Gospel of the Kingdom; Jesus is affirmed by the Evangelists to be the King. This Son of God and King of Israel certainly died, actually rose with His body, appeared to those who knew Him, and spoke and ate with them. This for the Evangelists ". . . is the accomplishment of the union between heaven and earth; it is no longer a word, it is a fact." Maurice describes the person and work of Christ mainly in the terms suggested by the fifth chapter of Romans, the Christ-Adam relation. He says that by Christ's obedience unto death He, as the second Adam, brought mercy to mankind in place of what was brought by the first Adam. Christ is the Lord and head of every man whether each man recognizes it and acknowledges Christ or not; for Christ's coming, humility, obedience and resurrection have in fact changed man's moral situation. The creeds accurately describe who Christ is and the character of His work. All men have witnessed to Him insofar as

they have needed and have sought the perfect man, a Prince, divine humanity. Christ is "the Man," the representative of all mankind. Man's constitution is that he is created in Christ. By His incarnation, death, and resurrection Christ revealed and established a spiritual and universal Kingdom of which all men are members, whether or not they acknowledge him.

The "signs" of this universal and spiritual society are baptism, the creeds, forms of worship, the Eucharist, the ministry, and the Scriptures.

The universal Church baptizes a child because the child has a human form and countenance which Christ bore, and because in renouncing the evil society which is opposed to humanity adults do not abandon their children to that society. Baptism is the token of the redeemed covenant family, ". . . the sign of admission into a Spiritual and Universal Kingdom, grounded upon our Lord's incarnation and ultimately resting on the name of the Father, the Son, and the Holy Spirit. . . ."

If by baptism we are acknowledged as spiritual creatures united to the supreme spiritual Being, by the creed, as an act of allegiance, we claim our spiritual position; we assert our union with that Being. When Maurice defends the creeds against various assailants, he does so on the grounds that they are declarations of "belief in a name, and not in notions." In fact, there is no road into "mere notionality" as certain and direct "as that of rejecting all common and united forms of utterance."

Prayer presupposes that a restoration has already taken place, since the very idea of "a Church which is not built upon the confession of a restored humanity is a contradiction in terms." Maurice writes: "The very essence of their prayers is this: a cry that those sins which they feel in themselves, under which they are groaning, which they have committed, may not be, as they have been, their masters, and the masters of the universe." The act which is most fit for man, most thoroughly joyful, is that of thanking and blessing God.

Given the necessity and validity of the Lord's Supper, Maurice declares that he must protect the Eucharist from misinterpretation by both the Protestants and the Romans. The Protestants, he says, continually lose sight of the finished sacrifice of Christ in their anxiety to assert the importance of human faith; and the Romans constantly try through a violent effort of recollection, assisted by visible images and presentations, to bring back the very event of our Lord's crucifixion. Maurice accepts the term "recollection" because there is nothing in it which is not applicable to "a Living Actual Presence. What I plead for is the duty of recollecting that presence in the Eucharist, *because it is there.*"

The ministry has a crucial, even decisive, function. "Upon the character of this agency must depend the whole character of the Kingdom itself," Maurice claims. The Gospels present Christ as training His disciples for an *office;* He breathed on His disciples after the resurrection, and He bestowed on them the gift of the Holy Ghost. The disciples understood that the powers thereby confirmed belonged to them officially and not personally. The "officers" were to bring before men the fact that all men are subject to an invisible and universal Ruler; the task of the disciples was to exhibit Him to men in that character and in those offices which He came to perform: they were to look upon themselves in no light other than as ministers. As Christ was the great absolver, so the priest truly absolves and does not merely preach forgiveness of sins.

The episcopate contains the various functions committed by our Lord to His immediate disciples. The bishops have all the needful power for performing these functions. The episcopal succession is rightly maintained "expressly as a witness of the permanent constitution of the Church, and therefore of the continued abiding of Christ in it, and of each Bishop in each age being his servant and the receiver of gifts and power directly from Him. . . ." Maurice makes a distinction, over against the Roman Church, between a "representative" and a "vicarial" doctrine of the ministry. Once ministers are made vicarial, the scheme of "Popedom," alien to the New Testament, is initiated.

The Scriptures not only interpret to us the signs of the universal and spiritual Kingdom, but are themselves such a sign. They become intelligible when seen as a unified witness to a permanent Kingdom. Their credit should not be sustained by the miracles they record, nor by the consistency of the facts they register, nor by their ideal truth. Although Maurice finds "monstrous and heretical" the idea that the Bible was dictated, he concedes a verbal inspiration in the sense that inspired thoughts find for themselves a suitable clothing in words.

The universal Church, far from being against national churches, vindicates their necessity. Catholicity, existing in different lands in national churches, corrects and teaches the nations, and it benefits from the nations it instructs. The universal Church witnesses against the dangers of nationalism in religion, and national churches hinder the universal Church from becoming despotic.

The principle of an eye for an eye and a tooth for a tooth lies at the heart of a state and explains what a state is. Vengeance must be somewhere, Maurice writes, "and the State is that which teaches each man that there is a Lord [to whom vengeance belongs] . . . whose authority he is bound to acknowledge and upon whose authority every act of private vengeance is an infringement." The office of the state is to restrain the acts of self-will; the office of the Church to bring out by loving methods the free-will of which the self-will is a base counterfeit. The office of the State is to punish the overt, foolish acts which proceed from private judgment and which disturb the commonwealth; the office of the

Church is to teach men how to rise above those private judgments and to attain that manly judgment which is one of the most important qualifications of a good citizen.

Maurice's thought and action engendered lively discussion among his contemporaries. Some of them, like Kingsley, John Stuart Mill (1806-1873) the social philosopher, and Alfred Lord Tennyson (1809-1892), the poet, were avid in their praise. Others were perplexed by Maurice's method of thinking, put off by his Christian socialism, or worried by his universalism. In any case, his manner of attributing actuality and objectivity to God's redemptive actions, his Christocentricity, his dialectical mode of thought and expression, and his declaration of freedom for Biblical criticism, have given Maurice a hearing beyond his own century, country, and denomination.

HISTORY OF THE DEVELOPMENT OF THE DOCTRINE OF THE PERSON OF CHRIST

Author: Isaac August Dorner (1809-1884)
Type of work: History of doctrine
First published: 1839

PRINCIPAL IDEAS ADVANCED

The history of the Christian Church is marked by the attempt to develop the doctrine of the person of Christ in a manner faithful to the teaching of Scripture, in which due recognition is given to the twofold nature, the divine and the human, united in one person.

There has been a tendency throughout the course of the history of the Church to deny one or the other element, or to mix them improperly.

The fullness of the Christian life can be attained solely when the conception of the nature of Christ is freed from distortions and is made to embody the insights developed throughout the course of centuries.

Isaac August Dorner's *History of the Development of the Doctrine of the Person of Christ* is a comprehensive and an exhaustive critical study of the original sources pertaining to the Christological problem. The work is divided into two main divisions; the first part is published in two volumes; the second, in three volumes. The first part of the book covers the history of Christian doctrine up to 381, by which time the essential elements in the human and divine person of Christ had been recognized. The second part deals with the development of the doctrine of Christ from 381 until 1800.

Dorner begins by claiming that although the idea of a union between God and man is found in some degree in almost every religion, the manner in which Christianity asserts the idea of the God-man is entirely unique. The universal and perpetual belief of the Christian Church is that the unity of the divine and the human has appeared in a personal and unique mode in Jesus of Nazareth.

Christianity gives expression to what is sought in other religions, and it embraces many truths which they contain, but the idea of the God-man, so peculiarly characteristic of Christianity, did not arise outside Christianity, but wholly from within. The idea of the God-man is original and essential to Christianity, Dorner writes; it is found nowhere else, and where it is lacking, Christianity has vanished.

Dorner insists that all genuine historical investigation leads to the conclusion that the cause of the Christian idea of the God-man is to be ascribed to Jesus' own consciousness of Himself, and His own self-disclosure to others. From the very beginning of its existence the Church accepted this basic Christian truth in its totality, although not in its fully developed form. The Church could not immediately give a precise theological definition of the contents of its fully developed faith, a faith that was already complete in all its parts. Consequently, the Church limited itself to such declarations as the immediate occasion required, declarations which were to some extent incomplete and therefore unsatisfactory to a later age, when the Church was called upon to repudiate unchristian positions and to assert the Christian truth in opposition to them. In subsequent ages the Church never sought to assert anything new; she merely had to maintain and freely utter that which she had always borne within herself.

The history of dogma, as Dorner conceives it, is concerned not with the doctrinal declaration of Christ and His Apostles, but with the faith that is developed into Church doctrine. Its task is to show how the objective testimony concerning Christ, given once and for all in Scripture, is disclosed to the consciousness of the Church under the guidance of the Holy Spirit.

It is to be noted, however, that the Pauline and Johannine form of doctrine, although of decisive and directing influence upon subsequent developments, does not differ essentially from that of the synoptic age of Christology. Within the canon of the New Testament there is no writing that does not presuppose the essential divinity of the Son, who stands in an ontological relation to the Father, and who, together with the Father and the Holy Spirit, constitutes the Holy Triad.

New Testament Christianity does not appear in precisely constructed dogmas, Dorner points out, but rather in the form of Christ's witness of Himself in word and deed, and of the faith of the Apostles testifying concerning Him, to which witness is added that of the Holy Spirit, to establish faith in those who have accepted it.

After Christianity had been established in human hearts, it became necessary to understand more exactly and conceptually what had been disclosed by the Holy Spirit through the Apostles. The attacks on Christianity largely contributed to the consolidation and conceptualization of Christian doctrines. The latter are, however, not merely a human product, for the knowledge of the Church also partakes of the divine Spirit.

Within the first period of Christological development, until 380, the ideas concerning the essential elements of the person of Christ were established. The unity of the Godhead and the manhood of Christ was presupposed. The true human body of Christ, its actual existence, its functions and natural affections, and the fact of His birth, death and resurrection, were subjects of the common conviction of the Christian world. With respect to Christ's deity, the divine in Christ was everywhere recognized, and the Christian community knew itself to be eternally reconciled and united with God in Christ. The problem, however, Dorner explains, was to understand the nature of Christ's human soul and to determine how the divine in Christ is related to the divine of the Father. The further task that was to be accomplished was to gain an understanding of the Trinity.

The Church successfully combatted opponents both of Christ's deity and of His humanity. Ebionism entirely put aside the view of the divinity of Christ and asserted that the truths of the Church held only for His humanity; Docetism, on the other hand, proposed to find the deeper meaning of Christianity by stressing the higher aspect, Christ's deity, at the expense of His humanity.

The Church maintained its witness both for the true Godhead and the true manhood of Christ. The two fundamental Christological heresies were defeated by the formulation of the doctrine of the Logos who became perfect man.

At the Council of Nicaea in 325, Dorner notes, the Church confessed the eternal hypostasis of the Son and His essential equality with the Father. It rejected the notion of hypostasis without deity, as taught by Arianism, a refined form of Ebionism, and it rejected the notion of a deity without a particular hypostasis, as taught by Sabellianism, a refined form of Docetism.

The Nicene Creed unconditionally claimed deity for the Son; it left unexamined, however, the questions of the precise nature of the hypostasis, the mode of its generation, and the basis of the Trinity in the Christian idea of God, and thereby it left room for the further doctrinal struggles of the Council of Constantinople in 381, and the Council of Chalcedon in 451.

The Church still needed to understand the living unity of the two aspects of the personality of Christ. Each period in the history of the Church was called upon to give its conception of this unity. The Church never wearied in its struggle against the tendency to detract from or to deny the individuality and reality of either the divine or the human nature. Some represented the divine nature as transformed into the human; others represented the human nature as transformed into the divine. Still others represented the one nature as tempered and modified by the other, so that the result was a mixture of both factors.

A second tendency that needed to be rejected, Dorner reports, was the view that regarded the two natures as mutually exclusive contrarieties, each of which possessed distinctive characteristics. Some suggested that the divine and human natures are one to the extent that the latter is the temple of the former. Others regarded the union as mechanical and appealed to the mere power of God as being able to conjoin and to form into one whole two natures which differ in essence and have no internal connection. Still others regarded the union as relative; they maintained that the Logos, who is present in all things, stood in a distinctive relation to the man Jesus, so that Jesus was honored by God with the rank of Sonship, a title which by nature belongs to the Logos. Others regarded the union as moral, consisting mainly in the sympathy with the divine which was experienced by the man Jesus.

The Church was to affirm that in Christ there is to be recognized a duality of the divine and human, and yet the two infinitely and essentially different natures which constitute this duality are united in one person.

The Council of Chalcedon, held in 451, repudiated those who tried to destroy the mystery of the divine economy by introducing a duality of sons. It rejected the notion that the Godhead is capable of suffering, and it refused to say that the two natures were intermixed, or that the form assumed by the Logos was other than human, nor would it listen to those

that claimed that previous to the union there were two natures, but afterwards only one. Instead it insisted that Jesus Christ was perfect in deity and perfect in humanity, with a body and a reasonable soul, of the same substance with the Father with respect to His Godhead, and of the same substance as ourselves with respect to His humanity, except that He was without sin. The peculiarity of the two natures was not abolished by their union, but remained unmixed, and undivided, combined, however, into a single person and one hypostasis, one and the same Son and only begotten, who is both God and man.

From the year 381 until the Reformation, Dorner writes, there was an increasing tendency to lay undue stress upon the divine aspect of the person of Christ. From 451 until the Council of Frankfurt in 794, the doctrine of the two natures formulated at Chalcedon received its logical completion. In the Middle Ages, from the ninth century to the Reformation, the dyophysite foundation of the Symbol of Chalcedon commenced to decay, and instead of Christology the Church occupied the central position, which led to the substitution of the saints, and the sacrifice of the Mass for the human aspect of Christ.

The magical character attached to the doctrine of grace in the Middle Ages had discernible consequences in Christology, Dorner claims. The human aspect became the garment of the divine; incarnation became theophany, and nihilianism (the idea that Christ, as human, was nothing) was substituted for the proper idea of a Godmanhood.

The Scholastics sought to show that it was not necessary for God to become man, and substitutes for Christology made their appearance. The human nature of Christ was treated as impersonal, and the personality of man, under Pelagian influence, was emphasized. Some theologians, like Thomas Aquinas, remained true to tradition, but returned to simpler mystical views of the person of Christ and lost interest in the rational development of Christology. Others again took up the position of Adoptianism, the view that Christ was the adopted Son, not the true Son. The result was a decay into skepticism and a blind subjection to the authority of the Church. Among the mystics the continuity of the process of development of Christology was maintained, but they too failed to advance beyond the impersonality of Christ's humanity, although they did regard the latter as the perfection of human nature.

It remained the task of the Reformation to formulate the real equiponderance of the two aspects of the person of Christ. In its doctrine of the *Communicatio idiomatum*, the Lutheran Church was not satisfied with the mere unity of the ego, and it did not allow the human aspect to be absorbed in the divine hypostasis. It declared instead that the main problem is to understand the union of the two natures, and it put forth much effort to effect a solution. For Luther the union is regarded principally as a union of natures, the result of which is the union of the person. The whole Son, in whom dwelt the whole deity,

assumed humanity. Everything human was thus appropriated by the divine nature, and the humanity of Christ received for its own that which belongs to the divine nature. Christ became man so that through him the man Jesus might become God.

The Reformed churches did not represent a new view of the doctrine of the person of Christ; they occupied the ground of the Council of Chalcedon and defended it against sects of every kind. With the Lutherans, they renounced Ebionism and Nestorianism, as well as the Doceticism of the Christology of Roman Catholicism. However, the Reformed churches did maintain that although the Word was united with a human person, He filled the world from the beginning.

Unfortunately, Dorner writes, the views of the Lutherans and the Reformed Churches did not prevent the rise of Socianianism and the subsequent decay of Christology into a one-sided subjectivity that finally resulted in the destruction of Christology by the subjective philosophy and defective Christology of men like Friedrich Schleiermacher (1768-1834).

It is to be hoped, however, Dorner concludes, that the evangelical Church may again be successful in reaching an agreement that fully embodies the Church doctrine concerning the person and the work of Christ. Dorner himself later worked out an elaborate Christology in Hegelian terms, in his *System of Christian Doctrine*, published posthumously in 1885.

THE ESSENCE OF CHRISTIANITY

Author: Ludwig Feuerbach (1804-1872)
Type of work: Philosophical theology
First published: 1841

Principal Ideas Advanced

Religion is the progressive attainment and deepening of self-knowledge; Christianity is a historically unique expression of this self-knowledge.

The study of God is at the same time the study of man; therefore, theology is reduced to anthropology, and anthropology is exalted to theology.

The basis of thought is matter, and the being of man cannot be understood independently of his biological existence.

God is the infinite universal essence of humanity, distinguished from the particular finite individual consciousness, which is always an inadequate representation of the species.

The essential significance of the doctrines of Christ, the Trinity, Revelation, and the Sacraments resides in their contribution to man's understanding of himself in his natural existence.

Ludwig Feuerbach's masterpiece, *The Essence of Christianity*, fell upon the official Christendom of the early nineteenth century like a bombshell. Its impact was felt by philosophers and theologians alike. It made explicit the anti-Hegelian presuppositions of Feuerbach's thought and provided a foundational reinterpretation of Christian doctrine. The anti-Hegelianism which is expressed is determined by a pervading existential attitude similar to that of Søren Kierkegaard (1813-1855), the Danish thinker who was attacking Hegel in Denmark at the same time. It was Feuerbach who cautioned his reader against wishing to be a philosopher to the neglect of being a man, and who urged him to think by existence rather than through abstraction. This existential attitude became the basis for his critique of orthodox academic theology.

Feuerbach found academic theology to be arid and sterile, and he sought to restate the essence of Christianity in such a way that it would become relevant for man's concrete, physical existence. He proposed a Christian realism, intended to illumine the being of man as he lives and moves in the marketplace. His concern was to make religion relevant and real, and to achieve this end he found it necessary to naturalize religion and to humanize God.

In the thinking of Feuerbach, religion is a process of enlightenment in which man progressively attains self-consciousness. This insight betrays Feuerbach's debt to his former teacher, Hegel, whom he later attacked. Viewed from one perspective Feuerbach is an anti-Hegelian; viewed from another perspective he is a neo-Hegelian. He is anti-Hegelian in his existential attitude as well as in his rejection of the dialectic of spirit as the ground of reality. For Feuerbach nature itself governs spirit, and matter becomes the basis of thought. Spirit is made dependent upon nature and the Hegelian dialectic is set upon its head in a way which reminds one of the anti-Hegelian protest of Marx. But both Feuerbach and Marx made use of the categories and basic insights of their chief opponent. Feuerbach's definition of religion as the progressive attainment of self-knowledge is clearly informed by the Hegelian definition of history as the progressive self-actualization of freedom working out that which it is potentially. Thus the anti-Hegelian protest of Feuerbach, when it comes full circle, leads to a neo-Hegelian naturalistic theology.

In such a theology the reality of God and the reality of man are convertible. Theology is understood in terms of anthropology, but this reductivism, argues the author, should not be taken in a negativistic sense. To make God relevant to our concrete, immediate existence, to make Him real, we must make Him human. However, in doing so, at the same time, we make man divine. Thus the reduction of theology to anthropology leads to an elevation of anthropology to theology.

To equate the divine nature with the human nature is not, however, to identify every human being as a god. The equation of God and humanity has to do with the essential humanity from which the individual representative is always in some sense alienated. The distinction between the divine and the human is simply indicative of the distinction between human nature in general, or the species, and the particular individual who is a member of this species. In no sense does Feuerbach speak of God as the particular individual. God is the universal essence of humanity. *"Man has his highest being,*

his God, in himself; not in himself as an individual, but in his essential nature, his species. No individual is an adequate representation of his species, but only the human individual is conscious of the distinction between the species and the individual; in the sense of this distinction lies the root of religion. The yearning of man after something above himself is nothing else than the longing after the perfect type of his nature, the yearning to be free from himself, i.e., from the limits and defects of his individuality," writes Feuerbach. God, understood as essential humanity, involves both a descriptive universal and a prescriptive ideal. God is the species, and as such He is the universal in terms of which every member of the class is able to understand itself as a member and thus to achieve self-consciousness. But this species which defines the particular is at the same time an archetype or an ideal. It is prescriptive as well as descriptive. God is the harmonium of human perfection. He is the ideal of humanity, and thus He is the ground of self awareness and the principle of self-actualization.

Having understood God as essential humanity one can then proceed to describe the nature of God in terms of His distinctive attributes. Feuerbach accepts the classical attributes which are found in the literature of the tradition. Love, justice, and personality, for example, can legitimately be attributed to God. Indeed, all the attributes which describe human nature can be applied to God insofar as God is nothing else than human nature freed from its individual limitations. All the attributes of the human nature *ipso facto* become attributes of the divine nature. Insofar as these attributes are purified by being freed from the limits of any particular individual, it must properly be said that God is not *a* being who loves, but He is love itself; He is not *a* being who exercises justice, He is justice itself; He is not *a* person but personality itself.

Feuerbach thus devotes himself to an analysis of the "essence of Christianity," and he finds in Christianity a historically unique expression of that knowledge of self which characterizes religion more generally. He is looking for the key to the riddle of the Christian religion, and he purports to extricate its true meaning from the accumulated mass of contradictions and delusions. The pivotal doctrine of Christianity is the doctrine of Christ, a doctrine which teaches that God is incarnate in the particularity of human existence. It is thus that Christ provides the final answer to the problem of the relation of the universal and the particular, the ideal of humanity, the real man. "The most unequivocal expression, the characteristic symbol of this immediate identity of the species and individuality in Christianity is Christ, the real God of the Christians," Feuerbach writes; "Christ is the ideal of humanity become existent, the compendium of all moral and divine perfections to the exclusion of all that is negative; pure, heavenly, sinless man, the typical man, the Adam Kadmon; not regarded as the totality of the species, of mankind, but immediately as one individual, one person." Christ takes up in Himself the divine essential humanity and a particular historical existence and thus becomes a powerful symbol of deified humanity. Christ is the symbol of the consciousness of the species and the unique instance of particularized divine perfec-

tions. To say with the Apostle Paul that we are all one with Christ thus means that we have ascended to the love of the species or essential humanity. Every one who is able to make this movement is a Christian; in a sense, he becomes Christ Himself. Every man must strive to become his own Christ.

In the history of Christianity, trinitarian and Christological considerations became interrelated. In distilling the essence of Christianity Feuerbach seeks to unravel the mystery of the Trinity, and to make the doctrine of the Trinity, like the doctrine of Christ, relevant for man's understanding of himself in his natural existence. The Trinity is a symbol for man's consciousness of himself in his totality. It indicates the inseparability and interrelation of distinct qualities and powers in the human psyche. The traditional images of the triadic structure of mind, will, and love illuminate this basic point. God as essential humanity is mind expressed as self-consciousness. But mind exhibits a three-fold structure in that mind is at the same time the subject of self-consciousness, the object of self-consciousness, and the relation of knowing itself as object. A similar triadic structure becomes apparent in the examination of will and love. A God who does not know His own being and does not will His own acts is a God without consciousness, who is thus reduced to an absurdity. The Trinity is the divine self-consciousness expressing itself in both diversity and identity.

Revelation indicates the movement whereby the particular existing man has disclosed to him the nature of his essential humanity. Every revelation is simply the revelation of the species to its member. In revelation man's universal being and possible perfections are disclosed to him, and we see once more that theology can be explained through anthropology. "That which comes from God to man," Feuerbach writes, "comes to man only from *man in God*, that is, only from the ideal nature of man to the phenomenal man, from the species to the individual. . . . And so in revelation man goes out of himself, in order, by a circuitous path, to return to himself! Here we have a striking confirmation of the position that the secret of theology is nothing else than anthropology—the knowledge of God nothing else than a knowledge of man!"

Remaining consistent with his thesis that the essence of Christianity can be explained through anthropological categories, Feuerbach interprets the sacraments of baptism and the Eucharist in terms of their natural significance. Baptism is understood as a celebration of the physical healing power of water and of nature. Water is the purest of all liquids and thus it provides us with the most appropriate symbol for the divinity of nature. Because of this natural quality and significance, water is consecrated as the vehicle of the Holy Spirit. The Eucharist also testifies to the creative powers of nature. The significance of the bread and the wine resides in their natural efficacy. In no sense do the elements contain a mystical manifestation of supernatural grace. There is operative neither the transubstantiation nor the consubstantiation of supernatural theology. What is given in the sacrament is the *sensuous* bread and the *sensuous* wine, elements which symbolize the creative forces of nature by dint of which our physical existence is nourished and maintained. Thus the relevance of the sacraments for man's concrete existence is set forth, and Christianity is once again seen in the context of its anthropological intent.

THE TRANSIENT AND PERMANENT IN CHRISTIANITY

Author: Theodore Parker (1810-1860)
Type of work: Transcendentalist sermon
First published: 1841

PRINCIPAL IDEAS ADVANCED

The doctrines and forms in which Christianity is expressed in every age are transient.

The core of Christianity, which is equivalent to natural religion, is the permanent element.

The truths in the teachings of Jesus are attested not by his personal authority nor by the Scriptures but by intuition.

Theodore Parker's *The Transient and Permanent in Christianity*, deliv- ered at the ordination of Charles Chauncy Shackford as minister of the

Hawes Place Church in Boston, May 19, 1841, established Parker as a leading proponent of transcendentalist views in American religion. This sermon reveals Parker's debt not only to Ralph Waldo Emerson, whose *Divinity School Address* at Harvard in 1838 had precipitated the transcendentalist controversy within the Unitarian movement, but also to the German proponents of higher criticism of the Bible.

Although the sermon appears to have created little stir among Parker's fellow Unitarians present for the occasion, several orthodox ministers in attendance published a summary of what they considered the more objectionable parts and demanded to know whether the Unitarians accepted or rejected such blasphemous sentiments. In the ensuing debate Parker reestablished the right of independent thought and speech in the Unitarian churches.

Parker begins his sermon with a tribute to the teachings of Jesus which, he says, have come down through the centuries despite the fact that Jesus did not write them down or found an institution to preserve them. Jesus entrusted them to the air in complete confidence that his words were for eternity. They have been translated into every tongue and have been the inspiration of countless men and women at all levels of society for eighteen centuries. The words of countless great men, though preserved in metal and stone and preserved by institutions, have died out; great kingdoms have risen and fallen; but the pure religion of Jesus has inspired a whole new civilization and the words of Jesus are as alive today as when he spoke them.

The pure religion taught by Jesus is fixed and certain, Parker claimed, and it grows more influential as men grow more wise. But this cannot be said of what men call Christianity. The Christianity preached, taught, and accepted by the people has taken on different forms in every place and time. Just as the forms which Christianity has assumed in past ages have changed and passed away, so will the forms it now assumes become outmoded. "Transient things form a great part of what is commonly taught as religion. An undue place has often been assigned to forms and doctrines, while too little stress has been laid on the divine life of the soul, love to God and love to man." Forms, no matter how beautiful or how useful, says Parker, are only the "accidents" of Christianity, not its "substance." The rationalizing Unitarians, for instance, have retained only two rites of the Christian church and these in very attenuated form. But it is possible that a future age may revive old forms or, indeed, invent new ones to suit its needs.

The doctrines of Christianity, says Parker, are just as changeable as its forms. Just as there is a "true system of nature," no matter how interpretations of nature may differ according to the power of observation of the individual, so there is "but one religion which is absolutely true," although man's understanding and interpretation of it continually changes. The doctrines of Christianity change from age to age and what is called heresy at one time is accepted as orthodox and infallible in another. At one time Arius is in the ascendant, at another Athanasius; some men are burned at the stake for affirming what other men are burned for denying.

Parker asserts in his sermon that inherited theological doctrines have come more from Judaism, heathenism, and philosophy than from "the principle and sentiment of Christianity." The doctrine of the Trinity, for example, is derived from philosophy rather than from religion and is so subtle that it cannot even be expressed.

Theological forms and doctrines are transient, here today, gone tomorrow. Only slowly and gradually is mankind by patient observation and reasoning working out a true view of nature, on the one hand, and of philosophy and theology on the other. Meanwhile, says Parker—making a point at the heart of transcendentalism— "the great truths of morality and religion, the deep sentiment of love to man and love to God, are perceived intuitively, and by instinct, as it were. . . ."

The transitoriness of doctrines can be illustrated by the way the Old and New Testaments have been treated over the centuries. There was a time when men were burned for holding to a scientific principle which conflicted with some part of the Old Testament. The Old Testament was considered to be miraculously inspired—infallible. Men were expected to believe that the legends of the Old Testament were literally true, that God spoke in human words, violated His own laws, and displayed all manner of fickleness. "Even now he is deemed an infidel, if not by implication an atheist, whose reverence for the Most High forbids him to believe that God commanded Abraham to sacrifice his son, a thought at which the flesh creeps with horror; to believe it solely on the authority of an oriental story, written down nobody knows when or by whom, or for what

purpose; which may be a poem, but cannot be the record of a fact, unless God is the author of confusion and a lie."

The Old Testament has not always been held in idolatry, says Parker. Jesus and Paul did not hold it so, and later Christian teachers have differed widely in their interpretations of the content of those books. Modern criticism, indeed, is revealing that the Old Testament books are often made up of materials from different authors and times and that the authors, as pious as many of them were, often were mistaken in their claims and predictions.

Further displaying his knowledge of developments in higher criticism, Parker points out that in much the same way the New Testament has been held to be the work of infallible writers. This has been true despite the fact that there are obvious differences between, for example, the Gospels of Luke and John, and that Paul and Peter are revealed as having had serious disagreements. Furthermore, the New Testament contains "accounts which shock the moral sense and revolt the reason, and tend to place Jesus in the same series with Hercules, and Apollonius of Tyana. . . ." Yet these books of the New Testament which were brought together by "caprice or accident" are insisted on as "the infallible word of God, the only certain rule of religious faith and practice." But, Parker points out, the Bible provides no foundation for this attitude; the authors of the various books reveal themselves as quite fallible men. In truth, attitudes toward the Bible continually change.

Another illustration given by Parker of the "transitoriness of doctrines" has to do with interpretations of the nature and authority of Christ. Some regard Christ as the infinite God; some believe him to be a combination of God and man; others look on him as a man like ourselves who sets an example of what we may be. Despite the existence of various interpretations, it is said that the truth of Christianity rests on the personal authority of Christ. But Parker does not see why a religious truth should rest on the authority of him who utters it any more than a scientific truth should depend on the person who establishes it. The truths of Christianity do not depend on the personal authority of Jesus any more than "the axioms of geometry rest on the personal authority of Euclid and Archimedes. The authority of Jesus, as of all teachers, one would naturally think, must rest on the truth of his words, and not their truth on his authority."

But these questions concerning the origin and form of the Bible and the nature and authority of Christ are not religious questions, says Parker, but theological. They are accidentals, having nothing to do with the truth of Christianity. For Parker, the truth of Christianity, which he, in effect, identified with absolute, natural religion, does not depend on Jesus. Parker is willing to go so far as to state that if Jesus had taught at Athens rather than at Jerusalem, if he had performed no miracles, if he had never been thought to be anything but human, if the Old Testament had perished at his birth, Christianity still would be true. Parker points out that the present views regarding the Bible are changing under the impact of higher criticism. But this does not matter really, for this is a question which concerns theology rather than Christianity. The truth of

Christianity is not dependent on the Bible nor on the personal authority of Jesus. Jesus was, says Parker echoing Emerson, the "organ through which the infinite spoke."

Next Parker carries his argument to its logical extreme. He says that if it could be shown (but he does not believe it can be) that Jesus never lived —that the Gospels are fabrications— none of the truth of Christianity would be lost. Much of the beauty and character of the Christian religion would be lost, certainly, but not the truth. Again stressing the intuitive path to religious knowledge, Parker says that Christianity is "true, like the axioms of geometry, because it is true, and is to be tried by the oracle God places in the breast. If it rest on the personal authority of Jesus alone, then there is no certainty of its truth if he were mistaken in the smallest matter, as some Christians have thought he was in predicting his second coming."

The Bible, according to Parker, is held in idolatry. It is treated as a fetish. But he believes the time will come when bibliolatry will give way before the recognition of what the Bible really is. Then its "puerile conceptions of God" will be seen as fictions and its beauty and depth of true piety will be appreciated. In poetic terms, Parker pays tribute to the Bible and its contributions to the lives of men through the ages.

The time also will come, he says, when error will be swept away and Christ will be seen for what he really is. "Then we shall see and love the divine life that he lived." Then men will see him as a brother, a son of God as they are sons of God. But if we mistakenly make a god of him, as did the early Christians, his significance for the life of man disappears. "His virtue has no merit, his love no feeling, his cross no burden, his agony no pain. His death is an illusion, his resurrection but a show."

Doctrines and forms, then, are transient. Opinions change in every age so that men of one age cannot truly appreciate the faith or the discords of another. "The contest about transubstantiation, and the immaculate purity of the Hebrew and Greek texts of the scriptures, was waged with a bitterness unequalled in these days. The Protestant smiles at one, the Catholic at the other, and men of sense wonder at both." Indeed, the time will come when our doctrines will be smiled at and our present theological controversies abhorred.

But while these great changes take place true Christianity—by which Parker means "absolute, pure religion" —remains the same from generation to generation. Its purpose is to unite men with God as Christ was united to Him in a life of obedience and goodness. But Parker is careful to add that it is a state of perfect freedom. Conformity is not demanded of men. Men should think uprightly but not necessarily alike. Unlike certain Christian groups, true Christianity does not insist on conformity but respects "individual genius and character."

Real Christianity, says Parker, encourages us to outgrow forms and systems of doctrines so that we can approach closer to truth; it makes us realize that the Bible is servant, not master; it makes us appreciate holy words of men of old, but it also makes us realize, more importantly, that God speaks to us through conscience, reason, and faith; it makes us realize that Jesus was a man whose sonship was won by faithful obedience to God and who by his teachings and the beauty of his dife helps us through life to within the gates of Heaven; it encourages us to create the Kingdom of God on earth in preparation for our entrance to the Kingdom on high.

Old forms, reiterates Parker, give way to new to keep up with changing times and each new form will capture some of the truth, but not the whole. There are always some who do not see the permanent element in religion and cling to transient things while suspecting and denouncing those who would do away with theological error. As always, so now, there is a clash between those who see through the transient forms to the permanent and those who do not. "The question puts itself to each man, 'Will you cling to what is perishing, or embrace what is eternal?' This question each must answer for himself."

CONCLUDING UNSCIENTIFIC POSTSCRIPT

Author: Søren Kierkegaard (1813-1855)
Type of work: Existential philosophy of religion
First published: 1846

Principal Ideas Advanced

Christianity proposes to base eternal salvation upon the temporal event of God's having become man, but this event lies outside the scope of historiography and every other kind of objective knowledge.

The absolute paradox of the God-man can be appropriated only in the passionate subjective inwardness of faith, which has the character of an infinite leap.

Since subjectivity is the truth and the purpose of individual existence, the highest accentuation of subjectivity answers and fulfills existence.

General religiousness, or the religion of immanence, develops existential pathos through resignation, suffering, and guilt; but, presupposing this pathos, Christian faith maximally accentuates subjective existence through relationship to the historical God-man.

Concluding Unscientific Postscript is the principal philosophical work of a thinker often named as the founder of existentialism. He could with equal accuracy be described as the greatest modern philosopher of *faith*—specifically of the Christian faith in the God-man, Jesus Christ. Kierkegaard was born and spent his life in Copenhagen where, though he never entered the ministry, he finished the course of theological study in 1840. Through wide reading he responded avidly to an immense range of aesthetic and intellectual stimuli, but in philosophy his leading ideas were especially conditioned by a preoccupation with and reaction against the system of G. W. F. Hegel (1770-1831). An exceedingly prolific writer, Kierkegaard brought forth much of his earlier authorship, up through the *Postscript,* under pseudonyms representing different stances within his own turmoil and development. The style is eminently personal. Seeking at all cost not to become a "paragraph in the system" (of Hegel), he aims through irony, humor, and "indirect communication" to evoke subjectivity, to touch the

reader's real existence. Severely critical of inauthentic tendencies which he discerned in the established Church, Kierkegaard was driven in the years just preceding his early death to the so-called *Attack upon Christendom.* This series of polemical articles registers the tragic denouement of one of the most passionate spirits in all literature. Kierkegaard collided violently with the modern age—and with all inauthenticity. But his collision was in the name and for the sake of Christ.

The *Postscript* received its title from the fact that it appeared as a sequel to a book about one-sixth its size which had been published two years previously (in 1844). In the earlier work, *Philosophical Fragments,* "the problem posed and formulated . . . , but without pretense of solving it, was as follows: *Is an historical point of departure possible for an eternal consciousness; . . . is it possible to base an eternal happiness upon historical knowledge?"* Writing under the pseudonym Johannes Climacus, Kierkegaard had undertaken to analyze the problem purely as a dialectician and not as a believing Christian. In fact, the *Fragments* is an outcome of the attitude of treating the problem simply in itself, without regard for the "historical costume" of Christianity—although it had been acknowledged that "Christianity is the only historical phenomenon which in spite of the historical, nay, precisely by means of it, has offered itself to the individual as a point of departure for his eternal consciousness. . . ." Against this backdrop the *Postscript* comes forward, in part, as the supplying of the historical costume, this being conceived as an inquiry into the "objective problem" of Christianity. But, Kierkegaard insists, the real difficulty lies in the individual's relationship to Christianity. Thus the bulk of the *Postscript* is devoted, not simply to the costume, but to a new dialectical assault on the *subjective* problem: "How may I, Johannes Climacus, participate in the happiness promised by Christianity?"

In the last quarter of the eighteenth century the problematic nature of the historical element in Christian faith had been expressed in the dictum of the German philosopher G. E. Lessing (1729-81): "Accidental historical truths can never become the proof of necessary truths of reason." Lessing had maintained that the historical nature of the object of faith created an "ugly wide ditch," requiring a "leap" of which he was incapable. In a crucial respect the subsequent movements of theological construction had all sought to resolve, or to avoid, the problem thus posed. Hegelianism in particular, in its theological aspects, circumvented Lessing's problem by representing the historical, in its conceptually essential meaning, as a necessary truth of reason, or, in other words, as logically deducible. Thus to

a thinking man, to whom mere faith would not suffice, no leap would be required after all. The essence of Christian truth, distilled from a mythical literalism, could be objectively demonstrated.

To Kierkegaard this approach seemed both comically and tragically wrongheaded. That men under the spell of an all-encompassing objectivity, forgetting the predicament of their individual sin and guilt, could propose to resolve the problems of life in pure theory, is comical, he comments. But it is also tragic, for the serious business of living is "the task of becoming subjective." Lessing had been right, Kierkegaard writes; the historical cannot become the proof for the necessary and eternal. A "leap" is precisely what is required. God alone can grant the condition for the leap. The subjective appropriation of the condition, or, what comes to the same thing, the leap itself, is *faith*. The Hegelians talk of going beyond mere faith. But has faith become so easy for everyone? Kierkegaard asks. Is it the elementary, childlike stage of truth, beyond which a mature speculative reason can now move? On the contrary, from the human point of view faith is infinitely difficult. It presents an insuperable obstacle to the understanding, whose role is not to go beyond faith, but to discern and hold fast the obstacle which serves as the occasion of faith.

Kierkegaard is at pains to clarify that he means specifically the Christian faith in the historical God-man. Such an object of faith presents what is really a double obstacle to the understanding. In the first instance, the historical aspect posits a breach which no objective research can span, since research at best yields only approximate results; whereas, for an infinite concern an approximation is still infinitely deficient. In the second instance, the affirmation that the Eternal has entered time is rationally absurd, the "absolute paradox." But this is precisely what differentiates Christian faith in relation to immanental religiousness, or "religiousness A," as Kierkegaard calls it. For "religiousness A" God is, as it were, everywhere in general, but nowhere in particular. Now this kind of God-consciousness, producing the pathos of resignation, suffering, and guilt (wherein the individual knows of God, but cannot relate decisively to God), is a necessary preamble to the Christian faith. But the peculiar nature of the Christian object of faith, the historical God-man, introduces a new level, the "paradoxically dialectic," or "religiousness B." Here, with the thought of an eternally decisive relationship to an indemonstrable and logically absurd event in time, it becomes meaningful to speak of faith. "For the absurd is the object of faith, and the only object that can be believed." That is to say, any other object would in some measure be accessible to objective *knowledge*. But, Kierkegaard writes, "without risk there is no faith, and the greater the risk the greater the faith. . . ." Not only of historiography, but of all empirical and speculative proofs, it must be said that "results are only rubbish. . . ."

By thus embracing Lessing's dilemma, Kierkegaard achieves a position from which some of modern Christianity's most troublesome difficulties can be constructively met. In the first place, as the *Philosophical Fragments* had spelled out, the problem of contemporaneity with the Christ event is resolved by shifting attention from the concrete *whatness* to the paradoxical *thatness* of the event. The original disciples were existentially no closer to the paradoxical object of faith than we are. For the Incarnation as such can neither be seen nor comprehended; and, as it demands of us an infinite leap, so it demanded no less of those who walked with Jesus in the flesh. By the same token, the *radical demand for faith* eclipses any difference, not only between the first century and the nineteenth, but between all sorts and conditions of men. The erudite and clever man has no advantage over the simple, since faith lays an unconditional and immeasurable claim upon all alike. This means, too, that the possibly debilitating effect of modern historical skepticism upon faith is forestalled. What historiography could or could not recover is no longer relevant, since the fulcrum of faith is not Jesus as an object of research but the witness to the Christ as the "absolute paradox" with respect to which all matters of concrete detail are incommensurable. In the decision of faith the *historicity* of Christ is posited. Kierkegaard's view hinges upon this. But no empirical, objective data can influence the decision one way or the other. Thus freed from hampering distractions, the issue of faith can assume again its full depth and seriousness. This, really, is Kierkegaard's leading motive: to restore to faith its authentic gravity. Made to appear irrelevant and contemptible by purveyors of intellectual progress, Christian faith (strictly *as* faith) was being left to recede into the backwaters of modern culture. Kierkegaard will bring it forward again—*as* faith, not as something "beyond" faith—as still the highest and most inexhaustible possibility that can confront an existing individual.

Hence the *Postscript* is a treatise in Christian apologetics, but the kind of apology it develops is inverse and dialectical. Instead of assembling objective proofs of Christian doctrine, it seeks to expose, indirectly and evocatively, the *congruency* between faith in Christ and human existence. It is in this enterprise that Kierkegaard becomes the author of the existential philosophy. The evolvement of his argument has two dimensions. On the one hand, *negatively*, he seeks to show that, contrary to Hegelian idealism, the rational is not the real; essence is not identical with existence. Real existence is a matter of radical individuality in anxiety, suffering, and despair; and philosophy, if it is not to become comical, must reckon with these categories. Ethics subsumes the individual under the universal, and immanental religiousness seeks God in the universal. But ethics and all forms of immanence founder decisively on the problem of *guilt*. Thus the individual is driven, by the dialectic of existence itself, to the alternative of guilty despair *or* the leap of faith which establishes a relationship to God in time (the God-man). This is the one dimension of the argument. On the other hand, *positively*, Kierkegaard sets forth a world view in which the development of maximal passionate inwardness is regarded as the aim and fulfillment of life in time. Again in opposition to Hegelianism, stress falls upon the individual subject in his responsible *freedom*. Inwardness is heightened by the existential pathos which culminates in guilt. But the highest conceivable accentuation of subjective inwardness is occasioned by

faith in the absolute paradox, by a decisive personal relationship to God's act in time. This commitment of faith is not something accomplished and thereafter simply possessed. It requires the constant engagement of one's whole existence; and it strains one's powers to their uttermost—including, be it noted, the powers of the understanding. Kierkegaard will not allow Christ to be had "in an aesthetical hodgepodge, just as though Christianity were wholesome fodder for simpletons because it cannot be thought, and as though the characteristic that it cannot be thought were not precisely the hardest to hold onto . . . especially for clever pates."

Now since "*an objective uncertainty held fast in an appropriation-process of the most passionate inwardness is the truth,*" the highest truth attainable for an *existing* individual," Christian faith provides eminently the conditions of truth. Such faith not only redeems from guilt; it fulfills the purpose of creation. But this congruency is not one that can be objectively exhibited; it too requires, and is posited by, the act of decision which faith is. Faith is quite consistent with itself, in that it remains empty until it is subjectively appropriated.

There is much, especially by way of personal reference on Kierkegaard's part, that cannot even be mentioned in a brief account of the *Postscript*. The inimitable style and method of approach cannot be conveyed at second hand. The book stands as one of the great instances of all time of faith seeking understanding and *vice versa*—and of the interplay between faith and understanding. No source has been more determinative for the contemporary Protestant understanding of the relations between faith and reason, with the possible exception of Immanuel Kant (1724-1804). Kant, too, was a philosopher of faith, for whom reason exhibited the essential human func-

tion of faith. By comparison with Kant, Kierkegaard's faith stands out as paradoxical, and as specifically the faith in the historical Incarnation.

CHRISTIAN DISCOURSES

Author: Søren Kierkegaard (1813-1855)
Type of work: Homilies
First published: 1848

PRINCIPAL IDEAS ADVANCED

Because of his ability to take thought for the morrow, man is tormented by anxiety.

Through affliction, he learns the hopelessness of finding joy in temporality, and he may learn to rejoice in the hope of eternity.

Merely nominal Christians fall under the condemnation of even those passages of Scripture in which they are accustomed to take comfort.

Only those who have personally committed themselves to Christ share in the hope of the Gospel.

Alongside his widely-known pseudonymous works, Søren Kierkegaard published in his own name an impressive list of religious books, which he called "edifying discourses." *Christian Discourses* stands in this series. Because he was never ordained, although he had received theological training, Kierkegaard scrupulously refrained from calling his writings "sermons"; and, only toward the end of his life, as his personal faith became more firmly established, did he venture to designate them "Christian."

Christian Discourses is a large volume, comprising four parts which might have been published as separate books, inasmuch as each part was conceived separately and developed along distinctive lines. It was a sound

insight, however, which led Kierkegaard to bring them under one cover; for, like the movements of a symphony, the parts offset and complement one another.

The first set of discourses, entitled "The Anxieties of the Heathen," is based on the well-known text from the Sermon on the Mount, in which Jesus exhorts His followers not to give thought to food and clothing, to their standing among men, or to the uncertainties of the future, "for after all these things do the heathen seek." Presumably, says Kierkegaard, one could determine what the anxieties of the heathen are by journeying to pagan lands. Another way would be to journey to a Christian land ("But what am I saying?" interposes the author:

"we are in fact living in a Christian land!") and note what anxieties are absent there. But the Gospel uses neither of these ways. Instead it points to the birds of the air and the lilies of the field, which are neither heathen nor Christian, and lets them answer the question. These creatures, although they have needs comparable to those of the heathen, do not have the anxieties of the heathen. Poor by any man's standards, they do not know the anxiety of poverty as the heathen do. On the other hand, because they do not pray for their daily bread, and hence do not know that God is their Father, they are not rich in the way Christians are. Birds are merely carefree.

Kierkegaard explains that it is *thought* which makes the difference. The birds take no thought, and therefore they do not know anxiety. The heathen supposes that taking thought is the way to overcome poverty, and thus he is burdened with the care of poverty. The Christian also takes thought, but not as the heathen do; his care is to relearn the ignorance of the birds and flowers, and so be freed from care. "For it requires no art to be ignorant," writes Kierkegaard, "but to *become* ignorant, and by becoming so, to be ignorant, that is the art. To this extent the Christian is different from the bird, for the bird *is* ignorant, but the Christian becomes ignorant."

Poverty, Kierkegaard points out, is not the real root of the heathen's anxiety. Man likes to think that his concern is the straightforward one of obtaining subsistence for himself and his family; but actually his chosen role of breadwinner is a means to bolstering up his ego, of vindicating his importance, and of making a place for himself in

the eyes of others. Meanwhile, he has no thoughts of God, and, in effect, he denies that he is God's creature.

So it is with all the anxieties of the heathen. The rich heathen is anxious in his abundance, and the man of rank is anxious in his pride. Unable to live for today, as the Christian does, he torments himself about tomorrow. "Tomorrow I shall perhaps hunger, even if I did not today; tomorrow a thief will perhaps steal my riches, or slander my honor, corruption my beauty, the envy of fate my good fortune—tomorrow, tomorrow!" The thought would drive him to madness if he did not find ways of busying himself in order not to think at all. At heart convinced that all the higher things of life are vanity, he manages to go on living, but in a dispirited fashion, having lost not merely God but his own self as well.

In the second set of discourses, Kierkegaard turns from the anxieties of the unbeliever to the joys of the believer. Taking as his text the saying of Paul: "We glory in tribulations also . . . ," he entitles this part of his discourses, "Joyful Notes in the Strife of Suffering." His theme is the contrast between man's temporality and God's eternity. The hope of youth, Kierkegaard says, lies in temporally finding the temporal; for example, the love of one's beloved. Suffering bereaves the youth of this hope as a storm strips the blossoms from a cherry tree. But suffering may be the occasion for a new hope to stir within the human breast, the hope of eternity: "O thou sufferer, whatsoever thou hast lost, thou hast lost only something temporal, it is impossible to *lose* anything else; and whatsoever thou hast lost, there is something to be gained, the eternal, which thou dost gain eternally."

Following the Apostle, Kierkegaard grounds the hope of eternity in God's fathomless love. Were it not, says Kierkegaard, for the love of God, man in his freedom would never exist. Were God merely omnipotent, man would be nothing, for omnipotence would crush him. "But God who creates out of nothing, who almightily takes from nothing and says, 'Be,' lovingly adjoins, 'Be something even in apposition to me.' Marvellous love, even His omnipotence is under the sway of love!" Hence, that "misfortune is good fortune" which tears our affection from this world and fixes it on God.

The third group of discourses is entitled "Thoughts which Wound from Behind—for Edification." From Kierkegaard's *Journal*, we learn that this was the first part of *Christian Discourses* to take shape in his mind. It has no unifying theme, but each discourse is based on some Scriptural passage with which Christians have come to feel comfortable, and gives the passage an uncomfortable application.

The Scripture says, for example, "Now is our salvation nearer than when we became believers." "When," Kierkegaard asks, "didst thou become a believer? . . . Test thyself therefore by means of this saying. It is a blessed comfort to dare to know that one's salvation is nearer than when one became a believer—but surely it is true that one must be certain one has become a believer. This saying therefore may serve to comfort, but also it may as it were come upon one from behind."

Again, the Scripture says, "The resurrection of the dead is at hand, of the just and of the unjust." People are eager for any kind of information about immortality, and thus they ask whether there really is a life beyond the grave, whether it is personal, whether people will recognize one another, and whether one will remember only his happy moments. Men regard these as serious questions. But what about the little matter of the just and the unjust? "Immortality is not a life indefinitely prolonged," says Kierkegaard; "but immortality is the eternal separation between the just and the unjust." The Scripture, Kierkegaard says, is as reassuring as it can possibly be to those who desire immortality: "Thou art immortal, whether thou wilt or no." One cannot ask for greater assurance—unless this "whether thou wilt or no" should prove disquieting!

The first three parts of *Christian Discourses* abound in flashes of that irony for which Kierkegaard is famous. An important aspect of Kierkegaard's mission, as he understood it, was to protest against the pseudo-Christianity of official Christendom. The fourth part, however, entitled "Discourses at the Communion on Fridays," is in an entirely different tone. Kierkegaard remarked, in his *Journal*, that the contrast between the third and fourth parts of *Christian Discourses* "is as sharp as possible and as searching: the one is like a commemoration of the Cleansing of the Temple—and then the quiet and most heartfelt of all acts of worship: a communion on Fridays."

The addresses of this group (two of which were delivered by Kierkegaard before a sprinkling of worshipers in the Cathedral on Fridays, with the noises of commerce dimly audible in the background) are faithful to the purpose of a communion meditation, and direct the hearers' thoughts to Christ memorialized on the altar. Of the two which he delivered, one is an application of the text, "Come unto Me"; the other, of the text, "My sheep hear my voice, and I know them, and they follow me." All the addresses emphasize the strictly personal character of the relation between the believer and Christ. Like the sun, Christ shines on all men; but, unlike the sun, Christ makes a distinction among those on whom He shines. Not all men are known of Christ, nor do all who come to the altar receive Him. "For physically," says Kierkegaard,

"one can point to the altar and say, 'Behold, there it is,' but, spiritually understood, the altar is *there* only if thou art known by Him."

Those who have studied the life of Kierkegaard remember that Holy Week, 1849, marked a crisis in this author's spiritual development, and that after that time he felt himself free to speak more directly about Christianity than he had before. *Christian Discourses* barely antedates this last of Kierkegaard's conversions ("metamorphoses," he called them), but in a sense also anticipates it.

CHRISTIAN DOGMATICS

Author: Hans Lassen Martensen (1808-1884)
Type of work: Dogmatic theology
First published: 1849

PRINCIPAL IDEAS ADVANCED

Dogmatic theology is an integral part of the Christian Church; a confessing Church cannot exist without doctrines and dogmas.

Dogma is a "truth of faith," and it receives its authority from the revelation of God witnessed to in the Holy Scriptures.

The essence of the Christian faith is Jesus Christ, who is the founder of the Christian religion as well as the redeemer of the human race.

The miracle of the Incarnation influences man by creating a new spirit within him, but at the same time the Incarnation is a cosmic event, affecting the entire history of the universe.

The Apostolic Church contained Christianity in its genuine and authentic form; by means of a reliable tradition this has been transmitted intact to the contemporary Church.

Hans Lassen Martensen was professor of theology at the University of Copenhagen, Denmark, as well as Bishop of the Danish State (Lutheran) Church. He was able, more than any of his contemporaries, to relate the dominant German theology in Europe to the theology of his native Denmark. His work *Christian Dogmatics* (which had as its subtitle in the British edition, A Compendium of the Doctrines of Christianity), published first in 1849, was considered to be the normative expression for Christian theology and for "true Christianity" in nineteenth century Denmark. Martensen looked upon theology as an integral part of the life of the Church. The theological task of the Church is to present, in a systematic way, the truths of the Christian faith. Martensen writes in the Introduction to Christian Dogmatics, "Dogmatic theology treats of the doctrines of the Christian faith held by the community of believers, in other words, by the Church. A confessing and witnessing Church cannot be conceived to exist without a definite sum of doctrines or dogmas. A dogma is not a doxa, not a subjective, human opinion, not an indefinite, vague notion; nor is it a mere truth of reason, whose universal validity can be made clear with mathematical or logical certainty: it is a truth of faith, derived from the authority of the word and revelation of God;—a positive truth, therefore, positive not merely by virtue of the positiveness with which it is laid down, but also by virtue of the authority with which it is sealed. Dogmatics is the science which presents and proves the Christian doctrines, regarded as forming a connected system."

The dogmatic theologian attempts to attain an intelligent faith, but always from within the Christian Church. This task, however, is never inseparable from a personal experience of Christian truth. Dogmatics begins not with doubt or speculation, but with the fullness and certainty of the Christian faith. Martensen wrote that "Dogmatics serves, therefore, not to rescue faith in the time of its exigency, but to glorify it. . . ."

Hans Lassen Martensen was dependent philosophically upon Georg Wilhelm Friedrich Hegel (1770-1831), the great German idealist. In Hegel's system, everything in history is considered to be necessary and significant. Nothing can be considered accidental or indifferent. The Idea, the Absolute, unfolds itself in history according to its own laws, with the result that, according to Hegel, every event in the "dialectical" development of history is free. Nothing external can intervene and disrupt the basic laws of historical development. Within Hegel's philosophical system, it is quite clear that revelation yields no truth which cannot be attained by speculative thought. Religion, for Hegel, represents an imperfect representational form of knowledge, whereas speculative thought (speculative idealism) represents a higher, perfect, conceptual form. Revelation, therefore, is considered to be a necessary historical event, a consequence of the self-unfolding of the Absolute in a particular time and place. It brings, however, no new truth with itself. For Hegel, there is no inherent contradiction between reason and revelation. The highest form of religion, Christianity, and the highest form of philosophy, speculative idealism, have really the same content. They vary solely in terms of the different forms they assume.

On the basis of this position, a number of Hegel's followers, David F. Strauss (1808-1874) (author of The Life of Jesus) and Ludwig Feuerbach (1804-1872) (author of The Essence of Christianity) among them, drew the obvious conclusions and maintained a skeptical attitude toward New Testament miracles and revelation. Martensen, who was Hegelianism's foremost representative in Denmark, was aware that within Hegel's system there could be no contradiction between reason and revelation, between the philosophy of idealism and the Christian faith. Martensen believed, however, that he could "go further" than Hegel by reconciling Hegel's philosophy with the orthodox New Testament faith.

The Christian faith, for Martensen, is only one aspect of the comprehensive world-view of the Christian. Reason, as well as imagination, is the organ of religious perception. No religion, therefore, and the Christian faith in particular, could succeed as a historical religion without developing a comprehensive and ideal view of the universe, "an imaginative view by which the invisible is blended with the visible," as Martensen writes.

Revelation is defined, therefore, as God's communication of Himself to His creatures. This revelation is direct and unambiguous because it is related to the spirit within man. In this way, the revelation is apprehended by a free, conscious, historical being. Revelation and history, therefore, are never to be separated. Martensen writes, "If we may, in truth, speak of a sacred, divine revelation, then there must be a history within history, there must be within profane history a *sacred history*, in which God reveals Himself as God; a history in which is revealed the sacred design of the world as such, in which the word of God so encases itself in the word of man that the latter becomes the pure organ for the former, and in which the acts of God are so involved in the acts of men that the latter become a perfectly transparent medium through which the former may be seen." Sacred history is seen to be the history of election, a deliberate selection of a people within profane history. First Israel is elected, and then Christ, who is the fulfillment of election.

The essence of Christianity, for Martensen, is Christ Himself. Christ is not only the historic founder of the Christian religion, but also the redeemer of the human race. The Incarnation is the fundamental miracle of Christianity, but also of world history. His presence in history is miraculous not simply because Christ is a moral and religious genius, but rather because Christ initiates a cosmic change in the universe. Christ begins a new development in the conscious life of man. The human race in its entirety receives a new spirit because of the revelation of Christ. Martensen emphasized, however, that the Incarnation which introduces this new spirit to man is the same event which created the Christian Church.

Furthermore, the Christian faith does not disturb the forces and powers resident in nature. Rather, the revelation of Christ and the Kingdom of Christ "pronounces the last potency of the work of creation." The new creation in Christ does not destroy nature, but anticipates a new nature. A new system of laws appears, a system which exhibits the harmony of the laws of nature and freedom. The present creation, Martensen insisted, which shows an "unappeased strife" between spirit and nature, is but a transitional period. According to Martensen, ". . . the point of unity between the natural and the supernatural lies in the teleological design of nature to subserve the kingdom of God, and its consequent *susceptibility* to, its *capacity of being moulded* by, the supernatural, creative activity. Nature does not contradict the notion of a creation; and it is in miracles that the dependence of nature on a free Creator becomes perfectly evident."

Christian dogmatics must be Biblical as well as confessional. The Bible itself, Martensen maintained, points to a *confessing* Church. In Martensen's lengthy discussion of the difference between Protestantism (the Evangelical Church) and Roman Catholicism, it is in the interpretation of the Holy Scriptures that the major point of controversy can be found. The Protestant looks at the Church and claims (as does the Roman Catholic) that the Spirit of the Lord is within the Church and is leading it to truth. But the perfect union of the Spirit and man, which is called Inspiration, and which constitutes the essence of the apostolate (that is, which assures the truth of the Christian Church), is assigned by the Protestant to the beginning of the Church. The Roman Catholic, on the other hand, holds to a living apostolate in the Church which perpetuates itself throughout all time. The Protestant admits the relative merit of tradition, but he insists, says Martensen, that the Holy Scriptures of the New Testament are the "only perfect, authentic and absolutely canonical expression of the original fulness of the apostolic spirit."

For this reason, the Apostolic Church contained Christianity in its genuine form. But Martensen believed that this authentic original form of the Christian faith had been transmitted to the present generation by means of a reliable tradition. The Reformers, particularly Luther, Martensen believed, saw this fact very clearly. The only perfect, trustworthy form of Apostolic tradition is found in the Holy Scriptures. But the tradition is transmitted in an authentic way only when it is controlled by the Holy Scriptures. Tradition is adequate only when it can be criticized on the basis of the Holy Scriptures. It is for this reason that the Lutheran Reformation was a Reformation which reasserted the primacy and authority of the Holy Scriptures for the Church.

The Lutheran Reformers took a positive attitude toward dogma and adopted the ecumenical "symbols," the Apostolic, Nicaean, and the Athanasian creeds, as the purest expression of the dogmatic tradition. Scripture and dogmatic tradition were *not* separated by the Reformers, but were simply put in their proper relation to each other. The formal principle of the Protestant Evangelical tradition is, therefore, the Holy Scriptures, in their indissoluble connection with the confessing Church. The external canon of Christianity, that which fixes something as normative or authoritative, whether Scripture or the Church itself, points directly to the internal canon, the regenerated Christian mind. It is here, in the Christian mind, that the Spirit of God witnesses with the spirit of man. Martensen maintained that "Only to that mind in which Christianity, in which the spirit of the Scriptures and of the church, is present as an inner principle of life, do the Scriptures and tradition unfold their contents; without this internal canon they remain unintelligible."

For Martensen, the Christian is governed by two principles, the subjective and the objective, the personal and the historical. Luther's consciousness of the "freedom of the Christian man" was the confidence that faith possessed the Spirit which leads to truth, as well as the conviction that the revelation of God in Christ was extended within the Christian Church.

Martensen's *Christian Dogmatics* is therefore based upon the Holy Scriptures, and it represents an attempt to construct a Biblically-oriented foundation for the Christian faith. The doctrines of the Church which Martensen dealt with and criticized were all related to their Biblical origins. The ecumenical symbols of the Christian Church were employed as well, in order, as Martensen said, "to hold to that type of sound doctrine which is therein contained." In this way, Martensen was convinced that he was preserving an association with the Apostolic Church. He believed, too, that the creeds of the Lutheran Church, in particular the Augsburg Confession, could be employed in order to provide "sound doctrine" for the contemporary Church.

Søren Kierkegaard (1813-1855), the existentialist philosopher-theologian, was extremely critical of Martensen (and Hegel) because he felt that there was an absolute contrast between philosophical idealism (Greek, Platonic, Hegelian) and New Testament Christianity. He interpreted revelation as the moment in which the divine comes into the human; that is, when the Eternal and the temporal meet. Revelation takes on the characteristics of something unanticipated and is thereby necessarily paradoxical. The only possible response to the revelation of God in Christ is one of faith, a "condition" which is given by God himself. Christianity is, for Søren Kierkegaard, the truth of revelation, which is given at a particular time (the moment of revelation) and in a particular form (the Incarnation). This revelation is *incompatible* with the dialectic method of speculative idealism. Idealism and Christianity are absolutely irreconcilable, Kierkegaard asserted. Reason cannot understand the revelation of God in Christ. Thought, Kierkegaard insisted, meets the unthinkable, the miraculous, the *Miracle*. The event of God in Christ transcends all of the categories of human reason and understanding.

Kierkegaard looked upon the idealism of Hegel as asserting that human beings possess the truth of salvation, that they are in immediate relationship to God, against which Christianity asserted that human beings do not possess saving truth. This is a contradiction which can never be reconciled, and Kierkegaard criticized Martensen for believing that he could create a synthesis of idealism and Christianity.

GOD IN CHRIST

Author: Horace Bushnell (1802-1876)
Type of work: Liberal theology
First published: 1849

PRINCIPAL IDEAS ADVANCED

Language is by nature symbolic and imprecise and must be used in a non-literal fashion.

The doctrine of the Trinity is not a description of God's ultimate being, but only of the modes of God's revelation to man.

The atoning work of Christ is not a "satisfaction" made to God, but a concrete expression of God's forgiving love.

A revival of religion can occur only when doctrinal differences are minimized and when tolerance and charity are shown in theological disputes.

Horace Bushnell lived the major portion of his life in New England and served for twenty-six years as pastor of the North Church (Congregational) in Hartford, Connecticut. Because of his formal education at Yale (Class of 1827) and his vocation as a minister, he was thoroughly acquainted with the theological issues of the day. He stood at the juncture of American theology when Calvinism had lost its great spokesmen, and the defenders of Unitarianism and transcendentalism occupied the center of the stage. His early training under Nathaniel William Taylor (1786-1858), Professor of Divinity at Yale College, made him conscious of the need to mediate between Calvinism and the increasingly popular "liberal" theology.

In 1848, fifteen years after he had accepted the pastorate of the North Church, Bushnell was invited to speak at the major centers of theological education in New England: Harvard, Yale, and Andover. The titles of the addresses he gave in 1848 and which are included in *God in Christ* are, "Concio Ad Clerum: A Discourse on the Divinity of Christ" (Yale), "A Discourse on the Atonement" (Harvard), and "A Discourse on Dogma and Spirit; or the True Reviving of Religion" (Andover). To supplement these three essays, Bushnell prepared, in 1849, a "Preliminary Dissertation on the Nature of Language, as Related to Thought and Spirit," which he included as the prefatory treatise in the collection of his essays. The four discourses make possible an appreciation of the distinctive contribution of this New England theologian to American theology; his later work was an elaboration of the theories developed in this one volume.

The nature of theological language was a central problem for Bushnell. The churches had become accustomed to tedious and arid theological controversy; the religious vocabulary of the past was no longer useful. He sought an understanding of language which would discourage literalism and irrelevance.

The theme of the essay was the proposition that infinite ideas cannot be contained in finite words. Language is more "an instrument of suggestion, than of "absolute conveyance for thought, since it acts suggestively, through symbols held up in the words, which symbols and words are never exact measures of any truth. . . ." Precise theological formulations are impossible; words are only symbolic. "Words of thought or spirit are not only inexact in their significance, never measuring the truth or giving its precise equivalent, but they always affirm something which is false, or contrary to the truth intended." To be sure, "language . . . has a literal character in regard to physical objects. . . . But, when we come to religion and mental science, our terms are only analogies, signs, shadows, so to speak, of the formless mysteries above us and within us." The theologian must freely use adjectives to give as full a picture of a word as possible; he must "multiply words and figures . . . to present the subject on opposites sides or many sides." In Bushnell's view, therefore, the interpretation of Scripture has more to do with poetry than with doctrine or dialectics. All forms of Christian doctrine, including creeds and catechisms, express the limited points of view and historical contexts of their authors and must, therefore, be open to change and re-examination; they must be seen as proximate statements, never as the full truth. Yet Bushnell did not sympathize with the Unitarian rejection of historical creeds; he argued that all available perspectives on theological mysteries contribute to our understanding.

In the address delivered at Yale, "The Divinity of Christ," Bushnell applied his understanding of the nature of language to the doctrine of the Trinity. What he came out with was satisfactory neither to the Unitarians nor to the orthodox Calvinists. Bushnell argued that the traditional statement that there are three persons in the Godhead is meaningless if taken in a metaphysical sense; belief in a real and metaphysical Trinity of persons in the divine nature produces only confusion in thought. He preferred to speak of God as one and to say that in Him

there is a "strict personal unity" of mind, heart, will, and consciousness. But with this as the starting point, how can we speak of Jesus as God? The answer is that although the doctrine of the Trinity is not a description of God's ultimate being, it is a description of the modes of God's self-disclosure. Words will not permit a description of the being of God; language is here unfaithful and always incomplete. But as God makes Himself known through revelation, we do find evidence of the Trinity, of the modes of His self-disclosure. Man could not have knowledge of God as He is, unless God chose to disclose Himself through finite form: "He must let forth His nature in sounds, colors, forms, works, definite objects and signs." This does not mean, however, that man will comprehend God as He is, for to know God fully would be to know only a "larger man than ourselves, and set this larger man in the place of Absolute Being." But since God does have the capacity for self-expression, a power to represent Himself in finite form, man can know Him in part. He makes himself known to us as Father, as Son, and as Spirit.

We have in Bushnell's thought what may be called an "instrumental Trinity"; the doctrine of the Trinity is a useful doctrine only when seen as the way in which God reveals Himself, not as a description of His absolute nature. Bushnell's arguments was as much opposed to what he considered to be the "tritheism" of the traditional formulations as it was to the superficiality of Unitarianism.

There is in Bushnell's essay a kind of agnosticism. His discussion of the issues confronting the Council of Chalcedon (451) where the doctrine of the two natures, divine and human, united in one person (Christ) was enunciated, avoids the essential problem. As he said, to investigate "the mystery of the person of Jesus, when it is given us only to communicate God and His love, is in fact to puzzle ourselves with the vehicle, and rob ourselves of the grace it brings." But his reason for not further exploring the nature of Christ was simply that language is not adaptable to such an investigation. Bushnell did not deny the Chalcedonian decision, or affirm it, but rather he asserted that Jesus "stands before us in simple unity, one person, the divine-human, representing the qualities of his double parentage as the Son of God, and the son of Mary." This was as far as he was willing to go.

At Harvard he turned to a discussion of the work of Christ, the doctrine of the atonement. The medieval theologian St. Anselm (c.1033-1109) had enunciated what is commonly called the "satisfaction theory of the atonement." To Anselm, God needed to be satisfied for the sin man has committed; the slate cannot be wiped clean without recompense and this is the work of Christ. Christ, being God and man, is the only one who can offer satisfaction. To Bushnell, this transfer of guilt and punishment from the condemned to the innocent is unjust and cruel. The theory of the seventeenth century jurist, Hugo Grotius (1583-1645), commonly called the "governmental theory of the atonement," presented equal difficulties. Grotius argued that without punishment for sin, which Christ has taken upon Himself, divine government of the universe would crumble; chaos would reign. But this theory, which

dominated New England theology during the period of Calvinist domination, was equally unsatisfactory to Bushnell, because it did not take into consideration the individual sinner. If man does not undergo a change himself, if he does not suffer through the pain of separation from God which is the result of sin, then the result is the "worst conceivable form of licentiousness." These theories did not express Bushnell's understanding of the justification of man by God. "Justification is that which will give confidence, again, to guilty minds; that which will assure the base and humiliated soul of the world, chase away the demons of wrath and despair it has evoked, and help it to return to God in courage, whispering still to itself—soul be of good cheer, thy sins are forgiven thee." The atonement by Christ was seen, therefore, as "interrupting the flow of justice by delivering men, or assisting them to deliver themselves from the penal consequences of transgression; . . . a confidence equally repugnant to justice, that God will freely accept, embrace, and even justify the transgressor who forsakes his sin." The purpose of the atonement was to make men penitent and eager for forgiveness, and to emphasize the "integrity" and "sanctity" of God's law. Christ accomplished these ends through His teaching, His obedience, and His sacrifice.

At Andover Bushnell turned his attention to the controversies engaging the New England churches. He made an impassioned plea for tolerance and charity among the theological disputants. While not denying the need for creative theological work, he regretted that the passion of discussion had led to a hardening of lines between parties and to division within the churches. Bushnell was convinced that it was dogmatism which had brought division. If the New England churches had embodied "the simple love of God under some such badge, for example, as the Apostle's Creed, it is very probable to me that the causes of the division would never have existed." Instead, disputes concerning the Trinity, the atonement, the nature of man, and the means of regeneration, abounded. Bushnell called for a revival of religion, but he insisted that this could take place only "through . . . an esthetic elevation in the sensibilities of our souls, which only the closest possible union of the life to God can produce."

Bushnell the transcendentalist came into focus at Andover. The Hartford pastor was actually minimizing the severe and obvious theological conflicts of his day. He himself must have known that although the Apostle's Creed could be subscribed to by all, Unitarian and Orthodox alike, its common acceptance would serve no purpose other than to discourage controversy. The warmth of Bushnell's own religious sensitivity, however, showed through in appealing style.

The publication of *God in Christ* precipitated further theological controversy. Charges of heresy were brought against Bushnell. Though he was supported by his own church, he was from this point on regarded with suspicion by the orthodox. Though later writings tended to bring him more in line with his inherited Calvinism, this volume marks Bushnell as the father of liberal theology in America.

TRAINING IN CHRISTIANITY

Author: Søren Kierkegaard (1813-1855)
Type of work: Existential exegetical reflections
First published: 1850

PRINCIPAL IDEAS ADVANCED

Christ is a contemporary reality present to every believer; existential contemporaneity rather than objective historical knowledge of His personality constitutes His essential significance for the Christian.

Christ disclosed in his contemporaneity is the God-man, who, in relation to the human understanding, appears as the Paradox and the Offense; as the Offense Christ appears in two forms: in His collision with the established order and in His claim to be God.

Christianity is not a doctrine; truth is a mode of being rather than a set of propositions and definitions; in the truth of Christianity the Teacher is more important than the teaching.

Christianity receives its genuine expression in the Church militant rather than in the Church triumphant; the task of the Christian is to be a follower of Christ rather than simply an admirer.

With the publication of his book *Training in Christianity*, Søren Kierkegaard openly launched his protest against the established Church. This protest reached its culmination in the publication of the *Attack upon Christendom* four years later, in 1854. In the former the author's protest was subtle and subdued; in the latter the protest became violent and envenomed. Although intermittently polemical in nature, *Training in Christianity* has for its central task a positive formulation of what it means to be a Christian in Christendom. Christendom, according to the author, has unwittingly done away with Christianity. The essential task thus becomes that of reintroducing Christianity into Christendom.

What does it mean to be a Christian? This is the lead question which directs the discussion of the author's work. Various answers are presented in which various themes are elaborated, but the theme of contemporaneity is central. To exist as a Christian is to exist contemporaneously with Christ. The Christian is he who acknowledges Christ as a present reality, as the object of his faith and as the pattern and paradigm for his ethical decisions. It is the existential rather than historical significance of Christ that provides the touchstone for the Christian. "For in relation to the absolute there is only one tense: the present. For him who is not contemporary with the absolute —for him it has no existence. And as Christ is the absolute, it is easy to see that with respect to Him there is only one situation: that of contemporaneousness. The five, the seven, the fifteen, the eighteen hundred years are neither here nor there; they do not change Him, neither do they in any wise reveal who He was, for who He is is revealed only to faith." Christ as an item of objective historical knowledge becomes a matter of indifference for the believer. He is not someone of whom we learn through a study of history. He is a living reality, seen through the eyes of faith, contemporaneous with each generation. His reality is such that it transcends both time and place.

This Christ of Christianity, disclosed in his contemporaneity, is the God-man, the Absolute Paradox, the Offense. It is for this reason that the understanding must come to a standstill in His presence. From the standpoint of human reason Christ as the God-man is not only a paradox but also an offense for reason and society alike. This offense takes two forms. In one of its forms it indicates a collision with the established order. Here the contradiction appears within society and can be elucidated through the use of social categories. The first form of the offense has to do not with the God-man as such, but with Christ as teacher who insists on inwardness and consequently rejects the empty externalism of the established order. At the time of His decisive revelation in Jesus of Nazareth this offense was disclosed in His attacks on the Scribes and the Pharisees, who at that time represented the established order. But this offense is not bound to a particular time and place; it constitutes a permanent and continuing revolt against God. Wherever a claim for the complete commensurability between the externals of society and the inward life of man is set forth, Christ appears as the offense who collides with this externalization and secularization.

The second form of the offense is

more decisive. Kierkegaard speaks of it as the *essential* offense. This has to do with the fact that Jesus, as an individual man, speaks and acts as though He were God. Furthermore, the offense is heightened in that Jesus is of the lowest class, subjected to humiliation, a lowly man, born of a despised maiden, son of a carpenter, friend of the poor and afflicted, the most impotent of men and, nevertheless, one who declares Himself to be God! Not only does He declare Himself to be God, but He invites all those who labor and are heavy-laden to come hither so that he might give them rest! He who himself is in need of help offers to help others, and asks even to help those who despise Him. It is here that the offense becomes explicit and occasions denial and rejection. It was this which led Peter to deny Christ. That a man should fall into humiliation, affliction, and ultimately into the power of his enemies is human; but that the one who declares Himself to be God should do so is an occasion for denial. The essential offense thus places the individual squarely before the God-man, tests his faith, and calls him to decision.

Clearly the penetration to the existential significance of Christ as the God-man and the Offense is not a matter of demonstrations and proofs. It is, says Kierkegaard, as though Christ were to say: "By way of proofs no man cometh unto me." Christ becomes the God-man in the act of existential faith, an act which must be repeated throughout the life of every individual and in every generation. Every generation has to begin anew with Christ. Faith is a repeatable existential possibility and is lost in the moment that it is transformed into a set of propositions or doctrines. Christianity is not a doctrine. The truth of Christianity indicates a mode of being or manner of existence rather than a sum of propositional assertions and definitions. "Christianity understood, the truth consists not in knowing the truth but in being the truth." Truth, existentially apprehended, is a way of life, patterned after Christ as the paradigm in the situation of contemporaneity. The God-man is the unity of God and a concrete individual in a concrete situation which has significance for every other concrete situation. The most fantastic distortion of all, according to the author, is to transform the concrete contemporaneity of Christ into a speculative unity of God and man *sub specie aeterni* (as did those who came under the spell of Hegel). There is no contradiction in the idea of the speculative unity of God and man in general, but there is a contradiction between being God and being a particular, concrete man.

The truth of Christianity is embodied in the life of the Teacher, as this life unites in itself the lowly existence of a humiliated and suffering man and the quality of eternity. It is thus that the Teacher is more important than the teaching. The teaching is already an abstraction from the truth of his existence. The error of Christendom, says Kierkegaard, is that it has done away with the Teacher, and only the teaching remains. Insofar as Christ as the Teacher *is* the truth of Christianity, all direct communication is rendered impossible. The truth of a teaching can be directly communicated, but the communication of the truth of the Teacher, or the truth of an Incarnate Existence as it is actually lived, requires indirect means. This is why

Christ lived and taught *incognito*, and revealed himself only to those who made the movement of faith and sought to follow his life of perfect obedience. But this faith and obedience of the follower was soon replaced by belief, and the next stage was to comprehend this belief as a doctrine. It was to this end that the help of philosophy, and more specifically Hegelianism, was solicited. Beliefs and doctrines cast in philosophical form are "reasonable" and directly communicable. But the truth of Christianity is precisely the Paradox and the Offense which is neither rationally intelligible nor directly communicable. It requires the inward transformation and appropriation which constitutes the peculiar quality of existential faith.

This existential faith and obedience constitutes the marrow of the Church militant, which according to the author must be clearly distinguished from the Church triumphant. The Church triumphant is the Church of established Christendom. It views Christianity simply as an extension of world-history, marking a higher stage in the development of the human race. Christianity becomes an intramundane process; the Church and the world become synonymous. In the Church triumphant it is easy to be a Christian for there is no essential difference between the Christian and the non-Christian. The offense of Christianity is transformed into a gentle doctrine of consolations which are there just in case man some time during his life finds need of them. In the Church triumphant the essence of Christianity is dissolved. The offense is secularized, human sin is attenuated, religious commitment is confused with

social commitment, and faith is externalized. In one of his more polemical and ironical passages the author writes: "Everyone is baptized as an infant; later, but while he is still a child, he is confirmed—presumably in order that as early as possible everything may be arranged about that sort of passport which is so necessary if one is to get through the world without receiving a reproof from the magistrate. And of everyone who as an infant was baptized, as a boy or a girl was confirmed, it is certain that he is a Christian—by consulting the parish register one can ascertain this." In short, the Church triumphant has reduced the Christianity of Christ to cultural Christianity. It is against this cultural Christianity that the Church militant must wage a continuing war. It is only in the Church militant that one can become a Christian, properly speaking. The Church militant accentuates the offense and teaches that love of God is hatred of the world.

Corresponding with the distinction between the Church militant and the Church triumphtant is the distinction between the "admirer" and the "follower." The admirer looks at Christ from a distance and sings praises of His noble qualities—at least on Sunday morning. The follower also admires Christ, but above all he seeks to resemble Him. He strives *to be* what he admires; he discerns that the object of his admiration makes a claim upon him. To be an admirer is easy; indeed it pays well. To be a follower is difficult. It entails resolute commitment and suffering, both of which receive their most intensive expression in the life of Him who is to be followed.

THE WORKS OF LYMAN BEECHER

Author: Lyman Beecher (1775-1863)
Type of work: Evangelical theology
First published: 1852 (Volumes I and II); 1853 (Volume III)

PRINCIPAL IDEAS ADVANCED

Calvinism rightly understood teaches the moral government of God over free, accountable subjects, who, although possessing the natural power of contrary choice, universally manifest a moral inability to live a holy life because of the bias to sin inherited from Adam.

Since men invariably, though voluntarily, sin in every act from the moment they become responsible moral agents, they are utterly dependent for their salvation upon the regenerating work of the Holy Spirit.

The democratic institutions of America depend upon belief in God and upon obedience to Him in accordance with the teachings of the Bible; therefore, atheism and its political consequences must be resisted.

America is a land especially blessed of God and the scene of considerable moral and social progress, but the times call for a revival of evangelical religion and a reform of morals which will eliminate the evils of national life, such as intemperance and dueling.

The *Works of Lyman Beecher* provides excellent insight into the issues, interests, and controversies which marked the life of an eminent American preacher and revivalist during the first half of the nineteenth century. A man of great eloquence and power in the pulpit, Beecher also became embroiled in the theological disputes which divided the Calvinistic divines of his time. Beecher began his ministry as a Congregational pastor and served in Litchfield, Connecticut, and Boston, Massachusetts, before entering the Presbyterian Church and assuming the presidency of Lane Theological Seminary in Cincinnati, Ohio, a post which he held from 1832 to 1851. As a pastor he acquired a reputation as a passionate crusader against such evils as intemperance and dueling, and in Boston he was one of the fiercest enemies of Unitarianism. His move to the West involved him almost immediately in a heresy trial in which he was accused of betraying the tenets of the Westminster Confession of Faith. The collection of Beecher's sermons and essays considered here, although not complete, brings together some of the most important writings of his career and reveals not only the workings of his own versatile mind but also something of the spirit of the age.

Calvinistic theologians of Lyman Beecher's day were engaged in heated controversy regarding the doctrines of original sin and human depravity. The federal theology of the Westminster Confession (1643-1648), which the Puritans brought to New England, taught that the entire human race was involved in Adam's Fall, both by direct participation and by legal representation, so that all men share his guilt and come into the world with a wholly corrupt nature. Jonathan Edwards (1703-1758), the initiator of a tradition which is commonly known as "the New England theology," set forth his own version of original sin in which he reaffirmed the unity of Adam with his posterity and defended the theory of inherited guilt and depravity. The successors of Edwards gradually moved in an Arminian direction in the interests of securing a better defense of human freedom and responsibility. Beecher was one of those in this tradition who contributed to the modification of the older Calvinistic and Edwardian views.

In particular, Beecher was associated with the views of "the New Haven theology," whose chief spokesman was Nathaniel William Taylor (1786-1858) of Yale Divinity School. Although claiming to be loyal to the essentials of the Edwardian view, Taylor actually moved a considerable distance from it in that he repudiated the imputation of Adam's sin to his progeny and denied that men come into the world with a nature that is already, in the strict sense, corrupt. The heart of his position was that all sin is personal and voluntary. However, men are born with a nature so deteriorated that all, without exception, will sin as soon as they attain the power of moral agency, unless or until grace intervenes. While sin is certain, it is not necessary, since men have the natural ability of contrary choice and lack only moral inclination. In short, Taylor's view was that original sin consists, not of the sharing of Adam's guilt or of his corrupt nature, but only of hereditary and perverted powers which manifest themselves at the dawn of moral consciousness in voluntary disobedience. These views, while paradoxical in na-

ture, provided a theology well suited for revivalistic purposes, and they enabled Taylor to defend more easily the moral government of God. Beecher agreed substantially with Taylor on these points and insisted that to do so was to be true to the real intent of the Calvinistic system.

While a majority of the Congregational theologians adopted the moderate Calvinism of Taylor, the Presbyterians were more evenly divided between the Old School men, who preferred the sterner views of human guilt and corruption, and the New School men, who found "the New Haven theology" agreeable. It was this conflict among Presbyterians which occasioned Beecher's heresy trial. Although Beecher was accepted into the Presbytery of Cincinnati upon his arrival to take up his duties at Lane Theological Seminary, the Old School moderator, Joshua L. Wilson, preferred charges against him, including among other things the charge that Beecher's concepts of man's native ability, human depravity, and the effectual calling of the Holy Spirit were heterodox. The trial began in June of 1835 and ended with Beecher's acquittal, since a majority of the judges held New School opinions. The two sermons which were entered as evidence against him ("Dependence and Free Agency" and "On the Native Character of Man"), a detailed record of the trial, and his lengthy defense (as published later in a revised form under the title, *Views of Theology*) are contained in Volume III of Beecher's *Works*. In his sermons Beecher's position is clear enough, and his basic agreement with Taylor is beyond question. However, in his defense before the Presbytery he used every semantic device and every subtlety of thought possible in an attempt to harmonize his theology with the Westminster Confession. The unwary reader can easily be led astray as Beecher maneuvers to make Old School language teach New School doctrines.

A great deal of Beecher's effort was devoted to establishing the distinction between natural ability and moral inability in Adam's descendants. In referring to natural ability Beecher meant to suggest that man, before and after the Fall, had all of the requisite capacities and faculties, such as reason, conscience, and will, to enable him to function as a free agent with the power of contrary choice. Beecher argues that only if man has such ability can God justly hold him responsible for his sinfulness in the moral government of the world. This means that men, even in their fallen state, can render obedience unto God in the sense that they can be loyal, for they sin, not by an inexorable necessity, but by voluntary choice. Moreover, in any given case of wrong choice the sinner could have and ought to have chosen otherwise than he did. However, while men since Adam's defection have the natural ability to live a life of holiness, they are characterized by a moral inability to do so. Moral inability is the lack of inclination in a free agent because of a contrary choice. In the fallen state all men come into the world with a nature so perverted that the will manifests a general and abiding decision against God which issues only in wrongdoing until the Holy Spirit acts to regenerate the sinner. In the strict sense, however, the children of Adam are not born guilty or with a nature that is already corrupt. Men are held accountable only for the sin

which proceeds from their own voluntary decision. Original sin, then, consists of the inheritance from Adam of a constitutional bias which, with unfailing certainty, becomes the inevitable occasion, though not the necessary cause, of sin and nothing but sin from the first moment that a person attains the power of moral choice. Thus, men are wholly dependent on the regenerating work of the Holy Spirit for salvation.

Volume I of Beecher's *Works* is dedicated to the working men of America and contains a series of lectures on "Political Atheism" and on intemperance. In the former Beecher is concerned not only with theoretical disbelief in God but also with the anarchistic, socialistic, and egalitarian social philosophy which he associated with it. Asserting that governments are necessary to restrain the evil propensities of men, Beecher defends private property and inequality of condition in society and argues for the necessity of a strong rule of law undergirded by a morally alert citizenry. He further maintains that the free institutions of America are dependent on belief in the Deity, warning that chaos, violence, and tyranny are the inevitable concomitants of atheism. Beecher does not identify his foes very clearly, but he does refer to the existence of certain anarchistic and atheistic societies in this country, to some revolutionary groups in Germany, and to the radicals of the French revolution who attempted to establish a new atheistic religion based on the worship of the goddess Reason. Running through this whole discussion is a sense that the present age is marked by great social and moral progress and that America has been divinely chosen to usher in a new era of human well being in the world.

In his rebuttal of atheism Beecher attempts to demonstrate the rationality, morality, and political relevance of the Bible. He presents the cosmological and theological arguments for the existence of God, maintains the necessity of a special divine revelation, argues for the inspiration of the Bible on the basis of prophecy and miracles, defends the morality and political philosophy of the Old Testament, insists that God's government of the world is moral, and urges that Jesus is the best friend the working man has.

The six lectures on intemperance in Volume I and the eight sermons in Volume II indicate some of the practical concerns of Beecher. After outlining the nature, causes, signs, and evils of excessive drinking, he urges a strictly enforced national prohibition of the manufacture and sale of ardent spirits. Beecher also condemns dueling and contends that if the people will withhold their votes from all political candidates who support it, the way can be opened for its abolition. An ordination sermon delivered in Massachusetts compares the "Evangelical System" (Calvinism) with the "Liberal System" (Unitarianism), arguing that the former is the faith once delivered to the saints and that the latter, as a system, tends toward laxity of morals. Something of the subtlety of Beecher's homiletical logic becomes apparent in the conclusion he draws from the Biblical premise that the righteous love the truth. Since the wicked portion of the populace uniformly detest Calvinistic tenets and

the most pious people of the land are agreeable to them, he maintains that this is evidence of the correctness of the "Evangelical System." While he is careful not to pronounce Unitarians as a body to be immoral, he does hint that those who are loose in their morality, as evidenced by their attendance at plays, dances, and masquerades, are more likely to be in the Unitarian than the Calvinistic camp. Following the sermon, there is a long defense of it which Beecher made in response to a Unitarian reviewer who maintained that Beecher's ideas were too Arminian in tendency to qualify as real Calvinism and that he had vilified the Unitarians by casting aspersions upon their morality. The sermon and the response cover one hundred and seventy pages.

Two sermons, "The Government of God Desirable," and "The Bible a Code of Laws," deal with the moral government of God, which is a basic theme of Beecher's theology. He contends that God's blessedness and man's eternal salvation are dependent upon the sovereignty of God over all things. By divine moral government Beecher means the rule of God over free, accountable human subjects on the basis of revealed laws maintained by appropriate rewards and punishment. In the remaining sermons Beecher asserts the necessity and practicality of a reformation in morals, defines the duties of local churches, specifies ways of combating the evil designs of Satan, and offers a plan for rebuilding some of the weak or abandoned churches of Connecticut.

ATTACK ON CHRISTENDOM

Author: Søren Kierkegaard (1813-1855)
Type of work: Criticism of secularized Christianity
First published: 1854-1855

PRINCIPAL IDEAS ADVANCED

The official established religion of Denmark is an utter contradiction of the Christianity of the New Testament; this contradiction results from the wealth and status enjoyed by the official state Church and its spokesmen.

Christendom is so dull, stupid, and lacking in both understanding and vigor that it cannot even answer attacks made on it.

The Christianity of the New Testament demands a radical break with the world.

Christianity is essentially an individual affair, both in its true expressions and in its protests against abuses.

The *Attack on Christendom* is a collection of materials written by the Danish philosopher-theologian Søren Kierkegaard in the last two years of his life. The first group of articles consists of twenty-one items published in the years 1854 and 1855 in a political journal entitled *The Fatherland,* followed by a short essay independently published on May 16, 1855, in Copenhagen, entitled "The Midnight Cry." The second set of materials consists of ten editions of a little paper entitled *The Instant,* published between May and October of 1855. The first nine of these bear the imprint: Copenhagen, Published by C. A. Reitzel's Estate and Heirs, Bianco Luno's Press. The last edition bears no imprint and is presumed to have been finished by its author just prior to his journey to the hospital with a fatal illness on October 2, 1955, and to have been released posthumously. The material was collected after Kierkegaard's death and given the title it now bears. Since it represents its author's sharp and sustained criticism of conditions in the Danish

Church during his lifetime, it has been judged by some commentators to be more in the nature of a popular diatribe than a serious theological work.

The first six of the twenty-one items from *The Fatherland* were written as Kierkegaard's reactions to a funeral eulogy preached by Professor Hans Lassen Martensen (1808-1884) for the deceased Danish Bishop Jakob Mynster (1775-1854). Mynster died on January 30, and Martensen delivered his tribute on the fifth Sunday after Epiphany (February 5, 1854) extolling Bishop Mynster as a "witness to the truth." Kierkegaard immediately penned his first attack upon Martensen but did not release it until December of that year, when Martensen was appointed to the chair left vacant by Mynster's death. Kierkegaard objected vigorously in this and the succeeding articles to the possibility that an official and comfortable ecclesiastic in the Church of Denmark could be a witness to the truth of Christianity as portrayed in the New Testament. The Christianity of the New Testament seemed to Kierkegaard to demand a breach with the world, while official clergy enjoyed the comforts of their dependence upon the world. Priests and deacons who are not in danger can hardly be considered witnesses to the truth. The fact that Martensen was appointed to the bishopric left vacant by the death of Mynster means that Kierkegaard's strictures were aimed at him as well.

The attack was prompted by, but not confined to, the Mynster-Martensen incident. The remaining fifteen articles from *The Fatherland* extended the attack to conditions in the whole established state Church. It was Kierkegaard's single thesis that the type of Christianity set forth in the New Testament simply did not exist in the Denmark of his day. It was Kierkegaard's purpose to prompt the honesty required to admit this fact. Kierkegaard suggested that honesty is required to see poverty as the fundamental requirement of New Testament Christianity. Anyone can know, he suggested, what New Testament Christianity requires, except priests who benefit financially from the fraudulent substitute they perpetuate in its name. The honesty of shoplifters and usurers, who admit selfish purposes, is to be preferred to the pretense of the clergy which uses pious platitudes to cloak its betrayal of the Gospel.

Kierkegaard told his readers that they should not feel guilty about absenting themselves from ecclesiastical functions. But he did not seek to organize a mass protest and his objection remains an essentially individual one. He invited others to make their own individual protests, but he had no interest in starting a rebellion.

In places Kierkegaard seems to be satisfied by the fact that he was not directly embroiled in the behavior he castigates. At other places he expresses guilt for his part in the total condition of Christianity in his day. He admits his melancholy for his involvement and his own need of punishment, yet he insists that nothing could be gained by punishing him with excommunication since his membership in the Church was of no importance. He briefly considers the consequences of joining the Roman Catholic Church, but he finds it no better than official Protestantism. His entire approach remains an intensely individualist insistence that the New Testament demands poverty, risk, and suffering on the part of Christians. Moreover, he flatly argues that grace cannot be a substitute for lack of rigor in the Christian life.

The material in the second part of the collection is entitled *The Instant*. The significance of the title lies in Kierkegaard's understanding of the existential meaning of the present moment. The writing is not detached, for it partakes of the polemical present. Kierkegaard expresses a dislike of the present even though he is called upon to live in this conflict. He bids farewell to detachment with a flourish of sorrow.

The existential meaning of the present also signifies the decisive character of the attack Kierkegaard was making on the Christian institutions and behavior of his contemporaries. He turns the premise to suggest that the real attack on Christianity in his day was being made by the priests who were urging men to take Christianity lightly. He admonishes the Danish people to "Take an emetic!" in order to get rid of the false kind of Christianity to which they had been introduced by the thousand functionaires, or official clergymen.

When Kierkegaard becomes the object of counterattack he interprets the outbursts as proof that he was correct in his criticism. The New Testament predicts that men who defend the Gospel will suffer persecution, and Kierkegaard comforts himself by the implications in his own case. He renews his criticism of state Christianity with its temporal comforts and promise of easily earned eternal blessedness. Kierkegaard doubts that any further gain for true Christianity can be made until the state religion has been swept away. He ridicules the idea that the state, a human and temporal institution, can use the official cult as a protection for the divine. He blames the idea of a state church for the fact that the gate to Christianity has been made wide and deceptive. The idea of establishment is "ridiculous" and the name "God" is transformed from a symbol of awe and majesty into mere "twaddle."

"Thanks be to you, ye Government Clerks," he writes, "ye Counselors of Chancery, Counselors of Justice, Counselors of State, and Privy Counselors, thanks for the enormous amount of scribbling ye have had to do to arrange for His Majesty's subjects all and sundry in a cheap and comfortable way the attainment of eternal blessedness; thanks be to you, ye clerical counselors; truly ye have not done it for naught, for ye have your percentage; yet after all it is no more than reasonable that ye should be thanked."

Kierkegaard takes the words from Matthew 23:29-33 and Luke 11:47ff., in which Christ castigates the scribes

and Pharisees for supposing that if they had lived in the days of their fathers they would not have shed the innocent blood of the prophets, and Kierkegaard turns the words upon the Danish clergy of the nineteenth century. He suggests that the priests should keep silent rather than kill or criticize the prophets of the present times. He implies that if Christ were to come again He would heap upon the Danish clergy the same bitter criticism He gave the scribes and Pharisees in his day. The priests are especially guilty for they have perverted the image of Christ by picturing the Christian life in terms of comfort and money.

Kierkegaard treats the idea of the state and the idea of Christianity in antithetical terms. Although the strength of the state is directly proportional to numbers in population, Christianity is vital with an inverse relation to numbers and its strength is dependent upon the intensity of devotion found in the few. "One single true Christian is enough to justify the assertion that Christianity exists." Because the state and Christianity stand in sharp juxtaposition the state should get out of the religious domain. It should no longer support priests or underwrite theological education. This opposition of Kierkegaard to a state religion should not be confused with more recent theories of separation, for Kierkegaard's view is based upon a radical individualism and a distrust of the state's influence on religion rather than upon a judgment that separation of the two realms is best for the general life of both.

Kierkegaard's bitterness toward the official clergy appears in such a variety of forms that only by reading the book will the reader sense the depth of the antagonism. Any state supported functionary in religion will spoil what he teaches. The private practice of religious preaching might mean that most practitioners would starve. The clergy do well to ask the public to include them in its prayers, for they most certainly need them. But despite the variety of form which Kierkegaard's criticism takes, it retains a common and even repetitious theme.

A true Christian, Kierkegaard holds, is more rare than a genius, yet the evangelists of Danish Christendom win thousands of converts in a short time. Whereas Christ won a dozen followers in three years, the popular evangelists of the nineteenth century "win" as many as three thousand in an hour! The author blasts the Sunday orators who make a popular success of preaching poverty. These "silken and velvet orators" create tears and put them in a bottle. It is this dangerous and even dishonest destruction of Christianity undertaken in pretense of its

support that elicits Kierkegaard's most profound disgust. "Persecution, maltreatment, bloodshedding," he writes, "has by no means done such injury, no, it has been inestimably beneficial in comparison with the radical damage done by official Christianity, which is designed to serve human indolence, mediocrity, by making men believe that indolence, mediocrity and enjoyment of life is Christianity. Do away with official Christianity, let persecution come—that very instant Christianity again exists."

Kierkegaard's bitter criticisms called attention to grave faults, but he has been accused of excess and of lacking the spirit of love found in the New Testament. In his memoirs, Bishop Martensen made a reply to Kierkegaard, but the issues at stake between the two men, especially the issue concerning the individual's place in relation to the Church as the community which bears Christ's name, have not been resolved to this day.

THE NATURE OF THE ATONEMENT

Author: John McLeod Campbell (1800-1872)
Type of work: Soteriology
First published: 1856

PRINCIPAL IDEAS ADVANCED

Explanations of the work of Christ on behalf of men in terms of punishment by God and satisfaction of His justice are unacceptable to an enlightened conscience.

A moral and spiritual approach must be substituted for a legal approach, and this is supported by the witness of Christ in the Gospels.

Christ the Son offers to God the Father a perfect confession of, and repentance for, human sin; and the Father who delights in mercy accepts this repentance, and men are forgiven and share in eternal life.

The thesis which John McLeod Campbell incorporated into his volume on *The Nature of the Atonement* had cost him his ministerial status in the Church of Scotland. He stood at the bar of the General Assembly in 1831 and heard himself deposed as a heretic, by an almost unanimous vote, for holding and teaching views unacceptable to the Church about the significance of the work of Christ. His pastoral work as a minister was beyond reproach, and in personal character he was held in high regard by all. But he came to believe by the study of Scripture and reflection upon religious experience that the love of God was universal and not limited to the elect, and that filial, not legal, perspectives were best suited to explain God's relationship to men.

In 1856 he published his book *The Nature of the Atonement and its Relation to Remission of Sins and Eternal Life*. It was often republished and is regarded by some authorities as the most significant work on the subject by a British writer of the nineteenth century. He lived to receive an honorary doctorate from the University of Glasgow, a testimonial to his worth from many of the most noted people in Scotland, and to know that his views were being accepted by an increasing number of churchmen.

The purpose of the book is to isolate from among the many aspects of the atonement the one which had most significantly engaged his attention, namely, what the atonement of Christ was in itself, rather than the extent of its influence or the sum of its achievements, although he fully recognized that these are all intertwined. Previous expositions, he believed, did not satisfy the enlightened conscience of the age, nor did they do justice to the teaching of the New Testament. He makes much of this appeal to what he calls "internal evidence"; that is, the way in which the moral consciousness will respond affirmatively to the truth when truth is presented to it. This self-evident principle of validity constitutes the authority to which the Scriptures themselves appeal, the fact that the divine revelation of truth arouses an answering witness in the spirit of man. In this experience is the strongest evidence for the truth of the Christian faith.

Any serious man reflecting on himself in the light of the Gospel will discover that his self-consciousness confronts him with his personal involvement in guilt and with the kind of life he would hope to attain. These may be called the retrospective and prospective witnesses of conscience. The sense of sin is more than the superficial awareness of imperfection. It is the deeply disturbing realization that we do not love God and neighbor as we ought and that we need a remedy. What we long for is a new life principle within us, the eternal life of the Gospels, not primarily in future terms, but as a present experience of the life of God in the soul. This twofold testimony of self-awareness is the necessary preparation for understanding what the atonement is about.

The Christian message itself makes demands on us, and John McLeod Campbell points out that the first of these is that we recognize the truth that God delights in forgiving men their sins and guilt. This is a fundamental recognition which must precede atonement itself. God does not require to be appeased, propitiated, or changed in His attitude to man as if

He delighted in damnation. It is His desire to bridge the gap between the retrospective and the prospective witnesses of self-consciousness.

If this be so, then why should there be any need to proceed with a work of atonement? Could not God of His clemency simply pronounce general forgiveness and thereby end the estrangement? Why the necessity for atonement?

Such questions are serious issues and any answer must not ignore the fact of divine mercy. Indeed it is just the fact that we are dealing with infinite love and not just infinite power that is the key to the difficulty. Love is never cheap, but costly in sacrifice; it is willing to forgive sin, but it cannot ignore the power and reality of sin. The internal evidence of our spirit responds affirmatively only to a love that is really aware of what sin is, a love that does not bestow its favors promiscuously and gratuitously. Hence the necessity of a manifestation of love in depth, and this Christ reveals. The nature of the atonement, then, will be consistent with the nature of God as manifest in Christ, and it is at this point that previous explanations have been unsatisfactory. Campbell willingly concedes that all due weight must be given to the place of the holiness of God, the wrath of God, and the realities of law and justice in salvation, but they have been used in a misleading and erroneous way by theologians. Instead of being contributions to hope they have been construed as barriers. God is a Savior because He is holy and just, not despite His righteousness.

When he examined Martin Luther's commentary on the Epistle to the Galatians, McLeod Campbell gave his assent to the Reformer's expositions on redemption, grace, justification by faith, and especially on the personal appropriation of Christ as the indispensable core of the salvation. He found little, however, to enlighten him about the precise nature of the reconciling deed of Christ. Luther seems to assert the identification of Christ with man's curse and death, and His unity with eternal righteousness, leaving the two aspects of Christ's nature in apparent opposition and contradiction. The Savior bears the sin of the world, but it is not clear how this redemptive task was possible. That Christ became a sinner, as Luther's terms literally taken would imply, could not be true.

On the other hand, the prevailing Calvinism did not satisfy the enlightened conscience to which Campbell continually appeals. What he calls the earlier form, that of Jonathan Edwards (1703-1758), the New England divine, was deficient on two counts: (1) it restricted the atonement to the elect, those chosen by God from among mankind to receive salvation, and (2) it conferred on the elect a legal standing as if law and not love were the center of the Gospel. In its prevailing forms in the nineteenth century theologians had struggled to modify the details of the earlier Calvinist scholasticism, but they kept the same kind of language. Instead of describing divine justice as giving every man his due, the Calvinists spoke of God as a Moral Governor who demands only such punishment as will vindicate the principle of moral law; or they argued that Christ died for all men, but only the elect would be touched by sovereign grace to respond; or they held the view that the divinity of Christ gave infinite value to suffering of short duration, in place of the older view which understood divinity as making Christ capable of infinite suffering. Campbell is sympathetic to the motives which prompted such revisions and to the admission that the older theories had elements in them repugnant to a mature conscience. He believed, however, that this patching of the old garment was useless. Justice rather than love was still central, and punishment as a method of understanding the death of Christ still prevailed. "As long as Christ's sufferings are held to be *penal*," he writes, "which, even when the old form of words is most departed from, is the expression still used, I cannot see what difference it makes." He gladly acknowledges that the practical piety and pastoral care of many were better than their theories would suggest, but the nature of the atonement expounded needed a radical shift at its foundation from a legal to a filial base, from God as Judge to God as Father. This he proceeds to make by restructuring the atonement around the belief that men are erring sons to whom God the Father offers restoration through the work of His incarnate Son.

The atonement, it is argued, is to be understood in its own light; that is, in the light of the significance of the persons involved as grouped in family realities. The key is in the words of the fortieth Psalm and attributed to Jesus, "Lo, I come to do Thy will, O God," which is the very essence of sonship. When Christ suffered for sin, it was the suffering of infinite love in the face of human ingratitude, and not a primitive unloading of divine revenge and wrath from inexorable divine justice. The atonement has two aspects: (1) that involved in Christ's "dealing with men on the part of God," and (2) that involved in "His dealing with God on behalf of men."

The first, or retrospective aspect, as Campbell calls it, covers the Son's witness to, and vindication of, the love of the Father, so that He could say, "He that hath seen me hath seen the Father." This love must not be confused with an amiable tolerance of sin. Sin is condemned in perfect accordance with the idea of the wrath of God against it, and its enormity is confessed to the Father by the Son on behalf of all sons. In a memorable sentence Campbell asserts this key position, "This confession, as to its own nature, must have been *a perfect Amen in humanity to the judgment of God on the sin of man*." In a striking metaphor he holds that by this perfect response and repentence Christ "absorbs" the judgment of God and satisfies the claim of divine justice. At one time Jonathan Edwards had opined that justice demanded either "an equivalent punishment or an equivalent sorrow and repentance," but he had dismissed the latter alternative as inoperable. What Campbell does is to take it and demonstrate its validity. "We feel," he writes, "that such a repentance as we are supposing would, in such a case, be the true and proper satisfaction to offended justice."

The second, or prospective, aspect of this moral and spiritual interpretation of the atonement deals with what God desires men to become. The Father delights in answering the intercession of the Son by granting men remission of sins and eternal life. This remission is not a legal title, an imputed righteousness, but a spiritual state, an active sonship, bestowed here and now. Our own nature while in sin had this capacity of sonship, and we vaguely knew our need. It is Christ who reveals this "hidden capacity for good that is in man" by demonstrating it in His own life. We reproduce what Christ did on our behalf when we share His confidence in the Father's love, and walk as obedient sons. Campbell writes, "We get near to God just as the measure in which in the spirit of Christ we thus livingly adopt His confession of our sins—in this measure and no further."

When this understanding of the atonement became clear and convincing to Campbell, he confesses, it was like the appearance of light in a dark place and a relief to his spirit. His conscience responded to it eagerly, and it had the practical merit, he believed, of making the pastoral task of the ministry perspicuous and effective for human need. The very significance of the Christian Faith was transformed; unity and simplicity in perspective was substituted for a jungle of legal arguments that seemed to remove theology from the witness of the Gospels. This understanding was not clarity in the sense of removing all mystery from the ways of God to man, but it removed unnecessary and erroneous mystification arising out of the dominance of a conception of God as power and arbitrary will. It assumed a prior commitment to Christian faith, and it attempted to hold firmly to a natural sequence of explanations originating in the nature of God as Father, whose desire is to bestow eternal sonship on those who had rebelled against Him.

The Incarnation was the self-disclosure of the love of God, initiating a life which grew in a unity of obedience, a life which was truly a life of faith involving "the conception of a progressive development of the eternal life in our Lord's human consciousness." Even in the darkest moment of the Crucifixion, in "the cry of dereliction," this faith did not fail. Campbell protests with vigor against any idea of a staged performance, a planned legal transaction, an elaborate fiction of imputed guilt, a concentration on commerical balance sheet theories, in connection with the life of Christ. He believes that it is a commendable feature of his own explanation that it sees the nature of the atonement as one with the nature of the Christian life of obedient sonship, and that the relationship between the divine Father and the perfect Son provides a sufficient, consistent, and morally satisfying context within which justification and sanctification can be realized. The necessity of the atonement must be explained in terms of self-sacrificing love. To defend it in legal and punitive terms is to invoke "moral repulsiveness and intellectual contradiction." This appeal to self-evidencing light is the ultimate authority on which Campbell rests his case, a basis which he believes is the same as that by which Christ Himself commended His teaching. "If we consider the record of His personal ministry," he writes, "we shall see Him ever taking His hearers to a light already given in the Spirit, and in every man; to which light it is that He appeals in claiming to be received."

Attempts have been made to trace the antecedents of this position of Campbell, but such attempts have met with only debatable success. There are so many discussions on the work of Christ throughout theological literature that it would be surprising if none of the ideas of this Scottish theologian were present anywhere else. For example, there was a work by a fellow Scot, Thomas Erskine of Linthalen (1788-1870), called *The Brazen Serpent* (1831), which was probably known to Campbell, for the two men were friends; and it advanced some of the ideas of the moral repentance theory. Campbell does not mention this book, but he sees his own roots in independent study of the Bible and in reaction to Luther and some Calvinist divines. The truth of the matter probably is that serious questioning of traditional positions was being done by many Presbyterians who were separated from the Church of Scotland, men such as Edward Irving (1792-1834) and Thomas Carlyle (1795-1881), with whom Campbell was acquainted.

What is true beyond dispute is that *The Nature of the Atonement* was the first book on the subject by a competent thinker to work out in a careful and systematic way the particular thesis he defends. Campbell believed he was opening up new ground. Where he is conscious of borrowing he acknowledges it, and he clearly defines his departure from prevailing views. Others have attempted to improve on his exposition, and all subsequent writers have had to reckon with his pioneer labors.

CHRISTIAN NURTURE

Author: Horace Bushnell (1802-1876)
Type of work: Philosophy of Christian education
First published: 1860 (*Views of Christian Nurture*, 1846)

PRINCIPAL IDEAS ADVANCED

Children are amoral, not depraved, and they stand in need of Christian nurture.

The Christian atmosphere of the home and the religious and moral life of the parents are the formative influences on the Christian nurture of children.

The Church is a school for Christian nurture, and it is similar to a large family displaying the love of God to its members and to the world.

Through gradual Christian nurture the power and reach of the Kingdom of God on earth will be increased.

In 1846 the Massachusetts Sunday School Society published Horace Bushnell's *Views of Christian Nurture*, which, in a later and more widely read revised edition, was entitled *Christian Nurture*. Though the book has often been associated primarily with the field of religious education, it is in addition a theological essay.

Bushnell was born in Litchfield, Connecticut, educated at Yale College and the Theological School of Yale, and was at the time of the publication of *Views of Christian Nurture* pastor of the North Church (Congregational) in Hartford, Connecticut. When the 1860 edition of *Christian Nurture* was printed he had retired from his pastorate and was devoting his time to writing and traveling.

His attention had been directed to the subject of revivals and growth in Christian life ever since his arrival at Hartford in 1833. Bushnell was never a successful revivalist. The North Church in Hartford did not enjoy the fruits of periodic "awakenings," as did the First Congregational Church in the same town. During the early years of his Hartford ministry, Bushnell sought to encourage new declarations of faith, but he was notably unsuccessful; though, in 1834, forty-one new members joined his church, only four made a profession of faith in 1835 and only twelve in 1836. In that day a minister's success was measured by the number of conversions he brought about.

The battles over revivals had a long history in New England. During the First Great Awakening (1734-1735; 1740-1741) the Congregationalists split into Old Lights and New Lights, the opponents and defenders of the revivals respectively. Jonathan Edwards (1703-1758) was a key figure in these discussions and a supporter of the revivals; the Arminian theologian, Charles Chauncy (1705-1787), led the Old Light party. The issue remained alive for the next century. The advocates of revivalistic measures insisted that regeneration and conversion are the work of God and that such changes are not dependent on human effort. From the pulpit the New Light parishioners heard of their sinful, helpless plight; they were told that men are lost until God regenerates their souls and thereby encourages them to confess publicly their new "state." The Old Lights were less confident of the lasting effect of sudden conversions and thus minimized or resisted the call of the revivalist preacher. The theological basis of the Old Light position was Arminian; the opponents of revivalism believed in man's ability to determine himself. The conflict between the Old and New Light positions arose again during the Second Great Awakening at the end of the eighteenth century and dominated much of the theological discussion of the early decades of the nineteenth century. The New England churches, therefore, had been involved in these debates for a considerable period of time before Bushnell undertook an examination of the basic theological conflicts underlying the difference of opinion.

Until the time of Horace Bushnell, surprisingly little attention had been given in New England theology to the religious education of children. The young had been treated as adults; conversion was said to be their only hope. But during the 1830's and 1840's, partly as a result of the growth of the Sunday School movement, attention turned to the child, and theology had to be accommodated to the abilities of youthful apprehension. Theological reconstruction had to take place; the nature of religious experience had to be redefined. It was too much to expect children to experience divine separation, wrath, and judgment.

In this context Bushnell began to write and speak on the subject of Christian nurture. As he had been taught by Nathaniel William Taylor (1786-1858), Professor of Divinity at Yale College, Bushnell believed that the child was amoral, not depraved.

With proper Christian nurture no child need be forever lost and condemned.

The center for the development of the child's religious life is the home. The mother and father were, for Bushnell, the "natural and moral image" of God; the love of the mother for her child reveals the character of the love of Christ for all men. The impressions the child receives from his parents determines his religious development. Bushnell insisted that "a child is really not born till he emerges from the infantile state, and never before that time can he be said to receive a separate and properly individual nature." What happens to the child during this period of development shapes his attitudes and life.

Bushnell stressed the requirements laid upon parents to create the family atmosphere conducive to the proper nurture of children. Discipline of the parents is as essential as discipline of the children. He admonished parents to show that "religion is a first thing with you. And . . . not in words and talk, but visibly first in your love—that which fixes your aims, feeds your enjoyments, sanctifies your pleasures, supports your trials, satisfies your wants, contents your ambition, beautifies and blesses your character." Such is the nature of Christian education.

The child does not need to undergo a sudden conversion, but rather "the child is to grow up a Christian, and never know himself as being otherwise." The "organic unity of the family" is the natural organ for creating the Christian life and serves as the instrument for Christian or non-Christian ends. The relationships, opinions, prejudices, motives, and spirit of the home create the "atmosphere which passes into all and pervades all, as naturally as the air they breathe."

The Hartford pastor offered specific advice to parents on the conduct of family life. Good table manners, personal neatness, proper dress, avoidance of self-indulgence, observance of the Sabbath, punctuality, are all given mention. In the second half of his essay entitled "The Mode," Bushnell wrote a guide book for families desiring the Christian nurture of their children and of the adults themselves.

The role of the Church in this process did not escape his attention. In his own words, "The Church of God is a school, and the members are disciples, or learners." The Church is seen as a large family, seeking to manifest the love and spirit of Christ to the world. Baptism of infants and children is essential and once baptized they should be treated as members. It had been customary for ministers to regard baptized children as unregenerate, to stir them to a conversion experience. But Bushnell argued that children who have been baptized have been received into the covenant of the church; they deserve Christian nurture. "For there is a nuture of grace, as well as a grace of conversion; that for childhood, as this for the age of maturity, and one as sure and genuine as the other." The Christian expectation is that the child will develop in the faith and claim for himself the covenant into which he has been entered by his parents. In criticism of the practices of many New England churches, Bushnell argued that baptized children should be enrolled as Church members, subject to Church discipline, and that "when they come forward to acknowledge their baptism, and assume the covenant in their own choice, they ought not to be received as converts from the world, as if they were heathens coming into the fold, but there should be a distinction preserved, such as makes due account of their previous qualified membership; a *form of assumption* tendered in place of a *confession.* . . ."

An aim of Christian nurture was to broaden the power and reach of the Kingdom of God on earth. Though there is the Gospel command to convert the world, there is also the mode of increasing "Christian population." The Church needs to rediscover "that conversion over to the church is not the only way of increase; that God ordains a law of population in it as truly as he does in an earthly kingdom, or colony, and by this increase from within, quite as much as by conversion from without, designs to give it, finally, the complete dominion promised." Thus, the child growing up in a Christian family creates an influence which draws others into the circle, which, in turn, ever widens in scope and increases in number. This force generated by Christian nurture

will be "mighty enough to overlive, and finally to completely people the world." The Church would have a converting power on the outer world, while within its life children and adults would grow in the Christian graces. Here Bushnell was reverting to the older Puritan ideal of a society redeemed by the Church.

Christian Nurture met with strong opposition. Bushnell was challenged by members of his own Ministerial Association; Presbyterian and Episcopalian critics took note of the book and, though approving many of its criticisms of the necessity for conversion experience, argued that the Hartford pastor had minimized the role of special divine grace in regeneration and had concentrated too much on attempting to attract the lukewarm and "natural" man. It took the passing of another generation to see the import of this volume for American theology. Though the essay received notoriety in its own day, it became almost a handbook for religious educators in the early twentieth century.

THE LIFE OF JESUS

Author: Ernest Renan (1823-1892)
Type of work: Biography of Jesus
First published: 1863

PRINCIPAL IDEAS ADVANCED

The four Gospels are legendary biographies and therefore must be critically evaluated and imaginatively interpreted in order to sift the authentic material from pious embellishments.

Jesus, a person of infinite charm and conscious of a unique intimacy with God, began his ministry proclaiming a pleasing theology of love.

A rebuff from the Jewish leadership in Jerusalem was followed by an increas-

ing apocalyptic emphasis, a radical alienation from the world, and a final martyr-dom.

Jesus stands at the summit of the human race, the embodiment of mankind's purest idealism, and the perfecter of the world's absolute religion.

Publication of *The Life of Jesus* by Joseph Ernest Renan was one of the most important events in the nineteenth century attempt to write the biography of Jesus. No book in the long series of lives of Jesus was more widely discussed or the subject of as much controversy as this one, not even the *Life of Jesus* (1835) by David Friedrich Strauss (1808-1874), whose mythological and Hegelian interpretation of Jesus had acutely raised many of the issues that were to be in the forefront for many decades. Renan's rejection of the miraculous and his emphasis upon the legendary elements in the Gospel story gained him an immediate notoriety among orthodox Christians, but the long range significance of his book rests on other grounds. Not only was it the first work of its kind for the Catholic world and a charming literary achievement, but, more importantly, it also brought the problem of the life of Jesus to the attention of the entire educated world of his day. Running to ten editions during the first year after its publication, it was one of the most famous books of the century.

Generally speaking, the attempt to write a life of Jesus has gone through two periods, the pre-critical and the critical. The pre-critical period ran on into the eighteenth century and included the orthodox writings, which presupposed the Christian dogmas about Christ and accepted all four Gospels in their entirety as reliable authorities, and the rationalistic writ-

ings of the Enlightenment period, which presented a life of Jesus free from all miraculous and dogmatic considerations. The first produced the Christ of the creeds, and the second produced an idea of Jesus as an enlightened modern man and a teacher of ethics. The critical period can be conveniently said to begin with the work of Hermann Samuel Reimarus (1694-1768). The historians in this tradition based their work on a careful study of the sources and sought ostensibly to present objective accounts of the life and ministry of Jesus. The German scholars were in the forefront of the nineteenth century critical quest of the historical Jesus and have continued to take the lead in introducing new phases of this area of research. The twentieth century has given birth to a widespread conviction in New Testament circles that the prodigious attempt to write a biography of Jesus has been a monumental failure and that the whole Christological problem must be put in a quite different context due to the recognition that the Gospels are not sources of biographical data but testimonies of faith in Jesus as the Christ. Renan's *Life of Jesus* was an important stage in the development of the nineteenth century phase of the critical quest of the real Jesus of history.

A Frenchman by birth, Renan originally set out to become a Catholic priest, but a reading of the critical theology of the German scholars raised a serious doubt in his mind as to the truth of Christianity. He acquired a reputation as a man of letters and as an authority on the Semitic languages and Oriental archeology, and this reputation gained for him a commission from the French government in 1860 to make a research expedition into Syria. Here Renan wrote his famous work. He reports that under the inspiration of the actual sites of Jesus' ministry, the Gospels became alive, enabling him to see on the pages of a "fifth Gospel" a real and admirable human figure. Published in 1863, *The Life of Jesus* was the first in a series of volumes by Renan dealing with the origin and history of the early Church, but none of his subsequent works attracted extraordinary attention. The world remembers Renan only for his life of Jesus.

Two decisive issues in Renan's presentation of Jesus are his attitude toward miracles and his assessment of the Gospel sources. Renan does not rule out miracles as absolute impossibilities, but he does assert that no miracle has ever been satisfactorily shown to be authentic. Since none of the wonders reported by the New Testament took place under scientific conditions, they may be conveniently dismissed and viewed as the natural product of the mind of the age at work idealizing one of its greatest heroes.

In the light of the questions raised by the publication of Strauss' *Life of Jesus*, it became evident that anyone who desired to write a biography of Jesus had to come to some conclusions regarding the nature of the Gospel sources and the manner of their literary composition. Renan was familiar with the most advanced positions taken by the German scholars, and he devoted a considerable part of his first chapter to a discussion of his views regarding the nature and composition of the four Gospels. He regarded all the Gospels as legendary biographies; that is, as works containing a core of factual material embellished with a considerable amount of pious fiction. The original documents underlying the Synoptic Gospels are discourses about Jesus brought together by Matthew and a collection of narratives prepared by Mark from the preaching of Peter. These documents, mixed with other sources and connected in some way with each other, form respectively the present Gospels of Matthew and Mark. Luke is a later work of less historical value compiled from second-hand sources, including no doubt the sayings of Matthew and the narratives of Mark. The Fourth Gospel presents a distinct case. The long discourses are not genuine, but some of the narratives and settings have the sure ring of authenticity.

The Gospel materials, then, according to Renan, must be critically evaluated and interpreted by the biographer. What is called for is an imaginative and sympathetic grasp of the personality of Jesus in its fullest dimensions so that the data provided by the Gospels can be harmoniously combined to form an organic whole.

Jesus was born, according to Renan, in Nazareth of Joseph and Mary and was taught the Hebrew language and religion in the local synagogue school. Knowing little about the political realities of his time, Jesus absorbed the eager hopes of Israel for a blissful future and saw in the splendors of the natural beauty around him a transparent symbol of an ideal order of existence. After the death of Joseph, Jesus continued for a while to work as a carpenter, but soon, under the inspiration of an extraordinary consciousness of God, he set out to call men to the practice of the pure religion of the heart, a religion which consists of intimacy with and imitation of the beneficent Father in heaven. Renan describes Jesus as an amiable carpenter, filled with an infinite sweetness and charm, wandering happily about Galilee and teaching a delightful theology of love and the brotherhood of man.

Attracted by the reputation of John the Baptist, Jesus and his intimates journeyed to the wilderness of Judea to receive baptism and to join for a while the followers of John. The encounter with this stern, pessimistic preacher tended to make the gentle idealist deviate from his path, but after the arrest of the Baptist, Jesus returned to Galilee and to his own message, now more conscious of his own originality and better informed in the ways of preaching and mass leadership. The idea of an imminent revolution which would establish the Kingdom of God on earth became more prominent in his message. As Renan describes the early ministry, much vagueness accompanied Jesus' thought of the coming new order, but it was conceived as a spiritual transformation to be brought about largely by the conversion of the poor and the outcast, although apocalyptic ideas of divine intervention hovered around the dark edges of his thinking. Jesus regarded himself as the Son of Man, who, as prophesied by Daniel, would be the herald and heir of the new Kingdom; he allowed the people to adore him as the Messiah and the Son of David.

Gathering about himself an inner circle of disciples, Jesus moved about the territory in and about Capernaum and the Sea of Galilee preaching a pleasing message of love and light in the presence of a natural environment which inspired only noble thoughts. He rode through throngs of admirers on a gentle mule, and he taught the poor of the bliss that was to be theirs. With his followers Jesus enjoyed the simple joys of life. What Renan presents at this stage is a sentimental pastoral idyl in which fair maidens, laughing children, and carefree fishermen surround Jesus and are daily intoxicated by the elevated joy which vibrates through them under the spell of the charming prophet, the azure sky, the peaceful pastures, the delicate flowers, and the shimmering sea.

The spell of this idyl was broken by a visit to austere, fanatical Jerusalem with its proud priests and formal religion. Jesus found there little sympathy and much coldness. Revolting against the legalistic, sacrificial worship of the Jews, he returned to his native Galilee by way of Samaria with a new revolutionary fervor and an intensified apocalyptic note in his preaching. The sweet theology of love was complicated by predictions of a stormy end to history and the inauguration of a new age amid fiery clouds and stern judgment. The scene grew progressively darker as Jesus became so attached to his transcendent expectation that he was alienated from the realities and cares of the world, and a strange desire for martyrdom took possession of him. During this same time he was forced against his will by popular pressure to become a miracle worker. Legend soon added greater supernatural deeds to his actual healings, and perhaps the family of Mary and Martha actually co-operated to help

make possible the miracle of the raising of their brother Lazarus. Jesus was
never fully absorbed in his apocalyptic
expectations, however, for at the very
height of his preoccupation with them
he was establishing the foundations
for a continuing Church. He taught
the disciples secretly and instituted
among them, long before the last week
in Jerusalem, the breaking of bread
and the drinking of wine in a fellowship meal.

After some eighteen months Jesus
returned again to Jerusalem to spend
the last half year of his life. Public
success had given increase to the opposition and unbelief that had existed
from the beginning in some quarters.
The opposition was led in Jerusalem
by the Pharisees and the defenders of
the established religious order, which
was radically threatened by the pure
religion of the heart advocated by Jesus.
The drama hastened to its end amid
controversy, intrigue, personal struggle, betrayal, and the continuing adoration of Jesus by the faithful. The religious leaders condemned Jesus for
corrupting the religion of Moses and
they convinced Pilate of his disloyalty
to the state. After his crucifixion and
burial, rumors began to fly that Jesus
had risen.

Renan offers no certain explanation of how belief in the Resurrection
arose, but he thinks that in some way
it must have been connected with the
imaginative mind of Mary Magda-
lene, from whom Jesus had cast out
seven demons.

In Renan's view the greatness of
Jesus is to be seen in the fact that he
introduced a new spirit into the world.
His purity of heart, his perfect idealism, his vision of a world filled only
with love and tenderness, and his conception of a worship concerned only
with the intimacy of the human spirit
with God, enshrine the best that mankind has ever conceived. Jesus gave
the world a religion free from fixed
dogmas and hindering rituals, the essence of which is the communion of a
pure heart with a loving God whose
presence fills the world. He stands at
the summit of the human race as
the greatest triumph of the human
struggle for nobility. Whatever the future brings, Renan is sure that "Jesus
will not be surpassed. His worship
will constantly renew its youth, the
tale of his life will cause ceaseless
tears, his sufferings will soften the
best hearts; all the ages will proclaim
that, among the sons of men, there is
none born who is greater than Jesus."

APOLOGIA PRO VITA SUA

Author: John Henry Cardinal Newman (1801-1890)
Type of work: Autobiography and Christian apologetics
First published: 1864

PRINCIPAL IDEAS ADVANCED

*God is manifested through nature and history; He is especially present in the
sacraments and in His Body, the Church.*

The Protestant emphasis upon the subjective experience of God has led to the neglect of objective truth, and has resulted in schism.

The Anglican Via Media, though an attempt to recover the holiness, apostolicity, and catholicity of Christ's Church, is mistaken because the Establishment is schismatic in origin.

The only bulwark against rationalism, skepticism, and atheism is the Church of Rome.

In the apology which he delivered before the Athenian assembly, Socrates said that he had to answer, besides the charges expressly brought against him by Anytus, a host of false accusations which had been circulating for many years. Newman's case was much the same. The ostensible purpose of the *Apologia pro vita sua* was to refute a pamphlet written against him by the clergyman and novelist, Charles Kingsley (1819-1875). But Newman recognized that there was no point in simply dealing with the particular arguments Kingsley had brought against him. It was a "bias of the court," he claimed, "that prepossession against me, which takes it for granted that, when my reasoning is convincing it is only ingenious, and that when my statements are unanswerable, there is always something put out of sight or hidden in my sleeve." For three decades Newman had been advocating religious beliefs which, to the majority of Englishmen, were more Romish than Protestant. When, at the age of forty-four, he joined the Catholic Church, the bitterness knew no bounds. There were many who could say, "I told you so!" There were others who charged that all those years Newman had been a Jesuit, secretly assigned to the task of winning converts from within the Anglican Church. The *Apologia* is mainly an attempt to persuade people of the genuineness of his profession by recounting the history of his opinions. The book is, in effect, a spiritual autobiography. Only in the introductory and concluding chapters is attention paid to Kingsley's pamphlet.

A precocious youth, imaginative, and carefully schooled, Newman was converted to the religious life in the autumn of 1816, about the time of his entrance to Trinity College, Oxford. Among the books which he read at this time were William Law's *Serious Call to a Devout and Holy Life* (1728), which impressed him with the unmitigated warfare between the Kingdom of God and the Kingdom of Darkness, and Thomas Newton's *Dissertation on the Prophecies* (1758), which convinced him that the Pope was Antichrist. It was also at that time he discerned "that it was the will of God that [he] should lead a single life." Thus far the influences on his life had been primarily Protestant and Puritan; only after he was made a fellow of Oriel College, in 1821, where John Keble (1792-1866) and Edward Pusey (1800-1882) were also fellows, did he become concerned with the task of recovering for the Establishment the marks of the true Church (holiness, apostolicity, and catholicity) which led to the Oxford Movement.

Among the factors that entered into Newman's thinking at the beginning of his public life were the following: a strong anti-Erastian sentiment "against the profanation of Christ's

Kingdom, by that *double usurpation,* the interference of the Church in temporals, of the State in spirituals," an appreciation of the sacramental system, "that is, the doctrine that the material phenomena are both the types and the instruments of real things unseen," and a mystical sense, deriving from the Alexandrian philosophies of Clement and Origin, of the divine presence "hidden behind the visible things . . . whose robe and ornaments those objects were."

So spiritual an interpretation of Christianity might have disposed a man to retire to some rural chapel and let the world take its course. The fact that Newman could never bring himself to hide his light and that he spent his long lifetime clashing with the earthly-minded, first in the Anglican and later in the Roman communions, helps account for the difficulties which his behavior constantly raised. No one perceived more clearly than did Newman himself the paradox of an unworldly soul cast in a worldly role. After quoting a letter which he had written in 1837, where he entertains the notion that John Bull is in fact one of the "angels, principalities, and powers" of which apocalyptic writers were accustomed to speak, he comments: "I am aware that what I have been saying will, with many men, be doing credit to my imagination at the expense of my judgment —'Hippoclides doesn't care;' I am not setting myself up as a pattern of good sense or of anything else: I am but vindicating myself from the charge of dishonesty." The paradox appears in the very fact that, instead of pouring out his life story to God in the form of a *confessio,* as many have done, he was moved to write an *apologia.*

Here, in fact, seems to be the key to Newman's spiritual development, that, as opposed to Protestant individualism and subjectivism, which tended to make religion purely an affair of man's inner life, Newman recovered a sense of the objective and social character of divine revelation, as manifest in history, particularly in the sacraments, the dogmas, and the discipline of the Church. Against the maxim, "The Bible and the Bible only is the religion of Protestants," he came to hold that "the sacred text was never intended to teach doctrine, but only to prove it, and that if we would learn doctrine, we must have recourse to the formularies of the Church," and gave up subscribing to the Bible Society. As to the doctrine of justification by faith, he maintained that, although in Luther's mind it was a paradox, in Melanchthon's it was a truism with which no one, either in the Anglican or the Roman Church, would disagree. The principle of "private judgment" seemed to him the essence of impiety, leading to rationalism, liberalism, skepticism, and atheism.

During the years of his association with the Oxford Movement, Newman was mainly concerned with recovering what he and his associates believed was the essential teaching of the Anglican Church, which they viewed as a *via media* between Protestantism and Romanism. His contention was that Protestants are heretical, particularly in their teachings concerning the Church and the sacraments, and have cut themselves off from the Apostolic succession. But for many years Newman also contended, with scarcely less emphasis, that the Roman Church was corrupt and idolatrous in its veneration of saints and particularly in its subservience to the pope. The Anglican Church, at least in its seventeenth century form, had preserved both apostolicity and holiness. Admittedly, in the eighteenth century, it had been influenced by Protestantism and by rationalism, and it had lent itself to national and imperial aims. But, in the eyes of Newman and his associates, these elements were alien elements which had to be expurgated so that the true dogma and liturgy might be restored, and the independence of the Church from civil policy recovered. Such was the tenor of innumerable articles, sermons, and scholarly works which appeared in the 1830's.

A series of pamphlets called *Tracts for the Times,* to which Newman was a leading contributor, was the main source of controversy. In 1841, Tract 90 of the series, which sought to demonstrate that the Thirty-Nine Articles, the official Anglican statement of belief, could be interpreted as teaching Catholic doctrine, created such a stir that Newman's bishop prevailed on him to conclude the series.

By this time, however, Newman had begun to have second thoughts. For one thing, he was no longer certain that the Roman Church was reprobate, and he had set about working for a reunion between the Churches of England and Rome. Again, he had come to ask whether the Anglican Church were not in schism, the same as the Calvinistic and Lutheran groups. He believed that it could truly claim apostolicity and even holiness (at least with as much right as Rome), but he was not satisfied that it could claim catholicity. Finally, the opposition which the Oxford Movement had encountered from the Anglican hierarchy and from the great majority of

the denomination gradually brought him to the conclusion that there was no ground for hoping that the Establishment would ever again possess the marks of the true Church.

Having arrived privately at these conclusions, Newman was understandably embarrassed by his public position. Many of his younger associates, driven by the logic of their position, were going over to the Roman Church—a move which, for some months, Newman opposed on the grounds that it was an undue exercise of "private judgment" and that Anglicans ought to submit to their own Church discipline and pray for the day when the Churches would be one. For himself, Newman proposed to resign his important position as vicar of St. Mary's Church, Oxford, and retire to a lay standing within the Anglican communion. In fact, he did move in this direction, in 1843; but in 1845 he professed faith in the Roman belief, and he resigned all his connections at Oxford. A year later, in Rome, he was ordained a priest of the Roman Catholic Church, and, after some years, returned to England and to the kind of animosity which called forth the *Apologia.*

As Newman viewed the controversy twenty years later, he and his friends had been engaged in a last-ditch stand against "liberalism," whether religious or political. He knew and feared the inroads which higher criticism and post-Kantian idealism were making into the Church. But he was no less alarmed at the prospect of a Parliament dominated by economic interests and a hierarchy dominated by Whig appointees. "Against the anti-dogmatic principle I had thrown my whole mind," he writes; "I was one of those who had kept it at bay in Oxford for so many years; and thus my very retirement was its triumph. The men who had driven me from Oxford were distinctly the Liberals; it was they who had opened the attack upon Tract 90, and it was they who would gain a second benefit, if I went on to retire from the Anglican Church." This is one of the few places Newman expresses any regret. He had an impressive following in Oxford, which, however, would not follow him from Anglicanism to Romanism, "but would at once leave Anglicanism and me for the Liberal camp." To this disillusioned following, Newman felt that he owed an apology, a reasoned defense, even though it involved admitting that when he had argued for the Anglican Church as the *via media,* he had not read the Church Fathers critically enough.

No doubt many who were attracted to the Catholic revival in Newman's time were influenced by romantic sentiments and the desire to escape from the prospects of a bourgeois civilization into an imaginary past. But this was not the case with Newman. Perhaps it is more illuminating to think of him as a successor to Edmund Burke (1729-1797). Newman very much disliked being called a "conserva-

tive," a term which does not apply very well to Burke, either; but in an age which made a fetish of free-thinking and individuality of belief, both Newman and Burke stressed the need for roots, and the importance to the individual of respect for the past and of obedience to authority. Intellectually, too, Newman belongs to the same tradition as Burke, along with Bishop Joseph Butler (1692-1752), a tradition which opposed to a facile rationalism a system of reasoning based on probability. Newman writes: "I say, that I believed in a God on a ground of probability, that I believed in Christianity on a probability, and that I believed in Catholicism on a probability, and that all three were about the same kind of probability, a cumulative, a transcendent probability, but still probability; inasmuch as He who made us, has so willed that in mathematics indeed we arrive at certitude by rigid demonstration, but in religious inquiry we arrive at certitude by accumulated probabilities—inasmuch as He who has willed that we should so act, cooperates with us in our acting, and thereby bestows on us a certitude which rises higher than the logical force of our conclusions."

ECCE HOMO

Author: Sir John Robert Seeley (1834-1895)
Type of work: Biography of Jesus
First published: 1865

Principal Ideas Advanced

The life and work of Jesus are plainly understandable if viewed without theological presuppositions.

Jesus proposed to revive theocracy (the rule of God on earth), but on a broadly humanitarian foundation.

Jesus' work had two parts: calling men into the new society, and legislating for them.

Faith is the only requirement for entering the society; love is the only law.

Jesus' ideal society agrees in many points with that of philosophical moralists, but whereas their systems have remained abstract ideals, Jesus has brought His into existence by appealing to concrete loyalties.

Ecce Homo is an outline of the life and work of Christ. The author states in the Preface that the book was written to satisfy his own mind concerning a historical character, who, in spite of all the books that had been written about Him, both from the side of faith and from the side of unbelief, remained incomprehensible. The book appeared anonymously, but it was later acknowledged to be the work of John Robert Seeley, who in 1869 became a professor of modern history at Cambridge University.

Seeley rejected the view of certain rationalistic historians, such as David F. Strauss (1808-1874), who maintained that the Gospel account of Christ is an invention of "the consciousness of an age." He took the Gospels as authentic "biographies," and attempted, by the use of constructive imagination, to present Christ as a character of history, setting to one side the claim of the Church that Christ was God Incarnate. Foreseeing the criticism which his work would receive in orthodox circles, Seeley stipulated that in *Ecce Homo* he would deal with only one side of Christ's work, His foundation of a new social and ethical system, and he promised that in a future volume he would treat of Christ as the founder of a new theology and religion. The second work never appeared; and, standing by itself, *Ecce Home* did much to promote the view

that Christ was merely the founder of an improved system of morality.

According to Seeley, the life and work of Jesus are easy to understand, once theological assumptions are set aside. "No other career ever had so much unity," he says; "no other biography is so simple, or can so well afford to dispense with details." This is owing to the fact that, from the time of His temptation, Jesus followed a well thought-out plan. Attaching Himself to the prophetic tradition in Israel, He proposed to reinstitute a theocratic society, but to do this with due regard to the altered circumstances of the age in which He lived. Because there was no longer any possibility of recovering Israel's national autonomy, Jesus conceived the idea of constituting God's Kingdom on a broadly humanitarian basis. Contemporary Jewish thought conceived of the Messiah as a new David. Jesus conceived of the Messiah as a new Abraham, and a new Moses. As a new Abraham, He must gather people into the theocratic society; as a new Moses, He must legislate for them. These, according to Seeley, make up the two aspects of Jesus' program. If we keep them in view, all the details fall nicely into place.

At the time of His temptation, Jesus grasped the secret of success. He was conscious, as other great founders have been also, of possessing miraculous powers. But whereas other leaders have thought in terms of their own pre-eminence and used their superiority to enhance their leadership, Jesus resolved to use His powers only for the good of others. "This temperance in the use of supernatural power," says Seeley, "is the masterpiece of Christ. It is a moral miracle superimposed upon a physical one. This repose in greatness makes him surely the most sublime image ever offered to the human imagination. And it is precisely this trait which gave him his immense and immediate ascendancy over men." The mere working of miracles was not enough for His purpose. He won men's loyalty and devotion by combining greatness and self-sacrifice, by dedicating His extraordinary powers to beneficent uses only, and by deliberately disarming Himself when his own interest was attacked. In this way Christ could put Himself forward as "the Founder and Legislator of a new Society," without falling into the traps in which other leaders have been caught.

Christ's "call" for men to join Him in the new theocracy was as original as the method by which He established his sovereignty over them. As Jesus went among men summoning them to enroll in His Kingdom, He did not ask them to disassociate themselves from other groups to which they belonged. Usually founders have been exclusive in their demands; Christ was infinitely comprehensive. He did, however, demand that men "follow him," that they "change all their prospects," and "adopt a new mode of life." Seeley comments: "In this way, without excluding any, Christ suffered the unworthy to exclude themselves."

According to Seeley, the one condition for membership in Christ's Kingdom can best be denominated "faith." Seeley argues, however, that the faith which Christ required is not that which the Church has ordinarily insisted on. Christ insisted on personal loyalty, on faithfulness. The Church has too often misplaced the emphasis and has demanded something more like credulity. The critical mind of modern man, says Seeley, has great difficulty with religious dogma. Indeed, he says, if the important issues of life could be settled by reason alone, one would have to decide in favor of the philosophers rather than Christ. But the philosophers have misunderstood the human condition, for they have failed to effect any worthwhile change, because they have been unable to alter the direction of human motives. It is here that Christ proved wiser than the philosophers. He saw that the only effective way to change men's lives is to encourage them to form concrete, personal attachments to a man of conspicuous goodness. Even the worst of men can be changed into good men by vowing "obedience in life and death to such a person," and by joining their lives with those of "others who have made the same vow."

But besides calling men into a new society, Christ further had the task of legislating for His followers. Seeley points out that with the rise of the Roman Empire, old ethnic moralities had everywhere outlived their usefulness. Not merely Jews, but Greeks, Italians, and other national groups were confused and frustrated by the emergence of an international state. Previous codes had rested upon the distinction between one's friends and one's enemies. Christ minimized this distinction and inculcated in His followers a new "enthusiasm for Humanity."

In the plain sense of the word "law," Christ was no lawgiver, says Seeley. Instead, He gave men "character," instilling into their souls a new governing passion, and holding Himself before them as a model for them to imitate. Seeley acknowledges that, prior to Jesus, virtuous men had on rare occasions risen to the heights which He subsequently demanded; but what had heretofore been regarded as exceptional and praiseworthy was henceforth, among Christians, to become the ordinary mainspring of action. The new word *agape,* translated "love," was brought into existence in order to indicate the law which Christians were to obey. To the question as to how love can be commanded, Seeley replies that, strictly speaking, it cannot. But, says Seeley, love is really native to the human breast; and what can be commanded is that men rid their minds of prejudicial ways of thinking, particularly of the habit, inculcated by natural groups, of regarding outsiders as enemies. If one learns to think of all men as brothers, his kindly fellow-feeling toward them will become habitual, and his character will become like that of Christ.

Seeley distinguishes two aspects in the new morality. The first has to do with the alleviation of physical suffering. Seeley calls it the "law of philanthropy." No other rule is more plainly deducible from the law of love than the duty to feed the hungry and care for the sick. The second, which takes away nothing from the first, is "the law of edification." This law has to do with the moral and spiritual development of mankind, with the duty to raise every man into the society of

the humane. Seeley remarks that, while in the earlier stages of the Christian movement, philanthropy consisted chiefly in relieving distress, and edification in preaching the Gospel, the morality implicit in such practices is now obsolete. Christians must, he says, engage in active social reform, investigating and remedying the causes of evil, particularly with a view to "the removal of all such social abuses as destroy natural affection, and by doing so kill Christian humanity in its germ." Nor, he says, is it enough for individuals to contribute financially to a Christian organization; if the Church is to be the representative of Christ's Kingdom in the world, its members must comprise an active society in which each individual is "ready to work in the service of humanity."

As Seeley understands Christ's teaching, it coincides with the utilitarian philosophy of John Stuart Mill (1806-1873). Christ does not censure men for seeking pleasure, but shows them, rather, that "the *summum bonum* of human life, the secret of happiness and of all enduring good," lies in actively promoting the happiness of others. It is a mistake, Seeley thinks, to surround the new society which Christ came to establish with the customary aura of piety. What Jesus intended was merely to institute in actuality what philosophers have often talked about in an ineffective fashion; namely, a community of healthy-minded men, in which the happiness of each would be the happiness of all.

Ecce Homo was roundly condemned by numerous important Church leaders as a repudiation of the divine character of the person and work of Christ. For example, the well-known Congregationalist minister, Joseph Parker (1830-1902), responded with a book called *Ecce Deus* (1868). New Testament scholars, on the other hand, have mostly ignored the work because it does not take account of "Higher Critical" methods. Some churchmen, however, have maintained that Seeley grasped with unusual clarity the essential character of the mission and message of Jesus. Bishop Charles Gore is an example. In *Christ and Society* (1928), he wrote, "There is still no book about the teaching of our Lord which can rival *Ecce Homo.*"

AN EIRENICON

Author: Edward B. Pusey (1800-1882)
Type of work: Ecumenical theology
First published: 1865

PRINCIPAL IDEAS ADVANCED

The doctrine of the Church of England is Catholic in all points.

Its differences with the Church of Rome are confined to points at which Rome has departed from the teaching of the Apostles and of the ecumenical councils.

The theoretical teaching of the Roman Church is closer to Catholic truth than its practical teaching.

A union of all the Churches could be effected by a new ecumenical council.

In the year 1864, Henry Edward Manning (1808-1892), originally an important figure in the Tractarian Movement, who went over to the Church of Rome in 1851, published an open letter to Edward B. Pusey, charging the Anglican Church with responsibility for the increase of infidelity in England. John Keble (1792-1866), another leader in the Tractarian Movement, celebrated for his poetical work, *The Christian Year* (1827), expressed the view that Pusey should reply to Manning. *An Eirenicon* is, thus, "A Letter to the Author of 'The Christian Year,'" and is subtitled *The Church of England a Portion of Christ's One Holy Catholic Church, and A Means of Restoring Visible Unity.*

To the immediate charge that the Anglican Church is responsible for the spread of rationalism and unbelief in England, Pusey replies that if this is the case then the Roman Church is responsible for the spread of infidelity in France and for the anti-clerical movement in Italy. But Pusey declares that he is less interested in assessing blame than in forming a united front against these developments, and he charges bad faith in Romanists who seek to weaken the Anglican position out of a desire to proselyte members. One of the criticisms which Manning made against

Pusey was that, contrary to his Tractarian principles, Pusey had lately been cultivating the friendship of Evangelical Christians. Pusey admits that this is the case. Without sacrificing his Catholic convictions, he has sought to unite with Protestant groups in matters where there is agreement. Such a policy, he argues, has a two-fold advantage: it strengthens the Christian cause; and, by breaking down traditional barriers, it opens the way for better understanding between Catholic and Protestant groups.

Manning had taken up a statement by Pusey to the effect that "the Church of England is in God's hands the greatest bulwark against infidelity in this land," and he had affirmed the contradictory; namely, that it is "the cause and spring of" that unbelief. Manning had argued that the Church of England rejects much of the truth which the Catholic Church receives, and that such truth as it retains it detaches from the authoritative voice of the Church.

Pusey replies, in the first place, that the claim which he made for the Church against infidelity was not original with him, but had been made by "one of the deepest thinkers and observers in the Roman Communion." Pusey is willing, however, to add that he did not intend to say that the Church of England is the best possible bulwark against infidelity, but that, as a matter of fact, it exercises a greater influence against unbelief than either Romanism or dissent.

Pusey then proceeds, in careful detail, to argue that in essential points the English Church does not differ from that of the Roman and Eastern communions. The attitude of the English Church to the sacraments, for example, is entirely Catholic. The English Church affirms the real presence of Christ in the Mass, and it maintains that the sacrifice which the Church presents on the altar is the same as that which Christ pleads in Heaven. Nor does the Church deny that there are seven sacraments, except that it agrees with the Eastern as against the Roman communion as to the proper interpretation of extreme unction.

On certain doctrines, such as the Immaculate Conception, the fires of purgatory, and the efficacy of indulgences, Pusey admits, the difference be tween the Anglican and Roman beliefs is rather wide. But he maintains that even in the Roman communion there are different interpretations of these doctrines, and that often the theoretical teaching of the Church differs widely from her practical teaching. As an example, he cites a Roman devotional writer who says that Christ in the sacrament of Holy Communion is as much disposed to reject sinners as to accept them unless the Blessed Virgin intercedes for them. "We must then go to a sacrament solely of mercy," this Roman writer urges, "wherein Jesus Christ exercises no judgments. This sacrament is the most Blessed Virgin." "So then," Pusey comments, "it seems as if the Roman Church must either advance in her theoretical teaching, or recede in her practical teaching." Pusey finds the same gap between official and popular Romanism when it comes to the subject of images, to prayers for the dead, and to purgatory. The Anglicans, like the Greeks, are willing to accept what is ancient and Catholic in all these doctrines; they reject only abuses which, as a matter of fact, many Roman theologians also reject.

In support of his charge that the Church of Rome practically tolerates what it officially rejects, Pusey cites at length from the *Histoire ecclésiastique,* by the Roman Catholic scholar Claude Fleury (1640-1725). Fleury acknowledges that great changes were introduced into the constitution of the Church after the tenth century, as a result of the acceptance by its leaders of the pseudo-Isidorian Decretals. Most of the prerogatives which modern popes claim, says Fleury, are contrary to the usage of the early Church and have no other foundation than these forged documents, which, at the height of the Middle Ages, were supposed genuine. Since the Renaissance, Fleury says, Roman Catholics have admitted that the documents are false, but they have done nothing to revise the system built upon them. Had they done so, Fleury avers, the Protestant revolt might have been prevented.

Pusey and the Tractarians were, of course, maintaining something very similar to what Fleury says. In general, they argued that the practice of the ancient Church was violated by medieval innovations, and in particular they found fault with the claims of the bishop of Rome (who was supported only by the forged Decretals) to exercise authority over other bishops and over councils. It is on these grounds that Pusey meets the charge by Manning that the Anglican Church has no adequate authority for its teaching. "We ourselves have," he says, "equally with those in the Roman Church, infallible truth, as resting on infallible authority." He has reference to the "infallible authority" of the Scriptures and the ecumenical councils. The Roman Church, on the other hand, has "a tendency to hold cheaply by Holy Scripture, as being comparatively unimportant to them, who have the authority of an infallible Church, forgetting that the authority of the Church depends upon Holy Scripture." Furthermore, in claiming the seal of infallibility for its own rulings, irrespective of the consensus of the Greek and Anglican communions, it is acting on a "quasi-authority."

Pusey entitles his letter *An Eirenicon* because he means it to emphasize those doctrines which Anglicans and Romans hold in common, with a view to an eventual reunion of the two denominations. He says, "I have never expected to see that external unity of intercommunion restored in my own day; but I have felt it to be an end to be wished for, and prayed for." In the interests of this development, he reviews the correspondence which took place in the early eighteenth century between Archbishop William Wake (1657-1737) and the French scholar Louis DuPin (1657-1719). DuPin examined in detail the more controversial of the Anglican Thirty-Nine Articles and concluded "that the controversies between us may easily be settled, if only the fairer Theologians are heard on both sides, if dictating is avoided, and we are led, not by party-spirit, but by love of seeking the truth."

Raising his sights to envisage a possible reunion not only with Catholics but also with Protestants, Pusey agrees that the Anglican communion is in a unique position to bring union to pass. This truth, he says, did not escape the notice of so zealous a Romanist as Joseph De Maistre (1753-1821), who said, "If Christians ever in fact reunite, as everyone urges them to do, it seems that the Church of England must initiate the movement. We [the French] are too far removed from the sectarian groups, and have no way of reaching them; but the Church of England, which touches us with one hand touches with the other those whom we cannot reach; and, although it is condemned by both parties, and in fact does present the slightly ridiculous spectacle of a rebel which preaches obedience, still, it performs a valuable function, and may be compared to a catalyst which is able to bring into combination elements which by their nature have no tendency to unite."

Pusey argues that union could be realized by means of an ecumenical council. At such a council, he says, the Anglican Thirty-Nine Articles, the Roman Decrees of the Council of Trent, and other denominational creeds drawn up at the time of the Protestant revolt, could be retracted, and a new platform laid down on which all could agree. The difficulty with the Greek Church over the expression "filioque" in connection with the doctrine of the Procession of the Holy Spirit is of a different sort; no doubt each party would continue to use the formula to which it has become accustomed, but this could be done at the same time that unfortunate misunderstandings were erased. What is mostly desired, according to Pusey, is public explanations of the sort that are commonly given privately by Roman teachers to converts who have difficulty with some of the popular variants of the Church's faith.

For the most part, Pusey bases his argument with Manning on historical precedents, and he appeals to theological authorities who, if not accepted by Manning, might exercise weight with persons born in the Roman Church. In one place, however, he appeals not to authority but to religious experience. In disputing whether the Anglican sacrament of Holy Communion is real or not, he says, "I do not believe that God maintains the faith, where there is not the reality. . . . Heretics, who are really cut off from the Body of Christ, receive the Sacrament, though not the grace of the Sacrament. We have the witness that we have really the true Body and Blood of Christ and the grace of the Sacrament: 1) from the knowledge of those who receive it. God would not allow His own to be deluded in such a matter as this. 2) In the supernatural lives of grace, led by persons, the life of whose souls is Christ in the Holy Eucharist." Pusey goes on to say that God gives to each according to his faith. He distinguishes the kind of piety which characterizes Presbyterians from that which characterizes Anglicans. "Presbyterians have what *they* believe; we, what *we* believe. But they who have observed pious Presbyterians and pious English Catholics, have discerned among our people a spiritual life, of a kind which was not among theirs; in a word, a sacramental life." He justifies the English practice of confession in the same way. As a clergyman who has seen the change in those whose confessions he has heard, he finds the validity of Anglican absolutions self-confirming: "God, the Author of truth, has set his seal upon them."

Before Pusey's long letter had gone to press, two events took place which prompted him to add a lengthy Postscript. One was the elevation of Dr. Manning to the position of Archbishop of Westminster. The other was the appearance of a new Papal Encyclical which, says Pusey, disclosed "how advanced, above all which was known formerly, is the present theory of Papal Infallibility." There is no use any longer in pretending, he says, that the pope claims infallibility only in matters of faith and morals. As now interpreted, the pope's infallibility includes everything declared by him "to regard the Church's right discipline and general good," such as political judgments, injunctions contained in letters to individual persons, syllabi of errors, and statements of fact unconnected with former revelation. Pusey argues that the extent of the claims can only prove embarrassing to the pope's defenders, and he brings forward numerous historical instances which suggest that popes have erred. Nevertheless, the Encyclical, taken together with the promotion of Dr. Manning, who was noted for his zeal as a champion of papal infallibility,

cooled Pusey's hopes for closer relations between the two denominations.

When *An Eirenicon* appeared, it was answered by J. H. Newman (1801-1890), another former Tractarian, who had preceded Manning into the Church of Rome, in "A Letter to the Rev. E. B. Pusey on his recent 'Eirenicon.'" Newman's answer dealt particularly with Pusey's charges of Mariolatry, but it held out little which the Anglo-Catholics could accept. Pusey answered Newman in two further eirenicons, which appeared in 1869. The Vatican Council of 1870, however, which made papal infallibility a matter of faith, and finally denied the possibility of an appeal from the pope to an ecumenical council, made clear to Pusey that union was no longer possible. Pusey continued to work for union with the Eastern Orthodox and with the Wesleyan Churches, but he found little to encourage him.

JOHN PLOUGHMAN'S TALKS

Author: Charles Haddon Spurgeon (1834-1892)
Type of work: Popular moral essays
First published: 1869

PRINCIPAL IDEAS ADVANCED

A sturdy commonsense allied to a Christian character will bring the greatest measure of durable happiness to mankind.

Proverbial wisdom is the bearer of the experience of the past for the practical affairs of the present.

Charles Hadden Spurgeon, English Baptist preacher, came from yeoman stock, and in his formative years he

absorbed much of the homespun lore of the English countryside. His popular *John Ploughman's Talks, or Plain*

Advice to Plain People, was as native to the agricultural scene in the Victorian era as a patchwork quilt. There is nothing complicated or esoteric in the religion his book advocates, nothing scandalous in its proverbial wisdom that would eliminate it from the cottage bookshelf, and nothing so uncouth as to bar it from the library of the manor house. The pithy sagacity of John Ploughman spoke to the follies and foibles of human affairs with a plainness, and even bluntness, that carried its own moral force.

The talks originated in 1869 in the form of penny broadsheets entitled *John Ploughman's Almanack.* After 365 issues with a daily proverb and comment, the series came to a close. The requests for the resumption of the talks were so many and so clamorous that Spurgeon began again, and the series continued until his death in 1892, and then for a few years more on the basis of material which he left. The book known as *John Ploughman's Talks* is a selection from these sources.

Spurgeon, reared as a Congregationalist, but converted to the Baptist Church in his teens, was invited to a London pulpit when nineteen years of age, and he remained in the same church all his ministry. Before he arrived the congregation had been searching in vain for a pastor, and their invitation to an Essex lad seemed a desperate move. But in a matter of weeks the place was crowded, all 1200 seats. Exeter Hall with room for 4500 was taken; then the Royal Sussex Gardens Hall with accommodation for about 12,000. Spurgeon filled them all in succession Sunday after Sunday. For a church home, his congregation erected the Metropolitan Tabernacle with 6,000 capacity, and it was filled several times a week for over thirty years.

C. H. S., as he was familiarly called, was a phenomenon of some magnitude in the world of Victorian oratory. He was not a scholar in the technical sense, nor was he a social prophet calling for justice in the industrial sweat shops, nor did his style of speech or writing achieve linguistic excellence. His strength was in his ability to handle an audience, in his forthright utterances on evangelical themes, and in his ability to use an unsophisticated style with direct decisiveness. The printed editions of his sermons sold by the millions, and an enterprising American literary agency offered him $1,000 in gold for each lecture he would deliver in the United States, but he never could be persuaded to cross the Atlantic.

His output in print added up to some 135 volumes, including the sermon series, *John Ploughman's Talks,* and the companion volume, *John Ploughman's Pictures.*

A sample of the titles of items within the *Talks* sufficiently illustrates the territory within which the book moves: To the Idle, On Seizing Opportunities, Things not Worth Trying, A Good Word to Wives, Men With Two Faces, Tall Talk, Things I Would Not Choose. In each of these essays there is an outpouring of simulated rustic wisdom in an abundance of maxims, analogies, proverbs, and anecdotes. By heaping saying upon saying, a cumulative effect is achieved that compels the reader to do some homework by way of self-examination. The whole is unashamedly didactic, consisting of preachments in favor of an earnest moral character which scorns hypocrisy, sham, waste, sloth, and impiety.

Here is the Protestant Puritan ethic in clear unmistakable form. It is robust, assured, and outspoken, even though at times it rises little higher than prudential morality and a worldly wise sagacity. Many familiar aphorisms are liberally strewn across the pages; thus, we read about cutting one's coat according to the cloth, locking the door when the horse is gone, counting chickens before they are hatched, and the like. We are conducted, as it were, up the village street, invited to enter the local bethel, allowed to overhear the market day conversation, and permitted to sit around the open hearth fire. Much of what we hear is the fruit of experience, the wise counsel that knows the popular sins and their all too common consequences.

John Ploughman uses all the tried and proved devices to communicate his pronouncements. Sarcasm, exaggeration, sharp contrasts, emotionally weighted words, and appeals to religious authority make their appearance without apology. He speaks in utter sincerity and neighborly concern, suspicious of the concrete jungles of the city, and innocent of the technical problems of the statesman.

The ideal in Spurgeon's book is what has been called Victorian respectability—but in the good sense of that ill-used phrase. Moral earnestness, diligence, and honest toil, accompanied by an abhorrence of vulgarity, licentiousness, malevolence, and injustice, are marks of the life that is pleasing to God and beneficial to human welfare. John has a strong preference for England and for Sussex in particular. He asserts with pride, "To keep debt, dirt and the devil out of my cottage has been my greatest wish ever since I set up housekeeping."

Though not a spectator of eternal ideas—as was Plato's philosopher—John Ploughman was a shrewd critic of life as he saw it around him, and as he reflected on it behind his plough. Others might plough a crooked furrow; his was straight. If some of his neighbors preferred to be conformist, he was sturdily independent. "I take my leave," he says, "to look about me and speak my mind, for a cat may look at a king, and a fool may give wise men some good advice."

Biblical precedents, warnings about the miseries of the wicked, and remarks concerning the sheer stupidity of the profligate are used to castigate the drunkard, the shrew, the spendthrift, the character assassin, the homebreaker, and the Judas. "It is not a very good sign," says John, "when the fox walked into the hen roost and said, 'Good morning to you all, my very good friends.' "

For John Ploughman and his friends, "home" is one of the great words in the English language, and it inspires a recurring topic in John's counselling program. Allied to the thought of home are the kindred topics of family, wife, and children. Here personal relationships are most intimate, and emotions most intensely felt for good or ill. "Our lane is the most beautiful for twenty miles around, because our home is in it." It is not the size of it or any other physical property, but the love and understanding that is in it that makes a home so desirable. In a homily called "Home," the ploughman sage is eloquent in his denunciation of all who undermine what makes home so precious to him. The beer shop comes in for rough opposition, for in it, John Ploughman says, men waste their time and money to the detriment of their families. Beer is "so much fools' milk to drown their wits in." Husbands who do not take their share of responsibility receive little sympathy from John Ploughman: "If the father drops the reins, the family coach will soon be in the ditch." Likewise a wife can be a power for good or ill, for she is either wise or foolish in her domestic cares. One of the talks is entitled "A Good Word for Wives," for the author is of the opinion that wives are the subject of injustice in some country sayings. No doubt there are many bad wives who make a bethel into a bedlam, but the Bible can supply only one Jezebel. The cause of a husband's grumbles may often be of his own making: "The rottenest bough cracks first, and it looks as if the male side of the house was the worse of the two, for it certainly has made up the most grumbling proverbs." The foundation of a blessed home is mutual love and piety: "When home is ruled according to God's word, angels might be asked to stay a night with us, and they would not find themselves out of their element."

The cartoons which accompany the text of the *Talks*, as in some other works of Spurgeon, such as the three volume *Lectures to My Students,* add greatly to the power of the sayings they illustrate, and lighten the admonitions with a touch of humor. The drawing of two optimistic souls trying to pour water into a sieve raises a smile, and one showing the credulous friend who tries to take a bull by the horns, with less than happy results, supplies a useful visual aid to the text.

Hundreds of thousands of copies of the *Talks* were circulated all over the world, and Spurgeon compiled a companion volume called *John Ploughman's Pictures* in which the cartoons were featured. "There is no particular virtue," he wrote, "in being seriously unreadable." It was this quality of semi-humorous and folksy common sense that made the *Talks* so popular. Spurgeon was deliberately making use of a medium other than the pulpit, and he said of his talks, in the Preface, "I have aimed my blows at the vices of the many and tried to inculcate those moral virtues without which men are degraded."

THE CHRISTIAN DOCTRINE OF JUSTIFICATION AND RECONCILIATION

Author: Albrecht Ritschl (1822-1889)
Type of work: Systematic theology; soteriology
First published: 1870-1874

PRINCIPAL IDEAS ADVANCED

Christ and His work can be adequately understood only in terms of, and from the standpoint of, the community which He founded.

Based on God's revelation in Christ, the Christian religion resembles an ellipse, one focus of which is redemption from sin, the other of which is the impetus to moral effort in the universal kingdom of God.

Justification, which is equivalent to the forgiveness of sins, means acceptance into God's fellowship; regarded as effective in the life of the believer, justification is to be conceived also as reconciliation.

As the import of theological conceptions lies always in the voluntary activities called forth by revelation in the believer, so the meaning of Chirst is confirmed in the traits of Christian existence: trust in God, peace, patience, humility, thanksgiving, and love-motivated action.

During the last third of the nineteenth century no name was more prominent in Protestant theology than that of Albrecht Ritschl. Professor at Bonn and then at Göttingen for twenty-five years, no one did more than he to shape the characteristic trends of Protestant Liberalism. Son of a prominent churchman in Berlin, Ritschl attended the universities of Bonn, Halle, Heidelberg, and Tübingen. In the early work in New Testament theology he followed the lead of the historical theologian F. C. Baur (1792-1860), who was influenced by the philosophy of G. W. F. Hegel (1770-1831). But by 1857 Ritschl had rejected the Hegelian view and begun developing his own systematic theology on the basis of Friedrich Schleiermacher (1768-1834) and Immanuel Kant (1724-1804), combining the former's method and redemptive interest with the moral stress of the latter. The first volume of Ritschl's major work appeared in 1870, and was translated by J. S. Black in 1872, under the title *A Critical History of the Christian Doctrine of Justification and Reconciliation.* The second volume, published in 1874, concerning the Biblical substance of the doctrine, has not been translated into English. The concluding volume

reviewed here, also appearing in 1874, gives Ritschl's constructive statement. Intended as an exhaustive monograph on one theme, the book is, as Ritschl remarked, "an almost complete outline of Systematic Theology, the remaining parts of which could easily be supplied." The formidable style of the work has made it somewhat inaccessible, but through it Ritschl, as a theologian's theologian, has exercised profound influence upon his contemporaries and successors.

In full swing in the 1870's was the so-called "Life of Jesus Movement," which sought to reconstruct objectively the facts about the "real Jesus" as He was prior to the religious interpretations of the New Testament writers. Although Ritschl too had called for a return from the historical development of dogma to the original Christian norm, he rejected the "Life of Jesus" project on the ground that "We can discover the full compass of . . . [Jesus'] . . . historical actuality solely from the faith of the Christian community." Thus the Apostolic—especially the Pauline—witness to Christ is a functional component of the norm. But it is also necessary for the theologian, or anyone who would understand Jesus historically, to share the community's faith. The historical *and* Biblical Christ is the objective ground, and participating, subjective faith is the indispensable means of standing upon it. In striving exclusively for the correlation of these two poles, God in Christ and faith, Ritschl regarded himself as carrying through the intention of the Reformers.

Historical and contemporary theology has allowed rationalistic metaphysics to override the Christian revelation; at least, there has been failure to maintain Christ's authority throughout the theological system. However, Ritschl cannot approve the endeavor of some to return to a theology so purely Biblical as to amount to no more than a concatenation of texts; to follow such a limited course would be to ignore the task of clarifying Christ's relation to human existence in general. Another criticism of preceding theology is that it has almost always presented a biased version of Christianity, sometimes favoring the moral and sometimes the religious-redemptive aspect, despite the fact that, as in an ellipse, these foci equally determine the whole. Furthermore, the theological tradition has been wont to present doctrinal propositions apart from the evaluating will, feelings, and active life of the believer. Ritschl's own theological program aims to avoid the separation of doctrine and life.

Following his introduction, Ritschl undertakes the definition of justification and reconciliation. The two ideas are inseparable, yet complementary. Justification, the Pauline way of putting what for Jesus was the forgiveness of sin, means that God accepts the sinner *in spite of* his guilt. This is the objective basis of reconciliation, which consists of a new life in fellowship with God and in relation to one's fellow men. But justification, as the phrase "by faith" indicates, cannot be construed as absolutely nonsubjective. Like every religious notion, its meaning implies the personal involvement —the value-judgments—of the believer: in this case, a turning to God in trust and penitence. But these subjective conditions are not a law for the sinner to fulfill; they are spontaneously implied in his response to God's gracious offer of pardon. Similarly with respect to the assurance of forgiveness (or of election), such assurance is not something that can be objectively established, as it were, outside the subject. One cannot abstractly prove to oneself that one is sure of God's mercy. Certitude is given only in the spontaneous subjective act of responding to the message of Christ.

Ritschl next develops the presuppositions of the doctrine of justification and reconciliation. Fundamental is the distinctive Christian understanding of the personal God who has created the world and seeks to realize in the world His purpose of righteous love. In the history of theology this understanding has been obscured both by metaphysical notions of God as a neutral ultimate, and by legalistic ideas of God as the indifferent rewarder of good and evil. But Christians worship the "Father of our Lord Jesus Christ." Knowledge of God is not neutrally theoretical but of infinite interest to the knower. And the divine righteousness, when grasped Biblically, means not unconcerned retribution but God's unswerving faithfulness to His loving purpose. The Kingdom of God obtains wherever, and in whatever measure, the purpose is realized. Eternal Life is life in time which shares in the realization of the purpose and is thus everlastingly upheld in the divine will of love.

Justification's negative presupposition is sin, which expresses the felt disparity between man's actual state and God's will. Ritschl stresses the claim that the idea can be developed properly only by reference to Christ as the human criterion under the judgment of which the rest of us stand. To express our own lack of merit was the purpose of the doctrine of original sin, which, however, was like using a "boulder to kill a gnat." Ritschl proposes the "kingdom of sin" as a substitute notion, thereby signifying the collusion in sin by which all are influenced and to which all contribute. Sin is not reducible to ignorance but is conditioned by it, at least in inception. It is forgivable except in the hypothetical case of resolutely conscious defiance of God's will of love—a defiance which is the sin against the Holy Spirit.

The third main presupposition of justification is Christ's person and work. These two aspects of the total meaning of Christ cannot be separated. The description of the person in terms of human ideality and of divinity can be validated only through the effects He has upon us; that is, in terms of His work. That God was active in Him in a unique way cannot be doubted, but in the absence of any theoretic understanding of how this was the case, the practical import of His Godhead is "the worth to be put on those human achievements of His which suffice for our salvation." Ritschl insists that the estimate of Christ is to be based on the Biblical picture of His historical life, not on speculations about pre-existence or

postexistence. The exalted Lord who reigns is the man who is victorious on the Cross through unbroken trust in God. Christ's will and purpose so coincide with God's intention that through Christ the sinner receives the word of reconciling pardon as well as the imperative which demands moral action in the Kingdom.

Having developed his presuppositions, Ritschl essays a "proof" of the "necessity" of justification and of basing it upon the work of Christ. He does not envisage a detached rational argument for Christianity. For "the proof is nothing but a demonstration of the harmony of the ideas which are bound up together in the Christian view of the world and the Christian view of the self. The man who altogether rejects this system of ideas will find their proof meaningless too." Ritschl proceeds from the basic fact of man's practical concern for his ultimate worth or meaning. Religion roots in this concern, and the idea of God corresponds to the way in which personal worth is estimated, grounded, and eternally guaranteed. In other words, God, by definition, means that power upon which man's meaning and destiny depend. But sin and guilt vitiate the divine-human relationship; and until they are removed as obstacles to fellowship with God, man's personal worth and destiny stand in jeopardy. Hence the necessity of justification and reconciliation. How, though, were the divine forgiveness and purpose to be made real among men except through their concrete revelation in a historical personal life mediated through community? Without such revelation, forgiveness and purpose would remain, at best, abstract speculations. But in Christ God's gracious pardon and Kingdom-forming purpose have established themselves as practical realities; they have actually been bestowed upon men. The work of Christ in establishing His community has accomplished the archetype, and also the vessel, of God's eternal purpose. In identifying with this purpose, and through being accepted, in spite of sin, into the Body of Christ, the individual finds the answer to his own deepest needs (the guarantee of his ultimate worth and meaningfulness) precisely in and through what Christ has done for him. Thus, in Ritschl's view, the "proof" is completed with the exposition of the integral mediating role of the historical Christ.

The concluding part of the book sets forth the "consequences" of justification and reconciliation. One of Ritschl's constant emphases is that the meaning of theological notions must be manifested in practical life—in the spiritual and moral activity of the personal subject. He isolates the marks of Christian existence which are grounded in and derived from Christ. A key idea is lordship over the world, sublimely exemplified in Christ on the Cross. Through unshakable trust in God the Father, men bear suffering, the world's contempt, and even violent death with patience and humility.

Such faith in God, freeing one from all selfish worldly pursuits, issues in spontaneously prayerful thanksgiving and in love-motivated action. One can act "in" the Kingdom of God, for by faith one affirms the universal sovereignty of God; so to act is to partake, in time, of the life eternal.

No brief summary can do justice to the incisiveness, subtlety, and detail of Ritschl's massive tome. With masterful competency in Biblical scholarship and in the history of theology, he sharpens his views against the diversifications of the whole tradition in which he stands. His own central thrust emerges from the interplay of two concerns: the redemptive and ethical normativeness of the Biblical, historical Christ, and the practical character of religious affirmations, both as answering to real needs of human existence and as manifest in the actualities of man's will, feeling, and course of life. A widely influential Ritschlian school flourished for decades after the master's death. More recent theology has seen sharp reactions against him. Yet his greatness is reflected in the fact that so much of subsequent theological discussion, even when explicitly anti-Ritschlian, has proceeded from one or another elements in his combination of themes.

COLLOQUIA PERIPATETICA

Author: John Duncan (1796-1870) [Edited by William Knight]
Type of work: Theological conversations
First published: 1870

Principal Ideas Advanced

God is apprehended within the soul of man; God is the archetype of human existence.

Evil is the privation of the good; although God is the author of all things, He cannot be the author of sin, for sin has no author.

A balanced Calvinism avoids extremes of Arminianism and Antinomianism, for the will of man chooses the good only because of the efficacious operation of the grace of God.

Mysticism is not altogether false; it errs only when it attempts to destroy the logical.

Dr. John Duncan, known to his students and admirers as "Rabbi Duncan," was born at Aberdeen in 1796. Having left the Secession, he entered the Established Church and studied theology at the University of Aberdeen (1817-1821). There, under the influence of his professors, he was brought out of "Spinozism" or any other form of naturalism. Dr. Duncan later told how he "danced on the brig of Dee with delight, when he was convinced that there was a God." In 1825 he was licensed to preach, although he accepted the Westminster Confession only as "articles of peace." Shortly afterwards he experienced a conversion under the influence of Caesar Malan of Geneva and his own biographer, David Brown. Malan sought by syllogism to bring inquirers to assurance of faith. His words to Duncan, "See, you have the word of God in your mouth" flashed through him like a shock of electricity. Duncan says of the outcome: "Next day as I sat down to study, and took my pen in my hand, I became suddenly the passive recipient of all the truths which I had heard and been taught in my childhood. I sat unmoving for hours, and they came and preached themselves to me. There was no investigation, but the presenta-tion of the truth to me passive." Assurance of salvation by syllogism was shattered in Duncan's later experiences of tormenting doubts as to the sincerity of his faith. The influence of the eccentric Dr. John Kidd of Aberdeen and the searching experimental preacher Dr. John Love contributed to the ripening of Duncan's personal piety and doctrinal thought. The writings of the Puritan, John Owen, and the Dutch Master of Federal Theology, Herman Witsius, gave a distinct cast to his theological studies.

In 1836, Duncan was ordained as pastor of Milton Church, Glasgow, and was married the following year. A skilled Hebraist, he was sent by the Church of Scotland in 1841 to minister to Jews in Hungary. After the disruption of the Church of Scotland in 1843, Duncan was appointed Professor of Hebrew in the New College of the Free Church at Edinburgh. Although his absent-mindedness and other eccentricities were not conducive to effective language teaching, his influence on the thought and piety of his students was incalculable. He was himself the "good specimen of the Patristic Scholastic Puritan" which he judged John Owen to be.

Colloquia peripatetica consists of

notes of conversations with Duncan, made by William Knight, Professor of Moral Philosophy in the University of St. Andrews. The colloquia are miscellaneous, ranging over many aspects of philosophical and practical theology. The peripatetic flavor of Duncan's dialectic exemplifies what he says about Aristotle in one of the colloquia: "He is by far the compactest and most precise writer we have, in any literature. He is the *beau ideal* of the precise. Two things I wonder at in Aristotle— the extent of his acquirements and the exactitude of his writing. . . . He could see, I suppose, as far as a mason could see into a wall that he had built, and that is a good deal farther than other people see into it." The charm of the *Colloquia*, however, is due to its Socratic and Platonic as well as to its peripatetic character. Duncan admired Aristotle, but he loved Plato: "Plato goes peering up, often into cloudland; yet I like to follow him into the mist, for when I don't see through it, I generally think *he* does. It is a good thing to go up now and then into the mist, if we do not, like Ixion, embrace the cloud."

The *Colloquia* opens with the remark, "I am a philosophical sceptic, who have taken refuge in Theology." God is the starting point for Duncan's thought, which is deductive from that postulate. Dr. Knight asks, "But as we are not divine, how do you get *up* in the first instance?" Dr. Duncan replies, "I cannot tell you; *only, I am up.* Probably it is by instinct. Say, if you choose, that reason has overleapt itself. I find that I cannot bridge the gulf between the creature and a Creator, the many and the One, in my ascent, so I endeavour to do so in my descent." To the charge of circularity

in reasoning, Duncan retorts, "No: there is no circle; for God is apprehended within the soul of man, as the archetype of existence. We do not infer His being from what we are. We cannot rise to Him thus. But He is himself within us. *His* voice, not the voice of consciousness, may be heard."

Duncan believed in reason and respected it as the creature of God, but he was doubtful of the philosophies. Reason is of use to show its own impotence and to welcome a revelation. The results of the Scottish Common Sense philosophy are valid, but not philosophically. Duncan believed in axioms (including the mathematical and logical laws); in the senses which report the external world; in objectivity (including the existence of other minds); in testimony (under which is to be ranked the evidences of a historical revelation); and in the syllogistic nexus. He believed in common sense, but not in a philosophy of common sense which he branded as "can't-help-myself-ism."

Belief in God presses multifariously upon man, Duncan declared. Its origin is neither here nor there, but everywhere. There is a knowledge of God which all men have, and a knowledge possible only to the new creature. The operation of the Holy Spirit must be recognized as the source of a faith in God which is more than parrotism and traditionalism. Consequently, not all conviction can be due to demonstration.

George Berkeley and David Hume, though in error, were profounder than the Scottish philosopher Thomas Reid (1710-1796), Duncan believed. Objectivity reached through the immediate perception of matter may be true for the percipient alone. An absolutely universal truth is needed, Duncan emphatically asserts; "I would despise humanity, were it not so." Plato was on the track of this truth with his theory concerning archetypal ideas, but the final answer is found in the creation of man in the image of God; as cast in the divine image, man possesses a universal element in his nature.

Duncan thought much and deeply on the nature and origin of evil. He stoutly defended the Augustinian thesis that evil, including sin, is a privation. God is not the author of sin, because sin has no author. The privative view of sin enabled Augustine to escape from Manichaeism and supported Samuel Rutherford's strong position that God is the author of all entitive acts. Though sin is positive as well as privative, its privative nature is its profoundest. Sin aims at deicide. It seeks to slay Being at the root.

Whence comes sin? Not from God, but *from naught*. At this point the causal nexus is broken, for sin is causeless and irrational. The causal nexus fails also to bind the will of God *qua* will. As *moral* the divine will is necessarily holy, but it is free *qua* will. The determinism of Jonathan Edwards is rejected, as hazarding a speculation on will *qua* will, and therefore on all will, divine and human. Yet the question of free will may not be dismissed as an insoluble problem of metaphysics. Four ultra theories, two on either side of the controversy, are repudiated: liberty of independence and liberty of indifference, on the one hand, and freedom from co-action without or within the will, on the other. The liberty which is the ground of accountability is more than the latter and less than the former theories maintain. Independency is Epicureanism. God is remotely the cause

of the action's causality. The *permission* of sin by God, as Rutherford said, is adorable, while the *actual fact* of sin is abominable. As to the permission, some of God's attributes would not have been displayed had sin not been. Duncan says paradoxically: "In a certain sense I am a tremendous freewiller. My predestination is all free will." There was no necessity that the perfections of God should be displayed. Edwardian determinism leads to the *necessity* of creation. Yet Edwardian theology, despite this metaphysical blot, is steeped in the affections.

Duncan once remarked "There's no such thing as Calvinism." Calvin simply pieced together teachings of St. Augustine, St. Remigius (c.438-c.533), St. Anselm, and Luther. Duncan called himself a *high* Calvinist, while deploring the miserable narrowness of some Calvinists. He also repudiated the "hyper-Calvinism" which he characterized as all house and no door. His breadth included a willingness to turn Thomist commentator on one occasion. He quotes Aquinas as saying, "Deus voluit hoc propter illud, sed non propter illud voluit hoc Deus," and comments: "There is a relation of *propter*ty between the two things as the objects of divine volition. There is much more in this distinction of Aquinas than meets the eye at first glance; though the vulgar mind will call it a distinction without a difference."

The *Colloquia* represents Calvinism as a *juste milieu* between Arminianism and Antinomianism. Arminianism robs God while Antinomianism fanaticizes man. Moral power in the will is to be admitted against the Antinomians, but disowned against the Arminians. That God works half of salvation and man the other half is the Arminian error. That God works all, and man does all, is true. As metaphysicians we are compelled to fall back on the Apostle Paul's statement, "Work out your salvation, for it is God that worketh in you." One colloquium, warning against the loose use of the word "heresy," notes that Amesius in his *De conscientia* discussed the question whether Arminianism is a heresy. Duncan's zeal for the moral law overcame him in another colloquium, in which he suggests that there is only one heresy, and that is Antinomianism. F. D. Maurice's ethical theory is branded as pure illegality, a charge which Maurice repudiated in the preface to his work on conscience, in which he magnanimously paid tribute to Dr. Duncan's learning and worth, in return for the latter's censure on his writings.

Several of the colloquia exemplify what one of them refers to as the attempt to say the unsayable. Two kinds of perplexity are distinguished: one when the theme itself is slippery as an eel and glides from us altogether; the other when, in our attempt to solve a perplexity, or to grapple with it, it gives out its mystery as if it were throwing out a great cuttlefish blackness about itself. Duncan's colloquia studiously avoid the meaninglessness they censure, while they exhibit an abundance of paradoxical expressions in their effort to express the deepest mysteries of the Christian faith. Thus, Duncan says: "Mysticism is not altogether false. Mysticism only errs when it enters into the province of logic to destroy it; as logic errs when it trespasses into the domain of intuition to fetter it. Whenever we worship, we acknowledge that there is a region above us, at once known and unknown, half-clear and half-dark."

SYSTEMATIC THEOLOGY

Author: Charles Hodge (1797-1878)
Type of work: Calvinistic apologetics; soteriology
First published: 1871-1873

PRINCIPAL IDEAS ADVANCED

Theology is an inductive science in which the systematically arranged data of the Old and New Testament constitute the basis of man's knowledge about God, man, and man's final destiny.

The writers of Scripture exercised their own talents even though the authors were infallible instruments of the Holy Spirit; what the writers of Scripture wrote is the Word of God.

Although our knowledge of God is imperfect and partial, sufficient information has been revealed to insure the possibility of man's redemption from sin and to guarantee man's eternal salvation.

Charles Hodge was born in 1797, and he taught at Princeton Theological Seminary from 1822 until shortly before his death in 1878. His *Systematic Theology* is representative of orthodox Protestant theology as far as doctrine is concerned, but Hodge's views of the nature of theology itself are original and provocative.

In Volume One Hodge defends the thesis that theology is a science. The Bible itself, however, is not a system of theology. Nevertheless, the truths which the theologian has to collect, arrange, and exhibit in their internal relations to one another are contained in the Bible. What nature is to the natural scientist, the Bible is to the theologian. The Bible is a storehouse of facts about God; the theologian applies the inductive method to these facts. Facts are to be carefully collected, and the theologian is to seek the greatest comprehensiveness possible. Theological principles are not to be impressed upon the facts, but are to be derived from the data of the Scriptures. The latter constitute the facts of theology. Theology is, therefore, concerned with nothing other than the facts and principles of the Bible.

Hodge argues that to hold that the task of theology is to exhibit the facts of Scripture is not to rule out the possibility of natural theology, although what nature teaches concerning God and our duties is revealed more fully and more authoritatively in God's Word. The Bible is the sole infallible source of knowledge of things divine. Hodge repudiates the claims of rationalism, mysticism, and Romanism that reason, or an inner supernatural light, or an infallible Church are superior or co-ordinate avenues to theological knowledge.

The Scriptures of the Old and New Testaments are infallible, Hodge declares, because they are the Word of God, and they are the Word of God because they were given by the supernatural inspiration of the Holy Spirit. The latter exerted an influence upon the minds of certain select men so that they became the organs of God; what God said, they said. The sacred writers were not machines, but living men. Their being inspired as the organs of God in no way interfered with the free exercise of their distinctive mental characteristics as individual writers. The writers of Scripture impressed their peculiarities upon their productions as though they were under no special influence. God spoke in the language of men, and He used men as His instruments, each according to his own special gifts, according to his own nature. Although the inspired writer wrote out of the fullness of his own feelings and thought, and used the language and expressions which he found most natural and appropriate, what he wrote was what the Holy Spirit moved him to write.

As a Christian theologian, Hodge is concerned with the doctrine of God, with our knowledge of His nature and attributes, with the Trinity, the divinity of Christ, with the nature of the Holy Spirit, the divine decrees, the doctrines of creation and providence, with miracles and angels. He is concerned further with anthropology and soteriology, the subject matter of Volume Two; with the origin of the soul, the unity of the human race, with man's original state, the fall into sin, and with the divine plan of salvation through the person and work of Christ. He is concerned with regeneration, faith, justification, sanctification, with the moral law, with the means of grace, and finally, in the concluding section of Volume Three, with eschatology, the doctrine of last things, and with the state of the soul after death, the Resurrection, and the Second Coming.

The theologian's task is to study the Scriptures, Hodge writes. The theologian is supported in his efforts by the fact that all men have some innate knowledge of God, for men are sentient, rational, and moral beings. In addition, the traditional arguments for the existence of God, except for the ontological argument, in spite of the objections of Hume and Kant, serve to prove what theists hold to be true concerning God.

That God can be known does not mean that all that is true concerning God can be known. We cannot form a mental image of God, Hodge declares, nor can He be comprehended in such a manner that we can know His essence and all His attributes. Although our knowledge of God is partial and imperfect, it is true as far as it goes. To the extent that our idea of God is determined by the revelation He has made in the constitution of our nature, in His works, in His Word, and in the person of His Son, God is really what we believe Him to be. He is an infinite, eternal, and unchangeable Spirit, whose being includes wisdom, power, justice, goodness, holiness, and truth.

The triune God is the creator of man, Hodge insists. Man's body was formed by the immediate intervention of God, and his soul was derived from God. Man consists, therefore, of two distinct principles, a body and a soul: the one corporeal, the other spiritual. The soul is not a form of the divine life, or a series of acts, or an unsubstantial force; it is, rather, a real subsistence, an entity or substance. Man is a created spirit in vital union with a material organized body.

Man was originally created in a state of maturity and perfection, Hodge writes. The body of Adam was free of disease and the seeds of death. Its constitution contained nothing that was not conducive to the highest happiness and well-being of man. The distinguishing characteristic of man is that he is created in the image and likeness of God. As God is a spirit, so the human soul is a spirit. God thus endowed man with the essential attributes of spirit; namely, reason, conscience, and will. It is because we are like God that we can know Him and are capable of having communion with Him. Man was created in a state of original righteousness, in perfect harmony, and endowed with knowledge and holiness.

After the creation, God made a promise of life to Adam, upon the condition of perfect obedience, and He attached the penalty of death for disobedience. Man's state of probation ended in an act of disobedience, the account of which is neither allegorical nor mythical, but truly historical. Man's Fall resulted in the immediate execution of the righteous judgment of God, in man's expulsion from the Garden of Eden, and in the loss of man's original righteousness.

The sin of Adam and Eve injured not only themselves, but also all their descendants, who are, therefore, rendered incapable of performing any spiritual good. The redemption of fallen man can, take place only because God Himself has graciously accomplished it through the person and work of Christ Jesus.

The incarnation of the eternal Son of God was not a necessary event arising out of the nature of God, Hodge declares, but an act of voluntary humiliation.

Jesus was truly man, with a real material body, in every respect like the bodies of ordinary men. He also had a rational soul; He thought and reasoned like other men. Nevertheless, He was truly God. He was perfect man and perfect God and still one person—two natures united in hypostatic union, but not mingled or confounded.

The name of Christ is the only name by which man can be saved. The design of the incarnation of the Son of God was to reconcile man unto God. Christ is the only Mediator between God and man.

Christ is truly a priest, writes Hodge, in that He alone has liberty of access unto God. Sin could not have been taken away by any sacrifice other than His. For it is only through Him that God is propitious to sinful men. Christ once offered Himself as a sacrifice to satisfy divine justice, and thereby He reconciled us to God. Christ suffered vicariously; He suffered in the place of sinners; He was their substitute. The guilt of the sinner is expiated, and the justice of God is propitiated. For Christ's work was of the nature of a satisfaction; it met all the demands of God's law against the sinner, so that the sinner who believes in Christ is no longer condemned by the law, but is delivered from the power of sin and Satan and from all evil. The sinner is thus restored to the image and fellowship of God. His guilt is removed, and his soul is quick-

ened with a new principle of divine life.

According to Hodge, the success of the whole scheme of divine redemption rests upon the fact that Christ rose from the dead with the same, although a changed, body. The ascended body of Christ as it now exists in Heaven is glorious, incorruptible, immortal, and spiritual, and yet it retains all the essential properties of a body.

Man's salvation is accomplished by the grace of God, which works a subjective change in the soul, thereby causing a spiritual resurrection, and a new birth or regeneration. Regeneration is an act of God, an act of His power, in which God is the agent, a quickening of the soul, a communication of a new principle of life. The first conscious exercise of the renewed soul is faith, the persuasion of the truth of the facts and doctrines recorded in the Scriptures, on the testimony of the Spirit of God.

Christ is the special object of saving faith, says Hodge, since by receiving the testimony of God concerning Him, the salvation of the sinner is secured. For faith is the condition on which God promises to impute unto men the righteousness of Christ, so that when they believe, they are no longer condemned, but are justified by a forensic act, in which God declares that justice has been satisfied so far as the believing sinner is concerned.

The act of justification is followed by a process of sanctification, a supernatural work of grace, whereby the principles of evil infecting our nature are increasingly removed and the principle of spiritual life grows until our acts, thoughts, and feelings are brought under control, and the soul is brought into conformity with the image of Christ. The soul is led to receive Jesus as its Savior, and is delivered from the guilt and power of sin. The soul of the believer is united to Christ; it participates in His merits, and it becomes the abode of the indwelling Holy Spirit, the source of a new spiritual life, a life that bears fruit in good works, in the keeping of God's holy law.

According to Hodge, the ordinary channels of God's grace, of the supernatural influence of the Holy Spirit, are the Word of God, the sacraments of baptism, the Lord's Supper, and prayer. It is by these means that God communicates to the souls of men the life-giving and sanctifying influences of the Spirit.

After death, after the dissolution of the body, the soul continues its conscious existence in an intermediate state, until the resurrection of the body, at the Second Coming of Christ. The Second Coming is marked by the resurrection of the just and the unjust, the Final Judgment, the end of the world, and the consummation of the Kingdom of Christ.

The Final Judgment is a definite event, Hodge declares, when the eternal destiny of men shall be finally determined and publicly manifest. Each person shall be assigned his final abode, in Heaven or in Hell. The righteous will then enjoy the incomprehensible blessedness of Heaven, which arises from the vision of God and which flows from His infinite love. The saints will enjoy the secure and everlasting possession of every good, and they will be entirely exempt from all sin and sorrow. The wicked will enter into everlasting punishment, the sufferings of which will arise from the loss of earthly goods, and the presence and favor of God, from the final withdrawal from them of the Holy Spirit, from the despairful operations of conscience, and from positive afflictions, which, although not literally fire, are nevertheless perpetual. As there are degrees in the glory of the blessedness of Heaven, so there will be degrees in the suffering of the lost.

The theology of Charles Hodge has exercised and continues to exert considerable influence on orthodox segments of the Protestant Church. It is characterized by a thorough treatment of opposing views and by a minimum of speculation upon matters on which there is little Biblical evidence.

LITERATURE AND DOGMA

Author: Matthew Arnold (1822-1888)
Type of work: Critique of theology
First published: 1873

PRINCIPAL IDEAS ADVANCED

Since the language of the Bible is fluid and literary, a knowledge of culture is necessary to an understanding of the Bible.

Dogmatic theology falsifies the meaning of the Bible, for such a theology rests on the logical development of metaphysical ideas about which there is endless disagreement.

The object of religion is conduct; religion is morality heightened by emotion. Religious beliefs are not scientific; they are instances of "Aberglaube," or extra-belief, the literary expression of hope.

Jesus showed that righteousness and happiness are one by exhibiting a sweet reasonableness, a method of inner examination, and a secret of self-renouncement.

Matthew Arnold's *Literature and Dogma* is both a plea and a demonstration. It is a plea for a literary reading of the Bible, for an understanding of the Bible as an expression of human aspirations and expectations, and it is a demonstration of such a reading. The result is a sensitive and suggestive interpretation of the Bible, particularly of the New Testament.

Arnold's argument together with his interpretation has relevance in the twentieth century, for a division persists between those who take the Bible literally and build dogmatic theology upon it and those who take the Bible as a literary work and build their lives upon it.

Arnold was disturbed by the decreasing power of influence of the Bible, and he attributed the Bible's decline to the effect of dogmatic theology. He wanted to find an experimental basis for the Bible, a way of verifying its message, and he deplored the theologian's reliance on unverifiable assumptions. He decided that if the Bible were properly read as a literary expression of hopes and ideals, it could then be experimentally tried by putting into action the suggestions to be found within it.

It was not enough for Arnold to declare that the Bible has to be read as a literary work. He had first to consider how a proper reading of the Bible is possible. The answer, it seemed to him, is that one can read the Bible only after having acquainted oneself with "the best that has been known and said in the world"; that is, with culture. If a man immerses himself in letters, he acquires a "flexibility of spirit" which, together with "the judgment which forms itself insensibly in a fair mind" as a result of culture, provides the reader with a new perspective on what he reads.

Armed by culture, a man can recognize the language of the Bible as being literary, not scientific, language. Arnold points out that such terms as "grace," "new birth," and "justification," terms which St. Paul used "in a fluid and passing way, as men use terms in common discourse or in eloquence and poetry, to describe approximately, but only approximately, what they have present before their mind," have been used by theologians "in a fixed and rigid manner, as if they [the terms] were symbols with as definite and fully grasped a meaning as the names *line* or *angle*. . . ." Once one realizes that theologians have misread the Bible, the irrelevance and logical austerity of dogmatic theology can be accounted for.

The term "God" is central in religious writings, Arnold points out, and yet, he declares, no other term is more ambiguous. The difficulties of understanding the word are multiplied when those who use it suppose that it has a definite and precise meaning. Theologians have constructed an elaborate and presumably Biblically justified conception of God as "an infinite and eternal substance, and at the same time a person, the great first cause, the moral and intelligent governor of the universe; Jesus Christ consubstantial with him; and the Holy Ghost a person proceeding from the other two." But, Arnold writes, this "scientific" idea is nothing more than a fanciful construction by men who are not cultured enough to be able to read the Bible. When one considers that religion is concerned primarily with conduct and that conduct is three-fourths of life, when one regards religion as "morality touched by emotion," then one finally realizes that the term "God" has been used to call attention to "*the enduring power, not ourselves, which makes for righteousness.*" Arnold attributes the difficulties which come out of theology to the failure of theologians to recognize the moral relevance of the term "God" as used in the Bible. He quotes with approval Luther's definition of God as the "best that we can know."

Arnold claims that Israel's original comment on experience is a true comment: "*Righteousness tendeth to life.*" The belief was that the Eternal, the enduring way of things, is such that a man is truly himself, truly lives, and is truly happy, only if he is righteous. As time went on, however, this basic idea —that righteousness tendeth to life —which was more an expression of hope and a comment on experience than it was a metaphysical generalization, tended to be perverted by the expectation that eventually the righteous would prosper in some material and political fashion and that the ungodly would go down to obvious defeat. The idea that righteous living is *living* in the best sense of that term was obscured by the idea that righteousness somehow leads to an *outer* victory, a triumph of the outer and not merely of the inner man. Thus, the idea of the Messiah arose. But the idea of the Messiah is not an experimental idea; it is "a kind of fairy-tale. . . ." Such an idea, the idea of a Messiah, a belief for which there is no justification in experience, Arnold calls "Aberglaube" or "extra-belief." Extra-belief is "the poetry of life"; it expresses human hopes and resolutions, and since it is poetry, it must be understood as poetry.

By the time of Jesus Christ righteousness was no longer associated with happiness; the impulse which emotion had given to righteousness had been lost. Arnold describes Jesus' task, then, as that of restoring to righteousness "the sanction of *happiness.*" To accomplish this end, Jesus had to turn attention to the inner man. Judaism had come more and more to emphasize the outward manifestation of righteousness, the act according to the law, but Jesus turned the attention of His followers to "heart and character," to matters of motive, sentiment, and intention. He taught with such "sweet reasonableness" that by His manner He made righteousness attractive; in finally understanding the reasons behind rules, the followers of Christ found themselves refreshed in spirit and made happy. Jesus also encouraged self-renouncement, a turning from the ways which lead to the destruction of the self, and a turning to the ways of righteousness, a way already exemplified by Christ's mildness and sweet reasonableness and by His concern for the inner self. The sanction for righteousness became, then, not the utility of obedience—if you obey, *then* you will be happy—but the love and happiness which Christ inspired by his presence, by His method of inwardness, and by His secret of self-renouncement. In loving Christ, men loved righteousness, and in the love of Christ and of righteousness they were happy. Happiness became the consequence, but not the motive, for those who followed Him. The motive was love, not happiness, and thus happiness became the sanction of the righteousness which that love encouraged.

But just as the Old Testament idea that to righteousness belongs happiness, or that righteousness brings life, gave way to the *Aberglaube* of the Messiah, so the New Testament idea, which was the sanction of the Old Testament faith, gave way to the *Aberglaube* "of a phantasmagorical advent of Jesus Christ, a resurrection and judgment, Christ's adherents glorified, his rejectors punished everlastingly."

Once Christianity succumbed to the temptation of "extra-belief," it lost the strength that came from reliance on internal evidence. The emphasis then fell on prophecy and miracle. What was wrong with this fall within Christianity was not the introduction of *Aberglaube*; Arnold agrees with Goethe in regarding *Aberglaube* as "the poetry of life." Poetry has its uses; it enables the imagination to construct a possibility to which the heart can give assent. But poetry has its dangers also, particularly for those who forget that it is poetry with which they are concerned, imaginative and not scientific language.

The fall was not to *Aberglaube*, but to prophecy and miracle.

Arnold argues that is is a mistake to rely on prophecies for evidence in support of Christianity. Prophetic language is ambiguous; the description of an act is adaptable to the language of prophecy; men sometimes act in full knowledge of what has been prophesied; and translations tend to emphasize, as prophetic, passages which were in all likelihood innocent of prophetic intent. In any case, the truth of predictions has nothing to do with the essential emphasis upon conduct and righteousness. Even if there have been prophets, men able, through supernatural support, to know of the future, the meaning of the Christian religion does not come from them.

Nor can Christianity find its proof in miracles. Men forget—and many never realize—that the idea of God is not a metaphysical but a moral idea; the idea is concerned with the character of conduct, not with the structure of reality. But ordinary minds are very much impressed by events which seem to depart from the natural course of things, and many persons are inclined to suppose that a religion which encourages extraordinary events must somehow be a true religion. Anthropomorphic language suits the sentiments of conventional minds, and the supposition of miracles, a supposition suggested and encouraged by anthropomorphic language, confirms the metaphysical faith which tends to accompany the blind use of poetic language.

But, Arnold declares, there is a persistent and tenacious critic of prophecy and miracle; that critic is the *Zeit-Geist*, the Time-Spirit, the mind of man enlightened by experience. One can understand very well how hope and imagination can combine to foster belief in prophecy and miracle; the creative impulse which moved Shakespeare moved also the writers of the Old and New Testaments. The critical and experienced mind, the mind trained by culture, can find every reason for believing that in the accounts of prophecies and miracles the poetic imagination is at work, but no mind can find criteria by reference to which rival miraculous claims can systematically be tested. The only truth which may reside in the accounts of miracles is the psychological truth that those who err tend to become ill, while those who recognize their crimes and receive forgiveness tend to become healthy again. Jesus was a man capable of freeing others from the sense of guilt. Enlightened by the *Zeit-Geist,* the critic understands that the account of the Resurrection, for example, is not so much a fragment of history as it is an expression of hope. In effect, writes Arnold, the Biblical narrators, for all their simplicity and good faith, are really saying, *"Behold a legend growing under your eyes!"*

Despite the fact that the writers of the New Testament were not aware of their literal acceptance of extra-belief, and despite the possibility that Jesus Himself did not apprehend the full significance of His conduct and was Himself affected by the *Aberglaube* which determined the descriptions of His acts, the meaning of the New Testament becomes clear to one who takes the difficult road of literary criticism. The New Testament record is inconsistent, ambiguous, and puzzling; it is full of the "poetry of life." But, properly understood, it presents Jesus as one who asked men to look into

themselves and to renounce whatever is not worthy of the self.

Jesus spiritualized the *Aberglaube* of Israel — the belief in a Messiah—by His method of inner searching and His secret of self-renouncement. But the method and the secret need the support of His "sweet reasonableness," a matter of disposition which He could not bequeath to His followers. When that sweet reasonableness is missing, the method and the secret fail, and what should be read as a call to the Spirit becomes a metaphysical hint to be deciphered by dogmatic theologians. Perhaps the most tragic consequence of the failure to read the Bible properly is the Christian's coming to believe that resurrection from physical death is the final reward of religion. The idea that the "dying" which Christ encouraged is an inner dying of the unrighteous self and that what was demanded by Him was not a physical but a spiritual crucifixion and resurrection—a death of the old spirit to make new life possible—is an idea lost to anyone who takes the language of the Bible literally.

When readers suppose that the Bible is to be read as history or metaphysics, there is the danger of their giving up the Bible altogether, for time will show that much of what the Bible says is either false or improbable—insofar as it is meaningful at all. But if the Bible is read as a literary attempt to endorse the righteous life and to commend the method, the secret, and the sweet reasonableness of Christ, the Bible can survive scientific attack, for such an attack is then seen to be irrelevant.

In taking the Bible seriously as a literary expression of that spiritual reconstruction which Christ made evident, Arnold performed a service to the Christian reader. His work reveals a sophisticated, a *cultured*, awareness of the uses of language. Philosophers and theologians who are coming to the Bible with a fresh appreciation of the varieties of linguistic uses—an appreciation made possible by twentieth century philosophical investigations—can find a fresh and resourceful tutor in Matthew Arnold.

SCIENCE AND HEALTH WITH KEY TO THE SCRIPTURES

Author: Mary Baker Eddy (1821-1910)
Type of work: Principles of Christian Science
First published: 1875

PRINCIPAL IDEAS ADVANCED

By denying evil and by stressing the primacy of the mind, one can overcome illness and death.

God is Mind; since God is infinite, all is Mind.

Jesus redeemed man from matter, sin, and death by giving man a true sense of love.

Sin and suffering are the result of the false belief in the existence of matter; matter is nothing, an illusion.

Along with its author, Mary Baker Eddy, and the religious body, Christian Science, which is built upon it, *Science and Health with Key to the Scriptures* occupies a unique position in modern religious thought. It is practically impossible to understand any one of the three separately, for to a most unusual degree the lives of the author, the book, and the church are interwoven one with the other. Mary Baker Eddy, who was born in obscurity in rural New Hampshire in 1821 and who was at her death in Boston in 1910 internationally known as the founder of Christian Science, poured into the countless editions of her constantly revised book the totality of her religious, philosophical, and practical world views.

There is no difficulty in understanding Mrs. Eddy's opening statements on the discovery and mission of Christian Science: "In the year 1866 I discovered the Science of Metaphysical Healing, and named it Christian Science. God has been graciously fitting me, during many years, for the reception of a final revelation of the absolute Principle of Scientific Mindhealing. This apodictical Principle points to the revelation of Immanuel, the everpresent God,—the sovereign Omnipotence, delivering the children of men from every ill that flesh is heir to."

The first edition of one thousand copies contained 456 pages divided into eight chapters dealing with the following subjects: Natural Science, Imposition and Demonstration, Spirit and Matter, Creation, Prayer and Atonement, Marriage, Physiology, and Healing the Sick. Later editions were much amended and contained additional chapters on such themes as Animal Magnetism, Christian Science Practice, Teaching Christian Science, together with an important section entitled "Key to the Scriptures" which provides Mrs. Eddy's original interpretations of Biblical teaching and terminology. The variations among the editions not only reflect the progressive refinement and extension of Mrs. Eddy's theological position but also chronicle her reaction to the many and varied responses the public was making to her developing religion.

Promotion of the work was of great interest to the author who insisted that each loyal follower obtain the newest edition and discard the old. An idea of the significance of this is suggested in the fact that just twenty-two years after the first appearance of the book, it had passed into 124 editions. Judgment regarding the nature of the author's indebtedness to writers and thinkers other than herself is influenced by the position taken toward Mrs. Eddy and her movement as a whole. Some reject any suggestion of influence other than divine inspiration; others are convinced that the book reflects quite clearly a direct indebtedness to other writers, among them Phineas Quimby, an itinerant New England mental healer (1802-1866), John Ruskin (1819-1900), and Thomas Carlyle (1795-1881). However the matter is viewed, it is certain that whatever the sources for the extensive work, everything which Mrs.

Eddy presents is marked with her own distinctive touch.

The major themes of Mrs. Eddy's work reflect her convictions in three important areas: psychology, philosophy, and theology. Her psychology has as its dominant theme that of mental prophylaxis or mind-healing. By denying evil, by positive thinking, by stressing the primacy of the mind, indeed, by denying the objectivity of the material world, one can overcome illness and death by recognizing them as illusions. Mrs. Eddy writes, "The notion that mind and matter commingle in the human illusion as to sin, sickness, and death must eventually submit to the Science of Mind, which denies this notion." This position receives philosophical and theological support in the identification of God, good, mind, and all: *"God is Mind, and God is infinite; hence all is Mind."*

The fundamental position of *Science and Health* is that "All is Mind and Mind's idea." Since God, perfect goodness and the only reality, is Mind, then sin, sickness, evil, and matter are not real. Matter and evil can thus be identified. The only reality is the world of the mind; there is no objective world. He who would progress in an understanding of these teachings must learn by doing; he must demonstrate that life itself is God. "Hold perpetually this thought," Mrs. Eddy writes, "that it is the spiritual idea, the Holy Ghost and Christ, which enables you to demonstrate, with scientific certainty, the rule of healing, based upon its divine Principle, Love, underlying, overlying, and encompassing all true being." (Present editions of Mrs. Eddy's work conclude with a long chapter of one hundred pages entitled "Fruitage" in which nearly a hundred testimonies are given to the healing effected through acceptance and practice of the teaching in *Science and Health*.)

The first subject presented in the current authorized editions is prayer, which is interpreted as a subjective state whose value is hindered by audible expression. In keeping with this view the only spoken prayer at Christian Science services is the Lord's Prayer accompanied by Mrs. Eddy's verse by verse explanation of its "spiritual sense." The phrase, "Deliver us from evil," is interpreted as "Deliver us from the evil one" which "is but another name for the first lie and all liars." Mrs. Eddy's version demonstrates succinctly the nature of her entire work: "Our Father-Mother God, all harmonious, Adorable One, Thy kingdom is come; Thou art ever-present. Enable us to know,—as in heaven, so on earth,—God is omnipotent, supreme. Give us grace for to-day; feed the famished affections; And Love is reflected in love; and God leadeth us not into temptation, but delivereth us from sin, disease, and death. For God is infinite, all-power, all Life, Truth, Love, over all, and All."

Turning next to the atonement and the Eucharist, Mrs. Eddy presents a moral influence theory of the former, and the latter is seen not as commemorating the evening meal before the day of Jesus' crucifixion but rather the morning meal which Jesus had with His disciples after His resurrection. By giving man a truer sense of love, Mrs. Eddy claims, Jesus redeemed man from the law of matter, sin, and death by the law of the Spirit. Mrs. Eddy rejects both "erudite theology," which is said to provide a ready pardon for all sinners by means of Jesus' crucifixion,

and Spiritualism, which uses Jesus' death as a means of proving that spirits can return to earth. Jesus' crucifixion and resurrection are proof that death is a mortal dream, and thus they provide the supreme vindication of the divine Science. The material disappearance of Jesus assisted the disciples to move from belief to understanding, a movement which is the real meaning of Pentecost.

The brief teaching on marriage as a legal and moral temporary provision to be accepted until "it is learned that God is the Father of all" is followed by a refutation of the errors of Spiritualism on the basis of the irreconcilability of mind and matter. In the next chapter animal magnetism is identified with hypnotism and mortal mind, and is soundly rejected. The chapter on science, theology, and medicine contains the central propositions of the book: "1. God is All-in-all. 2. God is good. Good is Mind. 3. God, Spirit, being all, nothing is matter. 4. Life, God, omnipotent good, deny death, evil, sin, disease—Disease, sin evil, death, deny good, omnipotent God, life." Disease is healed by knowledge of or belief in Mind or God.

The chapter on physiology reiterates the lack of affinity between mind and matter and the power of truth to cast out the ills of the flesh. Evil is seen as nothing, as having neither power nor reality, yet as self-assertive. The perspective changes with great frequency from what appears to be true to mortal mind and what is actually true from the standpoint of Science. Thus one finds the author repeatedly claiming that although sin and suffering are real, they are illusions.

In the chapter "Science of Being," Mrs. Eddy further supports the basic teaching regarding the unreality of matter, and she summarizes the teachings of Christian Science. Again, error is defined as illusion having no real existence; since *"Truth is real . . . error, Truth's unlikeness, is unreal."* Divine metaphysics explains matter away and only "Spirit" is recognized.

The reader must decide when Mrs. Eddy is speaking descriptively and when normatively, as when she states that "As for spiritual error there is none." Hostile critics have heaped scorn upon both style and content in this work, and even the most charitable admit to difficulties in gaining precision of understanding.

The thirty-two tenets offered as the platform of divine metaphysics or Christian Science reiterate the themes already mentioned here. The third one is typical and illustrates both the thorny nature of the problem with which Mrs. Eddy wrestled and the kind of answer she proposed: "The notion that both evil and good are real is a delusion of material sense, which Science annihilates. Evil is nothing, no thing, mind, nor power. As manifested by mankind it stands for a life, nothing claiming to be something—for lust, dishonesty, selfishness, envy, hypocrisy, slander, hate, theft, adultery, murder, dementia, insanity, inanity, devil, hell, with all the etceteras that word includes."

It is easier to point out the ineptness of asserting the nothingness of that for which fifteen words denoting fifteen painfully familiar actualities are available than it is to solve the problem of evil. No reader familiar with the life and work of Mrs. Eddy can escape the poignancy of this representative passage any more than he can escape in his own experience the necessity of coming to terms with the same problem.

After considering various objections to Christian Science, Mrs. Eddy concludes with chapters on the practice and the teaching of Christian Science; she provides a recapitulation of her ideas, and an appendix of commentary on approximately one hundred verses of Scripture, together with a glossary of key Biblical terms.

LECTURES ON PREACHING

Author: Phillips Brooks (1835-1893)
Type of work: Homiletics
First published: 1877

PRINCIPAL IDEAS ADVANCED

Preaching has in it two elements, the truth preached and the personality of the preacher.

The preacher must be a whole person, able to enter into the most varied relationships with his fellow men.

The truth preached is the divine-human Christ, who said, "I am the Truth";

and preaching is the continuation of His witness that God is the Father of all men.

The goal of preaching, which is that of saving the souls of men, must guide the preparation and delivery of sermons.

Phillips Brooks delivered his *Lectures on Preaching* under the Lyman Beecher Lectureship at Yale Divinity School while he was rector of Trinity Episcopal Church in Boston. Brooks's thesis is that preaching has two essential components: the truth proclaimed, and the personality of the man who proclaims it. Christianity, for Brooks, is a "personal force," stemming from the Jesus who was both human and divine. Christ's loving proclamation of the universal Fatherhood of God transformed the lives of those whom He touched; and, witnessed to by His disciples, Christ's proclamation has been powerful to the ends of the earth. Jesus chose preaching as the method of spreading his Gospel. Preaching would serve for the dissemination of any truth equally well, but, says Brooks, it is especially adapted to the Gospel because "that truth is preeminently personal."

Because Brooks considers the man to be inextricably bound up with his message, he devotes the same number of lectures to "The Preacher" as he does to "The Sermon." The task of the theological seminary, he says, "must be nothing less than the making of a man. It cannot be the mere training to certain tricks. It cannot be even the furnishing with abundant knowledge. It must be nothing less than the kneading and tempering of a man's whole nature till it becomes of such a consistency and quality as to be capable of transmission."

The first task awaiting the potential minister is that of "winning a true self." Brooks warns against the tendency of most ministers to conform to the clerical "type." But he finds equally objectionable the way in which some try to pattern themselves on one or another outstanding preacher. The kind of development necessary is that which comes from a constant openness to God and to man, to divine truth and to human need. The first quality required in an effective preacher is "personal piety, a deep possession in one's own soul of the faith and hope and resolution which he is to offer to his fellow-men for their new life."

Great care should be exercised in the screening of ministerial candidates, writes Brooks. Above all, the ministry requires "whole" men, because it brings a man into almost every conceivable relation to his fellows. There are no specific ministerial duties. A minister has no contract which says what he is to do and where his responsibility ends. He is totally at the service of those who need him.

Brooks repudiates the view that the ministerial functions can be parceled out, so that one man can be a preacher and the other a pastor. Good health, both of body and soul, are of first importance; so are a disciplined mind and cultivated manner: "For a good sermon there must be a man who can speak well, whose nature stands in right relations to those to whom he speaks, who has brought his life close to theirs with sympathy."

Few callings, says Brooks, offer more challenge to greatness or grant more in the way of personal rewards than the ministry, but the dangers of failure are correspondingly great. Because the minister is, in most cases, responsible to no man for the way in which he employs himself, the temptation to sloth and indulgence always besets a preacher. Moreover, he is almost totally exempt from severe and healthy criticism, in spite of the willingness of gossips to find out his little faults and let him hear of them. That the young minister will be self-conceited is altogether likely, and when he gradually learns that men do not share his views concerning his worth, he runs the risk of becoming resentful and blaming the age and its aversion to preaching. There is no deliverance from this fault, says Brooks, except to fall back upon God, who is able to make us as ready to fail for Him as to succeed. However, Brooks adds, success can also have the effect of humbling a man, if it opens to him the deeper meaning of his work and lets him see that more is at stake than his personal ambition.

It is wonderful, says Brooks, to hear a minister talk about "my congregation!" This way of thinking contains much folly, but, at the same time, deep truth. A young minister, especially, is likely to attribute almost mystical qualities to the group which he faces as he stands in the pulpit and to forget that his congregation is composed of individual men, women, and children, whose thoughts are widely variant from one another's, and even further from his own. On the other hand, says Brooks, there is something hallowed in the relation of a preacher and his congregation. A preacher becomes a better man as he stands before the congregation; and the congregation ("this strange composite be-

ing"), if it sees that its minister is totally devoted to it, stands devotedly with him, and follows him as far as it is able. Even here, however, lies a danger; for the congregation will spoil the minister by its indulgence if he is not on his guard.

As the messenger must be one whose life is from day to day being molded by the power of Christ, it follows that the message will be nothing more nor less than the witness to others of the love that has transformed the life of the messenger. Preaching, says Brooks, is essentially witnessing: "However the Gospel may be capable of statement in dogmatic form, its truest statement we know is not in dogma but in personal life." The Incarnation itself is the personification of Truth. Jesus said, "As my Father has sent me into the world, even so have I sent you into the world." Preaching is, thus, the continuation of the Incarnation, of His life who said, "I am the Truth."

The minister must never lose sight of the truth that the purpose of preaching is always the salvation of men. The sermon is not intended to be a work of art for men to admire or contemplate—although it comes to be regarded as such both by the minister and by the people whenever it loses its purpose of persuading and moving men's souls. Again, the sermon is not intended to be a lecture in which Christ and the Gospel, faith and the Church, are made the subject of a discussion. Much preaching, Brooks complains, is "preaching about Christ as distinct from preaching Christ."

What salvation means in the concrete may not be the same for every minister; whether it has to do mainly with sin or with suffering, with the individual or with society, with the present world or the world to come, is a matter to be decided. "The first thing for you to do," says Brooks, "is to see clearly what you are going to preach for, what you mean to try to save men from. By your conviction about that, the whole quality of your ministry will be decided." In general, the goal of preaching is always to bring men to Christ and Christ to men: "The sermon is God's message sent by you to certain of your fellow-men." When, as he inevitably must, the minister undertakes to speak on social and political issues, he does so not as an expert in these disciplines, but as "the messenger of Christ to the soul of man." He is ready to speak on any contemporary topic, but his sermon will never be mistaken for a newspaper editorial. The minister is nothing apart from the authority of the Word which he is given to proclaim.

Although the Lectures on Preaching are concerned with broad principles and not with homiletical details, the book has much to impart in the way of practical advice on sermon-preparation. As between the practice of preparing intensively for each week's sermon and expending the same industry in wider studies, Brooks favors the latter. A congregation can always tell the difference between a sermon which has been "crammed" and one which is the result of seasoned thought and wide experience. Brooks maintains, however, that sermons ought to be carefully prepared during the preceding week and not gotten up on Saturday night. He is not impressed with the arguments for extemporaneous preaching, and he maintains that if a sermon is genuinely extemporaneous when it is written, it will still have that quality when it is spoken. The

main question, says Brooks, is whether the sermon springs freshly from the preacher's heart and mind, and whether it is responsive to its audience. If so, a man's sermon will be "like the leaping of a fountain and not like the pumping of a pump."

Speaking of the selection of sermon topics, Brooks recommends following the calendar of the Church year. It is flexible enough to permit each man all the liberty he needs, while providing the kind of direction which will help him to preserve a proper symmetry. The actual selection of a text or a topic should, says Brooks, arise from a sympathetic and wise perception of what the people need. This, he adds, will not come as a sudden impression resulting from a casual conversation or a parish visit or the need to convince some critic. "It is the aggregate effect of a large sympathetic intercourse, the fruit of a true knowledge of human nature, combined with a special knowledge of these special people, and a cordial interest in the circumstances under which they live." Brooks urges that a minister particularly remember the large group in his congregation who are only loosely attached to the Church. He calls them "seekers." If you preach to these, he says, you will be preaching to all.

Brooks warns ministers against what he calls "the haunting incubus of the notion of great sermons." Pastors who think of sermons as oratorical masterpieces care for their sermons and not for the truth they have to proclaim or for the people whom they have to help. The man who is thinking every day about Christ and man, about the Bible and the world, will not have difficulty each time he enters the pulpit in saying things that are relevant.

Most of the discussion as to the merits of different kinds of sermons (doctrinal, topical, textual, expository) is beside the point. Different things need to be said, and said in different ways. The best sermon, says Brooks, is simply "the time's best utterance." A preacher must be a man of his age, in sympathy with those things in it which are praiseworthy, but aware also of its besetting sins. Even so, if he is constrained by too narrow a conception of the sermon, he is prevented from achieving his full effect as the spokesman of God to his generation.

In a lecture entitled "The Ministry for our Age," Brooks takes account of the anti-religious world-view that was becoming more and more prevalent. He saw clearly that the main difficulty was not the conflict between science and theology but the fact that

men had become preoccupied with the machinery of life to the neglect of its ultimate meaning. In particular, they had lost a sense of personal values and of the certainties that are necessary to give direction to life. He counseled preachers against trying to argue down the atheist or the materialist. To argue with them, he said, is to misunderstand their need. They do not really believe these doctrines; their trouble is that they have lost the ability to believe anything else. The only way the minister can help them is by declaring the facts of spiritual life. It is possible, Brooks says, to declare spiritual truths today with as much certainty as in any of the "ages of faith." The truths are as new as ever, and men are as ready as ever to feel their truth. "The world," writes Brooks, "has not heard its best preaching yet."

LECTURES ON GODMANHOOD

Author: Vladimir Solovyev (1853-1900)
Type of work: Christian social philosophy
First published: 1878

PRINCIPAL IDEAS ADVANCED

Secular humanism is doomed to failure because it does not unite man to the unconditioned, which is the source and end of his being.

The external freedom which Western civilization has brought needs to be supplemented by the internal freedom which positive religion can give.

The union between God and man, which is sought throughout the history of religion, is realized in Christianity, by means of Christ's becoming man.

The *Twelve Lectures on Godmanhood* was originally a series of public addresses given by Solovyev at St. Petersburg in his capacity as a member of the Ministry of Public Education. The

lectures were phenomenally successful, filling the large hall where they were given, and drawing such intellectual leaders as Fyodor Dostoevski and Leo Tolstoy. In spite of his youth, the author, who had previously been a fellow at the University of Moscow, and had studied at London and at Cairo, spoke with authority on philosophy and history. A zealous Christian, but not a clergyman, he also impressed men by the ascetic purity of his life, as we easily understand when we learn that Dostoevski used him as the model for Alyosha in *The Brothers Karamazov*.

The *Lectures on Godmanhood* is a synthesis of many strands of thought: Western philosophy, Buddhism, Platonism, the Church Fathers, the Hebrew Cabala, the mysticism of Boehme, and the speculation of Schelling and Hegel. Solovyev was disposed to find truth everywhere, and his great passion was to unify the world in truth and love. Having sensed the growing pessimism and nihilism of Western secular thought, Solovyev had turned to religion to find the organizing principle of life. He maintained that the conception of *Sophia* (Wisdom), preserved in Eastern Orthodoxy, contains the central and all-comprehending revelation which will unify creation by uniting it to God.

Although the reader may be tempted to see in Solovyev's lectures simply a Russian version of the romantic philosophy of Johann Fichte (1762-1814), Friedrich von Schelling (1775-1854), and G. W. F. Hegel (1770-1831), he will do better to begin by viewing it as an emendation of the Positive Philosophy of Auguste Comte (1798-1857). Comte had labored for a new society which should have for its foundations the laws of positive science and for its goal the unity of mankind. It was, in Comte's opinion, one of the positive laws of society that mankind passes through three stages: the theological stage,

which is a constructive or positive moment because it possesses a unifying faith; the metaphysical or critical stage, which is a destructive moment, and divorces thought from action; and the positive stage, which is once more constructive, but, unlike the theological stage, promises to be permanent, because it puts man's critical capacities to work in serving society. Solovyev, like Comte, put thought at the service of life and of action, and he regarded it as his vocation to "transform the world." But, in his opinion, positive or empirical knowledge was no more successful than the rationalism it was meant to replace in arriving at the knowledge of reality which is essential for man's spiritual life. Nor did a socialism based on the promise of satisfying man's egotistical wants offer any more hope for unifying mankind than did competitive society. In Solovyev's opinion, socialism and positivism were not new moments in the history of mankind, but closing phases of the godless, humanistic movement which came into existence with the breakup of Catholic Europe. The next, and final, moment in the history of mankind must be a revival of positive religion. Such a revival need not involve a return to the past. It is a law of history that only one function can be developed at a time. Accordingly, in the religions of the world, man realized the divine idea in the realm of spirit; then, in Western secular civilization, he realized the divine idea in the realm of nature. What remains, Solovyev argues, is to bring religion and civilization together in a new synthesis in which truth shall find its foundation in the knowledge of God, and brotherhood shall be realized through the love of God.

According to Solovyev, the failure of secularism is a result of the attempt to comprehend the conditioned world of sense experience while remaining agnostic about the unconditioned being on which the sensible world depends. Nowhere is this failure more apparent than in the secular view of man. Solovyev sums up the new humanism in the mocking formula: "Man is a hairless monkey and therefore must lay down his life for his friend!" There is nothing in secular thought to justify the high value which Western civilization places on human life; nor is this surprising if, as Solovyev holds, the value of human existence lies in the link which it provides between the creature and the Creator. Like Comte, Solovyev was completely devoted to the service of humanity, but the humanity which he served was not an empirical collection of individual men but a transcendent reality, man's ultimate and perfect state, which Solovyev called *Godmanhood.*

Because our active life cannot be divorced from knowledge, we must, says Solovyev, bring philosophy and religion to bear upon the human problem. The result is a novel blend of Hegelian dialectics and gnostic intuitions. Reality, says Solovyev, is organically one, a whole made up of parts. The principle of organization is that of tri-unity. We can discover this principle in the human soul, as Augustine showed, where within the unity the self we distinguish being, knowing, and willing. But the same principle is present in the blade of grass and in the Divinity. Moreover, it is this principle which enables men to understand the relationship which exists between God and the world within the All-

encompassing. For, in Solovyev's ontology, the world is the eternal image or counterpart of God, the essence or content which is implied in primal being. The world is God's *alter ego,* necessitated by that logic (Hegelian) according to which "being" implies "essence," and "unity" implies "plurality." Thus, the world must be differentiated from God. But because the identity of being is more fundamental than any diversity, God and the world are bound to each other by ties of eternal love. Once again, the whole scheme can be understood in terms of being, knowing, and willing: God is, the world is God's perception of Himself, and the All-encompassing whole is God's self-affirmation.

As has been suggested, the triunitarian motif may be traced repeatedly, both within the Deity and within the world. The familiar Trinity of Christian theology exemplifies the principle within divine unity, but, unlike the world, God is beyond all diversity, movement, or change. A corresponding trinity may be traced within our world of diversity and change. The first moment, comparable to the being of God, is inchoate matter, the world "without form and void," in which each material particle asserts its own identity irrespective of every other. The second moment, comparable to the Logos or Reason of God, is mind or intellect; it is the world of Platonic essences, but also of angels, who are pure intellects. The third moment, corresponding to the Holy Ghost in the divine Trinity, is the world soul, which in mystical theology is called Sophia. This third moment brings together matter and mind in an organic whole.

Solovyev triumphantly concludes

that man and man alone is the synthesis of the physical and the mental, of chance and logic, of lawlessness and love. But it is not man considered as a collection of empirical individuals who achieves this synthesis; rather, it is man as a corporate whole, of which the individuals are the cells of a greater organism. Man, then, is the temporal image of God, the consummation of the world; in him the whole of creation is recapitulated; and by man's free will, creation makes its movement back toward reunion with God in the All-encompassing.

The estimate of man at which Solovyev arrives has many points in common with the optimism of Renaissance humanism, as shown, for example, in Pico della Mirandola's (1463-1494) famous poem "On the Dignity of Man." But it is modified, in Solovyev's case, by a profoundly Russian sense of the radical character of evil. Man, as the lord and priest of nature, should bring the whole creation into harmony with God. That he does not is due to the freedom which is inherent in the creature and to the consequences of the disobedience of the Adam, the father of mankind. Made in the likeness of God, Adam, "or the world soul in him," was not satisfied with being the passive recipient of God's essence, but strove to become the foundation of his own being; in thus asserting himself, Adam fell away from God. As a further tragic result, man lost the harmony which was natural to his own being, and fell under the domination of matter. For in matter, according to Solovyev, self-assertiveness tends to prevail, and this is the cause of sin and suffering.

Still, with his eternal part, man strives for unity and truth; such is the theme of history, the underlying motif of religion and morality. But, aside from pointing to unity as man's goal, history has been futile and tragic. Only as Christ, in whom Logos and Sophia are joined, "descended into the stream of phenomena" could mankind and the world be restored to harmony with itself and to unity with its Creator. For Christ is not one individual among others; as the Second Adam, He is "the universal being, embracing all the regenerated, spiritual humanity."

Solovyev sought to show that all the wisdom and virtue of previous history came together in Christianity. He denied that there is such a thing as a false religion, although a religion becomes unfruitful when it turns fanatical and exclusive. In every religion, he said, there is a "sudden appearance of truth," partial though it be. Primitive religion, for example, found God in nature, but too exclusively; hence, the religions of India were useful insofar as they freed human personality from nature, but they erred in going to the opposite extreme by denying reality to nature. The failure was the unfortunate result of confusing the world and God. The Greeks and the Hebrews affirmed the transcendence of the unconditioned, but in different ways; the former affirmed God as object; that is, as essence or idea; the latter affirmed Him as subject; that is, as will and personality. Both the Greek and the Hebrew emphases were needed; Alexandrian philosophy brought them together, and developed the idea of the Trinity. Christianity, coming soon after, recapitulated the whole development. Christianity contains the ascetic principle of Buddhism, the idealism of the Greeks, the monotheism of the Hebrews, and the trinitarian understanding of the Alexandrians. To these, however, it added that which brings all the others to their fulfillment, lifting them from the ideal into the actual, inasmuch as it proclaims the Incarnation, or, as the Russians prefer to say, the "inhumanization" of Christ, in whom the disaffected world is effectually reunited with God.

Thus, to the positivism of secular philosophy Solovyev opposes "the truths of positive religion." When he wrote these lectures, he inclined to the view, shared with Dostoevski, that Eastern Orthodoxy holds more promise than Roman Catholicism or Protestantism. He praised the steadfastness with which Rome binds men to the Absolute, but he complained of the use which it makes of force. He praised the Protestant emphasis on freedom of conscience, but he deplored its tendency toward subjectivism and individualism. The Russian Orthodox Church, he maintained, preserves the positive values both of Catholicism and of Protestantism, while avoiding their respective faults. In later years, this judgment was modified, and Solovyev came to place more hope in the Roman than in the Russian Church, so far as the world mission of Christianity is concerned, even going so far as to become a communicating member of the Roman Catholic Church, in an effort to help heal the schism between the East and the West. The most immediate result of his life and labor, however, was the revival, around the turn of the century, of Christianity among young Russian intellectuals. Sergius Bulgakov and Nikolai Berdyaev are prominent examples.

THE GRAND INQUISITOR

Author: Fyodor Dostoevski (1821-1881)
Type of work: Christian ethics
First published: 1880, in *The Brothers Karamazov*

PRINCIPAL IDEAS ADVANCED

In opposition to Christ, who refused to do anything which would take away from the freedom of men, the Grand Inquisitor maintains that the masses can never be happy until they are relieved of the burden of freedom.

Socialism supposes that once men have bread they can be entrusted with freedom, but the socialist experiment will fail, and the Roman Church, which understands that men must also have miracles and someone to worship, hopes to complete the harmonious ant-society which the socialists have begun.

The Russian Church, which preserves the spirit of Christ, is destined in the long run to win over the socialist and the Roman way.

The *Grand Inquisitor* relates, in the form of a legend, how Christ was received when he visited Seville during the height of the Spanish Inquisition.

Dostoevski includes the story in the novel *The Brothers Karamazov*, as part of the explanation which the brilliant and sensitive university graduate Ivan Karamazov gives to his younger brother, Alexey, of his rebellious attitude with respect to the human condition. Ivan is incensed at man's cruelty, especially toward children, and on this ground he charges that God ought not to have given man free will. Alexey, a novice at the monastery, protests that before we accuse God of recklessness in giving man freedom, we must remember that God consented to suffer in His own person the consequence of men's cruelty. This prompts Ivan to relate his "legend," of which the purport is that, at least in Western Christendom, the Church has for many centuries been attempting to take away the freedom which God gave men, and for which Christ died.

Ivan's story of the "Grand Inquisitor" is essentially an independent statement, which brings to the highest artistic expression a dilemma which has tormented many minds in our own times nearly as much as it tormented Dostoevski.

The setting of the story is the sixteenth century, when, as Ivan explains, it was not uncommon for authors to describe heavenly personages as coming to earth. Christ's visit is not His promised coming in glory; rather, in answer to the fervent prayers of that century of religious conflict, Christ deigns to come once more in the form of a servant to reassure men of His way. Strangely, for He wears no insignia and has no one to herald Him, everyone recognizes Him as he moves silently in their midst with His gentle smile of compassion. Healing virtue radiates from his garments. The crowd weeps and does homage to him. Then the cardinal, the Grand Inquisitor, approaches and commands his guards to take Him. The people tremble before the Inquisitor, but they make no protest while the guards lead Christ away. Afterwards, they bow before the high churchman and receive his benediction.

That evening, the Grand Inquisitor visits Christ in the prison cell and accuses Him of coming to hinder the Church's work. Christ is to be burned at the stake the next day. Christ is silent throughout the interview, and thus he appears to justify the Church's claim that He has surrendered all authority to the pope. The Inquisitor, an old man of ninety, reveals the secret which he has kept in his heart for many years. Having tried in his youth to follow Christ's teaching, he has long since concluded that such teaching is impractical. A few elect souls can follow Christ's way, but it is too difficult for the masses.

As the Grand Inquisitor understands the Gospel story, the spirit of destruction who tempted Christ in the wilderness was more realistic and practical than any man, than even the Son of Man Himself. In rejecting the Devil, Christ persisted in His high opinion of human nature. He refused to purchase men's obedience by giving them bread, or by accepting the crown which they proffered him, or by bowing to their love for miracles; He hoped, rather, to win their hearts from rebellion by the power of truth and justice and of love freely given. Satan saw this ideal as a cruel mockery. Men want bread more than they want freedom; indeed, they are so weak that if they have freedom they will never have bread. They want someone before whom they can bow down and worship, someone in whose name they can conquer the world and force all men to believe and worship as they do. Moreover, they demand miracles, and they will not believe in a God who disdains miracles; they will shift their loyalty to the first charlatan who will concoct wonders for them to gape at.

The Inquisitor explains that the Catholic Church, having seen the impossibility of Jesus' way, has acted with the insight of a master psychologist. The Church has taken away men's freedom, and men have loved it for that very reason. "I tell Thee," the Inquisitor says to Christ, "that man is tormented by no greater anxiety than to find someone quickly to whom he can hand over that gift of freedom with which the ill-fated creature is born." Men readily bless the Church for giving them a steady objective in life, and they are readily persuaded that their only freedom is to come through submission to religious authority, especially when they are reminded of "the horrors of slavery and confusion" which their former freedom entailed. Leaders of the Church have consented to take upon themselves the freedom which knowledge of good and evil imposes upon men. Like adults in the midst of children, the priests have incurred anxiety and guilt, but in doing so they have allowed the weak and lustful to live out their lives in innocence and happiness. "Judge us," he says, "if Thou canst and darest."

The Grand Inquisitor protests that he too has dwelt in the wilderness and eaten roots. He too has prized the freedom which Christ taught and has striven to stand among the elect. "But

I awakened and would not serve madness. I turned back and joined the ranks of those *who have corrected Thy work*. I left the proud and went back to the humble, for the happiness of the humble." Christ, he concludes, in returning to the world, hinders the Church's work; therefore, He deserves to be burned as a heretic. When he has finished speaking, the Inquisitor waits for his prisoner to answer, but Christ, after looking at him intently in silence, approaches in silence and kisses the Inquisitor on his "bloodless aged" lips. The old man is visibly moved and, opening the door, says, "Go, and come no more. . . . Come not at all, never, never!" Christ departs.

In the mouth of Ivan, the story raises the utmost doubt respecting the teaching that man's crowning dignity is the gift of freedom. Even if one supposes that in the distant future men shall learn to live together in freedom and harmony, one cannot justify the wretchedness and torment which freedom has brought in its train. And it is not even certain, especially to one without faith, that eternal harmony is in store. Ivan's lack of faith especially torments him and the Inquisitor. Alexey has said, "Your Inquisitor does not believe in God, that's his secret." "It's perfectly true," replies Ivan, "that that's the whole secret, but isn't that suffering, at least for a man like that, who has wasted his whole life in the desert and yet could not shake off his incurable love of humanity?" Unlike the Inquisitor, however, Ivan has spent no time in the desert. He can only dream of a distant time when men will be happy in a socialist paradise. Meanwhile, to his anguished mind, Satan appears with other proposals. Is not a man who knows that there is no God, himself a God among men? And why is such a man bound to pity his fellows? Such is the further logic of "the spirit of self-destruction and non-existence," which was to prove Ivan's undoing.

There are other dimensions to the story. A theme which interested Dostoevski, together with other Russian writers (for example, Vladimir Solovyev) is the relationship between Eastern and Western Christianity and their respective roles in the future of mankind. Dostoevski belonged to the Slavophile group, which maintained that, despite the glaring incompetencies of the Russian Empire and the corruptions within the Orthodox Church, the spirit of Christ was profoundly at work in the lives of the Russian people, from which it would one day rise up and take the leadership of mankind away from Europe.

The Western Church, Dostoevski held, has long since forsaken the Gospel and has put its hope in the secular power which it inherited from ancient Rome. The Roman Church, says Dostoevski, proclaimed itself a state at the time of Charlemagne; Protestantism never reversed this step. Thus, in the West, a prisoner condemned by the State is condemned absolutely; there is no Christian society, apart from the civil order, which continues to claim the criminal as a member. As a consequence, the criminal rarely repents. Society triumphs over him by force, and he, in turn, considers his crime a legitimate protest against oppressive authority. In the East, according to Dostoevski, the situation is different. The civil power has, indeed, taken into its hands the judgment of men, but alongside the law courts the Church remains, which continues to minister to the criminal as to a precious son; and though, for many centuries, the Church has bowed to the Empire, it cherishes the hope of a time when the Empire will be diminished and all jurisdiction will pass to the Church.

As we learn from *The Diary of a Writer*, which comes from the same period as *The Brothers Karamazov*, Dostoevski was greatly interested in the reforms then taking place within Roman Catholicism, particularly in those reforms suggested by Christian socialism. For Dostoevski, atheistic socialism was merely an expression of denigrated Protestantism. The atheistic socialist had lost his faith in God and in the dignity of man. But, as one of the characters of *The Brothers Karamazov* says, "The socialist who is a Christian is more to be dreaded than a socialist who is an atheist." The reason becomes apparent in *The Grand Inquisitor*. Atheistic socialists have for their slogan, "Feed men and then ask them for virtue!"; with this slogan they draw men away from the Church. Dostoevski predicts that they will have a temporary success. With much bloodshed they will build their tower of Babel, "not to mount to Heaven from earth but to set up Heaven on earth." But they will not succeed. The reason is, they have only the wisdom of men, and the socialists err in supposing that after they have fed men they can give men freedom. The Church of Rome is wiser, having learned that freedom is worse than hunger, and that he who wants to deliver man from his anguish must also give him miracles and someone to worship. In this way, says the Inquisitor, the Roman Church is destined to triumph over socialism and to complete the tower of Babel, "uniting all in one unanimous and harmonious ant-heap. . . . For having begun to build their tower of Babel without us, they will end, of course, with cannibalism. But then the beast will crawl to us and lick our feet and spatter them with tears of blood. And we shall sit upon the beast and raise the cup, and on it will be written, 'Mystery.' But then, and only then, the reign of peace and happiness will come for men."

This triumph of cynical power is, of course, horrible to contemplate; Dostoevski regularly opposes to it what he calls the Russian approach, which is moral and Christian. "In Europe," he writes in *The Diary of a Writer*, "such an approach is inconceivable, although there, sooner or later—after floods of blood and 100 million heads—they will have to recognize it because in it alone lies the solution."

WHAT I BELIEVE

Author: Leo Tolstoy (1828-1910)
Type of work: Christian ethics
First published: 1882

Principal Ideas Advanced

Whereas civilization is based upon the belief that personal life is the true life, Christ taught that this belief is illusory and that obedience to God's will and service of mankind is the true life.

Christ's commandments, including "Resist not evil," are not impossible for man to keep, because they are natural to man and because keeping them will bring general and eternal peace.

The attempt of man to attain and defend personal good, by resisting evil and taking the product of other men's work, is the source of war, poverty, and misery.

When Tolstoy was in his early fifties, he quit writing novels for a number of years and devoted himself to the study of religion, writing his *Critique of Dogmatic Theology* (1880), and his *The Four Gospels, Harmonized and Translated* (1882). These bulky works have little interest for the general reader. But *My Confession* (1879), which serves as a preface to the former work, and *What I Believe*, which sums up the whole enterprise, deserve a permanent, if humble, place in the religious literature of mankind.

What I Believe is sometimes published under the title *My Religion*, not unsuitably in view of the fact that the Russian word *vera*, which appears in the Russian title, connotes a religious creed.

Tolstoy turned to religion in an effort to find the "meaning of life." In *My Confession*, he relates that as he approached the age of fifty he began to be plagued with the questions "Why?" and "What Then?" He possessed six thousand desyatinas of land in Samara. What then? He was educating his children to be gentle-folk. For what reason? A few more literary successes and his name would take its place with Shakespeare and Molière. What of that? At first, he tells us, these questions were merely interruptions; he continued to have enthusiasm for his work, telling himself that, were he to take the time, he could find the answers. But, like the symptom of a mortal disease, the question "What then?" grew more insistent, and Tolstoy was forced to admit that he did not know the answer. This brought his life to a standstill. He could no longer live without being able to give a reason for what he was doing. He consulted science and philosophy, but in vain. The only philosophers who seemed to face up to the problem were Solomon (in Ecclesiastes), Buddha, Socrates, and Schopenhauer, all of whom averred that life is meaningless and that death is a release from suffering. Men of affairs were of no more help, for however vigorously they pursued their respective goals, none of them knew why they were doing so. Because it seemed to him that certain humble folk found in religion a reason for their way of life, he concluded that in the end one must have a faith in order to live. For this reason he returned for a time to the Russian Orthodox Church, performed its rituals, and studied its theology. But the more he learned about official Christianity, the more he was disgusted. It was, he said, like a bag of stinking mud, in which a pearl is hidden, which has always been covered with mud. He was discouraged until, at last, he persuaded himself that the pearl could be had without the mud, and that, cleansed of dogmatic accretions, the Gospel could shine with the same lus-ter that drew men to it in the beginning.

What I Believe presents to us this pearl of great price, with Tolstoy's account of how he managed to find it, and his explanations of how so precious a gem came to be, for all practical purposes, lost to mankind.

The passage in the Sermon on the Mount in which Jesus says, "Resist not evil," first brought home to Tolstoy the force of the original Gospel. Suppose Jesus really meant what he said! If so, His view of life was radically different from what His followers are accustomed to suppose it to be. Civilization and morals, religion and politics, are based on resisting evil. If Jesus meant what these words say, He was demanding a complete revaluation of all values. Suddenly, Tolstoy says, everything in life fell into place, like pieces of a broken statue which one had been trying vainly to reconstruct, when, although the pieces fit, the statue which they form turns out to be a different one from what had previously existed. (Like other sectarians, Tolstoy supposed that he had found the whole truth in a single Biblical passage.)

Whereas men are accustomed to believe that Christ came to bless their personal lives, Tolstoy writes, the fact is that Christ tells us our personal lives cannot be saved. Trying to save our lives, we are quick to resist everything that threatens them and to seize anything that might help to save them. But we cannot save them no matter how hard we try, and our frantic efforts in this direction are the cause of most of the evil in the world today. Tolstoy does not make "nonresistance" the center of Christ's Gospel; he merely says that, in his own case, it was

Christ's teaching of nonresistance, and the bold contradiction between this teaching and the precepts and practice of the Church, which served as a key to open the Gospel to his understanding.

Actually, the command, "Resist not evil," is only one of the five commandments which, according to Tolstoy, sum up the teaching of Christ. They are all found in the fifth chapter of Matthew, in the passage in which Jesus contrasts his righteousness with the righteousness of the Pharisees. "Ye have heard it said by them of old time . . . but I say unto you. . . ." Human laws, says Tolstoy, are always conditional. For example, Moses forbids killing, but he immediately qualifies the command and mentions circumstances in which killing is lawful. So with divorce, and with other prescriptions. Christ, on the other hand, proclaimed divine laws, which admit no qualifications. Thus, He forbade all killing, all divorce, all oath-taking, all vengeance, and all discrimination between one's own nation and other nations. The Jews, especially Paul, failed to understand that Jesus was repudiating their law. They thought that when He said that not "one jot or tittle shall pass until all be fulfilled" he was speaking of the law of Moses. Thus, they glossed His teachings, putting into the text qualifying phrases. For example, when He said, "Be not angry," they added, "without just cause." Similarly, when He forbade divorce, they added, "except for cause of adultery." These changes show that they entirely misapprehended Him. When He said that the Law shall not pass away, he was referring to the Eternal Law laid down by the Creator for the direction of mankind. That Law upsets every maxim of human prudence. For him who has ears to hear, it announces that as long as men seek to satisfy their personal desires, life is futile and evil, and that the only way to diminish suffering and to find peace and joy on earth is to obey the will of God and thereby to serve the good of mankind.

Man must have a faith to live by, yet there are, says Tolstoy, two rival faiths. One is faith in the possibility of personal life, both here and hereafter. This is the faith professed by the Church and by secular culture, in spite of what the world's wisest men have said about the vanity of this way of life. The other faith starts with the recognition that our personal lives are perishable and demands that, forsaking our illusory goals, we obey the will of God and devote ourselves to the well-being of humanity. This is the faith Christ taught. According to Tolstoy, Christ said nothing to encourage the popular belief in the continuing life of the individual after death. He spoke, instead, of the resurrection of the *son of man,* by which He meant, not an individual person, but humanity as such. "The true life," says Tolstoy, "is only the one which continues the past life and which cooperates with the good of the contemporary life and with that of the future life. To be a participant in this life, a man must renounce his will for the purpose of fulfilling the will of the Father of life, who gave it to the son of man. . . . But the will of the Father of life is not the life of a separate individual, but of the one son of man who lives in men; and so man preserves life only when he looks upon his life as upon a pledge, a talent given him by the Father, that he may serve the life of all, when he lives not for himself, but for the son of man."

Tolstoy takes up the objection that this plan is unworkable. Those who suppose this, he says, simply do not realize how hard and unworkable the world's way is. Christianity has had its martyrs, but they are negligible by comparison with the victims of onward-marching civilization. Not without reason did Jesus say that the Christian's yoke is easy and his burden light. Tolstoy calls upon the reader to compare the sufferings endured by Christians with the suffering which the cultured and godless classes perpetuate from generation to generation through their sterile and profitless regimen. If universally practiced, Christ's commandments would mean the return of mankind to a healthy, hardworking life, closely attuned to nature. As to the solitary believer who ventures to turn his back on civilization, Tolstoy counts the suffering such a man must bear as being unimportant so long as the solitary believer's life and death "serve the salvation and the life of all men." But Tolstoy argues that even the enmity of the world is hardly enough to counterbalance the positive gain in peace and joy which comes from forsaking the illusions of civilization and living according to God's will and the principles of nature.

Tolstoy does not rest his teaching upon any authoritative claims for Jesus, as if He were a divine messenger. On the contrary, he maintains that there is a rational clarity to the Gospel which agrees with the truth of nature and with the light of reason in man. In this sense, he maintains that the Gospel is eternal and universal. The Church, which formerly moulded European and Russian life, he believes, has ceased to serve any good purpose. It is, he says, like the umbilical cord which carries nourishment from mother to fetus, but after the infant is born, the cord is fit only to be decently buried. Tolstoy regarded the European world of his day as being like a new-born animal, trying to find its own way; its energetic life was possible only because it was still living on its mother's fluids. Tolstoy hoped that Europe would shortly develop its own conscious spiritual foundation based on the recognition of "the rational teachings about the good life" which Christ first made clear. This teaching, in his opinion, "cannot fail to be accepted by men, not because it is impossible to deny that metaphysical explanation which it gives (everything can be denied), but because it alone gives those rules of life without which humanity has not lived and cannot live, and not one man has lived or can live, if he wants to live like a man, that is, a rational life."

EVOLUTION AND RELIGION

Author: Henry Ward Beecher (1813-1887)
Type of work: Christian evolutionary theory
First published: 1885

Principal Ideas Advanced

Man is not a fallen saint but a risen animal.

Christian religion is the product of a long, divinely inspired, human quest for higher spiritual and moral life; hence, what the theory of evolution discloses about the development of the natural order is true of the realm of the spirit as well.

Orthodox theology has unnecessarily alienated sensitive religious men by insisting upon the centrality of creeds rather than life, and by demanding absolute allegiance to primitive dogmas which are repugnant to man's increased moral and intellectual sensitivities.

A purified religion, focused on life and receptive to God's continuing revelation of truth, would be able to command the allegiance of all good men and thus to resume its place as a dynamic force for human growth.

The Reverend Henry Ward Beecher was eminent for his eloquence, his social concern, and his ability to relate Christian religion to the thought and life of his times. Because of his liberal stands on social issues and because of his considerable ability as a popularizer of the best sort, he was perhaps the most influential preacher of his day. From the pulpit of Plymouth Church in Brooklyn, New York, and in numerous books, he skillfully translated complicated philosophical, theological, and scientific ideas into language which the ordinary man could understand. _Evolution and Religion,_ comprised of twenty-six sermons preached over the course of several years "discussing the bearings of the evolutionary philosophy on the fundamental doctrines of evangelical Christianity," is typical of his work.

Convinced that Christianity has been an evolving religion, and that God reveals Himself to man continually through the thought and life of the present day, Beecher was wholeheartedly an expositor of the "new Theology," a liberal theological movement of the late nineteenth century led by

Horace Bushnell (1802-1876), and he helped to turn the popular religious mind in the liberal direction by his powerful preaching of these doctrines. A Christianity responsive to the findings of science was his central concern, for he regarded religion as a search for all truth wherever it be found.

The theology which had developed among these liberals in the nineteenth century was such that there was no serious conflict with the new theory of evolution. Liberalism had already made its peace with modern thought. Liberals had come to understand God's revelation in terms of inspired human thought, and they argued that wherever truth be found, God is speaking. Since the voice of science is one of the voices of God, it must be listened to with reverence. The great traditions of religion, the Bible, and later reflections on moral and spiritual truths, are all products of a long and patient human search for truth and life. As man grows, religiously and otherwise, he has to put away childish thoughts, rejecting what he has discovered to be outmoded and accepting new truth, whatever its source. What science discovers is religiously valid and presents to modern man new ways of describing how God has actually worked in and upon mankind. Liberalism as a whole stressed the immanent working of God (God's working *in* things) rather than, as the Orthodox tradition did, His transcendent working (God's working *on* things from outside).

As Beecher saw it, then, he was not engaged in modifying Christianity to fit new scientific ideas of evolution; rather, he was engaged in using new ideas to interpret what religion had already known: that man has undergone spiritual growth. The theory of evolution did not force Beecher to change his ideas of God and man, for early in life he had come to believe in man as a growing being. Beecher writes, "Later I began to feel that science had struck a larger view, and that this unfolding . . . in spiritual things was but one application of a great cosmic doctrine, which underlay God's methods in universal creation, and was notably to be seen in the whole development of human society and human thought." The scientific doctrine, then, merely fit in with the already known facts of spiritual and intellectual evolution, and showed them to be parts of a general cosmic process. The theory of evolution traced, on the natural level, the same patient workings of God to create a higher order of life that religion had already traced on the spiritual level. Hence, the publication by Charles Darwin (1809-1882) of his *Origin of Species* (1859) and *Descent of Man* (1871), works which established the theory of evolution scientifically, and the writing of Herbert Spencer (1820-1903), who presented similar doctrines in philosophical form and who was directly influential on Beecher, served not to weaken but rather to provide confirmation for Protestant liberal theology. Evolution replaced the outworn science which had become so troublesome for modern Christianity and in so doing allowed morality and the true spiritual life to emerge more clearly as the concerns of religion.

Beecher has provided several summaries of his theology, the shortest of which follows: "These four truths— the fact of sinfulness; the fact of regeneration, its need, its reality, its possibility; the life-giving Spirit of God, that helps a man out of this lower into the higher stage; and the fact of the holiness into which man may come by the aid of the Spirit, concurrent with his own will—these are what I call the executive doctrines of Christianity. . . ." Other summaries mention also the redemptive work of Jesus as teacher and inspirer of men, and the achievement of miraculous powers over nature by men whose spirituality has been fully realized. As for the rest of the traditional doctrine, Beecher once said, "If, besides all that, the Church wants to carry baggage and baggage-wagons, and all sorts of furniture and all sorts of ordnance, and is able to do so, it may. There is no law by which a man should not go to battle now with Saul's armor on, but he would be a fool to sweat under Saul's armor on a midsummer's day. So that all of the churches or the people may be just as foolish as they please, if they do not set themselves up for models. . . ."

According to Beecher, much that orthodox Christianity has believed is badly in error. Man did not fall from some primitive paradise; rather, he has risen from primitive animality by a long process of moral and spiritual growth. The orthodox view was that Adam fell, passing on to all his descendants a corrupt nature which rendered all their works odious and left them spiritually unclean, thereby requiring a bloody sacrifice so that God might be free to welcome man again. Moreover, the orthodox view held that God predestined some men to salvation, condemning all others to eternal torment in Hell. According to Beecher, these doctrines are both false and morally repugnant.

The fact of the matter, Beecher insists, is that man did not descend; he *ascended*. Through centuries of gradual discovery and exploration, man has broken free from primitive superstition and moral crudity, and has created for himself, by the inspiration of God, lofty theological ideals and a way of life which leads to true morality and the spiritual life. Jesus did not come to save man by buying man's salvation; rather, He came to inspire men by His teachings and His example, showing clearly to men that there is a spiritual power which can regenerate them by raising them up to spiritual sonship. Sin is man's failure to do the things that he knows he should do: it is his failure to grow in spirit, his willingness to remain fleshly. Regeneration, which is the process of spiritual growth, takes place only as man is inwardly transformed; hence, regeneration is accomplished *in* man and cannot be applied to him from outside by magical rites such as baptism. As men develop their spiritual lives, they rise to such heights of nearness to God that they develop godlike powers over nature which enable them to perform what seem to ordinary men to be miracles. At death, according to Beecher, most men are extinguished, but those who by their efforts to grow in this life have become fit for further growth enter into another stage of life and ascend spiritually.

The view that religion has undergone spiritual evolution is confirmed, according to Beecher, by modern theories concerning the Scriptures and the doctrines of the Church. Scholars have concluded that the Bible is a very human document, the result of gradually growing spiritual insight, rather than an infallible transcription of words which came from God. The Bible, properly interpreted, records man's gradual discovery of moral and spiritual truth. Much of the Biblical writing reflects primitive ideas about man and his universe, and these ideas are consequently not binding upon present generations; the lasting truths of Scripture are its great examples, the power of its ideas and ideals. To achieve a separation of what is false and outworn from what is perennially valid is to liberate religion. As Beecher has eloquently stated it, modern theology will "free the Sacred Scriptures from fictitious pretensions made by men, from clouds of misconceptions, and give to us the book as a clear and shining light, instead of an orb veiled by false claims and worn-out philosophies."

The history of Christianity has been further complicated by the fact that too many theologians have chosen for crucial emphasis doctrines which are primitive and morally crude: use has been made of arbitrary selections of proof texts which are contraverted by the more advanced insights of the Bible itself. Every party to every theological dispute has his own set of texts to appeal to, and "there is scarcely a square league that has not a separate sect in it, and all of them cry, 'Thus saith the Lord!' " Because so many of the doctrines heretofore selected for emphasis have been barbarous, because such quarrels are divisive, and because they result from and contribute to a preoccupation with creeds instead of life, religion has been badly distorted and has lost much of its effectiveness.

Religiousness is to be measured, Beecher writes, in terms of what one does, how one puts into practice moral and spiritual truths, not in terms of what theological creeds, forms of government, or religious rites one believes in. It is by their fruits that men are known to be Christian or not. Beecher even went so far as to say that no church had the right to make *any* rules or regulations which would prevent a man of good religious life from participating in the activities of the church. Rather, churches must change their ways so that all godly men can be included.

Religion is the product of a long spiritual evolution, the creation of a divinely inspired effort to find what is true and noble in life. Orthodoxy has threatened continued growth by its insistence upon the infallibility of the past, and by requiring that men continue to believe things which are not only untrue but religiously offensive. The evolutionary process continues, and a religion which is to be responsive to God must grow; it must listen to the voice of God in the present as well as in the past, in order that it may once again become a vital means to the spiritual growth of mankind. Man stands on the threshold of a new age and he must give himself wholeheartedly to the task of shaping his further spiritual growth, for the Kingdom of God, the seeds of which were planted long ago, is now almost fully come. Thus the theory of evolution, as a statement of a general principle of the cosmos, illuminates man's knowledge of both nature and spirit, contributing to his understanding of both the past and the future. A religion in which this awareness has become articulate can help man to rediscover the regenerative powers which reside in God.

The Church is a necessity for religious life, Beecher agrees, but if it is to meet the religious needs of modern men it must become more spiritual and inclusive, less dogmatically inclined and less factional. In his final sermon, Part I, Beecher gave voice to his hope for the Church, saying ". . . I hope yet to see the day when that proverb will have died out of the memory of man: 'I know they are Christians, they quarrel so.' "

SYSTEMATIC THEOLOGY

Author: Augustus Hopkins Strong (1836-1921)
Type of work: Protestant orthodoxy
First published: 1886; new and enlarged version, 1907 (Volumes I and II) and 1909 (Volume III)

Principal Ideas Advanced

The times call for a defense of the old evangelical doctrines of sin and grace against a growing tendency to deny them.

The key to such a defense is provided by the philosophy of ethical monism, which teaches that reality consists of a single substance, God, whose divine life is partially and progressively manifest in the universe through the agency of Christ the Logos, in and through whom all things are unified.

Such a monistic and idealistic world-view enables the theologian to take into account the scientific theory of evolution, the philosophical emphasis on the immanence of God, and the conclusions of a sane higher criticism, while at the same time preserving the fundamental truths of the Biblical revelation.

Augustus Hopkins Strong's *Systematic Theology* has been the most widely used textbook of theology produced in America by a Baptist theologian. Published originally in 1886, seven editions appeared in the next two decades. In the meantime Strong, president of Rochester Theological Seminary for forty years, underwent a change in his philosophical orientation and issued a new and enlarged version of the system in three volumes during the period 1907 to 1909. A one-volume outline containing all of the major propositions, but eliminating all bibliographical and illustrative material as well as the index, was published in 1908 under the title *Outlines of Systematic Theology*. Strong's *Systematic Theology* continues to be widely read today in conservative circles and has recently been reprinted both in England and in the United States.

Strong believed that he had discovered a way of uniting philosophical and theological truth in a version of metaphysical idealism which he called ethical monism. This outlook is heavily dependent on the personal idealism of the German philosopher Hermann Lotze (1817-1881) and is closely re-

lated to the thought of such American idealists as George Trumball Ladd (1842-1921) of Yale University. More fully explained in *Christ in Creation and Ethical Monism* (1899), Strong's view is that there is one basic spiritual substance, God, who is partially and progressively expressed in the various finite and temporal grades of the created world. Strong's metaphysical monism, however, is qualified by the doctrine of psychological dualism which teaches that human personality is distinct from matter, on the one hand, and from the transcendent personality of God, on the other hand. The creator is Christ, the Logos, who is the organ of divine self-consciousness and self-determination. This means that Christ is the ground of unity in the universe and the organizing principle of all truth and reality, thus guaranteeing that reason and Scripture are harmonious though distinct sources of knowledge. Matter is the spiritual product of the divine will manifesting itself in the form of force under the law of necessity; finite mind or personality is the expression of God under the law of freedom. Reality, then, is one organic spiritual life grounded in the eternal transcendent personality and will of God, whose infinite being is partially manifested through the creative agency of Christ, the divine reason, in the various levels and kinds of finite existence.

Strong did his work at a time when the leading theological centers in America were moving toward liberalism, and his writings reflect this struggle. Unable either to give up his modified Calvinism or to turn his back completely upon the newer currents of thought in philosophy and science, Strong attempted to present the old doctrines in a modern intellectual setting. His ethical monism took into account the prevailing idealistic tendencies in philosophy and reflected the growing emphasis on the immanence of God and the progressive development of nature and history; yet his essential loyalties were given to a Calvinistic type of Protestant orthodoxy. Strong accepted evolution and higher criticism in principle but insisted on the historicity of Adam, the plenary inspiration of the Bible, and the Mosaic authorship of the Pentateuch. While maintaining that no scientific or historical error had ever been shown to exist in the Bible, he did leave the door open for Biblical criticism by an admission that inspiration does not necessarily guarantee infallibility in matters not essential to religious truth.

With regard to method Strong was in the scholastic tradition of the older Protestant dogmatists. His system of theology consists of a series of propositions arranged around the main doctrinal headings and outlined to the finest detail. Strong employs a rationalistic and proof-text approach in supporting his views. As an idealist he affirms the organic unity of truth and stresses the power of reason to buttress

Scriptural teaching. Natural theology is supplemented by a fuller disclosure of religious truth recorded in the Bible, which is the court of final appeal. Deductive and inferential reasoning is accompanied by numerous quotations from the Scriptures. Strong makes extensive references to opposing views and refutes them systematically. Containing a wealth of homiletical and illustrative material, his presentation abounds with copious quotations from philosophers, theologians, poets, and other writers, whose views support his own or call for counterargument.

Theology, according to Strong, deals with God and His relations to the universe. Its sources are the world of nature as it is apprehended by reason and the Bible. God is an infinite, perfect Spirit, whose existence is a rationally intuited first truth logically prior to all other knowledge. In Strong's opinion, the classical arguments for the existence of God, while not demonstrative, do provide cumulative evidence of a corroborative nature.

A priori reasons suggest the probability of a revelation of God, and the Bible provides such a revelation, attested by miracles and fulfillments of prophecy. Rational considerations prove that the authors of Scripture are honest men, credible witnesses to divinely-given truth; furthermore, the nature and unity of the Bible, the moral superiority of the New Testament, the character and testimony of Christ, and the marvelous success and beneficent influence of the Christian enterprise all point conclusively to the supernatural character of the Biblical writings.

Strong argues that inspiration is the divine influence which makes the Scriptures a source of truth sufficient for salvation. The Bible bears the marks of its human authorship and is not necessarily correct in matters not essential to salvation, but because of its supernatural inspiration it does constitute an infallible rule of religious faith and practice.

The attributes of God fall into two main classes, Strong argues. The absolute attributes (life, personality, self-existence, immutability, unity, truth, love, and holiness) belong to God independently of His relationships with the world. The relative attributes (eternity, immensity, omnipresence, omniscience, omnipotence, and the transitive dimension of truth, holiness, and love) belong to God considered in relation to the creation. Holiness is the supreme moral attribute and the norm of love. God exists as one essence manifested in three eternal and distinct persons; both the tripersonality and the unity of God are essential elements in the inscrutable but not irrational doctrine of the Trinity.

Strong claims that although by the decrees of God certain events of the universe have been made certain, God is in no way responsible for sin or for voiding the free agency of man. Creation is the absolute origination of the universe without the use of pre-existing materials. Preservation is the maintenance in existence of created beings and their powers. Providence is the directing of all events toward the end planned for them. Instances of special providential action, miracles, and regeneration are simply extraordinary cases of God's working among men and are not contrary to his general direction of the universe according to law. Both good and evil angels exist and are, in different ways, agents of the providential agency of God.

While man has a brute ancestry, he appears on the scene as a fully moral and self-conscious being, and the whole human race is a unity descended from a single pair. Strong argues that man consists essentially of body and soul and possesses the moral powers of conscience and will. Created originally in the image of God and thus characterized by personality and holiness, man lost his state of original righteousness and communion with God by his mysterious, self-chosen revolt. Sin is any lack of conformity to the moral law of God, whether in act, disposition, or state, its essential nature being best defined as selfishness. Sin proceeds from a corrupt nature inherited from Adam, whose original transgression constituted the fall of the whole human race, since all men existed in organic unity with and were seminally present in him. Thus, all men suffer the consequences of depravity, guilt, and penalty, although infants are saved by a special act of grace which regenerates them at the point of death.

God wills to save man by the redemptive act performed by Christ, who is one person with a fully human and a fully divine nature. Prophet and king as well as priest, Christ makes atonement by suffering for sinners the punishment demanded by the holiness of God, thus satisfying the demands of justice and making possible the operation of grace. As the creator and the immanent life of the human race Christ is organically one with it. Therefore, He can, as the incarnate Logos, suffer the punishment due to mankind for the racial sin of Adam. This unity of Christ with the race also explains how the benefits of Christ's death can be appropriated by the repentant sinner. The incarnate Christ reveals and completes historically the work of atonement which the eternal Logos accomplishes in the divine realm both before and after Calvary. According to Strong, the Holy Spirit makes effectual in the lives of men the salvation objectively made available by Christ. God eternally elects certain of the lost to be the recipients of saving grace, and this election is accomplished through the efficacious calling of men by the Holy Spirit and the establishment of a spiritual union between Christ and the believer. The components of redemption viewed from the standpoint of its beginning are regeneration (the divine side of the new birth), conversion (the human side of regeneration and involving repentance and faith), and justification (the divine judicial acquittal of the sinner). The components of redemption viewed from the standpoint of its continuation are sanctification (growth in holiness accomplished by the Holy Spirit) and perseverance (the human side of sanctification).

The universal or invisible Church consists of the whole company of regenerate persons in all ages, while the individual church is a local group of believers who have voluntarily united themselves together. The proper government of the church is congregational, and the proper offices of the church are two: bishop, presbyter, or pastor and deacon. Two ordinances have been given the local church as visible signs of the saving truth of the Gospel. Baptism is the immersion in water of a believer, while the Lord's Supper is the eating of bread and the drinking of wine by baptized believers; thus, the regenerate person is united with Christ by whom the spiritual life is nourished.

The Christian life is not completed in this life but awaits a consummation in the life to come, Strong believed. After death both the righteous and the wicked exist consciously in an intermediate state and experience a foretaste of their ultimate destiny. The final events to occur will be the millennium, the second coming of Jesus, the Resurrection, and the Last Judgment, all of which are outward visible happenings. The Resurrection will reunite the souls of all the dead with appropriate bodies, and the Last Judgment will send the wicked into everlasting though not necessarily physical torment and the righteous into everlasting and unimaginable joy.

In short, what Augustus Hopkins Strong offers in his *Systematic Theology* is a standard Baptist version of a Calvinistic type of theology based on a scholastic method and set within a context of a version of metaphysical idealism. While Strong's ethical monism seems to be only remotely connected with the development of most of his doctrinal convictions, it did function in his own mind as an overall vision of reality which enabled him to incorporate rational and revealed truth into one harmonious system of thought.

A STUDY OF RELIGION

Author: James Martineau (1805-1900)
Type of work: Philosophy of religion
First published: 1888

PRINCIPAL IDEAS ADVANCED

From the principle of causality, which the intellect employs to interpret external phenomena, the natural world is resolved into the effect of one wise and mighty will.

From the sense of duty, by which the conscience finds a sacredness in life and puts a divine construction on a large portion of internal experience, man's affinity with a supreme omnipresent righteousness is discovered.

From the relation between causality and duty it is evident that the two are separate only in apprehension; in reality, causality and duty meet in one Being, perfect both in thought and holiness.

A *Study of Religion* by James Martineau is a critical examination of the source and content of religion. The work contains four books, published in two volumes. The limits of human intelligence are discussed in Book One. Book Two is devoted to a discussion of theism; Book Three reviews the opposing system of pantheism, and discusses determinism and free will; Book Four deals with the life to come.

Martineau is unwilling to identify God with nature, but he does not seek to propound a religion without God. The belief and worship of that supreme mind and will which directs the operations of the universe and sustains moral relations to man is the very essence of religion, he claims. Such a supreme mind not only exists, but notwithstanding the skeptical conclusions of Kantian and post-Kantian philosophy, He is also knowable. Martineau challenges the assumption that our intellectual apprehension is limited to the data of sensation and to the *a priori* conditions that lie in the mind itself.

A human being is more than a collection of faculties and susceptibilities which coherently treat and interpret phenomena without access to anything beyond. It is logically possible that our cognitive faculties are constituted in accordance with things as they are. Nothing stands in the way of trust in the reliability of our instinctive trust in a world beyond the content of consciousness. Through experience we have access to other persons and to an external world, to objects not to be found within consciousness. The outer world is not merely an illusory postulate of thought; the external world is a complex of actual events which condition experience and are affected by experience.

Religion is concerned with what is higher than man, Martineau suggests. God is conceived as a supreme mind, a mind superior in scope and creativity to all finite minds. What we seek to know of the divine can be subscribed under two relations: the relation of God to nature; that is, God as cause; and the relation of God to man; that is, God as holy.

To understand God as cause, the meaning of the causal relation must first be ascertained. No static thing can ever play the part of cause, except as the seat of change, or as partner in a change. Nor is the causal relation to be resolved into a mere arrangement of feelings and mental images. When God is spoken of as cause, what is meant is that there is but one universal cause, the infinite and eternal seat of all power, an omniscient mind, ordering all things for ends selected with perfect wisdom.

Just as the causal aspect of the divine nature is opened to us by our own will and extended into the sphere of nature, so the moral aspect of the divine nature is disclosed by conscience, and is then applied to human relationships. From knowledge of ourselves, says Martineau, we gain knowledge of God. From our volitional experience, we can infer objective causality; from our moral experience, we can infer an objective authority.

Our knowledge of an infinite and righteous cause of all is the result of an immediate intuition, Martineau claims; such knowledge is on the same footing of certainty as our apprehension of the external material world.

According to Martineau, the conscience supplies the moral nature with a special sphere of cognition. Whenever we are confronted by two incompatible courses of action, our moral intuition provides us with the certainty that one of the alternatives is superior in excellence. The more excellent course is not marked by greater pleasure or advantage, or by greater seemliness or beauty, but its excellence consists in a greater degree of *rightness,*

which demands our assent and commands our obedience.

Such superiority may be disregarded by us, but when the lesser course is followed we are haunted by a sense of disloyalty. We accuse ourselves and know that our offense is not a private mistake. We are cast down by guilt. The springs of action are differentiated to the conscience by an element of value. The superior terms in the scale of right claim us by their *authority;* they tell us that we *ought* to follow them, that they are binding on us, that they are presented to us by a Being higher than we, and that we sin in neglecting them. We are in fact responsible for doing our duty; that is, for conforming our voluntary life to the preferential scale of obligation, as its parts emerge into consciousness.

The moral law, writes Martineau, is imposed by an authority foreign to our personality; it may be obeyed or disobeyed. The right is not determined by social vote; the authority which forces itself upon us is not simply the embodiment of public opinion, an ideal aggregate of sentiment which bestows praise and blame on what aids or is detrimental to human interests. Neither self-love nor collective self-interest is sufficient to account for the idea of right. The inherent differences between right and wrong are more than subjective fancies. They are urged upon us by an objective power with which their validity is identified.

According to Martineau, we are introduced immediately in the act of conscience to a being higher than ourselves, which causes us to know the right. There is a perfect analogy between the dualism of perception, which confronts us with an objective world, and the dualism of conscience, which confronts us with an objective higher mind. The integral meaning of the moral law is reached when the latter is seen as implicit in a perfect mind, which communicates to us and by exercising its power over our affections draws us into divine communion. The very constitution of our moral nature is intelligible solely when viewed as a response to an objective perfection pervading the universe with holy law. The moral differences that we feel have their verification in reality, in an eternal holiness. The conscience reveals the living God, an infinite objective perfection, not merely a set of moral ideals.

The theism developed upon the basis of causality was outward, in the cosmos, but the reference now is inward, in the human soul; the divine agency is here seen in the moral law, not in the laws of nature, which are laws of invariable necessity, but in the laws of variable possibility and freedom.

By our conscience, says Martineau, we can apprehend certain attributes of God. God is identical with the *highest*, the supreme term in the hierarchy of spiritual natures; He is the eternal life of moral perfection. By analyzing the elements of ideal perfection, we recognize the attributes that may be ascribed to God. We thus reach conceptions of God by probing our moral nature, for God's attributes are the transcendent forms of human aims and prayers. Benevolence towards sentient beings must, for example, be ascribed to God. From the constitution of our humanity we learn that God its author is loving, merciful, and compassionate. In the infinite disposer we recognize justice toward moral beings. The conscience of mankind refuses to believe in the ultimate impunity of guilt. No objective belief has more than a subjective guarantee, but there is no less reason to accept our conscience as delegate of a sovereign righteousness, than to regard our bodily dimensions as limited from universal space. Since moral effects surely must flow from a moral source, we may discover the reflections of an eternal justice in our own ethical discriminations. However vast the distance between God and man, we may suppose that God is sympathetic to devoted minds. Related spirits are joined by a common creative aim, intent on what is pure and good. Religious experience affirms that the silent soliloquies of the heart are happily interrupted, for divine words flow in and break the loneliness.

According to Martineau, the revelation of the all-perfect is not simply to the individual but to all mankind; one harmony vibrates throughout the universal medium of spiritual existence; God stands in one relation to all, breathes the same inspirations, gives the same warnings, and invites the same affections. Our united human nature constitutes the Kingdom of God; for it has no offenses which are not sins and no penalties which do not express His will. As nature constitutes one intellectual organism, so humanity constitutes one moral organism. The whole domain of knowledge and duty can thus be seen to be suffused with the divine.

Martineau claims that there is a unity of God as cause and God as perfection. While it is possible to find the origin of our primary religious ideas in the two sides of our nature, the intellectual and the moral, God's attributes are inseparable. Intelligence, power, self-existence, benevolence, justice, holiness, and sovereignty over men are attributes of the one causal and holy God. We ourselves unite in our own persons a subjection to the outward physical order and to the inward moral law, writes Martineau. The moral order and the physical order are organically blended in real existence. External nature is not foreign to the system of moral laws. The moral system to which we belong corresponds to the righteousness of God. A certain range of contingency is surrendered to the free will of finite beings, for God does not necessitate a good; moral evil is thus possible.

Neither pantheism nor determinism is compatible with the theism here defended, since the former invalidates all personal relations, and the latter all moral relations, between the human and divine mind.

The universe presents us with a grandeur that is divine only when we read the causality behind phenomena. And when we find our duty invested with a supernatural light, we are subdued by its sanctity. The embrace of the all-comprehending God transforms each object into a religious object. The same transition, from the empirical to the transcendent, brings the future life under the surveillance of religion.

Martineau suggests that the question of a life to come centers in the interpretation of death as affecting the individual. From the physiological point of view, there is no way of knowing that the individual soul does not survive the dissolution of the body, for the universe may well contain means of individualization other than the present human body. Martineau believes in the immortality of the soul, not as a demonstrable truth of science, but as a supreme article of an abiding faith in the reasonableness of God's work. From the moral point of view, two inferences seem to force themselves upon us, Martineau suggests: first, that there are everywhere indelible marks of a morally constituted world, moving toward righteous ends; and second, that nowhere do we find the fulfillment of the latter, so that the unfinished character of ourselves and of our world implies a justifying and perfect sequel. It is, therefore, reasonable to believe, Martineau concludes, that we stand in divine relations which indefinitely exceed the limits of our earthly years.

THE ASCENT OF MAN

Author: Henry Drummond (1851-1897)
Type of work: Christian evolutionary theory
First published: 1894

PRINCIPAL IDEAS ADVANCED

The scientific account of evolution is the story of creation as told by those who know it best.

Naturalists err in interpreting nature from the standpoint of the atom; theologians err in separating man from his environment.

Any evolutionary account must consider the place of soul and spirit in the world, for the universe is an expression of God's will.
There is no inherent opposition between science and religion.

Henry Drummond's Lowell Lectures published in 1894 as *The Ascent of Man* are of value today less for their specific teaching than for what they reveal of an important type of response to the challenge the theory of evolution presented to religious thought in the late nineteenth century. The title reflects the theme which is constantly reiterated throughout the book: the theory of evolution supports a positive interpretation of man's progressive *ascent;* the theory need not be castigated as insisting upon the *descent* of man from some primeval ape.

Drummond's purpose was a corrective one: to re-examine the notion of evolution which had been given to the modern world. The impetus for his work lay in the author's deep-seated conviction that a more balanced, broader, and deeper evolutionary theory was needed as a standard for the thought of his day. His aim was to speak to neither the specialist nor the theologian but to an audience of laymen; he wanted to describe the basic phases in the ascent and arrest of man's body, the dawn of mind and language and the struggle for life. Finally, he wanted to offer an interpretation of all these matters.

Henry Drummond, a gifted Scotsman, preacher of a practical Christian religion, and a teacher of science, was a person with a compelling and passionate concern for achieving a reconciliation of science and theology in the service of Jesus Christ. Drummond enjoyed very great fame as a lecturer on religious themes presented in an unconventional manner, utilizing the latest intellectual methods, and permeated with a contagious faith in God and the reality of religious experience. He was possessed of a commanding appearance and a penetrating gaze which caused one who knew him to say: "No man could be double, or base, or mean, or impure before those eyes." He was so influential that Christian work among students in England, America, Germany, Australia, Japan, and Russia owes a direct indebtedness to his inspiration. On tours to college campuses Drummond made deep impressions upon his audience. His most famous and lasting work is the sermon on love, which has become a classic and best-selling work under the title, "The Greatest Thing in the World." Of his other works, *Natural Law in the Spiritual World* (1883), the most widely read religious work in the world in its day, and *The Ascent of Man* are the most important.

The problem of the ascent, or evolution, of man is at once the noblest and most practical of all studies, Drummond asserts. The scientific account of evolution is, after all, simply "the story of creation as told by those who know it best."

The critical modern reader notes in these lectures the absence of any discussion concerning the propriety of associating a cosmological theory of creation with a scientific account of evolution. Drummond accepted the science of his day as providing definitive answers to the problem of man's creation and evolution. Thus, Drummond's work is interesting and informative as much for what it does not say and for what it takes for granted, as for its positive claims.

Despite Drummond's enthusiasm for science, he was not uncritical in regard to it. He points out, for example, that evolutionary theory as an attempt to explain the development of life quite naturally tends to express the predilections of the particular thinkers who contribute to evolutionary theory. But science is self-corrective, for criticism within scientific circles is more severe than the irresponsible charges which come from the outside.

Drummond advises suspension of judgment concerning Darwinism. He describes his age as "the age of the evolution of Evolution," and he suggests that because of the constantly changing content of scientific thought, and in consideration of the humility, tolerance, and lack of dogmatism which often accompany scientific work, evolutionary theory be accepted in general in order that it might continue to emerge ever stronger from its many immersions in "the crucible of criticism." Evolutionary theory for Drummond was no mathematical proposition which may be declared true or false; it is the product of a method of looking upon nature, of a way of intellectual life.

The error of his time Drummond sees as too little rather than too much attention to evolution. The naturalists make the mistake of interpreting nature from the standpoint of the atom, while theologians err in separating man from his environment. Deploring those "defenses" of science and religion which have the effect of removing the rational basis of religion and the legitimate crown of science, Drummond protests unnatural religion and inhuman science. Both scientist and theo-logian need to enlarge their views, the former to include the whole man in all of his moral, social, intellectual, and religious dimensions, and the latter to include man as human being in a world setting. Drummond's unfailing gift for expressing such notions in an appealing manner is illustrated in the following passage: "The man who is busy with the stars will never come across Natural Selection, yet surely must he allow for Natural Selection in his construction of the world as a whole. He who works among star-fish will encounter little of Mental Evolution, yet will he not deny that it exists. The stars have their voices, but there are other voices; the star-fishes have activities, but there are other activities. Man, body, soul, spirit, are not only to be considered, but are first to be considered in any theory of the world. You cannot describe the life of kings, or arrange their kingdoms, from the cellar beneath the palace." That his admirers appreciated such rhetoric and the ideas it expressed is suggested by the fact that whole blocks of tickets for the lecture series were bought by speculators and sold for fabulous prices and that many persons were turned away. One writer described the published lectures as "the New Testament of the science of evolution, as Darwin's work was the Old."

Drummond would have agreed that the importance of his efforts lay not in the detail which make up the chapters tracing through nature the struggle for life (individualism) and the struggle for the life of others (altruism). It is well that specific detail should be rendered obsolete as new insights develop. What is essential is the recognition of the validity of the evolutionary insight which permits nature to be seen as the garment of God, His revelation and expression of His will. It is not to be supposed that Drummond's work was a facile reconciliation of the very real tensions facing those who were struggling to reconcile the apparent dichotomies between the traditional religious and the new scientific views. He knew the issues in both science and theology. One of his significant contributions was in making articulate the perplexities facing the thoughtful person of his day.

Drummond was very much aware that his was not the time for grand summations. He was cautious with regard to statements about the manner of development of the course of evolution. He doubted that it would ever be possible to determine whether the ascent of man took place in a continuous and uninterrupted rise or by steps abrupt and steep.

Drummond's concern was one which characterizes that of deeply discerning minds in every period: to re-late scientific and religious insights in a way which pays honor to them both. Not for Drummond was the practice of giving to religion the left-overs of science with the result that God becomes the symbol for what science has not yet been able to understand. For Drummond, "nature is God's writing and can only tell the truth," while evolution is God's method of creation. The immanent God of evolution "is infinitely grander than the occasional wonder-worker who is the God of an old theology." While readers today may properly take exception to certain aspects of both the science and the theology which Drummond used in his remarkable harmonizing of the two, no one can read *The Ascent of Man* without sensing the appealing enthusiasm and sincerity which were the result of Drummond's having actually achieved for himself the reconciliation of the mind and the heart about which he so eloquently spoke.

IN HIS STEPS

Author: Charles Monroe Sheldon (1857-1946)
Type of work: Novel, or social tract
First published: 1896

Principal Ideas Advanced

Since Jesus is truly an example for mankind, it is possible to follow in His steps but only if one is willing to follow Jesus in making the sacrifices that such a course of action may require.

The task of the Christian who wants to be obedient to Jesus in his present life is defined by the question "What would Jesus do?"

Charles Monroe Sheldon, a successful minister and author of many books, has accomplished what few men have: he has written a book which can truly be said to have helped change the world. It has been estimated that *In His Steps*, subtitled "What Would Jesus Do?" sold at least thirty million copies within the half-century following its original publication in 1896 and that it has been translated into at least twenty-one languages. Originally read chapter by chapter on Sunday evenings to the Christian Endeavor Society of the Central Congregational Church of Topeka, Kansas, and published simultaneously in serial form in the *Chicago Advance*, the book entered the public domain because of a defective copyright, a fact which may have contributed to its popularity among publishers.

In terms of its influence as a social tract, *In His Steps* has been ranked alongside such American classics as *Uncle Tom's Cabin*, and it has been described as having nearly brought on all by itself a national movement for social reform, despite such defects as its highly sentimental and romantic form.

The book is not a literary masterpiece, being neither particularly well-written nor profound in its characterizations. That it was written as a series of Sunday night readings accounts for a somewhat laborious repetition of themes since each episode had to be nearly complete in itself. *In His Steps* is a series of episodes strung together on its subtitle's theme "What Would Jesus Do?" There are too many subplots, many of which seem overly sentimental to modern readers, and many themes are introduced which are never adequately developed; hence it is not its literary perfection which accounts for the power of this book.

What does account for the book's influence is its call to a deepened conception of Christian discipleship. The book proclaims that there is something wrong about the fact that there are Christians who claim to follow Jesus without themselves sacrificing anything, who are able to enjoy all the good things of life, even profiting financially from social evils, without feeling that there is anything religiously wrong about their activities. *In His Steps* consists of a series of episodes involving people who, feeling this wrongness, renounce their ordinary ways, resolving to apply the example of Jesus to their own lives by walking in His steps, doing what Jesus would do were He in their place.

The hero, Henry Maxwell, a minister known for his polished sermons but for little else, is the pastor of the First Church of Raymond. Maxwell is an ordinarily decent man, warm-hearted and sincere, but with typically little social conscience, as is shown by his remark at one point in the book that this is the first time he has ever shaken the hand of a laboring man. The situation, then, is that of a quite ordinary Protestant church at the end of the nineteenth century, undistinguished in every respect. What causes it to become distinguished is the fact that some of its members undertake a radical adventure.

The crisis introducing the story is the appearance of an unemployed printer who raises in a dramatic way the question, "Do ordinary Christians really follow in His steps? Do Christians really apply their Christianity to the problems of society?" This man has lost his job because of the introduction of machines, and although he has looked long for other employment he has found none. His wife is now dead and his child is placed in another's home because of his poverty. Profound questions are raised as to whether our so-called "Christian" society is really what it pretends to be. Maxwell, shaken when the printer dies in his home, proposes to his congregation the following Sunday that they respond to the challenge in the following way: that for a period of one year they try to follow Jesus *completely* by doing what Jesus would do were He they. The story then recounts what happens during the course of that year to a few of those who volunteer to walk in His steps.

Not all sweetness and light ensues, for what Sheldon offers are tales of sacrifices which really hurt. The lovely church soloist Rachel Winslow, refusing an opera career, decides to devote her talents to bringing musical enrichment to the lives of the poor. A railroad superintendent responds by leaving his excellent job, thus alienating his family, because he discovers his company in wrong-doing. A bishop and a prominent minister in Chicago, influenced by Maxwell, leave their prosperous positions to open a settlement house. An heiress and her brother, both socially useless, find meaning in sacrificing their wealth to better conditions among both poor and rich. In most of these cases, families are broken up because there are members who protest these steps as extremist, impractical, and out of step with the requirements of modern social as well as religious life. In a deeper sense, however, there *is* peace and tranquility, as those who follow in His steps find former values fading and new values bestowing character and nobility upon their once rather useless but pleasant lives.

Many of the problems posed are unambiguous, easily solved in terms of simple moral action, such as: Should

a Christian rent space for a saloon? Should the college president and minister enter into the practical business of political reform, or should they remain aloof, isolated in their intellectual and spiritual interests respectively? Sheldon also shows at times a realistic wisdom about social and spiritual problems, realizing that they cannot all be disposed of by the exercise of will power. The movement to close the saloons fails. The editor in deciding to create a Christian newspaper is forced by his conscience to stop printing accounts of prize fights, to cancel liquor and tobacco advertising, to refuse to print family scandals, and to drop his Sunday edition—measures which cause his readership to dwindle. His appeal to fellow Christians to support his newspaper arouses some response, but the newspaper is delivered from its financial difficulties only by a large endowment given by an heiress who has joined the volunteers; hence it is never clear whether the author intends to say clearly that such ventures are economically feasible. Lastly, Maxwell's movement awakens some response outside his own congregation, but it does not silence all opposition, nor does it immediately lead to a renewal of the whole church, as might have been expected in a more simple-minded, completely sentimental book.

The novel, in other words, ends ambiguously. Henry Maxwell hoped that the movement would spread, that the knowledge of what is possible for those who fully follow in Jesus' steps would inspire Christians throughout the nation to take up similar work, but he also knew that the task was difficult and that resistance was great. One church, his own, had been radically changed; his community had been alerted to do battle for social betterment, and a few outsiders had been touched, but he had doubts as to whether his movement would ever spread beyond its present level of success, and even as to whether the progress made would in the long run be really significant.

About one form of success, however, the author is quite clear. Those who follow in His steps, carrying out their resolves to do what Jesus would do in their places, find meaning and joy in life. Several dramatic changes are briefly sketched, for example that of Rollin Page, society man, who is at first spurned by Rachel Winslow because he has no purpose in life, and is later converted at evangelistic meetings in the slums at which Rachel was singing. With a new sense of purpose for his own existence he sets to work redeeming his fellow club-men, becoming fully a man, and winning her admiration and love in the process. This is but one of a number of similar tales recounted in the book.

There are failures, also. Jaspar Chase, introduced as a young novelist whose love was also spurned by Miss Winslow, falls into unhappiness. In contrast to Rollin, who found life in following what Jesus would do, Jaspar is unable to carry out his pledge. Having finished a novel which is entertaining but socially useless, and knowing that Jesus would not have published it, Jaspar's will is not sufficient to his need. He falls into a pattern of cynical success. Similarly, in a wealthy family with two daughters divided, one daughter finds happiness and love in teaching cooking to the poor, while her sister, rejecting such a life, turns to security and a loveless marriage. Sheldon thus makes clear his conviction as to the seriousness of the choice between inconsequential worldly success and the deep joy that comes from serving God with all one's heart and strength by plunging into the fight for a Christian society which provides social justice for all.

The ethic displayed can be shown in terms of the following list which states "what Jesus would probably do in Milton Wright's place as a business man": He would engage in business primarily to glorify God rather than to make money; He would regard profits as a trust to be used for the good of humanity; His relations with His employees would be loving and helpful, with their interests, their well-being, the good of their Souls, taking precedence over the making of money; He would do nothing even questionable in His business dealings; and unselfishness would direct His business activities, shaping His relations to employees, customers, and to the general business world. This list fairly represents the type of reform that the author intended to inspire for his times.

The particular social adversaries are the saloon, tobacco, prize fights and billiard halls, slums and unemployment, but the major enemy seems really to be the complacency of churches. The book is primarily an effort to show Christians that to follow in Jesus' steps is to do what Jesus would do about social evils, regardless of personal cost. It is a book written by a Christian pastor for his congregation and Christian readers everywhere in which the author describes a path of active discipleship which could change the world.

Although the book tends toward an individualistic approach to social reform, there are more communal notes sounded at times. Stress is laid repeatedly upon the corporate life of the church as a source of strength and guidance. Weekly meetings of the volunteers help to guide and strengthen those who have undertaken this serious task, and there is a strong sense of mutual help and comfort. The power of the vote is emphasized as a means to social reform. Sheldon's own age was an age of crusades to change society by changing the individuals in it, and although he was a child of his times he sometimes took into account the need for more powerful means of social change.

Recognition of the fact that social conditions shape men and that to transform men one must transform their environments (the "Social Gospel") came relatively late to Christianity, and *In His Steps,* perhaps more than any other book, helped to popularize this insight. It was aimed both at problems created by indolence and wealth and at problems created by habitual vice and degradation. The indictment is primarily directed not at the struggling poor but at the indolent and unconcerned rich who sit in complacent comfort, deriving financial profit from the vices of modern life, yet think of themselves as walking in Jesus' steps. In the tradition of the great prophets, Sheldon challenges the consciences of those who "are at ease in Zion" (Amos 6:1).

THE CHRISTIAN PASTOR

Author: Washington Gladden (1836-1918)
Type of work: Pastoral theology
First published: 1898

PRINCIPAL IDEAS ADVANCED

The priestly conception of the Church as distinct from society must be replaced by the conception of society as an organism, with the Church as one of its parts.

The old distinctions between sacred and secular, clergy and laity, worship and work must be abandoned.

The pastor's office is that of teacher, leader, and friend to the whole community; his task is to preach the good news that God is organizing a divine society on earth, and to lead the people in social work.

The supernatural power of God's redeeming love works through nature; individual salvation consists in possessing a character harmonious with spiritual laws, but the individual cannot be saved except in relationship with society.

The Christian Pastor is one in the important series of volumes, by different authors, known as *The International Theological Library.* Gladden's book covers the subject of practical theology in all its aspects, but because a separate volume in the series is given to the subject of preaching, Gladden does not dwell at length on that topic.

The full title of the book, *The*

Christian Pastor and the Working Church, indicates the perspective within which Gladden approaches pastoral theology. One of the first advocates in this country of the "social gospel," and active in municipal affairs in Columbus, Ohio, where for thirty-six years he was pastor of a Congregational church, Gladden sought to awaken in his readers a sense of the Church's responsibility "to spiritualize the whole of life." "We have seen," he says, "that the new and higher conception of the church is that it is primarily a working body; that it is formed not mainly of those who seek to be fed and ministered unto, but of those who are working together to extend the Kingdom of God."

Although Gladden's own background was that provided by New England theology, he read widely in the literature of all communions. His book, indeed, abounds in lengthy quotations from such standard authors on pastoral theology as Horace Bushnell, Patrick Fairbairn, J. J. Van Oosterzee, and Alexandre Vinet. In spite of, or we might almost say because of, his conception of "the Working Church," Gladden produced a broad-gauged work which any pastor can read with profit. Many pastoral practices that were new in his day, such as the emphasis on pastoral counseling, have become accepted parts of the pastor's work two generations later. But they are nearly all dealt with in this book, and by one who had the advantage of being able to compare them with the different conceptions of the ministry that prevailed a hundred years ago. The book's chief limitations, from a practical standpoint, stem from the fact that it treats of the pastorate ex- clusively from the vantage point of the city church.

A main objective in Gladden's book is to break down the antitheses which have grown up in the Church owing to sacerdotalism. The priestly type of church quite deliberately insists on the distinction between sacred and secular, between the clergy and the laity, and between the Kingdom of God and the world. Even the reformed churches, which in principle have rejected most of these ideas, still follow them as a matter of habit. Gladden proposes that these distinctions be done away with. He insists that there must be no division between the Church and the community of which it is a part. The human community, he says, is an organism, with many specialized parts, of which the Church is one. But specialization of function does not mean separation of life. On the contrary, says Gladden, it is the function of the Church to sanctify every department of human life; and, if the Church fails, permitting the community about it to decay, then nothing can preserve the life of the Church.

From this conception of the Church's task, it follows that the minister must be no narrow churchman, but very much a man of the world. The notion that ordination sets him apart from other members of Christ's Church in any sense other than that he is to be their leader, teacher, and friend, Gladden rejects. Of the various names (priest, parson, pastor, minister) that are used to designate his office, Gladden prefers "minister," because, in its original intention, it signifies "one who serves."

What distinguishes the minister's activities from those of other leaders of the community is that all that he is able to do with and for men, as leader, organizer, and fellow worker, has a spiritual basis. Before all else, he is a spiritual teacher, who has the appointed task of awakening in men the desire to serve by means of the truth which it is given him to impart. This truth is the Gospel of the Kingdom of God, the Good News "that God is organizing on earth a divine society; that the New Jerusalem, whose walls are salvation and whose gates are praise, is rising here upon sure foundations." Because it is his task to "discern this Kingdom, to recognize the silent forces which are building it, to interpret its legislation," the pastor must have time for study. But he will be less interested in prying into traditional problems of theology and apologetics than he will in informing himself concerning such subjects as economics and sociology. He has not, it is true, to become an expert in the technical aspects of these subjects, but because industrial and urban developments involve "human relations," he has an active interest in them.

In a chapter entitled "The Pastor as Friend," Gladden says that the minister ought to be one of the most widely acquainted men in a community. Businessmen, teachers, professional men, workers, and school children should recognize him on the street and greet him as a friend. Gladden wishes to be rid of the old image of a parson as a kind of religious functionary, whose visit demands a special decorum, spiritual conversation, and official benedictions. Even when calling upon the sick, he should go simply as a friend, and he should offer prayer only when he is sure that the patient desires it. As a city pastor, Gladden recognized that more and more the pastoral call was being replaced by the demand for personal counseling. "The pastor offers less of personal service because the sacerdotal character of the minister is fading out, and the brotherly character is more strongly accentuated." This was written, however, before the day of the amateur psychologist, and the best thing that Gladden knew for a pastor to say in cases of marital difficulty is: "You two must live together. . . . Separation is not to be thought of. . . . The problem for each of you is to win and compel the respect, the affection, of the other. You can do it if you try. You had better die than fail. Go home and begin today." Such words, he testifies, have saved many a household, and thereby prevented children from growing up homeless.

Just as the sacred is not to be separated from the secular, so the worship of the Church is not to be set over against its work. In worship, as in work, the pastor is one with his congregation; they are priests together before God. Nothing is more fruitful of misapprehension than the supposition that those who sit in the pews form an audience, which has come to hear the preacher and to enjoy the choir. Gladden expresses approval of liturgical forms so far as these help involve the congregation in the service; he regards the choir as existing primarily to lead the congregation in singing the hymns, and he states his opposition to any kind of music which tends to draw attention to the performer and which interferes with the worship of God.

But the Church, as Gladden sees it, exists not merely for worship, but also for work; and he adds that the latter is in no way secondary to the former. In discussing "institutional churches," which were just then coming into prominence, Gladden deplores the tendency on the part of some, even those kindly disposed to the innovation, to speak apologetically of reading-rooms and bowling alleys, as if they were secular additions. "They are not merely means of getting people under religious influences," he says; "they are means of grace, every one of them —helps to a godly life—just as truly as is the prayer meeting itself." Gladden wants these things to be kept in mind when new churches are built. The churchbuilding should be adapted to "the newer conception of the church as a working body," and it should have provisions for class rooms, social rooms, committee rooms, and any special accommodations the particular church's work requires.

Gladden claims that the most important meeting in the church year is the congregational meeting, at which reports from the various organizations are received. In a working church, the organizations are central. Gladden deals with these in appreciative detail, giving separate chapters to the Sunday School, mid-week service, committees, social gatherings, women's work, and youth groups. When a person joins the Church, he should do so with the understanding that he is to take on some responsibility. Gladden was not interested in activity for its own sake. He refers to the familiar complaint of the minister in a growing community of thousands who need to be reached. The minister's first thought, he says, quoting Dean Gott, is that to reach those thousands is impossible; his second thought is, "Through Christ I can do all things"; his third thought is that he can secure help through organization. "Into this teeming multitude,

ever coming and going, diffuse yourself that you may concentrate yourself through an army of church-workers, and unite them with your parishioners and yourself in Christ."

Gladden was not unmindful of the importance of pressing home the message of salvation to individual souls, but he construed redemption and regeneration in terms of character building. There are multitudes, he writes, for whom no salvation is possible, unless they completely reverse the whole course of their lives; it is the preacher's mission to bring about this change, wherever possible. The older theology, says Gladden, distinguished between preaching law and preaching grace, but this distinction no longer holds, because we now know that spiritual laws are natural laws, and that love is the foundation of law. The dogma of the "new birth" is no mere mystical extravagance, but a psychological fact. It occurs daily, both within and without the Church, most frequently under the mysterious workings of human love. Gladden had little sympathy with "revivals and revivalism"; he preferred the path marked out by Horace Bushnell in *Christian Nurture,* who, in the chapter entitled "The Out-Populating Power of the Christian Stock," argued that the Church need only "hold its own" to speedily gain possession of the world. Here, as elsewhere, Gladden appeals to the organic principle. Wholesome character can thrive only in a wholesome society.

Gladden advises ministers to accentuate the practical and the positive, and to leave speculation and doubt alone. "When a man begins to preach the Gospel the great underlying verities of the Kingdom of Heaven ought to be settled in his mind beyond questioning; it should not be necessary for him to keep convincing himself that they are true." The minister has as his fundamental postulate the existence of the spiritual realm. He believes that love and not law is at the heart of things, that God is a personal being who loves men and in fellowship with whom men find grace and strength in time of need, and that man is a free spirit who chooses his own destiny. When members of his congregation have difficulties with what they call "the supernatural," the minister will point out that what is supernatural is not *anti*-natural, and that there is no antecedent reason why there should not be a power active in our lives and in the world about us that we cannot understand. He will further point out that the only proof possible that there is a God is the practical test of living in fellowship with Him.

The spirit of Gladden's own ministry, and that of the ideal of *The Christian Pastor and the Working Church* is, perhaps, most perfectly expressed in Gladden's hymn, "O Master, let me walk with thee, in lowly paths of service free."

CHRISTIAN MYSTICISM

Author: William Ralph Inge (1860-1954)
Type of work: Apologetic theology
First published: 1899

PRINCIPAL IDEAS ADVANCED

The witness of Christian mysticism constitutes the strongest evidence for the truth of the Christian religion.

Christian mysticism, following in the path of St. John and St. Paul, is preserved from the pessimism and nihilism of Oriental mysticism.

There is a mysticism which experiences God in the external world and in sacramental acts, as well as a mysticism which finds Him within the human soul.

Although in the form of a brief history of the subject, Dean Inge's Bampton Lectures on Christian mysticism are in substance "a contribution to Christian apologetics." The author seeks to show that where men's minds are illuminated by the revelation of God in Christ, they have a saner, more profound "sense of the tremendous issues of life in the world wherein we move," and he argues that it is on this ground that Christianity must base its case. On the practical side, he maintains that a return to "the fundamentals of spiritual religion" is required if the theological and liturgical forms of the Church are to meet the needs of our times.

Mysticism, according to Dean Inge, is only one form of man's "consciousness of the *beyond*." What distinguishes it from other types of religious experience, as well as from art and philosophy, is its attempt to "realize" the *beyond* as present in the soul and in nature. In Christian mysticism, where it is true to its New Testament origins, reality is experienced in relation to the image of Christ; in Inge's view, it is this relationship to Christ which has kept Christian mysticism "sound and sober." St. John's teaching that Christ is the Eternal Logos manifest in the flesh has preserved in Christian mystics a due reverence for reason, on the one hand, and for nature and life on the other. Similarly, St. Paul's teaching that a man's "old nature" must be crucified with Christ before that man can rise to newness of life in Christ has made the Christian mystics aware of the supreme worth of human personality.

Historically, however, Western mysticism has suffered incursions from non-Christian sources. One of the worst blights, according to Inge, has been the influence of Indian Pan-nihilism, which infected the philosophy of Plotinus (c.204-c.270) and, even more directly, of Pseudo-Dionysius (c.500), whose works were authoritative for both Eastern Orthodoxy and medieval Catholicism. It was, Inge holds, an error in Plotinus' philosophy when he declared that "the One," which for him was the fount and origin of all things, is beyond distinction. Westerners, world-weary and frightened at the collapse of their own civilization, were too ready to adopt the pessimism of the East; moreover, the doctrine of nirvana received specious support from the deadly seductiveness of the "blank trance" to which Plotinus was subject. According to Inge, this aberration is not required by anything in Plotinus' philosophy, who had himself observed

that "he who tries to rise above reason falls outside it."

Inge has little affection for the Middle Ages. The "negative theology" which it learned from Pseudo-Dionysius was, he says, to blame for "nearly all that repels us in medieval religious life": hostility to civilization, contempt for the family, abuse of the body, and absorption in solitary contemplation. However, the mischief attributable to the negative theology must be measured against the vicious consequences of the Roman Church's emphasis on miracles as the basis of belief in God. The more superstitious and magical aspects of medieval religion may be considered simply as survivals from primitive animism, but the fact that they survived in a Christian atmosphere is only to be understood in view of the sharp distinction which Roman theology makes between natural and supernatural, between reason and grace. The distinction is first fully developed by Richard of St. Victor (d.1173), one of the greatest mystics in the Middle Ages, who, although conceding that reason is a useful guide for bringing the generality of men to God, maintained that the supernatural grace which the mystic receives is completely beyond reason. According to Inge, this distinction between the rational and the mystical is both unphilosophical and unscriptural; far from leading to a "truer and deeper view of the actual," it introduces into the lives of men a lawless and disturbing force which threatens every genuinely human interest.

The little-known English mystics of the fourteenth century, Walter Hilton (died 1396) and Julian of Norwich (c.1342-after 1413) finally shook off "the chains of Asiatic nihilism." Of the former, Inge writes, "It is, I think, gratifying to observe how our countryman strikes off the fetters of the time-honoured Dionysian tradition, the paralysing creed which blurs all distinctions, and the 'negative road' which leads to darkness and not light." John ("Meister") Eckhart (c.1260-c.1327) and his successors among the German mystics had, indeed, moved to identify the Divine Logos with the Father. But Inge finds "something wrong with a system which ends in obliterating the distinction between the Creator and His creatures." Julian is a welcome contrast: "I saw no difference," she writes, "between God and our substance, but, as it were, all God. And yet my understanding took, that our substance is *in* God—that is to say, that God is God, and our substance a creature in God."

So far, we have spoken only of those mystics who seek to realize God's presence within the soul. Those are no less mystics, according to Inge, who discover His presence in nature, which they take to be "a world of symbolism, a rich hieroglyphic book," where things visible half conceal and half reveal invisible mysteries. Ancient astrology, the Greek mystery religions, the Jewish cabbala were all expressions of nature-mysticism. Such mysticism has been abused as shamefully as the speculative kind, but in able and devout hands, it is no less fruitful. Among its more creditable exponents are Jakob Boehme (1575-1624), and William Law (1686-1761), who in his mature life was a follower of Boehme. Inge cites with commendation a passage in which Law denies that there is anything supernatural in the whole of Christianity. "All our redemption," says Law, "is only nature set right, or

made to be that which it ought to be." Law goes on to affirm that distinctions between right and wrong, truth and falsity, blessedness and misery are ultimate, and that nothing supernatural can change them. Inge does not limit the mysticism of nature to those who follow the path of prayer and mortification. The Cambridge Platonists of the seventeenth century, and several nineteenth century poets (notably, Wordsworth, Tennyson, Kingsley, and Browning) are eminent representatives of this order. Inge ventures to suggest that the task for the twentieth century is "to spiritualize science," which lags behind philosophy and the arts, and has not yet "found her God." He sees no reason why scientific workers who approach nature with the same earnestness and intensity which engage poetic and religious men should not be rewarded with a comparable revelation of God's wisdom and power.

According to Inge, the Christian sacraments are best understood in terms of the mysticism of nature. Although the plain man prefers to believe either that the sacraments are magical rites or that they are commemorative observances, the true view is that they are symbolic acts. For the mystic, the commonest acts of life are sacramental; that is, they enable us to realize our privileges as children of God. The sacraments of the Church are "divinely-ordered symbols, by which the Church, as an organic whole, and we as members of it, realize the highest and deepest of our spiritual privileges." It is, he believes, one of the assets of the Church of England that its teaching on this subject, as on many others, corrects the inadequacies of Romanism and Protestantism, neither of which by itself "possesses enough of the truth to satisfy the religious needs of the present day." In the mysticism of St. John and St. Paul, the Church of England possesses the "fresh springs" of spirituality by which it can retain its eternal youth.

Inge does not wish to maintain that mysticism is the whole of Christianity. The faith of the Church is grounded in historical events, and depends for its continued existence upon religious institutions. A "vague spirituality tempered by rationalism" would not carry men very far, but a proper appreciation of the Church's mystical heritage, Inge believes, leads to three conclusions that should "have a calming and reassuring influence upon those who, from whatever cause, are troubled with religious doubts."

First, there is the high degree of unanimity among those pre-eminent in saintliness that God is a spirit, that human spirits can hold fellowship with Him, that in Him they meet with perfect truth, beauty, and goodness, and that they "come to themselves" in proportion as they draw near to Him. This testimony cannot be set aside, any more than can the testimony of specialists in any other subject.

Second, although the mystical experience cannot guarantee the truth of historical events, such as are attested in Gospel history, still it must be the living experience of Christ which vests sacred events with their eternal meaning. To maintain that the truth revealed in Christ is the very truth of God is, says Inge, to make a statement which, strictly speaking, only God can make. All that we can intelligently mean by such a statement is that, when we read the Gospels, our spirit is persuaded that "here are the words of eternal life."

Third, mystical experience gives us the only satisfactory answer to our questions concerning man's ultimate destiny. That part of our life is bound up with the future of mankind upon earth, Inge gladly concedes, but man's spirit "beats against the bars of space and time," seeking its true home in "some higher sphere of existence." Only through the most inadequate symbols can we represent to ourselves what such a life would be, but the faith is "enthroned in the centre of our being . . . an earnest of a final victory over the grave."

PRACTICAL CHRISTIANITY

Author: Rufus Matthew Jones (1863-1948)
Type of work: Practical ethics
First published: 1899

Principal Ideas Advanced

What is vital in religion is not belief in certain doctrines, participation in certain formal rituals, or obedience to a moral code, but a direct, immediate, personal experience of God which floods the soul with peace, joy, and power, and leads to a new life of holiness and active love.

The heart of Christianity is its witness to a God of love who has manifested Himself among men in the perfect human-divine personality of Jesus Christ and who, as life-giving Spirit, works in the world to transform mankind into the Kingdom of God.

The only real internal proof of Christianity is the soul's immediate awareness of being drawn into a spiritual union with God, and the only real external test of the genuineness of Christian experience is a transformed moral life which overflows with love for the neighbor expressed in helpful deeds of practical service.

The Church is a spiritual organism whose mission is to proclaim the salvation available to men in Christ and to continue the practical ministry of aiding stricken humanity that Jesus began when he was on earth.

Undoubtedly, Rufus Jones is the most outstanding personality, religious leader, and writer the Society of Friends has produced in America during the last hundred years. Jones was the author of fifty-seven books. *Practical Christianity: Essays on the Practice of Religion* was the second book he wrote and the first one to set forth an interpretation of the Christian life. It provides excellent insight into the nature of the practical, experiential Christianity which he so well represented both in his personal life and in his many writings. His concern in this early book, as indicated by the title of his last book written nearly half a century later, is to present "a call to what is vital in religion." He magnifies the importance of the practical application of Christian teachings and of the actual doing of the will of God in human life. Constantly manifesting a disdain for abstract theory and mere talk about Christianity, Jones calls men to "practice the presence of God" in daily affairs and thus to find empirical validation of the claim of Christianity to be an authentic revelation of God. Throughout the pages of this book one encounters a deeply religious personality who has caught the spirit of the sect's tradition and who writes as one who knows at firsthand whereof he speaks as he defines practical Christianity and invites men to respond to its stirring challenge.

Rufus Jones was a mystic in his personal religion and a liberal in theology. The impact of modern knowledge convinced him that new ways of thinking about the Bible and religious authority were necessary, and thus he felt most at home with the exponents of theological liberalism. However, since, as a good Quaker, he stressed the authority of a direct, personal experience of God, he was convinced that no possible development in science, philosophy, or historical research could undermine the abiding essence of Christianity. With his faith grounded securely in the immediacy of experience, he could sincerely urge a free and open spirit before the facts in order that new truth for new situations might be forthcoming. One of his greatest fears was rigidity in belief and the freezing of traditions into hard and fast forms. The only test of orthodoxy, as he saw it, was the quality of man's moral and spiritual life, not the formal creed which he professed intellectually.

Mysticism meant for Jones essentially an unmediated personal awareness of the reality and goodness of God which fills the soul with peace, joy, and love and supplies life with new meaning and moral power. He put the emphasis on the practical, ethical, and social aspects of religious experience rather than on quietistic states of private ecstasy. The Christian life consists of a vital, personal encounter with God in the depths of the inner life, and the Christian spirit manifests itself in the doing of the divine will in the everyday world of people and events. The genius of Christianity is its power to draw men into intimate fellowship with a God of love revealed in the perfect human-divine life of Jesus Christ and to send them out into the world filled with the envigorating Spirit to do battle for a Kingdom of God in which all men will live as brothers. Jones, then, espoused a Christ-centered, ethical mysticism which stressed the practical results of religion in the struggle for human betterment. His was a robust, activistic, optimistic faith centered in a God who works ceaselessly among men to bring them into spiritual union with Himself and to make His Kingdom a reality here and now.

The second edtion of *Practical Christianity* (1905) contains a collection of sixty-six short chapters, the great majority of which are about three pages long. Most of these essays had appeared previously as editorials and are here put together in no apparent order. Various topics ranging from Christian recreation and diversion to the doctrine of the Trinity are dealt with in independent chapters, and no

common theme is pursued from one to another. Most of the chapters, however, deal with some aspect of the Christian life. Jones's focus of attention seldom gets away from the practical side of Christian belief, and even when he does occasionally venture to discuss topics such as the Trinity, the Incarnation, or the atonement, he attempts to relate this to the concrete experience of the believer.

Central to any interpretation of Christianity is an understanding of the being and nature of God. Using, with very few exceptions, the ordinary language of the man on the street, Jones states the Christian view of God in practical terms. However, he does dare in a few instances to provide some insight into the meaning of the trinitarian doctrine. God is the Father in Heaven whose inner essence is love. Since love implies a beloved object, God has from eternity generated the Son, who is the express image of His person. This is the Logos, the self-revealing aspect of God. Yet, the Father and the Son, along with the Holy Spirit, are one in the same way that a ray of light exists in indivisible unity though it appears to us as light, color, and energy. This brief and tentative hint as to what the Trinity means is the closest that Jones ever comes in this book to an approach which borders on theological speculation. Since God could not disclose Himself to human beings in any other way, He manifested Himself in person at a particular point in time in the life of Jesus Christ, who is both a perfect man and a partaker of the divine nature. The Incarnation is a mystery beyond comprehension and must not be made into a metaphysical puzzle. However, if human minds could be sufficiently enlightened, it would become apparent that humanity and divinity are not incompatible. The practical meaning of the doctrine is that God has come among men in person and in power to make them sons and eternal heirs of His Kingdom. In confrontation with Christ men come to know who God is and what they are and may become in fellowship with God in Christ.

The Spirit of God is working constantly among men, Jones writes; the Spirit floods into life, drawing persons into spiritual union with Christ and remaking them into new creatures. The Christian is Spirit empowered. Religion is not a burden to be carried by human effort; religion is rather a matter of being lifted up to new heights of joy and moral achievement by a power that breaks into life from without and makes it over from within so that all things are seen in a new light, and love of others becomes the spontaneous expression of a Spirit-filled soul.

Salvation is not a judicial transaction whereby the guilt of inherited sin is removed from the soul thereby making it eligible for bliss beyond death. Instead, salvation is a matter of being transformed here and now so that life becomes patterned after the teachings and example of Jesus. To be saved is to live in direct, immediate fellowship with God and in organic unity with Christ through the power of the life-giving Spirit. Salvation means more than morality, for salvation involves a holy life and obedience to the will of God. Holiness in the Christian life means genuine emancipation from the power of sin, and the perfection of one's deepest motives. To be holy is to hate sin and to love the will of God

with such absoluteness that perfection of moral character becomes a reality here and now. The life of holiness is possible because of the intimacy of fellowship between the soul and Christ and because of the flow of the Spirit into the heart of the believer. The believer is organically related to Christ as the branches of a plant are related to the vine. In such union the aims and ideals of Christ are infused into the life of the Christian in such a way that the individual becomes an instrument of the divine purpose in the world. The believer's supreme motive is to serve his Savior by working diligently to relieve the burdens of the oppressed and to make the good life a reality for all.

The Christian life is incomplete without the communion of the soul with God in worship. To worship is to enjoy God in the intimacy of spiritual fellowship. The Friends way of gathering to sit in silence to listen to God is of inestimable value, but it needs to be supplemented by speaking and teaching on the part of those who, having listened, have heard a helpful word from God. The Sabbath should be set aside for such worship and the refreshing of body and spirit.

The Church is an organic community of individual believers who have been drawn into union with Christ through the Spirit. It is not an institution directed by a hierarchy which imposes dogmas and traditions by power and by might. It is a free fellowship of believers animated by the love and spirit of Christ. It exists to proclaim the power of God unto salvation and to invite men to receive new life by becoming a part of the Christian organism. Moreover, it is part of its mission to continue the ministry of practical aid to hurt humanity begun by Jesus himself. The Church should exert its influence to bring about such reform of society as will enable every person to attain his fullest possible development. The only test that can be applied to the Church is that of determining whether it does actually serve as an agency of proclamation of the Gospel and as a center of social action which improves the quality of life on earth.

The brief essays in this volume set forth a view of the practical meaning of Christianity as one outstanding Society of Friends leader sees it. In the longest chapter in the book Jones attempts to interpret the historical significance of the Society of Friends movement itself. Christianity began with the revelation of God in the divine-human person of Christ and with the offer of new life through the grace and power of God. The Friends movement emerged in seventeenth century England as a part of the great emancipation from the tyranny of an ecclesiastical institution which for centuries had smothered the dynamic Gospel of grace by restricting the approach to God to certain defined channels. The original message of the Friends was that salvation is a matter of a personal relationship between a man and God, that Christ brings new life to the soul, and that the witness of this is to be found in the immediate awareness of intimacy with God and in the actuality of a transformed life. Here was a call for firsthand religion based, as was modern philosophy, on the testimony of the immediate self-consciousness of the individual. The movement stressed freedom from external authority and tradition, experiential knowledge of God, the priesthood of all believers before God, and the reality of salvation in this life. The ultimate goal becomes perfected men living in a perfected society ruled by the pervading Spirit of God who draws men into organic union with Christ and into loving fellowship with the total community of believers.

Rufus Jones has presented in *Practical Christianity* an exposition of the message of the Quakers for the present age. The purpose of the sect as Jones sees it is identical with the purpose of this book, which, in his own words, is "not to develop or defend a theory, but to attract persons to a type of life—to set men actually to practising the presence of God."

WHAT IS CHRISTIANITY?

Author: Adolf Harnack (1851-1930)
Type of work: History of theology; liberal Continental theology
First published: 1900

PRINCIPAL IDEAS ADVANCED

The essence of Christianity is found in the Gospel proclaimed by Jesus Christ, the leading features of which were (1) the Kingdom of God and its coming,

(2) *God the Father and the infinite value of the human soul, and* (3) *the higher righteousness and the commandment of love.*

This sublime message, which received its personal realization and its impelling force from Jesus himself, ought not be obscured or perverted by speculative Christological theories about His person; the Gospel, as Jesus proclaimed it, has to do with the Father only and not with the Son.

The greatest transformation and corruption of the Gospel occurred during the early Patristic period, when, under the impact of Hellenism and the threat of Gnosticism, the Christian religion developed into Catholicism; Protestantism represents an attempt to reform the Church and its message according to the pristine Gospel.

Adolph Harnack, Professor of Church History at the University of Berlin from 1889 to 1921, was the most distinguished Patristic scholar of his generation. His *What Is Christianity?*, the book which resulted from a series of open lectures on *Das Wesen des Christentums* during the winter of 1899-1900, attracted an extraordinary response, and by 1927 it had appeared in fourteen editions and had been translated into fourteen languages. The amazing success of the work cannot be attributed simply to the author's immense erudition in the field of history of doctrine or to his ability to present the subject matter in a lucid and interesting fashion. Rather, the book stands as a classic expression of the so-called "liberal" Continental theology, which was deeply rooted in the thought of an earlier German Protestant theologian, Albrecht Ritschl (1822-1889). As an expression of liberal theology, the book aroused bitter opposition as well as eloquent praise.

Harnack's purpose was to answer the pressing question: What is Christianity? His interest was that neither of the apologist nor of the religious philosopher, but of the historian. The materials for his investigation are at once simple and exhaustive: Jesus Christ and His Gospel. However, the focus is not limited to the New Testament period alone, but extends to the differing historical forms assumed by the Gospel during the course of history. Harnack's intention was to discover the permanently valid truth inherent in the Gospel, regardless of the historical form. He of course realized the limitation faced in any such inquiry; namely, the fact that in history absolute judgments are impossible.

The author's first task is to distinguish the leading features of Jesus' own message as set forth in the four Gospels in the New Testament. What is the "Gospel" according to the Gospels? Harnack concedes that the Gospels offer no biography of Jesus, but he believes that they do supply reliable information concerning Jesus' teaching, how His life issued in the service of His vocation, and the impression He made upon His disciples. His teaching, which is really the heart of the matter, can be summed up under three headings, each of which actually contains the whole: (1) the Kingdom of God and its coming, (2) God the Father and the infinite value of the human soul, and (3) the higher righteousness and the commandment of love.

Harnack recognizes that there are two different views of the Kingdom of

God in the Gospels: the external rule of God that is anticipated as a purely future event, and the internal rule of God that is already present. It is Harnack's opinion that Jesus rejected the former, traditional view and proclaimed the latter: the Kingdom that comes to the individual, the rule of God in the heart. As such, declares the author, "it is God himself in his power," which means that the Kingdom is a gift from above that confers a purely religious blessing and is the most important experience a man can have. One's whole existence becomes permeated and dominated by the living God through this inner link.

Another way in which Jesus expresses this truth is by His declaration that God is the Father of all mankind, and that, as the Father, He is infinitely concerned for His children. Every human soul is precious to God. Indeed, declares Jesus, the very hairs of one's head are numbered! Since God is the Father, then all His children are brothers; consequently, Jesus taught men to live the humble life of brotherly love. Ethics in the Kingdom involves far more than attention to external religious forms and technical observance; what is demanded is a "higher righteousness" that stems from man's inmost disposition and intention, the inner motive of love.

Having defined the main elements of the Gospel as Jesus declared it, Harnack next examines certain problems related to that Gospel. Concerning the relation of the Gospel to the world, he argues that world-shunning asceticism has absolutely no place in the Gospel; Jesus teaches that His disciples should live in the world but struggle against three great enemies: mammon, care, and selfishness. What Jesus demands is not ascetic withdrawal, but the self-denying and self-sacrificing love that serves the world. In regard to the social question, or the relation of the Gospel and the poor, Harnack eschews both the view of Jesus as the great social reformer and the view that He had little or no interest in social and economic conditions. Harnack contends that the Gospel is a powerful social message, proclaiming solidarity and brotherliness in favor of the poor, but this message is bound up with what Jesus said about the Kingdom of God and the infinite value of the human soul. It contains no law bidding us forcibly to alter the conditions of the age in which we happen to be living.

How is the Gospel related to the law? Here Harnack reminds us that the Gospel is fundamentally above mundane questions, such as the question of public order, since the Gospel is concerned primarily with the souls of men. Nevertheless, the Gospel is not unrelated to constituted authority and legal ordinance. Jesus did not disparage the law, but He did insist that everyone has certain rights and that His disciples should share in the administering of God's justice. However, the basis for this administering is to be, not force, but free obedience to the good; not legal constraint, but the ministry of love. Harnack claims that the attitude of Jesus toward work, and questions of civilization, is basically the same. While labor and the progress of civilization are precious and worthy of great effort, they do not comprise the highest ideal; namely, the Kingdom of love. We live, not in so far as we work, but in so far as we love and are loved.

Professor Harnack's final pair of questions are the most controversial:

the questions of Christology and of creed. In regard to the first, he contends that what is important is not some doctrine about Jesus' person and dignity, but Jesus' message. Harnack's central claim is this: "The Gospel, as Jesus proclaimed it, has to do with the Father only and not with the Son." However, this circumstance does not mean that Jesus is a merely incidental factor in connection with the Gospel. On the contrary, He was its personal realization and its strength. Nevertheless, His message is the touchstone, a living force that has become efficacious and of critical importance for all time, and it should never be confused with a creed or a system of doctrine or a philosophy of the universe. To place a "Christological" creed before the Gospel, declares Harnack, is to reverse the order of values. No man can think rightly about Christ until he has begun to live according to Christ's Gospel.

The second half of the book is an inquiry into "The Gospel in History." What happens to the Gospel when the Christian religion (which for Harnack means one thing only: "Eternal life in the midst of time, by the strength and under the eyes of God") enters the course of history? The author's investigation begins with the Christianity of the Apostolic Age, traces the development into Catholicism, delineates the characteristics and achievements of the Greek Catholicism of the East and the Roman Catholicism of the West, and ends with a discussion of Protestantism.

Christian religion in the Apostolic Age was characterized, first, by the recognition of Jesus as the living Lord, whose sacrificial death for sinners put an end to all blood-sacrifices and made an atonement that shames and purifies us, and whose resurrection and ascension to the right hand of the Father brings to mankind the certainty of eternal life in and beyond time, and establishes faith in the value of personal life. Second, religion for the members of the new community was an actual experience involving the consciousness of a living union with God through the gift of the Spirit. Finally, the members led a holy life in purity and brotherly fellowship, and in the expectation of Christ's return in the near future. They were mistaken in this expectation, of course, but it nevertheless proved efficacious in lifting them above the world and in helping them to distinguish between what is of time and what is of eternity.

It was also during the Apostolic Age that the Apostle Paul delivered the Christian religion from Judaism. Conceiving the Gospel as the message of effected redemption and present salvation that abolished the religion of the Law and pertained to all individuals, Paul gave the Gospel a new language intelligible to all men, transformed it into a universal religion, and laid the groundwork for the Church. Although Paul did not violate the inner and essential features of the Gospel, his modifications in the realm of ecclesiology, Christology, and Scripture were, according to Harnack, not altogether salutary.

One of the main contentions of the author is that the greatest transformation of the Christian religion took place in the second century, when it developed into Catholicism. With the waning of the original enthusiasm, a religion of law and form arose; with the influx of Hellenism and the union of the Greek spirit with the Gospel, faith was intellectualized as doctrine; in its struggle against Gnosticism, the supreme illustration of the Hellenization of the Christian faith, the Church put its teaching, worship, and discipline into fixed forms and ordinances, and excluded everyone who would not yield them obedience. Thus the Church itself obtained an independent value as an institution and became a religious power.

Greek Catholicism, argues Harnack, is little more than a continuation of Greek natural religion: a Greek product in Christian dress rather than a Christian product in Greek dress. Its characteristic traditionalism, intellectualism, and ritualism have little to do with the Gospel; only its monasticism preserves a Christian element in the Church. The Roman Church of the West shares with the Eastern Church these corrupt features of Catholicism, but it has also been profoundly affected by the Latin spirit and the Roman world empire, on the one hand, and the spirit and religious fervor of St. Augustine (354-430), on the other. The latter proved to be an inward resuscitation of Pauline experience and doctrines, but the former turned salvation into a form of contract under definite conditions, revelation into law, and the Church into a legal institution claiming divine dignity. Although the internal and external elements in this *"complexio oppositorum"* continue to struggle for union, Harnack's judgment is that the inward influence of Augustinianism is overwhelmed by the institutional Church, with its exercise of governmental power under an infallible Pope. In this form, he asserts, Roman Catholicism is simply the transformed continuation of the Roman world empire and, as such, is a total perversion of the Gospel.

Protestantism is to be understood as a reformation in regard to the doctrine of salvation and as a revolution in regard to the Church, its authority and apparatus. Here religion is freed of alien accretions and critically reduced to its essential features: the Word of God and faith. The Church is divested of its priestly system, external authority, sacramentalism, ritualism, and double morality, and becomes again a spiritual community of faith, a universal priesthood constrained only by the Gospel. The Reformation had its bad features, however, especially in the Church's affiliation with the State and in the onesided emphasis on faith to the exclusion of "good works." During the post-Reformation period a Biblical scholasticism and doctrinal orthodoxy further weakened the force of the Reformation. Harnack ends the book with a plea that the Protestant Churches grasp again the Christian religion of the Reformation: the Gospel in its simplicity and purity. He argues that theology alone will not avail; firmness of Christian character will also be required. But his attitude is optimistic, like that of other liberal theologians of his day, and he ends by affirming "the forces and the standards which on the summits of our inner life shine out as our highest good."

THE PHILOSOPHY OF RELIGION

Author: Harald Höffding (1843-1931)
Type of work: Philosophy of religion
First published: 1901

PRINCIPAL IDEAS ADVANCED

That which expresses the innermost tendency of all religions is the axiom of the conservation of value.

In its golden ages a religion provides its adherents with a comprehensive explanation of existence, but as religion develops it meets challenges which force it to relate to competing value systems and to reassess its own nature.

Essentially, religion is concerned with the valuation rather than with the comprehension of existence.

The criterion for judging religion lies in the ethical sphere: What effect does the religion have on the conduct of the believer?

Neither religion nor science can solve the riddles of existence, but both must proceed vigorously with their critical tasks.

The *Philosophy of Religion*, by the Danish professor Harald Höffding, has earned a permanent place in the scholarly world for its thoroughness in developing the idea of religion as the conservation of value. Höffding's work may be understood in the context of the discipline that is indicated by the title of his work: the philosophy of religion. This discipline employs the tools of critical analysis and evaluation upon the general subject of religion, without known bias to any particular form religion may take. Religion and its thought comprise the subject matter of the philosophy of religion as Höffding understands it.

The distinction between religion reflecting upon its own problems from its own presuppositions and religion as the object of critical and disinterested investigation is crucial in Höffding's understanding of the philosophy of religion. Only when other aspects of the spiritual life—science, art, moral and social life—begin to emancipate themselves and to claim free independent value does the religious problem in the sense used by philosophers of religion arise. In its great and classic periods of inception and organization, religion has either ignored these other areas or assessed them from its own point of view and its own standards. Only when these other aspects develop their own standards of judgment and value does the opportunity exist for the development of philosophy of religion. Spiritual discord is a pre-condition of the philosophy of religion. This book is addressed neither to the satisfied nor to the anxious, neither to those whose minds are made up, whether positively or negatively, regarding religion, nor to those who are afraid to think about religion. Höffding's work is addressed rather to the seekers after truth.

Höffding's work is an example of that type of scholarly ideal which essays objectivity by renouncing any ready-made philosophical system as the point of departure for the investigation of religion. Acknowledging that internal harmony and consistency are the signs of truth within all spheres, he accepts them for his discipline. His goal, however, is not to bring religion into relation with an already concluded philosophical scheme, but rather to illuminate and elucidate the relation of religion to the general spiritual life of which religion itself is a mode or form. The philosophy of religion has the goal of discovering the means by which religion can continue to deepen and enrich the spiritual life as it develops.

The three main divisions of Höffding's work follow from his interpretation of the history of religious ideas: the epistemological, the psychological, the ethical. In its golden ages religion supplies men with a comprehensive explanation of existence. But when an independent science arises, a new mode of explanation is available and some attempt at harmonization must be made. The attempt to discover the relationship of religion to science involves the consideration of the ways of knowing and of validating knowledge which each employs. This first phase of investigation is the epistemological phase.

If it turns out that religious ideas do not solve the riddles which science faces and, indeed, are made irrelevant by the success of science in its ever-increasing sphere, the question arises as to what significance religious ideas do actually possess. The investigation turns naturally to a consideration of what the ideas mean in the experience of the individual holding them. This phase of investigation is the psychological phase. If religious ideas lose their status as claims to knowledge, their value must lie elsewhere. Höffding

discovers their value to lie in the conviction that no value perishes out of the world. Religion in its innermost essence is concerned not with the comprehension but with the valuation of existence. "Religious ideas express the relation in which actual existence, as we know it, stands to that which, for us, invests life with its highest value."

The third phase of the investigation of religious ideas is the ethical phase; the question concerns the ethical significance of the belief in the conservation of value. What effect does the religious idea have upon human conduct? This question is fundamental for Höffding, for the ultimate criterion for judging religion must originate within the ethical sphere where spiritual accounts are finally balanced.

The "problem of religion" rises when faith and knowledge are distinguished from one another. Roman Catholicism does not make a rigid distinction here and thus recognizes no "problem" within the intellectual sphere. A distinction between faith and knowledge implies an interruption of the unity of the spiritual life. The question as to whether any compensating value may be ascribed for the presumed loss of unity indicates the centrality of the question of value for religion. The concern for value is not limited to the human world but extends also to the cosmological level. One has to ask about the relationship between man's highest values and the laws of existence. It does not matter for Höffding's thesis what values are being held and conserved, but that religion is the concern for values is axiomatic. Value is defined as "the property possessed by a thing either of conferring immediate satisfaction or serving as a means to procuring it."

Höffding describes two types of thinking present in human experience: the scientific and the religious. The task to which he sets himself is to investigate the presuppositions and forms which constitute the basis of each. Understanding involves reducing something hitherto unknown to the known. Kinds of understanding comes from identity, rationality, and causality. Scientific causality seeks to relate causes to a series of effects; the longer and more continuous the series, the better. Scientific work is a work of personality. Religious causality does not demand natural causation; its interest lies not in discovering an inner connection between events, but in regarding all events as expressions of one identical power. Though there are thus basic differences in the "explanations" of science and religion, they may meet and unite if their origin in personal experience and their differences in intention are kept in mind. Höffding, a neo-Kantian who was obligated to Kant for the distinction between explanation and evaluation, was well versed in science as well as in religion; he felt it improbable that science and religion would be able in the long run to develop independently of each other, though he was not optimistic about their relationships in the near future. In his opinion, the empirical sciences have not fostered the habit of mind which would make co-operation with religion easy, and religion has been centered on traditional concepts which fail to meet the newer spiritual needs.

In response to the traditional cosmological argument for God as the first cause which is not itself an effect of any antecedent cause, Höffding accepts and extends Kant's criticisms. It is not possible to reason from finite effects to infinite causes. Höffding's theory of knowledge forces him to reject the notion of creation in any sense in which creation is used in scientific thought. The inexhaustibility of experience makes it impossible to arrive at an objective conclusion to knowledge. In contrast to Kant, Höffding states that we have no right to reject the possibility that the inconclusiveness of experience and of knowledge may be attributable to the fact that being itself is not complete but, rather, continually developing. An absolute conclusion to knowledge would involve the annulling of the distinction between knowing and being, subject and object, but it is precisely this distinction which is the condition of all knowledge.

The failure of thought, be it scientific or religious, to reach absolute objectivity does not cause Höffding to despair: "To cease thinking is not the same as to begin understanding." He accepts the analogical method as providing the only auxiliary available, though it is not without considerable problems itself. Science, psychology, religion—all use analogy in the attempt to understand experience, and yet it is clear that at a critical point all analogies fail when an attempt is made to move from the finite to the infinite.

The failure of analogy is especially clear in the arguments as to the personality of God. If the term *personality* is used to describe God, either it is used in a sense quite different from its ordinary use, or else God is necessarily limited in ways which traditional religion finds difficult to accept. It is important to note that Höffding does not move from an acceptance of the impossibility of absolutely objective knowl-

THE PHILOSOPHY OF RELIGION   831

edge to the conclusion that the "unknowable" is entirely different from everything that appears in experience. There is no foundation for this belief, he asserts; on the contrary, there must be some connection between the ground of being and the experience of men who possess being. The very fact of our thinking forms part of existence and must be accounted for in any conclusion. Religious thought is tasked with acknowledging its inherent limitations while proceeding vigorously with critical reflection upon the relation of the part and the whole. This is the task of what Höffding calls "Critical Monism." The function of religious ideas is not to explain special events or to afford conclusions for scientific thought, but to serve as symbolic expressions for the feelings and aspirations of men in the struggle for existence.

Having dealt with the epistemological significance of religious ideas, the book moves to an examination of the actual constitution and origin of religious ideas regardless of their use or validity. The central portion of the work deals with the psychological study of religious experience, religious faith, the development of religious ideas, dogmas, and symbols, the axiom of the conservation of value, and the principle of personality.

In the distinctly religious states of consciousness the quest for knowledge is less dominant than the desire to express and to react, to symbolize. Religious experience ought to be given encouragement and freedom of expression in view of the fact that no conclusion is to be reached. The religious feeling is that which is determined by concern for the fate of values in the struggle for existence. Religious faith involves the struggle to hold fast to the relation between reality and value. Conservation of values is faith's object, and the existence of faith is itself a witness to the axiomatic nature of the concern for conservation of values. The concept of God may be understood as the principle of the conservation of value in reality, and it is the fundamental predicate of all religious judgments and quests.

Höffding concludes the central section of his work with an extensive discussion of the principle of personality, which he terms a necessity within the religious sphere. Since personality invests all other things with value, as centers of value personalities must possess independent and immediate value as ends themselves. No absolutes must be permitted to exercise dominance over personality and its freedom: "It is homogeneity and schematism, not differences and peculiarities which have to justify themselves." The distinctive movement in religion is to personality rather than to dogma, Höffding insists, and Protestantism is the illustration of this truth.

Concluding with an investigation into the relationship between ethics and religion, Höffding shows that it is religion which is based upon ethical ideas. As men discover ethical problems and develop ethical sensitivity, so their gods assume ethical characters. Man's gods grow with him and are symbols of his highest values. The transition from nature religion to ethical religion is the most significant in the history of religion. Mature religious insight assumes an independent human ethic. The "other world" is always derived from this world.

It is not surprising that with this critical emphasis on the human dimension of religion Höffding should arrive at an agnostic attitude toward traditional dogmas and a negative opinion of much popular religion. Where once religion was the pillar of fire showing the way for the human race, it now too often assumes the role of "the ambulance which follows in the rear and picks up the exhausted and wounded." Even though religion cannot solve the great riddles of life any more than can science, it is no less significant, for it is concerned with the "inner experience of the relation between values and reality in conjunction with the need for an emotional and imaginative expression of the content of this experi-ence." It is to the cultivation of this dimension that the Church is called. Each man is tasked to make of his life a work of art, and religion, as faith in the preservation of values, and ethics, as discovery of the principles accord-ing to which the discovery and pro-duction of values occurs, are two of tools for realizing the art of life. "To live eternal life in the midst of time, that is the true immortality, whether or not there is any other immortality," writes Höffding. He concludes by stressing the point that the idea of the continuity of all forces and values is that toward which each religious move-ment strives.

THE GOSPEL AND THE CHURCH

Author: Alfred Loisy (1857-1940)
Type of work: Biblical criticism; apologetics
First published: 1902

PRINCIPAL IDEAS ADVANCED

If Christianity is to meet the intellectual challenge of our times, it must take its stand on the developed Christianity of the Church.

Harnack's attempt to recover the "essence of Christianity" by stripping away historical accretions is mistaken.

The original Gospel was not an ethical doctrine concerning the nature of God and man, but the proclamation of the approaching Kingdom of God.

The organization, creed, and worship of the Church developed naturally from the Gospel as it found a place in the Hellenistic world.

Only through the means provided by the living Church can modern man enter into relation with Christ and with the Father.

Alfred Loisy was a French Roman Catholic priest and Biblical scholar whose modernism led to his excommu-nication in 1908. *The Gospel and the Church,* which was written in reply to Adolf Harnack's *What is Christianity?* (1900), is an attempt on the part of a progressive Catholic theologian to meet the "great religious crisis" which, Loisy says, Christianity faces as a result of modern developments in the politi-cal, intellectual, and economic realms.

Loisy argues that it is a mistake for the Church to try to meet the crisis by a minimizing apologetic, like that of Harnack, which reduces the Gospel to a single principle, more ethical than religious. Instead, one should take his stand on Christianity as we know it and show "how necessary and useful is the immense development accomplished in the Church" to adapt the primitive Gospel to the needs of men in widely different historical circumstances.

Many of the criticisms which Loisy directs against Harnack's book will be supported by modern Protestant scholars, whether liberal or conservative. Loisy charges the German scholar with confusing theology and history when Harnack tries to maintain that the essence of Jesus' teaching is the proclamation that God is a merciful Father to mankind. Warning that "the historian must resist the temptation to modernize" the Gospel, Loisy says, "It is his own religion, not that of the gospel, which Herr Harnack expounds and defends when he announces that 'God and the soul, the soul and its God, are the whole contents of the gospel.'" If there is to be a historical reconstruction of early Christianity, says Loisy, it must proceed without doctrinal commitments. The scholar must not assume at the beginning that what he himself regards as the true religious system will be found in its pristine form on the lips of Jesus.

Harnack's distinction between the "kernel and the husk" seems to Loisy an unfortunate metaphor. It suggests that the Gospel is a fruit, a kind of metaphysical essence, which can be abstracted from the concrete experience of men. Moreover, in identifying the kernel with what is "personal," and the

husk with what is "traditional" in the teaching of Jesus, Harnack adheres too closely to outmoded rationalistic conceptions of human nature, as if the individual were independent of society and the soul unaffected by the needs of the body.

Loisy maintains that it is more in accord with the historical outlook to think of the Gospel as a seed than to think of it as a fruit. It is not by peeling away the supposed accretions that surround the Gospel that we shall come to understand Christianity, but by observing its origins, its characteristics, and its developments. "Let us regard the Christian religion in its life, observing by what means it has lived from the beginning and is still sustained; let us note the principal features of this venerable existence, convinced that they lose nothing in reality or importance, because today they are presented to us under colours that are not those of a former time." This means, according to Loisy, that we must first see Christianity in its Jewish setting, and then trace its development as it moves into the ancient and into the modern world, always with a view to finding those features which are recognizable throughout the whole of its career.

Loisy inclines toward the interpretation of primitive Christianity later popularized by Albert Schweitzer, according to which the original Gospel was rooted in Jewish apocalyptic hopes, and consisted in the proclamation of the near approach of the Kingdom of God, together with Jesus' belief that He was the Messiah whose death and resurrection were essential to His future glorification and rule. So far from finding the center of the Gospel in eternal moral truths, Loisy says that the ethical teachings of Jesus and His attitude toward society (the family, wealth, the state) were inseparably bound up with his conviction that civilization was soon to be destroyed and that a new order, divinely constituted would take its place.

Loisy concedes that at this point rationalism and faith part company, and he concludes that rationalizing theologians, who, like Harnack, are disposed to see in Jesus a moral and spiritual teacher, are running counter to plain historical evidence. Harnack places Jesus higher than Socrates. But, says Loisy, on the basis of the record, Jesus cuts a pitiable figure alongside philosophy's greatest martyr. His piety cannot be disentangled from His dreams, and He "died the victim of error rather than the servant of the truth that was in Him." Such, at least, is the judgment at which clear headed rationalism must arrive.

Because it is a closed system, with its own presuppositions and logic, rationalism cannot be refuted by faith. But that, says Loisy, is poor grounds for confusing the point of view of reason with that of faith. Rationalism, religion will maintain, simply breaks down when it attempts to understand the great mysteries connected with "God and the providential destiny of man." These are disclosed only to faith, and they find their expression in symbolic representations. "The concrete symbol, the living image," says Loisy, "not the pure idea, is the normal expression of faith, and the condition of its moral efficacy in man and in the world." Seen in this way, the mission and the message of Jesus are signs not of folly but of wisdom of the highest order. Jesus went voluntarily to death in the confidence that He had chosen the way in which His destiny would be fulfilled. His

faith was rewarded in a way and to a degree that no philosophical historian can fail to recognize.

Because the Gospel was a living faith and not a metaphysical teaching, it must find expression in concrete, historical terms. Nothing, says Loisy, could make Jesus other than a Jew, or eliminate from His teaching fundamentally Judaistic modes of thought and expression. By the same kind of necessity, when the Gospel spread outside of the Jewish world, it took on many of the characteristics of its new environment. "The gospel will always need a body to be human," Loisy insists; and when, after a century and a half, we find that the followers of Christ constitute a tightly organized cult, with a priesthood, a law, a ritual, and a creed, we ought not to lament how much the Gospel has changed, but ask rather whether these developments were not inevitable if the Gospel was to achieve its purpose. We do not discover the essential character of a man, Loisy reminds us, by going back to the cradle.

Harnack gives a particularly unsympathetic picture of the development of the Roman Church, which, he says, became merely a political organization. Loisy protests that this is unfair, that the spiritual mission of the Church has always set it off from that of the empire or the state. The fact that the Church is organized along lines comparable to a state is another matter, and the question arises whether it makes any sense to talk about a human society which does not have the characteristics of an organization. Loisy charges Protestants with talking nonsense when they speak of the primitive Christians as forming a purely spiritual fellowship. He points out that Jesus set apart the twelve disciples and that the early churches took over the pattern of the synagogue. He further maintains that if the Church of the second century had not had strong and able administrators, it would almost certainly have been absorbed into the general religious milieu of the times. "Does it not follow," he asks, "that the Church is as necessary to the gospel as the gospel to the Church, and that the two are really one, as the group of believers were during the ministry of Jesus?" There is no point, says Loisy, in attempting to justify the forms which Christianity has taken by making an appeal to Jesus' own teachings or those of His immediate followers. One need only ask whether the Church through the centuries has stood for the "essential elements of the living gospel"; namely, the idea of a heavenly Kingdom, of a divine Messiah, and of a world-wide mission.

Loisy answers in a similar fashion Harnack's complaint that the Gospel has been turned into a dogma. While Loisy admits that the Gospel itself is not dogma, he finds it inevitable that, as men reflect upon their faith, dogma develops out of the Gospel and, henceforth, Gospel lives in dogma. Pauline theology, he says, was essential if Christianity was not to remain essentially Jewish; Johannine theology was essential if it was to make its way in the Hellenistic world. But Loisy denies that, when theologians began to state the faith in Greek terms, Christianity was changed into philosophy. Indeed, he denies that theology is a science in the true sense of the term, maintaining that "the logic of faith," dealing as it does with images, is incommensurate with the logic of science. Such developments as the trinitarian and Christological dogmas were part of an attempt to bridge the gap between the new religion and Greek ways of thought. "It was not erudite research that determined their character, but the instinct of faith in souls otherwise saturated with the Greek spirit."

Pure spirituality in worship, according to Loisy, is as unrealistic as fellowship without organization and Gospel without theology. Harnack has alleged that the kernel of the Gospel became so overlaid with rites, relics, images, and mysteries taken over from pagan religion that it soon appeared "not as a Christian creation with a Greek thread, but as a Greek creation with a Christian thread." But, says Loisy, if Christianity is to be a religion, and not a kind of "mystic philosophy," it must have particular liturgical forms. Loisy argues that the important question is not whether the forms are borrowed from pagan sources, but whether, in being taken over by the Church, the forms are taken into the life of the faith. All worship approaches the Creator through the image of the creature. But in pagan worship, says Loisy, the association of human features with divinity was detrimental to man's understanding of God, because it undermined the sense of God's transcendence. "Christianity," he says, "avoided this confusion, while satisfying, by the worship of Jesus and the sacraments coordinated therewith, that need of deification which seems inseparable from human nature. . . . It has been able to do so without falling into polytheism or man-worship, because it distinguishes, in the object of its adoration, the Eternal God and the human nature in which this God was manifested on earth."

Loisy does not deny that there are many things in the Roman Catholic

Church which stand in the way of modern man's acceptance of the Gospel. He is mainly concerned to argue for what he calls the principle of development within the faith. The Church, Christian dogma, and Christian worship are not deformations of the Gospel, but its natural product; and if, due to the changes in our times, certain traditional ways of thinking must be revised, then let them be revised. But, Loisy maintains, Christianity endures only by the force of its past, nor is there any way in which modern man can enter into communion with Christ and the Father except through the living Church.

Loisy was, undoubtedly, over-optimistic about the readiness of the Roman Church to accept change. (His book was immediately condemned by the Archbishop of Paris.) He maintained that even the conception of "ecclesiastical authority" needed to be further reflected on. In any case, he says, those who have followed the progress of Christianity from the beginning cannot doubt that change will continue to take place. Religious symbolism, by its very nature, is always inadequate, striving after perfection. The historian sees in the teachings of the Church an "interpretation of religious facts, acquired by a laborious effort" through many centuries; although their substance is divine, their structure and composition is human. "It is inconceivable," he says, "that their future should not correspond to their past. Reason never ceases to put questions to faith, and traditional formulas are submitted to a constant work of interpretation wherein 'the letter that killeth' is effectively controlled by 'the spirit that giveth life.' "

THE VARIETIES OF RELIGIOUS EXPERIENCE

Author: William James (1842-1910)
Type of work: Psychology of religion
First published: 1902

PRINCIPAL IDEAS ADVANCED

A working definition of religion sees it as "the feelings, acts, and experiences of individual men in their solitude, so far as they apprehend themselves to stand in relation to whatever they may consider the divine."

Temperament has much to do with the nature of religion, as the distinction between the optimistic and healthy-minded, and the pessimistic and sick-minded, indicates.

The mystical state is distinguished by the qualities of ineffability, illumination, transiency, and passivity; although mystical experience carries authority only for the mystic, it helps to break down the exclusive authority of rationalistic states.

The traditional metaphysical descriptions of God have no practical significance, but they are important as restatements of religious experience.

From the time of their delivery in 1901-1902 at the University of Edinburgh, James's Gifford Lectures, as collected in *The Varieties of Religious Experience*, have enjoyed both critical and popular acclaim. Scholars have found this pioneering work in the psychology of religion an inexhaustible source of insight and stimulation. Ordinary readers have enjoyed the direct conversational style and the interesting illustrations with which the book abounds.

William James studied physiology at Harvard, but he soon turned to psychology, which he proceeded to change from "mental philosophy" to a laboratory science. His restless mind led him from the laboratory to the study of religious experience and psychic phenomena. The subtitle of the work under consideration, "A Study in Human Nature," reveals the nature of his interest. The choice of first-person accounts of religious experience as sources for his study indicate James's consistency with his own experience-centered philosophy of pragmatism. Through twenty lectures it is personal experience which serves as source of observation and court of appeal.

James begins his lectures with a direct confrontation of current theories which interpreted religion "scientifically" on the basis of its alleged sexual and neurotic origins. Pointing out the fallacy of judging solely on the basis of origins, James insists that the real significance of religious experience is determined by its results. He scorns "medical materialism" which easily disposes of St. Paul's vision as the result of a lesion of the occipital cortex, while St. Teresa of Avila is viewed as a hysteric, St. Francis of Assisi as a hereditary degenerate, and George Fox as

simply sick. James argues that if organic conditioning be influential in religious emotion, so it must be in every other sphere including that of scientific theorizing. To single out religion for derision and rejection on this account would be illogical and arbitrary, and James declares that he would not tolerate such action in either science or religion.

A good part of the appeal of James's work is the result of his devotion to personal religion "pure and simple." He largely ignores institutional religion, systematic theology, and philosophy of religion. Cautioning that religion defies exact definition, he interprets "the divine" as "only such a primal reality as the individual feels impelled to respond to solemnly and gravely, and neither by a curse nor a jest." The experience-centered method leads to the conclusion that religion is not only vitally important but actually essential to human life in that it "makes easy and felicitous what in any case is necessary."

Characterizing religion in the most general of terms as belief in an unseen order, and the supreme good as the harmonious adjustment to that order, James examines the "psychological peculiarities" of the belief in the reality of the unseen. Brief references to Kantian and Platonic doctrines and to more personal anecdotes are used to support the thesis that psychological certitude is infinitely more significant in religion than is rationalistic certainty. Reasons are cogent in religion only when one's articulate feelings have already been impressed in favor of the conclusions to which reason leads. "The unreasoned and immediate assurance is the deep thing in us, the reasoned argument is but a surface exhibition," declares James. James intends neither to approve nor to disapprove dependence on feeling, but only to point out that the priority of feeling is a fact.

Since the kind of religion one has is thus determined more by temperament than by intellectual acceptance or rejection of various "proofs," James proceeds to make his famous delineation of two major temperamental types of religious outlook: the healthy-minded (tough-minded) and the sick-minded (tender-minded.) Seemingly unable to write a dull page, James affords the reader a rich diet of fact and opinion as he documents his contentions with vivid first-person accounts of religious experience. Responding to criticism that his work over-emphasizes the bizarre, James notes that his purpose is to emphasize the enormous diversities of the spiritual lives of men. He castigates as stupid those of the "deadly respectable" type who bar phenomena which they are incapable of experiencing themselves.

In his conclusions regarding the sick-minded in religion as opposed to the healthy-minded, James characteristically commends the latter as being splendid provided it works. It ceases to work, however, when inescapable melancholy comes. Thus optimistic healthy-mindedness is charged with inadequacy because the evils it refuses to account for are an integral part of reality. Often it is the evil in life which opens one's eyes to the deepest levels of truth. The universe is more complex than either healthy-minded optimism or sick-minded pessimism alone allows for. Since all verifications are simply experiences which agree with systems of ideas that men's minds have formed, it ill becomes anyone to insist that only one such system of ideas is true. No one view, be it religious or scientific, is exhaustive of reality's riches. Perhaps the method of alternating between various approaches depending upon the seeker's temperament and his goal is most desirable. The religion of the healthy-minded is the religion of the once-born, and a simple algebraic sum of pluses and minuses suffices for their religious accounting. The religion of the sick-minded is far more complex and mysterious. The most complete religion is one in which the pessimistic elements are best developed. Buddhism and Christianity as religions of deliverance in which the person dies to an unreal life before being born into real life—that is, is "twice-born"—are commended.

In their extreme forms healthy-minded religion is naturalism, and sick-minded religion is salvationism. Consideration of the latter leads to a consideration of the divided self and the experience of conversion. James interprets conversion as a normal adolescent phenomenon occurring as one passes from a small universe to the wider intellectual and spiritual life of maturity. Two types of conversion are distinguished: volitional and self-surrender. In response to the question as to whether conversion is a divine miracle or a natural process, James turns to the current field of consciousness theory which stresses the wide variety of individual differences in mental states. The nature of one's religious conversion will depend in large part upon the character of his field of consciousness. Whether or not one interprets the religious experience of conversion in orthodox terms, mere transcendency proves nothing about either the divine or the diabolic. Only the effect of an experience in the life of the individual can attest to its origin. The most significant fact about conversion is not its duration or even its type, but its effect upon the life of the person involved.

His emphasis upon the practical fruits of religious experience prompts James first to describe and then to evaluate the characteristics of saintliness, a state of being which he sees as involving conviction regarding the existence of an ideal power or God, a willing self-surrender to its control, a sense of elation and freedom, and a movement of the emotional center toward loving and harmonious expression. Practical consequences of saintliness are asceticism, strength of soul, purity, and charity. Genuine firsthand religious experience always appears to observers as possibly arising out of madness and as leading to heresy. Ecclesiasticism, which grows up about a primary experience, tends to stifle the spontaneous religious spirit, but the bigotries of organized religion are due less to religion than to its intellectual partner, the spirit of dogmatic dominion. The corruption of excess afflicts the fruits of religion as it does all other human products. James is hesitant to pronounce the saintly type as the "ideal" type for every man, for there are many functions to which men are called. But even though some saints lose their heads and thus become failures biologically, they may be successes in the sense of being leavens of religion and righteousness in the world. Testing religion by practical common sense and through the empirical method, James finds it soundly occupying its towering place in history.

It is not until the sixteenth and seventeenth lectures that James considers those mystical states of consciousness from which personal religious experience springs. He distinguishes the qualities of ineffability, illumination, transiency, and passivity within the mystical state. Following documentation of these characteristics, he observes that while mystic states carry authority for him who has them, they do not do so for anyone else. Since it is not possible to argue from psychic states, it is always necessary to subject positions based on the authority of such states to rigorous scrutiny. Often when psychological certitude is confused with epistemological or rational certainty, one is asked to accept the validity of a proposition solely upon the basis of another's psychic state. But even though one ought to be cautious of knowledge claims based on mystical experience he ought to be appreciative of the tendency of such experience to break down the exclusive authority of rationalistic systems which may overlook man's emotional dimensions. For James, feeling is primary in religion. Mysticism has more affinities with music than with conceptual speech, and in speaking of mysticism James demonstrates a degree of empathy quite remarkable in a scientific examination. He speaks of musical and mystical whispers which hover in the mind and mingle with the operations of our understanding "even as the waters of the infinite ocean send their waves to break among the pebbles that lie upon our shores."

Having found mysticism too private and variable to stand as universal authority for the claim of religion to be objectively true, James then investigates religion's claims from the standpoint of philosophy. Both philosophical and theological formulas are secondary products, whereas feeling is primary in religion. But philosophy's essential role is to redeem religion from the kind of mystery, paradox, and unwholesome privacy which detracts from its objective validity. Myth, superstition, dogma, creed, metaphysical speculation, party rivalry—all are spontaneously and inevitably engendered by religious experience, and all need the ministration of philosophical examination. James hopes that his work will contribute something to this "science of religion." Yet philosophy itself is scarcely a perfect tool, for it fails to banish differences, and it founds schools and sects just as feeling does. The philosopher finds arguments to fit his prior convictions just as the preacher does who writes his sermon and then searches for his text.

After briefly surveying other characteristics of religion, including aesthetic elements, sacrifice, confession, prayer, and the phenomena of automatisms, James concludes his lectures with a recapitulation of the major themes of his lectures. He expresses his dismay at the amount of emotionality which he finds in his manuscript, and he thus proposes to close with the practical question as to the dangers inherent in the religious element of life. Protesting that it should not be assumed that all men should have identical religions, he rejects the notion that modern science should develop a religious creed for all men. Scientific objects are abstractions, too, and only individualized experiences are concrete. Since religion deals with concrete personal experience, it is nearer to truth than those disciplines which deal with the cosmic and the general. A common nucleus of religion may be discerned, however, in the feeling of uneasiness about something wrong and in the desire to seek deliverance from the wrong through connection with higher powers.

Few persons read James without having been enriched through contact with a truly large mind and spirit, as revealed in his edifying, stimulating, and provocative essays.

CHRISTIAN THEOLOGY IN OUTLINE

Author: William Adams Brown (1865-1943)
Type of work: Liberal theology
First published: 1906

PRINCIPAL IDEAS ADVANCED

Revelation is continuous with reason, and the natural with the supernatural.

Jesus Christ reveals God in Christ's consciousness of divine Sonship, and in His embodiment of God's moral purpose, the Kingdom of God.

The world is adapted to the Christian end, and history is its progressive fulfillment.

Sin is selfishness, and it is overcome by the redemptive power of Christ in history and, ultimately, in eternity.

Christian Theology in Outline gives expression to the Ritschlian theology as modified by American optimism and social idealism. William Adams Brown pays tribute to a former teacher, Adolf Harnack (1851-1930), and to William Newton Clarke (1841-1912), as honored friends in whom systematic theology has reached its freest and clearest expression. But it is William Adams Brown's own capacity to clarify and organize ideas and to give them effectual expression that makes his *Christian Theology in Outline* a permanent point of reference for this form of Christian theology.

Following his own account of it, the theology may be characterized as modern, empirical, idealistic, and progressive. Great confidence is manifested in modern philosophy and science, in "our better psychology," and in the present progress of the Christian ideal in the world. Systematic theology is described as "the philosophy of the Christian life." Consistently with this position, no authority, ecclesiastical, creedal, or Biblical is recognized, although Scripture, the creeds, and traditional doctrines are freely used and interpreted to express the meanings of the new theology. It is a theology which accepts the historic Christian faith in God the Creator, in Christ the Incarnation of God, and in the salvation of man from sin, and translates this faith into terms of the Christian experience, or the consciousness of the Christian.

The place of the historic Jesus is central and primary in this theology. He is the Incarnation of God not in a metaphysical sense, but in His moral character and purpose and in His unclouded consciousness of Sonship to God. There is nothing miraculous or supernatural in the Incarnation. God is immanent in the world and in all men, in the noblest of whom we have the clue to His will and purpose; Jesus Christ is in this sense the supreme revelation of God.

While the Christian's knowledge of God comes to clarity and completeness in Christ, it is broadly based on the whole of human experience. No line can be drawn between reason and revelation, or between the natural and the supernatural. All things reveal God and give some knowledge of God. Both science and philosophy contribute to the idea of God which, however, reaches its ultimate expression in the historic person of Jesus Christ. Christian faith is really faith in the *idea* of God which is given its definitive form in Christ. It is based not on mystical experience or on speculative thought but on the practical needs and nature of man. The idea of God is also the Christian ideal, and belief is complete trust in it. Brown freely accepts the "moral value" interpretation of the idea of God. As will be seen, God is regarded by Brown as being objectively real, but He is the "unseen" reality who is manifested in the personality of Christ and in the religious consciousness of the Christian. Such revelation is possible because God is moral personality; He is a Christlike God.

While all speculative theology is rejected, Brown nevertheless recognizes the validity of the philosophical conception of the Absolute. God is beyond our comprehension as He is in Himself. The doctrine of the Trinity therefore is accepted; God is the Absolute, the ultimate source of all being and life; God is the self-revealing one, known to men through His revelation in nature, in history, and, above all, in Christ; God is the self-imparting one, known through experience in the consciousness of man. The conception of God thus formed through Christian experience, and, more generally, through the experience of the race is empirically verified "partly in the response which the idea meets in the individual consciousness, partly in its growing supremacy over the reason, the conscience and the religious feeling of the race."

The objective reality of the God so conceived is postulated or assumed as are the general assumptions of science or moral theory. God is creator of the world. Creation for the Christian is based primarily upon "experience of the new life in Christ, of which we are daily partakers through his Spirit." Brown claims that creation is best conceived intellectually, in accordance with scientific knowledge, "as a permanent process, expressing that continual relation between phenomena and their spiritual ground which is the form in which the idealistic philosophy conceives of the reality of the world." But the real meaning of creation for the Christian is in the end or purpose of God in creating the world. This end is generally defined as the Kingdom of God; more specifically, it is the "production of beings like the good God, and their union with himself in the fellowship of holy love." The spirit of the time and the whole outlook of Brown are revealed in this statement: "It is because the world as we know it to-day ministers to such a spiritual end that we believe it had its origin in the will of the holy and loving Father whom Christ reveals."

Jesus Christ is both the revealer of God and the redeemer of man. The core of the revelation is the eternal purpose of God which is the Kingdom of God, "the all-comprehending theological conception" of the Christian faith. Jesus revealed this purpose in His own life and character, and He established the Kingdom in history. The Kingdom of God is a society of men living by the ethic of love: this is God's "end." Therefore Christianity is a teleological religion, the perfect ethical religion, and all its meanings are to be determined by this basic conception. The religious form of the Kingdom of God is the consciousness of sonship to God, and its moral form is the life of love and service. The Kingdom is found in history as the progressive realization of the Christian ideal, and the Church is the divinely appointed means for its realization. The world itself is "adapted to the Christian end." This is frequently indicated by the term "the divinity of the world." The Kingdom of God is not, therefore, as with Ritschl, a supramundane reality, but an actual fellowship growing in history and destined to embrace all men. The power of this development finds its historic source in Jesus and in the influences that come from Him through the preaching of the Gospel and through the life and witness of the Christian community.

Christ is also redeemer. The great obstacle to progress of the Kingdom of God is sin, and sin is selfishness with all its by-products in the life of man. By His moral example, through the preaching of the Gospel and the influence of Christian fellowship, Christ calls men to repentance of their sins and to participation in the life of love, which is participation in the Kingdom. Such repentance is salvation. Sin is primarily an individual thing, but it is also a social fact and heritage. There is no such thing as an individual acting independently of social influences; his moral freedom must be understood in the light of his union with other persons, and also of the universal sovereignty of God. Brown rejects the "libertarian" doctrine and accepts the "determinist" view of man's moral development, which is realized only through union with other persons, and which takes place under divine law and control. The freedom which man enjoys in his spiritual life is freedom from the "blind" necessity of nature. But, Brown claims, "spiritual influences, as well as physical, are at God's disposal, and through the use of these he is certain to accomplish his end." Upon the basis of divine sovereignty so conceived, the progress of the Kingdom of God in history is assured, together with its ultimate triumph in the future life.

Implications of Brown's doctrine of divine sovereignty are carried out in several directions. Sin is not the arbitrary misuse of human freedom, for it is included in the purpose of God. Its role in the divine purpose is educational; the experience of sin and the conquest of it through Christ is a way to the highest and richest development of personality. The certainty of God's ultimate victory and the full realization of His Kingdom rob sin of any final power over human life.

Real freedom of choice, or self-transcendence, is rejected by Brown because it would mean a limitation on the power of God in the world. It is always a person who chooses, and a person is what he is in a social context. The idea also of a sheer act of will as such is incomprehensible. But the self-identification of the person which is re-vealed in choice is involved in sin, and this involves freedom. It is freedom, however, not of a momentary act, but of the total life of the person as exhibited in all his choices. In Brown's words, two things are affirmed in the light of this dilemma: (1) "In the secret places of the human spirit takes place the strange change by which the non-moral is transformed into the moral. . . . It is the mystery of all beginnings"; (2) Christ revealed sin "for the first time in its true nature as an offense against the loving Father who ever seeks the highest good of his children, and in whose love, supremely manifested in Christ, is found the ground for faith that sin shall finally be overcome."

The progressive realization of the Christian ideal in history is one of the proofs of the truth of the Christian religion. The Christian faith is destined eventually to win all men. This expectation is based both on the purpose of God and on the common nature and need of men. But so many influences obstruct the progress of the Kingdom in this world that complete victory will come only in the future life. In this victory the Cross of Christ has a decisive part to play. His suffering on the cross revealed His full fidelity to God, but it also showed that the way to moral victory is through suffering and sacrifice. And it is a revelation of the pain endured by the good God and loving Father because of the sin of men. It is the cost to God of His own forgiveness and of our reconciliation.

So essential to the perfection of moral personality and the realization of the Kingdom of God are the endurance of suffering and the conquest of sin that both suffering and sin will continue in the life to come. That life will not be static goodness, but a life of growth and progressive attainment. However, there remains as certain, Brown claims, the final consummation (I Cor. 15:28) "when Christ, his mediatorial work complete, shall surrender his authority to the Father that God may be all in all."

A MUCH ABUSED LETTER

Author: George Tyrrell (1861-1909)
Type of work: Christian apologetics; pastoral counseling
First published: 1906

PRINCIPAL IDEAS ADVANCED

One can be a good Christian without giving intellectual assent to the theology of the Church.

The Church "invisible" is not confined by the historical limits of Christianity; yet the Church "visible" is the highest expression of the divine purpose in history.

The life of the Church is a hidden, subconscious force, and is inadequately expressed in theology.

Faith is a kind of divine insight by which each man apprehends Unseen Reality.

The Catholic Church, if it is to continue to witness to Divine Reality, must abandon its reliance on authority and its claims to infallibility.

George Tyrrell went over from the Anglican to the Roman Church in 1879 and became a leading member of the Jesuit order. His counsel was much sought after by educated Catholics who found difficulty in reconciling the teachings of the Church with modern learning. For the help of one of these, a professor of anthropology, Tyrrell composed a long letter, in which he declared that one can be a good Christian—even a good Catholic—without giving intellectual assent to the theology of the Church. Because the kind of problem raised by the anthropologist was one which he met often, he reproduced the letter for private circulation. Contrary to his intention, it was made public in an Italian translation, with the result that he was expelled from the Society of Jesus and excommunicated from the Roman Church. These events led Tyrrell to publish *A Much Abused Letter*, which includes the text of the original letter, an account of the controversy which it occasioned, and numerous explanatory notes.

Tyrrell is careful to explain that the letter was never intended for the general reader, and that those who published it were administering indiscriminately a medicine which was intended for a limited group. He maintains that the advice which he gives in the letter, although it may seem scandalous to those who are strangers to the world of intellect, is the kind regularly given in the confessional by priests who are accustomed to dealing with cases of this sort. Persons who are ignorant of Biblical criticism, of history, and of anthropology are unwilling to believe that there is any conflict between theology and the sciences, but the truth of the situation is well known among educated persons, both lay and clerical. If the conflict causes no concern to the more worldly type of Catholic, it is serious enough to compel those who, like the anthropology professor to whom the letter is directed, consider it their moral obligation to withdraw from the Church.

Tyrrell explains that his method in dealing with such cases is an indirect one. Instead of attempting to resolve the questions which the scientist raises, he undertakes only to show that intellectual doubts need not stand in the way of religious faith. Tyrrell insists that he is not indifferent to truth and that he does not wish to encourage indifference in others, but he points out that as a confessor he has to minister to people who, when it becomes impossible for them to accept the pronouncements of the clergy, imagine that they are guilty of mortal sin. By his indirect method, he frees them from this misconception, trusting in positive spiritual forces to bring about recovery, just as a physician, having removed a foreign particle from the body, trusts nature to heal the wound.

The metaphor of healing is suitable, in view of Tyrrell's general philosophy, which is closer to that of Henri Bergson than to that of Thomas Aquinas. The divine Being, Tyrrell maintains, is a creative force which we feel within ourselves and recognize in humanity

everywhere. He approves Matthew Arnold's description of it as the "Power that makes for Righteousness." Although we cannot think of it as other than personal or spiritual, we must not narrow it to the dimensions of our comprehension, as if it were defined by our human aspirations. Men, he says, are free either to resist this divine force or to obey it; but only in obedience to it can they find rest and peace.

Tyrrell holds that we can recognize the operation of this force in all branches of the human race, "whom it binds together into one mystical body and brotherhood and shapes to a collective presentment and revelation of itself, and to a society for the furtherance of its own ends." This mystical brotherhood is the Catholic Church, understood, however, as the invisible rather than as the visible institution; for it is only of the former that the motto holds good, *Extra ecclesiam salus nulla* (No safety outside the Church). "We do not worship Humanity, with the Comtists," Tyrrell explains, "but we worship the Power that is revealed in human goodness of every sort." He suggests that wherever men have sacrificed themselves for what is just and noble, there the mystical Christ is present, "and every member of that society is in his measure a Christ or revealer in whom God is made flesh and dwells in our midst." On the other hand, says Tyrrell, there is much to be said for keeping up communion with the visible Church. In spite of all its defects, Roman Catholicism remains "at once the highest expression or determination and the most effectual instrument of the life of religion." Her creeds embody the religious experience of a great sector of mankind. If we do not take them too literally, but see in them rather the "impression of itself which the Infinite has left" upon men's minds, all her doctrines will appear to us as "determinations of one and the same presentment of the Eternal Goodness," like pieces of stained glass through which the colorless light of God's truth is made comprehensible to our eyes.

Tyrrell insists that his correspondent's quarrel is with the theologians and not with the body of the Church. Drawing upon the distinction between the conscious and the subconscious, he suggests that the statement of doctrine which the theologians are accustomed to give is comparable to the ego's interpretation of the soul's motives, and that, consequently, theological doctrines are often mistaken. Theologians, he says, stand to the Church in the same relation as political leaders stand to a nation; the business of politicians is to bring to consciousness the unformulated mind of the people, and, so far as they do this correctly, they are instrumental in civilizing and improving the masses; but all too frequently the political leaders divorce themselves from the will of the people whom they are supposed to represent and become a separate class whose interests conflict with those of the body politic. In the same way, says Tyrrell, the theologians have mistaken their true function in that they have supposed that the intellectual systems which they devise are the substance of religion. Tyrrell is careful, however, to distinguish between the ecumenical creeds or symbols of the Church, which were a spontaneous expression of the Church's life, and the dogmas of the schools. It is the latter, he maintains, that are the source of such difficulties as those mentioned by the professor of anthropology.

Everything depends, says Tyrrell,

upon a correct understanding of what is meant by faith. One must distinguish between "the facts of religious experience" and "their analysis and expression." It is ridiculous to suppose, with the clerical party, that it is the latter which is necessary for salvation. When Christ rebuked men for their lack of faith, He was not accusing them of harboring heretical beliefs, but complaining about their want of "that deeper intelligence which is conditioned by moral dispositions." Faith, then, is man's grasp of that which lies beyond sense and reason. By faith we see God only darkly, to be sure, but nevertheless it is a "seeing for oneself; not a believing in hearsay." Faith is "a rudimentary faculty relating us to a world which is as yet 'future' and 'beyond' in respect to our clear consciousness." In moments of faith, we "gaze with God's eyes and from the standpoint of the whole." A life based on faith is one lived in the light of these moments, in consequence of which a man's horizons are lifted beyond mere selfish goals. It is a life which, united to the divine energy that surges through the world, becomes an instrument in the service of universal ends. Expressed in Christian terms, this is as much as to say that faith gives rise to hope and to love.

Tyrrell maintains that the Roman Church will have to undergo radical changes if it is to continue to be a bearer of divine truth. Its claims to infallibility, its lazy appeal to authority, its practice of hurling anathemas will all have to go. "Already," he says, "their authority-theory is stretched to snapping-point, and self-strangled by inherent contradictions and preposterous consequences." He compares the condition of the Church in our times with that of Judaism at the time of Christ. The Jews quoted the Prophets to show that Judaism would at last conquer the world. They were right, but only in a sense which they did not understand. "Judaism was to live a risen and glorified life in Christianity." Similarly, Tyrrell says, the theologians may be right in another sense than they suppose when they look for the Church to embrace humankind. Catholicism, like Judaism, may have to die in order to live again in a more prefect form.

Tyrrell's *Letter*, together with his spirited stand in the face of Vatican censure, marks the high-tide of modern-ism within the bounds of the Roman Church. In 1907, Pope Pius X (1835-1914) issued two sharp decrees commanding bishops to "purge their clergy of modernistic infection." Although the movement did not lack other spokesmen, notably Baron Friedrich von Hügel (1852-1925) and Alfred Loisy (1857-1940), Tyrrell's untimely death silenced its most effective spokesman, but not before he had vindicated his stand in two other important books, *Through Scylla and Charybdis* (1907), and *Christianity at the Crossroads* (1909).

THE QUEST OF THE HISTORICAL JESUS

Author: Albert Schweitzer (1875-   )
Type of work: History of New Testament criticism
First published: 1906

Principal Ideas Advanced

For 130 years scholarship has been engaged in a quest to discover the historical Jesus obscured by centuries of Christian dogma.

These attempts have generally failed in that they have portrayed Jesus as a man relevant to the modern world rather than as a man holding a vastly different world-view.

Jesus was thoroughly a man of His own time, in that He believed that history was about to come to a cataclysmic end and that the Kingdom of God was to be established.

Although the historical Jesus cannot be adapted to modern conditions, His spirit transcends His time and inspires men today.

Had modesty permitted, Albert Schweitzer could very well have entitled his great book, originally entitled *Von Reimarus zu Wrede, From Reimarus to Schweitzer*, for in it he seeks to trace the eschatological interpretation of the life of Jesus from the time that it emerges in the writings of the deist and Biblical critic Hermann Samuel Reimarus (1694-1768) to Schweitzer's work, *The Mystery of the Kingdom of God*, published in 1901. The original title also alludes to the skeptic William Wrede (1859-1906).

Schweitzer's interest in the history of scholarship concerning the life of Jesus grew out of a course of lectures he delivered in 1905 while a member of the theological faculty at Strassburg. He became so fascinated with the subject that he went on to the full-scale study embodied in *The Quest of the Historical Jesus.*

Surprisingly enough, Schweitzer believes that *hate* was a great motivating force in the historical investigation of Jesus in German scholarship from Reimarus to his own day. It was not that the scholars hated Jesus, but rather that they hated the tyranny of the dogma which surrounded the church's conception of Jesus, and they used historical investigation as a weapon in fighting it. They were anxious to rid Jesus of the "supernatural nimbus," to "strip from Him the robes of splendour with which He had been apparelled, and clothe Him once more with the coarse garments in which He had walked in Galilee."

Even David Friedrich Strauss (1808-1874) whose career was ruined by the persecution which followed publication of his revolutionary *Life of Jesus* (1835-1836) never ceased to be proud of his accomplishment. As Schweitzer points out, the critical work done on the life of Jesus "has been for theology a school of honesty. The world had never seen before, and will never see again, a struggle for truth so full of pain and renunciation as that of which the Lives of Jesus of the last hundred years contain the cryptic record."

The great key to the understanding of Jesus, according to Schweitzer, is eschatology; that is, the belief that God is to intervene in human history by bringing it to a cataclysmic end. It was Reimarus, professor of Oriental Languages at Hamburg (whose theological fragments were published by the noted German author Gotthold Lessing in 1778), who first introduced the question of eschatology into the study of Jesus. Since Reimarus was the first person in eighteen centuries to gain an inkling of the importance of eschatology in the life of Jesus, the scholars of his day were not prepared to realize the importance of his views. After Reimarus another hundred years elapsed before Johannes Weiss (1863-1914) once again brought the problem of eschatology to the fore—where it has since remained.

In the intervening years, the world was treated to various approaches to an understanding of Jesus. Schweitzer patiently works through these schools of thought and isolates those elements which he believes contributed insight concerning the difficult task of separating the historical Jesus from the other elements included in the Gospels.

Each of these schools of scholarship attempted to make Jesus at home in contemporary life. In a real sense Jesus was created in the image of the creators.

Schweitzer produced his record of the history of the quest of the historical Jesus at the very point he believed crucial for the resolution of the problem. By the beginning of the twentieth century two approaches were contending on the field, what Schweitzer labeled "thoroughgoing scepticism," on the one hand, and "thoroughgoing eschatology," on the other. As diverse as these approaches to the problem are, Schweitzer believed that they combined to destroy the "modern view" which was prevalent at the end of the nineteenth century.

The modern view presented Jesus as

an enlightened teacher who sought to spiritualize the earthly, political conception of the Messiah expected by the Jews. According to this view, Jesus attempted to found an ethical Kingdom of God on earth. When, however, He failed in His effort at enlightenment and lost the popular following which was initially His, He resolved to die at Jerusalem to seal his mission and thus carry it to victory.

The modern view of Jesus as the ethical reformer began to crumble with Schweitzer's forceful presentation of the challenge made by the schools of thoroughgoing skepticism and thoroughgoing eschatology.

The thoroughgoing skeptical school is best exemplified by the work of William Wrede. In *The Messianic Secret in the Gospels* (1901) Wrede held that the Gospel of Mark, although it was in time of composition closest to the events it recounts, cannot be accepted as history. Wrede took the position that this Gospel must be approached with great skepticism. The fact that Mark pictures Jesus as a Messiah who kept His messiahship a secret indicates that the historical Jesus never claimed messiahship but considered Himself to be a teacher. The Messianic elements were read back into Jesus' life by the early Christian community. Indeed, the eschatological framework of the Gospel of Mark is the creation of the early Church and is not a valid picture of the world-view which Jesus held. Wrede insisted that the very fact that there is a patent lack of connection between the various sections of Mark's story indicates that the author never really knew the circumstances of Jesus' life but was imposing his own interpretation on material which had come down to him.

Schweitzer attempts to show that, although Wrede presents a serious challenge to New Testament scholarship with his skeptical view of the sources, there is an alternative theory which better explains the material with which the scholar is confronted. Instead of viewing eschatology and the secret messiahship as something imposed on the record by the Gospel of Mark, Schweitzer believes that they shoud be accepted as historical elements. Furthermore, Schweitzer believes that the reliability of Mark should not be questioned because of seeming breaks in the narration, for the Gospel reflects the situation as it was. Schweitzer's view is that Jesus imposed His own dogmatic eschatological interpretation of history on the natural events of His day and that our failure to grasp this fact has kept us from understanding the true impact of eschatology on Jesus. "Eschatology is simply 'dogmatic history'—history as moulded by theological beliefs—which breaks in upon the natural course of history and abrogates it."

If one reads the story with this in mind, what formerly appeared as puzzling actions on the part of Jesus, now become clear. Jesus was not at all concerned with the attitude which the multitudes or, for that matter, other important elements of society, showed toward Him. He was interpreting events in an eschatological manner. Thus when, after His baptism by John, He enjoyed initial success in His native Galilee in preaching the coming of the Kingdom of God and suddenly withdrew to the north for a "period of inexplicable concealment," Jesus was not motivated by the standards of "success" in this world but by His dogmatic eschatological view of what was needful.

Schweitzer, in fact, denies that success as a "teacher" was of any concern to Jesus, for Jesus did not consider Himself to be a teacher. Using the thoroughgoing eschatological approach, Schweitzer argues there is little didactic material truly present in the message of Jesus. Actually, Jesus did not exhort people to prepare for the coming of the Kingdom, but instead He announced its coming. He did not expect to be understood by all but only by those who had been predestined by God for entrance into the Kingdom.

That predestination is an important element in Jesus' interpretation is shown by such statements as. "Unto him that hath shall be given, and from him that hath not shall be taken away even that which he hath" (Mark 4:24-25). "Many are called but few are chosen" (Matthew 22:1-14). Thus, even the Beatitudes are not to be taken as injunctions or exhortations designed to convert people in time for entrance into the Kingdom of Heaven but rather, writes Schweitzer, as statements of fact: ". . . in their being poor in spirit, in their meekness, in their love of peace, it is made manifest that they are predestined to the Kingdom. By the possession of these qualities they are marked as belonging to it." In other words, one cannot earn the Kingdom; one is predestined to it. The so-called "reward" sayings among Jesus' teachings are not really such if set before "a background of predestination."

Schweitzer believes that Jesus' public career lasted just a few months. He points out Jesus' references to sowing and reaping and contends that there is a symbolic and temporal connection between the coming of the harvest and the coming of the Kingdom. The end is truly at hand.

When Jesus sent out the Twelve to announce the coming of the Kingdom, he did not expect to see them again in this life. In sending them forth he fully expected to loose the final woes and strife which were associated with the Parousia (appearance) of the Son of Man (supernatural Messiah). Jesus, however, was mistaken in His expectation. The disciples returned and still the Son of Man and the Kingdom had not appeared. It was this disappointment which motivated Jesus to take a new direction. He no longer expected the preaching of repentance to bring in the Kingdom; thus, He decided to go to Jerusalem to die.

Schweitzer is convinced that Jesus identified Himself with the Son of Man whose appearance on the clouds of Heaven was to usher in the Kingdom. The Messianic consciousness of Jesus, Schweitzer believes, is apparent in all He does. Jesus, however, never revealed His secret to the people. His entrance into Jerusalem was as a secret Messiah. The people were obviously not aware of His belief, and, says Schweitzer, did not greet him as the Messiah. If they had taken Him as the Messiah, the charge would have been brought against Him in His trial— something that was not done. The High Priest could produce no witnesses to say that Jesus claimed messiahship; the attempts to convict Him were based on other grounds. Only when all else had failed did the Priest, using information supplied by the disciple Judas, accuse Jesus of Messianic pretensions. Jesus finally was convicted because of His own admission.

Jesus' death, then, was not the result of historical necessity but, rather, was grounded in dogma—in His own conviction that He had to die for the predestined in order that the Kingdom might come.

So it is, argues Schweitzer, that the figure of Jesus created by nineteenth century scholarship is critically exposed both by thoroughgoing skepticism and by thoroughgoing eschatology. No matter which of these two schools is finally proved to be right, the Jesus of nineteenth century scholarship is destroyed. Just at the point in the history of the quest for the historical Jesus where we "were already stretching out our hands to draw Him into our own time, we have been obliged to give up the attempt and acknowledge our failure." Not only can we not transport Him and make Him a part of our time, we must be prepared "to find that the historical knowledge of the personality and life of Jesus will not be a help, but perhaps an offence to religion."

But although the historical Jesus was captive to His world-view and cannot be adapted to our own time, Schweitzer does not conclude his *Quest* on a note of frustration. On the contrary, he claims that despite the tremendous chasm between the world view of Jesus and our own, despite the fact that "Jesus as a concrete historical personality remains a stranger to our time," the spirit of Jesus transcends His day and reaches out as an inspiration to men in ours.

The old names for Jesus—Messiah, Son of Man, Son of God—mean nothing to us. We are incapable of devising a name that describes His meaning for us: "He comes to us as One unknown, without a name, as of old, by the lakeside, He came to those men who knew Him not. He speaks to us the same word: 'Follow thou me!' and sets us to the tasks which He has to fulfill for our time. He commands. And to those who obey Him, whether they be wise or simple, He will reveal Himself in the toils, the conflicts, the sufferings which they shall pass through in His fellowship, and, as an ineffable mystery, they shall learn in their own experience Who He is."

PERSONALISM

Author: Borden Parker Bowne (1847-1910)
Type of work: Systematic theology
First published: 1908

PRINCIPAL IDEAS ADVANCED

The knower and the known are not alien to each other in their natures.
The world which is known is the world as ordered by minds.
Nature must be understood as affected by a dynamic cause; such a cause must be a unified and creative Will and Intelligence.
The creative Intelligence is best understood as the ground of ordered experience; He is an infinite Person who provokes a creative response in finite persons.

Borden Parker Bowne's whole scholarly life as a philosopher was immersed from 1876 on in teaching at Boston University, where he became the first dean of the Graduate School. Strongly influenced in his thought by Hermann Lotze (1817-1881), Immanuel Kant (1724-1804), and George Berkeley (1685-1753), he dissented from each significantly. As he said, "I am a Personalist, the first of the clan in any thorough-going sense." The author of several books and many articles, Bowne was constantly concerned to defend the vitality of experience as a whole from the pontifical claims of the Christian supernaturalism, evolutionary naturalism, psychological associationism and materialism, and the ethical utilitarianism of his day.

In *Personalism* (the Norman Wait Harris Lectures at Northwestern University for 1907) Bowne found it possible to summarize and to epitomize his more elaborate studies in *Theism* (1902), *The Theory of Thought and Knowledge* (1897), and *Metaphysics* (1898).

Persons do not make themselves, he claimed, nor do they create the common world of experience they take for granted, or the laws of reason which allow them to communicate in this common world. The world is, to be sure, an orderly world on which persons can depend. But an orderly world need not be a nonmental world. One must not jump to the conclusion, as do realists and naturalists, that this world can exist in entire independence of persons. From the outset it must be clear that science and practical daily living need a trustworthy world, but by no means a self-sufficient realm of nonmental beings.

We must ask what the nature of the trustworthy world is, Bowne writes, and we can do no better than to start with the undeniable datum, the knowing experience of persons. Knowing is itself a unique event unlike any other known fact. For its very nature consists, inscrutably, in referring to something other than itself, a something it does not create by such referring. Once more, however, one must not jump to the realistic and naturalistic conclusion that since knowing refers to something other than itself, it refers to something nonmental.

What knowing presupposes, Bowne suggests, is a not-me (or not-us) that is in interaction with me (or us). But in interacting with the knower the object to be known obeys its own nature. Realization of this fact leads to a far-reaching conclusion. For if the human mind, in knowing the object not of its own making, meets the conditions of that object and knows it, then the object, in turn, evidently meets the conditions set by the nature of the knowing subject. The knower and the known are not alien to each other in their natures.

Still further conclusions must be drawn: "No knowledge, whether of the ideas of another or of anything else, is imported ready-made into a passive mind, but the mind must actually construct knowledge for itself." The object as known and the object to be known are never one or identical. The nature of the mind is to think; the nature of the object is to be. The known object is the thought object. The knower *thinks* the object to be known; he does not "embrace" it. In other words, what happens in the knowing process is not that things as thought pass into a passive mind. Upon the occasion of interaction, the mind responds in accordance with its own laws and "creates" its own known world. Just as the thoughts of a teacher as expressed in his words are read back to a teacher in accordance with the understanding capacity of the student, so what we know as "the physical world" is our human reflective response to the "real" world. Our world is not identical with the real world that supports this humanly known world.

More analytically: each knower is bombarded with a flux of discontinuous impressions which as such certainly are not the world as we know it. If in the midst of this flux there were no abiding knower to interpret these discontinuous impressions, and if the knower had no rational principles in accordance with which he could organize these incoming sense data, there would be no "world" of sense but only the meaningless maelstrom of unassorted sense-impressions: sounds, colors, smells, and other sense data. Thus the world we know, in order to be a world and not chaos, must be a world as organized by the patterns of understanding intrinsic to the knowing mind. The world as we know it, the "phenomenal" world, is not a "material" world, and certainly not the real world. It is the world as ordered by minds that interact with the real world.

Yet this is only one side of the story, the side neglected by realists and naturalists. The other side, neglected in Kant's doctrine that the real world cannot be known, is that the mind cannot impose its phenomenal construct on a reality completely alien to it. The phenomenal world exhibits the rational structure which persons impose upon it, to be sure, but that

rational structure does not itself create the real objects with which persons interact. The world as known is the world persons construct on the basis of the reality beyond thought. The phenomenal world is not a mask of the real world; it is that world as manifested to minds which find it cooperative with their natures.

Is the real world made up of nonmental entities and events spread out in nonmental space and time? Bowne finds no reason for introducing nonmental entities in order to explain either persons or their knowledge. He admits that he does not prove beyond a shadow of a doubt that such nonmental beings cannot exist. But he finds them unnecessary, unexperienced supports for the actual phenomenal world as ordered in accordance with human categories and as steadfastly serving human purposes. That nonmental, unintelligent, unpurposive entities would interact supportively with intelligent minds is hard to believe, Bowne suggests. And for intelligent minds to be produced in a world made up of unintelligent entities which in turn can be known by them—this seems the least likely way to explain what one actively confronts in experience; namely, ordered world. Why not, then, postulate, more economically and empirically, a unified Intelligence as the productive cause both of human minds and of the order of events it puts at their disposal?

Again, Bowne does not assert that just because the phenomenal world expresses the structure of the knower, all existents are mental. He insists that there is an order of being beyond human intelligence. But why try to explain the known, knowing beings and their ordered world, by nonmental beings, if to do so creates rather than solves problems? His fundamental contention is that since persons can find identities in and through change in the experienced world, and since persons can find that world meaningful, what is ultimately real must have not only an affinity with persons but also the kind of self-identity and unity that persons exemplify.

What happens to space and time on this view? Bowne would be willing to postulate that the cosmic Intelligence operates via a nonmental space and time world, if he could find evidence for such a world in experience. But, in Kantian fashion, he finds that we do not experience space as an infinite, three-dimensional, all-embracing, nonmental reality, nor time as an infinite, all-embracing being independent of mind. Space, in fact, is the form that pervades all "outer" experience, while time pervades both inner and outer. The objects in dreams are as much "in space and time" as are any others. There is no more experiential ground, then, for supposing that we need an independent "real" space and time "in which" to live than to suppose that the space and time of our dreamobjects need "real" space and time.

Does this not mean that space as known is an illusion or a mask that we put on reality? Not for a moment, Bowne insists. If we stay close to experimental fact we note a specific spatial order. There must be something, then, in the dynamic structure of the real that imposes this and not some other order upon us. And the same reasoning applies to time.

We run into trouble, Bowne writes, only when we try to *picture* how a spatial order might "copy" the real, or how a nonspatial Being can manifest

itself as spatial in our experience. The facts as known must stand: the space-relations and the time-sequence as known are what they are, and hence they cannot be identical with the nonphenomenal world. Instead of trying to put either finite or infinite mind "in space" why not simply realize that minds are where they act? Minds, by their very nonspatial nature, cannot fill some vacuum with bulk.

If we pass from space and time in general to individual substances such as stones, apples, and chairs—substances which presumably exist independent of persons—we uncover similar picture-thinking philosophy, Bowne claims. For actually we do not bump into solid, unified objects; we sort out our experiences into dependable sequences, and we selectively organize different clusters into a world of things having the continuity which certain sequences of experiences impose on us. Once more, these phenomenal things are not outright creations of persons, but the constructs which persons develop in response to the continuity and structure of the supporting dynamic realm beyond themselves.

What, then, does it mean to talk about nature, if we stay close to experienced data? Nature is the continuous, organized world of objects in spatial and temporal continuity; it is a common world, exhibiting dependable laws of sequence and concomitant change, a world that reflects the interplay of finite minds and a dynamic realm beyond themselves. To call nature a causal world is to emphasize the dependable order and continuity among our experiences. But order and cause are descriptive. If we are to explain the fact that we do not make the continuity and establish the order we find in experience, cause must be given another meaning, namely "productive" or "dynamic" cause.

What shall we conceive such a productive cause to be? We experience a dynamic cause in our own wills, and we experience continuity when our wills carry out one purpose. Bowne, reasoning by analogy, suggests, then, that the order, lawfulness, and continuity we discover in the processes of nature can find no better explanation than that they exhibit the working-out of the purposes of a creative Will. If we postulate a unified Will and Intelligence, we can say that the real world, not the phenomenal world, is the activity of the Creator on a cosmic level; the real world is His thought in action; the Creator is both thought and deed.

The phenomenal world of nature, concludes Bowne, is the world as we construct it in response to the continuity, unity, and variety of the presentations the cosmic Person produces in us in accordance with our receptivity. His cosmic activity is not necessarily restricted to such presentations as we have, for He may well produce a cosmic order without any relation to us. Yet we can trust the connections we have inferred from the past only because this world-order, far from being a mere succession of causes, is the manifestation of one unified, purposeful Creator.

The plurality-in-order that we know as our world is "posited" by the Creator without loss of His own unity. He remains immanent in the world that manifests him, but His nature is not exhausted by it. He is both immanent and transcendent; He is the ground for our system of common experience which testifies to a basic affinity between finite intelligence and deeds and infinite Intelligence and Deed.

The controlling analogy in conceiving the infinite Person is the finite person and his kind of unity. This unity is irreducible; abiding through change and time, it is self-equivalent. Otherwise knowledge such as we have would be impossible. But this unity cannot be explained by the very categories that express its unity. The person, then, is the category of categories, Bowne suggests.

The person also experiences admittedly mysterious self-determination or free-will—a phenomenon that must not be reduced to some form of mechanical order. Freedom and order, rightly conceived, are far from inimical to each other. Freedom is the unity of the person in choice-action: it is not an abstract power unrelated to desire or intelligence. Since the unity of the person is not a collection of will, intelligence, and desire, will is "the power to form plans, purposes and ideals and to work for their realization." As such, freedom initially and always is the freedom to work in relation to order.

The vision of man, world, and God that spreads before us becomes clear only as we see man, with the created autonomy granted him, working out the concrete significance of his freedom in a world order that at once limits him and gives him the opportunity for fulfillment. Freedom would effect nothing did it not live in a realm of order. Freedom does not create rational law but uses it to guide whatever thought and action is open to the individual's nature in a given world order. For the personalist, then, the natural order is not an order in terms of which the individual's intelligence and freedom can be explained away. The natural order is the objectification of interaction of both finite and infinite persons. Finite persons are not reducible to an impersonal order or to a qualityless parade of nonmental events. But the world in which finite persons express their will and intelligence is common ground with the Infinite Will upon whose living will and purpose they depend for the basic form and order of their existence. To try to *picture* this relation of the free creative person to the Creator is to court failure by attempting to think of the person as a part of a larger whole. But the inalienable unity of thought, will, and feeling as found in finite persons cannot be merged into an Absolute One without blurring the fundamental fact that persons live in independence and dependence.

Thus, reversing the argument and moving from God to nature and man, the world-view that emerges can be briefly stated as follows: The infinite Unified Will and Intelligence, or Person, creates finite unities of will and intelligence and allows them relative independence within the larger realm of dynamic order that constitutes His world. The capacities, cognitive and otherwise, of finite persons are not alien to this larger order of thought and will with which they interact, and they depend upon that underlying order for the relative phenomenal world they construct in accordance with their cognitive-volitional capacities.

The phenomenal world of space, time, and things is not a world out of all relation to the constant intelligent willing of the cosmic Person, but neither is it identical with Him. There is no sufficient reason for imposing, between the cosmic Person and finite persons, an orderly realm of nonmental entities. For all we could empirically mean by such entities is certain dependable forms and systems of experience that persons find they can develop in response to the inferred steady activity beyond themselves. Why not, then, asks Bowne, hold that the system of experience presupposed by common sense, science, and philosophy is a system grounded not in impersonal or nonpersonal forces, but in the interplay between the dependable creativity of the cosmic Person's active will and the creative response of free, intelligent, finite persons?

Reality, Bowne concludes, is composed of a purposive system—a whole of purposers, and not a whole of parts without freedom or creativity. The infinite Person manifests Himself in a dynamic order that sustains and directs in basic ways the constructive response of finite persons. They in turn, with their delegated freedom and intelligence, can create within that dynamic order a phenomenal and moral world that expresses in different ways the interaction between man and God.

The concrete world-order at any time is the product of the interplay between the Creator and His orderly activities and the constructive responses of persons who make of the cosmic data what they will, within the limits of their powers. According to Bowne's personalistic world-view, finite persons can fulfill both themselves and the purpose of God only as they will purposes born of reason and love in their relations to one another and to their Creator.

OUR CALLING

Author: Einar Billing (1871-1939)
Type of work: Systematic theology
First published: 1909

PRINCIPAL IDEAS ADVANCED

The nature of the Christian faith is such that it permits itself to be made contemporary; that is, to become relevant to the modern world.

The Christian's "calling," or vocation, must be seen in relationship to the overall history of the Bible, in which God has made Himself known.

Man is capable of contributing to the building of God's Kingdom on earth.

By means of our calling, that is, in the fulfillment of those tasks to which God has called us, particularly to the service of our neighbor, we participate in the building of His Kingdom.

Man is a participant in the creation of God's Kingdom only by virtue of the fact that he is a forgiven sinner.

Einar Billing, who was professor of theology at the University of Uppsala, in Sweden, as well as Bishop of the Lutheran State Church, was one of the most influential thinkers in his country. His contribution to Swedish theological thought (unfortunately, he is not well-known outside his native land) is based upon an analysis of the Bible and of the thought of Martin Luther. *Our Calling*, which is one of Billing's major theological works, demonstrates his reliance upon the Bible and Luther in the presentation of the doctrine of vocation.

The study of the Bible provided Billing with material for theological works dealing with the nature of ethical thinking in the early Christian Church and with the doctrine of the atonement. In his analysis of the Old Testament Billing discovered in what way the ethic of the Hebrews is continued in the New Testament. In his study of the New Testament and the atonement, Billing considered different theories of the atonement within the Christian Church. The Bible, Billing discovered, proposed a world view, including a concept of history—"history as the drama of revelation"—which was antithetical to the Greek world view. The God of the Bible cannot be compared to the God of Classical Greek philosophy, Billing claims. God is an acting God in the Bible; He is constantly revealing Himself to individuals in history. According to the Old Testament, He led the Jews from Egypt in the Exodus, and He called the prophet into being to bring the immediate knowledge of His will. In the New Testament, Jesus Christ is the bearer of the news that God is ultimately concerned about man. This "good news" takes the form of God's coming into history in the person of Jesus Christ. Thus, the essential element in the Bible is the historical element, by means of which God makes himself known. Revelation is historical.

On the basis of his reflections, the task of theology became very clear for

Billing. Theology must relate the Biblical confessions of faith regarding God's activity in history to the present day and the modern world. It must do so, however, in terms of the reality of the situation. Another distinction between the Bible and Greek philosophy then became clear; the Greeks, unlike the Biblical writers, always became lost in abstractions.

Billing believed that even Luther could be understood only on the basis of the *setting* in which his ideas were expressed. Luther is a part of a period in theological history, and his work is important to the Christian church only if it is analyzed historically. The words Luther used, Billing found, had undergone a change in meaning. This fact alone motivated Billing, the Luther-scholar, to look more carefully at the Reformer in terms of the world in which he lived. Not everything in Luther has equal value, Billing asserted. His teachings do not become normative simply because he uttered them. However, Luther's significance for the Christian Church lies in the fact that in his discussion of the New Testament he gave an insight which is constantly being verified in the experience of believers. Luther's historical significance, according to Billing, lies not in the particular ideas he expressed, but in the fact that he interpreted and preached the Gospel more accurately than anyone else in his time. What does not relate to the central motif of Luther, that God has revealed himself in Christ, is only of *secondary* historical interest. Billing insisted that one can understand Luther solely from this theological point of view and that one is likely to misinterpret Luther if this presupposition is not maintained. Luther, too, Billing felt, was to be the ob-

ject of the investigations of the theologian, and again the theologian was to make Luther's insight into the nature of the Christian gospel relevant to modern man.

Billing saw a direct line between the Bible and Luther. Luther's theology was simply a reduplication or rediscovery of the Pauline (and early Christian) faith. Just as Luther had taken the Bible and made it come alive in his world (as Paul had done with the Old Testament), so too must the modern Christian make the past come alive, and make the Word of God speak to the present situation.

Billing's methodology is important as a background for his work, *Our Calling.* Into his Biblical-historical view, he introduced the Christian doctrine of calling or vocation.

Billing maintained that there is a continuity between the acts of God in history, the present-day activity of God and the Kingdom of God which is to come. However, Billing maintained that man participates in the construction of the Kingdom. Unlike Luther, who at times insisted that the Kingdom is to be identified with the Church of Christ which shall stand when the world shall fall, Billing believed that man is able to contribute to the creation of God's Kingdom. Man's contribution to the Kingdom involves necessarily the nature of man's *calling,* said Billing. The Kingdom shall not be fulfilled automatically, although God has assured us that it will be consummated. Rather, Christian man is responsible for bringing about its fulfillment. Billing wrote: "God builds his kingdom in time through the centuries. God has by virtue of his forgiveness called us to participate in the building of His kingdom. By means of the orders of our world he has given us our vocation. Very rarely are we given any prior knowledge of how our rather insignificant deed contributes to the kingdom. . . ."

Billing could not, however, find a similar conception of vocation in Luther's theology. The relationship in Luther between faith and works and vocation is very clear: faith evokes love, and love expresses the good deeds which belong to one's calling. There is not in Luther a *final* goal to which these good deeds are directed, and there is no way by which specific good deeds can be related to a larger whole. Billing, however, saw that the relationship of the doctrine of the forgiveness of sins and the doctrine of God's kingdom provided such a unity. He wrote: "In the forgiveness of sins, we experience our escape from the Egyptians. We know, therefore, that God will lead us to his eternal kingdom. The divine ordinances which we encounter during our lifetime show us their intention to carry us towards that goal. Furthermore, deep within each of them is a message of grace. . . . If we faithfully and patiently permit the forgiveness of sins to force us back once again upon the forgiveness of sins, then in the midst of darkness (even a 70 year exile, when all hope was lost) a kingdom shall spring forth. . . . But only the calling, which God himself has given us, makes this possible for us."

Billing observed that the aim of the good deeds of the Christian is "to aid another, that is, to serve one's neighbor." But the good deed, the giving aid to another individual, is related directly to the Kingdom of God. Although Billing could not find within Luther the relationship of the Chris-

tian doctrine of vocation to the Kingdom of God, he nonetheless believed that Luther had intended to emphasize such a relationship and Billing regarded himself as simply carrying forth the consequences of Luther's own work.

Our Calling relates the doctrine of vocation directly to the idea of the Kingdom of God. Nonetheless, Billing's conception of vocation is dependent upon the Christian doctrine of the forgiveness of sins. We can understand the relationship between vocation and the forgiveness of sins, said Billing, when we conceive of the forgiveness of sins as the action of the living God in approaching man. But this fact compels each individual to approach another individual. This is the nature of our vocation. God initiates the act of response in relation to our neighbor. As we go to our neighbors, we become co-workers with God. In this way, God molds our lives so that they become related to God's activity in history.

Billing reintroduces his conception of history at this point. Long before most men could rightfully talk about their calling, Billing wrote, a people, the people of Israel, had a specific calling. They received their calling by virtue of God's act of election. The people of Israel knew, therefore, that there was a purpose to their history, and that God would lead them to the fulfillment of His election. Their vocation was to co-operate with God in this fulfillment. Vocation in an individual's life, therefore, said Billing, corresponds to what was the nature of history for Israel. History is always "the message of grace." Vocation is an example of this history, but in a personalized sense. Vocation reveals again that God has entered history on behalf of man, to save him. Billing could say, therefore, that "vocation is the forgiveness of sins." In vocation, "there is the gift of God's son, the forgiver of sins." "In vocation, one finds the gospel." It is clear that faith in the living God of history is the primary element of Einar Billing's conception of vocation.

The doctrine of vocation is therefore closely related to Billing's study of the ethical thinking of the early Christian Church, as well as to his study of the atonement. In contrast to the Jewish ethic, which distinguished between God's righteousness and mercy, the Christian in the early Church unified the concept of the righteousness and love of God. However, Billing said, the nature of the election of the Jews by God excluded forever the possibility that a distinction could be made between God's righteousness and mercy. The prophets saw this clearly, as did Second-Isaiah. The fact of election means that God's righteousness and His love *concur*. The history of the Jews in the desert, the miracle of the Red Sea, all indicate clearly that God's election meant that His love was identical with His righteousness. The tragedy of the Jews, for Billing, was that they made their relationship with God dependent upon what He would do for them. On this basis, they could then make a distinction between the different ways in which it appeared God was dealing with them. Only then could they distinguish between God's love and His righteousness.

Jesus' message attempted to reconcile these divergent characteristics of God. Jesus Himself is motivated solely by the Father. His work is an integral part of God's election. He forgives sins in the name of the Father. He, therefore, has united in His person, (and in His death and resurrection), the themes of the mercy and righteousness of God. Billing found, furthermore, that Paul had seen very clearly this unity in God's nature.

The difference between the Old Testament and the New Testament is therefore simply that in the Old Testament, election (the unity of mercy and righteousness) is of a people, the people of Israel, whereas in the New Testament, election is of an individual, Jesus Christ. In the New Testament, the forgiveness of sins, which Christ offered, corresponds to the Old Testament experience of the Jews' being led through the Red Sea. Because of Jesus Christ, God's revelation is concentrated about a *person* rather than a people. By means of Christ's resurrection, God has extended His activity through the history of all mankind and through every century. God is not changeable, however. He does not act in one way in relation to the Jews and another way in relation to Christ. God's will is a unity of grace and judgment, love and justice, which work together on the basis of the one overarching principle—the *forgiveness of sins*. The central meaning of God's election is that man, sinful man, who does not deserve it, is nevertheless forgiven by God.

The Church is important to Billing in relation to the doctrine of vocation. It is within the Church that God's acts in history are brought into their clearest focus. In the Church, the forgiveness of sins becomes a "present" possibility. For Billing, the Church of Sweden is the promise of God to the Swedish people that their sins are forgiven. The baptism of a child is a witness to the presence of God in the present world. The Church is a reality in the world because it is itself dependent upon the Christ who died for it; God, in Christ, continues to relate Himself to man through the Church. Since in the Church the history of the living, active God, is made known, the Church is "the bridge" which makes Biblical history part of contemporary history. The Church and voca-

tion, Billing says, "seek for an association" with modern man.

Vocation, therefore, is not primarily to be thought of as a *task* given to man by God. Rather, it is a gift which God has given man by virtue of the forgiveness of sins. Vocation "creates man's life" and provides the connection between Israel's history and that of modern man.

THE PERSON AND PLACE OF JESUS CHRIST

Author: Peter Taylor Forsyth (1848-1921)
Type of work: Christology
First published: 1909

PRINCIPAL IDEAS ADVANCED

Concentrating on the way Christ's person is demonstrated by His benefits, fruitful Christological reflection starts with the conviction that in Christ's action we experience God's action upon us.

The dichotomy between the Jesus of history and the Christ of faith is a false one because even the writers of the Gospels believed in and worshiped a risen, glorified, and redeeming Christ.

When the dogma of the Incarnation is taken out of the realm of the speculative and is made a matter of personally ethical religion, it describes not a union of two static natures into a person, but a moral act which unites God to man and man to God.

Christ's redeeming act consists in the way this God-man and man-God movement is traced by the self-emptying (kenosis) of the eternal Son and his self-fulfillment (plerosis), by which He regains through His human obedience what is His by right.

Peter Taylor Forsyth studied at the university of his native town, Aberdeen, Scotland, and he spent a semester in 1870 under the theologian Albrecht Ritschl in Göttingen. He held pastorates in London and Manchester before becoming pastor of the important Emanuel Congregational Church in Cambridge. From 1901 to 1921, For-

syth was the principal of Hackney College, a Congregational Seminary. It was in this capacity that in 1909 Forsyth delivered the lectures to the Congregational Union of England and Wales which were subsequently published as one of the most representative statements of Forsyth's thought, *The Person and Place of Jesus Christ.*

According to Forsyth, correct reflection about Christ's person starts with the conviction that in experiencing Christ's actions we experience God's actions upon us. The benefits of Christ demonstrate His nature. The deity of Christ is at the center of Christian truth because it alone makes the Christian experience of redemption conceivable, and redemption in turn is Christianity. Such theology and such thought about Christ is evangelical, lay, and theocentric. "All Christology exists in the interest of the evangelical faith of the layman who has in Jesus Christ the pardon of his sins and everlasting life," writes Forsyth; "We are all laymen here." Yet the lay mind which in these matters everyone shares, must be called back from some deceptive preoccupations. "Lay" has become increasingly not the antithesis of "sacerdotal" but of "theological," as the lay mind has become more and more detached from the Bible. We have become "more concerned with man's religion than with God's salvation," Forsyth claims. It is not enough for Christianity to be merely Christocentric, for it is possible to have a religion which claims Christ's centrality but which actually aims at developing the innate spiritual resource ascribed to a splendid race of mankind. This is an anthropocentric Christianity which is subtly less Christocentric than egocentric. What must be specified is a theocentric faith in which man lives, in Forsyth's terms, "for the worship and glory of God and for obedience to His revelation of Himself; which is not in man, and not in spirituality, but in Christ, in the historic, superhistoric, Christ."

Forsyth elucidates his views about the "Jesus of history" versus "Christ of faith" problem. In this scheme, set forth by an influential part of nineteenth century scholarship, the "Jesus of history" was the religious figure of the Synoptics whose religion involved the "Fatherhood of God and the brotherhood of man." The "Christ of faith" was what the disciples and Apostles made out of the simple Jesus of Nazareth. This view of Christ is recorded most prominently in the Pauline and Johannine literature. In opposition to this dichotomy, which Forsyth believes is a false and impossible one, Forsyth follows the German theologian Martin Kaehler, who is described as the most powerful theological mind on the subject, and says one cannot distinguish between the Jesus of history and the Christ of faith. What may be called Pauline Christianity was the faith of the earliest Church we know of, and it was the faith even of the writers of the Gospels. "Jesus was for the Apostles and their Churches not the consummation of a God-consciousness, labouring up through creation, but the invasive source of forgiveness, new creation, and eternal life," Forsyth writes. In essential matters the Apostolic documents are prolongations of the message of Jesus.

All who extol Christ's greatness affirm some great unity of Christ with God. Forsyth designates three ways this has been done: Socinianism explained Christ's greatness in terms of His being God's perfect prophet, and Arianism did so in terms of His being God's plenipotentiary. Athanasianism, although including the positive aspects of the other two, went on to affirm that in Christ there was God's real presence. If for the first Christ was man, and for the second, superman, for the third he was the Lord from Heaven. At stake was man's salvation, for a mere prophet or a half-God could not redeem the soul created by the whole God. God must be the immediate doer in Christ's saving actions. On this score, the Church decides among these alternatives according to whether or not she counts herself an aided or a purchased people.

Christ, the whole Christ, was mindful of His own divinity and included it within His own Gospel. Leaving aside the Johannine self-testimonies, Forsyth says he is willing to use only the Matthew 11:27 passage concerning the Father's exclusive knowledge of the Son and the Son's exclusive knowledge of the Father. An exposition of this passage leads, according to Forsyth, to the conviction that Christ believed His Sonship to be unique in kind, and it leads further to the doctrine of His pre-existence; that is, His existence eternally as the Son of God. In the Synoptics, Christ's witness to Himself is part of His preaching about the Kingdom. Only in the completion of the Cross did Christ become the object of the preaching recorded in the Gospel, because only then was He perfected as Redeemer. Then the Spirit was released for men even as men were then released for the Spirit. The consequence was that Christ's own preaching about the Kingdom was replaced by the Apostolic preaching about Christ, and he became identified with the Kingdom.

When Forsyth looks at the testimony of the Apostolic inspiration, he distinguishes between the material and formal aspects of revelation. The material aspect of revelation was a person, Christ. The formal aspect of revelation was its completion in the Apostolic interpretation or inspiration. The material revelation took effect in the New Testament, and the New Testament is not solely the product of revelation but is a part of it: the formal element of it, as Christ was the material element.

Both the Bible and the Church are products of the Gospel; both are sustained by the Spirit, the one through faith, the other through inspiration. What Forsyth calls positive revelation has three component parts: the incarnate fact (God entering the world), the interpretive notice of that fact in the Apostles, and the same fact enshrined in the soul of the believing Church. The Apostolic inspiration was, Forsyth writes, "a certain action stirred by the heavenly Christ in the soul, by which his first elect were enabled to see the moral, spiritual, and theological nature of the manifestation with a unique clearness, a clearness and explicitness perhaps not always present to Christ's own mind in doing the act." Insofar as the Bible is witness to revelation but is not revelation itself, it is final but not infallible.

Forsyth reserves an important place for "experience in the Soul." Protestantism is, he says, a blend of two currents: the Reformation and the Enlightenment; or three by another reckoning: "classical Protestantism," emphasizing the objective tendency; "romantic Protestantism," emphasizing the subjective tendency; and the Enlightenment. The goal for Protestantism is not to correlate the views of the Reformation and the Enlightenment, but to correct itself with an emphasis on the practical relations between God and the soul arising not out of reason or romance but out of the "renovation of faith by the piety and genius of men like Spener, Francke, Schleiermacher, and Wesley." The personal experience of Christ, Forsyth claims, is not visionary and mystical but moral, personal, and mutual. Christ works a change in one's life comparable only to birth. This experienced salvation is not a passing, subjective impression, but an objective relationship, even a transaction effected by the Spirit as God in action.

Dogma is "the collective expression of a Church's belief," Forsyth writes, and to moralize dogma is to change it from a speculative notion to a personally ethical religion. Dogma is necessary to the Church, but it has to be revised from time to time to keep pace with the Church's growth as a living body in a living world. The dogma of the Incarnation needs especially to be moralized: a view of the Incarnation is needed which is ethical and dynamic instead of metaphysical and static. The Greek Fathers described the Incarnation too much in terms of cosmic and natural forces, and in terms of the metaphysical and miraculous. "Union" is too physical a term to describe the Incarnation; the Incarnation was not an act uniting two natures into a person, but one uniting two natures through the moral act of the person. Ethical categories (such as society, history, personality) have taken precedence over categories of being (such as nature and substance). Forsyth insists that "The ethical notion of the true unity as the interpenetration of persons by moral action must take the place of the old metaphysic of the union of natures. . . ."

Sketching the outlines of such a moralized Christology, Forsyth shows successively how it involves (1) a doctrine of the pre-existence of Christ, (2) a doctrine of the self-emptying, or *kenosis,* of Christ, and (3) a doctrine of the self-fulfillment, or *plerosis,* of Christ. For Forsyth, the clue to the relation of God and man in the person of Christ is the relation of God's movement toward man and man's movement of active passivity toward God. "On the one hand we have an initiative, creative, productive action, clear and sure, on the part of the eternal and absolute God; on the other we have the seeking, receptive, appropriative action of groping, erring, growing man." This God-man, man-God movement is traced by the self-emptying of the pre-existent Christ and His growing self-fulfillment or "reintegration."

Accounting for Christ's uniqueness in terms of the Virgin Birth is no longer viable, according to Forsyth. Forsyth chooses to handle the problem in terms of another doctrine, that of Christ's pre-existence; and in doing so, he claims to be following the lead of St. Paul. Forsyth's point is that the special relation to the Father could not have arisen in time. Christ's victory in history is the index of a choice and conquest in the Godhead itself; Christ's obedience as a man was only a detail of the supreme obedience by which He became man. Christ never ceased to have a unique relation to the Father. It was this unique relationship which constituted, which was the very essence of, His personality of absolute Sonship: this can be said of none of us. It is clear that Christ saved primarily because He was God.

The reality of Christ's moral conflict as man was ensured by His kenotic ignorance of His inability to sin. This self-emptying was not the renunciation of eternal and divine attributes such as omniscience, nor was it the conscious possession and concealment of them. By this "self-retraction," which term might be better than "self-emptying," the history of Christ's human growth became the history of His recovery by gradual moral conquest of the mode of being from which He came. It was a reconquest: Christ "won by duty what was his own by right." The reason for this *kenosis* was our redemption, Forsyth claims; "He who is the end of all, humbles himself to be the means, that he may win all."

Forsyth opposes his view of the *kenosis* to those views which concentrate on the negative, resigning char-acter of the Incarnation. Besides the subjective repudiation of Christ, we must note, Forsyth writes, "the growth, the exaltation, of his objective achievement, culminating in the perfecting at once of his soul and our salvation in the cross, resurrection, and glory." This positive growth of Christ was the growth of human redemption in which the agent of creation became the very soul it pleased Him to make. By this self-fulfillment, Christ presented as His satisfaction to God the perfect, holy Humanity.

THE RELIGIOUS A PRIORI

Author: Ernst Troeltsch (1865-1923)
Type of work: Philosophy of religion
First published: 1909

PRINCIPAL IDEAS ADVANCED

Religion is independent of morality and philosophy.

Religion rests ultimately upon certain intuitively apprehended and self-evident truths, which are religious in character; this body of truths is the religious a priori.

The religious a priori *is the regulative, creative, epistemological, and ontological principle of religion.*

The religious a priori *is being realized in the development of the historical religions of the world.*

The *Religious A Priori* formed the basis for what Ernst Troeltsch called the "science of religion" (*Religionswissenschaft*). Troeltsch was very much dependent upon the philosophy of Immanuel Kant (1724-1804), and in agreement with Kant he argued that values are justified only when they exhibit an immanent rational necessity and can also satisfy the demands of universality. Religion, Troeltsch wanted to show, rested ultimately upon certain intuitively apprehended and self-evident truths, which are religious in nature. To demonstrate this, it was necessary for Troeltsch to employ the critical philosophy of Kant. In the *Critiques,* Kant proposed the idea of the *a priori* character of experience. In the first *Critique, The Critique of Pure Reason* (1781), Kant attempted to discover *a priori* constituents of theoretical knowledge. In the second *Critique, The Critique of Practical Reason* (1788), he performed the same task for practical knowledge; that is, in relation to our knowledge of good and evil. However, when Kant came to the question of religious knowledge, he insisted that the procedure had to be modified somewhat. Religious knowledge, Kant believed, is dependent upon our knowledge of good and evil; that is, it is a product of our practical reason. Because of this, Kant never recognized any separate *a priori* in religious experience; he insisted, rather, that the only genuinely *a priori* element in religion is the ethical element.

Troeltsch was not at all satisfied with Kant's refusal to give an independent place to religion in the *a priori* structure of man's experience. Religion, he insisted, possessed its own existence and could not be subsumed under morality or any other human experience. For this reason, Troeltsch sought to find the religious *a priori*. He sought to demonstrate that the fundamental affirmations of the religious consciousness are ultimate truths of reason which are intuitively apprehended and immediately evident. He wanted to give religious knowledge a firm and independent foundation of its own.

Religion cannot be identified with cosmological speculation, Troeltsch wrote in 1905 (in *Psychologie und Erkenntnistheorie in der Religionswissenschaft*). Consequently, Troeltsch was interested in demonstrating "the nature of truth within the religious consciousness itself." He approached this task in two ways: first, by reference to religion as a psychological and sociological phenomenon; second, by considering the source of religious truth.

According to Troeltsch, in his *Die Absolutheit des Christentums und die Religionsgeschichte,* 1901, the first problem for religion, when one considers religion as a phenomenon of consciousness, lies in an examination of religion as an aspect of empirical psychology. In this study, the religious phenomena are studied as much as possible in their unreflective stage; that is, before they have been influenced by or related to any other experience. It was one of Troeltsch's fundamental assumptions that all vital religion arises in the uncultured classes, where no distinction is made between symbol and reality; the imaginative pictures of religion are entirely unquestioned there. Religion is always born absolute. It necessarily assumes the form of a divine "revelation," absolute in its claims, and everywhere authoritative. Reflective religion is, on the other hand, critical, rational, individualistic, and aristocratic. The "naïve" type of religion shows too that the affective side is the most vivid and intense of all the constituent parts of the religious life. Thus, for Troeltsch, religion is primarily a state of feeling (*Gefühlsgehalt*), although the religious consciousness is found to contain three constituents—conation, cognition, and affection. Real religion for Troeltsch is therefore an identification of the finite with the infinite, but an identification in which the infinite is related to the root of all life, immediate, spontaneous, and unconditioned. The religious "feeling" is a feeling of the infinite, attainable only through the activity of a free agent. The fundamental presupposition of religious experience is, therefore, personal creative faith in the living God.

The second task in Troeltsch's program to determine the independent nature of religion within the consciousness of man deals with the question of the truth of one's religious beliefs. His inquiry is concerned with the validity and objectivity of those experiences one calls religious. We must find an instrument, Troeltsch urged, which will enable us to distinguish the true and the valuable forms of religious experience from the illusory and subjective. The empirical investigation of religion (religious sociology or psychology) must now give way to a rational analysis of religion (religious epistemology). The task of religious epistemology, said Troeltsch, is to find the rational within the phenomenon known as religion, and the valid within the actual religions of the world. Once again, Troeltsch was willing to let Kant define the "true" epistemological method. In every area of experience it was Troeltsch's desire, following Kant, not only to distinguish the genuinely *a priori* elements within experience, but also to apply this method to the religious experience.

Troeltsch insisted that the modern study of religion must follow in principle Kant's critical method. It must seek the *a priori* law of consciousness which finds expression in the phenomena of the religious life. Only in this way can the *truth content* of religion be apprehended. Furthermore, a method or an instrument will thereby be obtained which can be used to criticize further the psychological manifestations of religion.

Troeltsch was, however, critical of Kant's "narrow" definition of the *a priori*. Kant seemed to think that it was possible to offer a complete or "closed" system of the *a priori* conceptions operative in every sphere of experience, but Troeltsch argued that all systems of the *a priori* are provisional and are subject to constant revision on the basis of new experiences. Troeltsch claimed that one can never assert finality for any system of categories.

Troeltsch criticized Kant's conception of the *a priori* structure on one other point. He argued that there was a difference in the way Kant used the *a priori* of the theoretical reason from the way he used it for the practical reason. In the area of morality, Kant represented the *a priori* as the whole of morality. Kant seemed to speak as if the bare abstract formula of the categorical imperative were sufficient by itself and could be equated with the entire moral experience. Furthermore, in the realm of religion, he spoke as if the simple awareness of a moral order were the entire legitimate content of the historical religions of mankind. Troeltsch insisted, rather, that the ethical and the religious *a priori* are both abstractions from the realities themselves. The religious *a priori* served to determine that which is necessary and universal in the empirical religions of the world.

Troeltsch agreed that values are justified only when their rational necessity as universally valid concepts has been demonstrated. On this basis, he proceeded to construct a critique of religion (the religious *a priori*); that is, to find those constitutive principles without which there could be no religious experience. While the religious *a priori* is similar to the *a priori* in logic, ethics, and aesthetics, in terms of the concept of necessity, there are nevertheless essential differences. The major difference may be seen in the association of the ethical, the aesthetic, and the religious *a priori*, as distinguished from the theoretical or logical *a priori*. "I have emphasized," Troeltsch affirmed in *The Religious A Priori*, "the distinction between the *a priori* of science and that of the ethical-religious-aesthetic forms of value judgment." The distinction between "theoretic logic and the practical logic of the ethical, aesthetic, and religious" must be maintained, he continued. The theoretical or logical *a priori* deals with experience in an abstract way; that is, it seeks to unify experience in terms of mechanical causation, which gives a picture of reality that is purely phenomenal. Theoretical science provides laws and concepts which can be used to control the actual empirical qualitative world of experience ("die naturwissenschaftlich-kausalgesetzliche Vernunft"). The ethical, aesthetic, and religious *a priori*, on the other hand, deal with concrete vital powers, with the creative activity of historical personalities ("die geschichtswissenschaftlich-wertgesetzliche Vernunft"). There is in our historical experience, Troeltsch asserted, something which is more than phenomenal, which is in fact, "metaphysical." There is in our historical experience the emergence of a power from within "which realizes an interior whole of spiritual values." Religious knowledge is therefore not merely a description of pious feeling as it was in Friedrich Schleiermacher (1768-1834), but it is metaphysical, proceeding from the epistemological subject, whose judgments of value bring us into association with all reality and with God, who is the absolute worth and root of all life.

The religious *a priori* is, therefore, related to the "unity" of our mental life. As a result of his psychological and epistemological analysis of the religious experience, Troeltsch claimed to have found the *a priori* conditions upon which the possibility and the fact of reality itself must depend. The religious consciousness of union with the infinite is an experience which relates the finite individual to the entire development of life. The "revelations" of the great religious personalities disclose this relationship of the finite to the infinite.

To summarize, Troeltsch's conception of the religious *a priori* may be seen in the following: (1) The religious *a priori* is the *epistemological principle* of religion. The religious *a priori* indicates the fact that there are immanent rational elements in consciousness, which we recognize to be unconditionally valid, and which relate us to God, the source of all value; (2) The religious *a priori* is the *ontological principle* of life. The religious *a priori* gives a basis to the logical, aesthetic, and ethical experiences of life, and relates these to the unconditioned, the absolute consciousness, which is beyond all phenomenal manifestations; (3) The religious *a priori* is an *epistemological* and *ontological principle* which is *being realized* in the historical development of religion; that is, religion is recognizable only through history. The religious *a priori* discloses itself in the religious experience as the norm of the religious experience. It is the standard by which the various historical religions are to be appraised, as well as the criterion by which the prevailing religion is justified and propagated and its vitality critically regulated.

Troeltsch found that his concept of the religious *a priori* gave to the religious state of feeling (*Gefühlsgehalt*), which is itself a purely irrational, alogical, experience, its fundamental quality of rational necessity. In this way, he discovered, the characteristic ideas of religion are born. By means of the religious *a priori* he came upon the epistemological and metaphysical root of the presupposition for all religious experience—the idea of God. This idea, which received its content only in union with the historical religions of the world, is an ontological concept which signifies the reality in which all things exist, the reality "in whom we live and move and have our being."

THE MEANING OF GOD IN HUMAN EXPERIENCE

Author: William Ernest Hocking (1873-   )
Type of work: Philosophy of religion
First published: 1912

PRINCIPAL IDEAS ADVANCED

Whatever is real for man is so by consent of his will, but the universe cannot be defined as merely the fulfillment of man's will.

God is known in experience; the original source of the knowledge of God is the experience of not being alone in knowing the world.

God as the Absolute Other promotes human morality by allowing man to escape reference to himself alone.

The vision of God which is provided by the mystic experience supplies the basic reason for the irrational loyalties which give life value.

Religion aims at producing a prophetic consciousness whereby man is enabled to act by reference to the divine.

William Ernest Hocking's *The Meaning of God in Human Experience* is important as a carefully reasoned attempt by an American idealist to strengthen the idealistic conception of religion by attending to pragmatic criticism and by relating experience to human action. Hocking argues that pragmatism revealed the weakness of classical idealism to be its inability to do the "work" which religious truth must do if it is to be worthwhile to man. It was Hocking's conviction that a new idealism might be fashioned which would finish the task left un-

finished by classical idealism; namely, the task of giving direction and content to worship by finding the way to the concrete and the particular.

If the meaning of God can be found in human experience, Hocking argues, the generalizations of idealist philosophers will finally make sense. Hocking attempts to study religion through its effects; he develops the notion that religious truth is a function of the active will; he claims that the experience of God arises originally as the experience of not being alone in the world; and he concludes that it is through the experience of God that man develops a concern for others and a motive for acting on their behalf.

In initiating his pragmatic study of religion, Hocking concedes that there is the danger of reducing all concerns with the "Other-world" to a present concern for men in their social relationships on this earth. But he argues that there is an interrelationship which unites the religious concerns for this and the "Other" world, and he contends that the interrelationship is best understood through experience and human action. History shows that religion begins by giving culture its content; finally, culture becomes the whole of religion. An understanding of this development is provided, Hocking claims, once it is realized that only creativity satisfies instinct, and only religion can call forth a unifying creativity.

Religion can be distinguished from art, according to Hocking, for art undertakes infinite tasks, "infinitely distant," while religion "involves a present possession in some sort of the very objects which the Arts infinitely seek." A religious man acts *as if* what he sought were already present; he conducts himself *as if* the knowledge and the immortality he seeks were already realized; he knows, in present experience, what could be attained and realized were he to confine himself to the course of nature, "only at the end of infinite progression."

Religion could not, through experience, achieve meaning and value, were feeling not an integral part of the religious experience. But Hocking is not content to reduce the religious experience to feeling alone. Although intellect cannot do the kind of work which religion demands, feeling cannot exist independently of theory. In Hocking's

words, "a *feeling does no work apart from its guiding idea.*" What is needed, then, is a conception of religion which shows ideas organically unified with feeling.

Proceeding from the central belief which is common to all idealistic theories, namely, the belief that experience alone is real, and that all knowledge of reality is through experience, Hocking advances the idealistic theory of knowledge by maintaining that reality is in part a function of will. He rejects the idea that the objects of religious knowledge are static and wholly independent; on the contrary, he argues that the objects of religious knowledge are in process of development, and that they are responsive in both character and reality to man's will. But although Hocking claims that whatever is real is so by man's consent, he goes on to argue that the real objects of man's knowledge are not merely fulfillments of his will; the objects of religious knowledge are not creations of will, although they would not be real for man were man not actively responding to them in experience. Hocking writes: "The universe fulfills my will; but it is not definable as the fulfilment of my will; it is *That Which* fulfills my will. . . . The universe has its own soul, and its own counsel which is not mine. This is its independence."

Hocking calls attention to man's desire for unity and an absolute. Optimism seems to require a monism; although a unity might be conceived as possibly being bad, an organization of many factors into a unity satisfying to the creative mind is what men require if they are to be content. Man requires the Absolute, Hocking claims, but the Absolute must not be a denial of human experience or a mysterious static entity which is in itself eternally removed from all finite values. The Absolute functions to provide a unity which man ultimately desires; it provides the terminus of man's search for truth; the monism of the world gives meaning to pluralism. Consequently, "God . . . must needs also be the Absolute," and as the Absolute, God can be of worth to man only to the degree that the meaning of God can become clear in human experience.

But how is God to be known in human experience? Hocking calls attention to the feelings of fear and awe with which men have in the past met the changing events in nature; he agrees with other writers who have argued that the experience of God seems sometimes to be provoked by moments in which man regards himself as threatened by nature and as in need of assistance. But the experience of God would not arise, Hocking goes on to argue, were not the negative aspects of experience taken as negative in virtue of the supposition that there is a positive side to be sought. Hocking finds the original source of the knowledge of God to be "an experience which might be described as an experience of *not being alone in knowing the world,* and especially the world of Nature."

In a fascinating passage which anticipates the perspective of later Christian existentialists, Hocking describes religion "as the healing of an alienation between man and his world . . . the healing of a breach which religion itself has made. . . ." In developing the conception of the "Other," who may turn out to be either an enemy or a companion, man develops, through experience, the conception of God. To fear God, to be in awe of God, to seek God—all of these states presuppose the experience of God as the Other.

Hocking does not rest with the conception of God as the Absolute and the Other; he continues by insisting that God is Other Mind. But mind is ordinarily known only through knowledge of body; all that we meet in experience are natural bodies. Hocking does not succumb to skepticism at this point; nor does he allow himself to be satisfied with accepting the hypothesis of other minds (and of Other Mind) *as if* that hypothesis were true. He expresses the desire to show how knowledge of other minds is possible. The answer is that knowledge of other minds, like knowledge of any reality, is partly a matter of the consent of will; we know because we desire to affirm what presses upon us for acceptance.

It becomes relevant for Hocking, then, to examine what knowledge of Other Mind we desire. Knowing what we desire to know, we may find that we already know it through the consent of will. Hocking decides that what any experience of Other Mind must contain is a social experience of a common world. When one person has the conviction of identity with another mind, the conviction is no illusion; the world of experience which the two selves share is a common world; changes within one person's experience of nature are changes for the Other. "I have sometimes sat looking at a comrade," writes Hocking, "speculating on this mysterious isolation of self from self. Why are we so made that I gaze and see of thee only thy Wall and never Thee?" But then the discovery comes: "But I *am* in thy soul. These things around me are in thy experience. They are thy own; when I touch them and move them I change thee." The conclusion is triumphant: "This world in which I live, is the world of thy soul: and being within that, I am within thee."

Hocking argues that the idea of a social experience, the idea of Other Mind, is an idea which rests on the social experience of Other Mind. The epistemological problem concerning other minds arises only because the experience of other minds makes the problem possible. Hocking is emphatic: ". . . my idea of Other Mind is at the same time an experience of Other Mind."

Hocking's next step is to argue that the experience of Other Mind is not to be identified with the experience of the presence of any other individual person or group of persons. The experience which constitutes for any man the knowledge of nature and of other minds is a knowledge of God. Hocking writes, "My current social experience, the finding of any fellow finite mind, is an application of my prior idea of an Other; in a sense, an application of my idea of God. It is through the knowledge of God that I am able to know men; not first through the knowledge of men that I am able to know or imagine God." Hocking's ontological argument for the existence of God, then, consists of an appeal to the experience on which any experience of nature or of other minds depends: the experience of the Absolute Other, of God.

The moral value of the experience of God arises from the circumstance that God by presence alone draws man from a self-centered concern. In being Other Mind, God continually challenges man to a self beyond himself; the individual finds himself only through abstraction from a universal

social experience. Even the knowledge of the Son depends upon a knowledge, through experience, of the Father. "Without the Father, the Son is a mere man," Hocking writes; "for the incarnate is always bound and infected by the finite thing it touches."

For Hocking, worship or prayer is the attempt to approach God to know through experience the attachment to the Other on whom all experience centers. Through the vision of God—which is to say, through the experience which gives value and being to all experience—man acquires that love which motivates him in all his actions henceforth. "The vision of God must give the reason for all the irrational attachments of life, all the sacrifices of self to brother, state, or cause. It furnishes the answer to the last Why of duty." And because of the pervasive power of that vision, Hocking argues, man finds himself being loyal to God and man; from knowledge and love of the One, man turns to knowledge and love of the many.

The mystic experience which worship engenders (or is) is prophetic, Hocking claims. Since the experience of God is an experience which incites man to creative action, it is anticipatory; it looks forward to experiences yet to be won through action. And since the religious experience is prophetic and creative, it is an experience in which the individual shares in the reality of the divine. Through creative action the individual works toward a unification of history; the religious man discovers or creates a meaning which endows human action with new sense. The religious institution, as Hocking describes it, encourages the individual not only in his social and moral relationships, but in his response to the world. What religion seeks to provide through creative experience, writes Hocking, is a "unified and responsible world, one which cares for the individual in his concrete character, and will bear out his rightful will to endure. . . ."

The influence of William James (1842-1910) is clear in this book during the early chapters in which Hocking refashions idealism according to the pragmatic ideal, and the spirit of Josiah Royce (1855-1916) makes itself felt in the later chapters in which Hocking develops the idea of God from the idea of community experience. Hocking acknowledges his debt to his "honored masters," but the product of his labors is an original work, a unified and responsible view of man's relationships to God; as such, the book contributes to that prophetic consciousness by which the labors of various men come together in a unity which is both enlightening and encouraging.

THE SOCIAL TEACHING OF THE CHRISTIAN CHURCHES

Author: Ernst Troeltsch (1865-1923)
Type of work: Christian ethics
First published: 1912

PRINCIPAL IDEAS ADVANCED

The Christian Gospel is not primarily ethical but religious.

The churches' ethical and social ideals have developed out of the relationship between the Church and the world.

The two main themes of the Gospel have given rise to two distinct types of Christianity: universalism, which stresses the universal scope of salvation through the Church; and individualism, which holds fast to the sectarian demand for individual perfection.

Because the ethical and social ideals of the churches have been developed in response to varied world-situations, there is no absolute Christian ethic that waits to be applied, but in each age it must be formulated anew.

Social structures rest upon economic and not upon ethical foundations, but men with religious and ethical convictions can change social structures.

As a teacher of theology, Ernst Troeltsch stands in the tradition of Friedrich Schleiermacher (1768-1834) and Albrecht Ritschl (1822-1889), for he holds that Christianity is rooted in the religious feeling which is common to all mankind. In *The Social* *Teaching of the Christian Churches* Troeltsch argues that the original Christian Gospel contained no explicit ethical or social teachings, but consisted in the purely religious vision of the Kingdom of God, according to which, out of purity of heart, men should seek only to know God and to do His will. The fact that the first disciples came together upon the death of their Master inevitably led, however, to the formation of a social structure, with the consequence that ethical principles and a social philosophy soon made their appearance. It is Troeltsch's contention, moreover, that as the Christian community has moved into different world situations, it has modified its principles to suit changing circumstances. Thus, while Christianity has been a perennial inspiration of ethical and social renewal, the abiding source of its influence is religious. In Troeltsch's opinion, it is a mistake to look to the New Testament, or to any period in the history of the Church, for an absolute Christian ethic. Rather, the Church today, facing an altered world situation, must work out fresh approaches to the problems confronting it. Since in this task much depends upon the correctness with which the Church understands the economic and social needs of the new age, a clear apprehension of the history of its previous successes and failures is necessary.

According to Troeltsch, the original Gospel contained two distinct ideals which have made their presence felt throughout the history of the Church and are mainly responsible for the variety of social expressions within Christianity. These ideals, which find expression in the commandments to love God with all one's heart and to love one's neighbor as oneself, are *individualism*, with its emphasis on inward purity as the prerequisite for the ultimate blessedness of seeing God, and *universalism*, with its insistence on the equality of all men in God's sight. These two motifs, reconcilable in the abstract, have been something less

than compatible under the conditions of human existence. Thus, when Christians have been concerned to make salvation accessible to all sorts and conditions of men, they have tended to neglect the requirement for individual perfection. On the other hand, when Christians have concerned themselves with the ideal of personal holiness, they have tended to lose sight of the goal of universality.

Troeltsch maintains that the two motifs of individualism and universalism have given rise to two distinct types of Christian thought, each with its characteristic sociological expression. Church-type Christianity has pursued the goal of universality while sect-type Christianity has emphasized individuality. The sect, as Troeltsch views it, is not a mere schism of the church, nor is it an undeveloped form of church-type Christianity, but it is a rival expression of the same Christian faith. According to Troeltsch, the relation between Church and sect is complementary; each stresses one of the aspects of Jesus' teaching. Christianity requires both if its Gospel is to be fully effective in the world. Moreover, the two forms interact, and they stimulate each other. Historically, the church-type is the more fundamental, whereas the sect-type, which comes and goes, has provided the dynamism necessary to bring the Church into new relations with the changing world.

As Troeltsch understands it, church-type Christianity, with its concern to make salvation accessible to entire populations, has interpreted the Church as an objective embodiment of a supernatural power in the world. It has provided itself with an authoritative clergy, which ministers salvation to all comers through the sacraments and the

Word. Recognizing human weakness, it emphasizes grace rather than law, but it provides men with an other-worldly ethical code, designed to guard them against the more prevalent perils of the flesh. The church-type regularly compromises with "the world," under the theory that the present age is the result of man's Fall and will one day be destroyed. Meanwhile, it tries to keep alive the ideal of inwardness and spiritual perfection by encouraging its members to strive for a higher devotional life. According to Troeltsch, the church-type emerged in Patristic times, and, although the Roman Catholic Church is its most complete expression, the Reformation Churches (Lutheran, Reformed, Anglican) were essentially of the same type. Further, there is a tendency for sects, as their membership grows, to pass gradually into the church-type, as, for example, the Baptist and Methodist groups.

Historically, sect-type Christianity has most often arisen in protest against the abuses of church-type Christianity. Men impressed with the demand of the Gospel for purity of heart are likely to judge that, in its emphasis upon universality, the Church has departed entirely from the spirit of its Lord. Sect-type Christianity, therefore, tends to deny the objectivity of the Church as an institution, to break down the distinction between clergy and laity, and to emphasize the necessity of individual believers working out their own salvation by inward discipline. Sociologically, sects tend to be small, intimate groups, composed of members who have demonstrated in their lives the seriousness of their profession. They interpret the universality of the Gospel in terms of love for the breth-ren, and they tend to view the world with indifference, if not with active hostility. According to Troeltsch, the spirit of sect-Christianity has been present in every age of the Church's history, from the Donatists and Montanists down to the present time. The beginning of the modern sect-movement, however, is traced to the Gregorian reforms of the twelfth and thirteenth centuries, at which time the Roman see was making its most strenuous efforts toward universality. Numerous sects also appeared at the time of the Protestant Reformation.

Any account of the Christian ethical and social philosophy is bound to be complicated by the fact that church-type and sect-type Christianity emphasize opposite poles of the Christian message (not to mention here the mystical-type, which, in Troeltsch's analysis, constitutes a third important variant). It is further complicated by the fact that the Church has faced different economic and social conditions in each period of its history, and it has responded to them concretely.

In the ancient world, the Christian movement encountered a highly developed social system in process of deterioration. Its response was mainly that of passive acquiescence. Following the way marked out by Paul, it accepted the Roman Empire as a provisional institution of divine justice for sinful man; in the same way, it made its accord with the social structure of the time, including the institution of slavery. The Church looked upon itself as a new society in which the demands of brotherly love and equality must be respected, but the larger social and economic situation, even after Christianity became the official religion of the Empire, was not its concern.

With the rise of new territorial regimes in Europe, the situation was altered. Monarchs, ambitious to bring their peoples the benefits of civilization, welcomed the help and guidance of the Church. Laboring under crude conditions, the Church of the early Middle Ages was offered an unexampled opportunity to mold a civilization according to ethical principles. According to Troeltsch, the Church's lack did not lie on the ethical side, nor did it want the highest motivation; its failure to accomplish more was due to its not understanding economic and social processes and the dependence of ethical achievements upon those processes.

A change took place at the height of the Middle Ages, when Gregory VII (c.1021-1085) and his successors undertook to recover the leadership from the territorial churches. The high catholicism of Innocent III (1160-1216) and of Thomas Aquinas (c.1225-1274) rested upon a historical achievement—the existence in actuality of a Christianized Europe. This made a difference in social theory. No longer was the Church thought of as being in opposition to the world, but as perfecting the world. In the new synthesis, ethical, social, and political foundations were ascribed to natural law; the Church considered that its task was not to criticize or revise these foundations, but to bring them to their intended perfection by means of supernatural grace.

With the passing of the feudal order and the rise of nationalism and an urban economy, the Christianized institutions of the Middle Ages ceased to suffice. At this point, says Troeltsch, following in the main the thesis of Max Weber's *Protestant Ethic and*

the *Spirit of Capitalism* (1905), it was the Calvinistic churches which proved resourceful, taking a constructive attitude toward such problems as urban government, international competition, and a money economy. Lutheranism, in Troeltsch's judgment, faltered before this new undertaking when it accepted on principle a division of function between the Church and the secular order. The sects, on the other hand, commonly representing the lower strata of society and fired with apocalyptic visions, stirred up radical and Utopian movements which continued to gain momentum even after the sects had disappeared. According to Troeltsch, the social ethic of contemporary Protestantism is an amalgam of Calvinistic and sectarian principles; he calls this combined ethic "ascetic Protestantism." It stands for separation of Church and State; for democracy, independence, and love of liberty; for zeal in one's calling, concern for humanity, and the reform (rather than the overthrow) of existing social institutions. Meanwhile, says Troeltsch, the Catholic Church has revised its social outlook, while retaining its medieval foundation. Accepting capitalism and industrialism, it has strived to remedy the impersonality and servitude of modern society by recalling men to the principles of natural law, and by working to restore such features of the organic society of the Middle Ages as the family, the guild, and the social class.

Troeltsch maintains, in opposition to historical materialism, that the spiritual life of man is independent of economic and social conditions. The Gospel preached by Jesus and the early Apostles had a religious origin and cannot be explained in terms of the class struggles and political oppressions of the time. In the history of the West, religious and ethical beliefs have interacted with social and political forces to help determine cultural change. The teachings of the churches have, to be sure, been influenced by economic conditions, but the reverse is also true.

Nevertheless, according to Troeltsch, the Church must learn from modern social science the impressive truth that the foundation of society is always economic and not ethical. This means, on the one hand, that if Christianity is to achieve the fullest moral and spiritual development of men, it must concern itself with the need for changes in the social constitution. On the other hand, it also means that Christian reformers have to divest themselves of many naïve notions about the possibility of achieving the kind of changes which they desire.

Reviewing the situation in 1911, Troeltsch concluded that the churches had lost most of the influence that they formerly exercised. Ascetic Protestantism, which had done so much to shape modern bourgeois society, had ceased to be a source of fertile directives; Catholicism, in seeking to restore an organic pattern of society, was blind to historical actualities; Christian Socialism, the heir to sect-type radicalism, nourished dreams of Utopian transformations, but had no sense of the brute reality of economic and social forces. The prevailing social philosophy of the day, said Troeltsch, was not Christian, but an expression of the new rationalistic individualism which owed its foundations to the principles of Newtonian and Darwinian science. But Troeltsch regarded the situation as unstable. "Radical in-

dividualism," he said, "will probably soon be an interlude between an old and a new civilization of constraint. This individualism may be compared with the process of taking the materials of a house which has been pulled down, sorting them out into the actual individual stones, out of which a new house will be built. What the new house will look like, and what possibilities it will provide for the development of Christian ethics and of Christian social philosophy, no one can at present tell. Christian social philosophy will bring to the task both its common sense and its metaphysical individualism; but it will have to share the labour with other builders, and like them it will be restricted by the peculiarities of the ground and of the material."

Troeltsch suggests that five main ethical values have emerged in the history of Christianity; these values will, undoubtedly, find their place in any new formulation of the Christian social ideal. First is the conviction, arising out of its belief in a personal God, that the human personality is worth while; to this is added its conception of a fundamental social relation between man and man, based on its belief in God's all-embracing love; a solution to the problem of equality and inequality, rooted in the voluntary acceptance by man of his responsibility in the social order; a high realization of charity, or the spirit of active helpfulness, without which no social order can long endure; and, finally, a conviction of the validity of human aspirations, not as conditioned by the relativities of earthly life but as founded in the original purpose of creation. Possessing these guiding persuasions, says Troeltsch, the Church has no need of fixed programs or Utopian goals. "The truth is," he concludes, "the Kingdom of God is within us. But we must let our light shine before men in confident and untiring labour that they may see our good works and praise our Father in Heaven. The final ends of all humanity are hidden within His Hands."

THE PROBLEM OF CHRISTIANITY

Author: Josiah Royce (1855-1916)
Type of work: Philosophy of religion
First published: 1913

PRINCIPAL IDEAS ADVANCED

The central features of the Christian religion are the idea of a spiritual community of the faithful, the idea of the inescapable moral guilt of the individual, and the idea of atonement for the sin and guilt of mankind.

The Christian doctrine of life, understood as the coherent interpenetration of these three essential ideas, is metaphysically grounded as a community of interpretation within the world, which is a universe of signs and interpretation.

This interpretation of Christianity is both faithful to the distinctive essence of the Christian religion and ethically and religiously significant for the modern man.

The *Problem of Christianity* first appeared as a lecture series delivered at Manchester College, Oxford, in the winter of 1913. This work constitutes the mature reflections of Josiah Royce about those religious problems which first drove him into philosophy and which persistently engaged his attention. These meditations reveal the author's special concern with the Christian faith, and most especially with the spirit of the Church. At the same time, these contemplations are philosophical in character and have their immediate origin in the author's work on the philosophy of loyalty. The philosophy of loyalty is an absolute ethic which implies and depends upon the concept of community as its meta-physico-ethical foundation. Thus, the historic Christian religion has to be interpreted for modern man, while modern religious philosophy needs an interpretation of the historic Christian community. The interpretation of Christianity involves the convergence of the religious and philosophical aspects of our remembered history and, consequently, a method which is neither apologetic, skeptical, nor indifferent in its attitude toward the Christian religion.

The concept of "problem" is an important clue to Royce's method of analysis. It is Royce's intention to interpret to his fellow men a common religious inheritance for the sake of the future. This intention expresses itself in the activity of formulating the historic Christian religion as a "problem" for modern man. The concept of "problem" is connected with grasping the essential Christian ideas in their coherence. A "problem" is formulated in the understanding of these ideas as an interpretation of life, rather than as an empty metaphysical or theological dogma. The question of the philosophical truth of these ideas as an interpretation of life also functions as a "problem." All of these problems are unified in the problem of Christianity, Royce's own venture of interpretation. The concept of "problem" thus indicates the method of Royce's philosophy of religion.

Royce begins his examination of the essential concepts of the Christian religion in their human significance with the idea of a beloved community. Man is naturally a social creature. Furthermore, because the community is an organism making demands upon its members, the individual can be obligated or devoted to the community as such. Devotion to the community is the condition of the ethics of loyalty; the ethics of loyalty, in turn, implies the concept of a beloved community, the community as a source and object of devotion. Human devotion is ordinarily directed toward a particular community, although the social history of man shows the emergence and development of the ideal of a universal community.

The Christian idea of community becomes important in connection with the universalization of the idea of the beloved community. The Christian idea has one of its most important sources in Jesus' idea of an active love based upon the love of God for man rather than upon man's self-abnegation.

Hence the ethical significance of the Kingdom of God. Yet the Christian idea of the universal community comes to full expression only in the Pauline doctrine of the Body of Christ. The concept of the Kingdom of God is an incomplete sketch of a universal community because it is lacking in ethical rules for practical decisions.

In the doctrine of the Body of Christ, Paul articulates the concept of a new entity which counsels the love of neighbor as neighbor because the neighbor is a fellow member of the visible community, which is based upon the hope that this community will actually become universal, and which thereby becomes a form by means of which Christian love assumes the ethical aspect of the spirit of loyalty. Thus, the Christian achieved the idea of a beloved community. Still this essential idea must be interpreted for modern man because the idea was originally connected with the expectation of the imminent end of the world.

The second essential idea of the Christian religion is the idea of the overwhelming moral burden of the individual. This idea has its natural origin in the fact that in human nature there are many tendencies which the moral consciousness views as evil. Conduct is learned within the social environment. Social training teaches the individual knowledge of "the law" and at the same time intensifies self-consciousness as opposed to "the law." The dialectic of internalized social tension tends to breed an ever greater sense of guilt and a growing division within the will. The dialectic of moral guilt essentially expresses the Pauline doctrine of "original sin," because it describes that moral situation in which one cannot save himself. The Pauline doctrine of original sin, stripped of its antiquated language, is essentially the idea of the overwhelming moral burden of the individual.

The problem is resolved by means of the doctrine of grace or the idea of a beloved community. The individual cannot of himself effect his own wholehearted union with the natural community. He can be saved from his predicament only through faith or loyalty in the beloved community, a universal community of grace which is both existent and lovable. But a community which is so beloved is possible only by divine grace. We can choose to be loyal only insofar as we find ourselves already within the community of grace and choose to remain loyal. What is the origin of such a community? How can there be an actual universal community which transcends the natural bonds of communities of law? Royce concedes the mystery of the origin of such a community. He can speak only of the miracle of a leader who loves and who has the power to create what He loves. In Pauline language, the beloved community is the consequence of the work of Christ. The spirit of Christ is the origin of the beloved community. Beyond this mystery, this miracle, we cannot penetrate.

A still deeper problem than that of the overwhelming moral burden of the individual faces the beloved community. If it is possible to choose loyalty to the beloved community, it is also possible to choose disloyalty. Disloyalty is shown in the act of betrayal. The problem of the traitor is not merely the problem of social alienation, of an individual's being unable to save himself through the attitude of loyalty. The traitor, remembering his act of disloyalty, finds himself in a kind of spiritual damnation. He has committed a sin which neither he nor the community can forgive. As long as time continues, nothing that he can do will ever erase the deed. He is condemned to "the hell of the irrevocable." Yet, Royce claims, there may be a way in which the traitor can be reinstated within the community. The guilt of the traitor may be atoned, not by denying or seeking to obliterate the traitorous deed, but rather by overcoming it. If a faithful and suffering servant of the beloved community acts in response to the evil deed so as to help create a better world than would have existed if the evil deed had not been done, then atonement is possible. The act of atonement does not remove the evil deed, but rather transforms its meaning by a creative and thereby reconciling efficacy. For every traitorous deed of Judas in the history of the beloved community, there can be an atoning work of Jesus, the suffering servant.

These three doctrines of community, guilt, and atonement, together constitute the Christian doctrine of life. The doctrine of life is both a mode of living and a way of salvation. It involves a creative attitude toward the human will in that it seeks the raising of the human self from its natural level to the level of grace by means of the definition of the ideal community. It implies the creation of a universal community which, throughout its history, realizes new forms of morality within the Christian spirit and seeks continually the triumph of good over evil through deeds of loyalty and atonement.

In the second volume of *The Prob-*

lem of Christianity Royce turns to a consideration of the metaphysical bases of the Christian doctrine of life. This is both an inquiry into the metaphysical foundations of the essence of Christianity and an articulation of the metaphysical aspect of Royce's own method of delineating the essence of Christianity. The metaphysical inquiry thus has both its ontological and its epistemological aspect. Through Royce's ingenuity these two aspects are held together in his account of what might be called the metaphysics of the Holy Spirit.

Consider, for instance, Royce's treatment of the relation of time and community. Individuals are differentiated in their perceptions, feelings, and acts. The fact that people function collectively in a common social nexus does not necessarily mean that they form a community; they may be nothing more than a mob. Community by definition requires a common interpretation of a remembered past for the sake of an ideal expectation. Time is of the essence to community also with respect to the transformation of the irrevocable deed of guilt by the succeeding act of atonement. There is a community only insofar as there is a temporal continuity serving as the foundation for present acts of cooperation.

The concept of interpretation requires further analysis. Why does the community require interpretation? How does interpretation form the basis of community? Royce declares that his theory of interpretation is based upon Charles Sanders Peirce's (1839-1914) theory of signs, but is a novel application of it. Like Peirce, Royce describes interpretation as a triadic function in contrast to the dyadic char-acter of perception and conception. In perception or conception there is merely the perceiver and the perceived, or the thinker and the thought. Interpretation, however, implies that which is to be interpreted, an interpreter, and a society for whom the interpretation is made. The datum of interpretation is thus a sign to be interpreted *by* someone *to* someone. Furthermore, any factor in one triadic order of interpretation may serve as the datum for a further interpretation. Consequently, interpretation as a theory of signs is itself an infinite social process. Interpretation is necessary for community because individuals are unique in the individuality of their perceptions, conceptions, and action. Interpretation arises from the will to interpret, and it has as its aim the ideal unity of community.

Insofar as individuals are real and are characterized by the will to interpret, the theory of signs is also a theory of reality as social process. In this respect the world always appears as a situation requiring interpretation. An interpretation of the world is true in proportion to the adequacy with which the community of interpretation realizes its ideal unity. Furthermore, any interpretation of the world becomes at the same time a sign for further interpretation. Thus, the world as social process consists of signs and interpretation. "The world is the interpretation of the problems which it presents."

The world understood as social process is profoundly connected with the fact of historical change and with the task of interpretation. This task of interpretation Royce takes upon himself when he treats the problem of Christianity, interpreting the essential

Christian doctrine of life to modern man. Modern man, the man who epitomizes the historical education of the human race, is not the same as the man of the New Testament world. The future vitality of the Christian religion depends upon its adequate interpretation to modern man. Yet modern man longs for a universal community, and this search depends for its realization upon the interpretation of the essence of Christianity. In his interpretation of the problem of Christianity, Royce exhibits the ethic of loyalty in the realm of philosophical action.

THE IDEA OF THE HOLY

Author: Rudolf Otto (1869-1937)
Type of work: Phenomenology of religion
First published: 1917

PRINCIPAL IDEAS ADVANCED

The essence of deity cannot be defined conceptually.

The idea of the holy depends on understanding the features of the experience of the numinous, that which transcends comprehension.

By the feeling of mysterium tremendum *man knows the power and majesty of the holy.*

By the feeling of fascinans *man knows the appealing fascination of God.*

An awareness of the nonrational elements in the deity is found in every religion, for mankind is endowed with a pure a priori *capacity for experiencing the holy; but the numinous has been most fully realized in Christianity, for the holy has been made manifest in the person of Christ.*

The Idea of the Holy endeavors to describe the nonconceptual elements of religion. According to Rudolf Otto, religion is rational in that it ascribes definable attributes to the deity; it is nonrational or suprarational in that the essence of the deity is not exhaustively defined by any such ascription.

The nonrational aspect of religion does not admit of a conceptual definition. The nonrational is the innermost core of religion, the experience that is peculiarly religious, the experience of the holy that can be evoked but not defined. The awareness of deity transcends comprehension in either rational or ethical terms. To describe such awareness Rudolph Otto coined the word *numinous.*

The primary purpose of *The Idea of the Holy* is to analyze the numinous into its elements, and to explore the conditions under which the consciousness of the numinous has arisen.

The numinous is felt to be objective and outside the self. It is more than merely a feeling of dependence. To be understood it must be experienced in oneself, in a creature-consciousness or creature-feeling, when a person feels himself overwhelmed by and responds to an overpowering might.

The nature of the numinous, that aspect of deity which transcends or eludes comprehension in rational or ethical terms, can only be suggested by the way it is reflected in the mind in terms of feeling. The numinous is not identical with feeling; it is rather what evokes certain affective states.

The deepest and most basic element of strong religious emotion is the feeling *mysterium tremendum*.

The adjective *tremendum* connotes more than is usually understood by fear. It implies marking the holy off by a feeling of peculiar dread; it contains an element of awfulness, of awe, of religious dread, evoked by the awe-inspiring object as it is experienced directly. Man feels that certain aspects of the deity are absolutely unapproachable; he is overwhelmed by the absolute overpoweringness, the awful majesty of the deity. He feels submerged and as nothing. He feels the urgency or energy of the numinous object which he expresses symbolically in terms of will, force, wrath, and in the idea of the living God.

The substantive idea *mysterium* refers to more than what is merely an uncomprehended and unexplained secret; it is here the "wholly-other." It places the mind in a stupor and fills it with wonder and astonishment. What is mysterious lies beyond the usual, the intelligible, and the familiar. The character of what is "wholly other" is incommensurable with our own character, and it is in this feeling of the "wholly other" that the numinous is experienced.

The numinous experience is not exhausted by the element of daunting awfulness and majesty; such experi-ence also contains something uniquely attractive and fascinating, the element of *fascinans*. The deity may appear as an object both of dread and of fascination. Man is entranced and captivated by the mystery. The numinous exercises a supreme fascination, analogous to the sublime in the field of aesthetics.

Man's reaction to the numinous is the occasion of his awareness of sin and atonement. As he feels submerged into nothingness, his self is devalued; the holy appears as a category of value. For when the numinous reality is a fact of consciousness, man spontaneously depreciates himself and is aware of his own "uncleanness" and "sinfulness." Such awareness does not arise from the consciousness of a violation of a divine commandment; it accompanies rather the awareness of the deity. It belongs to a special category of valuation: the feeling of absolute "profaneness."

To understand what this profaneness is a person must himself be in the spirit, for profaneness is felt only when a person knows himself to be a creature in confrontation with that which is above all creatures.

Such an encounter enables him to pass upon the deity a judgment of appreciation diametrically opposite to the profane; namely, the ascription of the category of the holy, a category that belongs to the numinous alone.

The recognition of the holy need not be accompanied by the sense of moral demands. The holy is inwardly recognized as commanding our respect; it is extolled as a value beyond all conception, as a power that received praise because it is absolutely worthy of praise. The deity is valued subjectively because of its fascination; it is valued subjectively because it is august.

The awareness of sin and the need of atonement develops when numinous unworthiness or disvalue is centered in moral delinquency. The need of atonement arises when man feels that his profaneness makes him unworthy to stand before the holy, that he might even defile it by his presence. Man's desire for atonement is expressed as a longing to transcend his unworthiness as a creature, as a profane rational being.

Christianity, more than any other religion, has expressed the need for atonement, not because it has developed the conceptual theory that the righteousness of Christ is imputed to the sinner, but because the Christian experiences the atonement as an incomprehensible grace whereby God permits access to Himself.

The essential nature of the consciousness of the numinous can be clarified by examining the way in which it is outwardly expressed and is transmitted from mind to mind.

The numinous cannot be taught, but where the spirit is present and there is an inborn capacity to receive and understand it, it can be directly induced, incited, and aroused.

The sense of the numinous is indirectly evoked by feelings that seem to be opposite to the numinous in significance. Thus, the fearful and loathsome may give rise to genuine feelings of religious awe. Terror and dread may be replaced by a feeling for the grand and the sublime. The terrifying, the baffling, and the miraculous may awaken man's sense of the *mysterium*. The numinous is also evoked by art and by the sublime; it appears in music, in magic, and in silence.

The feelings of the nonrational and the numinous are found in every religion but they are pre-eminently present in the Old and New Testaments.

In the Old Testament, mystery moves in all its potency. In Yahweh the numinous dominates the rational, and in Elohim the rational overshadows the numinous. Moses marks the beginning of a process in which the numinous is rationalized and moralized until it becomes the holy in the fullest sense in the Prophets and the Gospels. In Deutero-Isaiah the stage of a universal world-religion is reached; Yahweh in His pre-Mosaic form is transcended.

The Old Testament champions of the living God, the God of anger, love, and the emotions, unwittingly defended the nonrational core of the Biblical conception of God against excessive rationalization. They erred, however, in that they misconceived the numinous character of such attributes and regarded them literally instead of admitting them only as figurative "indications of something essentially non-rational."

In the New Testament, apprehension of the numinous reaches its consummation in the Gospel of the Kingdom, for the Kingdom is absolute greatness, the wholly other, contrasted to the world of here and now.

The numinous experience is to be found in the garden of Gethsemane and in the Christian confession "I believe in Jesus Christ risen from the dead." To speak of the "Resurrection" is to speak of a mystery. To hold to the mystery of the risen Christ necessitates the rejection of two interpretations; namely, the supernaturalistic notion that the empty tomb was evident to the senses, and the rationalistic notion that the faith in the Resurrection grew out of the subjective impression made by Jesus on His disciples.

Both the rationalists and the supernaturalists ignore the important fact about this experience; namely, that it was a mystery, a mystery which, with the certainty of eternal truth, discloses the numinous.

The numinous is present in the writings of Paul, when he speaks of predestination, and it is also present in the writings of John, when he writes of the Spirit; it is seen in Roman Catholic forms of worship and dogma, and it is also found in the works of Luther and of Schleiermacher.

The permeation of the rational by the nonrational deepens the rational conception of God. To disregard the numinous elements leads to the impoverishment of religion, but when the numinous is permeated by elements signifying rationality, purpose, morality and personality, a fuller idea of the holy emerges. The "holy" now appears as a complex category that combines rational and nonrational components; the "holy" is a purely *a priori* category. Rational ideas of absoluteness, completion, necessity, substantiality— ideas of the good as objective value— are evolved not from sense perception but from an original, underived capacity of the mind implanted in the "pure reason." (Otto's view here is markedly Kantian.) The nonrational elements in the category of the holy are also absolutely pure. The ideas of the numinous and the feelings that correspond to them refer to what is deeper than pure reason, to the *Seelengrund* (the bottom of the soul). Sense impressions are simply the occasion, the stimulus for our awareness of the numinous.

The facts of numinous consciousness point to a hidden substantive source, to a pure reason in the profoundest sense, to a depth beyond the pure theoretical reason and the pure practical reason of Kant.

The discovery that man has an innate predisposition to religion provides the key for an insight into the historical origin and development of religion, from its cruder phases to its most mature Christian form.

Man possesses a faculty of divination, a faculty of genuinely cognizing and recognizing the appearances of the holy. Instances of divination are to be found in primitive Christianity, as, for example, when the disciples of Jesus experienced the holy in His person and life; He became a revelation of the holy. Divination is also to be found in Christianity today, for even modern man recognizes the holy and responds to it. It makes no difference that the records of Christ's life are fragmentary, filled with uncertainties and with legendary elements. Christianity has undergone significant changes since the time when it was simple, unpretentious religion. Nevertheless, contemporary Christianity retains the essence and inner meaning to be found in the religion of Jesus; Christianity continues to be a religion of redemption and salvation, a redemption to be fulfilled by God in the promise of His Kingdom hereafter, and yet to be experienced here and now in the present experience of His Fatherhood.

Otto writes that any man can experience Christ as holiness made manifest, not by demonstration or by applying some conceptual rule but by pure contemplation, by the submission of the mind to a pure impression of the object, out of which there arises the pure feeling of "recognition of holiness," the intuition of the eternal in the temporal.

The holy is thus an *a priori* category of the mind, and yet it is manifest in outward appearance. The ultimate criterion of religion is to be found neither in what a religion has done for a culture nor in any external feature. The innermost essence of religion is the idea of holiness as such. Rudolph Otto argues that holiness is found supremely in Jesus, who is more than a prophet: "He is the Son."

The Idea of the Holy is a part of that contemporary theological tradition which places religious intuitions beyond rational criticism, beyond the results of Biblical exegesis and higher criticism, in the realm of religious feeling. The book has contributed to the widespread tendency of religious thinkers to emphasize the nonrational element of religion. It may be regarded as a modification and outgrowth of the liberal tradition within Protestantism.

A THEOLOGY FOR THE SOCIAL GOSPEL

Author: Walter Rauschenbusch (1861-1918)
Type of work: Christian social ethics
First published: 1917

Principal Ideas Advanced

Just as the social gospel needs theological grounds to be effective, so theology needs social concern to be vital and relevant in the modern world.

The social gospel is neither alien nor new; it exists as an authentic part of the Christian faith and seeks to focus religious interest on contemporary ethical problems.

By its stress on the pervasiveness of sin in the corporate and collective efforts of men and on social salvation, the social gospel is a corrective to the one-sided focus on personal sin and individual salvation.

The doctrine of the Kingdom of God is central in a theology for the social gospel.

Occasionally a book is hailed as the epitome of an entire movement. This is the case with Walter Rauschenbusch's *A Theology for the Social Gospel.* Walter Rauschenbusch was one of the most distinguished leaders of the influential "Social Gospel Movement" which was prominent in American Church life from 1875 to 1930. His

name is synonymous with that movement.

Rauschenbusch published his first book in America in 1907 (earlier he wrote *Leben Jesu,* 1895, and three other works in German) in order to discharge a debt. The book was *Christianity and the Social Crisis,* and the debt he owed, in his own words, was "to the working people on the west side of New York City," whose life he had shared for eleven years as pastor of the Second German Baptist Church, on the borders of "Hell's Kitchen."

In his last and greatest work, *A Theology for the Social Gospel*, Rauschenbusch never ceased to feel that he still owed "help to the poor and plain people" who were his friends. This volume consists of lectures delivered under the auspices of the Nathaniel W. Taylor Foundation at Yale Divinity School. The author sought to construct a systematic theology large enough to match and vital enough to back a social gospel. He wanted to furnish intellectual grounds for the social gospel. This meant no less a task than to conceive Christian doctrine in social terms and to relate the Christian message to the regeneration of the social order.

Thus, the book gives the lie to those who charge that the social gospel is without theological foundations and convictions. Rauschenbusch writes with power and passion. Some of the passages in this book read as if they were straight from the prophetic writings of Amos or Isaiah. This modern prophet brought to his task a disciplined intellect, which shows signs of his professorship for twenty-one years at Rochester Theological Seminary. Never turgid in style, his scholarship is blended with the social compassion and zeal which characterized his vigorous ministry.

Many of the issues that the author deals with in this book have a familiar contemporary ring. He stressed the importance of relating theological thought and social concern. Failure to relate theology and social ethics means that the choice is between an "unso- cial system of theology and an irreligious system of social salvation." The social gospel without theology is ineffective, but theology without social relevance is dead. The interplay and interdependence of theology and ethics will result in a purifying influence upon theology. When ethics inspires theology, religion is more sensitive to ethical righteousness. But lest it become sterile intellectualism, theology always stands in need of the kind of rejuvenation that ethics can give to it. Hence, the social gospel is a reformatory force within theology.

Often the social gospel is pitted against a personal gospel of individual salvation. This debate between a personal or social gospel remains unresolved today. It is true that the social gospel movement centered attention on the social side, perhaps as a corrective to the preoccupation of conservative Christian thinkers who stressed personal salvation. However, among the best thinkers of the social gospel movement, and particularly in the thought of Rauschenbusch, the social gospel and individual salvation are not mutually exclusive.

Religion seeks nothing less than the wholeness and unity of life, Rauschenbusch claims. It speaks to man's total existence, both personal and social. When the Gospel becomes narrowly individualistic and places excessive emphasis on personal salvation and on the sin in the individual human heart, it fails to comprehend the pervasiveness of sin in man's collective efforts and in the institutions of society. It is against this oversimplified view of individual sin and personal salvation that much of the polemic of the social gospel movement was waged.

Walter Rauschenbusch argued that

theology must be related to the human situation. Great religious thinkers who wrote seminal theological treatises were leaders whose ideas responded to the challenge of specific situations. Thus, St. Paul wrote in the context of a fresh religious experience and of practical problems facing particular Christian communities. Luther's doctrine of "justification by faith" grew out of his profound religious experience and of the great social, political, and religious upheaval of his time. In like manner, the social gospel is a response to the "consciousness of vast sins and sufferings and the longing for righteousness and a new life."

The social gospel concentrates religious interest on the major ethical problems of social life. It despises the tithing of mint, anise, and cumin, and it seeks to deal with the weightier matters of God's law, with justice and mercy. It is neither alien nor new, but authentic as a vital part of the historic Christian faith. It is found in the Old and continued in the New Testament. Far from its being alien or novel, the gospel rests on the most ancient and authentic foundation of the Apostles and Prophets. The social gospel restored the doctrine of the Kingdom of God that John the Baptist and Jesus proclaimed, a doctrine which was obscured and forgotten by theologians who developed their system along individualistic lines.

Rauschenbusch's major aim is to examine theological doctrines to discover how the social gospel affects them and to see how these doctrines could give more adequate expression to the social gospel. He deals extensively with the doctrines of sin and redemption. He also considers such theological topics as the Kingdom of God, God,

the Holy Spirit, revelation, the sacraments, eschatology, and the atonement.

In his discussion of sin, Rauschenbusch acknowledges that one of the widespread criticisms of the social gospel is that its exponents fail to appreciate the power of human sin and tend to put the blame for wrongdoing on the social environment. Although he stresses the social reality of sin, Rauschenbusch himself never fails to recognize sin in its personal dimension. Sin is defined as selfishness, sensuousness, and godlessness. It is always revealed in contrast to righteousness. The view that selfishness is the essence of sin is more in harmony with the social gospel than the notion that sin is rebellion against God.

Rauschenbusch explains the nature of sin in the following passage: "The sinful mind, then, is the unsocial and anti-social mind. To find the climax of sin we must not linger over a man who swears, or sneers at religion, or denies the mystery of the trinity, but put our hands on social groups who have turned the patrimony of a nation into the private property of a small class, or have left the peasant labourers cowed, degraded, demoralized, and without rights in the land. When we find such in history, or in present-day life, we shall know we have struck real rebellion against God on the higher levels of sin."

Traditional theology has overworked the doctrine of original sin. Rauschenbusch contends it has overlooked the fact that sin is transmitted through social customs and institutions, through traditions which the individual absorbs from his social group. A theology for the social gospel must argue that original sin is partly social. It is transmitted from generation to generation not only by biological propagation, but also by social assimilation. The result is corporate sin or a "Kingdom of Evil."

Despite our common involvement in a Kingdom of Evil in which we share a collective guilt, the social gospel holds forth the possibility of personal and social salvation, and the necessity of redeeming the historical life of man from social wrongs. Salvation involves a transformation in which man turns from self to God and humanity. Man's selfishness is replaced by a loving spirit in conformity to the loving impulses of the spirit of God. Faith becomes not mere belief or the submission of the mind to affirmations of dogma; rather, faith means prophetic vision, hope in a righteous and fraternal social order, and affirming our fellowship with God and man.

The doctrine of the Kingdom of God is central in a theology for the social gospel. With it, the task of redeeming the social order and of proclaiming and applying social morality has a firm footing. The doctrine of the Kingdom occupied a chief place in the teachings of Jesus, but it was reduced to a pathetic remnant in the course of Christian thought. As a result, the ethical force and revolutionary ferment of Christianity was weakened. The Church was left without a corrective force, and salvation was viewed in terms of an individual's relation to the Church and to the future life, but not in relation to the task of saving the social order.

Contrary to much popular misconception, Rauschenbusch did not hold the naïve view that the Kingdom of God would soon be ushered in on earth by dint of man's own labors. Others in the social gospel movement may have thought in such optimistic terms, but Rauschenbusch wrote that the Kingdom of God was initiated by Jesus Christ and will be brought to fulfillment by the power of God in His own time. He believed that the Kingdom of God is always both present and future: "The Kingdom of God is always coming, but we can never say, 'Lo, here.'" Rauschenbusch did express hope, however, in the progressive development of mankind toward the Kingdom of God. The living marks of the Kingdom are worth of personality, freedom, growth, love, solidarity, and service. He regarded our labor for the Kingdom here and now as preparation for our participation in it hereafter.

Rauschenbusch indicates how the social gospel is related to the doctrine of God by his contention that man's conceptions of God are shaped by the social conditions of his environment. Under tyrannous conditions the idea of God is apt to be tainted with despotism and to stress God's right of arbitrary decision. When Jesus called God "our Father," he democratized the conception of God. As long as economic and political despotisms prevail, the triumph of the Christian idea of God as a loving Father will never be final. The transcendent conception of God as dwelling on high, apart from human life, is a natural basis for autocratic ideas about God. The view that God is immanent in humanity, and that He moves and lives in the life of mankind, is the natural basis for democratic ideas about him. God is the ground of all social unity; He transcends all human barriers so that all become unified by a spiritual oneness and social solidarity.

The work of the Holy Spirit gives

evidence of the social nature of religion. Old Testament prophets were not solitary figures, but were surrounded by religious groups to whom and for whom they spoke in moments of inspired social consciousness. Genuine prophecy arises where fervent religious experience combines with a democratic spirit, a strong sense of social injustice, and free utterance.

Rauschenbusch was convinced that the era of prophetic Christianity had just begun, and that the "social gospel is the voice of prophecy in modern life." American Christianity stands forever indebted to the eloquent and prophetic voice of Walter Rauschenbusch. He made Christian faith relevant to the abuses, injustices, and social miseries growing out of the industrial revolution during the first few decades of the twentieth century.

THE PLAN OF SALVATION

Author: Benjamin B. Warfield (1851-1921)
Type of work: Calvinist apologetics
First published: 1918

PRINCIPAL IDEAS ADVANCED

The basic issue with respect to the nature of God's plan of salvation is between the naturalists, who hold that man saves himself, and the supernaturalists, who maintain that God saves man.

The entire organized Church—Orthodox Greek, Roman Catholic, and Protestant, whether Lutheran, Reformed, or Arminian—opposes naturalism by confessing that whatever part man plays in the saving process is subsidiary and is itself the effect of the divine operation; it is God and God alone who saves the soul.

The fundamental issue among supernaturalists concerns the immediacy of the saving operations of God: Does God save men by the immediate operations of His grace (as the evangelicals contend), or does He act upon men only through instrumentalities established for that purpose (as the sacerdotalists maintain)?

The Plan of Salvation was written by Benjamin B. Warfield, who was a Professor at Princeton Theological Seminary from 1887 until 1921. During his lifetime Warfield was considered by many to be the leading orthodox protestant theologian in the English speaking world.

The Plan of Salvation is concerned with an examination of those divine activities which center around, and have as their proximate goal, the salvation of sinful man. That God acts upon a plan in all His activities is a presupposition of theism. To believe in a personal God who has immediate control of the world He has made is to believe in a plan underlying all that God does, including what He does to save man. For believers, therefore, there can be no question as to the reality of God's plan. The only question that can arise concerns the nature of God's plan. The latter question has been answered in many different ways, not only by non-Christians, but by Christians themselves. The first chapter of the present work surveys and critically examines views which have been held by large parties in the Church. It is followed by separate chapters on autosoterism, sacerdotalism, universalism, and Calvinism.

The most profound division with respect to the plan of salvation is for Warfield the cleft between the naturalists and the supernaturalists. The issue here is whether God has planned to leave man completely responsible for saving himself, or whether He has planned to intervene and thereby to bring salvation to man. In other words, does God save man or does man save himself?

The naturalists have maintained that salvation is from ourselves. Such a doctrine of autosoterism, self-salvation, is in effect the denial of the true God and the gift of His grace.

The influence of the notion that salvation can be secured by man's own wisdom and power was first systematically presented in the Christian church by Pelagius (c.360-c.420), the British monk and theologian, whose system is characteristic of such ideas of salvation which have succeeded it.

Pelagius built a complete autosoteric scheme upon the central principle of the plenary ability of the human will; since man has been endowed with an inalienable freedom of will, he is fully competent to do all that is required of him. Pelagius denied any "fall" suffered by mankind. Man does not inherit any sin or weakness from his past history. He is born in the same condition of innocence in which Adam was created, and throughout his life he continues in the same condition in which he is born. Adam's Fall is at most a bad example which no one need follow unless he so chooses. Even our own past sins do not in any way abridge our ability to keep God's commandments and to be henceforth free from sin. Man can at any moment cease all sinning and be perfect from that very instant. To this great gift of freedom God has added the gifts of the Law and the Gospel to point to the way of righteousness and to persuade man to walk in it. The gift of Christ supplies expiation for past sins for all who will do God's will, and it sets a good example. Everyone who turns from his sins and acts righteously is accepted by God and rewarded according to his deeds. The grace of God, in the sense of inward help from God, is not needed. The Pelagian meaning of grace refers solely to the fundamental endowment of man with an inalienable freedom of will, together with the inducements God has given man to choose the good.

According to Warfield, the entire Christian Church has taken an official stand against naturalistic Pelagianism. The class of supernaturalists is divided, however, into two main divisions, the evangelicals and the sacerdotalists.

The sacerdotalists and the evangelicals agree that salvation is wholly from God. They differ, however, in that the former hold that God operates indirectly upon the human soul though instrumentalities, as the means by which His saving grace is communicated to men; whereas the latter insist that the welfare of the soul depends directly and solely upon the grace of God.

The sacerdotal principle finds expression in the Roman Catholic Church. The Church teaches that what God does for the salvation of man He does through the mediation of the Church, to which, having endowed it with powers adequate to the task, He has committed the whole work of salvation.

The Roman Catholic Church does not regard itself as having superseded Christ's work, but as having taken over that work. The Church believes itself to be a reincarnation of Christ whereby His redemptive mission is continued and completed. Christ perpetuates His offices as prophet, priest, and king through the Church, which interprets doctrine with infallible authority, mediates between God and man, provides the propitiatory sacrifice of the Mass, and secures the absolute obedience of its members.

With respect to the actual salvation of individual men, the sacerdotalists maintain that God wills the salvation of all men by an antecedent conditional will and that He provides for their salvation in the Church by its sacramental system. The actual work of the Church, however, is accomplished through second causes by which the application of grace is effected. Those who are saved by obtaining the sacraments, and those who are lost by missing them, are saved or lost by the natural working of secondary causes rather than by divine appointment.

Evangelicals refuse to follow the sacerdotalist in their separation of the soul from the direct contact with and immediate dependence upon God the Holy Spirit as the source of all grace. The evangelical is convinced that God deals with each sinful soul directly and for itself. There is in Protestantism, however, a tendency to construe the saving activities of God universally instead of individualistically. Evangelical

Arminianism and Evangelical Lutheranism hold that what God does with respect to salvation, He does not for individual men as individuals but for all men alike as men, without distinction. Such a position is, however, fraught with difficulties. For if God alone works salvation and works on all men alike, all men without exception must be saved. However, if salvation depends in part upon man, then evangelicalism must be abandoned in favor of the naturalism of autosoterism. If God's gracious activities are not extended to all men alike, then universalism must give way to particularism. Consistent evangelicalism and consistent universalism are incompatible unless all men are saved. Such a solution, however, contradicts the clear teaching of Scripture that not all men are saved. The attempts that have been made to overcome this difficulty inevitably lead by one path or another to the destruction of the supernaturalistic principle by transferring salvation from God to man.

In opposition to all attempts to understand the operations of God as directed toward universal salvation, Warfield defends Calvinism as the most consistent form of Christianity. Calvinism maintains that the saving operations of God are not directed to those individuals who are not saved. Calvinism is frankly a particularism. The Calvinist insists that in His saving operations God deals solely with those who are actually saved. The acceptance of the supernaturalism of salvation and of the immediacy of the operations of divine grace necessitates the acceptance of particularism; and the denial of particularism is tantamount to the denial of the immediacy of divine grace, that is, of evangelicalism, and of the supernaturalism of salvation, that is, of Christianity. To reject particularism is logically to reject Christianity.

Discrimination is placed by some Calvinists, the Supralapsarians, at the root of all God's dealings with His creatures. The very fact that God has any creatures at all is evidence of discrimination. In fact, everything God decrees concerning His creatures He decrees in order that He may discriminate between them. The decree of "election" by which men are made to differ is therefore placed *logically prior,* in the order of decrees, to the decree of creation, at least insofar as the latter is concerned with man as such. The decree of election is thus logically prior in the order of thought to the decree of the Fall.

Other Calvinists, the Sublapsarians or Infralapsarians hold that election is specifically concerned with salvation, so that the principle of particularism, in the sense of discrimination, belongs in the sphere of God's soteriological, not in that of his cosmical, creation. Election is regarded as logically prior to those operations which concern salvation, but not to those which concern the Creation or the Fall. In the order of decrees, election is placed at the head of those decrees of God which look to salvation, but election falls into position in the order of thought *after* the decrees of Creation and the Fall. The latter refer to all men alike, since all men have been created and all have fallen. The decree of election precedes the decree of redemption and its application, but it follows logically after that of the Fall.

Still other Calvinists are post-Redemptionists. Because of the Scriptural teaching concerning the universal reference of the redemption of Christ, and because of their desire to base the universal offer of salvation on an equally universal provision, the post-Redemptionists postpone the introduction of the particularistic principle to a point within the saving operations of God. They therefore introduce the decree of election, in the order of thought, after the decree of redemption in Christ.

Post-Redemptionists, who are also called Amyraldianists or Hypothetical Universalists, differ among themselves in that some hold to a Congruism or Pajonism, that is, to the principle that grace comes to those upon whom the Holy Spirit operates in His gracious suasion in a fashion that is carefully and infallibly adapted by Him to secure their adhesion to the Gospel. It can thus be said that men voluntarily come to Christ and are joined to Him by the free act of their own unrenewed wills, even though only those come to Christ whom God has selected so to persuade to come to Him that they certainly will come of their own free wills.

Warfield recognizes Supralapsarians, Infralapsarians, post-Redemptionists, and Pajonists as Calvinists insofar as particularism is concerned, but he rejects the post-Redemptionists as inconsistent Calvinists who turn away from a substitutive atonement by holding that Christ died to open the way of salvation to sinners rather than to die in their stead. Pajonists depart even further from pure Calvinism in that their view also denies the whole substance of that regeneration and renovation by which, in the creative work of the Spirit, we are made new creatures.

There is for the true Calvinist no antinomy in saying that Christ died for His people and for the world. Unless it is Christ who actually saves His people, there is no reason to believe that there will ever be a saved world. His people may be few today, but the world will be His tomorrow.

It is the Calvinist alone who has warrant to believe in salvation, whether of the individual or the world. Both rest upon the sovereign grace of God, and for Warfield all other ground is shifting sand.

THE EPISTLE TO THE ROMANS

Author: Karl Barth (1886-   )
Type of work: Biblical commentary
First published: 1919

PRINCIPAL IDEAS ADVANCED

The voice of the Apostle Paul has relevance in our times.

Paul's theme of the "power of the resurrection" is a sign of judgment upon all things temporal, and a sign of hope in the Coming World of God.

Christian religion and morality fall under judgment with all things temporal, but they direct us to God's grace and to man's obligation in response to grace.

There are two reasons why Karl Barth created a stir in theological circles with his Biblical commentary *The Epistle to the Romans.* In the first place, he challenged the theological specialists by venturing to write a commentary with a different aim from the one usually pursued by those devoted to modern objective, historical scholarship. Barth did not reject the methods of Biblical criticism, as conservative scholars do. But he was inclined to treat lightly the notion of historical objectivity, and he denied that there is any theological worth in commentaries which have no higher goal than to reconstruct the minutiae of the Biblical period. Especially he deplored the practice of making modern liberal humanism the criterion for judging the contents of Biblical writings. Turning his back on the professional exegetes, he declared it his purpose to let the Apostolic message break with full force upon our age, which, in his opinion, needed to hear once again the Gospel message.

The second reason why Barth's commentary attracted attention is that the message which he discovered in Romans turned out to be a violent attack on the whole nineteenth century spirit of liberalism, progressivism, and humanism. It is true that voices had been raised against these optimistic notions before Barth's work appeared, and, following the first World War, many voices joined his. But Protestantism, which had in many quarters become simply the official expression of the spirit of the age, could remain complacent as long as these troubled liberal spirits and "enemies of the people" remained outside the Church. But Karl Barth was a promising young theologian, a member of an eminent family of scholars, and the pastor of a rural church in Switzerland; when he ventured to suggest that Western culture is no more acceptable in God's sight than that of Nineveh and Rome, theologians had to stop whatever they were doing and answer him. His book rapidly went through several editions, and its author, appointed to a professorship, shortly became the dean of Protestant theologians.

Barth's *The Epistle to the Romans,* although it bears little resemblance to the technical commentaries of modern research, is nonetheless in the great tradition of Biblical exegesis. The author has written with a host of works at his hand, and he is in a position to report not merely what Paul says but also what others have understood by the Apostle's words. But he never allows the details of scholarship to dull the edge of his exposition. Perhaps the reader marvels most that a man can sustain a single theme over so many pages without exhausting the resources of language and imagination. For, in a sense, Barth's *The Epistle to the Romans* is a *tour de force.* Barth, in writing as if Paul had only one message, has displayed no little genius, not merely in the singleness of mind with which he holds to a paradoxical thesis, but also in the subtlety with which he implements this theme by reference to the Apostle's writing. Much of the power of the work derives from the relentlessness with which it presses its one astonishing claim. Yet Barth, in a later preface, his *Shorter Commentary on Romans,* acknowledges that there is greater variety (though also greater monotony) in his *Romans* than he had acknowledged, and that were the commentary to be rewritten, many threads then unnoticed would have to be unraveled.

The theme of the Biblical book of Romans, according to Barth, is "the infinite qualitative distinction" between time and eternity, or between man and God. Wherever God's revelation appears, it will appear as judgment (*krisis*) upon the world. Consequently, eschatology is central to Christian theology. At least, such is Barth's assumption in regard to the theme; in answer to objectors, he appeals to the work for confirmation: "If Paul was not primarily concerned with the permanent *krisis* of the relation between time and eternity, but was dealing with some other theme, the absurdity of a false assumption will become clear in the course of a detailed examination of the text."

The key, perhaps, to Barth's reading of Paul lies in his identification of Paul's "gospel" with the Resurrection of Christ from the grave. "The Gospel of the Resurrection is the action, the supreme miracle, by which God, the unknown God dwelling in light unapproachable, the Holy One, Creator, and Redeemer, makes himself known." But the Resurrection is not to be viewed as an ordinary miracle, a "supernatural" event; that is, as an event which, although exceptional so far as our experience is concerned, is nevertheless relative to it. On the contrary, the Resurrection brings us to the ultimate limit of human experience; it confronts us with "the Primal Origin" in the presence of which all our creaturely notions and expectations are dissolved and reconstituted on a different foundation. For the Resurrection of Christ is the intersection of eternity and time, a moment in which the absolute antithesis between man's righteousness and God's righteousness becomes manifest.

The power of the Resurrection manifests itself in two ways. First, it condemns all human "possibilities," shatters all human hopes, and shakes the foundation of every human enterprise. In the light of God's eternity, all human light is darkness. There is, indeed, what Barth calls the "wisdom of night," an awareness of the tragedy of man's condition. But no advantage comes of such awareness because it lacks the power of grace; hence, despairing of every "possibility," men resign their humanity and plunge themselves into sensuality and greed; or they fasten determinedly upon science, morality, statecraft, or religion in order to secure for themselves an island in the sea of despair and thereby to preserve at least one "possibility." Even religion, which Barth calls the "last human possibility," the one to which man flees when all else has failed, stands under eternal judgment, for religion attempts "with criminal arrogance" to mix together the temporal and the eternal.

There is a second way in which the power of the Resurrection manifests itself. Besides condemning all human "possibility," the Resurrection also discloses the divine "impossibility." That Jesus of Nazareth should rise from the dead is, in Barth's words, *"the* possibility which possesses all the marks of impossibility."* Thus, instead of leaving mankind to perish in the hopelessness of his temporality, as does the "wisdom of night," the Resurrection awakens in man "the memory of Eternity." Christ's resurrection was not the first occasion of eternity's breaking into time; history shows different points at which men were enabled to

take the divine perspective on themselves. Even in paganism, there were those who saw in the corruptible a "parable of the incorruptible," and concluded that, "though the world is incapable of redemption, yet there is a redemption for the world." The Resurrection does not overthrow these "signposts"; rather, it establishes them and gives them direction. For here is proclaimed the invisibility of God and the reality of that "new creation," uninhabitable by flesh and blood, for which our whole creation groans. In His death, Christ is completely at one with our tragic condition; in His resurrection, He foreshows God's "decision to erect His justice by the complete renewal of heaven and earth."

Barth warns us against holding either of these ways without the other. For man, the truth of Eternity must always be dialectical. Barth finds a dialectical movement in Romans itself in that a chapter devoted to the righteousness of men is followed by a chapter devoted to the righteousness of God; a chapter devoted to history is followed by one devoted to the Coming Day; a chapter devoted to the ambiguity of religion is followed by one devoted to the decisiveness of Grace. For this reason, one should not read the commentary by snatches. Indeed, a person needs to know the substance of the whole book in order rightly to assess the meaning of any part, which, in a sense, is as true of Paul as it is of Barth. As every Bible student knows, Romans falls into two parts; the former part (Chapters 1 to 11) dealing with doctrine, the latter (Chapters 12 to 16) dealing with ethics. Barth is especially concerned lest his readers try to understand his commentary on

Paul's doctrine without his commentary on Paul's ethics, or vice versa.

We have seen something of the ambiguity which, according to Barth, is characteristic of religion. As the "last human possibility" it speaks both a "yes" and a "no"; that is, it partly affirms the world and denies God, and it partly denies the world and affirms God. Genuine religion, according to Barth, always bears the impress of revelation. In every oracle, rite, or sanctuary is some vestige of an erstwhile manifestation of eternity. Such religious appurtenances are, however, no more than burned-out craters or empty canals. They belong entirely to this world; though religious persons depend on the appurtenances of religion, nothing transcendent or eternal is to be found there. Should we, then, abandon religion? Yes, in the sense that we must not have any faith in it. But, in another sense, we must never abandon religion; as the "last human possibility," religion bears witness of our sinfulness and rebellion and prompts us to call out for forgiveness. Contrary to what many suppose, religion brings uneasiness and dread, not peace and contentment. Its ultimate expression is a nameless fear, together with the question, which it can never resolve, "What are we then to do?" In this sense, religion is a proper attitude for man. The difficulty lies in sustaining it without becoming self-righteous and supposing that God is obliged to visit us because we wait on Him.

Christianity, it must be remembered, is a religion, and falls under the same judgment as the rest. Because the Church is the place where the invisible was once and for all transformed into a visible thing, its members and particularly its leaders are under constant temptation to suppose that the divine presence tabernacles here in time. Barth was greatly impressed by Dostoevski's story "The Grand Inquisitor" (in The Brothers Karamazov, 1880). In the sinister churchman there represented, Barth saw the Church's perennial effort to "humanize the divine," and its ambition to substitute a kingdom of this world for that Kingdom which flesh and blood cannot inherit. Thus, the Church is guilty of "criminal arrogance." On the other hand, those who attack the Church ordinarily do so on the assumption that they possess some righteousness or hope which is superior to that which the Church holds out, and this is even more arrogant. We must, says Barth, hold the Church and the Gospel in tension. In condemning the Church, we must preserve our solidarity with it, realizing that we condemn ourselves. This is the real tribulation of the Church, to know its guilt, and to recognize its guilt as unavoidable. But precisely in tribulation there is hope— the hope of the Resurrection in which God justifies himself by justifying the ungodly.

Barth finds much the same kind of ambiguity in ethics and in politics as he finds in religion. The keynote of Christian ethics, as he reads Romans, is "disturbance." The Resurrection disturbs life, because obedience to the power of grace therein revealed demands that one attack the world, one's fellowmen, and one's own self. On the primary level, revelation discloses to man the dominion of sin over his life, and also the fact that sin's dominion has no other foundation than man's freedom. With this discovery it becomes impossible for man to live, either as a conservative or as a revolutionary, either in the world or in flight from it. In ethics, as in dogmatics, the only conclusion is *soli deo gloria*. One can only sacrifice his life and wait for God's judgment. On the secondary level, there is, according to Barth, a positive and a negative "possibility" set before the Christian. On the positive side, obedience to the Resurrection demands that, while living under the conditions of this world, man shall bear in his body the marks of the divine transformation of the world; that is, his life must become legible as a protest against human *eros* and as a parable of divine *agape*. This requirement, however, issues in no scheme of reform and gives no ground for moral indignation. Our love for men, says Barth, is itself trivial, but it is a parable of God's love for men. On the negative side, obedience to the Resurrection demands of man that he live humbly and that he avoid the pretense and ambition, and, in a word, the "titanism" which characterize the wisdom of this world—taking all care, however, lest he become arrogant and in warring against the titan make himself a titan.

Following Paul's words about ruling power, Barth has a word concerning the believer's duty toward the state. He calls the state "the great negative possibility." It is "great" because it gathers to itself the totality of human pretension, and it is "negative" because it arrogates to itself the possibility that belongs only to God. Barth says that revolutionaries are justified insofar as they find intolerable the pretenses of any existing order, but they are con-

demned when they raise their hand against it, because in doing so they are presuming to execute a judgment that belongs to God. What the revolutionary actually intends, according to Barth, is to obviate the necessity of the Resurrection and to actualize the "impossible possibility" by man's strength alone. It is better, says Barth, to choose the "possible possibility" which is proportionate to our situation, the possibility of living in contentment under the usurpation and of leaving judgment to God. This view, however, is far from justifying the legitimist, who seeks to identify God's justice with the existing order. The ultimate antithesis to the "great negative possibility" is not the "possible possibility" of the political reactionary, but the "great positive possibility" of love. The possibility of this "possibility" places the reactionary in the wrong, along with the revolutionary; in loving, one cannot wish for either the old or the new, but only for The Coming World.

Barth finds an interesting contradiction in the ending of Paul's Romans. Where the Apostle enjoins his followers from making their Christian freedom a stumbling-block to weaker brethren, Paul is, says Barth, letting Romans "dissolve itself." This ultimate perception of the ambiguity of man's condition forbids any man, even the Apostle, setting up a scheme of dogma and ethics. Nothing is to be done but to point to the Resurrection. Thus, there should be no Paulinism—and *a fortiori* no Barthianism, as Barth is the first to acknowledge.

THEOLOGY AS AN EMPIRICAL SCIENCE

Author: Douglas Clyde Macintosh (1877-1948)
Type of work: Scientific theology
First published: 1919

PRINCIPAL IDEAS ADVANCED

Religious experience at its best provides the empirical ground for a scientific theology.

The presupposition peculiar to theology is the assumption that God exists; it is left to scientific theology to determine the properties of the divine object.

The empirical data for scientific theology come from revelations of the divine, as in the person and work of Christ, and in the Christian experience of salvation.

The one fundamental attribute of God, from the point of view of empirical theology, is absoluteness; theology also discovers God to have such moral attributes as holiness, justice, love, and mercy.

The theologian has always been eager to justify his profession, but the urge was especially strong in the early twentieth century when the growing eminence of science threatened to put theology into the shade forever. Douglas Clyde Macintosh, who at the time of writing *Theology As an Empirical Science* was Dwight Professor of Theology at Yale University, attempted the defense of theology not by maintaining, as theologians often do, that the attempt to understand God, although unscientific, is the most significant effort to be made by the mind and spirit of man, but by insisting that theology is itself, or at least *can* be, an empirical science. To be sure, Macintosh did not suggest that the data of theology are of the same sort as those which provide the physical sciences with their content and starting-point; he maintained, rather, that the data of an empirical theology come from "religious experience at its best," but he did regard religious experience as reliable and as subject to formulation and development through use of the inductive method.

Although nontheological scientists might quarrel with Macintosh's use of the term "science"—and, indeed, he anticipated such criticism—no one who has read Macintosh can deny that he has made every reasonable attempt to clarify and organize religious experience and to realize its implications. Perhaps the data of a "scientific" theology are not as hard as Macintosh supposed, but given the sorts of experiences which Macintosh regarded as indicating the presence of the divine, whether or not fashioned by the faithful expectations of the believer, it is reasonable to conclude that knowledge about the implications of religious experience is possible. It was to much the same systematic development of religious ideas, on the basis of religious experience, that the British philosopher H. D. Lewis was later to devote his effort in *Our Experience of God* (1959).

Macintosh begins his inquiry with an analysis of theological method. He discusses traditional theology, with its emphasis on ecclesiastical and Biblical sources; rationalistic theology, with its emphasis on *a priori* truths to be developed deductively; mystical theology, paradoxically attempting to derive knowledge from ineffable experience; eclectic theology, drawing upon various sources and experiences which more limited theologies count on exclusively; and, finally, scientific theology, the "new" theology, not yet born, but the voice of the future.

Macintosh quotes with approval T. H. Huxley's remark, "If anyone is able to make good the assertion that his theology rests upon valid evidence and sound reasoning, then it appears to me that such theology must take its place as a part of science." Macintosh also assents to the words of William James: "Let empiricism once become associated with religion . . . and I believe that a new era of religion as well as of philosophy will be ready to begin."

The problem, then, is not *whether* theology should be empirical, but *how* it is to be empirical. Macintosh suggests that a scientific theology is possible if theology turns from religious pragmatism to a scientifically critical pragmatism. He distinguishes between a partial working-out of an idea and "that working which constitutes full verification. . . ." To use James's terminology, which Macintosh does not adopt in this context, religious pragmatism can become scientific only if it becomes "tough-minded." To be tough-minded the theologian must be content with nothing less than the rigorous procedures of the empirical scientist; like the physical scientist, the theologian must identify his data and frame his inductive generalizations in

such a way that they can be justified by reference to the data.

A scientific theology will begin, Macintosh suggests, with an examination of the presuppositions of theology. The fundamental assumption which the scientific theologian makes is that God exists; he justifies his presupposition by reference to revelations of the divine to be found in religious experience; his central effort becomes that of discovering the properties of God, and he does not, like the agnostic or skeptic, waste time attempting to prove what only religious experience can make convincing. Just as the physical scientist assumes the existence of material substance, and has some basis in experience for his belief, so the theologian assumes the existence, but not the nature, of God.

Having examined the presuppositions of his science, the theologian then turns to the task of collecting empirical data on the basis of which his laws will be constructed. Finally, on the basis of the laws, theological theory will be devised. Theory construction involves taking advantage of those intuitions provoked by religious experience, taking as a practically necessary hypothesis whatever man's religious and moral needs demand, and framing theories as to the nature of the religious object—God—whose existence prescientific experience insisted upon.

According to Macintosh, sciences other than theology may provide theology with well-established results which can serve as theological presuppositions. Thus, the physical facts of the universe, as established by the physical sciences, may be taken for granted; the immensity of the universe, the conservation of energy, the evolution of man and society—these discoveries become the presuppositions of theology. Of special relevance to theology, however, are the findings of those scientific activities we may call the history and psychology of religion. The central historical claim on which Christian theology depends is the proposition that Jesus of Nazareth lived and that He regarded Himself, at least on occasion, as a Messiah sent by God to prepare for the Kingdom of God. Macintosh regards this claim as probably true, relative to the evidence of history; there may be disagreement as to the precise influence of the Messianic idea on Jesus, but the arguments of all parties appear to come together when the claim is made that Jesus lived, that He acted compassionately, that He preached the love of God and man, and that He died for His beliefs.

Other presuppositions of theology, according to Macintosh's account, are the beliefs that man is a free agent (that is, that his acts are not completely determined by heredity, environment, character, and ideas), the belief that immortality is possible (which is to be presupposed together with the idea that immortality is morally imperative), and the belief that sin (wrong-doing) has evil consequences.

A scientific theology must be based on empirical data, Macintosh insists; and the empirical data for theology are those experiences which may reasonably be taken as revelations of the divine. The author rejects primitive, traditional, and rationalistic accounts of revelatory experience. Like Lewis (whose *Experience of God* has been mentioned), Macintosh begins with the experience of the *presence* of the

divine; the divine is revealed to the individual, and only after the revelation of the divine is it possible to frame normative notions, ideas of value.

The divine has been most clearly revealed in the person and works of Christ, Macintosh asserts. A critical examination of historical evidence, together with a consideration of what religious experience suggests in regard to the interpretation of the evidence, leads one to the empirical conclusion that Christ exhibited a divine quality of personality; He was deeply religious, and He depended on God for moral support and received reinforcement in response to prayer. Macintosh does *not* believe that a scientific theology can justify the further claims that Jesus, because of His essentially divine nature, can be identified with God; that the spirit of Jesus existed before Jesus the man began his earthly trials; that it is possible to be in direct communication with Christ through prayer; and, finally, that Jesus could not be equaled or transcended in spiritual quality by another man. (Earlier in his discussion of empirical theology Macintosh declared the belief in the Virgin Birth to be scientifically indefensible.)

Macintosh describes the atoning work of Christ as a revelation of the divine through the moral and religious teaching of Christ and through His acts; Jesus revealed the divine in that He was Himself saved from sin through religious dependence, and He was moved by holy love.

The Christian experience of salvation provides further empirical evidence of the divine. A man knows through experience that his dependence on God is not merely emotionally satisfying; it is practically effective.

In framing the laws of empirical theology, Macintosh writes, one is able to rely on certain "constants." What he calls "the Constant" of empirical theological laws is God Himself, "the necessary objective Factor in religious experience, . . . the Object of active religious dependence, . . . the Source of salvation, i.e., of religious deliverance from evil." Certain variables also must be taken into account: the quality and degree of the individual's responsiveness to the divine, and the religious adjustment involved.

Macintosh then offers as the principal laws of empirical theology two sets of laws: primary theological laws, which he defines as "the laws of volitional experiences," and secondary theological laws, which include the laws of emotional, intellectual, physiological, and social experience. The laws may be described in general as indicating the responsiveness of God to the efforts and reasonable petitions of men; one receives moral power, victory over temptation, peace, joy, and love from Christian effort and success.

It now becomes possible for Macintosh to proceed to the *a posteriori* definition of God's nature. Having begun with the presupposition of the reality of the divine object, and having won through empirical investigation a knowledge of certain laws having to do with the exercise of divine power, it becomes possible to theorize in regard to the divine nature. Macintosh's theories are concerned with the moral and metaphysical attributes of God, with the relation of God to the universe, with eschatological matters, and with the problem of evil.

The fundamental moral attribute of God, according to Macintosh, is *absoluteness*. By "absoluteness" Macintosh

does not mean what the absolute idealist means; namely, the completely nonrelational, nonrelative, nonconditioned character of the divine. Macintosh uses the word "absoluteness" in what he calls a "pragmatic and empirical sense" to mean "absolute satisfactoriness as Object of religious dependence, absolute sufficiency for man's religious needs." Empirical theology justifies the claim that God is morally ideal, that He is perfect relative to human needs.

Macintosh analyzes the moral absoluteness of God into the "immanent" attributes of holiness and love, and the "transitive" attributes of justice and mercy, or righteousness and grace. These attributes entail God's granting to man the opportunity for working toward the moral ideal. Since the moral struggle involves freedom, man is free and God becomes both judge and redeemer.

An empirical theology shows that God is not only good, but great. To make His greatness clear, it is necessary to determine God's metaphysical attributes. Once again, the fundamental attribute is God's absoluteness, His being the "absolutely dependable Object of dependence and Source of salvation." But God is known empirically not only to be what man needs Him to be, but also *not* to be what man needs Him *not* to be. Thus, there are negative attributes as well as positive attributes to be determined. The mystics and rationalists have been in error, or at least have not been empirical, in uncritically assigning to God such negative attributes as incorporeality, invisibility, incomprehensibility, immutability, and infinity. An empirical theology shows that the matter is by no means so simple. God cannot be thought of in purely corporeal terms, but since the physical universe may be an expression of the divine spirit, it is possible that there is a divine body. God is invisible considered as spirit, but considered as body, as the physical universe which is moved by His spirit, He may be considered to be visible. God is not completely comprehensible, but it does not follow that He is in no way comprehensible. The situation is much the same as regards other negative attributes; there is no need to think of God as completely impassible (without feeling), as in no way mutable, as completely out of time, and as absolutely unconditioned. In fact, if God is to be the absolutely dependable object of religious devotion, He must be responsive in feeling to man's needs, and He must be able to work within the limits of time and space.

Turning to the positive metaphysical attributes, Macintosh insists upon God's aseity; that is, on His ultimate self-dependence. But God need not be considered to be in every way omnipotent; all that is needed is divine power sufficient to meet the needs of man; it would be idle, as well as empirically meaningless, to assign the power to resolve contradictions to God. God's knowledge is absolutely sufficient relative to man's needs, but it need not be supposed that God possesses useless knowledge. God is immanent to the extent that His presence is needed; He is transcendent in that He is a real source of spiritual power. He is a personality in that He is a rational being, self-conscious and self-directed. He is almost certainly a unity, for no more than one absolute God is necessary. God is a trinity relative to the attempt to conceive the divine

One from the practical Jewish point of view (as the Father), from the mystical-philosophical Greek point of view (as the Son), or from a point of view which emphasizes spirit (as the Holy Ghost). Finally, it is possible to know that God exists, whatever His complete nature might be, if one proceeds scientifically from religious experience at its best and most revealing.

Once the attributes of God are agreed upon, it becomes possible to draw certain conclusions concerning the relation of God to the universe. Empirical theology, as Macintosh conceives it, justifies the claim that God preserves and creatively controls the universe He created. But creative control does not involve divine interruption of natural order; a scientific theology is not likely to be sympathetic to the idea of miracles.

Certain eschatological conclusions also follow deductively: a future life is necessary to the consummation of Christian salvation; God's justice and mercy will continue to affect the spirit of man; Heaven is the transcendent reality which makes realization of the moral ideal possible.

Finally, an empirical theology has something to say about the problem of evil. Macintosh asserts that "a world of human free agency is the best possible kind of world." Yet a world of free agency is one which permits suffering through sin and error. Order in the world would seem to entail sensation, thought, free will, and moral salvation; thought corrects sensation; freedom makes creative thinking possible; salvation corrects the errors of thought and action. But salvation demands development of the spirit beyond the present life; thus, immortality is morally necessary. The conclusion seems to be that evil is a necessary accompaniment of the best possible state of affairs, but there is no empirical justification for claiming that the Devil exists.

ON THE ETERNAL IN MAN

Author: Max Scheler (1874-1928)
Type of work: Phenomenology of religion; social criticism
First published: 1921

PRINCIPAL IDEAS ADVANCED

Religion is an autonomous activity of the mind, an activity independent of conscience and reason; by means of this faculty man knows God as personal Creator and Redeemer.

The collapse of European culture is due to the loss of religious knowledge, a loss which has resulted in an inverted sense of value.

The hope for the future lies in repentance and renewal, in the recovery of objectivity in ethics and in philosophy, and in the emergence of a new hierarchy of value, with Christian faith in the highest place.

The essays which make up *On the Eternal in Man* were written by Max Scheler in the closing years of the first World War. Three of them are technical investigations in the same phenomenological vein as the author's celebrated studies on "resentment" and on "sympathy." They are entitled: "Repentance and Rebirth," "The Nature of Philosophy and the Moral Preconditions of Philosophical Knowledge," and "Problems of Religion: The Renewal of Religion." These studies are followed by two popular lectures, entitled "Christian Love in the Twentieth Century," and "The Reconstruction of European Culture," which serve to point up the relevance of the foregoing investigations to the crisis in contemporary civilization. The relevance is never far to seek, for, as was the case with Augustine, Pascal, and Newman, Scheler's intelligence was always at the beck of his restless heart, and few thinkers were more deeply concerned than he with the sickness that had plunged Europe into war.

Scheler's thesis is presented in the central essay, "Problems of Religion," a book-length study which deserves to be set alongside Rudolph Otto's *The Idea of the Holy* (1917) as a major contribution to the phenomenology of religion. Scheler protests the inadequacy of the genetic accounts of religion which have been put forward by anthropologists and psychologists; he denies that their way is the only scientific way of viewing religion. He likewise denies that the truth of religion can be assimilated either to ethics or to metaphysics. It is his claim, rather, that religion is an autonomous activity of the human spirit, with its own evidence and logic, and with a distinct kind of object. For the most part Scheler's findings agree with those independently arrived at by Otto, for whose work he has unstinted praise. There is, however, this important difference between them, that Otto, laboring upon the foundation of Kantian subjectivism, traces the formal elements of religious thought to the constitution of man's mind, whereas Scheler takes his stand in the older, Augustinian tradition, and maintains that in religion, as in other kinds of knowledge, man discovers the *a priori* in the world of objects.

Scheler holds that Augustine was correct in stating that man has his knowledge of essential being by divine illumination, but that Augustine was prevented from doing justice to this truth because he possessed no philosophical technique other than that of the Neoplatonists. Because of Neoplatonism, Western thinkers have tended to look upon religious and philosophical truth as, either wholly or partly, identical. What is needed, Scheler argues, is a new philosophical technique which will enable reflective men to recognize the uniqueness of religious insight without taking anything away from the independence and authority of reason and conscience, and *vice versa*. It is Scheler's opinion that philosophical phenomenology, as developed by Edmund Husserl (1859-1938), provides a method by which Augustine's insights can be fully exploited.

Following Husserl's method, Scheler has developed, in a separate volume, *Der Formalismus in der Ethik und die materiale Wertethik* (1913-1916), a phenomenology of morals, maintaining the point of view best known to

the English-speaking world through Nicolai Hartmann's *Ethics* (1926). According to Scheler and Hartmann, values constitute an objective hierarchy, disclosed to man by means of conscience. Within this hierarchy, says Scheler, the *summum bonum* or highest value is personality; but, because it is no function of the moral judgment to disclose reality to us, conscience is silent on the question whether Ultimate Being is personal.

The faculty by means of which man knows reality is reason or intelligence. But, Scheler argues in the essay entitled "The Nature of Philosophy," one must distinguish carefully between the conditional knowledge given to us by common sense and experimental science, and the unconditional knowledge which is proper to philosophy. The former, for all its practical value, does not reveal to us the nature of reality, because of limitations such as those imposed by our physical make-up, the limited purpose to which it is directed, and the presuppositions which it borrows from its cultural era. Man can, however, free his mind from these limitations by means of the phenomenological technique of "bracketing" them. When he does this, his reason is in a position to investigate essential Being, and to discover certain ultimate truths, notably the following: that there is something, that there is knowledge of it, that some beings are dependent on others, that there is a Being which is not dependent on any other. Philosophy, viewed in this manner, is knowledge of reality. Still, it is a limited knowledge, restricted by the nature of the intellectual act, which can apprehend only essences and their relations. Thus, although philosophy apprehends being, it is unqualified, in the nature of the case, to apprehend being as personal.

Religion, says Scheler, arises out of a third noetic capacity in man, as natural to him as conscience and reason, and even more fundamental; for, in the religious act, man discerns the lineaments of mind and will in the world about him, and, at the same moment, knows that he possesses mind and will himself. Thus, through religion we are able to make existential judgments which intellect and conscience, limited as they are to beholding static essences, cannot make. Philosophy, for example, distinguishes between absolute and relative being, but it is religion which, through the sense of dependence, enables us to affirm that the world is in fact dependent upon God's will and purpose. Or, to return to what was said above concerning the *summum bonum*, through conscience we can see that personality is the highest value, but only through the religious response to divine revelation can we affirm that the Supreme Being is personal.

On these foundations, Scheler proceeds to show the validity, not merely of a natural theology, based on the evidences of mind in man and in nature, but also of a positive theology, based on the revelation of God's will through the disclosures of *homines religiosi*, who, according to Scheler, comprise an important class of leaders, distinct from geniuses, but in many ways comparable to them. Scheler writes as a Roman Catholic, and his purpose at this point of the work is to make intelligible the submission to authority which is fundamental to Christian orthodoxy. Persuaded of the actuality of man's Fall and his depend-

ence for restitution upon divine grace, Scheler tries to do, in modern terms, substantially what Anselm (c.1033-1109) attempted in *Cur deus homo*, even going so far as to offer proof of the necessity for an infallible Church and the impossibility that Christianity should ever be superseded. There are marks of amateurism, however, in Scheler's discussion of theological matters; and the reader is not especially surprised to learn that, in subsequent years, Scheler moved away from many of these traditional notions.

Scheler's efforts to recover objectivity in the realm of spiritual truth is the major thesis of his work, but what he has to say by way of diagnosing Europe's trouble and prescribing for its cure is important as an application of his ideas to the needs of the times.

The horror of World War I was sufficient evidence to sensitive minds that European culture was in deep trouble. Those who wanted to place the blame on Prussia, or on monarchism, or on the armament makers were, in Scheler's opinion, mistaking the symptoms for the disease. The real blame rested on Western civilization, a blame shared in by the Allies and the Central Powers alike. Spokesmen from the Far East were inclined to lay the fault at the feet of Christianity. Scheler's reply is that Christianity cannot be blamed because, since the Middle Ages, Christianity has not determined European culture. On the contrary, humanitarianism has been in revolt against theism, welfarism has taken the place of love of man, and class spirit has disrupted the communal tie. Fundamentally, the trouble is a breakdown in world-order. When modern man dethroned God, he lost his "world" at the same time. Scheler traces the deterioration from century to century, laying the blame partly on Renaissance secularism, and partly on Protestant subjectivism. The eighteenth century, according to Scheler, still revered many Christian values, but these gave way in the nineteenth century to "realism" and "historicism." Thus, according to Scheler, although Christianity was still on many lips at the beginning of the War, Machiavellian policy dominated European life and thought.

Such, in Scheler's diagnosis, is the apostasy of Europe which resulted in world war. The only hope for the future lies in *repentance*. For, says Scheler, contrary to much modern psychology, repentance is a positive act, by means of which guilt is disposed of and past happenings are constructively integrated into a new life-purpose. Without repentance, deterministic despair will paralyze an individual or a society; but by means of repentance, advance to new spiritual levels is possible. Such, we may say, is Scheler's theodicy. Sin and guilt are very much a part of human history; but where these are followed, as they can be, by grace and remission, man emerges a higher being than before he sinned. Scheler claims this is especially the case where the guilt and the repentance are corporate, and he expresses the belief that a new European community will be born if the world crisis issues in collective repentance.

Believing as he did in the objectivity of moral and philosophical truth, Scheler assigned to conscience and to intellect important roles in the reconstruction which lay ahead. Much depended on man's ability to overcome the debilitating effects of French positivism and German transcendentalism. The objective hierarchy of values must be rediscovered, and, so far as possible, made the basis for a new social order, with the economic man subordinated to the citizen, and with the citizen duly respectful of the genius and the *homo religiosus*. Human society, says Scheler, must rest on spiritual foundations, and if it is to flourish, its development cannot be left to economic forces or to political necessity.

Scheler thought, in the months following the Armistice, that the self-knowledge gained during the war might be sufficient to arouse in men the determination necessary to rebuild civilization. Among youth groups and in new political unions, there were signs which he read as pointing toward an authentically human order; and, at the same time, there were signs that the Church might throw off its subservience to bourgeois interests and exercise the leadership needed to bring these secular movements into a living relation with God, whose redeeming grace can alone release from guilt and malice. The war had, in addition, taught many the spirit of sacrifice, and it had showed the possibilities of co-operative activity, which he hoped, would lead to a kind of guild socialism; guild socialism, in turn, combined with mutual disarmament and political federalism could bring about a new society, based *on the eternal in man*.

CHRISTIANITY AND LIBERALISM

Author: John Gresham Machen (1881-1937)
Type of work: Orthodox Protestant polemics
First published: 1923

PRINCIPAL IDEAS ADVANCED

An examination of the teachings of liberalism in comparison with those of Christianity shows that at every point the two movements are in direct opposition.

Liberalism differs from Christianity in its view of God, of man, of the seat of authority, and of the way of salvation.

Whether it is true or false, liberalism is no mere heresy—no mere divergence at isolated points from Christian teaching; it proceeds from a totally different root, and it constitutes, in essentials, a unitary system of its own.

J. Gresham Machen was on the faculty of Princeton Theological Seminary from 1906 until 1929. From 1929 until his death in 1937, he was Professor of New Testament in Westminster Theological Seminary, an institution that he helped establish. Machen devoted his life to the scholarly defense and exposition of orthodox Protestantism as contained in the Westminster Confession of Faith. Machen's *Christianity and Liberalism*, first published in 1923, sets forth the difference between historic Reformation Protestantism and liberalism or modernism. The book is the clearest and most able statement of the conflict between historic redemptive Protestantism and the modern non-redemptive "liberal" religion.

Machen compares the liberal and the orthodox views of doctrine, of God and man, the Bible, Christ, salvation, and the Church to show that modern liberalism has in fact relinquished everything distinctive of Christianity.

Liberalism frequently regards differences in doctrine as unimportant; it argues that creeds are simply the changing expression of a single Christian experience. From the liberal point of view, creeds are all equally true, if they express Christian experience. Christianity is not a doctrine but a way of life. The liberal puts his trust in the person of Jesus, rather than in what Jesus did; in Jesus' character rather than in the message of His death and resurrection.

Orthodoxy, in contrast to liberalism, contends that Christianity has a doctrinal basis. What Christianity is can be determined by looking at its beginnings. At its inception the Christian movement was not just a way of life, but a way of life based upon a message, upon an account of facts; that is, upon doctrine. The Apostle Paul, for example, certainly did not advocate an undogmatic religion. To remove Paulinism from Christianity is not a solution, the orthodox believer argues, because Paul was not an innovator, as is clear from his relationship to the church at Jerusalem and to the original companions of Jesus. The primitive Church was concerned with what Jesus had done. It was the proclamation of an event that was to redeem the world. Two elements are contained within the Christian message: the narration of the facts, that is, history, and the narration of the facts together with the meaning of the facts; that is, doctrine.

Jesus' disciples did not distort Christianity by basing it upon an event, for Jesus Himself did the same thing. The message Jesus proclaimed in Galilee was the coming of the Kingdom, an event, or a series of events. Jesus not only announced an event, but He announced the meaning of the event. Jesus' teaching was rooted in doctrine because it depended upon the presentation of Jesus' own person, in His Messianic consciousness.

To maintain the doctrinal basis of Christianity does not mean that Christianity is irrelevant to life, nor does it mean that all points of doctrine are equally important, nor does it mean that conservatives and liberals must live in personal animosity, although specifically Christian fellowship between them is impossible, Machen insists.

The rivalry between Christianity and liberalism is further in evidence in the contrasting views of God and man. Modern liberalism frequently is indifferent to any conception of God; it would merely feel His presence. Some liberals would become acquainted with God only through Jesus. Some liberals, though perhaps a decreasing number, think of God as a personal God, as a Father. Liberalism as a whole, however, has broken down the sharp distinction between God and the world, and when it is not consistently pantheistic, it tends toward pantheism.

The liberal view of man follows quite naturally from its doctrine of God. Liberalism has lost the awareness of sin and has supreme confidence in human goodness. Liberalism is rooted in the predominant pagan spirit of present-day Western civilization, a spirit which finds the highest goal of human existence in the harmonious development of existing human faculties.

Orthodox Christianity, in contrast to liberalism, holds that the knowledge of God is the very basis of religion. Theism, the knowledge of one Supreme Person, Maker, and active Ruler of the world is at the very root of the religion of Jesus. Jesus believed in the real existence of a personal God. Neither Jesus nor the New Testament supports the modern view of the Fatherhood of God, and its corollary, the brotherhood of man. What is distinctive in the New Testament teaching about the Fatherhood of God concerns only those who have become followers of Christ. Liberalism has lost sight of the very center and core of Christianity by eradicating the distinction between the creature and the Creator. Liberalism denies the transcendence of God, but orthodox Christianity holds that God is immanent in the world not because He is identical with the world but because He has created it and continues to uphold it.

According to the views of Machen, Christianity regards man as a sinner; unlike liberalism it begins with the consciousness that man is under the just condemnation of God and that his condition can be changed solely by the grace of God, after which change the Christian can proceed to develop every faculty in a higher Christian humanism founded not upon human pride but upon divine grace.

The two great presuppositions of the Christian message, the fact of sin and the presence of the living God, are disregarded by modern liberalism. The divergence between Christianity and liberalism is, however, not limited to presuppositions, but it affects the message itself. This is not surprising when it is remembered that the Bible is the Book through which the Christian message is delivered, and that the modern liberal rejects the notion that the Bible is a true revelation from God, free from error, and that it is an infallible rule of faith and practice. The liberal does not regard the Bible as trustworthy. He may at times give the false impression that Jesus is his authority in religious matters, but the words of Jesus which are regarded as authoritative are only such words as the liberal is willing to select. Jesus is not the real authority, then; the real authority is the liberal principle by which the selection within Jesus' recorded teaching is made. The real authority for liberals, Machen contends, is "Christian experience," and since individual experience is diverse, such authority is no authority at all.

The foundation of liberalism is the shifting emotions of sinful men. Christianity, on the other hand, is founded upon the Bible. Some Christians accept the central message of the Bible although they believe that the message itself rests upon the authority of reliable witnesses without the supernatural guidance of the Spirit of God. The view which Jesus Himself seems to have had of the Bible not only holds that the contents of the Bible are unique, but that the writers have been preserved from error. The Spirit of God did not dictate the Bible in a mechanical fashion. The doctrine of plenary inspiration, espoused by Machen, does not deny the individuality of the Biblical writers; nor does it ignore their use of ordinary means of acquiring information; nor does it involve a lack of interest in the historical situation which gave rise to the books of the Bible. It simply holds that the Bible is free of error; the account that the Bible gives is true, Machen argues, because the Spirit of God kept the writers from falling into error.

Christianity and liberalism are also sharply opposed in their attitudes toward Jesus, Machen points out. Christians stand in a religious relation to Jesus; liberals do not. To the liberal, Jesus is an example for faith; to the Christian, Jesus is the object of faith. Liberalism regards Jesus as an example and guide; Christianity, as a Savior. Liberalism regards Jesus as the fairest flower of humanity; Christianity regards Jesus as a supernatural Person, indeed as a person who was both God and man. Liberalism rejects the Jesus of the New Testament; it rejects His miracles, and finds in Jesus the highest type of humanity, a man who made such an impression upon His followers that after His death they could not believe He had perished but experienced hallucinations in which they thought they saw Him risen from the dead. The Jesus of the New Testament, in which Christians believe, performed miracles; He is the Savior who voluntarily entered into this world for our salvation, suffered for our sins on the cross, rose again from the dead, and continues to make intercession for us. The imitation of Jesus has a basic place in the Christian life, the orthodox Christian agrees; but the Jesus who can serve as an example is the Jesus of the New Testament, not the Jesus of modern liberal reconstruction. The New Testament Jesus, the Jesus accepted by Christians, primarily offered man, not guidance, but salvation.

To the extent that liberalism is willing to speak of salvation at all, it finds salvation in man; Christianity finds it in an act of God. The message of the Christian Gospel is that God has saved man. A cardinal doctrine of modern liberalism is that the world's evil may be overcome by the world's good.

Christianity teaches that Jesus is the Savior, not because of what He said, not even because of what He was, but because of what He did, because He took upon Himself the guilt of man's sins and bore it, on the cross, in his stead. The atonement taught in the New Testament is a vicarious atonement.

The liberal view of the death of Christ is that it had an effect upon men, not upon God. The liberal is correct in holding that the death of Christ is an example of self-sacrifice which may inspire self-sacrifice in others; it is also true that it shows how much God hates sin and how much He loves men, but these truths are swallowed up in a greater truth, a truth which liberalism denies; namely, that Christ died for man in order to present him faultless before the throne of God.

Christianity is dependent upon history, Machen insists; it is based upon something that happened; it offers tidings of something new; it is exclusive in its claim that Christ is the only means by which man can be saved, so that the Church has the responsibility of proclaiming the Gospel to everyone. Liberalism denies that a person can suffer for the guilt of another, but in so doing it forgets that Jesus was no ordinary person, no mere man, but the eternal Son of God.

Liberals persist in speaking of the sacrifice of Christ as though it were made by someone other than God, thereby forgetting that according to the Christian doctrine of the Cross, it is God Himself, and not another, that makes the sacrifice for sin. The atoning death of Christ, and it alone, makes sinners righteous in God's sight. On the basis of Christ's redeeming work, the Christian dies unto sin, and lives unto God. The work of Christ is applied to the individual Christian by the Holy Spirit. The believer is thus regenerated, and stands in a new relation to God by an act of justification.

The Christian is saved by the object of his faith, by Christ, so that an act of God becomes the beginning of his new life. The regeneration and justification of the sinner is followed by sanctification. In principle the Christian is free from the present evil world, but in practice the battle has just begun.

According to Machen, the liberal regards religion as a means to a higher end; his program has little place for Heaven, and this world is really all in all. The liberal believes that applied Christianity is all there is to Christianity; the Christian believes that applied Christianity is the result of an initial act of God, that man exists for the sake of God, and not conversely.

True Christians are united into the brotherhood of the Christian Church; the true brotherhood of man is the brotherhood of the redeemed, the

Church invisible, which finds expression in the Church visible.

The greatest menace to the visible Church, Machen concludes, comes not from its external enemies but from the presence within its membership of a type of faith and practice which is anti-Christian to the core. It is highly undesirable that liberalism and Christianity should be propagated within the same organization.

THE FAITH OF THE CHRISTIAN CHURCH

Author: Gustaf Aulén (1879-   )
Type of work: Theology
First published: 1923

PRINCIPAL IDEAS ADVANCED

Systematic theology can be a descriptive science, though the nature of the description must be adapted to the faith being described.

The holy God saves, judges, and creates, as His love overcomes His wrath and other powers hostile to man, and thus establishes its sovereignty.

In Jesus Christ the love of God was incarnate, became triumphant on the Cross, and thus delivered man, who, under the dominion of the risen Christ, is incorporated into fellowship with God.

The Church, in which Christ continues to be present and active on earth through word and sacrament, will ultimately be transformed into God's perfected Kingdom of glory.

Gustaf Aulén first wrote *The Faith of the Christian Church* in 1923 while professor at the University of Lund, Sweden. The book has since undergone several revisions reflecting the development of Aulén's thought during his professorship and his subsequent episcopate. The book begins with a discussion of faith and theology, after which sections on the doctrine of God, the doctrine of redemption, and the doctrine of the Church follow. Aulén points out that no particular section is exclusively devoted to eschatology (the doctrine of the last things), since eschatology as an essential dimension is implicit throughout the system.

The task of systematic theology, according to Aulén, is not to demonstrate the truth of the Christian faith, nor to prescribe what Christians must believe. It is rather the critical scientific task of describing the Christian faith, which Aulén insists is a given objective reality which can be made the object of scientific study. It is therefore not God Himself who is being described, but the relationship between God and man characteristic of the Christian faith, and the concept of God presupposed in that relationship.

The correlate of faith is revelation. God is revealed in nature and history, but the decisive revelation is in Jesus

Christ. This revelation must be understood in a broad context. No limits may be drawn about it, but no God is recognized other than He who reveals Himself in Christ.

In defining the content of the Christian faith, Aulén distinguishes between "motifs" and "forms of expression." There is a primary meaning (motif) of the Christian faith to which one must penetrate, a meaning which remains the same though forms of expression change, and is not to be identified with any particular form of expression, whether ancient or modern.

The primary meaning of the Christian faith is Biblically determined. Nevertheless, Aulén affirms, the Spirit of God has continued its activity after the closing of the canon, so that tradition has a legitimate place in so far as it expresses and interprets anew what is manifest or latent in the Biblical message. Tradition can be understood as a series of confessions, the first of which, namely, the New Testament confession of the resurrection of Jesus Christ, has been canonized. The two other primary confessions of the Church, according to Aulén, are the ancient Church's confession of the Incarnation, and the Reformation confession of justification by faith and grace alone.

Since our language is necessarily spatiotemporal, faith affirmations must be symbolic. Such affirmations involve inescapable tensions. The Christian faith affirms that although God is involved in history, He is above all change; although He is sovereign, evil is real; although sin is a human condition, it is voluntarily entered; although faith is divine, man can attain it. Such tensions must neither be eliminated nor embraced for their own sake; they reflect the tension-filled unity of divine revelation.

Aulén divides his discussion of the doctrine of God into two sections. He first discusses how God is conceived in the Christian faith, and then he discusses the activity of God. Holiness provides the background against which God is conceived. God is wholly other, unconditionally majestic, the one upon whom man is unconditionally dependent. The most fundamental thing, however, that can be said about God is that God is love. God's love is spontaneous, creative, self-giving, and unfathomable. This love must in turn be related to God's justice and power. Aulén is critical of theologies in which the tensions of love, justice, and power in God are rationally resolved. On the other hand, sheer irrationalism, whereby contradictory divine attributes are affirmed, is equally inacceptable. According to Aulén, tensions are resolved only as love itself struggles with opposing forces, asserting its predominance over wrath, and defining the meaning of divine sovereignty.

Just as three fundamental ideas, love, justice, and power, are involved in the concept of God, so also God's activity is threefold, in that He saves, judges, and creates. God saves through establishing fellowship between Himself and a sinful and lost humanity. To achieve fellowship God must overcome the hostile power of man's egocentricity. The possibility of salvation lies entirely in the divine will and not in any human quality. The decisive encounter between God and the forces opposing Him has occurred, but the battle continues. Each individual Christian experiences fellowship here and now, but remains a sinner. The

Kingdom of God, in the sense of God's perfect dominion, therefore transcends history.

The love which saves also judges those who refuse to tolerate it. Yet there is no punishing activity which does not ultimately serve the saving activity. Aulén states that the ultimate destiny of those who stand under judgment lies beyond "the boundary line of faith." Faith is unable to decide between condemnation, annihilation, or the final return of all things to God (*apokatastasis*).

When one speaks of God's creative activity, one is not primarily concerned with a theory of origins. Creation has a beginning, but it also continues, and it has a goal. God's redemptive activity is continued creation. Creation is therefore that work of divine love through which God manifests His sovereignty in relation to existence. Since providence is continuous creative activity, providence cannot be distinguished from creation.

God as creator opposes all that ruins and destroys. The law of creation (of which natural law is a reflection) is nothing other than the law of love revealed in Christ. While moral evil is always in radical antithesis to the divine will, physical evil cannot be wholly separated from the divine will. God does not will everything that happens, but since He is sovereign in grace and judgment, He wills something in everything that happens.

Aulén's discussion of the doctrine of redemption divides into a section devoted to the act of God in Christ, and a section devoted to God's work in us. The meaning of the Incarnation, according to Aulén, is that the divine love, and thus God Himself, is incarnate in Jesus Christ. The Incarnation

is perfected on the cross. Aulén states that the Virgin Birth is not to be used as a rational explanation of the Incarnation.

The work of Christ, with which Aulén is primarily concerned, is the reconciliation Christ achieved by destroying and subjugating the hostile power of evil separating God and the world. The Cross is therefore understood in terms of struggle and victory. The emphasis is placed not on satisfaction offered on man's behalf to God, nor upon the sufferings of Christ that are to move man to repentance. Aulén speaks rather of Christ's victory over powers, such as sin and death, which are opposed to God, and also of Christ's overcoming of God's wrath itself.

The work which Christ finished on the cross does not need to be repeated. His exaltation in the resurrection, ascension, and session at the right hand of God unveils, reveals, and realizes the victory contained in his finished work. There is no significant difference, according to Aulén, between this continuing work of Christ and the work of the Spirit.

Aulén's discussion of God's work in us deals with sin, forgiveness, and faith. Sin, according to Aulén, has no meaning apart from reference to God, for sin is whatever separates God and man. Sin may be defined positively as egocentricity, negatively as unbelief. Aulén maintains that all sin is original sin, with actual sin as its external manifestation. Sin cannot be explained by reference to the Fall, for the original estate and the Fall belong to each individual. Faith, however, is more concerned about the nature of sin and its subjugation than about its origin. Forgiveness of sin is that act of divine love through which sinful man is subdued and incorporated into fellowship with God. Though man is forgiven, his unworthiness remains. Indeed, forgiveness makes for a more acute consciousness of sin. Man then participates through forgiveness in the eternal life of God, and thereby he gains power to struggle against sin and to serve his neighbor; he becomes an instrument of the divine love.

Faith is a work of God, but it also involves unconditional trust on man's part. Aulén points out that it is important that the divine and the human not be regarded as being independent; man's activity can never be separated from God's activity. Struggle is necessary even for man sustained by faith; hope is therefore the eschatological dimension of faith.

Aulén contends that the Christian Church, which appears as a living reality in and through the exaltation of Christ, is not to be understood as a society of qualified persons, but as a fellowship created by the Holy Spirit. The Church exists wherever faith discovers the dominion of Christ.

The Church is one, holy, ecumenical, and apostolic. Christ working through the Word and the sacraments is the source of its unity. This unity must be acknowledged and the divisions created by men must be overcome. However, there can be differentiation in structure of organization, in the way the faith is described, and in patterns of religious life; such differentiation does not destroy the basic unity which is of the essence of the Church. The holiness of the Church can be seen only by faith. The Church is holy because Christ is present in it, but the Church is also sinful. It shares with its individual members the am-

biguity of being both holy and sinful. The Church is ecumenical (the word Aulén prefers to express the catholicity of the Church), because the finished work of Christ is universal. No boundaries can be drawn to limit the activity of the Spirit. The Church is finally apostolic in the sense that it constantly needs new messengers to proclaim the living Word, who in turn must stand in continuity with the first authorized messengers of the Lord, and with the fundamental work they accomplished.

The Church, in Martin Luther's words in his *Large Catechism*, may be described as "the mother who bears and fosters every individual Christian." Though there is a direct and immediate relation between each individual and God, individualism in the sense of isolation is a sin from which the individual must be delivered. Here the Church becomes "a solidary interrelationship of blessing which is opposed to and struggles with the solidary interrelationship of sin."

In identifying the means of grace, means which are constituent factors of the church, Aulén with Friedrich Schleiermacher (German theologian, 1768-1834) adds prayer to the Word and the sacraments. Prayer, Aulén insists, is not solely a human act; it is also God's approach to us and may thus properly be regarded as a means of grace.

The Word of God is best understood as a message whereby the divine love is self-imparted. There is no standard by which the Word can be judged, but the Word itself convicts man through its own content and character. This Word, which is incarnate in Christ, is anchored to the Bible. The Bible's authority does not depend upon theories of its inspiration, but upon "the fact that the Christian faith is Christocentric, that Christ is the central content of the Scripture, and that every message about the act of God in Christ is derived from and determined by the message of Scripture."

The divine love can be self-imparted not only through the Word, but also through actions. The Church has several holy actions, two of which, baptism and the Lord's Supper, have been identified as sacraments because they comprehensively express the central content of the Gospel and are organically connected with the Christ event.

Aulén calls baptism the sacrament of prevenient grace, since baptism makes it evident that God's love seeks man before man seeks God; the validity of infant baptism is thereby established. In this way also all man-made hindrances to membership in the Church are removed. Yet the fellowship with God given in baptism must be actualized. The Church is obligated to sustain fellowship; at the same time each individual member should spend his entire life living out the implications of his baptism.

In the Lord's Supper Christ actualizes the sacrifice which began with the Incarnation and was completed on the cross. The significance of this sacrament depends entirely on the real presence of Christ. This presence must neither be unduly spiritualized nor unduly materialized, for the former misconception obscures the Cross, while the latter obscures the Resurrection. The primary gift of this sacrament is communion with Christ, in which gift other gifts, such as forgiveness, life, and salvation, are included. In this sacrament Jesus Christ is the true celebrant, using human servants as means. At the same time, the Lord's Supper is the Church's most important act of prayer, while those who participate are consecrated for a life of loving sacrificial service.

Prayer, according to Aulén, is both man's turning to God and God's approach to man. The purpose of prayer is not to change God's will, but to be a means through which God's will is done. Such a view does not, however, imply resignation, but rather a militant and conquering faith.

Aulén regards the ministry as also one of the constituent factors of the Church, because the ministry is a necessary instrument in the activity of the Word and the sacraments which establish the Church. All Church members have a dual obligation, to make use of the means of grace and to practice neighbor love, both of which obligations are also privileges.

Aulén concludes by discussing the Church in the light of the Christian hope. The life of the Church is ultimately eschatological in character, since the fellowship with God experienced in the Church is eternal in nature. Faith therefore looks forward to the ultimate perfection of the Church in the Kingdom of Glory. There is continuity between the militant Church and this Kingdom of Glory, in the sense that the struggling Church is transformed into the finished dominion of God, but there is also discontinuity, since God's perfect dominion will be accomplished by an act of God's eternal power which will involve radical transformation of the present order. Thus, the Christian hope avoids both world-denying pessimism and evolutionary optimism.

I AND THOU

Author: Martin Buber (1878-   )
Type of work: Religious existentialism
First published: 1923

PRINCIPAL IDEAS ADVANCED

Man finds fulfillment through personal encounters, but to become a person, he must also relate himself to an objective world.

To know a thing, a person, or a proposition, as an object is to know it as nothing more than an it to which one is related.

To know a thing or a person, not as an object, but through a direct, mutual encounter, is to have established the I-Thou relation.

Since, whenever we stand in the relation of I and Thou, the Eternal Thou speaks to us through the temporal instance, true religion involves discovering what God demands of us in the present moment.

Martin Buber's *I and Thou* is one of those exceptional works which know no ordinary boundaries of classification. Although Buber is a Jewish philosopher, his work has so illuminated the Christian faith—by providing an existentialist account of what he calls the "I-Thou" relation—that more than many works written by Christians, *I and Thou* can properly be called a masterpiece of Christian literature.

Buber is more interested in tearing down barriers than in erecting them, as is shown in the following instance which he recounts in *Between Man and Man*, a later work which particularly supplements *I and Thou.* At an international meeting early in 1914, when a delegate arose to protest that too large a proportion of the representatives were Jewish, Buber rose to the defense. "I no longer know," he writes, "how . . . I came to speak of Jesus and to say that we Jews knew him from within, in the impulses and stirrings of his Jewish being, in a way that remains inaccessible to the peoples submissive to him. 'In a way that

remains inaccessible to you'—so I directly addressed the former clergyman. He stood up, I too stood, we looked into the heart of one another's eyes. 'It is gone,' he said, and before everyone we gave one another the kiss of brotherhood."

The anecdote sheds light on Buber's attitude toward Christianity. His Judaism is of the unorthodox kind which, through the centuries, has turned a deaf ear to rabbinical authority. This appears from the emphasis he places on the prophetic voice in his Old Testament studies, and in his appreciation of the eighteenth century Jewish pietistic movement known as Hasidism. Even today, living in Jerusalem, he makes no pretense at keeping the ceremonial law. It is, therefore, not surprising that Buber is disposed to listen to the Christ of the Gospels, and to find in Christian writers, from the Apostle John to Søren Kierkegaard, authentic witnesses to divine truth. Indeed, to many Christians it appears that Buber's most characteristic teachings are directly derived from the New

Testament. In any case, it is difficult not to agree with Buber's English translator, R. G. Smith, when he says, "In *I and Thou* the two traditions interact and illuminate one another in a remarkable and moving way."

It is, however, to be noted that the point of the anecdote of 1914 is not that Jew and Christian found in Jesus a common ground of meeting, but that when Buber directly addressed his opponent, so that they looked deep into each other's eyes, a meeting took place which could not have been achieved on the secondary level of argument and discussion. Communication gave way to communion. In Buber's words, "The discussion of the situation between Jews and Christians had been transformed into a bond between the Christian and the Jew. In this transformation dialogue was fulfilled. Opinions were gone, in a bodily way the factual took place." Here we have a good illustration of the two fundamental dimensions of human experience, delineated by Kierkegaard, but brought to a new clarity by Buber; namely, the relation between *I* and *It* and the relation between *I* and *Thou*. The "change from communication to communion" is a transition from the *I-It* relation to the *I-Thou* relation. The former, according to Buber, is not, in the full sense of the word, a relation; he uses the term "experience" for the *I-It* type of knowing. When I know a thing, a person, or a proposition, in the mode of an *it*, I make it an object; I am related to it, I experience it, but it is unaffected by the relation. When I know any of these in the mode of *thou*, neither is an object for the other, but each "has to do with" each in a living mutuality. Ordinary communication between man and man

is indirect, inasmuch as that which passes between them is an object for each one. But in a moment such as that described by Buber, when the object and its relations are allowed to fall to one side and one self encounters another self, direct relation or communion is established.

Although the *I-Thou* relation is recognizable by most of us in the encounter between man and man, Buber maintains that essentially the same relation can exist between man and nature, and between man and spirit.

The word "nature," of course, stands to civilized man for the ordered cosmos, for the world of *It*. Our technical reason has laid hold of nature's uniformities and has taught us to regard the whole as a complex of identifiable things. But this has not always been the case. For the primitive, as for the child, nature is perceived much more directly, not as a complex of things but as expressions of a *Thou*. Moreover, in favorable moments, even civilized man is able to recover that elemental relation. Buber uses the example of a tree. One can classify it, analyze it, and subdue it to one's practical and scientific schemes; on occasion, however, without giving up any of this hard-earned knowledge, one finds oneself and the tree caught up into an unspeakable union. The experience is never more than a fleeting one, but it is qualitatively the same as that closer union between man and man made possible by speech. For this reason, Buber calls the sphere of our relation with natural entities the "pre-threshold" or "preliminal" stage.

When Buber speaks of our relation with spirit, he has reference not to angels or to disembodied souls but to creative works which embody form. Since at this stage the relation is not directly man to man, but beyond such a relation, Buber calls the stage "superliminal." A saying of some old master, when it is not the object of critical inquiry but that which is received in "the indivisible wholeness of something spoken," is an example of that which allows man to encounter spirit. Buber tells of confronting a Doric pillar in a church wall in Syracuse. He encountered the pillar as "mysterious primal mass represented in such simple form that there was nothing individual to look at, nothing individual to enjoy," and he reports that he did all that could be done; he "took [his] stand, stood fast, in the face of this structure of spirit, this mass penetrated and given body by the mind and hand of man."

Of course, the spoken word and the carved column readily harden into things, thereby becoming objects alongside other objects in the world of It. But they are unlike most things in that they have built into them a disposition to "change back again and again" and to draw man out of the world of It and into the world of Thou.

There is something melancholy about the human situation, Buber comments; the melancholy arises out of the fact that man cannot dwell for more than a fleeting instant in the union of pure relation. At the same time, the key to man's greatness is that he is able to move back and forth between the exclusiveness of I-Thou and the inclusiveness of I-It. The history of civilization, as well as the growth of individual persons, is dependent upon the "progressive augmentation of the world of It." Both our technical knowledge and our awareness of ourselves as individuals as distinguished from the group and as persons as distinguished from other kinds of being depends upon the primary distinction between subject and object and upon the fixed relational order which we discover in both the external world and the private world of the self. The human situation is melancholy, according to Buber, because the more articulation we introduce into the world of It, the farther we remove ourselves from the unity of the world of Thou. On the other hand, without this differentiation, neither the I nor the Thou can come to its highest realization; while relation cannot arise between two independent Its, neither can it arise in an undifferentiated One.

It is the primacy of relation and the fact that genuine relation can take place only between two persons that distinguishes Buber's religious philosophy from mysticism. As an example of the perfect union between man and God, he cites Jesus' words in the Fourth Gospel, "I and my Father are one." Here is no mystical absorption, no declaration of identity between the self and the divine One, but the exclusiveness of personal encounter. "The Father and the Son, like in being—we may even say God and Man, like in being—are the indissolubly real pair, the two bearers of the primal relation, which from God to man is termed mission and command, from man to God looking and hearing." According to Buber, mysticism is the end-product of the false kind of spirituality which results when man lives entirely in the dimension of I and It and loses touch with the dimension of I and Thou; the world of I and It tends to fall into two parts, the objective world of matter and causality and the subjective world of feelings and ideas.

In Buber's opinion, much of what passes for spirituality, including religious feeling, is a kind of subjectivism, which exists in alienation from nature, from society, and from the everyday world. (Buber himself passed through the mystical stage, which he regarded as a necessary step on the way to the *I-Thou* philosophy.) Mysticism is an attempt to recover unity, but it is spurious because it denies the world and seeks salvation "within the self-sufficient interior life of man." Only when man recovers the other dimension of *I* and *Thou* is he delivered from subjectivism and solipsism. The *I* of the *I-Thou* relation is not an individual, isolated from other individuals and from the world of events; he is a person, whose life consists in the relations of faith, hope, and love. He lives in community with other man, but the relation which binds him to other *thous* also binds him to the *Eternal Thou*.

Buber agrees with Søren Kierkegaard that, as between man and man, the *I-Thou* relation is exclusive; but he denies that this is the case between man and God. In this manner he hopes to remedy the one-sidedness (as he views it) of Kierkegaard's teaching. The Danish philosopher seemed to be saying that in order to serve God one must break off every relation that binds Him to the world, whether it be ties of marriage, vocation, or politics. Buber, on the contrary, wants to show that love to God is inclusive of all other loves. He uses the example of the relation of a poet and his reader. The reader does not meet the *whole* of the poet in any poem, but he neverthe-

less meets him in each poem. Similarly, while we do not meet God *in His entirety* in any one of our encounters, in each meeting we encounter the *Eternal Thou*. God "speaks" to us through natural events, through history and biography, through situations which demand of us that we act. Hence we should not turn away from the creature, for through fulfilling our responsibilities to the creature we perform our service to the Creator.

Because we are as likely to meet God at the workbench as at the altar, Buber finds much religion inadequate. Once, he tells us, he was much given to religious exercise. One day, after having spent the morning in his devotions, he was visited by a youth whom he had never met. The young man asked several questions and went away. Only later did Buber learn that his visitor had come to him in despair and had gone away with his deepest questions unasked. Buber thereupon concluded that he had failed the young man. Had he given himself fully to this meeting, he would have guessed the questions which his visitor was not able to ask. Henceforth, he renounced that kind of religion which draws one's attention away from the ordinary, and he resolved to occupy himself at all times with whatever occupation he had at hand. He calls this incident his "conversion."

Not only religion but also morality is taken up in this new point of view, which calls us to live intensively in the present moment and to recognize each new moment as a gift fresh from the Creator which lays on us the responsibility of making of it the best we can. This acceptance of responsibility is, from one point of view, what Buber understands by faith. Each situation in which we find ourselves is a new one. There are no rules to guide our action, as moralists, with their reliance on custom and reason, are accustomed to suppose. Each enterprise involves the risk of novelty, and calls for faith. But he who accepts his responsibility from God does so with hope. He who lives in the present is conscious of freedom and creativity. Necessity, the twin of intelligibility, belongs to the world of It, which is always past, and never exists. Necessity does not govern the present, and he who dares live in the present and to choose the way that is momentarily opened to him by God does so with hope. Furthermore, he who willingly responds when God speaks to him does so with love; in Buber's language, love is responsibility for a thou, whether a dog, a child, or one's fellow in a crowd. Love involves awareness of the other in the concreteness of his being and dares to wish the being of the other for just what he is. This, indeed, is the meaning of the commandment, "Love thy neighbor as thyself." The commandment does not mean that one should love one's neighbor as one loves oneself; it does mean that one should love one's neighbor by encountering him as one like oneself. In making oneself responsible for others, one performs the sacrifice of love: "A newly-created concrete reality has been laid in our arms; we answer for it. A dog has looked at you, you answer for its glance, a child has clutched your hand, you answer for its touch, a host of men moves about you, you answer for their need."

LOVE, THE LAW OF LIFE

Author: Toyohiko Kagawa (1888-1960)
Type of work: Christian ethics
First published: 1924

PRINCIPAL IDEAS ADVANCED

The experience of sacrificial love, which Jesus awakens in men's hearts, enables men to understand the nature of God, the world, and man.

Love is the principle underlying organic and social evolution; physical love tends to develop into psychical and, finally, into ethical love.

Love of individuals is an expression of a Cosmic Will.

The individual can realize his potentialities only as part of an organic whole to which he is bound by a social will.

When Toyohiko Kagawa was a high school boy he discovered, through personal conversation with a mission-teacher, the transforming power of divine love in his heart. Turning his back on a family inheritance and on his former Buddhist faith, he gave up studying for a diplomatic career and attended a Presbyterian seminary in Kobe (from 1905 to 1908), where he began his lifelong practice of living and working in slum districts. In the midst of a busy life as evangelist, labor organizer, and youth leader, Kagawa found time to write dozens of books, including several novels and volumes of poetry. The present work, which, literally translated, is entitled "The Science of Love," was begun with a view to counteracting the lax views of marriage that were then finding a vogue in Japan; but as the book unfolded in his hands, it turned into a comprehensive philosophy.

Kagawa does not claim that Jesus himself had any "philosophy of love." "Jesus," he says, "loved men without formulating any theory of love." Nevertheless, says Kagawa, it is the concept of sacrificial love which Jesus awakens in men's souls that provides the means for understanding the world and man's place in it. By creating a new dynamic within the heart, love enables man for the first time to recognize his kinship with his Creator, according to the principle expressed by the Apostle John, "Everyone that loves is born of God, and knoweth God; he that loves not does not know God, for God is love."

Nineteenth century vitalistic philosophers, such as Schopenhauer, were, in Kagawa's opinion, on the right track when they maintained that an unconscious Universal Will surges through nature, goading it on by an irresistible passion. However, Kagawa finds Schopenhauer too theoretical in his account of love, because he viewed love from the outside, as it manifests itself in evolution and in art, and did not experience it practically in his heart.

Kagawa credits Kant with first making clear the distinction between "two kinds of perception, the external and the internal," and with showing that it is only through the latter, conscience, that the Absolute is revealed. But Bergson, in Kagawa's opinion, gives an even more adequate account of the Absolute, because he grasps better than Kant the fact that the Absolute is "pure continuity" and is perceived only through an intuition of the inner self. It is Kagawa's reliance upon a kind of Bergsonian intuition that has led some writers to speak of him as a mystic.

Kagawa identifies God with evolution. "The man who says he believes in evolution but not in God, deceives himself," says Kagawa; "for it is a matter of difference in terms, not of variation in essence." When we speak of God we are using the language of subjective experience; when we speak of evolution, we are using the vocabulary of objective science. But, according to Kagawa, there is no ground for believing in evolution, in the sense of progress, except the experience of God which man has in his soul. "Thus," he says, "the idea of progress is subjective effort reflected objectively. When man begins to glimpse the first rays of the dawning hope of progress, he for the first time becomes assured that there is evolution in the cosmos; but when this hope is wanting, he thinks of the changes tending toward complexity in the cosmic structure merely as fetters binding mankind." The theory of evolution, he says, is a faith —"the greatest faith since Abraham." Theoretically expressed, it is the "belief that the God who is from the beginning becomes the final God."

To maintain that God is love is to believe that the evolution of the world manifests the effort of a cosmic will to "lift all and save all." Kagawa cites the argument of the Russian revolutionist Pëtr Kropotkin (1842-1921), to show that evolution could never have taken place if the struggle for existence had not brought forth a mutual aid on the part of individual creatures. This "unreasoned impulse" found in the animal world is not yet love, but love grows out of it; for example, love between the sexes, and the love of parents for their children.

Kagawa distinguishes three grades of love on the human level: physical, psychical, and ethical love. These are not exclusive, and, in the natural order of things, the first tends to develop into the second, and the second into the third. For example, sexual attraction tends to become refined into passionate love, which, because it overlays sexual desire with ideal elements, must be accounted psychical. Moreover, as passionate love develops, it may reach a point at which the sexual element disappears, as in the romantic love of St. Francis and St. Claire. The latent presence of this sacred love in physical attraction is, according to Kagawa, merely one instance of the presence throughout the cosmos of the higher, divine love, which found its perfect expression in the life and death of Jesus. For, as Kagawa understands it, the essential characteristic of this higher love is its readiness to sacrifice itself for others.

In Kagawa's philosophy, the theory of evolution finds its counterpart in an organic theory of nature and of society. Defining society as "the assembling of imperfect individuals for the purpose of securing something more nearly perfect," he says that there are as many kinds of societies as there are kinds of love. From physical affinities based on race and the struggle for survival, men tend to pass to psychical affinities based on economic and cultural wants, and then on to moral affinities based on the recognition of the divine life in every creature.

Kagawa's discussion of law and government presupposes this theory of society. In an organism, different parts have different functions, which, if they are not defined, may lead to conflict and disorder. Law exists to expedite the functioning of the social organism. As society evolves from one stage to another, law too evolves; and because evolution is gradual, different kinds of law exist side by side. Criminal law is an example. Kagawa finds that, while both physical and psychical societies are intolerant of nonconformists, ethical societies, because they value every person for his own sake, seek to reclaim social failures. Kagawa recognizes a similar development in international law, and he looks forward to the emergence among civilized peoples of a free society based on moral affinity. Kagawa's philosophy is not that of an "absolute optimist." He denies that there is any economic or political solution to the problems of war and crime. These can be solved only step by step, as more individuals experience inner awakening, and as sacrificial love replaces physical and psychical love.

Kagawa criticizes the individualism of representative nineteenth century ethical thinkers. Tolstoy, for example, had declared that the doctrine of social organism is injurious to the dignity of the ego; but Kagawa argues that blindness to the "supra-egoistic elements of self-consciousness" prevented Tolstoy from understanding the nature of love. Love, says Kagawa, does not begin in individuals; it is a social will, which comes to consciousness in individuals; ultimately, it is an expression of the cosmic will; that is to say, of God. Kagawa criticizes the perfectionist ideal of T. H. Green, the utilitarianism of John Stuart Mill, and the hedonism of Walter Pater on similar grounds. One and all, they fail to see that, apart from his fellows, the individual is a fragment, and that personality is total only in society. "Society," he says, "is an aggregation of individuals who supplement each other and cooperate in order to become stronger, more nearly perfect. It is the hundreds of millions of human beings who would share in striving after God-like perfection."

Kagawa's profound sense of social mission has its basis in his organic view of the world. Just as the cooperation of many has brought about all the beauty and excellency in the world, so it follows that the weakness of the few is a threat to the well-being of all. "It is a fundamental principle," says Kagawa, "that if there is anywhere in the universe a single flaw, the whole universe suffers. . . . If there were only one sinner in the universe, all creation would suffer sorrow and pain—God and I alike would suffer, and thereupon would be born spontaneously the energy which lifts up the sinner." Kagawa uses the example of a blood cell which spontaneously sacrifices itself to heal a wound; similarly, he says, men in whom a sense of moral affinity has been awakened are stirred to devote their lives to sacrificial labor whenever they find evil and pain. Such was the divine love which took Jesus to Calvary and prompted the parable, "Unless a grain of wheat falls into the earth and dies,

it remains a single grain; but if it dies, it bears much fruit."

Redemptive love constrained Kagawa to spend most of his life with people in the slums. Studying the needs of the poor at close range, he found that those who worked could be helped by labor organizations, but that those who were physically or spiritually disqualified from working could be helped only by neighborhood movements. Kagawa divided his energies between the two. It was through his efforts that the first labor unions were formed in Japan. Labor organizing was illegal at the time, and Kagawa and his associates were put in prison; but they persisted, and the laws were changed. Kagawa also carried on settlement work in Tokyo, Osaka, and Kobe, making each project an experiment in some aspect of social betterment. He stressed the fact, however, that no program and no amount of financial support can succeed in neighborhood work except where men and women of moral force are willing to sacrifice everything and to live among the persons whom they are trying to help. "These folk," he says, "do not have the health that the laboring classes have." Their trouble, he claims, is a kind of moral bankruptcy, and hence anyone who tries to help them must endure threats, misunderstanding, and even bodily harm. But the task is simple, at least, in principle: "It is simply being kind to one's neighbors." It may mean nursing a castaway child, teaching an old man to read, teaching a woman to sew, or giving advice in personal matters.

The possibility of reclaiming adult slum dwellers seemed to Kagawa very slight. While ministering to them as to the incurably ill, he placed his hope in salvaging the young (those under twelve) by emphasizing health and nutrition, mental therapy, and education. Kagawa's theories of education are based on the principle of "unfolding the child's whole nature." Education, he argues, is a psychological activity, and consists in "calling forth the original nature of man." Kagawa looked in this direction, rather than toward economics and politics, for the "socialization" of the world. He believed that capitalism must be abolished, and that government must be based on love instead of on the interests of special groups. But he maintained that this change can never be realized while the souls of men are famished and in distress. The proletariat must be emancipated "through the spirit of love and mutual aid," and enabled to live "always with its ideals firmly in mind" if society is to be reconstructed and a higher type of humanity created.

The strength of Kagawa's convictions and his unflagging zeal come from his deeply religious persuasion that the love which he finds in his own breast is "the motion of the unseen cosmic will." "It is not the *ego* which loves others," he says; "love is rather the motion resulting from the prior winding up of the mainspring." For Kagawa, the desire which draws the whole creation forward is the "wish to become divine." God is, in his view, the absolute value, and the morality of self-sacrifice and nonviolence is an absolute and eternal rule: "For those who eternally evolve there is an eternal cross."

RELIGION IN THE MAKING

Author: Alfred North Whitehead (1861-1947)
Type of work: Philosophy of religion
First published: 1926

PRINCIPAL IDEAS ADVANCED

Religion in its profoundest aspect, manifested clearly and fully only at the level of rationalization, consists of the intuitions of the individual in his solitariness.

The intuitions of rational religion, while they constitute the sources of religious insight, are not self-evidently authenticating but require metaphysical criticism for the verification of their truth.

The idea of God as the source of all actual order in the world and as the measure of the ideal harmony of the world is the metaphysical correlative of the intuitions of permanence and the hope for the realization of values experienced in rational religion.

Religion in the Making marks a transition in Whitehead's thought. Previously he had written works dealing with the philosophy of science. Subsequently he was to write metaphysics. *Religion in the Making* is a reflection of the older epoch in Whitehead's written thought inasmuch as it is an examination of the role of religion in the development of Western thought, an examination parallel to his analysis of the role of science in the Western tradition in *Science and the Modern World* (1925). *Religion in the Making* is at the same time an anticipation of the new epoch in Whitehead's thought because it contains a sketch of a religious metaphysics which finds its most systematic statement in *Process and Reality* (1929).

That this transitional work is Whitehead's most sustained treatment of religion shows that a religious factor plays an important formative role in the shaping of his thought. Because his efforts were those of philosophic thought, the focus of his analysis is upon religion as a constitutive factor in human experience rather than upon Christianity as a religious faith. He writes as a philosopher of religion rather than as a theologian. He writes, furthermore, as a philosopher of religion eager to arrest the development of what he sees to be the erosion of the traditional religions.

Nevertheless, numerous aspects of Whitehead's thought make it clear that he is chiefly, though not exclusively, concerned with the Christian religion. His analysis of the evolution of religion from ritual to emotion, myth, and reason is most relevant to Christian history. His criticism of dogmatism in religion is obviously applicable to Christian theology. The special attention paid to the metaphysical functions of God shows a Christian rather than a Buddhist interest. His plea for a search for ever more rational theological formulations expresses a feeling of the importance of Christian theology. His espousal of the idea of persuasion, which admittedly finds one of its most winning expressions in the New Testament picture of Christ, discloses an inheritance from Christian ethics. In all of these aspects, Whitehead's philosophy of religion reveals its Christian bias. It is no accident that Christian theologians have seen in Whitehead's thought new modes of expressing their faith more adequately.

The essence of religion, according to Whitehead, does not become apparent until religion has evolved to its rational expression. Only at the stage of rational religion does the inwardness of religious intuition stand sharply against collective emotions. Only at this point are the intuitions of religion themselves tempered by ethical insight. Only then do religious intuitions become fully capable of intellective elaboration. Indeed, to speak of religious intuition at all implies the context of rational religion. If Whitehead defines religion as "what the individual does with his own solitariness," he also makes clear that it is "not until belief and rationalization are well established that solitariness is discernible as constituting the heart of religious importance." Not until man's historical development allows him a genuinely cosmopolitan experience can a world-consciousness be produced and can religious intuitions be disengaged from the confining bonds of communal religion.

With the advent of rational religion religion's essential solitariness and its universal relevance become apparent. The source of religious insight becomes the direct intuitions of the in-

RELIGION IN THE MAKING

dividual, intuitions which claim to be universally valid. "Rational religion appeals to the direct intuition of special occasions," Whitehead writes, "and to the elucidatory power of its concepts for all occasions. It arises from that which is special, but it extends to what is general." Religion is peculiarly that type of human experience by which the juxtaposition of particularity and universality is understood. Religious intuition, insofar as it is genuinely intuitive, is the product of special moments of extraordinary insight. Yet religious intuitions, insofar as they are genuinely religious, are intuitions of what is permanent in the world. Religious intuition "brings into our consciousness that permanent side of the universe which we can care for."

Nevertheless, one cannot move simply from the special insights of religious intuition to their universal validity. The solitary individual may be the occasion of religious insight, but religious truth is not the self-evident product of such moments. Religious intuitions require metaphysical criticism because they must be correlated with other kinds of intuitions, because they cannot guarantee the adequacy of their own statement, and because they are inevitably infected by the historical circumstances of their origin. Furthermore, it is a primary metaphysical conviction of Whitehead that no single occasion is self-explaining. Rational religion originates from the intuitions of the solitary individual; but without reference to the world of other individuals, a solitary person cannot be uniquely individual nor can his intuitions be truly rational.

One other crucial factor enters into Whitehead's understanding of rational religion: the concept of value. Rational religion is that level of growth in religion characterized not only by a rational coordination of beliefs, but also by a purified understanding of the good. The world-consciousness of rational religion "rises to the conception of an essential rightness of things." Religion, in its earlier forms particularly, Whitehead argues, "is by no means necessarily good. It may be very evil." Only in rational religion does a purified and generally impartial view of value become possible.

Value pertains first of all to the self-valuation of the individual in his solitariness, then to the value of different individuals for each other, and finally to "the objective world which is a community derivative from the interrelations of its component individuals, and also necessary for the existence of each of these individuals." Hence, the intuitions of rational religion are intimately bound up with valuation and the realization of value. Hence, too, the intuition of permanence in rational religion is the intuition of a permanence which, as Whitehead states, "provides a meaning, in terms of value, for our own existence, a meaning which flows from the nature of things."

The social character of realized value is another reason why the individual in his solitariness and self-valuation may not simply accept his own intuitions and valuations normatively. For instance, he cannot legitimately appeal to a direct intuition of an omnipotent personal deity. If God is believed to be personal, this belief, for rational religion, must be inferential and not intuitive. Otherwise, God's person appears as an intuition incapable of generalization; God's existence becomes an essentially unverifiable supposition; and the goodness derivitive from God's person is arbitrary. The belief in a direct intuition of a personal deity is a relapse of religion into a prerational form.

With respect to the concept of value, Whitehead argues that the simple trust in individual self-valuation cannot explicate the problem of evil. Insofar as the world, seen as a social whole, exhibits a lack of complex self-consistency, it is evil. Hence, evil must be understood as the thwarting of intense social harmonies by recalcitrant realizations of partial values. Insofar as an actual entity is considered in itself, it is the realization of value. But insofar as it functions socially as a destructive agent with respect to greater possible realizations of value, it is evil. Appeal to the self-evidence of private intuitions, then, is no guarantee of the value of these intuitions.

At the same time, the intuitions of the individual are not necessarily arbitrary, and the self-valuation of the individual's solitude is not unqualifiedly evil. Evil is not intrinsic to the self-realization or self-valuation of the individual; evil arises from the maladjustment of this realized value to what might have been achieved in its world. Thus, self-valuation can also be the way in which a more complex harmony is introduced into the world. At any rate, it is Whitehead's conviction that evil is unstable and self-stultifying and that evil can be overcome by good.

A more complete account of the nature of the permanence discerned in religious intuition and of the possibility of the social harmony sought by rational valuation requires reference to Whitehead's view of the metaphysical functions of God. The idea of God is one of the three concepts Whitehead believes necessary for the elucidation of the world. The world consists of a multiplicity of temporal-spatial epochal occasions, each of which reflects in itself the other proximate occasions. This world requires the concept of creativity to explain the temporal succession of these occasions as being such that the succession exhibits the character of transition. Creativity is that characteristic of temporal success whereby one occasion can become a creator of a new creature. Whitehead says that the creatures exhibit the quality of creativity, though creativity cannot be conceived as an epochal occasion. Second, the world requires reference to a realm of ideal entities or forms in terms of which one epochal occasion can be relevantly related to other occasions. This ideal realm is itself a multiplicity of possibilities, any one or group of which is relevant to the relation between epochal occasions. The realm of ideal entities is not the same as the actual world because the epochal occasions in their creativity determine the way in which the ideal entities qualify the creative process. Third, the world requires reference to an "actual but non-temporal entity whereby the indetermination of mere creativity is transmuted into a determinate freedom." This is the function of God. Apart from God there would be no explanation of the actual order which the world does exhibit. Neither the principle of creativity nor the realm of ideal entities can explain this order because they are principles of potentiality and not powers of actuality. The succession of epochal occasions cannot explain this actual order in the world because epochal occasions are limited realizations of actuality which precisely in their multiplicity call for explanation.

These metaphysical functions, however, precisely correlate with the intuitions of rational religion. If religious intuitions are intuitions of the element of permanence in the world, God, in Whitehead's metaphysics, is that nontemporal actuality upon whom all actual order in the world depends. Nor is this metaphysical function lacking in its implication for values. As the nontemporal actuality upon whom order in the actual world depends, God partly determines the possibility of ideal entities for epochal occasions and partly conditions the creativity of the creatures. This is why the self-valuation of any epochal occasion is not wholly arbitrary. In its freedom of self-valuation, any creature exhibits a possibility which is never ultimately incompatible with God's harmony of apprehension. In religious language, as Whitehead explains it, "the kingdom of heaven is not the isolation of good from evil. It is the overcoming of evil by good. This transmutation of evil into good enters into the actual world by reason of the inclusion of the nature of God, which includes the ideal vision of each actual evil so met with a novel consequent as to issue in the restoration of goodness."

Though Whitehead's idea of God diverges significantly from important aspects of the Western religious tradition, Whitehead belongs to this tradition as its critic. He belongs to the Christian tradition because he does not fear to criticize what he believes to be its failures. He belongs to the Christian tradition also because he constructs a complex alternative to some of its chief doctrinal problems. Consequently, Whitehead's philosophy of religion must be considered an important event in the history of Christian thought.

FREEDOM AND THE SPIRIT

Author: Nikolai Berdyaev (1874-1948)
Type of work: Philosophy of religion; existentialism
First published: 1927

Principal Ideas Advanced

Spirit can never be understood in terms of a philosophy which accepts the categories of nature as ultimate.

Spirit reveals the freedom of its inner life in the symbolism of myth and religious dogma.

The Christian dogmas of the Creation, Fall, and redemption of the world represent the true life of Spirit.

The incarnation of God in a human nature and His resurrection from the grave contain the promise of man's victory over nature.

This spiritual hope is realized, not in technical progress nor in political union, but in the corporate experience of the Church.

In *Freedom and the Spirit*, Nikolai Berdyaev does not undertake to discuss either spirit or freedom in the traditional manner. His contention is that both philosophy and theology have erred in treating of spirit as if it were part of nature, subject to the categories of reason. If this error is to be corrected, an entirely new philosophy is needed which will start with spirit's knowledge of itself. Spirit knows that it does not derive its freedom from the world of nature; on the contrary, nature derives whatever meaning it has from the freedom which is spirit's very being.

According to Berdyaev, spirit represents a "breach in the structure of the psycho-corporeal monad." Spirit is not observable outwardly by scientific observation, but only inwardly, by reflection on the moral and religious experience of mankind. Refusing to be confined by the repetitious patterns which dominate matter, spirit is always striving to realize its own life more completely; and because spirit is essentially dynamic, it cannot make use of the static concepts of reason, but must devise a symbolism of its own. Thus, spirit invents the language of religious dogma and myth.

Religious symbolism, according to Berdyaev, makes possible a "revelation" of the secret inner life of spirit. The subconscious potencies of spirit disclose themselves in terms of the surface contents of mind, taking such natural and historical forms as lie near at hand. For example, the Biblical account of man's creation, his fall, and his redemption reveals to man that he is a child of two worlds: man is made of dust, but also he is fashioned in God's image; he is condemned to death, but also he is appointed to an eternal destiny. The Creation, Fall, and redemption, says Berdyaev, all transpired within the life of spirit itself; and it is a false philosophy which questions whether such spiritual events correspond with reality. Spirit *is* reality, and the symbols through which it comes to know itself are as real as anything in our experience.

Without denying that there are profound insights in all the world religions, Berdyaev holds that the Christian religion is the one through which free spirit has preserved its most authentic witness. Berdyaev considers "the mystery of the theandric humanity of Christ" to be the key to understanding both man and God; according to his view, the central reality of the religious life is the mutual interaction of God and man. The "humanizing of God" and the "divinizing of man" are both essential to spiritual development, and nowhere is this twofold movement so perfectly realized as in the coming of Christ, the God-man.

Nikolai Berdyaev's attachment to Christianity was "spiritual" and "free." He was not reared in the Church, and when he declared himself a Christian it was through no compulsion or authority. "I have come to Christ through liberty and through an intimate experience of the paths of freedom," he wrote in the introduction to *Freedom and the Spirit*. "Nor am I the only one who has passed through this experience. . . . Those whose religion is authoritarian and hereditary will never understand properly those who have come to religion through freedom, and through the tragedy immanent in their life's experience." Passionately engaged in Russian revolutionary activity, Berdyaev came to the conviction that secular humanism, which had prevailed from the time of the Renaissance, was no longer tenable, and that its collapse left no foundation for a belief in man's personal worth. Gradually he came to rely upon Christian revelation.

The Christ whom Berdyaev embraced was the silent figure who, in Dostoevski's *The Brothers Karamazov*, confronted the Grand Inquisitor. In this parable for our times, the Grand Inquisitor represents the socialist impulse (whether secular or clerical) which tries to relieve men's suffering at the expense of their liberty. The Inquisitor's professed love for the masses is a degrading pity. Christ refuses to palliate men's sufferings at the expense of their spiritual dignity. He shows his love by dying for them so that they may share in His resurrection. For it is only by participating in the risen Christ, whose human life is transfigured by the divine, that man can realize the life of free spirit.

The natural man, Berdyaev writes, knows only two kinds of freedom: the freedom of indeterminacy and the freedom of organized control. By the former he affirms his independence of nature and becomes, in fact, a spirit; however, as the story of Adam's Fall makes clear, man all too soon finds himself once again in bondage to the forces of nature. By bringing his life under regulations and social authority, he recovers a kind of independence; but in organized society his activity tends to become automatic, and regulation degenerates into tyranny. When the oppression becomes intolerable, man revolts and reaffirms his initial liberty. Thus, history is a "fatal dialectic" between two freedoms, a struggle from which there is no escape except that offered in Christ, "the new

Adam." Through Him a third kind of liberty is offered to us in which the other two are reconciled. Christ saves man's initial and God-given freedom from bondage to nature, not by means of the kind of human engineering favored by the Grand Inquisitor, but by uniting man's spirit to the Father of spirits, in the fellowship of all free spirits.

Berdyaev describes Christ's work as having universal scope. In His resurrection, the forces of nature are brought under the sway of divine love; all nature, like man, acquires the capacity of "divinization." Because He took true humanity upon Him, the whole race may be said to participate in His victory. On this account, Berdyaev is impatient with the historical churches, which, in his opinion, have been too apt to lapse into the freedom of organized control, and too little willing to claim the fruits of Christ's victory. Recognizing with St. Paul that not all men stand at the same spiritual level, Berdyaev concedes that the Church must accommodate its ministry to the "carnal" as well as to the "spiritual"; it must dispense milk to those who are unable to digest more substantial food. His complaint is that throughout the centuries the Church has catered exclusively to those weak in faith; thus, the Church has become authoritarian, rationalistic, and legalistic. At the same time, the Church has been singularly insensitive to the needs of the spiritually elite, with the result that great numbers of them have been excluded from its fellowship, to their loss, but also to the loss of the Church and of the non-Christian world. Thus, in the interests of preserving the authority of its doctrines, the Church has driven from its midst numerous gnostics, theosophists, and mystics, simply because they have claimed new knowledge of God. A similar rigidity in its social and political attitude has alienated from its fellowship progressive and liberal spirits whose genius has disclosed new depths in man's understanding of himself.

Impatient with the narrowness of institutional Christianity, Berdyaev broadens his definition of the Body of Christ to include such men as Goethe and Nietzsche. The actual Church, the Church Universal, is a spiritual company, never truly represented by "the visible historical church." But Christians ought not to be indifferent to the historical Church nor ought they to slacken their efforts to heal its schisms and to make it more representative of the Church Universal.

Berdyaev finds that in the history of the Church two classes of persons have been the bearers of revelation to their fellow men. He employs the term "mystic" to include them both. There are those whose calling is to holiness, persons ordinarily thought of as mystics; but besides these, there are mystics without any claim to holiness, whose calling is to prophecy. Among the holy mystics, Berdyaev believes, those who have experienced God within the compass of human experience are more truly Christian than those whose union with God has meant leaving their humanity behind. He cites with favor the saying of the German mystic and poet, Angelus Silesius (1624-1677), "I know that without me God could not endure for a moment. . . ." Among the prophetic mystics, Berdyaev includes an array of men whose "feeling for life and understanding of it" has been mystical, although

they have not brought their persons under religious discipline. Dostoevski is cited as a leading example; the list also includes Joseph de Maistre (1753-1821), Søren Kierkegaard (1813-1855), Vladimir Solovyov (1853-1900), and Leon Bloy (1846-1917).

As may be expected in one who stresses the dynamic quality of spirit and the community of God and man, Berdyaev is especially concerned with the problems of eschatology. He warns that secular progress, which involves the materialization and rationalization of human life, is purchased at the expense of spiritual freedom. Spirit develops only where changed circumstances, such as those in which modern man finds himself, call forth new revelations from the potential depths of spirit.

Berdyaev claims that spiritual gains are made and consolidated. For example, Christianity has impressed upon the Western soul a new compassion toward suffering in man and beast. God is no longer to be described as inflicting torment on brutish creatures. In fact, says Berdyaev, the notions of Heaven and Hell were never Christian, but pagan and naturalistic; and a true eschatology is not concerned with an afterworld but only with our "present spiritual orientation and moral will."

Berdyaev's ideas are those of an Eastern Orthodox Christian, particularly his conception of the corporate nature of redemption, called by the Russians *sobornost*. The Western Church, he believes, has overstressed the individual character of salvation. "The spirit of *sobornost*, the idea of the collective character of the ways of salvation, is opposed to this sort of individualism. In the Church we are saved with our brethren, all together." The universalism which Berdyaev calls for is qualitative, not quantitative. The Western experience of Christ differs from that of the East because of different historical circumstances, but variety is compatible with unity. Ecumenicity requires that the historical consciousness be subordinated to the eschatological and that the past be reinterpreted in terms of the future universal reign of Christ.

PHILOSOPHICAL THEOLOGY

Author: Frederick Robert Tennant (1866-1958)
Type of work: Natural theology
First published: Volume I, 1927; Volume II, 1928

PRINCIPAL IDEAS ADVANCED

Religious experience is experience interpreted from a religious point of view; such experience may be a source of intellectual, moral, and aesthetic inspiration.

The wider theological argument leads to belief in a purposive intelligence as the world's source and sustainer.

The world-ground is not infinite in the sense of being an indeterminate being; God is changeless in His self-identity and self-consistency; He is not to be described in terms of such static concepts as completeness, immutability, and timelessness.

The highest ideal we can conceive is that of a developing moral order; there must be the possibility of moral evil in the world.

Christ is the religious genius of theism; Christianity is the climax of the historical development of natural religion.

Since its appearance in two volumes in 1927 and 1928 Frederick Robert Tennant's *Philosophical Theology* has been recognized in the scholarly world by admirer and critic alike as a major contribution to natural as contrasted to dogmatic theology. Tennant, who taught science before becoming a priest in the Church of England, found in philosophy a means of reconciling the demands of science and theology. From 1913 to 1931 he was Lecturer in Theology at Cambridge University.

The nearly seven hundred pages of the *Philosophical Theology* are so uncompromising in their demands upon the reader that they have daunted many who might otherwise agree with the philosopher C. D. Broad that theologians and candidates for the ministry could not be better employed than in studying Tennant's work. He who makes the effort of following Tennant through the development of the argument will be rewarded for his effort, for he will have been guided through the intricacies of theological and philosophical problems by a most able teacher. Tennant's classical erudition influenced his literary style, and a subtle humor enlivens the pages at unexpected moments. An unrelenting concern for scientific accuracy, a philosophic judiciousness, and a mellow wisdom characterize the work.

The purpose of *Philosophical Theology* is twofold: to present the studies required for serious discussion of the grounds upon which theology rests, and to present the developed theistic interpretation of the world, man, and God toward which the examination of basic studies led. Volume One begins with a detailed examination of the major issues in psychology and philosophy, their data and method, the subject of consciousness and its elements, what is in the senses and what is in the mind itself, perception, imagination, memory, and ideation. Tennant acknowledges an indebtedness to James Ward (1843-1925), the English psychologist. Other chapters deal with theories of personality, value, thought and knowledge. The first volume concludes with considerations of induction and probability with reference to knowledge, belief, and faith. Only at the end of his investigation does Tennant turn to religious experience and to the nature and limitation of scientific knowledge.

Sensory experiences are the "humble beginning" of all human knowledge, according to Tennant. From the irreducible data of the senses, the *qualia* of sense which are not reducible to activity of the mind, man receives the opportunity for knowledge. Each man's experience begins with that consciousness which is prior to self-consciousness, the experiencing (*erleben*) of his embodiment. From this experience man becomes aware; he knows the fact of his being and in

this knowledge being and thinking meet. From this experience comes the conviction regarding embodiment, the notion of "having" a body which "has" experience.

The mind has both passive and active characteristics; it receives the stimulation of that which is over against it, but it responds, retains, assimilates, fuses, and differentiates the data in distinguishable manners. It is from the private (psychic) world of sense experience that the individual emerges in his quest for knowledge (epistemology) and for satisfaction regarding the nature of ultimate reality (metaphysics.) For Tennant it is extremely important to realize that the private world of the individual is the prerequisite of knowledge.

From the private world of certainty (psychological) one moves to communicate and to share meaningful observations about the realms of knowledge and truth. The presence of an ultimate or metaphysical reality underlying the phenomenal world is a postulation directly related to man's efforts to gain knowledge. This metaphysical reality cannot be known as the immediate private world of sense data is known, but reasonable speculation concerning its nature is permitted.

Tennant's theory of value is in harmony with his empirical approach to reality. He rejects value realism (the view that value is inherent in objects) and value absolutism (the view that values are nonrelational) just as he rejects metaphysical realism and absolute idealism. Values relate to persons and their individual experiences. A value is experienced as the object of desire. As desires are met, pleasure and pain result, and verdicts of "good" and "bad" are given. But as experience continues, life is discovered to have rewards other than mere pleasure, and pleasure itself becomes subject to a more discriminating assessment. The experiencing person begins to form concepts of value, to see goods become evils and evils become goods. He reaches a stage in which over-individual values are recognized and sought.

Concepts of values may be found to be at variance one with another, and the experient finds others who hold antithetical values. He becomes concerned with the truth; he wonders about the nature of supreme value; he aspires after a universal standard. The concepts may be manipulated in a way that ascribes metaphysical status to them, but here Tennant demurs. Perhaps, as in the knowing process one passes from a private world to a reality beyond, so in the process of valuation one may pass from over-individual values (those of a society) to the supreme value, but the experient cannot know that such progress is possible. He may not rightly hypostatize individual values into absolutes. One must be content with a psychological value-certainty which may indeed be reasonable and in harmony with the ultimate truth about value. Thus, Tennant concludes that there is no *a priori* absolutism in values. He offers instead an empirical ethics.

For Tennant, religious experience has as much cognitive value as any other experience rightly understood. He recognizes the emotional impact of religious experience, but he cannot grant to it status as an independent basis for belief in God. He argues that both science and religion have keys to reality and that both may be correct within their spheres. It is always the lock which determines whether the key shall fit. He rejects the mystical version of religious experience as confusing psychological certainty with epistemological certainty. He insists that the mystic inadvertently confuses these two, though Tennant admits the freshness, power, and sense of illumination that the mystic experiences. While there might be a mystical way of illumination, we cannot know that there is. No ineffable experience can be described. Every experience combines a given element and an interpretation of it. Tennant thus rejects views which describe religious experience as self-validating encounters with the numinous or the wholly other.

Tennant clarifies the cognitive value of religious experience by pointing out that even as science develops certain theories to account for facts of human dealings with matter and "nature," so religion develops theoretical constructs to account for human experience with factors in the "spiritual" realm such as value, beauty, goodness, and truth. Both science and religion require faith and belief.

In his second volume of *Philosophical Theology* Tennant moves from consideration of mental processes and knowledge into the realm of more strictly theological studies. His general problem is the validation of theistic belief. He presents two principal demonstrations of the truth of theism. The first is its essential continuity with the faith-venture in science and religion. He demonstrates this continuity from the reflective, the psychogenetic, and the analytic standpoints.

Tennant begins by defining law as a summary of past experiences which provides a basis for the prediction of future experiences. Law renders intelligible the manifold variety of nature. Any assertion of immutable and all-pervading law is logically and scientifically unwarrantable. Thus, Tennant rules out *a priori* law, and on the same ground he denies the *a priori* conclusion that all is ungrounded coincidence, that there is no law.

Tennant goes on to observe that science has not been successful in interpreting the world in totally mechanical terms. Indeed, the more developed science becomes, the more complex and varied are the explanations offered in hypothetical terms: "Every attempt thoroughly to mechanise Nature has involved resort to the mysterious and unknowable."

Continuing with an analysis of "explanation" in terms of the human desire for simplicity, changlessness, and rationality, Tennant sees it as human prejudice that men should hope for immutability in the real. He claims that to regard immutability as an attribute of deity is to prefer the material to the spiritual, for activity is as much a part of the soul as rest.

The world is such as to demand explanation in terms of purpose and design, Tennant claims. Theism as reasonable belief and as a philosophical theory of the world is a position which is based on facts of experience. Theism postulates an integrative and directive mind, and it thereby unifies the diversity of phenomena.

Tennant's teleology is new in that it seeks completion in a moral argument by which man is regarded as needing to work with nature. In contrast to the traditional form of "proving" the being of God by seeking to demonstrate a real counterpart to a preconceived idea, Tennant follows the empirical approach. He will, he says,

take the world as it is and attempt from it to read its message for better or for worse. If someone should protest that this is scarcely a lofty method for an elevated science such as theology, Tennant replies that, after all, we know other selves about whose existence we have unshakable conviction on similar grounds. No immediate (unmediated) knowledge either of other selves or of God is possible. Objects, be they other selves or God, are mediated inferences "provable" only by cumulative pragmatic verification.

According to Tennant, there are outstanding features in the world which call for a cosmic explanation: the world as an order amenable to thought, an order of progressive organic changes, an order of inorganic adaptations, an order which evokes beauty, an order instrumental to morality, an order of interconnected causes.

After examining in detail each of these features, Tennant is convinced that the only alternative to cosmic teleology "is to regard the self-subsistent entities of which the world is constituted, as comparable with letters of type which have shuffled themselves not only into a book or a literature but also into a reader commanding the particular tongue in which the book utters its unintentional meaning. If the inference from cumulative adaptiveness to design be non-logical, as is admitted, it at least is not unreasonable."

While we need not (and cannot) go further back than a creative spirit, we must go further back in explanation than the world because our minds are not satisfied with the notion that a nonintelligent world can create purposive beings. A purposeless world's producing the purposeful is scarcely a reasonable possibility. We are a part of the evolutionary process; we are of the world, and the purposeful demand we make is one the world itself has raised.

Through a complex synthesis of analogical discovery and ejective inference built out of the rapport of a socialized self and the ontal world and used by the self to interpret the experienced world, one gains an insight into the nature and being of God, Tennant claims.

According to Tennant, God is the creator whose being is transcendent to the world but who posits the constituents of the world. Creation is seen in terms of responsible volition. God is also viewed as the designer who constrains creatures in the general direction of evolutionary growth toward an environment suited to goodness, beauty, and truth. And if God's aim is to develop finite moral personalities, He must Himself be moral and thus respect the freedom of His creatures. One is able to read in the natural world the revelation of God's existence and purpose.

God's nature may truly be as superior to man's nature as scientific knowledge is to a worm's knowledge, but God's nature is like man's in that it involves intelligence, valuation, and volition. "God" is no generic term for universal reason, absolute morality, or a tendency making for righteousness. God is rather a determinate spirit, the source of beauty and love, as well as of the natural world.

There is only one method of reasonable inquiry concerning the knowledge that can be attributed to the supreme being, Tennant writes. The method is to begin with analogy, without which no discussion is possible, and then to eliminate from human knowledge such characteristics as are known to be humanly conditioned, subtraction of which will still leave what can legitimately be called knowledge. Tennant goes on to demonstrate this method which leads him to view God as the creator who gives His creatures freedom.

It is in this context of limited human freedom that Tennant offers his view of evil as inevitable in a world in which God permits authentic personal growth in human individuals. Final and unshakable answers are not possible. Indeed, God's purpose for us is to seek and to question rather than to have full light and certain knowledge.

Theism cannot countenance any doctrine of God's presence or man's life which destroys man's individual responsibility, Tennant insists. Any theory of God's relationship to man which appears to make that relationship personal is emphatically rejected.

For Tennant there is no discontinuity between religion and philosophical theology. The message of Christ, though grounded on other insights, is found to be identical with the world view reached by the indirective teleology Tennant employs.

Theistic belief is taken as the essence of Christianity, which is thus on a par, intellectually, with science. Christ is the religious genius of theism. Christianity is the climax of the historical development of natural religion. The theistic view to which Tennant has been led permits him the concluding observation that the cosmos is not a logico-geometrical scheme but rather "an adventure of divine love." For

many readers Tennant's name is revered precisely because through his

work they have been led to the same
conclusion.

SELECTED LETTERS

Author: Baron Friedrich von Hügel (1852-1925)
Type of work: Devotional letters
First published: 1927 (written 1896-1924)

PRINCIPAL IDEAS ADVANCED

Religion is adoration by the creature of the Creator.

*God as perfect personality is not finite but the absolute, unconditioned, ulti-
mate reality, a being of joy, pure and undefiled.*

*Mysticism needs to be inclusive of the three elements of religion—the institu-
tional, the rational, and the experimental-mystical—and the three corresponding
forces of the human soul—the sensational, the intellectual, and the volitional.*

*Suffering is the greatest grace; it deepens religious sensitivity and assists in
transforming the human personality.*

As friend, father, spiritual director
and critic, Baron Friedrich von Hügel
reflects within the *Selected Letters* of
1896 to 1924 his unique response to
the religious life. The letters are personal and yet candidly direct about the
life of the spirit in its quest for God.
The theme and mood of each letter
reveals the writer as a man passionately involved in this quest.

Friedrich von Hügel, Baron of the
Holy Roman Empire, was born in
Florence, Italy, May 8, 1852. His father, Baron Karl von Hügel, a member
of a noble Catholic Rhineland family,
was appointed by the Emperor of
Austria as ambassador to the Grand
Ducal Court of Tuscany. After several
years of service in Tuscany and Brus-
sels, the elder von Hügel moved his
family at the time of his retirement to
Torquay in England. This country became the permanent residence for

Friedrich von Hügel, although his
thoughts and many of his letters were
directed toward friends and associates
living on the Continent.

Friedrich von Hügel's education
was informal. Private tutors were appointed for his education. In England
young von Hügel was tutored to some
extent by the schoolmaster-geologist,
William Pengelly. The influence of
this tutoring and the natural inclination of von Hügel toward geology and
scientific research are evident in his
great regard for the discipline of both
science and religion. In a letter to Mrs.
Lillie, dated April 20, 1922, he compared science to a coral reef; like the
constant interaction between reef and
water, there is within science a process
of ceaseless search, an effort to discover error, and to substitute for error
something which is nearer to the truth.
Religion, on the other hand, is like a

golden shower from above, bestowing like rain the affirmation of belief in a definite God, a definite future life, and a definite loyalty to the Church: "Assimilate Religion to Science and you have levelled down to something which, though excellent for Science, has taken from Religion its entire force and good; and you have shorn Samson of his locks with a vengeance. On the other hand force Science up to the level of Religion or think that you have done so and Science affirms far more than, as such, it can affirm, and you, on your part, are in a world of unreality."

During his late teens, Baron von Hügel contracted typhoid fever, which left him with an extremely nervous and delicate physical constitution and with a deafness that increased through the years. Along with the disease came the death of his father. These two events temporarily shattered the bright world of the young von Hügel. However, it also provided the time and inclination to enter the circles of religious thought and devotion influenced by a Dutch Dominican friar, Father Raymond Hocking, and the Vicar of Saint Augustine in Paris, Abbé Huvelin. Special advice—short and concise—was given by Abbe Huvelin to von Hügel, which he in turn later included in some of his letters to friends in need of spiritual direction.

Von Hügel's marriage to Mary Herbert, daughter of Sidney Herbert (Gladstone's friend and ministerial colleague), opened the doors to the Catholic social-clerical world of London. It also afforded the opportunity for meeting the leading thinkers in English society interested in the religious and scientific issues of the day. Later, in writing to many of these leaders, von

Hügel expressed his own reactions to their opinions.

Three daughters, Gertrud, Hildegaard, and Thekla, were born to Baron von Hügel and Lady Mary. All of them received letters which may be found in this collection. They received their formal and religious education from their father. One letter in particular reflects this religious training. Thekla is quoted as being very insistent upon describing religion as primarily an "is-ness" not an "ought-ness." Her father was sympathetic and most likely responsible for this concept which found religion to be essentially evidential; he wrote that religion "intimates, first of all, that a superhuman world, a superhuman reality is, exists." Thus, the first and essential act of religion would be to adore, to proclaim this sense of God.

The death of the eldest daughter, Gertrud, resulted in the fine personal meditations on suffering included in Selected Letters. "Suffering can be the noblest of all actions," he wrote; "How wonderful it is, is it not, that literally only Christianity has taught us the true peace and function of suffering. The Stoics tried the hopeless little game of denying its objective reality, or of declaring it a good in itself (which it never is) and the Pessimists attempted to revel in it, as a food to their melancholy, and as something that can no more be transformed than it can be avoided or explained. But Christ came, and He did not really explain it; He did far more, He met it, willed it, transformed it; and He taught us how to do all this, or rather He Himself does it within us, if we do not hinder the all healing hands. In suffering, we are very near to God."

Von Hügel's daughter Hildegaard

writes about her father as one who considers suffering to be a splendid school, for it teaches one more than any amount of learning. It provides the opportunity for being near to the great realities, and from this, one can gain strength for work. Thus, suffering is the greatest grace.

Baron von Hügel's first scholarly effort in the field of religion was to study Greek and Hebrew in order to do research in the historical criticism of Biblical documents. "Certainly I have myself noticed in the Old Testament," he writes, "of which criticism is so much older, how stable and persistent is its general orientation, how more and more of detail are the questions which still arise. And I do not see why this principle, so universal in all the sciences, should turn out not to be operative in New Testament criticism also."

The weakness of Roman Catholic scholarship in New Testament criticism became apparent to him. He worked to obtain real respect for Catholic research, and from this task the principal struggle of his life emerged: "the defense of Catholic enlightenment in the face of obscurantists in the Church on the one side and her non-Catholic critics, especially in university circles, on the other." This struggle for Catholic enlightenment brought von Hügel into contact not only with the foremost English minds of the day such as William George Ward (1812-1882), John Henry Newman (1801-1890), James Martineau (1805-1900), George Tyrrell (1861-1909), Clement Webb (1865-1954), A. E. Taylor (1869-1945), Claud Montefiore (1858-1938), Evelyn Underhill (1875-1941), and Norman Kemp-Smith (1872-1958), but also with such Continental leaders as

Archbishop Söderblom (1866-1931), Ernst Troeltsch (1865-1923), Rudolph Eucken (1846-1926), and Alfred Loisy (1857-1940). Von Hügel was interested in the intellectual endeavors of those men and others who were writing in the religious and philosophical fields. Thus he became involved in a large correspondence—a great deal of which is found in the *Selected Letters* —with men and women of various countries to whom he wrote usually in their own tongues—German, French, Italian, or English. Into these letters he put the "most minute and conscientious labor."

This correspondence and personal acquaintance with the astute minds of Europe placed von Hügel in the center of the "Modernist Movement." Within the Roman Catholic Church, this movement produced several groups which opposed the authority of the Church in matters of criticism, scientific and historic. It also caused a division within these circles themselves when some members advocated extreme measures. Baron von Hügel, for example, supported the stand of Tyrrell and Loisy for Biblical criticism, but he diverged from them and from the "Modernist Movement" in general on the immanental view of religion. The Papal Encyclical of 1907 would have confronted von Hügel with excommunication if he had been forced to sign the anti-Modernist pledge which condemned all the efforts of Modernism. However, he was a layman and this fact spared him from signing the pledge. The fear of being excommunicated from the Roman Catholic Church remained with him throughout this period and this anxiety permeates some of his letters as he persuades and argues for the pure and ideal form of his Church: "Yet I cannot but note that Catholicism, *at its best,* still somehow produces saints of a depth of otherworldliness, of a delicate appealing heroism, and of a massiveness of spiritual wisdom, greater than I can find elsewhere."

Concepts concerned with the nature of God and the nature of religion permeate the majority of von Hügel's letters. In a letter to Maude Petre, von Hügel describes God as personal in nature. He rejects the charge of anthropomorphism and its resulting limitations when applied to the Infinite. To classify anything personal as rank anthropomorphism while accepting such concepts as thought, love, law, and substance as being above the anthropomorphic condemnation is, according to von Hügel, an illogical conclusion. All concepts knowable to man have the specific characteristics of the human thought which formulates them.

The necessary condition involved in this personalistic conviction regarding God is the distinction sensed within man between himself and God. This is realized especially by man in the religious experience of adoration and worship. Religion is adoration to von Hügel, adoration by the creature of the Creator: "And by religion I mean not some vague sentiment, or some beautiful thought, not even, though this is getting nearer to it, moral striving as apart from faith in, and realization of the great Spiritual Reality, God in Whose presence, and as Whose will, we thus strive to grow and be: but by and in self-donation, such self-commitment to a, to *the* Reality other than, yet immensely near to, ourselves."

God as perfect personality is not finite. Von Hügel writes to Maude Petre that the belief in a finite God is contrary to the affirmations of a wholehearted religion. Von Hügel's discussions concerning suffering and God are now classical expressions of the divine impassibility. According to von Hügel, suffering if correctly transformed by religious sensitivity may help in the development of human personality. There is no reason for ascribing suffering to the eternally perfect personality of the realized ideal. The serious difficulties, von Hügel insists, arising from divine impassibility are less than those connected with the concept of a suffering God. The only value derived from the concept of a finite God is that it points to the likeness between God and man. Beyond this conviction the value of the suffering God ceases. God is limited only by His relationship to creation. Ever beyond this relation, He remains the absolute, unconditioned, ultimate Reality, "as Being, as Joy Pure and Undefiled."

Von Hügel's total approach to religion indicates that the nature of God is apprehended by man's normal faculties of knowledge when these are properly directed to that end and suitably trained and assisted by divine grace. God's nature is not apprehended solely by means of intuition, nor is it grasped by some unique mystical faculty. A matured concept of God involves a keen sense of the objective, given, full reality of God which is obscured by the normal cognitive faculties of man.

Central to all von Hügel's letters is a mystical quality with which the author is usually identified. He carefully describes this mysticism in one letter to Father Tyrrell as having a place for the ingredients of the contingent world. It safeguards its own health by continual reference to the institutional and intellectual elements of religion. Von Hügel describes this type of mysticism as inclusive; that is, it stresses the inevitable mutual necessity and interaction among the three elements of religion and the three corresponding forces of the human soul. The institutional, rational, and experimental-mystical elements of religion and the corresponding sensational, intellectual, and volitional forces of the soul are indispensable to one another and to religion as a whole. It is extremely difficult to maintain the correct balance among these elements and forces. The problem of controlling one element and its corresponding force has appeared throughout the historical account of man, illustrating first the element's corrective dominance and then its dominant weakness. The only corrective to the wrong type of mysticism is another type—the inclusive—which brings into harmony the elements and soul-forces of the religious life.

Inclusive mysticism is religion at its best. Von Hügel describes it further in a letter to the Reverend H. Handley. All religion must have a world-fleeing and a world-seeking element, he writes. The spiritual life, often labeled the mystical life, cannot be measured by the world-fleeing element alone. There is rather the necessity of maintaining the two-fold movement of the spiritual life. This creates the true paradox and thereby the "divinely intended tensions" of the mystical way: "The two movements together —the tension thus generated between what thus conjointly produces a true paradox—are, I submit, of the very essence of our training, our testing, and our trail. . . ."

It is this training, this testing, and this trial which Baron von Hügel reveals so intimately in his letters. As a man of faith and an independent thinker, von Hügel, in attempting to answer questions of universal religious importance, provides spiritual direction for all Christians.

CHRIST AND SOCIETY

Author: Charles Gore (1853-1932)
Type of work: Christian social ethics
First published: 1928

PRINCIPAL IDEAS ADVANCED

Christ's mission of salvation included the establishment of a new social order.

The ethics of the Gospel was partly provisional, having regard to the initial stage of Christ's program, and partly permanent, having regard to a continuing community.

Historically, the Church never lost sight of its social mission until modern times when, confronted with the problems of the industrial age, it narrowed its concern to the salvation of individuals.

Contemporary churches are in no position to recover their social mission, but concerned Christians in various denominations should form associations for achieving political and social reforms.

Christ and Society is a series of six lectures delivered under The Halley Stewart Trust, which was founded in 1924 to further "research toward the Christian ideal in all social life." Bishop Gore, a member of the Anglo-Catholic wing of the Church of England, had for many years made his influence felt in behalf of the social message of the Church. In *Christ and Society* he reaffirms his conviction that Christ's mission was to establish a new social order in the world, and that the ultimate goal of history is the realization of the reign of God on earth. The Church, as Bishop Gore understands it, was instituted by Christ to be a spiritual brotherhood, with rigorous ethical standards, commissioned to bring God's Kingdom into being. Unfortunately, in our day the nominal churches have ceased to have the character of a spiritual elite; hence, small informal societies of persons who have a passion for humanity and for reform must be assembled to carry on the proper work of the Church. It is Gore's hope that such activity may do much to restore the fabric of the Church itself, permitting it to resume its leadership in world affairs. In *Christ and Society*, the next to the last of Gore's major works, the author presents the best summary of his thought on the "social gospel."

Gore wrote at a time when the ethical teachings of Jesus were being subjected to criticism. He mentions in particular the doubts raised in the minds of many by the "consistent eschatology" of Albert Schweitzer, according to whom Jesus' teachings provide only an "interim ethic" suited to those who are expecting the end of the world. Gore admits that many of Jesus' moral teachings have a heroic quality which makes them unsuitable for a settled Christian community, but he explains this characteristic of Jesus' teaching as representing only one stage of His program. For, in Gore's opinion, Jesus deliberately planned His ministry, taking account of the historical situation within which He had to work. The radical self-denial demanded by many Gospel precepts was asked of the chosen band of disciples, whom He selected, tested, and organized to be the nucleus of the redeemed society. This was only the first stage. The second stage, which would be instituted after His death and resurrection under the influence of the Pentecostal Spirit, was the formation of the Church. His apocalyptic utterances with respect to the destruction of apostate Jerusalem referred to a third stage. After this, in the uncharted future, would come "the complete and final victory or vindication of God" against the cosmic background of "a great final world-catastrophe, world-judgment and world renewal."

Gore devotes the greater part of his book to reviewing the social attitudes of the Church through history. He was justified in undertaking this task because Ernst Troeltsch's *Social Teaching of the Christian Churches* (1912) had not yet been made available in English. (The translation was published in 1931, also under the Halley Stewart Trust.) Gore has made some use of Troeltsch's work, but his standpoint is different from that of the German scholar. Troeltsch denied that the Gospel contains any recognizable ethical or social teaching, and his account of the Church's social teaching was meant to be an objective survey. Gore, on the other hand, holds that the Gospel does provide normative ethical and social principles, and he uses these as a standard for judging the Church's performance. Generally speaking, he gives the early Church high marks for its faithfulness to the Master's purposes. The early Church made fellowship fundamental, and it insisted that its members live up to the ethical and social principles of the New Covenant. After the Edict of Milan, the situation was changed for the worse: membership in the Church became more and more nominal; in its new position as a civil religion, the Church bowed to expediency on every hand, particularly in resorting to compulsion. But, Gore points out, almost as soon as the Church proved unfaithful to the teachings of the Gospel, monasticism gave a new and far-reaching expression to Christian social ideals.

Bishop Gore has no special enthusiasm for the Middle Ages. While not inclined to minimize the importance of the Church as a civilizing medium, he wonders that it fell so completely away from the principles of the New Covenant, while returning to those principles that governed the Old. Little could be expected of a Church which availed itself of the services of a Clovis and a Charlemagne, and into which men were "baptized in platoons." Still, Gore acknowledges, it never occurred either to the popes or to the scholars of the Middle Ages that it was not the task of the Church to build the Kingdom of Christ on earth. They were unfaithful, in many instances, to the Master's goals, and they disregarded this appointed means, but at least they insisted that no aspect of life ought to be carried on without reference to Christian principles.

The abandonment of "the idea of the Church as the representative of the kingdom of God and the lordship of Christ on earth," says Gore, occurred only in modern times. The breakup of medieval culture and the rise of nationalism and of the new urban economy brought about momentous social changes with which the Church was increasingly unable to cope. Gore rejects the view that the Reformation, with its emphasis upon individualism, destroyed the old moral order and opened the way for the moral chaos of the industrial age. On the contrary, he says, the Reformed Church tried, much in the same manner as the medieval Church, to impose religious controls on commerce and on politics. It failed because it went about the task in the wrong way, trying to enforce regulations on institutions even though it was unable to exert any real influence on the lives of men. Conscious of this failure, and faced with the fact of a secular state and a self-regulating economy, the churches (Catholic and Protestant alike) turned their backs on society and concentrated on the "salvation of the individual." An anti-Christian philosophy, based on the theory that man's only ultimate motive is the pursuit of his own self-interest, was, thus, permitted to dominate the whole new industrial order; and such protests as were launched against it came not from the churches but from individuals like Charles Dickens, and from groups like the

Chartists and the Christian Socialists.

Gore recognizes that modern secular culture has done a great deal for the improvement of the human condition. One can point to the higher living standard and to the spread of political democracy; these, to some degree, offset the evils of wage-labor, colonialism, and war. Still, he maintains, the present system is so unsatisfactory as to demand complete revolution; and, for this reason, he is pleased to join hands with a wide range of social crusaders, so long as they are not pledged to violence. Christians share their desire to give every individual a chance to make the best of himself, and their belief is that this can come to pass only when the present capitalistic and nationalistic system is replaced by one in which the wealth of the world is placed at the disposal of humanity and not usurped by any one class or race.

But, although Christians can join with liberals in many projects, they cannot surrender their distinctive faith. Modern emancipatory movements ordinarily proceed upon the same basic assumptions as does bourgeois individualism, differing only in their determination to distribute to the many the advantages hitherto enjoyed by the few, whereas Christians are committed precisely to the task of reversing "the inner spirit of selfish individualism." The new society which Christ came to establish presupposes that men's lives have been radically changed, that they live in fellowship with God the Father and with the brotherhood of Christians, and that they have become fellow workers with Christ in the labor of extending His dominion throughout the world. In a very important sense, says Gore, Christianity is "other-worldly." It is not otherworldly in the sense of being indifferent to "this" world, but in the sense of maintaining that "this" world needs another world to complete it. "This world is not the goal nor the end," says Gore, "nor can we rely on progress being maintained in this world. But history has a goal. One day God is to come into His own. One day Christ is visibly to reign in all the universe. One day we are to see the City of God; and the Church of here and now, which is the vestibule of the kingdom of God, will pass into the kingdom realized in its perfection."

Gore carefully avoids any distinction between natural and supernatural agencies. He sees in Christianity the fulfillment, not merely of spiritual forces which were previously at work in Israel, but, in a broad sense, of principles struggling to be born in all the great world religions. Moreover, he insists, the Church must have "its ears open to the moral ideals of each age and country," for these, at their best, are also "real expressions of the divine purpose and the divine wisdom." If we believe in "a permanent Gospel which speaks through all unchanging ages to the unchanging heart of man," we must, he says, "be able to recognize also a fresh 'movement of God' in each age." Gore tends to see in the widespread demands of people everywhere for "liberty, equality, and fraternity," such a movement of God. But he distrusts large scale mass movements and violent attempts to rectify wrong. "If we accept the teaching of past experience," he says, "we should expect the general alteration to arise from the influence in our society of groups of men, inspired probably by prophetic leaders, who have attained to a true vision both of the source of our evils and the nature of the true remedies; and who have the courage of faith to bind them together to act and to suffer in the cause of human emancipation until their vision and their faith come to prevail more or less completely in society at large."

Gore has confidence in the ability of small groups to alter the course of history. "There must," he says, "be thirty or forty or a hundred in every town, who are both believers in the Name of Jesus as the true redeemer of man, and are also sure that this redemption requires for its free course social and industrial reform and reconstruction of a radical kind." Let them organize, cutting across denominational lines, and not claiming to be representative of any church but "only of a state of mind and determination of action." They should join forces with others who are working for political and social reform. But they must never forget that change of laws and redistribution of wealth are not to be sought as ends, but have value "only so far as they are means toward the expression of the kingdom of God."

AGAPE AND EROS

Author: Anders Nygren (1890-   )
Type of work: History of Christian ethics
First published: Volume I, 1930; Volume II, 1936

PRINCIPAL IDEAS ADVANCED

The meaning of Christianity as a system of thought is best understood by determining its fundamental motif.

The fundamental motif of Christianity is Agape, God's spontaneous and unconditional gift of love to mankind.

Agape is incompatible with any other motif, but the history of Christianity reveals many attempts to synthesize it with Nomos and with Eros.

Nomos (law) is the fundamental motif of Judaism and Eros (man's egocentric and acquisitive love of the divine) is the fundamental motif of Hellenism.

St. Augustine determined the basic character of medieval piety by synthesizing Agape and Eros into Caritas, which is man's divinely inspired love of God.

Martin Luther attacked the Caritas piety of the medieval Church, broke the medieval synthesis of Agape and Eros, and returned to the motif of Agape as expressed in the New Testament.

Bishop Anders Nygren of the Church of Sweden, a former professor of theology at the University of Lund, is one of the foremost representatives of the so-called "Lundensian theology." Others in the movement are Bishop Gustaf Aulen, formerly a Lund professor, and Ragnar Bring and Gustaf Wingren, presently Lund professors.

The Lundensian school is distinguished by its theological method rather than by any novel theological conclusions. The Lundensians take seriously Immanuel Kant's attacks in *The Critique of Pure Reason* (1781) against the metaphysical presuppositions with which Christian theology had become associated. They see Kant's strictures as a reminder to the theologian that his task is to set forth objectively and descriptively a religion's understanding of how God and man come into fellowship with each other. The theologian's task is neither to defend the validity of religious experience nor to interpret this experience according to preconceived categories of philosophical or scientific analysis. The Lundensian method reflects also the influence of Martin Luther's belief that the Christian Gospel is its own authority. The theologian shows greatest respect for the freedom and authority of the Gospel when he limits himself to describing how the Gospel has been understood in its history.

The Lundensians in general, and Nygren in particular, hold that religions can be classified according to their answers to the question of the nature of the divine-human relationship. The study of these answers is called "motif research." The way to understand a religion is to determine the fundamental motif which it expresses through its thought and cultic practices. The method of motif research is appropriate for the study of any religion and not just for Christianity. Indeed, *Agape and Eros* is a comparative study of Judaism, Christianity, and various currents of Hellenistic religious thought. Still, the emphasis in this book is upon Christian

thought, and the method has been used very largely for the investigation of Christian theology.

Part I of *Eros and Agape* is a comparative treatment of the two motifs of Agape and Eros as these motifs are exhibited in their classic expressions. "Agape" is the Greek word used in the New Testament for describing the unique character of Christian fellowship with God, a fellowship which depends completely upon the unconditional divine love. Nygren's analysis of the New Testament Agape distinguishes four main characteristics: (1) It is spontaneous. (2) It is indifferent to the value of its object. God does not love the good man for his goodness nor the wicked man because of his wickedness. (3) Agape creates worth in its objects. (4) Agape initiates fellowship between God and man. Neither through merit nor repentance nor any other avenue is man able to come to God. Rather, God comes to man.

Nygren contends that the thought of both Jesus and St. Paul is controlled by the Agape motif. The chief difference between them is the latter's reluctance to speak of Agape as a human response to God, a reluctance which Nygren explains in terms of St. Paul's belief that human love can never be as completely unmotivated and spontaneous as divine love. St. Paul did, however, use Agape to refer to the Christian's love for his neighbor, for he saw the Christian as the instrument and bearer of Agape which flows out of God.

Plato (427-347 B.C.) and Plotinus (c.204-c.270) stated the Eros motif in the forms which most seriously challenged Agape, although there were numerous other Hellenistic religions and religious philosophies which also expressed the Eros motif. In Plato's thought Eros is the force which drives the soul upward from the material world to the world of absolute truth and beauty, the world of pure rational essences, or Ideas.

Plotinus, whose thought contains many Platonic elements and is described as Neoplatonic, sharply separated God and the physical world but provided for continuity between the two realms of being in the form of intermediate beings who emanated from God. The emanations represent a divine descent, but God in His essence remains aloof from the material world so that man by the power of Eros must ascend to God.

Eros is, in summary, that acquisitive, egocentric love by which man attempts to enhance the quality of his own being by possessing God. It is the upward movement by which man makes his way to God, whereas Agape is the downward movement by which God makes His way to man.

In Part II Nygren traces the seesaw history of the Agape motif once it had lost its initial clarity and depth and had begun to encounter the Jewish Nomos motif and the Hellenistic Eros motif.

The Apostolic Fathers and the apologists of the post-Apostolic period subordinated Agape to Nomos by picturing man's salvation as dependent upon his obeying the divine law of love.

Eros, however, was to present a more serious and persistent threat, and Nygren pictures Gnosticism as the form in which Eros presented its earliest serious challenge to Christianity. The Gnostic interpretation of Christianity, an interpretation which reached its peak of influence in the first half of the second century, pro-

vided for a divine descent in the form of Christ. Still, the Gnostic Christ descended from Heaven mainly to give men esoteric knowledge and an inspiring moral example which would enable them to save themselves from the lusts of the body. The Gnostic Christ was religiously significant in stimulating Eros rather than in giving rise to Agape.

Nygren sees the Agape motif coming to the fore again in the thought of Marcion (died c.140), but finally receding because of Marcion's heretical views. In the thought of Tertullian (c.150-c.230) Agape was subordinated to Nomos. After having been under suspicion because of its association with the Gnostic heresy, Eros was prominent in the thought of the Alexandrian theologians, Clement (c.150-c.215) and Origen (c.185-c.254). Irenaeus, writing late in the second century, affirmed the centrality of Agape, but in a form mixed with Eros. The Eros motif gained strength in the thought of the fourth century theologians Methodius of Olympus, Athanasius, and Gregory of Nyssa, and in the thought of these men Eros and Agape were related in a situation of compromise, without achieving a true synthesis.

True synthesis was to come in the thought of St. Augustine (354-430). Just as Agape seemed in prospect of disappearing from Christian thought it experienced a powerful renewal, but not without undergoing a transformation which was to be crucial in the history of Christianity. Nygren argues that Augustine's doctrine of love as Caritas effectively superseded the New Testament concept of Agape. Caritas was a uniquely new motif which was similar to but different from its two components of Agape and Eros.

Because Eros was the chief attraction for him in Neoplatonism, Augustine readily detected the centrality of love in Christianity. Nygren contends that Neoplatonism prepared Augustine to achieve deeper insight into the meaning of Christian love but that it also imposed limits on his understanding of Agape.

Eros alone, Augustine contended, is insufficient because the ascent to the divine which it inspires results in pride, and this pride prevents further ascent. The function of God's Agape is to break the power of pride. Caritas results when man's inherent Eros is combined with and transformed by the divine grace. Thus Agape enters the Caritas synthesis in the form of divine grace which enables man to ascend to God. Although it is primarily man's God-given love of God, Caritas may also have the neighbor as its object. Caritas includes self-love, but a self-love which is sublimated and spiritualized in love of God and neighbor.

Augustine's Caritas synthesis dominated medieval Catholic piety and held unchallenged dominion for a millennium. Gradually, however, tension between the two elements in the synthesis became so powerful that disintegration set in, with the Renaissance expressing the Eros motif and the Protestant Reformation expressing the Agape motif. Martin Luther (1483-1546) led the Protestant assault against Caritas. He objected to all egocentric features of medieval piety and insisted upon a radically theocentric fellowship with God. Luther taught that the great stumbling block to fellowship with God lies in man's temptation to strive for goodness and holiness in order to win this fellowship. This temptation is rooted in prideful unwillingness to live wholly upon God's forgiving mercy as freely given in Christ. Thus Luther returned to the New Testament motif of Agape and its emphasis on a divine-human fellowship which occurs on the human level to which God descends. Caritas piety pictured this fellowship as occurring on the divine level to which man must climb.

Luther's return to an unmodified Agape motif stemmed largely from his own religious difficulties with the idea of Caritas as the sublimation of self-love into pure love for God. His efforts to love God led him to the despairing conclusion that self-love lay behind these efforts. Thus Luther broke with Augustine's distinction between sinful self-love (which expresses *cupiditas*) and proper self-love (which is present in sublimated form in Caritas). Any scheme of salvation which depends in any degree upon any kind of self-love is egocentric.

It is a mistake, Nygren affirms, to say that faith stands at the center of Luther's thought whereas love stands at the center of Catholic piety. Fundamentally, Luther was concerned to establish Agape against Caritas because he saw in the latter a subtle expression of Eros. Eros blocks fellowship with God because—no matter how high-minded it may be—it is acquisitive and self-seeking. But through faith man becomes open to divine Agape and serves as a medium through which Agape touches the world.

Nygren's picture of Agape as radically opposed to all forms of natural human love, while widely influential in Protestant circles, has met challenges from both Protestant and Roman Catholic theologians. The Protestant theologian Paul Tillich, in his book *Love, Power, and Justice* (1954), distinguishes between Eros and Agape as two *qualities* of love rather than as two *kinds* of love. The English Jesuit scholar M. C. D'Arcy, in his book *The Mind and Heart of Love* (1945), takes issue with Nygren's characterization of Eros and Agape, claiming that the two forms of love are complementary, with Eros as the possessive love which belongs to the essential side of the self and Agape as the sacrificial love which belongs to the existential side of the self.

CHRISTUS VICTOR

Author: Gustaf Aulén (1879-   )
Type of work: History of doctrine
First published: 1930

Principal Ideas Advanced

In addition to the "objective" (Anselmian) and "subjective" (Abelardian) types of the idea of the atonement, there is a second objective type which may be called the "classic" idea of the atonement.

In the classic type the atonement is wholly the work of God and is achieved as God in Christ overcomes hostile powers which hold man in subjection.

Because of its predominance in the New Testament, in patristic writings, and in the theology of Luther, the classic type may be called the distinctively Christian idea of the atonement.

Gustaf Aulén's *Christus Victor*, which is a historical study of the three main types of the idea of the atonement, is an example of the application of the method of "the history of ideas" to historical theology. This theological method flourished during the past four decades at the University of Lund, Sweden, where Aulén taught until he was named a bishop. In using this historical method in *Christus Victor*, Aulén seeks to distinguish various "types," "ideas," or "views" of the atonement. He is primarily concerned that the reader should be able to recognize these types as they reappear in various periods of Church history. While some suggestions are given as to the origins of these ideas of the atonement, Aulén is less concerned with origins than with content. He holds, however, that it is significant to know which type is most characteristic of the teaching of the early Church.

In traditional histories of the doctrine of the atonement only two views have usually been presented, the "objective," or Anselmian, and the "subjective," or Abelardian, views. According to Aulén, however, there is another type of atonement doctrine in which Christ fights against and triumphs over evil powers (hence the expression "Christus Victor"), at the same time that God in Christ reconciles the world to Himself. This dualistic view Aulén calls the "classic" idea of the atonement, since it was dominant in Christianity for the first 1000 years of its history and was not displaced until the Middle Ages. The classic view was later restored by Luther, though his insights on this point were not accepted by his followers. Since the classic view is also objective, Aulén prefers to call the Anselmian view the "Latin" idea of the atonement. There are, then, two objective types (the classic and the Latin) as opposed to one subjective (or humanistic) type.

Aulén attributes the neglect of the classic view in recent times to the fact that both the orthodox and the liberals, although for different reasons, have failed to appreciate it. The classic view is not rational enough for the orthodox, while it is too mythological for the liberals, who react against its dualism and trace the idea to Zoroastrian sources.

Since the classic view can be clearly seen in the patristic period, and since our preconceptions do not blind us in studying the Fathers of the Church to the extent that they do when we read the New Testament, Aulén begins his study with the patristic writings. While Irenaeus, Bishop of Lyons (c.130-c.200), the first patristic writer who gives a clear and comprehensive doctrine of the atonement, places chief emphasis on the Incarnation, Aulén points out that in the classic view the atonement and the Incarnation are inseparably related. The Incarnation is necessary since only God can overcome the powers of sin, death, and the Devil. Through the life, death, and resurrection of Jesus Christ, whereby the life of man is recapitulated, these pow-

ers are overcome and God both reconciles man to Himself and is Himself reconciled. This recapitulation continues in the work of the Spirit in the Church and has an eschatological dimension.

Variations on this theme are found in the other patristic writers, though it is essential to understand correctly the imagery such writers use. Some say that the Devil, because of man's sin, has rights over men; others insist that the Devil is a usurper. All say the Devil is deceived. Some say a ransom is paid to the Devil, but that he is unable to retain it. Others prefer the thought of sacrifice. All are trying to say that God does not save man by almighty fiat, but participates by self-oblation in the drama by which men are freed. Those who say that the Devil is a usurper, yet has certain rights, are defending a limited dualism. The Devil is God's enemy, but the Devil is also the executant of divine judgment. To say that the Devil is deceived, is to say that the power of evil ultimately overreaches itself when it is in conflict with good or with God Himself.

The atonement, however, does not involve simply defeat of the Devil, for God is reconciled. Thus, the Devil and death are executants of the divine judgment. The emphasis on endurance of punishment and sacrifice shows the cost of victory for God. The paradoxical nature of this interpretation of the atonement prevents complete rational clarity, but Aulén suggests that there may be theological wisdom in not seeking to achieve complete rationality at this point.

After surveying the patristic period Aulén turns to the New Testament. He writes that we may assume it likely that the atonement view which dominates the patristic period should also be set forth in the Apostolic writings. One finds the Apostolic works are no more logically articulated in their ideas of the atonement than were the patristic. Nevertheless, one finds also a recurring theme of deliverance from hostile powers. Paul, in speaking of the powers which oppress man, emphasizes the Law more than do the Fathers, and he speaks of demonic *powers* rather than of the Devil. The Law is a hostile power not because it condemns sin, but because in so far as it contributes to legalistic religion it leads away from God. Divine love cannot be confined by the categories of merit and justice; it breaks through them. (Aulén attributes the early Church's failure to understand the hostile power of the Law to the controversy provoked by Marcion, a second century Christian heretic who wanted to exclude the Old Testament from the Christian canon.) Throughout the New Testament, in which it is emphasized that divine love itself is the agent of redemption, dualistic, or classical, concepts are prominent. In the Synoptic Gospels the exorcisms express the theme of triumph over evil powers, and the passion narratives tell how Jesus ultimately triumphs over the great adversary by succumbing to him and by giving His life as a ransom for many.

If the classic idea of the atonement is predominant in the New Testament and during the patristic period, how then is the origin of the Latin idea of the atonement to be explained? Aulén traces its beginnings to the Roman theologian Tertullian (c.160-c.220) and to Cyprian (c.200-258), who, in connection with their interpretation of the institution of penance, developed the ideas of satisfaction and merit. The

characteristics of the Latin theory of the atonement are that it is legalistic and that it emphasizes what Christ did as a man. Anselm of Canterbury (c.1033-1109) gives the Latin theory its most complete systematic formulation, emphasizing that because of man's sin satisfaction must be made by man, and this requirement is met by Christ's atoning deed. The earlier dualism, which held that there were hostile powers from which man needed to be delivered, was discarded. The atonement was interpreted in such a way as not to infringe upon the order of law and justice. The alternatives for God are either forgiveness, which would mean that sin would not be treated with sufficient seriousness, or satisfaction, which can only be achieved through the death of Christ, the God-man. In one sense, God's attitude is not changed in the process of the atonement, for it is His will that Christ should on man's behalf make the satisfaction divine justice demands. Yet Aulén argues that if satisfaction can make amends for sin, God's radical opposition to sin is compromised. Aulén also points out that when the atonement is so understood sin itself remains unremoved.

In the later Middle Ages the Latin doctrine of the atonement was dominant, though Anselm's insistence on its rationality was no longer maintained. Yet the fact that this Latin view of the atonement is so fully in accord with the medieval emphasis on penance and the sacrifice of the Mass causes it to remain as authoritative doctrine. Peter Abelard (1079-1142), on the other hand, represents a different point of view. According to Abelard, Christ is both a teacher and an example exciting meritorious love in man. But

Abelard saw no special significance in the death of Christ. However, his view does not exert any great influence during the Middle Ages, and it was not until later that his more subjective approach to the atonement was given much attention.

The next major development, as far as the doctrine of the atonement is concerned, was the revival of the classic idea in Martin Luther (1483-1546). Many interpreters of Luther have regarded Luther's teaching with respect to the atonement as being simply a continuation of the medieval Anselmian tradition. Aulén insists, however, that Luther's realistic imagery must be taken seriously. Luther speaks of sin, death, the Devil, Law, and wrath as tyrants that must be overcome. He refers also to the deception of the Devil, which is his way of saying that the God who reveals Himself and delivers man is at the same time hidden in that which is lowliest and most despised. This is God's "deceit," which leads evil to assail the good to its own undoing. According to Aulén, the three typical characteristics of the classic idea of the atonement are present in Luther's interpretation of the work of Christ. Luther stresses (1) the continuity of the divine operation, so that the atonement is wholly the work of God, (2) the close connection of the atonement with the Incarnation, and (3) the dualistic and dramatic aspects of Christ's sacrifice.

Aulén finds in Luther not only a restoration of the classic idea of the atonement, but also a deeper development of this idea. This can be seen in Luther's interpretation of the Law and the wrath of God as enemies which are overcome in the atonement. Because the demands of the Law are deepened to include not merely external commands but also the spontaneous obedience of love, legalism becomes impossible and the Law can be clearly recognized as an enemy. Since the Law can never provide the basis for man's relationship with God, it must give way to grace. The emphasis on the wrath of God as one of the enemies brings the conflict by which man is redeemed almost within the divine nature itself. The wrath is real, yet love must prevail. Aulén suggests that the wrath of God may be understood as transcended, so that though it is overcome by divine love it still remains latent in and behind the divine love.

Luther's view of the atonement, however, was not fully understood by his successors, and thus in Protestant orthodoxy the atonement continues to be interpreted in medieval terms. Later, during the periods of Pietism and the Enlightenment, the humanistic and subjective ideas earlier expressed by Abelard were emphasized. It was then believed that due to God's benevolence no atonement is necessary, as far as God is concerned; all that is needed is that man repent. Friedrich Schleiermacher (1768-1834), a German theologian who, according to Aulén, represents a subjective approach to the atonement, distinguishes between salvation and atonement, emphasizing the former. According to Schleiermacher, it is man's salvation that makes the atonement possible. Thus, the emphasis shifts from what is done by God to what is done in and by man.

Aulén concludes his study by contrasting the three types which he has distinguished. When they are compared as to structure, Aulén finds that in the classic type there is continuity in the divine operation, with discontinuity in the order of merit and justice. God saves man, but to do so He must do violence to the just demands of His own Law. In the Latin type there is continuity in the order of merit and justice, with discontinuity in the divine operation. In order that the demands of the Law might be justified, Christ suffers as man. Thus, at this crucial point the atonement is man's work rather than God's. In the humanistic type the whole emphasis is on man's approach to God, rather than on God's approach to man. There is accordingly no attempt to view the atonement as a divine achievement.

With respect to the problem that sin poses, Aulén claims that in both the Latin and the classic types sin is taken seriously, while in the humanistic type the power of sin is not so strongly emphasized. In the classic type forgiveness, however, has a positive meaning, implying the restoration of fellowship, while in the Latin type forgiveness implies only the removal of guilt. With respect to salvation, in the classic view justification and atonement are identified, and atonement and salvation coincide. In the Latin view, atonement makes salvation possible, but justification and sanctification are separate acts

having no organic connection. In the subjective type, salvation makes atonement possible and the change which takes place in man is emphasized.

As far as the Incarnation is concerned, in the classic type Christ is set forth as the man in whom God reveals Himself, carrying out His work of deliverance and atonement. In the Latin type, the connection between the Incarnation and the atonement is not as evident, while in the subjective type the whole emphasis is on the humanity of Christ. With respect to the concept, the classic type affirms dualism, yet insists that God is sovereign. In the Latin type, there is rational compromise of the opposition between God and evil, while in the humanistic type, God's opposition to evil is obscured.

Aulén finally reminds his reader that his intent in this book has been historical rather than apologetic. He has sought to describe three main types of the idea of the atonement, and he has not intended that his study should be a defense of the classic view. Yet Aulén does admit that in so far as the classic view is recognized as the authentic Christian understanding of the atonement, it is also in his opinion to this extent vindicated.

THE FAITH OF A MORALIST

Author: Alfred Edward Taylor (1869-1945)
Type of work: Moral theology
First published: 1930

PRINCIPAL IDEAS ADVANCED

Ethics has important metaphysical and theological implications, for what is and what ought to be may be distinguished but not divided.

The goal of the moral life is marked by a tension between the temporal and the eternal, and involves diminishing identification with the temporal and increasing participation in the eternal.

The historical religions have developed institutions to mediate and preserve their beliefs, and these institutions need not be regarded as irrational or scandalous by philosophers.

The prejudice against the historical and the individual on the part of many philosophers is unfortunate and, hence, the emphasis by Christianity on the historical as a real sphere of divine action is to be commended.

In the two volumes of his Gifford Lectures, *The Faith of a Moralist,* A. E. Taylor covers a wide territory of culture, philosophy, and theology. His vast scholarship produced a richly woven tapestry of mature learning. His stance in the first volume, entitled "The Theological Implications of Morality," is that of a professional teacher of ethics probing into the presuppositions and implications of the moral life to discover what, if anything, it has to say about the assertions of theology. Three issues, Taylor believes, are critical; first, how the moral ideal is related to time and the supratemporal; second, how it is related to human effort and the claim of divine grace; and third, how the question of autonomy should be handled in ethics and related disciplines.

His argument on the distinction between value and fact is fundamental. Ethics, some have said, has to do with values, ideals, and obligations and not with existences as such. Its sphere is that of the goodness or badness of what is. If this is so, the moralist would seem to be straying from his subject when he pronounces on what is, rather than on what ought to be. Ethics, it is argued, cannot be made to say anything about existence. Religion, however, if it is anything at all, certainly does say something about reality, for its object of worship must be taken as

a reality; its god cannot be known to be an illusion.

A. E. Taylor will have nothing to do with such a sharp disjunction between fact and value, and he asserts, "I regard it as the most important problem in the whole range of philosophy to examine this alleged want of connection between reality, actuality, existence or being, and goodness or value in a spirit of thorough criticism." Values, he argues, are always resident in persons, are more than mere ideas, and are always given together with facts. Therefore what they say is by no means unimportant to theology and metaphysics.

Human life is embedded in history, but this specter of the transitoriness of time need not be a frustration. The concept of time is a different thing in mathematics and morality. Mere before and after is one thing; past, present, and future is another. Man is unique in that he can survey the past, form expectations for the future, and respond to an ideal good which is present in all his moral striving. It is here that morality makes contact with religion, for God as "the absolute and final plenitude of good" can relieve our frustration. If the moral life is taken seriously, it involves aspiration and progress; and both imply time and its transcendence, attachment and detachment, in which the very salvation of the soul is at stake. Man in his pilgrimage may choose to follow the desires of the moment, or even to improve on the present and to tie his hopes to the march of history; but so long as he conforms himself to the temporal, the full ethical implications of the good will not be realized, for these implications point to the eternal, the goal of deiformity.

To argue thus is not to say that the moral end is clear and distinct after the manner of René Descartes (1596-1650), the father of modern philosophy. The moral ideal is not available to men through introspection; men come to know the good only as they are faithful to whatever light is already present. Morality involves faith.

Some reinforcement of the thesis that the moral life has religious ties comes from the experience of evil—a topic, says Taylor, that is often handled inadequately in ethical discussion. The experience of evil is exclusively human. Explanations in terms of environment, inefficiency, or outworn superstition will not do. The awareness of guilt and pollution can be evaluated adequately only in intrapersonal terms, as a breakdown of, indeed as an outrage against, an ideal which is actualized in God, the fount of all goodness.

How does a person go from badness to goodness? Moralists have tended to discuss both, but they have been less than satisfactory on how the transition is to be made. For religion, motivation is related to the grace of God, the divine initiative; and here again ethics leads up to theology. It would be a mistake, of course, to regard grace as eliminating human effort. Ethics can never permit the surrender of personal decision and striving. The position is rather one of response to the divine action so that, even in natural theology, there are directional signals toward God as redeemer, lover, and self-revealer.

Has the moral nature of man anything to say about the destiny of the individual? We do not have a blueprint of Heaven, and inferences have to be made with caution. At least, Taylor argues, we can note as of some interest that mankind as a whole believes in some kind of continuance of life after death. This ordinary belief is, however, limited in impressiveness. Kant's sophisticated argument that the balance of virtue and happiness demands immortality appeals to many, but does the moral imperative actually set up such a demand? If a convincing case can be made out for obligation as valid only within history in terms of an increase in individual happiness and social betterment, then obligation cannot be used as a witness to any life beyond history. Taylor prefers to argue, however, that the moral end is not exclusively concerned with a better world, but centers about the task of making better people, and this, in history, involves man's becoming less dependent on fluctuating circumstances, less identified with the temporal, more concerned with the eternal.

In fact, the concept of another world, if properly defined, is indispensable to moral endeavor in this world. The belief in eternal life has profound effects on the conduct of life. A moral person dare not make society, nation, or family his supreme loyalty. The alternative end may lack clear definition, but at least it can be said to be both present and future, immanent and transcendent, truly human and truly divine.

Great care must be taken to avoid defining morality in such a way that its end negates it. For example, if goodness is the result of successful conflict with evil, overcoming temptation, righting wrongs, putting the Devil to flight, then the struggle against evil would be an essential ingredient in the good life. When this fight is over and the victory won, goodness would vanish also. The correction needed here is to refuse to accept evil as necessary to good. The element of activity, adventure, and progress can still be present without the presence of evil. There can be progress *in* goodness as well as progress *toward* it. A life of service to God could mean the continual enrichment of personal life in moral activity.

A. E. Taylor proceeds to confront the positive religions in the second volume of his series. There is, he asserts, no philosophical religion, only religions that are historical and institutional, and these have four features: (1) they originate in some historical founder, (2) their message is believed to be revealed rather than discovered, (3) there is an authoritative medium of interpretation for the message, and (4) institutions are developed to sustain belief. All of them incorporate the three factors discussed in the first volume; namely, the existence of God, the grace of God, and participation in the life of God.

Many philosophers recoil from such religions and prefer to remain detached, because a historical religion is committed to association with contingent factors. Historical and empirical involvement creates tensions for the rational mind. As a matter of fact,

however, these very philosophical critics, Taylor points out, are deeply in debt to institutional religion for some of their own perspectives and may be in danger of discarding in the name of reason what in fact may be true by revelation.

The assault on the claims of the great religions, it must be admitted, has been impressively argued. Furthermore, Judaism, Christianity, Islam, Buddhism, and the like are in strong disagreement, and none seems to be able to establish its claim to be an exclusive medium of truth. In any case, the critics assert, the claim to revelation is incredible, and any pretension to finality is impossible where fallible human recipients are included. What really matters, it is said, is the practical function of religion in society and the moral quality of the life it stimulates, not its absurd doctrines which, as a matter of record, abound in scientific and historical errors.

These are serious charges, and Taylor is most anxious to give them their due while at the same time refusing to concede all that is claimed for them. A reasonable case can be made out for revelational religion, he believes, even in the face of such radical criticism. A conflict of claims between religions for example, does not mean that they cancel one another out. It could be that one is actually true. With regard to revelation, could it not be argued that genius is in the same vulnerable positions, for its appearance is also associated with insights into truth? In fact, the objections are too sweeping. It is not unreasonable to claim that revelation could be contextual and also final; the kernel and the husk can still be distinguished. Again, with regard to the contribution made by religion to morality, it is certainly true that religion has had an important moral effect, but this is true because of the theology behind religion. Indeed, the proper order is to make theology primary, and ethics derivative. Finally, the fact that proponents of religion have propagated some scientific and historical errors from time to time can be quite fairly charged to the fallible agents involved and need not imply the falsity of the religious truths they represent.

A really sore point of contention is the assertion, especially on the part of Christianity, that certain events of history are also facts of the faith by which one must be saved. This has been a sensitive point from earliest times. How can a faith claiming finality rest securely on a basis which is open to historical criticism? What if the records should prove to be false? Indeed some have argued that the mythical outweighs the historical in the Gospels.

Honest criticism, Taylor admits, must have its day in court. In fact, when its story is told, the divine Incarnation in a historical person is not weakened. On the contrary, the conviction that this is the strength of Christianity can be defended. The Apostolic message was never tied to biographical details; in fact, the message seems never to have made use of these details; it concentrated on the Crucifixion and Resurrection. Christians have never concealed the necessity of faith involved in the assertion of the Incarnation as divine revelation. "It is not the part of wisdom, which is always humble," Taylor writes, "to pronounce too confidently that there is 'nothing in' any conviction which has fed the spirituality of generations."

A special case of the historical factor is the matter of miracles, and this factor has provoked strong criticism. Undoubtedly miracles abound in religious literature, and few will dispute that great quantities of these stories of miracles are apocryphal. Must we say all?, Taylor asks. If reality were a closed system of natural law, Taylor says, this would end the argument; but, in fact, it is not so, as far as we know. Nature has its surprises as well as its regularities; and, if God exists, then He may very well act in ways that appear unusual and even startling to men. Such actions cannot be ruled out by a theist as either impossible or improbable. Miracles can be significant communication. Mistaken identification of the "numinous" quality of some events should not lead to a blanket rejection of all claims in regard to miracles.

Another feature of the positive religions with which A. E. Taylor deals in an incisive section is the assertion of an authority to which all must submit. This appears to be "treason to reason." All pronouncements, philosophers aver, should be scrutinized by rational analysis and their credentials evaluated. Undoubtedly, it must be granted, there have been so many utterances by religious persons that are highly questionable that discrimination is inevitable. On the other hand, the authoritative force of some experiences is common enough, such as in everyday sense perception of the natural world. Religious authority is the force with which religious experience is compelling independently of the mind's own action. The reports of such experiences, Taylor believes, are not necessarily accurate, and where asserted as authoritative these reports need scrutiny. Yet the sense of authority itself defies analysis. No better illustration of the paradoxical features of religious authority is available than in the function of conscience where the old rule holds true, that though conscience is not infallible it should always be followed.

Those who resent the authoritarian stance of the positive religions generally also object to the sacred procedures and structures which religions have developed to express their mission and to stabilize the approach to the supernatural. There are, of course, degrees of formality and convention all the way from the spontaneous Spirit-filled Apostolic fellowship to the elaborate liturgical spectacles of some modern churches. Support for or against forms and ceremonies has oscillated back and forth throughout Church history. Surely, however, there is nothing either religious or nonreligious about conventions as such. Life in general without habits would be intolerable. The true issue, Taylor argues at length, is neither fixed forms or spontaneous formlessness, but finding a mean that will be effective without being artificial. The aim of institutional procedures is to create an impression adequate to the theme, to contribute to significance. Human beings need orderly ways of doing things to channel affections and to sustain them. Thus, conventions appear in family life, in social and political action, in the administration of justice, as well as in religious activities. But conventions should never be so inflexible or so uniform as to prevent worship rather than promote it.

A special cause of scandal to some rationalists is the ritual of sacraments; that is, the use of objects of sense as media of spiritual benefit. To many this is nothing less than a relapse into magic. Taylor is insistent that this is not so, or not necessarily so. Belief in sacraments need not clash with the rational principles of metaphysics, for their present meaning is not tied to the more crude and primitive forms which engross the attention of the anthropologists. Again, it is not the material elements used that produce grace, but the divine will and the condition of the participant. Nor is it usual to hold that this is the only way the help of God can be found. Magic enters in only when some manipulation of material is believed to be automatically productive of some favor or curse. Such practices are certainly to be repudiated. Taylor is also opposed to precise enumeration of sacraments. "The effect on the Western Church of the hard-and-fast dogmatising of the divines of Trent, and the Reformers alike, about the number of the sacraments of grace and their immediate institution by Christ seems to me to have been wholly unfortunate," he writes. While the great moments of worship may come in sacramental acts, it is not in the power of man to tie God to a fixed number of ceremonies.

Again and again in the lectures the tension between the temporal and the eternal appears as the key problem. The historical and the superhistorical confront but do no oppose one another, and Christianity at least demands that neither be taken as illusory. The Incarnation demands time as a real element, though not necessarily as an ultimate element, in the divine purpose; dogmatism here, where knowledge is partial, would be reprehensible. A sane agnosticism befits an honest man. What we do know, however,

Taylor insists, we should try to make intelligible, and theology has its contribution to make to the search for truth just as much as do science and philosophy.

THE DESTINY OF MAN

Author: Nikolai Berdyaev (1874-1948)
Type of work: Christian ethics
First published: 1931

PRINCIPAL IDEAS ADVANCED

Ethics can be understood only in the context of man's created nature and ultimate destiny.

The suffering God alone can answer the problem of evil by revealing human creativity as of ultimate meaning in the completion of creation.

Ethics has beauty as its goal, the content of which must emerge through creative entry into the uniqueness of each situation.

For centuries, Eastern Orthodoxy has been of only historic interest to the West, even among Christian thinkers. The reasons for this isolation are two-fold. First, Eastern theological reflection has been ingrown and static. Second, there has been little interest in or capacity for creative dialogue with Western thought.

Consequently, the translation of the works of Nikolai Berdyaev into English, and particularly his chief work, *The Destiny of Man: An Essay in Paradoxical Ethics,* is to be heralded as a monumental first step in the establishment of creative theological dialogue between East and West. The results thus far have been considerable, both in fact and promise. For a Western Christianity thoroughly grounded in the emphasis of the Western Fathers on personal guilt and the atoning answer of Crucifixion, Berdyaev's reformulation of the emphasis of the Eastern Fathers on cosmic transformation through Incarnation and Resurrection comes as a welcomed addition. Immersed both in Western and Eastern philosophy, Berdyaev creatively relates Eastern process-thought and Western existentialism within a Christian framework shaped by the Kantian critiques.

For a contemporary theology presently obsessed with culture, Berdyaev must be recognized as one of the most original Christian thinkers on the meaning of culture and the arts. Finally, in the present social crisis, Berdyaev appears as one of the most outspoken critics of both Capitalism and Communism.

For Berdyaev, the modern dilemma has its basis in epistemology. "Man has lost the power of knowing real being, has lost access to reality and been reduced to studying knowledge." There can be no return to pre-critical metaphysics, but neither can man rest with the epistemological dualism made absolute after Immanuel Kant (1724-1804).

The only solution is an existentialist understanding of knowing: knowledge is a sympathetic penetration into the existence of the known. The error of modern philosophy was the attempt to become a science, to reduce all reality to phenomena, under the category of necessity. True knowledge is participation in the noumenal dimension. Theology is concerned with this realm, but its results are forced on it from without, through dogma accepted on authority. For the philosopher, however, such revelational facts are part of the world to be known and thus are true only if they become an inner experience. Philosophical knowledge, then, "is not revelation, but man's free cognitive reaction to revelation." Because philosophy deals with the mystery of being and life, it rests in spiritual experience.

Berdyaev's methodology is thus Augustinian, as opposed to the Thomistic method which he sees as thoroughly pagan: "Philosophy knows being in and through man and finds in man the solution of the problem of meaning, while science knows being as it were apart from man and outside him." Epistemology must discover who the knower is; and the intuitive discovery of the noumenal, spiritual self is the key to all knowledge; it is the penetration into being from within.

It is from this methodology that the nature of ethics, Berdyaev's primary concern in this volume, is to be derived. Like philosophy as a whole, ethics must rest on intuitive moral experience. It must be part of a living ontology centered in the interior knowledge of the doer. Since ethics involves all values (moral, aesthetic, cognitive), it embraces everything connected with human freedom; and since human freedom can be understood only in its relation to divine freedom, ethics can be understood only in terms of a total philosophical world view. "Ethics must be the theory of the destiny and vocation of man, and must inquire in the first instance into the nature of man, his origin and his goal."

It is at this point that the most difficult but fascinating portion of Berdyaev's understanding emerges. The primary problem of ethics is the feud between creature and Creator. Atheism is the honest attempt to come to terms with the fact of evil; there can be no transition to theism without an adequate theodicy. The traditional Christian understanding Berdyaev finds inadequate, for while it affirms human freedom as the cause of evil, this freedom is affirmed to be determined by God. Foreseeing that man would fall, God consents to create man. Likewise, in awaiting man's response, God is awaiting Himself, for even the response is predetermined.

For Berdyaev, the Christian understanding of God must begin not with Greek philosophical ideas of impassivity, pure actuality, and the like, but with an immanent awareness of the God of the Incarnation. From this perspective, the traditional theodicy is inadequate and stands in living contradiction to the suffering God of the Cross. Certain insights of the Christian mystics seem closer to the truth. Out of the Divine Nothing, the Holy Trinity is eternally being born; that is, God is not complete actuality, but He who acts. Because God exists, nonbeing takes on infinite possibilities in the creative imagination of God, and its fulfillment enriches God Himself. While God did not create nonbeing, whatever God creates must be created from nonbeing; that is, it must be created with freedom.

Consequently, man is the child both of God and freedom (nonbeing). While nonbeing consented to this creative act by God, man in his freedom rejected the Creator, yearning for nonbeing and thereby mixing being with nonbeing. This is man's tragedy, but also God's, for God longs for His friend, for man, to share in completing creation by bringing being from nonbeing through freedom.

God is all-powerful over being, but He is powerless over uncreated freedom. God cannot avert the Fall without destroying man. After the Fall, God does all that He can do. He appears not as Creator but as Redeemer. The Cross must not be understood juridically, as recompense for an autocratic deity, but as the supreme act of the suffering God, who descends into the abyss of nonbeing and participates in the world of demonic freedom. Evil can be enlightened only from within, or the positive possibilities of freedom are destroyed; redemption cannot be coercion.

The Fall itself points to this sublime destiny of creativity intended by God for His creatures. While the theologians use the Fall to humiliate man, Berdyaev sees it testifying to man's power, for man can rise against God Himself, transforming the world into an evil chaos. What belittles man is not his nature, but his evil use of freedom. In the Incarnation man is restored to his sublime nature, the image of the Creator God. Through spiritual experience, the Incarnation becomes

living fact. The God-man is not only a revelation of God, but also an anthropological revelation. This restored self is man's noumenal self, Kant's free self, which in the noumenal depths participates in the very life of God as well in the noumenal depth of all created reality. Thereby, through the inspiration of the Holy Spirit, man is opened in each new situation to its creative possibilities, transfiguring its nonbeing into being.

The Christian God is the Trinity, corresponding to the three-fold aspect of man's spiritual experience. When one ascribes to an Unmoved Mover all the attributes which one despises in man, man cannot help but revolt; only in the God of suffering love, yearning for his human "other," is human rebellion won over from within and freedom brought to its full creative possibilities.

It is from this understanding of man's destiny that ethics takes its meaning. Creativity is the divine-human vocation; and creation "means transition from non-being to being through a free act." The Fall created the distinction between good and evil. Good comes into being—and disappears—with evil. Thus, although the beginning and end of history is existence beyond the distinction, history is a tragic circle unless beginning and end are far from identical. Although Eden was the life of bliss, of instinct, the realm of the unconscious, man chose to abandon this ignorance in order to explore his destiny. Knowledge in itself is good, not sin, but man's choice was for nonbeing rather than a positive response to God's creative call. Once this choice is made, man must follow his destiny to its end.

The image of God in man could

have been preserved through limited consciousness, although consciousness is purchased at the price of the noumenal-phenomenal distinction. The real fall occurs when man makes this distinction absolute, surrendering to the necessity of the phenomenal realm. To do so is to forfeit freedom, the true self, and man's destiny as creator. This risk God cannot avoid; He must allow evil for the sake of the good of freedom.

This is the root of the tragedy of ethics. To legislate the good is to destroy freedom and to undermine the very good which one is intent on realizing. Ethics must correspond to the dynamism of existence; it must transfigure evil by enlightening freedom from within. True freedom is not in obeying laws but in creating new realities, in creating the good, not just in fulfilling it.

Such creativity is possible, Berdyaev believes, because the worlds of nature and spirit intersect in man. This is the existential meaning of the Incarnation, exposing "personality" as *the* moral principle. The "individual" is fallen; it is hardened selfhood. Personality is the melting away of the individual in communion with reality. The human task is thus to sublimate and reorient man's biological base through a revelation of man's spiritual, noumenal nature; this is to answer in freedom the divine call to creativity. Freedom is liberated creative energy.

Berdyaev's view is in radical opposition to much Christian ethics. Man is called not to reject his own self, but to love it as the image of God. The egoist is the one who has an aversion to the self. To love others as ourselves means to love the divine possibilities in our nature and to fulfill them; such fulfillment is through the mutuality of love.

In mutuality, the source of creativeness is revealed—the imagination. Through imagination, God created the world; through loving imagination, man enters into its completion, creating out of nonbeing images of beauty that have never before existed. In living dialogue with these images, the self and the other are mutually fulfilled. In ethics, imagination plays the part of talent.

Man is sick because he does not do what he wants to do. Not seeing this, Christian ethicists have seen only two possible ethics: the ethic of law (the Old Testament ethic of the Father) and the ethic of redemption (the New Testament ethic of the Son). A legal ethic cannot change human nature, for it only represses the unconscious. An ethic of society imposed on the individual renounces sin, but it cannot conquer it. In the primitive stages of humanity, such an ethic was necessary, and aspects of it are still necessary against demonic exploitation in the social sphere. Its highest achievement, however, is the concept of justice.

Once the distinction between good and evil appears, man thirsts not only for escape from evil, but also for escape from the very distinction. He thirsts for redemption. With redemption, morality is based not on ideas of the good but on the power of grace. The only law is that every moral action demands its own individual solution. Berdyaev writes, "Every moral act must be based upon the greatest possible consideration for the man from whom it proceeds and for the man upon whom it is directed." This is the heroic ethic of love, following the line of the greatest resistance to the world. It is to accept suffering positively, as the "fundamental law of life," for through suffering comes love and in love evil is illuminated from within.

These two ethics expose the dualism of man, in that they show that he belongs to the order of nature and spirit, law and grace. The Gospel and the world are utterly incompatible, and in this tragic tension the call to a third ethic is felt, the ethic of creativeness (the ethic of the Holy Spirit). In speaking ot talents that must be returned with profit, Christ spoke of man's creative vocation. Gifts from God are not to be passively awaited and received, but are to be performed actively as tasks. Genius feels that he is a means by which God works His own ends; he is a man possessed. Grace is inspiration, and freedom is response; their interaction is creativity. In creative work, the self is forgotten; one passes beyond good and evil and participates in the freedom of the Holy Spirit. Redemption, although utterly necessary, is negative; it is deliverance *from* sin. It is not an end but a means; it is *for* creativeness, for self-justifying fullness.

The ethic of creativeness neither destroys nor binds, but transfigures. Its stress is on motive, Berdyaev says, on the "selfless and disinterested love of God and of the divine in life. . . ." Each person must act as himself in the uniqueness of each situation, and not as one would have him act. Man must rise to divine creativeness, or the dynamism of his being will drive him into the destructive womb of nonbeing. Empty evil cannot be crushed; it must be reoriented. Sex, for example, can never be eliminated, but it can be creatively transfigured into the loftiest of values.

An ethic of negativity is self-destructive and existentially impossible, for it mistakes man's fallen condition for his ontic nature and ultimate destiny. The fallen creature desires, but on acquiring the object of desire, he tires of it; life is a continuous frustration. But in redemption the real nature of receiving is made known; in giving is the receiving real. Thus the true end of life is seen as not being the good, for good rests in dualism with evil. The final end is *beauty*. "Beauty is the image of creative energy radiating over the whole world and transfiguring it," writes Berdyaev. Creative intuition alone is an escape from sin, from necessity, from time; it is a momentary glance into eternity from which true beauty is inspired and to which in the end it will return with interest, to be completed as the enrichment of God Himself.

Because all ethical attainments are incomplete, ethics must ultimately rest in eschatology. The ethical vision of beauty shows that meaning is found only in terms of eternity, in that which conquers the nonbeing of death. Thus the fundamental principle of ethics is so to act as to conquer death by affirming the eternal possibility in every aspect of life. Christ's love means love for everything that lives, down to the very blades of grass. Either all must receive eternal life, or the world cannot be accepted and justified. Nothing is immortal in itself, but in the resurrection of Christ the hope witnessed to in life becomes a divine promise. This end to be, however, involves a demand. Berdyaev regards human creativity as having ontic significance; creativity makes possible "eternal, permanent, immortal goods and values which further the victory of eternity and prepare man for the end."

THE GROWTH OF THE IDEA OF GOD

Author: Shailer Mathews (1863-1941)
Type of work: American Protestant liberal theology
First published: 1931

PRINCIPAL IDEAS ADVANCED

Originating in the quest for security and moral direction through personal relations with the cosmic environment, the idea of God always reflects the prevailing social patterns of an era, and thus it must be understood through a study of its development in the light of the various mind-sets through which it has passed.

The evolutionary process described by modern science manifests something akin to purpose in its production of personality, and this fact provides the clue to a view of God viable for contemporary men.

God is the human conception of the personality-evolving and personally responsive factors in the universe upon which men are dependent for their fulfillment and with which religiously satisfying relations are possible.

Shailer Mathews's *The Growth of the Idea of God* is an excellent example of a widespread movement in twentieth century American theology which attempted to employ the methods and conclusions of empirical science in order to reinterpret the ancient Christian Gospel for the present age. One of the strong centers of this scientific modernism in the years following 1915 was the University of Chicago. Here Mathews and others constituted what has been called the Chicago school of theology, a group of men holding a variety of views but characterized generally by a socio-historical, empirical, and pragmatic approach to the study and interpretation of religion. Some of the other representatives of this left wing of liberalism were Shirley Jackson Case (1872-

1947), Gerald Birney Smith (1868-1929), Edward Scribner Ames (1870-1958), and John Merlin Powis Smith (1866-1932). All agreed that traditional Christian teaching had to be radically rethought if it were to compete for the minds of contemporary men. The present work attempts just this sort of modernizing with regard to a particular doctrine. It begins with an effort to discover by historical analysis the pragmatic meaning of the idea of God in human experience, and it concludes with a view of God which is thought to be relevant to the religious and intellectual needs of the scientific era.

Underlying this book is Mathews's conviction that religious doctrines are functional formulas which interpret the human experience of God in terms derived from the dominant social patterns of the age. This orientation leads him to affirm that the idea of God must be studied from the historical, social, and practical religious point of view and not from the standpoint of metaphysics. Philosophy has rationalized the idea of God but did not originate it. Religion, the human quest for aid, peace, and moral control through personal relations with the cosmic environment, has led men to speak of God, and society has provided the patterns in which this experience has been expressed. Since social patterns change, the forms of religious doctrines likewise change. God, then, is not an absolute metaphysical term with an unchanging content but is relative to the needs and the dominant social "mind-sets" of various cultural epochs. In short, the meaning of the idea of God is to be found in the history of the religious uses of that idea and in the study of the underlying social patterns which have structured it during the course of its development. Since through a combination of fortunate circumstances the idea of God has attained its most complex development in the Christian religion, Mathews concentrates on the background and growth of this social tradition.

The thesis of Mathews is that the ultimate origin of religion among primitive men is not to be found in fear but in the desire to establish help-gaining relationships with the mysterious powers on every hand on which human welfare was felt to be dependent. These relationships were initiated by approaching the gods in the socially approved ways of dealing with other persons, especially those held in high esteem. Certain persons were set aside

as being experts in bringing about proper adjustment to the gods; desire for reality in worship led to the representation of the venerated powers in various art forms; and finally the Gods were assigned the task of protecting and directing the mores of the group. In this way religion was born. The further development of religious ideas followed upon the increasing complexity of society and the emergence of civilization.

Hebrew religion, according to Mathews, had its roots in primitive practices, but over a period of one thousand years it underwent a remarkable growth and emerged with a high ethical monotheism. Lacking a philosophical spirit and the capacity for metaphysics, the Hebrews developed their unique religion by virtue of the special factors which characterized their social history. The distinctive faith of the Hebrews began to emerge when they adopted one god to be worshiped in exclusion to all others. The entrance into Canaan tore Jahveh loose from His mountainous home in the Sinaitic peninsula; the adoption of agriculture as a way of life led to an extension of His power over nature; the union of the tribes into a monarchy gave rise to a corresponding growth in the majesty and power of God; and finally the impact of other nations upon Israel suggested the idea that Jahveh is an international deity directing the destinies of all men. Thus, monotheism emerged and was given its classic statement in the writings of Deutero-Isaiah.

A cosmology adopted from the Babylonians explained the relationship of God to nature as that of Creator, and a pattern derived from Israel's political life interpreted the relationship of Jahveh to His people as that of Sovereign King, while the unusual insight of the Prophets gave rise to a view of God as a completely moral being. The emergence of the wisdom literature as a commentary on the practical problems of life, the development of legalism in an attempt to be obedient to the last detail of the divine law, and the emergence of apocalypticism under the pressure of persecution completed the major elements of the tradition into which Jesus appeared with His idea of God as a loving Father who desires all men to be brothers.

Mathews finds that the Graeco-Roman world had a quite different development. The Aryan peoples produced a popular polytheism and a philosophical monotheism. The latter was the product of the speculative genius of the great Greek and Roman thinkers who spoke in various ways of a unity of being and of a rational order underlying the multifarious processes of ordinary experience. While no clear-cut religious monotheism ever emerged to win universal adherence, a trend in this direction was furthered by the sense of power and unity generated by the Roman Empire, typified by the worship of the Emperor. It remained for Christianity to effect a union of Greek philosophical monotheism with Hebrew religious monotheism.

It is the view of Mathews that this union was accomplished by the widespread interpenetration of peoples throughout the Roman Empire and the transition of Christianity from Jewish to Hellenistic membership. A modification of Hebraic monotheism took place as Jesus was exalted to a divine status, and a complex struggle ensued in which the precise relationship of the divine Christ to the Creator-Father God of the Old Testament was worked out. The outcome was the formulation in the fourth century of the classical doctrine of the Trinity, which spoke of one God-substance existing in three persons. Mathews sees this orthodox formula not so much in terms of a triumph of superior logic or theological reasoning over alternative perspectives as in terms of a power struggle in which the strongest party was able to enforce its views on the whole Church. Although the doctrine of the Trinity contains insoluble philosophical difficulties due to the impossibility of treating analogies, symbols, and patterns such as paternity, sonship, generation, and procession as metaphysical truths, it did serve the important religious function of preserving a genuine though complex monotheism in which the same personal God is confronted in nature, in the life of Jesus, and in personal experience.

Mathews sees the growth of the idea of God from the fifth to the twentieth centuries as a reflection of the underlying changes which took place in the social structure of Western civilization. The theology of the Middle Ages took over the pattern of political sovereignty and presented God as an exalted feudal Monarch who orders all things by His omnipotent will. The Renaissance of the fourteenth and fifteenth centuries introduced an approach to God which saw Him immanent in the processes of nature, but, more importantly, it generated a line of development outside the Church regarding the idea of God which was to parallel from that time forward the theology within the Church. The Reformation, reflecting both political and economic factors, produced at its center a theology based on the absolute sovereignty of God patterned after the political absolutism of the emerging nation states. However, growing democratic tendencies in England and Holland were reflected in the gradual modification of the absolute divine decrees as, for example, in the rise of Arminian theology. The final triumph of democracy and a changed conception of God came about because of the demand of the bourgeoisie for economic freedom. In the last half of the nineteenth century God took on a humanitarian character and was presented in a growing liberalism as a loving Father, and adjustments to the patterns suggested by modern science were seen to be forthcoming in those social orders where freedom had made creative thought possible.

The contemporary era has been marked, according to Mathews, by the emergence of new religious patterns suggested by sociology, science, and philosophy. Out of a sociological background has come a humanism which stresses devotion to human values but which neglects the relationship of men to the cosmos which produced them. Numerous scientists have spoken of the reality of religion as the response to the mysterious spiritual powers which pervade the world of purposeful activity open to empirical observation. Present-day philosophers are characteristically oriented by scientific modes of thought and tend either to define religion as the pursuit of values or to speak of some sort of cosmic purpose based on the facts of creative evolution. All these conceptions abandon the patterns of traditional theology and make clear that

any contemporary view of God must be based on the scientific outlook.

At the conclusion of this study, which has attempted to illustrate the thesis that all ideas of God are relative to the social mind-sets of the various cultural eras through which it moved in its growth, Mathews sets forth his own conception of God. The many patterns in which the idea of God has appeared express relations between persons and their cosmic environment and therefore point to something real, although the reality does not correspond literally to the pattern. The problem, then, is to express this reality in contemporary terms. Mathews begins with the scientific description of a world process which has produced and continues to sustain personalities existing in organic relationship with the cosmos. The only explanation of this fact, Mathews urges, is that there are personality-producing factors in the universe. Moreover, these creative forces continue to function in the environment in which men live and offer aid to human fulfillment when proper adjustment is made to them. God is the conception men have of these personality-evolving elements in the cosmic environment upon which men rely for their fulfillment. The term includes both pragmatic and metaphysical elements in that it refers both to the functional concept and to objectively real activities in the cosmos. God viewed in this fashion cannot be thought of as a super-individual or as a metaphysical personality. However, since the fulfillment of human life requires the furtherance of such personal activities and relations as love, prayer, and worship, the cosmic environment which makes this kind of adjustment necessary must be thought of as personal in nature. Thus, it is legitimate to speak of God as Father, Great Companion, King, or even Almighty. The advantages of the conceptual view of God are that it (1) gives men confidence that their struggle for the good life is aided by the cosmos itself, (2) provides an objective foundation for morality in the dynamic structure of the world process, and (3) shows religion to be a means of gaining personal value through proper adjustment to the creative factors in the universe.

To summarize, Mathews argues that the socially-conditioned patterns used throughout human history to refer to God stand for something real in the very nature of things, and while the patterns change, God is forever the Cosmic Friend.

LECTURES ON CALVINISM

Author: Abraham Kuyper (1837-1920)
Type of work: Calvinistic apologetics
First published: 1931 (Stone Lectures, 1898)

Principal Ideas Advanced

Calvinism meets the requirements of furnishing Protestants with a world and life view because its principles provide a unique answer to the question concerning man's relation to God, to his fellow man, and to the world.

Calvinism provides the basis for political justice, and it insures the independence of the Church, the family, and other segments of life, from the encroachments of the state.

Each aspect of human society derives its authority from the sovereignty of God, rather than from the will of the people, or from the state; under God's grace, science, art, commerce, and politics will benefit from the exercise of the principles of Calvinism.

These lectures on Calvinism were delivered as the Stone Lectures in 1898 at Princeton University by Abraham Kuyper, who as a philosopher, theologian, and statesman successfully devoted his life to making the impact of Calvinism felt in the religious, political, and scientific life of his own country, the Netherlands.

Kuyper's *Lectures* are a battle cry against the advance of the spirit of the French revolution that regarded Jesus Christ as a scoundrel, and heralded the overthrow of the tyranny of the Bourbons as an emancipation from the authority of God. As an alternative to such an anti-Christian *Weltanschauung*, Kuyper sets forth the life-system of Calvinism, and applies its principles to religion, politics, science, and art.

Calvinism is not here equated with the dogmatic beliefs of any particular church or with any specific doctrine. It refers, first, to the historical course taken by the Reformation, so far as it was neither Lutheran, nor Anabaptist nor Socinian; second, to the system of conceptions that arose under the influence of Calvin in various social spheres; and third, to the political movement which brought political liberty in constitutional statesmanship, in Holland, England, and the United States.

Calvinism, an all-embracing system of principles, is able to do more than create a different Church-form. Calvinism can provide human society with a different form of life, with a unified *Weltanschauung*, or life-system, for it offers a peculiar insight, derived from a special principle, into three fundamental relations, our relation to God, to man, and to the world. Kuyper's lectures proceed to an analysis of these relations.

First, how does Calvinism interpret our relation to God? Calvinism does not seek God in the creature, nor does it isolate the creature from God, nor does it impose an ecclesiastical middle-link between God and man; it proclaims rather that God the Holy Spirit enters into immediate fellowship with man. There is no divine grace other than that which comes immediately from God to man. The Church is not an office or an independent institute; it is identical with the believers that constitute its membership. Every single believer can have the assurance of eternal salvation and live his life in the immediate fellowship with God, fully persuaded that his entire life is to be lived in the divine presence.

Calvinism's unique view of man's relation to God and God's relation to man is augmented by its own interpretation of the relation of man to man. By regarding human life as the immediate concern of God, it views all men, regardless of social or economic status, as lost sinners, who, as equal in the sight of God, are in consequence equal among themselves. No distinctions among men are to be recognized, except such as are imposed by God Himself, in that to some He gives authority and greater talents that they might serve those with lesser talents, and thereby also serve God. Calvinism could result only in a democratic view of life, in which nations are free, and every man, because he is a man created in the image and likeness of God, ought to be treated fairly, both politically and socially. Man is here placed on a footing of equality with man, not against God, but on his knees before God.

The third basic relation which determines the Calvinistic life-system is man's relation to the world. Calvinism rejects any dualism between a sanctified Church and a demonic world that must be taken into the protective custody of the Church. Calvinism honors man because of his likeness to the divine image; it honors the world as a divine creation. Particular grace works salvation; common grace arrests the corruption of the world and allows our life to develop outside the institutional Church to the glory and honor of God the Creator.

Under the influence of Calvinism, the institutionalized Church is nothing more than the assembly of believers; every sphere of life is emancipated from the dominion of the Church, but not from the sovereignty of God. Family life, trade, commerce, politics, science, and art are restored to their positions of independence. Man is not required to retire from the world in a monastery; his duty is to flee from sin alone. His task is to serve God in the world, in every phase of worldly life. Man is duty bound to discover and to develop the potencies hidden by God in nature and in human life. To do so is to keep the divine command given in Paradise: "Subdue and replenish the earth."

Calvinism is a life system and as such it is offered by Kuyper as the completed evolution of Protestantism, as providing principles which, when embodied in a form suitable to the requirements of our own century, can restore unity to Protestant thought and action. The benefits of Calvinism are to be found in every sphere. Its influence on religion, as such, stresses the fact that religion exists not for man, but for God; it operates directly from the heart, without human interposition; it is not partial in its operations, but affects the whole of our existence, and its character is soteriological, springing from the new man in Christ Jesus.

Calvinism regards the Church as a spiritual organism, with the starting point and center of its action in Heaven and not on earth. The Church on earth manifests itself in the form of local congregations of believers, living together in obedience to the ordinances of Christ; it is not an institution for the dispensation of grace. Its purpose is not human or egoistic; it exists merely for the sake of God, for the glory and honor of His name, to which end its members are called to conversion, worship, and moral purity.

Calvinism places the believer before the fact of God, not only in the Church, but also in his political life, in the domain of the state. The influence of Calvinism on political conceptions springs from its dominating basic principle: the sovereignty of the Triune God over the whole cosmos, including the state. For the magistrates derive their power by the institution of God, by reason of sin. Because of sin they are

indispensable, on the one hand, and because of sin, the people must ever guard against any assumption of power by the magistrates which would deprive the people of their personal liberty.

Sin alone has made the institutions of governments necessary, but the right to rule over men is a right possessed by God and by Him alone. Such authority does not belong to any man or to the people, nor does it originate in a social contract. The authority of earthly governments originates solely in the sovereignty of God, so that every magistrate rules solely by God's grace; the final duty of obedience to civil powers, no matter what form they take, is imposed by God Himself.

The sovereignty of God in the political sphere, recognized in the American revolution, is equally opposed to popular sovereignty, manifested in the French revolution, and to state sovereignty, propagated in Germany as a result of philosophical pantheism. To the Calvinist there is a court of appeal beyond that of the whims and desires of men, and whenever men have usurped the power that rightfully belongs to God alone, the Calvinist has not hesitated to appeal directly to the King of kings, and to overthrow the pretender to earthly power, by force, if necessary.

The sovereignty of God is in no way limited to its manifestation in the state. It is equally present in society as a whole, in the family, in business, science, and art, and in all other social spheres.

These social structures do not derive their existence from the state, Kuyper claims, but are endowed with their own form of authority; an authority which rules by the grace of God, not by the grace of the state. The individual social spheres possess their own individual sovereignty; they have nothing above themselves but God. The state cannot properly intrude; each social sphere is sovereign in its own domain.

The state bears the power of the sword of justice, to mete out punishment to the criminal; the sword of war, to defend its rights and interests against its enemies; the sword of order, to thwart rebellion at home. But state authority cannot properly be extended into any other social sphere. The life of science, of the family, or of commerce may never properly be enclosed by the stultifying tentacles of the state. This does not mean that the state can never interfere in these autonomous spheres of life. When the different social spheres clash, the state must compel mutual regard for the boundary lines; when power is abused, the state must defend the weak; and it must use coercion to see that each sphere bears its proper personal and financial burden for the preservation of the state. The state, however, must never forget that the source of authority for the social spheres of society is the same as that from which the state derives its own authority; namely, the absolute sovereignty of God.

The Calvinist, in fact, has not always been clear in his conception of the relationship between the sovereignty of the Church and the sovereignty of the state and has invoked the power of the state to defend the truth of his confessions. In principle, however, Calvinism recognizes that the magistrate has a spiritual duty towards God, in that he must recognize that it is from God that he derives his power, and that it is according to God's ordinances that he must rule the people. It is, however, the duty of the government to suspend its judgment concerning which temporal manifestation of the body of Christ is to be found most perfect in the eyes of God. The government must honor the complex of Christian churches as the multiform manifestation of the Church of Christ on earth. The sovereignty of the Church and the sovereignty of the state must both be recognized. The government is to see that the individual liberty and conscience of its citizens is respected, so that every man may serve God according to his own convictions. For the sovereignty of the Church is limited by the sovereignty of the free personality.

The benefits of Calvinism are not limited to the political sphere, Kuyper contends. With respect to science and learning, Calvinism has fostered, and could not but foster, a love of investigation. For its doctrine of the divine decree of God means that the entire cosmos, instead of being the plaything of chance, obeys law, a fact which permits science to ascend from the empirical investigation of phenomena to the laws and principles which rule them. Calvinism placed science in its proper domain by acknowledging that nature is God's handiwork; it delivered it from its unnatural bondage to the state and to the Church. Calvinism also provides an answer to the alleged conflict between faith and science by showing that such a conflict is not possible. The real point of dispute is between the assertion that the cosmos as it now exists is normal, that it moves by means of an eternal evolution from its potencies to its ideal, and the assertion that it is abnormal, that a past disturbance has taken place, and that a regenerating power alone can bring it to its final goal.

Kuyper contends that in the sphere

of art Calvinism did not produce a general art style because Calvinism reached such a high stage of religious development that its very principles prevented it from expressing religion in visible and sensible forms. In principle, however, Calvinism offers an interpretation of art which frees it from any slavish interpretation of nature. Art is a gift of the Holy Spirit, and it has as its vocation the task of disclosing to man a higher reality than he can find in this sinful and corrupted world. By releasing art from the trusteeship of the Church, Calvinism encouraged and advanced the development of the arts, especially in the fields of music and painting.

The significance of Kuyper's call to a return to Calvinism is not to be minimized. It has been more than sixty years since he delivered his lectures. The Free University of Amsterdam, which Kuyper founded, one of the six universities in the Netherlands, continues to flourish along the lines suggested by Kuyper in 1898. Outside the Netherlands, the Calvinists of the world still look to Kuyper and to his spiritual successors, to such men as Herman Bavinck, G. Berkouwer, and Herman Dooyeweerd, for leadership as they continue his struggle to bring the world to a recognition that God is sovereign in every sphere of life.

THE NATURAL AND THE SUPERNATURAL

Author: John Wood Oman (1860-1939)
Type of work: Philosophy of religion
First published: 1931

PRINCIPAL IDEAS ADVANCED

The natural is the environment as apprehended through the senses; the supernatural is the environment as apprehended through religious feeling.

Human progress has been made possible through man's apprehension of the supernatural, which, as eternal, provides him a footing amidst the flux of the natural.

The religions of mankind may be classified according to the manner in which they conceive of the natural and the supernatural.

Mysticism denies the natural and affirms the supernatural as undifferentiated unity.

Ethical and ceremonial legalism opposes the supernatural to the natural in an other-worldly fashion.

Prophetic monotheism discerns the supernatural in the natural and seeks a means of reconciling the ideal and the real.

The Natural and the Supernatural, as John Oman explains to the reader, is not a theological work, but merely "an attempt to lay a foundation for theology, by considering its method and its problems." Oman views the history of religion as the progressive victory within human experience of the supernatural over the natural. He maintains that the victory is most complete in Christianity, with its belief that God is personal and its confidence that "all things work together for good to them that love God."

Writing at a time when Anglo-Saxon religious thinkers were preoccupied with the problem of providing a spiritualistic alternative to naturalistic evolution, Oman reflects their concerns in his book. His work shows the influence of Friedrich Schleiermacher (1768-1834), whose *Discourses on Religion* he translated.

One of the most fruitful parts of Oman's work, still worth careful study, is his account of cognition, in the course of which he criticizes philosophical naturalism for too readily abandoning experience in favor of abstract principles of explanation. Abstract ideas are necessary, he says, as providing the framework within which reality is perceived, but they must never become a substitute for perception, as they are likely to do when one refuses to view the world except in causal terms. The child and the artist, says Oman, are on much firmer ground, because they constantly explore reality in its concreteness, thereby finding that it rewards their highest expectations. Naturalism, however, is no more culpable in this regard than traditional religion, and Oman finds it one of the striking features of Jesus' teaching that the truths which He discloses to us do not require the dead hand of authority to make them convincing. Higher religion, from Oman's point of view, is synonymous with higher truth.

Oman maintains that religious experience is just as much a part of the knowledge which we have of our environment as sense experience, and that it is equally important to human progress. Through the experience of the senses we know our environment only as a flux of varying impressions, but through religious experience we discover the abiding character of the whole. In Oman's terminology, the temporal world given us through the senses is the natural, while the eternal world given us through religious feeling is the supernatural. Our environment, says Oman, always includes both the natural and the supernatural: "the seen and temporal," on the one hand, and "the unseen and eternal," on the other.

Following upon this theory of cognition, Oman develops a spiritualistic account of the evolution of culture. In contrast with the prevailing naturalism of his day, which sought to explain all origins in terms of physical forces, Oman maintains that evolution involves a positive effort on the part of a creature to find a place for itself in its environment. If this thesis seems obscure when applied to organic evolution, it is plain enough when applied to the development of civilization. Progress, Oman maintains, depends on meaning, not on physical impulse; the history of civilization is the story of man's struggle to achieve more perfect relations with reality.

Oman explains the development of human culture through man's capacity to entertain free ideas. All perception includes fixed ideas, otherwise known as sensations and feelings, but man is unique in being able to engage himself with ideas which are not immediately given. These free ideas, says Oman, have made it possible for him to distinguish between the permanent and the changing in his environment, the eternal and the evanescent. Specifically, the idea of the sacred, apprehended through religious experience, enabled primitive man to rise above the determination of the natural, by providing him with "firm footing in the flux of experience," and by making it possible for him to "escape from mere immediate impression and natural desire." Primitive man sensed the numinous quality in birth, death, sexual union, and the more exceptional events of nature; his mind was awakened, as those of lower creatures were not, and he invented myths and rituals in response. So it has been with every advance in history; progress always involves the extension of the claims of ideal values over ephemeral ones, and only religion has the power to enforce these claims over the clamor of appetite and the fear of strife.

Because he conceives of religion as man's effort to win and hold faith in the supernatural in the face of the natural, Oman finds a basis for classifying religions in the manner by which these two are related. "When the Supernatural is submerged in the Natural, we have idolatry; when the Natural is submerged in the Supernatural, we have pantheism; when they are set sharply apart, we have deism; when they are related by some kind of moral victory, we have at least some kind of theism."

Primitive religion, says Oman, tends to find the supernatural diffused as an animistic force throughout the natural. Polytheism is an advance over animism, in that it introduces individuation into man's experience of both the supernatural and the natural; polytheism, thus, is associated with the rise of agriculture and of cities, and it constitutes a most important step in the development of civilization. Pantheism, on the other hand, is regressive. In its cosmic form, it identifies the supernatural with the natural, under such notions as fate and karma; in its acosmic form, it denies the reality of the natural and regards the supernatural as a self-sufficient unity. Deism, in Oman's sense of the terms, is the theory underlying the ritualistic and ethical dualism of Judaism, Zoroastrianism, and Islam. It is an advance over polytheism, in that it affirms the unity of the supernatural on the one hand and of the natural on the other, without sacrificing the concrete individuality of either; but because it distinguishes sharply between the sacred and the secular, deism represents an uneasy truce between the natural and the supernatural rather than a progressive victory of the supernatural over the natural. Theism resembles deism in affirming the unity of the supernatural and of the natural, but it differs in the way in which it brings these into relation. As expressed by the Hebrew Prophets, by Christ, and by the Apostles, theism opposes the ceremonial and legal outlook of deism, and it insists that the supernatural must find expression in the daily lives of men. It recognizes, as fully as deism, the presence of evil in the world, but it insists that the reality of the natural is dependent on the reality of the supernatural, and that faith in God gives victory over all evil.

According to the way in which they relate the natural and the supernatural, religions are either mystical or apocalyptic. Oman insists on reserving the term "mystical" for those religions which deny the reality of the natural. "A mystical religion is, as it always should be understood scientifically, one that seeks the eternal behind the illusion of the evanescent." Since, for mysticism, the natural is a delusive veil, and the concrete individual is a fiction derived from the senses and the appetites, the way to redemption for anyone lies in pressing toward absolute unity with the undifferentiated, unchanging Real. Oman maintains that, rightly speaking, there is no such thing as Christian mysticism; he argues that the whole apparatus of "negation, darkness, void, unknowing," and of "visions, raptures, ecstasies, physical manifestations, the large role assigned to the Evil One, and . . . of special cultivated emotions" is remote from theism and appropriate only to acosmic pantheism.

Those religions are apocalyptic, in Oman's sense of the term, which expect the Eternal to be revealed in the evanescent. Oman calls attention to the root meaning of the word *apocalypsis*, which literally signifies "revelation." As used by Oman, the term describes both deistic and theistic religions, since both affirm the reality of the world, and both look for manifestations of God's will and purpose in the lives of concrete persons. The difference is that deists, because they draw a qualitative distinction between the supernatural and the natural, think of these manifestations as special, miraculous interventions. Thus, deists believe in a special priesthood, a sacred literature, and a revealed code of conduct to arm the faithful for their journey through the world, while expectation of future judgment and heavenly reward gives them hope despite the presence of the world's evil. The theists, on the other hand, find God revealed in ordinary human relations and in great public events. Not only is nature obedient to God's voice, but history manifests His purpose toward mankind. Prophets and apostles have recognized the presence of evil in their own lives and in the lives of others, but they have considered evil to be the result of a failure to achieve positive righteousness rather than as the consequence of transgression of divine law, and they place their hope, not in their ability to achieve ethical or ceremonial perfection, but in the reconciling love of God, and in the response, however imperfect, which divine love finds in the human heart.

While Oman is inclined to describe the world in terms of progress and to see religion as the growing edge, he recognizes also the tendency for a culture, after it has achieved material prosperity, to fall away from its best insights. Religion, he says, is to be thought of not as a ladder which, once climbed by civilization, can be discarded, but as a pillar, on which civilization rests. "Some religion man must have," says Oman, "and when he fails to maintain a higher religion, he falls back on polytheism, meaning by that whatever gods there be that protect his body, his family, his property and his state, without exacting much self-denial in their protection." This fall within religion occurs even within Christianity, whenever, instead of sharing in God's perfection by forgiving others, men place their trust in "judicial ideas of pardon, mystical mechanical ideas of grace, and rules of belief and action which are ceremonial, in the sense of rules imposed from without and enforced by fear." A regressive religion is a "bad religion," Oman insists, and although he concedes that such religion has some use in conserving past gains, he maintains that it is an obstacle to further progress. A vigorous civilization, he says, must be striving for ideals that are beyond it, and these ideals, to be valid ones, must represent a truer apprehension of reality than has been possible before. High civilization depends upon high religion; for us, this can be nothing less than the increasing realization in our lives of the spirit of Jesus and the Apostles.

What Oman finds central in the teaching of Jesus is the conception of the universe as "in some sense personal." Against deism, which conceives of God as a potentate and proprietor who stands over the world and demands man's obedience, prophetic religion conceives of Him as a friend who, by means of the environment, seeks to manifest Himself to us in order to win our love and trust. Such, says Oman, is the best way to account for man's evolving experience of his environment. When ideals run beyond facts, and then, suddenly, facts comport with ideals, what is this, asks Oman, but a kind of personal intercourse? To those who are responsive, the world has never appeared dead or hostile; seeming chaos turns to order; obstacles prove a means to further advance, and even suffering can turn to joy. Such a world, says Oman, is "a realm of free children of God, and not a theater of even the most admirable puppets." Thus, the world cannot adequately be understood as anything less than an expression of a personal God.

THE VISION OF GOD: THE CHRISTIAN DOCTRINE OF THE *SUMMUM BONUM*

Author: Kenneth E. Kirk (1886-1954)
Type of work: Theological foundations of Christian ethics
First published: 1931

Principal Ideas Advanced

Worship, as the means by which men experience the vision of God and respond to it, is the central path to understanding and to the acceptance of Christian moral responsibility.

Self-fulfillment is an unsatisfactory motivation for Christian goodness; the search for pleasure, mystical ecstasy, or religious salvation turns the attention of the self inward and excludes devotion to God.

While formal codes embraced for their own sakes destroy the vision of God by robbing morality of its true center of attention, a spirit of reasoned orderliness is essential to the highest kind of service to God.

A Christian ethic should exhibit an element of rigor and devotion and be marked by some renunciation and sacrifice.

The Vision of God is the published form for the Bampton Lectures for 1928. To the lectures as delivered has been added extensive documentation. It is a historical and theological study of the relationship between worship and morality expounding the thesis that "the principal duty of the Christian moralist is to stimulate the spirit of worship in those to whom he addresses himself, rather than to set before them codes of behaviour." The book is not to be understood, however, as an antinomian tract, for it allows a place for lawful orderliness providing it is subservient to the vision of God. It is well to remember that its author earlier penned an introduction to casuistry entitled *Conscience and Its Problems* (1927).

The Vision of God defends the central thesis that worship, by focusing attention upon God, creates the only kind of disinterestedness which can enable the self to pursue the ethical life in creative abandon to God. Philosophical hedonism is not a sufficient foundation for Christian behavior because the effort of the self to achieve happiness may be just as fully an expression of selfishness as is crass worldly egoism. Formalism, which advocates obedience to rules for the sake of the soul's eventual reward, is equally unable to achieve the desired God-centeredness symbolized by worship. Only when obedience to rules becomes a means of expressing gratitude to God does it constitute an adequate Christian expression of moral concern. Such gratitude flows naturally and freely from the vision of God experienced in worship. Here lies the central significance of the beatitude in Matthew 5:8: "Blessed are the pure in heart, for they shall see God."

The argument of the book employs the juxtaposition of three terms: formalism, rigorism, and humanism. Formalism expresses itself as obedience to codified rules; rigorism prescribes for its adherents mortification and self denial, and is frequently a branch of formalism; humanism emphasizes possibilities for attainment, growth, and achievement through moral action. Formalism is an enemy of true Christian morality because it forces men into legalistic molds. Humanism is also unsatisfactory because it sometimes proceeds towards its goal without a sense of dependence upon God and it frequently makes the self central to ethical concern. Seeking to avoid humanism, Christians have sometimes embraced rigorism, especially at times when the Church has felt called to emphasize its distinctive separation from the world. But none of these alternatives to Christian morality can be adequate for one who would love God; Christian morality cannot be based on some generalized human ideal for such a foundation places a subordinate principle in the prime place reserved for the highest human experience of devotion to God.

A good proportion of the book is a detailed exposition of historical materials illustrating its main theme. Beginning with Old Testament and Hellenistic backgrounds which prepared the way for the vision of God as proclaimed in Christianity, the problems of New Testament interpretation receive early attention, and especially the sharp differences that have arisen over the interpretation of the teachings of Jesus. These differences are said to arise because rigorism and humanism stand side by side in the teachings of Jesus, so that even the Gospel writers themselves portray them differently. By focusing men's attention upon God and His Kingdom Jesus opened for His hearers a path leading to humility and purity; in doing so, He portrayed God's power and active concern for all the humanly meaningful aspects of experience. In the early Apostolic period the rigoristic elements in the teachings of Jesus became the foundation for an ethic in which the formalistic element was dominant, but the codes which expressed such rigorism were compatible with disciplined life in the world. Later the humanistic aspect was submerged to the rigoristic one and asceticism found its way into Christian practice.

It is clear that Kirk discerns a major gulf between the writers of the New Testament and the ethical thinking that followed soon thereafter. His sympathies are with the teachings of Jesus, the outlook of Paul, and the orientation of John. In Jesus he finds the centrality of the vision of God. In Paul the relationship of the believer to Christ is treated in much the same way in which Christ relates the believer to God. St. Paul was convinced that the vision of God was most perfectly given in Christ. John makes the vision of God a perpetual experience realized, not by individual mystical ecstasy, but through participation in the corporate vision of the Church. But soon after these early and creative Christian writings appeared, the Christian life was codified into a formal system. Both the way of life and the way of death are portrayed by the *Didache* (c.150), which gives a list of detailed prescriptions for behavior, obedience to which means salvation while violation means doom. Rabbinical patterns of teaching as well as the catalogued form of Orphic and Pythagorean ethical instruction undoubtedly influenced the development of this formalism and thereby eclipsed much of the creative originality of the earlier material. Kirk's objection to formalism is based upon the fact that it permits and even encourages a complacency concerning one's obedience to ethical standards, whereas the vision of God as given in the teachings of Jesus and the perspective of Paul gives no comfort to those who feel they have attained a sufficient level of virtue to merit a reward.

The rise of monasticism within the Christian tradition gave expression to the rigoristic impulse that frequently skirts the edges of the Christian ethic, most strongly so when the surrounding culture is at a low level of moral attainment. St. Jerome (c.342-420) was driven to monasticism in reaction to the excesses of fourth century Rome, and his converts renounced domestic responsibility. St. Antony of Egypt (c.251-356) undertook the same renunciation in individual terms and his attention focused on "holy ones" rather than on God. The anchorite thrust for ecstatic experience stands in sharp contrast to St. Paul's preference for love and knowledge rather than for mystical experience divorced from disciplined responsibility. Gradually the Church came to see that monastic renunciation was valid only for a few, a fact which Kirk uses to reinforce his conviction that domestic responsibility is a legitimate channel for the rigoristic impulse. Once this channel of responsibility is accepted it cannot be renounced, since to turn one's back upon family duties once they have been accepted is to violate duty to God. The book gathers several anecdotes from early monasticism which warn the family man against turning to monasticism.

Attempted reforms within monasticism are interpreted by Kirk as the effort of the Church to hold the rigoristic impulse in proper bounds. In its effort to set life in the ordinary world on an equal basis with monastic discipline the Church created a double moral standard of equally honored alternatives, even though the struggle to emphasize the equality was long and difficult. Even with the addition of manual work and practical service to the monastic way the assumption persisted that the monastic life was superior as a path to the vision of God. The fourth, fifth, and sixth centuries sought to bring monastic life into closer kinship with the life of ordinary Christians, but the efforts at reform had difficulty breaking through the rigoristic assumptions of the monastic impulse.

The author observes that even monasticism cherished the beauty of the world it sought to reject. Theological minds sought valiantly to reconcile the rigoristic impulse of monasticism with the humanistic concerns to be found in the Gospel. It was St. Augustine (354-430) who saw the implications of faith for social existence, and even though he was personally involved in the monastic system, his doctrine of the two cities created a theoretical foundation for Christians who were concerned about the cares, responsibilities, and achievements of the earthly city as well as for the good to be achieved on a higher level in the city of God. Influenced by historical conditions that placed him between the rigorist and the humanist alternatives, Augustine made his major contribution to Christian thought with a doctrine of grace which proved incompatible both with the earned salvation postulated by rigorism and with the trust in human achievements implicit in humanism. Kirk honors Augustine for this achievement and also St. Bernard of Clairvaux (1090-1153), who did much the same thing in devotional rather than theological terms.

In the demands which arose in the twelfth century for lay participation in Church life on the basis of full significance and equality as well as the development of mystical piety Kirk finds reinforcement for the idea that life can be disciplined without resort to monastic withdrawal, and he also finds confirmation of the contention that man's thrust to know God has a perennial place in the Christian tradition. St. Thomas (c.1225-1274) found meaning in the natural order, but only when that natural order was embraced in the cradle of a supernatural realm. Thomas placed reason above asceticism and opened the devotional life to all men. The latter achievement was carried even further by St. Ignatius Loyola (1491-1556), and St. Francis of Sales (1567-1622).

Kirk's treatment is predominantly concerned with Christian experience and thought prior to the Protestant Reformation. Modern Catholicism and Protestantism receive brief treatment. Kirk's distrust of the radical liberty which he attributes to the leadership of the Reformers is clearly apparent. He suggests that the Reformers instituted iron discipline in their own churches to offset the decline of inward discipline created by their radical theory of freedom. The rise of the radical left is treated as a protest against the same trend. The predominance of petitionary over adoration prayer in Luther is considered to show that Luther's vision of God was less adequate than it should have been. But post-Reformation Catholicism revived the invalid form of the double standard and likewise diminished the true vision of God in modern Christendom.

The treatise ends with a plea for a valid vision of God, in which worship and service are united, in which the corporate dimension of the search saves it from self-centeredness, and in which the nature of service to God is truly disinterested. The self can be taken out of the center of its own experience only by a vision of God. When the vision is clearly apprehended reasoned orderliness replaces formalism and vital devotion to the crucified and risen Christ becomes the channel of a dedicated service replacing the false kinds of rigorism which otherwise abound.

CHURCH DOGMATICS

Author: Karl Barth (1886-   )
Type of work: Dogmatics; Christian ethics
First published: 1932 (unfinished)

PRINCIPAL IDEAS ADVANCED

Knowledge of God is totally dependent upon God's making Himself known; God has revealed Himself in Jesus Christ, His incarnate Word, to be triune—the one Lord who exists eternally in the three modes of Father, Son, and Holy Spirit.

The one Word of God, which is heard and obediently acknowledged by man through God's gift of faith, has a threefold form: "revealed," "written," and "preached."

Dogmatics is the theological science in which the Church critically tests the content of its proclamation by the standard of the Word of God; it thereby asks for the "dogma" in the "dogmas."

Creation and redemption are inextricably conjoined in God's one work of grace; creation is the external basis of God's covenant with man, just as the covenant is the internal basis of creation.

The Church consists of those who, through the power of the Holy Spirit, participate in Jesus Christ—His life, death, and resurrection—and who, gratefully living the life of reconciliation in the light and truth of God, witness to Jesus Christ as the Savior of the world.

Karl Barth has become a legendary figure during his own lifetime. Initiator of the revolution against liberal theology, one of the leaders of the "Confessing Church" in its struggle against the Germanized Christianity advocated by the Nazi regime, and writer of what many consider to be the greatest dogmatics in the history of the Church, this life-loving Swiss theologian has been acclaimed by his admirers to be "the Church Father of the twentieth century." Whether Roman, Protestant, or Orthodox, no responsible theology can hereafter be written without taking into account the theological position which has been expounded by Barth in his monumental *Kirchliche Dogmatik* (*Church Dogmatics*).

Karl Barth was born in Basel, Switzerland, on May 10, 1886, the eldest son of Fritz Barth, who was a pastor of the Reformed Church and later Professor of New Testament at the University of Bern. Karl Barth received his theological education at Bern, and then in Germany at the Universities of Tübingen, Berlin, and Marburg. The teachers who influenced him most were Adolf von Harnack (1851-1930) and Wilhelm Herrmann (1846-1922), two outstanding exponents of liberal theology. Though possessing a mind that was never uncritical, Barth began as an advocate of the theological liberalism espoused by his teachers.

The foremost characteristic of liberal theology is its anthropocentrism. Attention is focused upon man—to be sure, pious, ethical, religious, Christian man—but, nevertheless, man. In such a theology God is not forgotten, of course, but even the divine is to be found through His essential connection with the human: in man's reason, in his innate sense of ethical obligation, and in the depths of his feeling. It is hardly surprising that, even in the nineteenth century, Ludwig Feuerbach (1804-1872) charged that liberal theology is really nothing more than anthropology, and Friedrich Nietzsche

(1844-1900) proclaimed that God is dead. These keen-witted philosophers detected that the "liberal" theologians, in their attempt to accommodate Christianity to the modern world views, were, at bottom, pseudo-philosophers. Nor is it surprising that at the beginning of the twentieth century theologians had turned their attention to such subjects as the history of dogma, the history of religions, and the communion of the individual soul with God. Anthropocentric theology foundered in a sea of historicism and psychologism.

The time was ripe for revolt. All that was needed was an incendiary occasion and someone to strike the match. The First World War (1914-1918) provided the occasion; it smashed man's illusions of grandeur and inevitable progress, and starkly revealed his tragic involvement with sin and evil. Karl Barth, who in 1911 had become a pastor in the Swiss village of Safenwil, lit the fire whose flames rapidly spread into a conflagration designed to purify and reform the Church according to the Word of God.

The book which catapulted Barth into the center of the arena of public theological controversy was his commentary, *The Epistle to the Romans*, a work he undertook in order to clarify his own thinking. Published in 1919, and in a second, completely rewritten edition in 1922, this volume, in which the author tried to interpret the message of the Apostle Paul for twentieth century man, marked the turning point from liberal theology to a theological movement which was loosely designated during the 1920's as the "Theology of Crisis" or "Dialectical Theology." This theology emphasized the "otherness" of God, or what Søren Kierkegaard (1813-1855) had called "the infinite qualitative distinction between time and eternity," the eschatological nature of salvation, the dialectic of God's "Yes" and His "No" to sinful man, and the paradoxical character of the Incarnation. Against liberalism's tendency to allow God and man to coalesce, the watchword of the new theology became: "Let God be God!"

On the basis of his *Römerbrief*, Barth, who had now spent ten years in the pastorate, was invited in 1921 to assume the chair of Reformed Theology at the University of Göttingen. Here he launched an academic career which was marked by moves to the University of Münster in 1925, to the University of Bonn in 1930, and, finally, after being dismissed from his post at Bonn by the Nazi authorities, to the University of Basel in 1935, where he continued as Professor of Systematic Theology until retirement in 1962. Barth is an indefatigable worker, and his literary output has been prodigious, embracing almost every discipline within the realm of theology.

The first half-volume of his *Church Dogmatics* appeared in 1932, and by 1959 the yet unfinished work had grown to twelve large books. The overall plan is simple. The author has designed the *Dogmatics* as a five volume work, although the length of his treatment has necessitated the subdivision of each into part-volumes for publication. Volume I is entitled "The Doctrine of the Word of God"; Volume II, "The Doctrine of God"; Volume III, "The Doctrine of Creation"; Volume IV, "The Doctrine of Reconciliation"; Volume V, "The Doctrine of Redemption."

The extraordinary length of the *Church Dogmatics* can be attributed to several factors. First, because this is truly a *Church* dogmatics, the author has incorporated extensive commentaries on Scripture and on the history of doctrine, in which churchmen of all ages and persuasions enter into critical dialogue concerning the truth of the Gospel. Second, because of his conviction that ethics and theology are inseparable, Barth has included major treatises on general and special ethics. The treatment of general ethics appears in Volume II under the heading "The Command of God," whereas a chapter on special ethics accompanies each of the volumes on creation, reconciliation, and redemption, elucidating the command of God from the viewpoints, respectively, of order, law, and promise. Finally, mention must be made of this theologian's circuitous style of writing, whereby he moves round and round a subject, relentlessly asking ever new questions and delving into different aspects in the belief that this procedure will finally allow the truth to disclose itself. In this way he seeks to serve the truth, rather than to master it.

Karl Barth begins his *Church Dogmatics* by defining the task he is undertaking: "Dogmatics," he states, "is the scientific test to which the Christian Church puts herself regarding the language about God which is peculiar to her." The material to be investigated is the present proclamation of the Church, pre-eminently in the form of preaching and sacrament, and the criterion to be used is the Word of God, which assumes a threefold form: the "revealed" Word, which was originally and conclusively uttered through God's revelation in Jesus Christ; the "written" Word, which is the attestation of the Prophets and Apostles in Holy Scripture; and the "preached" Word, which is the proclamation of the Church. The latter two forms are dependent upon the first, but in the hearing of the Word of God today all three forms are inevitably interrelated. The function of dogmatics within the Church is to test its proclamation by the standard of Holy Scripture and under the guidance of its confessions. The task is made necessary because of the fact that heresy arises in man's attempt to proclaim God's Word.

Barth insists that the Word of God is God Himself in His revelation, and that man's knowledge of God is utterly dependent upon God's revelatory action. There is no way from man to God, only the way of God to man. God has chosen to reveal Himself on the plane of human history in the man Jesus of Nazareth, and He continues to reveal Himself through the Church's witness to Jesus Christ. In the act of God's self-disclosure, to which there is a corresponding act of faith on man's part, God makes Himself an "object" for man, albeit an object unlike any other, since He remains indissolubly Subject and Lord. The reason of the man of faith is bound to and determined by this object, and thus revelation prescribes its own "epistemology."

"Prolegomena" is that part of dogmatics in which an account is given of its pathway to knowledge, and since the theologian must follow the way God Himself has taken to make Himself known, prolegomena becomes essentially the exposition of the revelation of God in His Word. Here Barth expounds the doctrine of the Trinity,

for in Jesus Christ God reveals Himself to be the triune God; namely, the one Lord who exists eternally in the three inseparably related but distinguishable "modes" of Father, Son, and Holy Spirit—or, in terms of the special activity appropriated to each: Creator, Reconciler, and Redeemer. It is the doctrine of the Trinity that distinguishes the Christian God from all falsely conceived gods.

In Volume II Barth discusses in succession God's knowability, reality, election, and command. He reiterates that man has no innate capacity for knowing God; the possibility of the knowledge of God cannot be discussed apart from its actuality. Since God has chosen to reveal Himself in the "sacramental objectivity" of the humanity of Jesus Christ, the Word made flesh, any idea of a "natural" knowledge of God is rejected. The triune God discloses His being in the act of His revelation, which means that God's being and action are inseparable. The living God, declares Barth, is He who loves in freedom, and His perfections are those of the divine loving (grace and holiness, mercy and righteousness, patience and wisdom) and those of the divine freedom (unity and omnipresence, constancy and omnipotence, eternity and glory). These perfections of His being are manifest in the freedom and love in which He elects Himself for fellowship with man, and man for fellowship with Himself. The doctrine of election, declares Barth, is the sum of the Gospel, for it is the Good News of the reconciliation between God and man that has been accomplished in Jesus Christ, who is at once the electing God and the elected man. In Jesus Christ God says "Yes" to sinful mankind and takes upon Himself the reprobation which man deserves. In this election of grace God makes known His claim upon man, revealing His eternal will and command, and this is the foundation of all theological ethics.

Volume III concerns the doctrine of creation, that is, the existence of a reality other than God, and Barth emphasizes that this doctrine, too, is a doctrine of faith. Creatureliness cannot be known in abstraction from the Creator, God the Father, whose overflowing love is revealed and actualized in the Incarnation. God's election of grace inseparably conjoins creation and redemption, and the author illustrates this by an exposition of the creation sagas in Genesis 1 and 2. In the first, creation is shown to be the external basis of the covenant, whereas in the second, the covenant is shown to be the internal basis of creation.

Man is the creature who is determined by God to be His covenant-partner, and the essential humanity of man is found in his togetherness as I and Thou, male and female. Barth finds in this togetherness the *imago Dei*, for it corresponds to an analogous relationship of I and Thou in the triune God Himself. Because the Word of God reveals man to be a sinner who perverts his own true nature, knowledge of the real man is disclosed solely in Jesus Christ, in whom the existence of man in his proper relationship with God is actualized. While natural sciences can provide much interesting and useful information concerning human phenomena, theological anthropology, stresses Barth, must be grounded in Christology.

The doctrine of reconciliation, which is the heart of the *Church Dog-matics,* receives masterly treatment in Volume IV. Barth endeavors to present all aspects of this doctrine, from Christology to ecclesiology, in their intrinsic relatedness, so that the wholeness of the work of reconciliation shines through. Thus he expounds the person and work of Christ in conjunction with the nature of sin, the objective results of the atonement, and the work of the Holy Spirit in the Christian community and in the life of each believer. Reconciliation, he declares, occurs in two great movements that take place simultaneously in the life, death, and resurrection of Jesus Christ, who in His own person is truly God and truly man. The first is a movement from above downwards: Jesus Christ is the Lord who humbles Himself and becomes a servant in order to do the work of atonement (His priestly office); the second is from below upwards: Jesus Christ is the servant in whom man is exalted into fellowship with God (His kingly office). The material content of the doctrine of reconciliation is exhausted in these two movements, but there is a final fact that must be emphasized; namely, that both are combined concretely in the person of Jesus Christ, who is the God-man, the eternal Mediator. Thus He Himself is the Guarantor and the true Witness of the reconciliation that has been accomplished conclusively (His prophetic office).

The Church is composed of those persons who, through the power of the Holy Spirit, acknowledge in faith God's saving action in Jesus Christ, gratefully live reconciled lives in the light of this truth, and assume the responsibility of witnessing to the whole world that Jesus Christ is its Lord and

Savior. Indeed, Barth calls the Church Christ's own earthly-historical form of existence.

Volume V, which deals with the doctrine of Redemption, has not yet been written. In it the author intends to discuss questions about the "Last Things," the final judgment, and the consummation of the world. If Karl Barth is able to complete his *Church Dogmatics,* we can be sure that this doctrine will be illuminated by the same Christocentric focus that has characterized all his theology.

THE DIVINE IMPERATIVE

Author: Emil Brunner (1889-   )
Type of work: Christian ethics
First published: 1932

PRINCIPAL IDEAS ADVANCED

Christian ethics is the reflective examination of human conduct as this con- duct is determined by the creating, judging, and redeeming will of God.

The ethical element is inseparable from the revealed element; the good is based on the Holy; and ethics becomes a part of dogmatics.

Legalism in ethics must be rejected, for it displaces the proper object of man's ultimate allegiance and violates the center of human personality.

The ethical meaning of God's revelation in history is that man is designed for community; the individual cannot be understood apart from the community, and the community cannot be understood apart from the individual.

Christian ethical responsibility becomes effectual in the various divine orders which constitute the human community: marriage and the family, the economic order, the state, culture, and the Church.

Emil Brunner's *The Divine Impera- tive* was published in German under the title: *Das Gebot und die Ord- nungen: Entwurf einer protestantisch- theologischen Ethik* (The Command and the Orders: An Outline of a Prot- estant Theological Ethic). The pres- ent English title was used only after consent and approval were given by Professor Brunner. The work was un- dertaken by the author because it was his belief that since the time of the Reformation no single work on ethics had appeared which made the Chris- tian faith central. To formulate such an ethic is the projected task in *The Divine Imperative.* Only in the Chris- tian faith, argues the author, do we find the final answers to man's ethical problems. This faith has its source in God, concretely known as Creator, Judge, and Redeemer. It is the con- tention of the author that during the development of Christianity this faith has received one of its most decisive historical expressions in Luther's for- mula: "Justification by faith through grace." Consequently, Brunner concludes that "the Christian ethic is not based upon a principle, but upon this process of Divine restoration, whose meaning is disclosed in 'justification by grace alone.'"

The pivotal point in any theory of ethics is the problem of the good. The major varieties of philosophical ethics in the Western tradition have been determined by their conceptions of value. Brunner examines these varieties—naturalistic ethics, idealistic ethics, ethics of self-realization, and utilitarianism—and finds that none achieves a real synthesis. Each approaches the problem of value in a different way, emerging with insights that are valid up to a point, correcting the errors and weaknesses of rival views, but falling into embarrassments of its own. Thus each version of philosophical ethics has its own particular contribution to make but so also does each have its special weakness. Brunner claims that the deficiencies of ethics point up the natural limits of the philosophical approach; at best philosophy is critical and regulative, but it can offer no final ethical perspective.

Kant's position in this tradition of moral philosophers is in some respects an exception for Brunner, and there are some evident similarities between Kant's "categorical imperative" and Brunner's "divine imperative." In both cases we find an "ethic of duty" in which responsibility is understood in terms of an obligation to a specified command or commands. But this structural similarity does not conceal significant differences as regards both the intention and final norm of the two approaches.

Brunner's criticisms of Kant are basically two. First, Brunner argues that Kant overlooked the Pauline and Lutheran teaching on the "enslaved will," and thus he fell into the error of Pelagianism. The author does recognize the import which Kant attached to the notion of "radical evil," but this radical evil is seen to be ultimately subordinated to a moralism and rationalism which attenuates the tragic implications of evil and precludes the necessity for divine grace. If the moral law commands that "thou *shalt* become a better man," for Kant the conclusion follows that "thou *canst.*" Brunner's second criticism is that Kant's ethic fails to give content to the "good will," and thus his ethic remains purely formal. Insofar as any ethical content is implicit, it must be understood in terms of the principle of well-being as the material principle which governs action. In the formulation of his theological ethic Brunner is able to avoid these errors of Kant's idealism. Human sin is taken most seriously as a fundamental fracture in human existence, requiring for its atonement an act of divine restoration, and the content of ethical action is supplied by revealed commands. The will of God becomes the basis and the norm of the good.

Although the basis for ethics is the divine imperative, this divine imperative should not be legalistically formulated, Brunner warns. The command of the will of God cannot be condensed into a tablet of moral laws without doing violence to the personal and existential relationship which should obtain between God and man. The Christian ethic requires the obedience of faith, but the obedience of faith is different from that of the obedience of law. The obedience of faith replaces all spurious claims for human autonomy and self-sufficiency. Man cannot live the good life on the basis of his own resources. His ethical independence is thus denied and he becomes dependent—but he becomes dependent on God and God alone. In turn this dependence on God frees man from the bondage to any religio-moral law. The Christian ethic thus leads to a life of freedom. This freedom, however, has a paradoxical quality. It is a freedom from external, legal constraints, a freedom which is rendered possible through man's absolute dependence on God. In the last analysis freedom means being rooted and grounded in God. To be free means to be able to enter into a relationship with God, who alone is sovereign. Ethical legalism vitiates this movement of freedom and surreptitiously introduces an ethic of self-righteousness (Pharisaism). Legalism, in teaching that man becomes good by following the law, neglects the basic sinfulness of man and instills a false confidence. An ethic based on justification by grace alone shatters this false confidence with its acknowledgment of the tragic fact of sin and the need for divine restitution. The ethical question is thus not simply a question in the sphere of conduct but is relocated in the sphere of personality as personality is defined in light of the structures of sin and grace.

An ethic based on the evangelical faith is indelibly social, Brunner insists. The ethical meaning of God's creating and redeeming activity is that man is designed for community. The concrete response to the divine imperative is a response by individuals in the life of their community. It is in the life of the community that we see the concrete realization of the moral commands. The essential structure of this community is a complex of I-Thou relationships. Its essential directive is love. This structure and this directive provide the basis for authentic communal responsibility. Responsibility is determined by the fact that the "I" is always confronted by the "Thou." The distinctive quality of man's communal existence is that the other can be addressed as a "Thou." The directive which gives this "I-Thou" existence its final meaning is love. "The *meaning* of this existence, however, as a responsible reciprocal existence, is *Love*," Brunner writes; "Every human relationship which does not express love is abnormal. In Jesus Christ we are told that this love is the whole meaning of our life, and is also its foundation. Here the Creator reveals Himself as the One who has created us *in* love, *by* love, *for* love. He *reveals* to us our true nature, and He *gives* it back to us."

The communal significance in Brunner's Christian ethic is made explicit in his doctrine of the divine orders of creation. He defines five forms or orders which constitute the communal topography of human existence: the order of the family, the order of economic life, the political and legal order, the order of culture, and the ecclesiastical order. The distinctive character of these orders is that they are orders of creation essentially based on nature. They exist because of the psychological nature of man. Their structure is recognized not by faith but by reason. Although Brunner is openly and sharply critical of the classical notion of natural law because of its tendencies toward legalism, his own theory of the natural orders exhibits a formal similarity to the classical idea. Insofar as God is the creator of nature, religiously and morally binding directives can be deduced from nature. The author formulates the argument that monogamy is the "natural" marriage relationship and is therefore sanctioned by the divine imperative. Two primary considerations lead him to this conclusion: (1) every human being is irrevocably the child of one man and one woman, and (2) genuine natural love is in its essence monistic, instinctually reactive against the intrusion of a third person. These factors indicate the intrinsically "monos" quality of the marriage relationship.

Man's economic institutions, like the institution of marriage, are founded upon a natural ordering of nature. God created man as a being needing economic organization. The provision of material goods is necessary for the preservation of life itself. Part of man's nature is thus that he is an economic creature, inextricably involved with various forces of production and exchange that structure his communal existence. A specific ethical implication of this fact is the assignment of dignity to economic activity. Economic activities, in that they arise from a natural order, are not "low" or "unspiritual." One of the contributions of Luther, the author maintains, was the restoration of the dignity of labor through his doctrine of the "calling" after this dignity had been obscured by the monastic ethic of the Middle Ages. However, there is another side to the natural orders which must not be neglected—the pervasive reality of sin. The natural orders, good by virtue of their grounding in the divine creativity, are nonetheless subject to the distortions and ambiguities of a sinful existence. This sin expresses itself as pride, and its effects can be seen in the economic order in the instances of exploitation and the false tendencies of specific economic programs to become ends in themselves, become absolutized, and demand ultimate allegiance. So whereas God as Creator requires of man that his first duty is to adjust himself to the natural orders, God as Redeemer requires of man that his second duty is to transform the existing state of affairs in view of the redemptive action of Christ and the coming of the Kingdom of God.

The state, like the community of labor, is a God-given order. The state arises from the self-consciousness of a people (Volk), united by a spatial environment, blood relationships, and a common destiny. Now the state, although equal in importance, is supplementary to the family and to the economic order rather than prior to them. With this insight Brunner purports to reject the idealistic view of the state (elaborated by Hegel in particular), a view which has an explicit emphasis upon centralized supremacy. The state as an empirical political unit is morally neutral. Hence, one cannot speak of a Christian form of the state, nor is there any justification for the institution of Christian political parties. However, man's relationship to the state does take on moral meaning when viewed in the religious context of creation, judgment, and redemption. Like all natural orders the state must be understood as an expression of the goodness of God's creation, as corrupted by the Fall, and as subject to the process of divine restoration. This implies a regulative principle by which two unfortunate extremes can be avoided: (1) a false secularization which views the state as intrinsically evil, and (2) a sentimental radicalism which obscures the state's bondage to sin.

The community of culture, as the fourth natural order, includes man's activities in the area of science, art, and education. Like the others, this order also is part of the divine purpose, comprising areas in which God's creativity expresses itself in human creativity. But the cultural creations of men and women not only manifest the rational nature created by God; they also exhibit the tendency to transform intellectual and artistic forms into absolutes which become idols and threaten both personal life and the life of the community. It is in the realm of culture that the temptation to erect a "Towel of Babel" becomes strongest. It is for this reason that faith must always take a critical attitude toward culture and attack all demonic claims for absoluteness in the fields of science, art, and education.

The Church constitutes the fifth communal order. A church is a place where two or three meet in the name of Christ to hear the preaching of the Word of God. According to the author, this definition constitutes the heart of the evangelical faith. A father expounding the Gospel to his family affords us an instance of the Church in action. Nothing else is necessary to make a house a real church. However, in the development of the worshiping community there is an increasing institutionalization required to enable it to realize its central purpose. This institutionalization may take the form of a state church, national church, or free church. Each of these forms meets special conditions and poses special problems. But in any of its institutional forms the Church must be understood as the earthly and historical manifestation of the Kingdom of God. It is thus that the divine mission of the Church becomes explicit. Nonetheless, the Church is not immune from error and corruption. As an expression of the Kingdom within history, the Church is subject to the conditions of sinful historical existence. The Church and perfection are mutually exclusive ideas. Those who comprise the community of the Church are still sinners, and therefore the Church like all other orders of creation remains an imperfect community, permeated with the distortions of sin. The Church, like the redeemed man, is *in* the world, although not *of* it.

THE TWO SOURCES OF MORALITY AND RELIGION

Author: Henri Bergson (1859-1941)
Type of work: Philosophy of religion
First published: 1932

PRINCIPAL IDEAS ADVANCED

Customary morality and static religion take their rise in a closed society understood as an extension of nature; creative morality and dynamic religion take their rise in an open society which transcends the structural permanence of nature.

The principle of obligation in customary morality functions primarily as a force of social cohesion; the principle of obligation in creative morality constitutes an aspiration toward an ideal through which the given social order is refashioned and vitalized.

Static religion provides the sanction for customary regulations, resists the individualizing and dissolving power of intelligence, and is riveted in the spatial determinations of nature; dynamic religion transcends the spatially bound spirits and deities of a religion of nature and finds its culmination in the mystical vision and action of exceptional personalities, such as the Christian mystics, who make the vital impetus (élan vital) effectual as a force of creative and transforming love.

Henri Bergson's approach in *The Two Sources of Morality and Religion* to the problem of the nature and origin of morality and religion is an empirical one; however, his empiricism must be understood in the broadest sense of the term. He appeals to experience, but this experience includes both the findings of scientific research and the records of the insights of the mystics. He makes use of the genetic approach in his description of morality and religion as universally given phenomena, and consequently he draws heavily from the discoveries in modern anthropology and sociology. Yet he is well aware of a possible misuse of the genetic approach insofar as it leads to the genetic fallacy. The genetic approach does not provide a criterion of evaluation. A description of origins cannot produce value judgments. Facts should not be confused with values.

The author begins his essay with a discussion of the nature of moral obligation. Moral obligation has been expressed in two ways in the history of mankind. On the one hand there are the obligations which arise out of a customary morality; on the other hand there are those which arise from a creative morality. In customary morality moral obligation functions primarily as a force of social cohesion. The directives which issue from it seek to perpetuate the existing social order, thus maintaining a given structure and equilibrium. This customary morality presupposes a "closed society" which in the author's words comes "fresh from the hands of nature." Customary morality is thus rooted in nature. Man was made for society just as the ant was made for the antheap. The distinctive feature of such natural phenomena as anthills and beehives is that each member is riveted to the given natural structure, and the task of each member is that of perpetuating the structure. The organization is fixed and invariable. A society of ants constitutes a "closed society." Although the author cautions the reader about overworking the analogy, he finds that it does convey a fundamental point. A "closed society" of human beings is similar to that of the ants in that the original structure of organization is perpetuated without consideration of critical questions concerning the need and nature of this structure. The preservation of society becomes the chief end of man. The morality of such a society must of necessity be a customary morality, one which finds its directives in the already established customs and mores. The power of motivation in such a morality comes from what Bergson calls "the totality of obligation." Obligation cannot be reduced to any one thing. Instinct and intelligence, passion and reason, habit and reflection interpenetrate in a proliferous configuration which in its totality defines the requirements of social life. The essence of obligation is thus quite clearly different from any requirements of an isolated and abstracted reason. Nonetheless, intelligence and reason are ever present, and specifically they are present in the task of legalizing the accumulated customs and habits. Customary morality thus becomes a morality of law.

Creative morality has its source in the aspiration toward an ideal rather than in the accumulated customs and habits which form the basis of obligation in customary morality. Such a creative morality requires an open rather than a closed society. In an open society the given organizational complexes are constantly subjected to critical questioning and evaluation. Instead of simply perpetuating the existing social order, creative or ideal morality seeks to change it. Customary morality is static, resistant to change and innovation; creative morality is dynamic, constantly striving to refashion and transform the given. The two moralities thus differ in essence; yet, at the same time, they are not wholly discontinuous.

The open society cannot dispense with customary regulations entirely. This would lead to chaos. Thus, it must seek to appropriate the stabilizing norms of customary morality and to find a place for them in its program of creative transformation. "Current morality is not abolished; but it appears like a virtual stop in the course of acutal progression. The old method is not given up; but it is fitted into a more general method, as is the case when the dynamic reabsorbs the static, the latter then becoming a mere particular instance of the former."

The dialectical relation between the old and the new, the static and the dynamic, is exemplified in the development of the concept of justice. Justice was first a social category, used as a norm to order the existing elements of a given society. But gradually justice emerged from social life and soared above to a transcendent and universal plane. Through this process of development its specific social function is not abolished, but this function receives its final definition through a principle which transcends the particular society. Morality thus becomes a "human" morality and is no longer simply a "social" morality.

Whereas customary morality becomes solidified into a morality of law, creative morality remains the morality of exceptional men. It is the exemplary life of the mystic, in particular, which supplies the touchstone. It is in the personality of the mystic that the *élan vital*, the fundamental principle of life itself, receives its most decisive expression. Creative morality is thus founded on the vital impetus, the dynamo in the process of creative evolution, which electrifies and inspires exceptional men in history.

Bergson's discussion of the nature of static and dynamic religion proceeds with an eye to this previously made distinction between customary and creative morality. Static religion and customary morality are coupled, as are creative morality and dynamic religion. The first function of religion, as that of morality, is social preservation. In primitive society morality is coextensive with religion. The whole of morality is custom, and religion provides the final sanction for customary regulations. Primitive religion thus takes precautions against any tendencies toward individualization by which the human intelligence may threaten the cohesion of the group. It is in light of this that primitive religion can be understood as "a defensive reaction of nature against the dissolvent power of intelligence." Primitive religion fights all forces which threaten group solidarity. This accounts for its static character. Like customary morality primitive religion is but an extension of nature, and such religion strives to maintain the structural and organizational permanence exhibited by anthills and beehives. Closely allied with the first function of static, primitive religion is the second function. This is its function as "a defensive reaction of nature against the representation, by intelligence, of the inevitability of death." Intelligence, through the process of generalization, discloses the universality and inevitability of death. Life is transitory and marked for destruction. Religion resists the implications of this generalization and instinctively affirms a belief in an afterlife. The idea that men live on as phantoms or shadowy replicas of what they were in this life is a natural belief present in all primitive cultures.

The static character of primitive religion can also be seen in its close alignment with magic, in spite of the essential difference between the two phenomena. In religion the individual seeks a relationship with a power conceived to be intrinsically personal; magic has to do with a mechanical manipulation of impersonal forces. Magic and religion thus go their separate ways and there can be no reduction of one to the other. Yet, the anthropological fact remains that in primitive religion the two phenomena are intertwined, and as a result of this mixture magic confers upon religion a static quality. This becomes evident through an inspection of the governing formula of magic, "Like is equivalent to like," which is itself convertible to the formula, "The static can replace the dynamic if it traces the pattern of the latter."

The more basic factor, however, in determining the static character of primitive religion is its bondage to space. Each spirit is bound to the spatial locality where it manifests itself. The multiple spirits in animism as well as the plurality of gods in polytheism are riveted to space. In the various religions this spatial quality is expressed in different ways. The gods depicted in the Vedic poems have their spheres of influence in the heavens, earth, and middle air respectively. Babylonian cosmology designates the sky as the realm of Anu, the earth belongs to Bel, and the sea is the dwelling place of Ea. In Greek religion we find again that the world is spatially dissected according to divine regions. Zeus is the god of heaven and earth, Poseidon is the god of the sea, and Hades is sovereign over the underworld. Static religion gives priority to the category of space.

Dynamic religion is a religion of time rather than of space. The vital impetus, which provides the ultimate basis for dynamic religion as it does for creative morality, permeates the entire evolutionary process and thus transcends every given spatial region. It thus supplants both animism and polytheism. The apex of this dynamic religion, as the author has suggested earlier, is mysticism. It is in the great mystics, particularly those of the Christian tradition, that dynamic religion attains its highest expression. The great mystic is defined by the author as that individual who is capable of transcending the limitations imposed on him by nature (matter and space), uniting with a divine reality, and transforming the given through the efficacy of human love and action. It is in Christian mysticism that such a movement is most illustriously exemplified. Greek and Indian mysticism never came to full fruition. The Greeks were too intellectual to be capable of mysticism. Plotinus, remaining faithful to this Greek intellectualism, never reached the final stage—the stage in which contemplation drives beyond itself to action. In Plotinus there is no union with a divine will and no consequent transformation of the human will. In Indian religion, mysticism is thwarted by a philosophy of pessimism which seeks not only to quench the fires of the will-to-live but also to depreciate everything finite and earthly. Complete mysticism is achieved only by the great Christian mystics. St. Paul, St. Teresa, St. Catherine of Siena, St. Francis, and St. Joan of Arc are listed as some of the most illustrious examples. Christian mysticism is a dynamic mysticism, a mysticism of action. It strives for a baptism of the will. The ecstatic union is not the point of culmination. The "vision of God" leads the Christian mystic to decisive action. The all-pervading directive in this decisive action is love. "God is love, and the object of love: herein lies the whole contribution of mysticism."

The mystic vision and the ensuing action evince an interrelated complex which is suprarational in character. Dynamic religion, like creative morality, transcends the merely rational and intelligible. This is why the author expresses some far reaching reservations regarding the religious significance of the "God of philosophy" (as had Pascal three centuries earlier). The God of the great mystics is not the God of the rational philosophers. Yet, according to the author, there is no complete break between reason and the mystic vision. Reason is transcended but not vitiated. Dynamic religion itself, although differing in essence from static religion, retains images and symbols borrowed from static religion which it then uses for its own propagation. Static religion is deepened with the new directive of love as expressed in the exemplary mystics, but its social function is not denied. It is transfigured but not abrogated.

THE LIVING GOD

Author: Nathan Söderblom (1866-1931)
Type of work: Philosophy of revelation
First published: 1933

PRINCIPAL IDEAS ADVANCED

Religious research indicates that the religion of revelation, of divine self-communication, is a definite type within the history of religions.

The Bible distinguishes between a general revelation of God and a special unique revelation of God in Christ.

The uniqueness of Christianity consists in the fact that God has chosen to reveal Himself in a special person of history, Jesus of Nazareth; the historic person of Jesus is, therefore, the full revelation of God on earth.

God's revelation is never finished, however, and can be seen in nature, history, and in the moral life; the continued revelation of God in Christianity is the continued action of the living Christ in the Church and in the experiences of men.

Nathan Söderblom in his Gifford Lectures of 1931, entitled *The Living God*, concerns himself with the problem of revelation. He believed in a general revelation of God. "There is a living God," he asserted on his death bed; "I can prove it by the history of religions." This idea of a general or "common" revelation is the integrating factor of his entire theological system, of which *The Living God* is the most mature expression. Söderblom believed that the Bible told of a general revelation of God to all men and of a special revelation of God to Israel and the Christian Church. A revelation of God could be found wherever real religion was found; that is, "wherever we find religious sincerity." Wherever God is known, no matter how imperfect and distorted the knowledge may be, it is God who has made himself known. Söderblom writes in *The Living God*, "Religious research distinguishes the religion of revelation as a definite type within the history of religions, and in the same way the Christian faith marks off a special sphere of revelation. . . . But a measure of revelation, i.e. of divine self-communication, is present wherever we find religious sincerity. That has been expressly declared by the belief in revelation within and without Christianity."

Revelation is defined as the action of the divine making Himself known. Therefore it is obvious, Söderblom argues on the basis of his research in the history of religions, that Christianity is not the sole depository for "the divine self-disclosure." Real religion is not a product of culture, but must depend upon a revelation of God. Belief in a general revelation of God is forced upon us, claims Söderblom, when we make a serious study of the non-Christian religions, no matter how debased, degraded, or "ignorant" they may be, and however loudly they may call for the Gospel of the Cross. The same God revealed himself to the Buddha, to Socrates, to Epictetus, to Christ, and to Mohammed. The originality and uniqueness of Christianity consists in the fact that "unique and absolute truth has in Christianity the form not of a rule, a law, Dharma, nor of ideas or theologies; Christian revelation has the form of a *man*." Söderblom continues, "God reveals himself in a human life. In Buddhism Gotama Buddha, the Revealer, reveals the truth about suffering; he reveals a rule or doctrine, Dharma, and the result is an order of monks, the Samgha. In Christianity Christ reveals not a doctrine, but his own heavenly Father."

With the myriad savior gods, hero cults, and divine beings found in the history of religions, why did the Christ gain such an important historical position among all the other saviors of antiquity? Söderblom, in The Living God, gives three reasons for the ascendancy of Christ: (1) the Israelitic-Jewish tradition and the Bible with its monotheistic exclusiveness and the overpowering experience of the zeal of God; (2) the personal character of Jesus Christ and His supreme religious power, both in His dramatic and pathetic death and also in the strength of His personal gifts; (3) the historical reality of Jesus Christ. Söderblom uses I John 1:1-3 in this reference: "That which we have heard, which we have seen with our eyes, which we have looked upon, and our hands have handled . . . declare we unto you."

In all religions there is revelation, but not everything in religion is revelation. The miraculous is not what we cannot understand, but that which only faith understands. A miracle, like revelation, is an indication of a "divine interference," an act of God. Growth in faith, Söderblom asserts, means seeing more of God's acts in history; that is, seeing more miracles. Revelation as divine self-disclosure is a miracle. It is not found in the realm of science, which is concerned only with causal events and relationships. God never appears as a secondary cause; that is, as a cause which the senses can perceive. Religious wonder does not consist in an external miracle, a break in the chain of causes, but is rather an interpretation of the natural connection as caused by God; it consists in the

experience of divine guidance and in the belief in a meaning and a goal for that which happens. Therefore the explanation of an event by science and an explanation by religion represent "two different ways of seeing." The former looks for causes; the latter, for divine purposes.

Söderblom suggests an agnostic position in reference to our understanding of revelation. We can never say, "Here is God and revelation!, There is man and Nature!" Even in the perfect revelation of God in the person of Christ the divine and human are commingled.

Söderblom's conception of revelation leads directly to the problem of whether God is personal or impersonal. The author makes a distinction between two kinds of mysticism—the mysticism of infinity and the mysticism of personality. Söderblom suggests that we compare Jesus with Buddha. Jesus is a prophet, Buddha a mystic; that is, Buddha defines communion with the eternal as a union, in pure ecstatic enjoyment, of all personal, conscious selves in a beatific state of Nirvana. Söderblom calls this view the "mysticism of infinity." Jesus, on the other hand, reveals communion with God to be a "prophetic experience." Knowledge of God is of a living, active, personal or superpersonal almighty power, of God as the Lord of life and history. This mysticism is the "mysticism of personality."

The difference between the two types of mysticism lies in the role which the person plays in each. Is the person repressed or extinguished in order to attain to the higher stages of the religious experience? Or is the person re-created and an eternal loving union with God realized, the person growing into a new man? Is the way to knowledge of the divine the *via negationis,* which leads, as Plotinus said, to the other side of existence, to where the "soul without being good or evil or anything," without consciousness of body or spirit, receives the divine? "Must we, with Hierotheus, reach the mysterious, silent stillness, which dissolves consciousness and form?", Söderblom asks; must we with the Areopagite, or Eckhart, or Ruysbroeck, arrive at the "divine darkness," "the nameless, formless nothing"? Or, is the way to God a way of affirmation (*via positionis*), a way which leads through complete self-renunciation and self-denial to a richer and stronger personal life, to the revelation of the divine will of love in the most glowing, most perfect, and most nobly formed personal life, Jesus Christ? The highest endowment of life is a personal love built on the foundation of a living trust in God. Such love is a warm, human reality, whether in suffering or in jubilation. Emphasis upon such love is entirely different from the motif of self-sacrifice in mysticism, which is the renunciation of all human relationships. The life of Christ demonstrates in a manner never surpassed how man may live confidently in relation to his fellowman and to God. The Christ of the Bible, however, does not become truly a revelation until the veil has been lifted from our eyes and we are led to see the divine life; that is, when we are able to see "the will of God beneath all of existence."

Söderblom maintains that religion is always a personal matter. The only effective answer which can be given to the religious question is found in the "discovery of the real sources and conditions of revelation in the life of the human spirit." However, the relation of one person to another in the mysticism of infinity becomes at best something impersonal and is associated with an illumination, or knowledge. The influence of personalities upon one another is fundamentally antagonistic to a mysticism which transcends time and history. Therefore, society and history are hindrances to the religious life and must be rejected in favor of the inner life. Mysticism, Söderblom claims, eludes the ancient and fundamental Christian question: How can we reconcile the fact that Christianity is indissolubly joined to a phenomenon in time, with the claim that Christianity is the absolute religion? Within revealed religion the person is an integral part of religion and is recognized as such. Revelation exists for the person. The unexpected has happened in the history of religions. Revealed religion has reached its perfection, not in doctrine or as a guide to salvation, but in a person, Jesus Christ. He is "the perfection of divine love and of human faithfulness."

Ethical relevance is not lacking in the mysticism of infinity, Söderblom concedes. On the contrary, the ethical is given a prominent place in the process of "purification," and in those means by which communion with God is attained. But in the mysticism of infinity the actual communion with God is affected "beyond good and evil." The individual's personal life is repressed rather than fulfilled in the communion with God. In the religion of the monks, which is an example of the mysticism of infinity, writes Söderblom, personality entirely disappears. The moral life becomes an ascetic practice, a self-discipline for the purpose of transcending every "creaturely" thing. It is not service of God with the positive "ideal," the Kingdom of God, in mind.

Furthermore, Söderblom writes, it is important to recognize that the mysticism of personality still contains unusual and abnormal physical and psychical phenomena, such as visions and ecstacies. God permits His power and love to be revealed in heavenly visions and raptures. Important religious experiences can be clothed in such strange forms.

Within that complex religious creation which is called Christianity, the mysticism of infinity has always remained, Söderblom claims. Historically, the mysticism of infinity is seen in the idea of the "consciousness of God," an idea which tended toward pantheism and abstract idealism. It is also seen in a conception of a Christ who is detached from history and becomes part of the mystic's inner life. Martin Luther, who for Söderblom was an example of a personal mystic, described "the communion of the Christian with God" according to the character of revealed religion, as contrasted with the sublime mysticism of infinity. Faith and confidence are expressions of personal relations. Basing his faith on Christ, on the revelation of God in Christ, not on any ambiguous or uncertain experiences of his own, Luther found his certainty of salvation. In the subsequent new life, resulting from faith in Jesus Christ, Luther found the distinguishing mark of personal religion. This, Söderblom remarks, was Luther's victory over mysticism.

Luther was able to identify the psychological experience which belonged to the mysticism of personality. The experience is the *terrores conscientiae*, (the "fear and trembling" of Søren Kierkegaard). The mysticism of infinity, however, seeks to unify man with God by destroying the creaturely nature of man. Only in this way, when the distinction is transcended between existence and nonexistence, between being and nonbeing, can union with God be achieved. The mysticism of personality, as expressed by Luther, cries out with the words, "Lord, spare me, depart from me! My guilt!" Here is man who cannot escape God—a God who is active, a God who crushes, but who also saves.

As we study the peculiar and distinctive forms of communion with God both within and outside revealed religion, Söderblom writes, we cannot escape the strong impression that in the mysticism of personality God conducts Himself in a manner entirely different from that observed in any other kind of religious orientation. God is active, intervening, self-communicating, attacking, revealing, standing forth in the life of the soul as in the world of history.

The "higher" religions represent a one-sided conception of the divine reality. Söderblom holds that the proper religion of revelation provides a richer knowledge of God. The religion of revelation, that is, the religion of the revealed God, the religion founded on Christ, knows much more of God. Therefore the Christian Church builds upon the experience of forgiveness of every regenerate soul.

Söderblom believes that the positive contribution of the mysticism of infinity is that in such a mysticism the divine is conceived to be other than that which is able to be expressed in conceptual terms. We cannot, asserted Söderblom, form an adequate conception of God. The God of Christianity is the "concealed God, revealed in

Christ." Christianity is communion with God through Christ. God can be conceived concretely only in the form of the Son. When Christ came, He had the power of making man's whole search for God an "antecedent of himself." The revelation of God in Christ complements what others have found, but it is this revelation which is the complete disclosure of the one God.

In conclusion, Söderblom makes the sincere piety of the individual the criterion for religious truth. Conviction about God, Söderblom claims, must build on an overwhelming personal experience of his reality, not on an accumulation of facts accessible to all. Religious knowledge is therefore subjective. Real piety is always "in its essence a secret of the soul, a revelation." In the sincerity of a heart in need of help there is something of God's revelation. The capacity to seek and find God is dependent upon the sincerity and seriousness of the seeker. Revelation requires a medium of expression, and the quality of the revelation depends on the quality of the personality receiving it.

NATURE, MAN AND GOD

Author: William Temple (1881-1944)
Type of work: Natural theology
First published: 1934

PRINCIPAL IDEAS ADVANCED

The emergence of mind in the process of nature suggests the hypothesis that the process itself needs Mind as its explanation.

The beauty and intelligibility of the world, and the phenomenon of morality are further evidence that the world derives from a transcendent Mind.

Transcendent Mind is personal; that is, it is governed by ideal purpose.

If the world is produced by Divine Personality, it is revelatory of Divine Character.

Like the angels which ascended and descended Jacob's ladder, the argument of Archbishop Temple's Gifford Lectures (Glasgow, 1932-1933, 1933-1934), follows a two-fold movement from nature to God, and from God to nature. In the first part, entitled "The Transcendence of the Immanent," Temple argues from the presence of mind in nature to the existence of a personal God in terms of whose purpose the world may be understood. In the second part, entitled "The Immanence of the Transcendent," he argues that only on the hypothesis that a personal God is revealing Himself in the world are the higher reaches of human experience meaningful. The title, *Nature, Man and God,* is well chosen, for it indicates what the author calls the "dialectical transitions of the argument": it is the problematic position of man in nature which leads our thoughts to God; and it is the revelation of God in the experience of man which at last enables us to understand and appreciate nature.

Nature, Man and God is a work in natural theology inasmuch as it does not rest its argument on the authority of revelation. The Archbishop was keenly aware of the tension which exists between the devotional and the critical frames of mind, or, in his language, between religion and philosophy. How shall we criticize that which, by its very nature, comes to us as authoritative? Temple's answer is, in effect, to take the notion of "criticism" in the Kantian sense. Given the higher religions, as part of human experience, what principles and categories are necessary in order to make them intelligible? Temple's argument is that the hypothesis of an Eternal Logos present throughout nature and history does make intelligible, not merely Christian beliefs, but the hopes and aspirations of all the religions of the world.

Although Temple calls himself a realist and is at pains to make clear his acceptance of "the new situation" in philosophy, his main argument, from the organic character of nature, and especially from the continuity between man's mind and nature, to Mind as first principle, has its roots in neo-Hegelianism. Temple follows emergent evolutionism in his account of the origin of mind, and he stresses the fact that in the beginning mind consisted simply in the organism's "responsive adjustment" to its environment. But, he argues, eventually there arose in consciousness a distinction between the self and the not-self; so that, while from one point of view minds are mere "episodes within the process," from another they transcend the process. Man "knows it while it does not know him."

But, the argument continues, that which transcends so much of nature can hardly be accounted for in terms of natural processes; yet, because minds are part of nature, if their origin is not explained, the world itself is not understood. Thus, it becomes reasonable to "test the hypothesis that Mind contains the explanation of the World-Process." This result marks Temple's first "dialectical transition." It is the hypothesis of "Immanent Theism."

The next step in the argument, which is to explore the extent to which Mind is immanent within nature, leads to an examination of values. In the pursuit of truth, beauty, and goodness, Temple argues, mind finds that the world is akin to itself and vindicates its interests and activities. Knowledge comes to have intrinsic value when, in addition to any instrumental use it may possess, mind discovers "its own principles in the world of its environment." The same is true in the mind's search for beauty; the aesthetic apprehension of nature and the appreciation of works of art both have as their foundation the meeting of mind with mind.

But the claims of truth and beauty, in which mind is related only indirectly to other minds, are secondary to those of moral goodness, for which the object is literally another mind. Obligation or duty, which in Temple's view is the foundation of morality, arises in social relations, and usually appears to the moral consciousness as a conflict between the interests of the self and the interests of the community. Moreover, this community does not admit of being sharply limited: as man progresses, "his mind finds what is akin to itself in the object, and he is on the way to learning that it is not only of a human community that he is a member, but also of a society which includes the myriad tribes of nature, animate and inanimate, because through all there lives and moves that Mind or Other akin to mind, with which in his Science and his Art man enters into fellowship." Thus, it is argued, man's most characteristic pursuits, which on the principle of the continuity of nature have to be viewed as immanent in the world, lead us to the view that the world owes its origin to a transcendent Mind.

In order to explain how mind can transcend process and create values, Temple examines the human personality, which, arising out of the flux, achieves a measure of self-determination by means of "free ideas." What chiefly characterizes man is that he is not determined by purely mechanical causes, but is guided by ideal considerations. Action determined in this way is called "purposive." In it lies man's "freedom," which is not indeterminism but "spiritual determination." "It is determination by what seems good as contrasted with determination by irresistible compulsion." Every organism is self-determined in the limited sense that it reacts to stimulation as an entirety; however, as Temple points out, nothing transcendent is involved, since the reaction is determined by the circumstances which exist in the present moment. Purposive action, possible only to personality, transcends the present and is determined by that which can have existence only in the future. Joining these considerations, then, to the previous conclusion, Temple affirmed that the world owes its origin to the purpose of a personal deity, or, in

the language of religion, of a living God. So he concludes the first series of lectures, "The Transcendence of the Immanent."

In the second series, entitled "The Immanence of the Transcendent," Temple develops his philosophy of revelation. His method is to employ the concept of Divine Personality as an explanatory hypothesis, one to be tested in terms of its ability to render intelligible the religious experience of mankind. Although Temple claims that a spiritual interpretation of the universe is more acceptable to general science in modern times than formerly, he holds that truth is better served when religion and science operate each within its proper province.

From the hypothesis that the world is the handiwork of a personal God, it follows that everything in nature is a "self-communication" of a purposive being, first of all to Himself, but also, because personality "exhibits itself supremely in the purposes of fellowship and love," to created persons. But although all of God's acts, as expressions of His freedom, are to some degree revelatory of His character, there is no reason to suppose that they are all equally revelatory. The Divine Logos, universally effective in the world, might act for centuries without disclosing the more personal aspects of His being; then, when the time is suitable, God may manifest Himself in more intimate ways. General revelation is thus the ground for special revelation which, according to Temple, need involve no breach with the ordinary processes of nature. For example, the birth of Christ from a virgin "is due to the same cause as other normal births, namely, the Will of this same Logos, now aiming at a special and unique result." The particularly revealing purpose of the one act does not make it any *more* God's act than other births, but merely makes it more fully expressive of Himself.

Temple distinguishes, even in the sphere of special revelation, between the revelation itself and the record of the revelation. The essence of revelation is "the intercourse of mind and event, not the communication of doctrine distilled from that intercourse." God reveals Himself in events, but an event is revelatory only when another person responds to it. For example, God spoke to the prophets of Israel through historical events; their words serve as the expression of their "personal apprehension of the Divine Character and activity as disclosed." And this apprehension is as much a submission of the will as it is an informing of the mind. Although it is true that many who read the words of the prophets are convinced that through those words God has spoken to their own souls, still "what is revealed is not truth concerning God, but God himself." Thus, revelation is not conceptual. Temple says, "I do not believe in any creed, but I use certain creeds to express, to conserve, and to deepen my belief in God."

Although God is not communicated through concepts, what is revealed is, according to Temple, intelligible. God is incomprehensible in the sense that what is Infinite can never be grasped by the finite, but this does not mean that His nature is unintelligible. Temple claims that there is "an impassable distinction between Creator and creature, Redeemer and redeemed," but he maintains nevertheless that "in so far as God and man are spiritual they are of one kind; in so far as God and man are rational, they are of one kind." Thus

Temple guards against superstition and fanaticism; in the long run, revelation must satisfy the deep-seated demands of human reason and conscience.

The claim that a transcendent purpose is manifest in nature and history raises a profound philosophical issue; namely, how the eternal can be understood as present in time. Temple discusses three traditional views. The first, which he attributes to Plato, holds that there is a one-way dependence of the temporal on the Eternal. The second, which is presumably that of Spinoza, is that Eternity is the totality of temporal events apprehended simultaneously. The third is the view, more appealing to imagination than to the reason, which conceives the Eternal as outside the world and time, and yet as persisting through it, so that time makes a difference to Eternity. Since none of these views was satisfactory to Temple, he developed a synthesis of his own.

Temple suggests that we be guided by what we know of human creativity and that we think of the world and history as grounded in God's will. God's thoughts are expressed not only in nature but also in the lives of men whom, however, He must control "according to the law of their being which he has imposed upon them"; that is, through what appears good to their unforced will and affection. Only in some such manner, Temple writes, is it possible to preserve the importance of the temporal and its characteristic meaning without surrendering "the complete and all-controlling supremacy of the Eternal." Temple calls this the "sacramental" view of the universe, because, like a sacrament, the world is viewed as "the effectual expression or symbolic instrument of spirit," yet in such a way that the natural order of things is given full cognizance. The Incarnation is the outstanding and unique instance of a direct expression of spirit through embodied existence. Christianity is the most "materialistic" of religions, Taylor suggests, in that it does justice to embodied existence.

BEING AND HAVING

Author: Gabriel Marcel (1889-   )
Type of work: Christian philosophy
First published: 1935

PRINCIPAL IDEAS ADVANCED

Man's capacity for thought sets him over against himself and the world.

In his anxiety to recover wholeness, he seizes upon the objects of thought and by their means tries to have the world.

Because thoughts are abstractions from being, a genuine recovery must come through concrete approaches, such as faith, prayer, and sacrifice.

The only way in which we can know being is by addressing it in the second person.

Metaphysics, like religion, is concerned not with a problem but with mystery.

The most direct paths for approaching mystery are through such spiritual means as fidelity, love, and hope.

Being and Having is a metaphysical diary, covering a period of five years, beginning in the Fall of 1928, shortly before Marcel's conversion to Christianity and his baptism into the Roman Catholic church. Besides the diary, Marcel has included several short essays, addresses, and book reviews which further develop the themes dealt with in the diary.

The title is taken from the two contrasting themes which appear as the author's thought unfolds itself. At the beginning of the work, Marcel is mainly exploring the problem of *being* (ontology); but as the investigation proceeds, he finds himself asking why modern man has characteristically avoided the problem of *being* in favor of the problem of knowledge and the problem of value. His answer to this question comes midway through the work when it occurs to him that the anti-ontological bias of modern thought is an expression of a fundamental attitude which he calls *having*.

Marcel's philosophy is unsystematic by its very nature, a chain of reflections rather than a set of conclusions, so that it is in his journals, dramas, and other occasional writings that one finds his ideas most authentically expressed. The present work, which is a continuation of his longer *Metaphysical Journal* (1914-1923), is a nuclear work; and if it lacks the organization of a system, it possesses the kind of unity which characterizes a successful improvisation.

Marcel was reared outside the Church. His philosophical training was mostly in the Neo-Kantian and Neo-Hegelian tradition. But his original work in philosophy, beginning as early as 1914, led him, with many of his contemporaries, away from idealism toward realism. Following his own line of development, Marcel found himself approaching more and more closely to religious faith. In time, partly due, no doubt, to the influence of such confessing Christians as Nikolai Berdyaev (1874-1948), Jacques Maritain, and François Mauriac, men of note who moved in the same intellectual circles as his own, Marcel declared himself at last "hemmed in" by Christianity; and, after submitting to instruction, he was baptized on March 23, 1929.

Even before he was converted, Marcel believed that the direct communion with reality called "faith" is experienced by some men, although he counted himself as one who was denied this experience. After he was converted, it seemed to him that to believe in the faith of others is itself a kind of faith. "The fact is," he told a group of Christian students in 1934, "that when we have already come as far as this, we are in an open and expectant state of mind which either implies faith or is faith." In his opinion, many who think of themselves as unbelievers are in this condition. He contrasts their unbelief with that of those persons whose minds are closed and unexpectant because they have embraced a set of preconceptions which on principle exclude faith.

Openness and expectancy character-

ize quite well Marcel's philosophical outlook. As he views the human predicament, man's capacity for thought poses a threat to his integrity. Descartes and his followers were mistaken, he says, in believing that thought is identical with being. On the contrary, thought abstracts from being, both as respects the thinker and the thought. In this sense, thought is "a sort of lie, or rather a sort of fundamental blindness." Knowledge, if it is based on a recognition of this initial blindness, is a return to being and a recovery of man's integrity. But none of us is disposed to begin with this recognition. In our anxiety at being alienated from being, we seize upon the abstractions of thought as if they were things, and then we fix them in a framework of ideal relations which we call the "world." Therefore, what we commonly call knowledge rests on self-deception, and it places a permanent barrier between man and reality.

These two ways of knowing are, however, merely expressions of two fundamental modes of responding to the ambiguities of the human situation. The kind of knowing which abstracts the ego and the object from reality and sets man up as a spectator of the world is, according to Marcel, a subtle form of the mode of *having*. To *have* anything implies, on the one hand, a kind of egotism. If I have knowledge, wealth, or power, my self is enhanced in its own eyes. On the other hand, to have implies a dualism between the ego and that which it calls the "world." What I have comprises a different order of being from myself, a world of things which are either objects of my passion or instruments for my exploitation. Marcel maintains that man's attempt to realize himself in the mode of *having* is self-defeating. "Having as such," he says, "seems to have a tendency to destroy and lose itself in the very thing it began by possessing, but which now absorbs the master who thought he controlled it. It seems that it is of the very nature of my body, or of my instruments in so far as I treat them as possessions, that they should tend to blot me out, although it is I who possess them."

As Marcel sees it, if man is to recover his identity and a fruitful relation to reality, he must find another way of responding to his environment. Instead of viewing it as a spectator, he must become a participant; instead of seeking to manage it, he must commit himself to the "creative intention that quickens the whole."

Man's relation to his own body is a ready example. I can either say, "I have a body," in which case I think of it as an instrument to be used for certain purposes; or, by diminishing the sovereign pretensions of the ego, I can say, "I am my body," and make this recognition the starting-point for finding my way back to *being*. For, says Marcel, "incarnation" is "the central 'given' of metaphysics." He continues: "To say that something exists is not only to say that it belongs to the same system as my body (that it is bound to it by certain connections which reason can define), it is also to say that it is in some way united to me as my body is."

To Marcel, the way of participation in being is what mankind has always known as religion. Like everything else in man's experience, religion is subject to ambiguity, and it easily slides into an object of *having*. But in its genuine expressions (faith, prayer, sacrifice) religion is the way in which man overcomes his alienation from *being*.

As early as 1918, Marcel argued, in the *Metaphysical Journal*, that what sets the religious frame of mind over against the scientific is that the religious man, like the lover, apprehends the Other as *thou*. The scientist, when he investigates a man, regards the object at hand in the "third person," grammatically speaking. This, says Marcel, does not exclude the possibility of a shift in perspective enabling the scientist to know the man in the "second person" as a friend. But, Marcel maintains, a contradiction enters when we try to apply the scientific attitude not simply to other entities, be they persons or things, but to the total environment, as if we ourselves were not involved in the very thing we try to reduce to the status of an *it*. "I would be prepared to say dogmatically," writes Marcel in the *Metaphysical Journal*, "that every relation of being to being is personal and that the relation between God and me is nothing if it is not a relation of being with being, or, strictly, of being with itself." This leads Marcel to declare that "God is the absolute *thou* who can never be converted into a *him*," and to conclude that the only knowledge man can have of God is through prayer.

In *Being and Having*, Marcel points out that the same distinction which we make between a *him* and a *thou* is preserved in the distinction between *thinking* a thought and *thinking of* a person or thing. In the former case, thought deals with ideas, which are abstractions from being. The error of the idealist or the essentialist consists in overlooking this fact. In the latter case, thought is engaged with concrete entities, and it stands in direct relation with aspects of reality which cannot be intellectualized.

With this new distinction in mind, Marcel returns to the subject of prayer. When we pray to God, he says, we *think of* God in a manner analogous to thinking of a person. Marcel writes, "When I think of a finite being, I restore, in a manner, between him and myself, a community, an intimacy, a *with* (to put it crudely) which might seem to have been broken." Something similar takes place in prayer: "To ask myself how I can think of God is to enquire in what sense I can be with him." There are obvious differences, says Marcel, between our relations with other persons and our relations with the One in whom we have our being. But he points out that even in the former case, to *think of* someone is an "active denying" of space and time, in the sense in which they involve separation. Thus, common experience points the way in which thought overcomes the fragmentation which, in its utilitarian mode, thought introduces into being.

Marcel observes that one of the characteristics of *having* is to view what lies beyond its current limit as a problem to be solved. It is a mistake, however, to carry over into our concrete relations with *being* the notion of a problem or the expectation of a solution. Here, he says, we are "in the realm of the metaproblematic, that is, of mystery." Whereas a problem lies before me as something that I can "lay siege to and reduce," a mystery is "something in which I am myself involved." There is, says Marcel, a temptation to reduce a mystery to a prob-

lem, as philosophy has traditionally done in speaking of the problem of being or the problem of evil. This, however, he claims, is "a corruption of the intelligence." A truer way of proceeding is to recognize that every genuine problem "conceals a mystery"; that is, implies something which cannot be reduced to a problem or treated as an object. For example, "the act of thinking cannot be represented and must be grasped as such." It is a mystery, and lies outside every explanatory system; but it is not, for this reason, unthinkable. We can *think of* it, even if we cannot *think* it.

Marcel concludes that the "mysterious" is the proper province of metaphysics, just as the "problematic" is the proper province of science. He further holds that, at bottom, metaphysics and religion, the way which leads to Being and the way which leads to Holiness, are in some hidden way identical. The approaches to "the ontological mystery," are, therefore, not principally to be found in exploring the presuppositions of science, but "in the elucidation of certain data which are spiritual in their own right, such as fidelity, hope, and love, where we may see man at grips with the temptations of denial, introversion, and hard-heartedness."

Marcel's account of these Christian "virtues" is perhaps the most illuminating part of his study. Faith, he says, presupposes fidelity, which, in turn is based upon commitment, an act of freedom by means of which man affirms his own being together with that of the Other. Love, Marcel interprets as a process of "decentralizing" the self, of becoming more completely "disposable," more open to others, more at one with the Other, less "autonomous," and more "free." Hope, he sees as the courage to turn away from the false promise of *having;* like the latter it yearns for salvation, for healing, for the re-establishment of order and peace; but it places its confidence not in programs and techniques, but in divine power and beneficence.

Religion would, of course, be no more than a delusion if it were merely a readiness on man's part for a response that never came. The believer "witnesses" that the Other is responsive. He can do no more than witness; because his whole person is involved, he cannot ask another to stand in his place and verify his experience. Witnessing, says Marcel, is a kind of fidelity. As such it involves a "mysterious union of necessity and liberty." At its root lies the recognition of something given. "In attesting," he writes, "I really proclaim, *ipso facto,* that I should be going back on myself, and —yes—even annulling myself, were I to deny this fact, this reality of which I have been the witness."

For many years Marcel wrote about the religious experience without being able to witness to it. On February 28, 1929, he says, "I at once fear and long to commit myself." The next entry, five days later, is: "I have no more doubts. This morning's happiness is miraculous. For the first time I have clearly experienced *grace.* A terrible thing to say, but so it is. I am hemmed in at last by Christianity—in, fathoms deep. Happy to be so! But I will write no more. And yet, I feel a kind of need to write. Feel I am stammering childishly . . . this is indeed a birth. Everything is different."

Marcel records experiencing "heavy weather" while studying the catechism preparatory to being baptized. He also confesses the misery he felt when confronted with the claims of Thomist philosophy. After having looked at Christianity from the outside for so long, he found it difficult to get used to seeing it from within. His main support was "the desire not to be on the side of those who betrayed Christ. . . . It is that part of the Gospel which is the spring of inspiration in my present state." He had the feeling, however, that each resistance which he made was cauterized away: "Is this an illusion?" he asks. At his baptism, he was tranquil. "My inward state was more than I had dared to hope for," he writes; "no transports, but peaceful, balanced, and full of faith and hope."

Five years later, he looks back on the experience. "Is faith an escape?" he asks, in an address to a group of students. An objective answer to the question is, of course, precluded. Marcel can only testify that in many cases it does not seem so. "For instance," he says, "I can assure you from my own experience that my faith was born at a time when I was in an exceptional state of moral stability and personal happiness. Otherwise I might have been suspicious of it."

Marcel's faith, in spite of his submission, remains free, however, in the same sense in which the faith of his friend Nikolai Berdyaev remains free. (See Berdyaev's *Freedom and Spirit,* 1927.) He declares that he has no interest in denominational religion, and he goes so far in one passage as to say that if his conviction (that God does not demand to be loved *against* Creation but rather *through* Creation) is heretical, "so much that the worse for orthodoxy." What he appreciates in the Roman Church is certainly not its exclusiveness, nor its claims to possess a universal and objective truth, but "the interdependence of spiritual destinies" which there becomes a reality.

"That," says Marcel, "is the sublime and unique feature of Catholicism."

JESUS THE LORD

Author: Karl Heim (1874-   )
Type of work: Christian existentialism
First published: 1935

PRINCIPAL IDEAS ADVANCED

Except for Christ, all men are prevented by the relativity inherent in human experience from knowing God, who is Ultimate Reality.

The Christian claims that by surrendering his will to Jesus as Lord, he comes to know God.

If man refuses to surrender his will to Christ, he tends to regard Christianity as an illusion; if he surrenders to Christ, he tends to explain man's natural predicament as the product of a Satanic will.

Karl Heim has spoken of the development of his theological career under the figure of a stream which must flow past a mountain. The stream of his thought flows in the direction of trying to make experience intelligible; the reality of Christ, like a mountain, alters the course of the stream but does not choke it off. It is Heim's opinion that contemporary Protestant theologians, in their zeal to recover the uniqueness of the Christian revelation, have too often failed in their responsibility to make intelligible the relation between faith in Christ and the remainder of human experience. In an effort to bridge the gap, Heim has written a series of volumes entitled *Christian Faith and Contemporary Thought.* The present volume is the second in the series, and it is central to the project inasmuch as it is here that the reader is placed most directly at the juncture of revelation and reason.

Heim argues in the first part of the book that left to his own resources man is in a hopelessly contradictory situation. Both in his efforts to understand the world and in his practical pursuits, he requires some kind of absolute; but due to the structure of empirical experience, he can never find it. Heim uses classical mechanics to illustrate his point. Leibniz is his authority for saying that rest and motion are essentially the same: were we to conceive of all the bodies in the universe remaining at the same distance from each other, it would be indifferent whether we said they were at rest or in uniform movement. To arrive at the conception of rest and motion as opposites, we must posit an original "state of indifference," and then destroy it. Thus, rest and motion are in polar relation to each other. But, Heim maintains, what is true of rest and motion is true of all the terms of our mundane experience. Polarity is an original relation which is basic to every other, and our sensible world is a breaking-up of an original "state of indifference" to which thinking endeavors to return. This is true of light and dark, sound and silence. It is also true of the fundamental relations of time (now and then) and of space (here and there). Everything in our world *is* because of something else. There are no ultimate causes or final goals.

Requiring, as he does, some absolute, man has proceeded in one of two ways to escape from his relativity. The usual way is to affirm the reality of the phenomenal world and arbitrarily to declare that some part or parts of it have original status. For theoretical purposes, man takes certain truths as self-evident and certain kinds of experience as primary; and, as a basis of conduct, he maintains the authority of certain axioms and the primacy of certain ends. According to Heim, this procedure is essentially idolatrous in that it accords to that which is relative an independence which could belong only to a Reality standing outside the relation of polarity; and, in fact, the dynamics of existence being what they are, men's idols are constantly being overthrown. But not their idolatry: even self-styled realists, such as Oswald Spengler (1880-1936), who mock the claims of philosophy and morality, and attempt to explain reality in terms of will, race, instinct, and power, are merely substituting new gods for old.

Such is one alternative—to affirm the reality of the phenomenal world and to deify some portion of it. But in times of widespread doubt and despair, sensitive individuals have discovered the other alternative, which is to deny

that the phenomenal world is real, and to force thought back in the direction of the unitary "state of indifference" implied in our manifold experience. This, according to Heim, is the significance of mysticism, both Eastern and Western. However, because the "state of indifference" is implicit in our experience of the phenomenal world, it too is involved in the relation of polarity. Hence, as an attempt to escape relativism and to find the ultimately Real, mysticism must also fail.

There is, according to Heim, no way in which man can escape the absurdity of his situation. The curse of polarity makes it impossible for him ever to bridge the abyss between phenomena and transpolar Reality. He cannot even speculate how this abyss might be bridged from the other side. Yet man cannot live without an ultimate.

This is the background against which Heim invites us to consider the claims of Christianity. The early Christians, whose testimony has come down to us in the New Testament, professed an experience of God which transformed their view of the world, brought joyous calm into their hearts, and gave them victory over death. Unlike other religions, early Christianity made no claims within the phenomenal world, set up no sanctuaries, proclaimed no laws, ordained no priesthood. Its faith consisted purely and simply in the surrender of men's whole lives to Jesus as *Lord*. In this way, it opened up a radically new perspective.

Heim acknowledges that the "category" of lordship was already present in the experience of the Hellenistic age, even as it has been revived by such twentieth century "lords" as Lenin, Gandhi, Mussolini, and Hitler.

But leaders of this sort remain within the sphere of the relative. Only in Christ does "lordship" find its fulfillment, for His leadership, unlike that of the others, "encompasses our whole existence, not only the fate of our body but also all our volition and cognition, not only our life until death but our entire future destiny for everlasting." In the experience of absolute surrender to Jesus as the "one true Leader," the early Christian found himself beyond polarity, face to face with God, the ultimately Real.

Whether obedience to Christ does in truth enable a man to transcend polarity poses a difficult question. Since the claim which Christians make is incompatible with our ordinary view of the world, it can be neither established nor refuted by argument, but only in practice. Thus, in Heim's terms, the fact of Christianity confronts man with a radical either-or. Either he surrenders himself totally to Christ, which involves surrendering his cognition along with everything else; or, he remains under some other leadership (perhaps his own) and refuses to surrender his mind to Christ. In the latter case he will never know whether the claim of the early Church was true. Only if he takes the step and surrenders wholly to Christ can he know the truth of the claim.

Heim, of course, has taken the step and is persuaded that the claim is true. But his aim in *Jesus the Lord* is not so much to persuade others to take the step as it is "reflectingly to develop and describe the content of faith in Christ." Accepting Christ, he maintains, gives rise to a wholly new world view. The Christian can only fall into confusion and error if he first embraces a system of philosophy and then

seeks to enthrone Christ in it. On the contrary, he must start with the experience of Jesus as Lord, and then employ his reason in discovering "what this fact entails for an understanding of the world and of human existence."

According to Heim, the first question for the Christian philosopher is why mankind is estranged from Reality. Is it man's fault, or is it due to his creaturely condition? Other religions say, in effect, that man is not to blame, and their salvation consists in an attempt to deliver him from suffering, misfortune, and finitude. Instead of regarding man as the victim of evil circumstances, Jesus regarded him as enslaved by a Satanic will, which He came to destroy.

Here, then, is the Christian's clue for understanding the human predicament. Satan stands for a will that is more fundamental than any of man's particular wants and wishes, for it is the will which originally prompted the act of enmity against God. By yielding to Satanic temptation, man freely declares his independence of his Creator, and this fundamental choice determines how he henceforth apprehends the world. Heim agrees with the thesis of existentialist philosophy, that the will or intentionality of the observer determines the structure of his world. Heim's special contention is that all men have been seduced into rebellion, and that what is for man the ordinary world of objective experience, with its polarity, relativity, aimlessness, and uncertainty, is the result of this rebellion. On this view, man is to blame for his predicament; and the choice by which he became imprisoned within it is so fundamental to his being that he cannot, by an ordinary act of will, reverse it.

Meanwhile, through surrender of his will to Jesus as Lord, the Christian sees the world in a wholly new light. "If our heart is with God while we are watching the object, then we can see it with pure childish eyes. Then all that we experience, do and suffer is in the light of fellowship with God." Actually, however, no man except the sinless Christ is able steadily to behold the world in its true light. The condition of the Christian is that of a man in whom two world-views are in constant tension. Original sin remains to plague him. No more than unbelievers can he escape the curse of polarity. But for the believer a new polarity has arisen which embodies hope: the polarity between our world of sin and death and the heaven and earth of God's intention. The Christian has experienced them both and knows that they are contradictory; but he also knows that God, who has revealed Himself in Christ, will finally resolve the contradiction; and he lives in the burning expectancy of that consummation.

A second question for the Christian philosopher is how God is able to reveal Himself within the compass of man's experience. In the first volume of this series, Professor Heim analyzes the nature of speech, making use of the distinction between I-It and I-Thou relations which the Jewish philosopher Martin Buber has explored in I and Thou (1923). The "word," according to Heim, is the means by which one self encounters the dynamic resistance of another "eternally foreign" self and seeks to change its world. The possibility of such an encounter presupposes a common "dimension," just as the meeting of two infinite lines presupposes the dimension of a plane; hence, speech takes place in the world of objects, although the word itself is not an object but an act. It is in this manner, according to Heim, that the early Christians conceived of God's revelation in Christ. God speaks to men, they said, through His Son Jesus Christ. It is important says Heim, that God speaks through a Thou. For, although Jesus enters our world of experience, and takes His place as a creature in the same frame with other creatures, the believer does not behold Christ simply as a figure of history. But, just as the spoken word is heard against the background of meaningless noise (and silence), yet is not heard merely as a sound, so Jesus, while intersecting our ordinary world of objects, is experienced not as an object but as an act by which God's will impresses itself upon ours.

Heim describes his world-view as essentially dynamic. Man's existence is constantly being renewed. He is in flight between the past, which is the world of "it," the objective world of our polar experience, and the future, which is determined only insofar as it is willed. What the future shall be depends upon a battle between wills, a battle not merely between the competing wills of men, who are all alike doomed to destruction, but between Satan and God, and correspondingly between those who are in rebellion against God and those who have submitted their lives to Christ.

THE PARABLES OF THE KINGDOM

Author: Charles Harold Dodd (1884-   )
Type of work: Theory and interpretation of parables
First published: 1935

PRINCIPAL IDEAS ADVANCED

The Kingdom of God, as presented in the parables of Jesus, was not intended as a future, eschatological event, but as a present fact, a realized eschatology.

In the ministry of Jesus the sovereign power of God had come to effective operation as a historical happening to which men should respond by repentance.

Christian thought finds a supreme crisis in the ministry and death of Jesus Christ, when history became the field within which God confronted men in a decisive way and placed before them a moral challenge that could not be evaded.

As one of the leading British Biblical scholars, Charles Harold Dodd examines the treatment of the theme of the Kingdom in recent scholarship and argues in *The Parables of the Kingdom* that the New Testament parables refer not to some esoteric future event but to a contemporary reality. The older world closed with the ministry of John; the new world begins with the Gospels and with the ministry of Jesus. Until the end of the nineteenth century the parables were treated as elaborate allegories, as teachings clothed in unintelligible forms. Instead, Dodd argues, the allegories are the natural expression of a mind that sees truth in concrete pictures. The parables are not esoteric doctrines but are metaphors or similies drawn from nature or from common life; as used by Jesus, the parables were vital parts of the proclamation of the Kingdom. (The break in the tradition of allegorical interpretation came with the publication of *Die Gleichnisreden Jesu* by the German scholar Adolf Jülicher in 1886.)

The typical parable presents one single point of comparison. Details are kept strictly subordinate to the dramatic realism. What we must assume is that Jesus meant to point to an inward affinity between the natural order and the spiritual order. Nature and the supernatural are one order, we must suppose. The sense of the divineness of the natural order, then, is the major premise of all the parables, Dodd is convinced. A parable is an argument, enticing its hearer to a judgment upon the situation depicted. In each parable there is a challenge, Dodd claims, to apply that judgment to the matter at hand. The way to an interpretation lies through a judgment of the imagined situation and not through the decoding of the various elements of the parable. We should expect the parables to bear upon the actual and critical situation in which Jesus and his hearers stood. How are we to apply the parables? The clue for the application must be found in such ideas as we may suppose to have been in the minds of the hearers of Jesus.

The Kingdom is a present fact. But the King is to be King of all the world. Israel looked for a temporal and political messiah, but instead, in an unsuspected way, God's sovereign power became manifest in Jesus. For him, sovereignty is something other than the scrupulous observance of the Torah. The Kingdom is a present fact, but not in a sense which could be recognized in the then current Jewish usage. Despite Israel's inability to recognize the Kingdom in this form, something critical had happened: the sovereign power of God had come to effective operation as a historical happening which men should respond to by repentance. In the very earliest tradition discernible in the New Testament, Jesus understood Himself as proclaiming that the Kingdom had at last come. The final Kingdom has moved from the future to the present.

Dodd's analysis yields the conclusion that in the ministry of Jesus the divine power was released in conflict with evil. The parables of the Kingdom must be taken as realized eschatology, as the impact of powers of a world-to-come manifest in a series of events, unpredictable and unprecedented, in actual process. What is new is that this Kingdom is to be revealed on earth, not in some later transformed age. Jesus conceived His ministry as moving rapidly to a crisis, one which would bring about His own death, the acute persecution of His disciples, and a general upheaval in which the power of Rome would make an end of the Jewish nation. His foresight was primarily insight. His predictions were primarily dramatizations of spiritual judgments. Jesus declared that the Kingdom of God had come. His words suggest, not any readjustment of conditions on this earth, but the glories of a world beyond this. Even before His death Jesus declared the Kingdom

to have come, so that it was not uniquely connected even with His death.

The Kingdom is God exercising His kingly rule among men, writes Dodd. Divine power is effectively at issue with the evil in the world, making an end to the enemy's kingdom. Judgment is the primary function and weapon of the Kingdom. In rejecting Jesus the Jewish nation was rejecting the Kingdom of God, and thereby it brought itself under the judgment of that Kingdom.

Paul understood that the death of Jesus fell within the Kingdom of God, as a part of the effective assertion of God's sovereign rule in the world. The course of events which outwardly was a series of disasters holds within itself, for those with insight, a revelation of the glory of God. That this could be so, that apparent disaster could actually be the coming of the Kingdom, is the mystery of the Kingdom of God. The final state is now a matter of actual experience, but it is experienced in the paradoxical form of the suffering and death of God's representative. Thus the Kingdom has come, but in a strange and unexpected guise.

The Scriptures also refer to the Day of the Son of Man, and it is not made clear that this Day is identical with the Day of Judgment. Yet in all our primary Gospel sources, Dodd writes, Jesus is identified with the Son of Man. "The Son of Man" must have been at some stage a current Messianic designation for Jesus. In the Gospels themselves the term is never used except in the mouth of Jesus. Interestingly enough, the term most familiar in the early Church, "Messiah," is recognized to be inappropriate in the mouth of Jesus. To apply the term "the Son of Man," with its apocalyptical and eschatological associations, to a living man is no doubt a paradox; but it is also a paradox to say that the Kingdom of God, itself an eschatological fact, has come in history. Both the death and the resurrection of Jesus, Dodd writes, are eschatological events.

Dodd contends that we are confronted by two diverse strains in the teaching of Jesus, one of which appears to contemplate the indefinite continuation of human life under historical conditions, while the other appears to suggest a speedy end to these conditions. A drastic criticism might eliminate the one strain or the other, but both are embedded in the earliest form of the tradition known to us. We must face the issue, and it may be possible to find a place for both strains, if we make full allowance for the symbolic character of the apocalyptical sayings. The symbolic method is inherent in apocalyptic sayings. Thus it is open to the reader to take the traditional apocalyptic imagery as a series of symbols standing for realities which the human mind cannot directly apprehend. However, in the teaching of Jesus the traditional apocalyptical symbolism is controlled by the central idea of the Kingdom of God. But Jesus declares that this ultimate, the Kingdom of God, has come into history, and He takes upon himself the eschatological role of the Son of Man. Thus, the absolute, the wholly other, has entered into time and space. And as the Kingdom of God has come, so also has judgment and blessedness come upon human experience.

According to Dodd's account, the imagery retains its signficance as symbolizing the eternal realities, which though they enter into history are never exhausted in it. The Son of Man has come, but it is also true that He *will* come. The Day of Man stands for a timeless fact. So far as history can contain this fact, it has become embodied in the historic crisis which the coming of Jesus brought into the world. Whether the subsequent span of the Day will be long or short, men will henceforth be living in a new age, an age in which the Kingdom of God, His grace, and His judgment stand revealed. Jesus points his hearers directly from the historic crisis in which they are involved toward the eternal order of which the crisis is only a mirror.

The ministry of Jesus cannot be regarded as an attempt to reform Judaism, Dodd declares; His ministry brings something entirely new into the world, which cannot be accommodated to the traditional system. But what of the group of parables which refer directly to the expected second advent of Christ? Did Jesus Himself teach His disciples to anticipate His second advent after a long and incalculable interval? The idea of this group of parables is really that of alertness and preparedness for any emergency, Dodd's examination suggests. We may then ask, what was the emergency which Jesus had in mind? We know that He saw in His own ministry the supreme crisis in history. But there is nothing in the parable itself against the view that the emergency He contemplated was in fact the crisis created by His own coming, and it is this view which Dodd adopts and urges as the best interpretation of the parables of the second coming. It was not to be some expected crisis in the more or less distant future, but simply His own first advent which brought the emergency for which men needed alerting.

The crisis which Jesus brought about was not a single momentary event but a developing situation. He did not speak these parables to prepare His disciples for a long though indefinite period of waiting for a second advent, but to enforce the necessity for alertness in a crisis then upon them. The growth of the interest in the expectation of the second advent, then, must have begun as soon as even a few years had elapsed since the Resurrection without bringing the expected consummation. The Kingdom of God had actually come, unexpectedly, incalculably, and Israel was taken by surprise. In all of these parables, Dodd suggests, there is the suggestion of complete unpreparedness for a sudden disaster. The predictions of the coming of the Son of Man or of That Day are to be regarded as running parallel with the predictions of historical disaster then upon them.

The coming of the Son of Man, then, in its aspect as judgment, is realized in the catastrophe which Jesus predicted as lying immediately in store —the persecution of Himself and His disciples, the destruction of the Temple and of the Jewish nation. It seems possible to give to all these eschatological parables an application within the context of the ministry of Jesus as it has been recorded. They were intended to enforce His appeal to men to recognize that the Kingdom of God was already present and that the day of judgment meant that, by their conduct in the presence of this tremendous crisis, they would judge themselves as faithful or unfaithful, wise or foolish. Then when the crisis had passed, the parables were adopted by the Church to enforce its appeal to men to prepare for the second and final world-crisis which it believed to be approaching. Thus the early Church transformed the original intent of the parables and set our present problem of interpretation.

The predominant interpretation of these parables makes them refer to future history and to the coming of the Kingdom of God in the world. If this is the way the parables are usually taken, and if Jesus declared that the Kingdom of God had arrived, these parables indicate that the Kingdom was present only in germ, and they allow for an indefinite period of development before consummation. This is one way of solving the problem, and yet, Dodd contends, the interpretation of the parables depends upon the view taken of the Kingdom of God. The view which he takes is that the Kingdom is neither an evolutionary process nor yet a catastrophic event in the near future, but a present crisis. Dodd argues that it is not that the Kingdom of God will shortly come, but that it is a present fact, in the sense that something has now happened in the ministry of Jesus which has never before happened. The parables would suggest, Dodd feels, that a crisis which had then arrived was the climax of a long process which prepared the way for it.

The parables represent the interpretation which our Lord offered of His own ministry, Dodd concludes. Jesus used parables to enforce and to illustrate the idea that the Kingdom of God had already come upon men, there and then. The inconceivable had happened. History had become the vehicle of the eternal; the absolute was clothed with flesh and blood. In the events before their eyes, then, God was confronting them in His Kingdom, in His power and in His glory. This world had become the scene of a divine drama, in which the eternal issues were laid bare. It was the hour of decision; it was realized eschatology.

The parables proclaim: this is the hour of fulfillment. Yet the Kingdom of God does come with judgment, it is still true to say. The disciples forsook Him and fled; but afterwards they rose out of failure into a new life and understood only then how the mystery of the Kingdom of God had been finally revealed in Jesus' death and resurrection.

The preaching of the Church is directed towards reconstituting in the experience of the individuals the hour of decision which Jesus brought, Dodd concludes. The Kingdom of God had come, and he who receives it as a little child shall enter in. The thought of Jesus had passed directly from the immediate situation to the eternal order lying beyond all history, of which the spoken word was clothed in the language of apocalyptic symbolism. The pattern of history, so far as its spiritual values are concerned, is exhibited in crisis rather than in evolution. Christian thought finds this supreme crisis in the ministry and in the death of Jesus Christ with its immediate sequel. The supreme significance of the crisis lies in the fact that here in history the historical process became the field within which God confronted men in a decisive way and placed before them a moral challenge that could not be evaded. We have warrant, Dodd is convinced, for affirming that God comes to meet us in history and sets before us the open but narrow door into His Kingdom. This is the present significance of the Gospel parables concerning the Kingdom of God and its coming, and they in turn serve as the central fact in the interpretation of Jesus, His person and His ministry.

A NEW CRITIQUE OF THEORETICAL THOUGHT

Author: Herman Dooyeweerd (1894–   )
Type of work: Christian philosophy
First published: 1936

PRINCIPAL IDEAS ADVANCED

Philosophy presupposes a religious commitment concerning the origin of the world, the nature of its unity and diversity, and the origin and the nature of the laws that govern it.

The alleged autonomy of theoretical reason is unmasked by an analysis of the theoretical attitude of thought and by a careful investigation of the history of philosophy which discloses various motives at work, ranging from that of form and matter in ancient Greece, to the motive of nature and freedom in modern humanism.

The Christian philosopher is properly guided in his philosophical investigations by the open acceptance of the Biblical motive of Creation, Fall, and Redemption in Christ Jesus in the communion of the Holy Spirit.

A New Critique of Theoretical Thought, in four volumes, is the major work of Herman Dooyeweerd, the founder of a new school of Christian philosophy in the tradition of St. Augustine. The work first appeared in Dutch in 1936.

Volume I deals with the necessary presuppositions of philosophy. Volume II develops a theory of modal spheres and treats problems of epistemology. Volume III is devoted to an elaboration of the structure of individuality within temporal reality and to the development of a Christian view of society. The fourth volume is an index of the entire work.

The central thesis defended by Dooyeweerd is that a religiously neutral philosophy is impossible. Philosophy can furnish a theoretical insight into the coherence of the aspects of our temporal world, if, and only if, the philosopher answers questions concerning the origin of the world and concerning his own relationship to that origin. Such a decision with respect to the origin of the world, both in its diversity and unity, is nontheoretical; it is religious, the result of an act of faith; it arises out of a religious community. The Christian philosopher is guided by the motive of Creation, Fall, and Redemption by Jesus Christ in the communion of the Holy Ghost. The spirit of apostasy from the true God, in contrast, leads the human heart in an apostate direction, towards the deification of the creature, to the absolutizing of the relative.

The classical Greek world was dominated by the motive of form and matter, which originated in the encounter of the pre-Homeric Greek religion of life with the later cultural religion of the Olympic Gods.

According to Dooyeweerd, the second manifestation of apostasy in Western thought has been guided by the motive of nature and freedom. Modern humanism has consciously or unconsciously absolutized the theoretical attitude of thought and has secularized the Christian idea of creation and freedom, thereby emancipating human personality from its religious dependence upon the God of Biblical revelation. Humanism has given rise to a polar tension between a "Faustian" passion to dominate reality by the method of science and the "Titanic" notion of practical freedom, expressed in the idea of the absolute sovereignty of human personality. Humanism is, therefore, characterized by a struggle between pessimism and optimism: individualism opposes an irrationalistic trans-personalism; universal validity opposes individuality; form opposes matter; theory opposes life; speculative metaphysics opposes skepticism; and the concept of function opposes the concept of substance.

Within humanism reason is made the origin of our world. Reason becomes the giver of law. At times the laws of the world are hypostatized. Under the primacy of the ideal of science, the result is a freedom-idealism which hypostatizes the categorical imperative. When reason is the law giver, the ideal of science leads to the absolutization of special forms of scientific thought (such as the mathematical, mechanical, biological, and psychological). When the ideal of human personality is given primacy the result may be the direction of transcendental thought, in its *a priori* syntheses, toward the idea of freedom. In Kant, for example, in relation to the experience of nature, transcendental thought is the formal origin of the laws of nature; but as practical reason, transcendental thought is the origin of the norms of moral freedom. In speculative metaphysics reason receives its final hypostatization and is identified in a theoretical or in a practical sense with the Deity.

Humanism leads to irrationalism when it hypostatizes individual subjectivity, Dooyeweerd claims. It may end in a biologistic vitalism, or in an irrationalistic dialectical spiritualism and historicism. An aspect of reality may then be absolutized, and the conception of general laws may be rejected.

The idea of the totality of our temporal world is conceived in many different ways by humanism, writes Dooyeweerd. The laws governing the external world may be absolutized. When the ideal of science is absolutized, a particular mathematical or natural scientific system of functional relations within an absolutized aspect of the temporal world may be made the common denominator in terms of which all other aspects of reality are then interpreted. When the ideal of personality is absolutized, the totality of the world may be interpreted in terms of the *homo noumenon*, or in terms of a totality of values, in which both theoretical and a-theoretical values are unified into a hierarchical order, established by the autonomous freedom of human personality. The totality of the world may also be conceived in terms

of an infinite succession of individual forms, in terms of feeling, or as the historical stream of experience. The absolute idealist conceives of the world in terms of the dialectical development of the absolute Idea through the totality of creative individuality, viewed, for example, in terms of an absolutized moral or aesthetic aspect.

According to Dooyeweerd, the interrelationship between the various aspects of reality is also regarded in such a manner that the modal laws of the world are absolutized. An absolutized aspect is then made the basic denominator of reality, and the result is mathematicism, mechanism, biologism, or psychologism. The laws governing the cosmos are at times regarded as a general concept of function, in which theoretical thought creates the genetic coherence of reality, and individual subjectivity becomes a dependent "exemplary" or particular function of this law. At other times the law in the sense of the universal law of nature is reduced to a transcendental thought-form, which determines the sensory material of experience, while at the same time the law in the supersensuous realm of freedom is identified with the pure will of human personality, thereby leading to an unbridgeable dualism between the laws of nature and the norms of freedom.

The laws of the cosmos may also be regarded as technical symbols which enable man to adapt biologically to nature. Man is then regarded as a creative individual who is not subject to a universally valid law, but is a law unto himself in nature, in culture, and in ethics.

Dooyeweerd asserts that the many forms of humanism seek their starting point immanently within the created world and are, therefore, irreconcilably opposed to Christian philosophy. Any attempt at synthesis between Christian and non-Christian thought is doomed to failure. A genuine Christian philosophy requires a basic presupposition which is the theoretical expression of the pure Biblical *Grundmotif*.

The neo-Augustinian recognizes the priority of faith and unmasks the alleged neutrality of theoretical reason as a dogma which masks the religious foundations of theoretical thought. But the Christian philosopher, writes Dooyeweerd, chooses Christ as the Archimedean point of his philosophy. The *cogito ergo sum* and the irrationalistic *vivo in fluxu continuo, etiam cogitans* is replaced by: *Ego, in Christo regeneratus, etiam cogitans ex Christo vivo.*

Christ is the new religious root of the entire temporal cosmos, Dooyeweerd states. From this foundation regenerate mankind derives its spiritual life, always subject to the central religious meaning of the law; namely, to love God and one's fellow men with all one's heart.

The Archimedean point of Christian philosophy is freed of the obscuring effects of sin, but this does not mean that the Christian philosopher is freed of error. The freedom of the Christian against errors is guaranteed solely by the constant subjection of his work to the Word of God which reveals us to ourselves.

As Dooyeweerd sees the Christian situation, the regenerate human heart is the center out of which Christian philosophy proceeds. The heart, in its Biblical sense, is the religious root and center of human existence. The heart is the fullness of the selfhood. It is within the heart, Dooyeweerd claims, that our temporal functions find their religious concentration and consummation of meaning. The heart transcends the boundary of cosmic time. Although the heart transcends the diversity of the aspects of temporal reality, and although it transcends temporal thought, within this diversity the heart is not to be identified with a complex of functions such as the metaphysical concept of the soul found in Greek and humanistic metaphysics. As the fullness of selfhood the heart is alien to any dualism between the body, conceived of as a complex of natural functions, and the soul, conceived of as a complex of psychical and normative functions.

Christian philosophy is emancipated from the polar tensions characteristic of non-Christian philosophy. By belonging to Christ, says Dooyeweerd, the Christian wages a daily battle against the temptation to absolutize temporal reality and to withdraw it from God. The basic religious motive which directs the labors of the Christian philosopher, the Biblical motive of creation, fall into sin, and redemption in Jesus Christ in the communion of the Holy Ghost, implies a conflict at the very root of our cosmos, the conflict between the kingdom of darkness and the Kingdom of God. It implies further that common grace checks the disintegrating activity of sin, because of the regenerate members of the human race, but it does not lead to antinomies in philosophy. It does result in an absolute antithesis with all philosophy dominated by apostate motives, and it leads also to a grateful recognition of the gifts and talents left by God to a fallen humanity.

With respect to the ultimate origin of the world, the Christian philosopher finds that origin in God's holy, sovereign, and creative will. All laws, and all things which are subject to law, originate in God's creative will. The cosmos is subject to God who stands above the cosmos as the sovereign Lawgiver. His law is the absolute boundary between Himself and His creation. All creatures are subject to it.

The Christian philosopher finds the totality of meaning in its direction of philosophical thought towards Christ, who provides the root and fullness of meaning of the cosmos. The Law is fulfilled in Him, and all subjective individuality is concentrated in Him. Nothing is indifferent; nothing in our temporal world is withdrawn from His dominion.

The very coherence in the modal diversity of our cosmos owes its origin to the divine world order. The intermodal coherence of our world, its unity, is not a construction of philosophical thought, but an enduring effect of God's sovereign power. Each mode, each aspect of our cosmos is under divine law. Each aspect of our world is a sphere of law, sovereign under God in its own domain. The structure of each aspect points toward and is an expression of the temporal coherence of meaning which points beyond itself to Christ. The integral coherence of meaning between the modal aspects of our cosmos is guaranteed by a cosmic order of time. There is no pre-logical natural reality *an sich*, separate from the normative aspects of reality.

The universe is ruled by God's laws, Dooyeweerd insists. In their modal diversity, God's laws constitute the universal valid determination and limitation of the individual subjectivity subject to them. Therefore, Dooyeweerd concludes, the Christian philosopher cannot tolerate any theoretical conception of cosmic reality which is emancipated from a Biblical starting point, for all such conceptions are dominated wholly or in part by apostate religious motives.

TRUE HUMANISM

Author: Jacques Maritain (1882-   )
Type of work: Philosophy of culture
First published: 1936

Principal Ideas Advanced

Man is a spiritual being who can find fulfillment only as he is completed by God; hence, a true humanism must be a theocentric (God-centered) humanism.

The tragedy of modernity is that in its discovery of man and the temporal order it turned gradually to anthropocentricity, a process which led inexorably to man's descent into sheer materiality and subjectivity and from which there is no escape except by a rehabilitation of man in God.

The hope of humanity lies in the creation of a new social order designed to preserve genuine human values which, although Christian in spirit, have autonomy from the Church and will thus elicit the co-operative working together of all men of good will, in order that all men can find fulfillment through God.

In *True Humanism* Jacques Maritain shows, by the depth of his analysis of the plight of modern Western society, the intellectual wisdom which has made him one of the most widely read of all modern Catholic thinkers. Originally a student of Henri Bergson (1859-1941), the vitalistic philosopher of creative evolution, Maritain was converted to Roman Catholicism in 1906. After pursuing an intensive study of St. Thomas Aquinas (c.1225-1274), the architect of modern Catholicism, Maritain began a prolific writing and teaching career as a Christian philosopher. Primarily a philosopher, Maritain has been wide-ranging in his interests, even serving at one point in the diplomatic corps, and the topics of his books range from the most difficult metaphysical philosophy to devotional treatises on the liturgy. His own position is that of a Neo-Thomist, one who attempts to apply and interpret St. Thomas's teachings in such a way as to take account of what has happened since St. Thomas's day. Perhaps no one has done more than Maritain in showing the continuing intellectual vitality of the Thomist tradition.

He writes primarily as a philosopher, and an appreciation of his work requires some training in Thomistic philosophy. *True Humanism* presupposes, and does not really adequately supply, a general knowledge of the basic principles of Thomistic philosophy; hence, the reader would be well advised to acquaint himself with Thomistic notions of revelation, man's Fall, supernatural grace, and natural law, prior to a reading of this book.

Humanism is defined as that which "tends to render man more truly human and to make his original greatness manifest by causing him to participate in all that can enrich him in nature and in history. . . ." True humanism, Maritain contends, is theocentric (God-centered), not anthropocentric (man-centered). The only true way to find man is to seek God, for man is the creation of God and can find his fulfillment only as he is led by God, filled with divine power, and illuminated by divine truth. Without God man is overcome by his defective nature and falls victim to error and selfish concerns. With God man is able to overcome his defects and to be raised to true knowledge and service. This theological insight can also be validated in terms of the cause of modern history. Modern society has proved to be destructive of what is best in man, and thus it provides historical testimony as to what happens to man when he loses God.

The historical side of Maritain's argument consists in his tracing the decline and fall of modern man from that moment when a separation of the supernatural from the natural first began. Ignoring the truth that grace bestows freedom, man began to think that he is free and glorious in himself. What began as a glorification of man degenerated in time into a denial of human dignity. The Renaissance celebrated the glory of man, the grandeur of truth, and the worth of the temporal order, but succeeding ages such as the age of liberalism chronicled man's descent. Liberalism, which Maritain describes as "a philosophy of freedom which makes of each abstract individual and his opinions the source of all right and truth," showed by its subjectivity and unchecked individualism that man had lost his moorings in objective truth and nobler strivings.

Developments in the late nineteenth century, especially the evolutionary hypothesis of Charles Darwin (1809-1882) and the psychoanalytic theories of Sigmund Freud (1856-1939), reduced man to the merely animal and degraded his nobler strivings toward higher values by presenting these as merely manifestations of basically animal instincts. His dignity and nobility surrendered, his nature interpreted by views which contradicted religious conceptions, modern man has been driven to the desperate expedient of sacrificing himself to the state in the false hope of receiving once again a meaning for life.

Maritain claims that a true philosophy of man knows that man as a child of God can be fulfilled only by divine grace. Grace is not some additional quality which merely crowns man's natural goodness; rather, it is a healing power which makes man whole, protecting him against his sinful propensities, guiding him toward truth, and bestowing the freedom and value which make man truly human. Only as man is vivified by grace can he become truly man.

Protestantism is not a tenable alternative, Maritain suggests. Protestantism is so much affected by man's depravity that it is unable to realize that grace liberates and transforms man. Protestantism understands grace and freedom to be antithetical; hence, in affirming God and grace Protestantism repudiates man's freedom and genuine dignity. Liberalism draws the opposite conclusion, that for man to be free he must reject God. Both positions in forcing an "either/or" instead of a "both/and" deprive man of his real fulfillment through grace.

Pure atheism is only in theory an alternative, for a pure atheism cannot be lived. Every will, whether it knows it or not, desires God when it desires the good, since all good is in God. To avoid God, then, one would have to cease to desire or affirm any values whatsoever. Citing the example given by Kirilov in *The Possessed* (a novel by Dostoevsky), who says just before his suicide that if God exists then all things depend upon Him and nothing can be done which is outside His will, Maritain observes that Kirilov's suicide is the logical outcome of his attempt to deny God completely.

Pure atheism, metaphysical atheism, cannot be lived, Maritain insists, but it is possible to have a social order which *believes* that it is radically atheistic when in its actual life it is not. In Russia, for example, there is an official atheism but nevertheless there is a practical involvement in genuine human problems. Russian life as it is lived is another form of the sin of idolatry, which is the refusal of man to regard obedience to God as the final aim of human life, and it is not, therefore, the radical opposite of Christianity. Because God is active in human life, and because man cannot escape seeking God in seeking the good, Maritain hopes that gradual modification of Marxist theories can be achieved. Because God offers grace in moments of crucial choices whether man believes in God or not, as the Russian people genuinely face practical problems and decisions a new truly human order may gradually emerge. Perhaps the Communist movement in Russian history, like liberalism in the West, marks a discovery of values which have been submerged, but a discovery which has been wrong-headed.

The tragedy of modern man is that the decline of man was not necessary. The concern for man and the temporal order, a concern which was implicit in Medieval Christendom, could have been made explicit within the Christian context. St. Thomas provided a proper way, and had modernity not departed from his synthesis a true humanism could have been created.

What man must do now, suggests Maritain, is to create a synthesis based on the insights of St. Thomas. A new Christian synthesis would include several points of difference from the medieval one. First, instead of the stress on conformity, there would be provision for a pluralism of communities and of interests within the wider whole. Second, instead of the temporal order's being primarily a *means* to the spiritual order, the temporal order would be regarded as autonomous, for although the temporal order is inferior in value to the spiritual, the temporal order has a legitimate sphere of its own; its concern is with the conditions which provide for the well-being of man. Third, coerced obedience would be replaced by persuasion. Instead of using secular power to enforce the claims of the spiritual, that power would be used to protect the freedom of persons. The freedom of the individual includes freedom of belief, expression, and practice, which means also the freedom of religion to integrate its own work with that of the state by assisting in public charity and providing Christian instruction. Maritain stresses also the freedom to own property and the freedom of women to return to their proper place in society, to the home and family. Fourth, instead of a diversity of social races (according to the aristocratic notions

of past times) there would be a unity of social race, an equality of essence. Blood and wealth would not be the basis for hierarchy; rather, ability alone would determine whatever hierarchies there need be. Fifth, rather than viewing the purpose of society as being that of building an empire for Christ, the aim of the new Christendom would be that of realizing a genuine fraternal community, which Maritain conceives as a kingdom of men built upon "the dignity of human personality and its spiritual vocation, and of the fraternal love which is its due. The task of the commonwealth will be the realisation of a common life here on earth, of a temporal system truly in conformity with that dignity, that vocation and that love."

Such an ideal of a new Christendom, allowing as it does the presence and interests of both believers and unbelievers, but allowing also the proper functioning of religion that is demanded by man's very nature, can provide a common program for all men of good will whether they have religious beliefs or not. Such a Christendom gives ample scope for the genuine discoveries of modern thought and life, the explicit concerns for man, his dignity, and his place as a temporal being, which medieval Christendom lacked, while at the same time re-establishing man on his proper basis. A true humanism is a theocentric humanism. It is humanistic in contrast to the humanism which was only implicit in the old Christian order; it is theocentric in contrast to the atheism and anthropocentricity of the modern secular order.

Such a new Christendom enables the Church to be free to carry out its own proper function, that of bringing man to God and thus bringing man to his own fulfillment. Maritain writes: "It is not for the Church but for Christians as temporal members of this temporal organism to strive directly and immediately to transform and act upon it in the spirit of Christianity." The Church, by its work, inspires the Christian citizen, but the Church as Church cannot be tied to specific social programs and still be loyal to its purpose. Christians as citizens must enter into the political and social arena, striving through united action to create a truly human social order.

Maritain was convinced, in writing this book in 1936, that the present order of civilization is dying: "Modern civilisation is a worn-out vesture: it is not a question of sewing on patches here and there, but of a total and substantial reformation, a trans-valuation of its cultural principles; since what is needed is a change to the primacy of quality over quantity, of work over money, of the human over technical means, of wisdom over science, of the common service of human beings instead of the covetousness of unlimited individual enrichment or a desire in the name of the State for unlimited power." Were St. Thomas living today he might very well urge such a Christian philosophy, a philosophy free from what is outmoded in order to be true to that wisdom of the past which is imperishable.

WORSHIP

Author: Evelyn Underhill (1875-1941)
Type of work: Liturgical theology
First published: 1936

Principal Ideas Advanced

Worship is the response of the creature to the revelation of the Creator.

Man's worship is part of the praise which the whole universe brings to God.

Because man is body as well as soul, his worship must involve physical and psychical dimensions.

Only trinitarian worship adequately responds to the revelation of God as transcendent, as incarnate, and as the sanctifier of the race.

In the sacraments, creaturely acts are endowed with divine grace and power. The perfect sacrament is the sacrifice of Christ, offered to God in the Eucharist.

Evelyn Underhill's *Worship* is an important contribution to the liturgical revival which began with the Oxford Movement in the Church of England and has gradually found its way into most of the major Protestant Churches.

Miss Underhill writes from the standpoint of Christian theism, having moved from the vaguely Bergsonian philosophy of her earlier work on *The Essentials of Mysticism* (1920) to the view of Neo-Scholasticism. Her book is not an anthropological investigation of worship the world around, but a loving exposition of Christian forms of devotion, forms which she finds foreshadowed, indeed, in the rites and sacrifices of other cults, but fully realized only in the services of the Church, specifically in the Divine Office and Holy Eucharist as observed in the Orthodox, Roman, and Anglican traditions.

For Miss Underhill, there are only two candid attitudes that one can take toward worship. One can regard it either as a tragically mistaken expenditure of human effort, or as the ultimate meaning and purpose of creation. Taking the latter alternative, she suggests that the deliberate praise which most peoples of the world accord to God must be extended until it envelops the whole of man's life. Nor is worship limited to man. As the angels and archangels pour out their lives in perpetual worship, so, if the world is of a piece, the lower forms of life must also be understood as rendering silent and unconscious praise to their Maker.

Christians, in attempting to understand their own religion, must not forget their bond with all creation. If, in virtue of our spiritual part, we claim kinship with the heavenly host, we must, on account of our physical aspect, recognize our affinity to lower forms of life. For this reason, Christians should not quarrel with the barbaric origins of many Christian practices. The history of sacrifice, for example, is replete with fear and cruelty. But, according to Miss Underhill, the important thing to remember is that ancient men, by the light that was given to them, were sincerely responding to "the impact of the Eternal." Although there is a tendency for the spirit of worship to degenerate into superstition and magic, worship initially is disinterested, an expression of man's desire to give back to God that which he has received; to be worthy of this high office, the gift must be costly. Old Testament worship includes many dreadful elements; for example, the binding of Isaac, and the institution of the Passover. Moreover, these very elements are taken up and sublimated in the Eucharist, where the unbloody sacrifice of the Son of God is daily celebrated. Christians must acknowledge the primitive roots of the Gospel, says Miss Underhill, in order that their worship will not become something thin, intellectual, and humanistic.

Worship, to achieve its full expression, must involve the entire psychological powers of man. Whatever truth the James-Lange theory of the emotions may have in general, it accurately describes the activity of worship, says the author, who quotes in support of her view a statement by the liberal Catholic theologian, Ulrich von Hügel: "I kiss my child because I love it," said von Hügel; "and I kiss my child in order to love it." Physical attitudes, rhythmical motions, sensible stimulants, unconscious associations are all part of the worship experience. This is true of single elements, such as kneeling or chanting; and the highest forms of worship are those in which the maximum of effective elements are brought together. It is a specious spirituality which, in the name of inwardness, would do away with ritual, lavish display, and apparently useless dedication of wealth.

Worship, however, is not merely a human invention, nor is its purpose the satisfaction of human needs. Worship, we are told, is the response man makes to the revelation of the Eternal. In one aspect, worship is the acknowledgment of the transcendence of God over everything that partakes of succession and change. But God is not merely transcendent; in the language of Neo-Scholasticism, He is "one who Acts," who discloses Himself to man in Christ and in the Church. Highest worship, therefore, must be trinitarian. While adoring eternal reality, it will also lay its gifts at the feet of Him who gave Himself on Calvary, and will offer up its praises to the Holy Spirit who transforms mankind into a holy community.

Miss Underhill discusses four main characteristics of worship, all of which, in her opinion, achieve their highest expression in Catholic worship: ritual, symbolism, sacrament, and sacrifice. Of these four, the notion of "sacrament" has especially interested Anglo-Catholic thinkers, involving as it does an extension of the "incarnational philosophy." A sacrament differs from a symbol, according to Miss Underhill, just as a significant deed differs from a significant image. Symbols are static; sacraments are dynamic. By means of the sacrament, "the Supernatural draws near to man in and through the natural." Common acts of daily living easily acquire sacramental significance, and by their means one after another aspect of creaturely existence is taken up into "the fabric of the worshipping life." Miss Underhill is inclined to favor a sacramental outlook on life over an ethical one, since the goal of Christ's redemptive act is not so much to change man's outward behavior as it is to sanctify the whole of life and to offer it to God. Christ, she says, is Himself "the major sacrament," and the Church, His Body, receives its life from the specific sacraments recognized by all the Catholic Churches. Miss Underhill notes

that some people want to embrace the notion of sacramentalism in a vague and diffused fashion, without acknowledging such high doctrines as baptismal regeneration and the real presence. But, she says, it is only by being canalized through special acts "held sacred, and kept for Himself alone," that God is able to make His grace and power felt by the religious soul.

Sacrifice, the fourth main aspect of worship, is both symbolic and sacramental. It is a token act, by which, out of pure love and gratitude, man seeks to make a gift to the One from whom all gifts come. Human charity responds to divine charity; and, like sacramental worship, it finds its perfect expression in the Mass, "the eternal movement of charity whereby the Son is self-given to the Father, and in union with Him, His Mystical Body, the Church—which is represented, but not repeated, under the conditions of time and space, in every Eucharist."

One of the most important aspects of worship, according to Miss Underhill, is its social dimension. The ideal is for the human worshiper to place himself in the company of "every creature which is in heaven and on earth and such as are in the sea"; and this sense should be preserved in the liturgy itself. For the rest, it is of utmost importance that Christians worship God in the congregation of the redeemed, and that, through corporate silence and various liturgical devices, such as the response, the whole body unite in one act of worship. Atomistic and subjectivistic piety are to be rejected, and so are those practices, such as the Low Mass, which permit the clergy to carry on the ceremony at the altar while the worshipers engage themselves in private prayers. Miss Underhill does not suggest that "personal" worship is by any means to be neglected, but personal devotion is not to be understood as a "private" affair. Plato's *Laws* are cited as showing that God "has ordered all things with a view to the excellence and preservation of the whole," and that the life of the individual exists "in order that the life of the whole may be blessed." The individual cannot achieve a deep and satisfactory devotional life in any other way than by repeating within his own daily life the great rhythms which are sacramentally achieved in the life, death, and resurrection of Christ, and which are repeated daily and annually in the worship of the Church.

In the second part of her book, Miss Underhill turns from the principles of Christian worship to consider different types of worship in the history of God's Church. Chapters are given to Judaism, to the Apostolic community, to Catholicism (East and West), to the Reformed Churches, to the Free Churches, and to the Anglican tradition. In the Preface, she notes that some of her friends criticized her for giving "too sympathetic and uncritical an account of types of worship" which are full of shortcomings. She explains, however, that her "wish has been to show all these as chapels of various types in the one Cathedral of the Spirit; and dwell on the particular structure of each, the love which has gone to their adornment, the shelter they can offer to many different kinds of souls. . . ." She tries generously to respond to the positive aspects of nonliturgical groups. Even those groups which repudiate the sacraments altogether—groups such as the Quakers—have, she says, something sacramental in the very austerity and bareness of their worship,

"a positive witness to the otherness of God, which may be more impressive, more suggestive of the unseen Holy, than the veil before the tabernacle or the sanctuary lamp." Moreover, she acknowledges the abuses which perennially accompany liturgical worship, and she understands the zeal, though she cannot help but lament the intemperance, of those who reject the ceremonies of the Catholic Church. It is a consolation to her, she writes, that Luther, Calvin, and Knox did not reject the liturgy as completely as did some of their followers, and she expresses satisfaction with attempts which are being made in Scandinavia, in Scotland, and elsewhere, to recover this aspect of their heritage.

Worship is one of the volumes of a series known as *The Library of Constructive Theology,* to which various authors have contributed. In the General Introduction, the editors remark that the present age is in revolt against authority, and that few people are content to rest their faith on dogma. We observe that this is the case with Miss Underhill. Her Neo-Scholastic philosophy does not lead her to accept the Roman doctrine of authority as the basis for her belief in the efficacy of the sacraments. Her case rests, instead, on the self-authenticating character of the Christian experience. The worship of God through the Eucharist proves itself to be the richest, most rewarding experience known to man. Other ways of worshiping God are not thereby repudiated but, rather, established in their various degrees; hence, a way is held open for all churches and all religions to join at last in one great divine society, at once prophetic and priestly, evangelical and eucharistic, historical and eternal.

THE COST OF DISCIPLESHIP

Author: Dietrich Bonhoeffer (1906-1945)
Type of work: Christian ethics
First published: 1937

PRINCIPAL IDEAS ADVANCED

The deadliest enemy of the Church is "cheap grace"; that is, grace understood as a general truth requiring only intellectual assent and used surreptitiously to justify a life void of discipleship.

Faith and obedience are inseparable; only he who believes is obedient, and only he who is obedient believes.

Discipleship means exclusive allegiance and bodily adherence to the person of Jesus Christ; it involves an obedient response to Jesus' call to follow Him and denotes both a breach with the world and a joyful sharing in His suffering love for the world.

The same Jesus Christ who called the first disciples into visible communion with Himself is alive and present today in the Church through the ministry of Word and Sacrament; as the crucified and risen Lord, He now calls us through the preaching of His Word, incorporates us into His earthly Body through baptism, and fosters and sustains our communion in that Body through the Lord's Supper.

Dietrich Bonhoeffer, a Christian whose life and thought are closely interwoven, lived during the tumultuous period of Adolf Hitler's Third German Reich. Son of a prominent psychiatrist and reared in the best liberal tradition, Bonhoeffer pursued his theological studies at the Universities of Tübingen and Berlin and at Union Theological Seminary in New York City. He enjoyed a brief career as Lecturer in Systematic Theology at the University of Berlin, but when Hitler came to power, Bonhoeffer soon became involved in the "German Church Struggle," in which he actively supported the "Confessing Church" in its opposition to the Nazi-backed "German Christians." At the height of the struggle, when he was the leader of a clandestine seminary in the Pomeranian village of Finkenwalde, Bonhoeffer wrote and published *The Cost of Discipleship,* which firmly established his reputation as a talented theologian. Later Bonhoeffer joined the underground resistance movement, which worked for the overthrow of Hitler's regime; his resistance activities led to his imprisonment in 1943 and to his execution on April 9, 1945, at the age of thirty-nine.

In his introduction to *The Cost of Discipleship* Bonhoeffer questions whether the modern Church has so obscured the pure Word of Jesus (by adding man-made dogmas, burdensome rules, and irrelevant demands) that to make a genuine decision for Christ has become extremely difficult. He proposes to tell how Jesus calls us to be His disciples, and his intention is not to impose still harder demands on already troubled and wounded consciences, but to show how anyone who follows the command of Jesus single-mindedly and unresistingly finds His yoke to be easy. Discipleship, asserts Bonhoeffer, means joy, and it is not limited to a spiritual élite, but is for every man.

The book is divided into two parts. The first is an exposition of the conception of discipleship that is to be found in the Synoptic Gospels, together with an interpretation of the Sermon on the Mount. The second part consists of Bonhoeffer's attempt to show how the terminology used by the evangelists has been translated into the language of the Church of the Apostle Paul.

Bonhoeffer opens *The Cost of Discipleship* with a powerful polemic against cheap grace, which he calls the deadly enemy of the evangelical Church. Cheap grace is grace as a doctrine or a principle, the forgiveness of sins proclaimed as a general truth, the justification of sin without the justification of the sinner. Cheap grace is the grace we bestow on ourselves, the grace by which we calculate in advance that our sins are forgiven and then conclude that there is no need for a life of obedience, no need for discipleship. The followers of Luther have turned his saying, "Sin boldly, but believe and rejoice in Christ more boldly still," into a *carte blanche* for sin. What for Luther was his very last refuge and consolation, after a lifetime of following Jesus Christ, has been perverted into a premise for obtaining grace as cheaply as possible. Happy are they, declares Bonhoeffer, who discover the truth that grace is costly just because it is the grace of God in Jesus Christ. "Such grace is *costly* because it calls us to follow, and it is

grace because it calls us to follow Jesus Christ. It is costly because it costs a man his life, and it is grace because it gives a man the only true life."

The call of Christ to discipleship demands the spontaneous response of obedience. Discipleship means adherence to Christ, and its only content is to follow Him. That is, discipleship offers no intelligible program for a way of life, no goal or ideal to strive after, no cause which we might deem worthy of our devotion. It offers only exclusive allegiance to the person of Jesus Christ, the living Son of God who became man. There can be no faith without following, no believing without obedience. Indeed, stresses Bonhoeffer, only he who believes is obedient, and only he who is obedient believes; it is unbiblical to hold either proposition without the other.

The single-minded obedience of the faithful disciple means self-denial and submission to the "law of Christ," which is the law of the Cross. The Cross is laid on every Christian, which means that he must expect to share in the suffering of Christ. There is a suffering entailed in the disciple's abandonment of attachments to the world and in the daily dying of the "old man" as a result of his encounter with Christ, but the more significant suffering is found in his bearing the burdens of others and thus participating in Christ's work of bearing and forgiving the sins of men. The disciple discovers that Christ's permission to share His suffering is really a token of His grace, for it becomes the way to communion with God. Suffering is overcome by suffering; the Cross brings forth joy.

The call of Jesus makes one an individual, for each man must decide and follow alone. Nevertheless, the disciple, who has broken all natural ties and relationships for the sake of following the Master, finds that he does not remain alone; through Christ he enters into a new fellowship that far surpasses what was lost. Christ is the Mediator, not only between God and man, but between man and man and between man and the world. Through His mediation the individual disciple is incorporated into a community, the community of the Cross. It is primarily to this community that Jesus addresses the Sermon on the Mount. The disciples are they whom He calls "blessed" in the Beatitudes, who by bearing the Cross in the life of grace are the salt of the earth and the light of the world, who live the extraordinary life of utter love, self-renunciation, absolute purity, truthfulness, and meekness. Yet the "extraordinariness" of this life is hidden from the disciples and becomes visible for the world alone. That is, the disciple never sees his "good works" and "better righteousness," because his eyes are directed solely to his Lord. He seeks merely to do His will, and therefore what seems extraordinary to the world appears to the disciple as the natural thing to do.

The life of the disciple is one of carefree simplicity: carefree because his trust is wholly in the Lord, and simple because his obedience is to only one Master. He need not look for complicated or hidden meanings in Christ's commands, nor is he given any special vantage point from which to judge the neighbor who is not a disciple. Since his righteousness is a gift deriving from his association with Christ, he can approach the unbeliever only as one to whom Christ comes, and therefore the disciple approaches others with an unconditional offer of fellowship and with the single-mindedness of the love of Jesus.

Following his expositions of the Sermon on the Mount and of the commissioning of the disciples as messengers equipped with the gracious sovereignty of the creative and redemptive Word of God (Matthew 10), Bonhoeffer raises the question of the possibility and meaning of discipleship for the Church, which no longer knows Jesus in the flesh. Does Jesus call men today to follow Him, just as He called Levi the publican? Bonhoeffer asserts that there is something strange about this question, for in the very asking "we are retreating from the presence of the living Christ and forgetting that Jesus Christ is not dead, but alive and speaking to us today through the testimony of the Scriptures." It is not the case that we who live today are worse off than the original disciples; indeed, we have a distinct advantage, for our call comes from the victorious and glorified Christ, who is present in the Church in bodily form and in His Word. The Church is indeed the Body of Christ, and through the ministry of Word and Sacrament the call of Christ goes forth and His gracious will is made known. Of course, our recognition of the Christ must be solely by faith, but this was precisely the same for the first disciples. "*They* saw the rabbi and the wonderworker, and believed on Christ. *We* hear the Word and believe on Christ."

Bonhoeffer points out that, whereas in the Synoptic Gospels the writers speak of the relationship between the disciples and the Lord almost exclusively in terms of following Him, St. Paul in his Epistles employs a new set of terms that depict the presence of the risen and glorified Lord and His work in us. It is Bonhoeffer's conviction that this difference in terminology involves no break in the unity of the Scriptural testimony and that neither set of terms is preferable to the other.

Where the Synoptists speak of Christ calling men and their following Him, St. Paul speaks of baptism. In baptism man suffers the call of Christ and becomes His possession; baptism betokens a breach with the world and the death of the "old man." Baptismal death means a daily dying in the power of the death that Christ died once and for all, and as such it is a death full of grace, for it means justification from sin and the gift of the Holy Spirit.

Just as the first disciples lived in the bodily presence and communion of Jesus, we are made members of the Body of Christ through baptism. "The word of preaching," emphasizes Bonhoeffer, "is insufficient to make us members of Christ; the sacraments also have to be added." Baptism incorporates us into the unity of Christ's Body, and the Lord's Supper fosters and sustains the fellowship in that Body. The Body is the Church, which is not to be thought of as an institution but as a person in a unique sense. The Church is essentially One Man, the new humanity of the risen Christ, and yet this one body of Christ includes all those members who through the Spirit are united with Christ and who participate in His suffering and glory.

Unlike truths or doctrines or religions, which are disembodied entities, the Body of Christ takes up space on earth. The Church is made up of living men and women, and this means that it is a visible reality. Bonhoeffer explains that the Body of Christ becomes visible in the preaching of the Word, in the sacraments of baptism and the Lord's Supper, in Church order, and in the daily life of the members in the world. The Christian gives the world a visible proof of his calling, not only by his sharing in the worship and discipline of the Church, but also by the new fellowship of brotherly love.

Where the Synoptists speak of the self-denying life of discipleship, St. Paul tells of Christians being drawn into the image of Christ crucified. In the life of suffering love they recover their true humanity and at the same time find a new solidarity with the whole human race. The new life in Christ is a life of joy, since those who share in His cross also share the glory of His resurrection. But, Bonhoeffer reminds us, the members of Christ's Body are oblivious to their own lives and to the new image they bear, for they look solely to their Head. Nevertheless, whether they realize it or not, in patterning their lives after that of their crucified Lord they have become "imitators of God."

THE PHILOSOPHICAL BASES OF THEISM

Author: George Dawes Hicks (1862-1941)
Type of work: Philosophy of religion
First published: 1937

PRINCIPAL IDEAS ADVANCED

All consciousness, including the religious consciousness, has an element of knowledge or interpretation.

Self-consciousness reveals the self or mind as a subject; things in nature are objects.

Minds and things are existences; qualities, ideas, and ideals are subsistences or essences.

We know existences through essences, the symbolized through the symbol.

God is known through the higher ideas, truth, goodness, and beauty, and through the sense of a presence that inspires reverence and trust.

George Dawes Hicks's *The Philosophical Bases of Theism* represents the Hibbert Lectures, delivered in 1931, as revised for publication in 1937. The author, who was one of the founders of the *Hibbert Journal*, develops the argument for a nontheological theism in its most cogent form. The philosophical point of view is that of post-Kantian idealism. Religion in its highest form is presented as belief in a supreme living and personal Mind. It is the business of philosophy to validate and interpret this belief. Religious experience is held to be the basis of the knowledge of God, and the revelation which comes through experience is described as a developing thing. Reason is present in all experience as interpretation, Hicks claims, and is therefore continuous with revelation. Philosophy carries this interpretation on in systematic and critical form. Philosophy is to religion what science is to common sense

As Hicks uses the term, religious faith is fundamentally a matter of knowledge, for all aspects of experience are elements of consciousness which is essentially knowing. "The transition from consciousness to self-consciousness is by far the greatest, by far the most momentous, advance ever made in the history of mind; or, indeed, for a matter of that, in the whole course of or-

ganic evolution." Man's knowledge of himself as subject, as even dimly distinguished from his knowledge of objects, is the key to his knowledge of spirit. The argument for a distinctive kind of knowledge upon which religious belief is based begins with this contrast between the subject and the object. Natural science deals with the relations of physical objects. But the knowing subject is not an object among other objects. The relation of the subject to the object is different in kind from the relation between objects in nature, which is a causal relation.

Even in physical science the idea of a purely mechanistic relation between objects in nature has been abandoned, Hicks argues. Physics has gone beyond the idea of simple efficient causation, and the doctrine of evolution has introduced a dynamic and developmental factor that suggests, if it does not prove, the presence of purpose. The organic character even of the atom means that there is an influence of the whole on the parts and their relations that is not mechanical. These developments strongly suggest the freedom and purposive presence of a divine Mind.

The affirmation of theistic faith is that we are in the presence of a spiritual environment as well as of a physical environment. We become aware of the latter through sense perception, and we are aware of the former through the religious consciousness which is native to consciousness of self. But basically all knowledge is the same. Consciousness involves interpretation as well as sensation and feeling. We see a tree as a tree; we see red as red (not blue) because implicit in our seeing is the idea of tree and red. It is the same in religious experience. Friedrich Schleiermacher (1768-1834) resolved religion into the feeling of absolute dependence; but feeling is never pure feeling, and the feeling of dependence involves an idea; namely, that the feeling is a feeling of dependence. Religious consciousness thus always has an element of interpretation, or knowing. Our knowledge of nature, however, is a knowledge of qualities as well as of quantities. The color and other qualities are objectively real; they are *in* the complex of objects and events that we perceive. Thus, the world of nature is not merely a collection of quantities; it has the qualities that we perceive it to have. The mind is not composed of those qualities, although it apprehends them. The elements of the divine, the spiritual elements of experience, truth, beauty and goodness, are also objective. They are elements in the spiritual environment which is the world of religious belief.

Religious experience, or the religious consciousness, gives us knowledge of the supernatural environment. The supernatural is known through the natural. Almost any event can be the medium or the occasion of the disclosure of the spiritual, but the form of apprehension is symbolical; we know the symbolized only through the symbol. This is not proved or demonstrated knowledge, but it is nevertheless genuine knowledge. The divine is not an element in our own consciousness, as claimed by Schleiermacher. Knowledge of the divine is not gained through the sense of the numinous, as Rudolph Otto (1869-1937) claimed; completely nondivine objects produce not only awe and a sense of the uncanny, but also other responses which create the feeling of the holy. Knowledge always involves intellectual form, for it is through interpretation of experience and events that knowledge is acquired of the objectively existent divine. Thus, religious knowledge is essentially like all other knowledge; religious knowledge is, in fact, the most comprehensive kind of knowledge.

Hicks's theory of knowledge, and of religious knowledge in particular, arises out of and expresses a certain metaphysics, which includes conceptions of (1) existences, (2) subsistences, and (3) essences. There are two kinds of existences, physical, and mental or spiritual. It is characteristic of both kinds that they are individual and concrete, and also that they are active. Objects in nature are physical existents; they are individual and active. Minds are spiritual existents; they too are individual and active. They exist in time, and are unique and changing. Minds are subjects; physical entities are objects. Human minds are individual existences; the divine Mind is also an existent being. Subsistences are realities that do not exist, such as laws of nature and ideals, especially the ideals of goodness, beauty, and truth. Goodness, beauty, and truth are eternal realities, as Plato declared them to be. But they are not God; neither are they merely subjective aspects of our consciousness. They constitute a realm of essences. But they are the true *via media* between minds, and between minds and objects. We know existences through essences. We know the natural world by a direct perception of its qualities as found concretely in individual objects. This is also the way we know the spiritual existence that we call God. The essences are spiritual, that is, mental; nature can be known because it is intelligible, or rational. But by that very fact nature points beyond itself to the intelligible source of its existence. Our knowledge of God, however, is enhanced by our apprehension of the higher aspects of experience, the values of truth, goodness, and beauty, and the sense of a presence that inspires reverence and trust. Thus, both directly and indirectly our knowledge of the divine Mind comes through the mediation of essences.

Ultimate interest in this philosophical essay is in the existent called God. It is noteworthy that Hicks does not himself speak of God as Spirit, but always as Mind. Reason and intellect are essentially instruments or forms of knowing, and while knowledge is taken to include the full range and depth of religious experience, such knowledge still has the essential character of rationality. God is Mind. As a spiritual or mental existent God is individual, active, and distinct from all other minds; He is not the absolute. Pantheism, wherever found, is rejected; for if God is the whole, then other minds are parts of Him. But the definition of mind excludes this possibility. Each mind is a distinct and separate subject.

Minds have knowledge of, and regard for, each other; but "other minds do not, therefore, enter into my being in any other manner or in any other respect," writes Hicks; "There is no such thing as confluence or overlapping of selves as existents." The same is true in the relation of the divine mind to human minds. Minds are essentially external to each other. The medium of their regard for and knowledge of each other, either man for man, or man for God, and God for man, is the world of essences; the truths, qualities, and values that are intelligible but not minds; such truths are subsistences but not existences.

God is the supreme personal Mind, Hicks writes, "a consciousness that knows all that we cannot know, that loves beyond our power of loving, that 'realizes' the good where our faltering efforts fail." The knowledge of God is not a "privileged experience," different from the normal rational experience of man. Hicks concludes, "The fuller the individual's life is of all that goes to constitute rich human experience the better equipped will it be for attaining knowledge of God. . . . If (man) brings to bear upon what is offered in experience his whole personal life in its concrete completeness,—intellect, reason, feeling, aspiration and love,—what ground is there for assuming that the divine reality will escape his ken?" It is Hicks's basic contention that in this wholeness of human experience and in its rational unification our knowledge of God is actually attained.

THE WISDOM OF GOD

Author: Sergius Bulgakov (1870-1944)
Type of work: Theology of culture
First published: 1937

PRINCIPAL IDEAS ADVANCED

The modern world faces the problem of recovering the religious meaning of culture, lost between secularist humanism and otherworldly religion.

The ancient doctrine that Sophia, or Wisdom, is the essence of God and also the essence of the creature provides a basis for this recovery.

In human culture, creation becomes aware of its sophianic character and its oneness with the Creator.

Secular humanism, having repudiated Sophia, must give place to the "true humanism" of God-manhood.

The Church must correct its dogmatic foundations in order to overcome its Manichean attitude toward the world.

Sergius Bulgakov was a priest of the Russian Orthodox Church, who was forced, because of the Revolution, to carry on his theological teaching in exile. *The Wisdom of God,* a brief outline of his theology, is a work which was prepared at the request of ecumenically oriented Western churchmen. Bulgakov is one of a group of Russian intellectuals who embraced Christianity after experimenting with its modern alternatives. Originally destined for the priesthood, he lost his faith, left the seminary for the gymnasium and the university, and became a Marxist, and eventually a professor of economics. Under the influence of Vladimir Solovyev (1853-1900), he made his way from materialism to idealism, then from idealism to Christianity. His ordination to the priesthood came in 1918, after many of his important works had already been published. Bulgakov, therefore, is hardly a conventional representative of Orthodoxy; he explains that "sophiology," his doctrine

of Divine Wisdom, is merely a development within Eastern Christianity, comparable to New-Thomism or Barthianism in the West.

According to Bulgakov, the great problem facing Christendom today is to recover the religious meaning of culture. In Europe, the problem dates from the time of the Renaissance and the Reformation, when the creative impulses of modern civilization became independent of the Church, and the Church withdrew from worldly concerns in order to preserve fundamental religion. In Russia, the problem became acute only in the nineteenth century, when the national culture was taking shape. Representatives of art and literature, confronted with the secularism of the West, were made deeply conscious of their own religious roots; but the Eastern Church was as unsympathetic toward their undertakings as were the Reformation and Counter-Reformation churches in the West. In Bulgakov's opinion, the problem still remains unsolved, for the liberal wing of Christendom has embraced the secularist solution and has abandoned God, while the conservative wing has continued to "excommunicate the world." Nor, according to Bulgakov, is there any possibility of a dialectical resolution of the antithesis: "We must discover how we can overcome the secularizing forces of the Reformation and of the Renaissance, not in a negative way or 'dialectically,' which is in any case merely theoretical and powerless; but in a positive way—through love for the world."

Bulgakov maintains that the "sophianic interpretation" of the world offers the only solution to the difficulty. Sophia, or Divine Wisdom, is, according to Bulgakov, the mediating principle which binds the world to God. On the one hand, Sophia is the very *ousia* or being of God, the divine substance which is one in all three persons of the Trinity. Not itself a person, or hypostasis, it is the divine nature, hidden in the Father, revealed in the Son, and beloved in the Spirit. But as Sophia is the life of the Godhead, so it is the hidden reality of the world, which was created "out of nothing," and has both its nature and existence from God. Since Sophia is not a person in the Godhead, but the nature common to the three persons, it can be realized outside the Godhead; and that is precisely what is effected in creation. Without being identical with God, the world is fundamentally divine in its nature. Bulgakov writes, "Wisdom in creation is ontologically identical with its prototype, the same Wisdom as it exists in God."

Although the principle of Sophia has deep roots in Christian devotion, as witnessed by the name of the famous church in Constantinople, and by its appearance in mystical literature and in Orthodox liturgy, Christian theology has failed, until recently, to take it into account. For example, the Nicene formulation of the Trinity makes use of the abstract and empty term *ousia* to designate the divine nature, and it makes no mention of Sophia, probably because early theologians mistakenly identified Sophia, the true name for God's nature, with the Logos, which is one of the divine hypostases. Similarly, the Chalcedonian formulation of the Incarnation, according to which Christ is a divine person with a divine and human nature, is content with a purely negative account of the hypostatical union between the two natures (*inconfuse, immutabiliter, indivise, inseparabiliter*), whereas an adequate understanding of the divine and creaturely Sophia would have made this union intelligible. So it is, according to Bulgakov, with all the main doctrines. For want of the key notion of Sophia, the Church has but rarely understood the doctrines which it affirms.

Of particular importance for the present crisis is the relation of Sophia to the question of human nature and destiny. Because man is a hypostasis, a person, like the members of the Trinity, it would not be correct simply to identify Sophia and humanity. But, just as Sophia is the nature which the divine persons share, so in humanity, Sophia is the essence which human persons share. On the creaturely level, where divine perfection is worked out imperfectly in time, the divine image in man is not realized at the beginning. When, at the creation, the Father made man in His image by His Word and Spirit, the divine perfections were present only potentially;

their actualization has been achieved through the entrance of the second and third hypostases into history, at the time of Christ's birth, and when the Spirit descended at Pentecost. Thus, the history of mankind, according to Bulgakov, is the history of the perfecting in man of his likeness to God. Bulgakov stresses the divine agency in history, but at the same time he seeks to preserve man's freedom. He does this by means of the doctrine of *kenosis*. According to the New Testament, Christ "emptied himself" (*heauton ekenosen*) of His divine glory when He became man. Similarly, says Bulgakov, the Spirit emptied Himself of His power when he gave himself to the Church at Pentecost. Thus, the three persons of the Godhead are active in the world, but in such a way that the world is not lost in the Infinite. Bulgakov underlines this point by calling his doctrine "pan-en-theism," in contrast to pantheism. But though insisting that man's will is independent of the divine, Bulgakov argues that the divine efficacy and "the compelling attraction of Wisdom" will win out over the willfulness of the creative. After all, says Bulgakov, evil is parasitical; essentially it is nothing, and it must "wither before the radiance of Wisdom."

Bulgakov holds that all human creativity, in thought, art, economics, and society, is the working out of Divine Wisdom on the creaturely level. He writes, "In man creation is to become aware of its own sophianic character and recognize it in intelligence, the seminal reason of creation, and its flower. And therewith man will recognize the likeness of the wisdom of God in himself." This development is, of course, not limited to Christendom;

but with the coming of Christ, man found new freedom and reached levels of culture undreamed of in the pagan world. For this reason, special attention must be given to the divorce between culture and religion in the Christian world. Supposedly advancing under the banner of humanism, modern culture has, in Bulgakov's opinion, surrendered the better part of humanity, and has fallen under the retrogressive forces of pagan sensuality and Satanic pride. For this, however, the Church is itself mainly responsible. With an inadequate doctrine of God, and an even less adequate doctrine of man, it has too frequently assumed an ascetic, almost Manichaean, attitude toward history and culture, and either sought to dominate the world through artificial constraint, or condemned it outright as a peril to men's souls. Modern civilization, in Bulgakov's opinion, is headed toward sterility and death unless it discovers some way to heal this breach, some mode of creativity which is both churchly and free. With Jacques Maritain, Bulgakov calls for another kind of humanism, the "true humanism," wherein man's potentialities find their fulfillment in God. But unlike the Catholic philosopher, who desires to see human nature complemented by supernatural graces, Bulgakov maintains that human nature is essentially divine, and his wish is to see that potentially divine come to its proper fruition. True manhood is God-manhood, says Bulgakov, borrowing Solovyev's expression; that is, it is manhood become conscious of its oneness with God.

Like others who draw their inspiration from Solovyev, Bulgakov holds that the Church is the center of human history: "God created the world for the sake of the Church. That is as much as to say that it is at once the ground and goal of the world, its final cause and entelechy." In the Church man finds true society, which eludes him in other kinds of association, and he realizes something comparable to the perfect love and communion of the Godhead. On the other hand, Bulgakov describes the state as "a kind of callosity on the skin of the social body—the Great Wen." Founded upon force, the state denies human nature and deals with man according to the principles of material necessity. Thus, although the Church is the best friend of culture, she is the sworn enemy of politics; and any concordat between them can be only a compromise, "embarrassing to the Church, which must always remain in relation to the State an anarchic force."

The Church, as Bulgakov thinks of it, is not to be identified with any of its historical manifestations. Though it has its visible embodiment, it transcends our empirical mode of knowledge. Thus, although Bulgakov was very much interested in "the several Oecumenical Movements of our modern religious world," it can hardly be said that he expected them by themselves to effect any important change; whatever change occurs must first take place within the churches

themselves, suffering as they do from the abiding antinomy between an acosmic affirmation of God's transcendence and an atheistic affirmation of the world. It is futile, according to Bulgakov, to suppose that any external "pact" between denominations can remedy so fundamental a fault. The first concern of the Church must be to find its own foundations, which it cannot do on the canonical or liturgical, but only on the doctrinal, level. But, according to Bulgakov, efforts to lead the churches back to the old creeds are foredoomed, because the creeds themselves are unstable. Even "incarnationism," which many churchmen seek to make the central affirmation of Christianity, is, says Bulgakov, not a primary doctrine, for it presupposes dogmatic assumptions about the nature of God and man which must first be dealt with. These presuppositions, long latent in Christian faith, have now been unfolded in sophiology. "The creaturely world is united with the divine world in the Divine Sophia . . . ," Bulgakov writes; "Godmanhood represents a dogmatic call both to spiritual ascesis and to creativity; to salvation from the world and to a salvation of the world. This is the dogmatic banner which should be henceforth unfurled with all power and glory in the Church of Christ."

THE CHRISTIAN MESSAGE IN A NON-CHRISTIAN WORLD

Author: Hendrik Kraemer (1888-   )
Type of work: Theology of missions
First published: 1938

PRINCIPAL IDEAS ADVANCED

Contemporary culture and the Christian Church are in crisis, both undermined by relativism; consequently, the Church must rediscover its absolute foundation if it is to have a mission to the modern world.

Christianity is utterly unique, founded in the revelation of divine forgiveness in Jesus Christ; all other religions are unaware of the permeation of all things by sin.

The fundamental need of man is for conversion to the new life of forgiveness; all missionary effort must thus be motivated in evangelism, however much such a call may issue in works of social service.

From the beginning of Christianity, Christian life has been characterized by the dialogue of worship and witness. Questions concerning the meaning of the Church and the mission of the Church are inseparable. It is not surprising, then, that the radical transition in Protestantism from Reformation orthodoxy to nineteenth century liberalism effected a radical revision not only in the understanding of the Church, but also in the conception of the Christian world mission.

In like fashion, it is to be expected that the emergence of neo-orthodox theology in the twentieth century would stimulate an equally radical reappraisal of "the Christian message in a non-Christian world." The liberal tended to understand Christianity as being a higher, purer form of a universal religious consciousness; consequently, the world mission was less a matter of evangelism and more a moral effort to better the social and physical state of the underprivileged.

Hendrik Kraemer's *The Christian Message in a Non-Christian World* is the most important single attempt to challenge this liberal understanding by vigorously insisting that the entire missionary enterprise be thoroughly evangelistic. Under Kraemer's influence,

theologian, missionary, and indigenous Church leader alike are being forced to rethink the entire missionary enterprise, from undergirding theology to practical program.

Kraemer's argument begins by appraising the condition of the contemporary world to which the Church is called to witness. The outstanding characteristic of our time is "the complete disappearance of all absolutes, and the victorious but dreadful dominion of the spirit and attitude of relativism." The problem of religious certainty, consequently, is the ultimate problem of modern man.

The spirit of secularism and relativism began as a courageous and exhilarating discovery of man's power, worth, and destiny to conquer the mysteries of nature and life. Yet, glorious and important though this process was, it has ended in the self-destruction of man. "Man, being rooted in God, destroys himself by destroying God." Man has not really abolished God, however, for every effort to do so has resulted in the creation of another god. The need for the divine Word belongs to the very essence of man. Even though the conscious hunger of our time is for a more untrammelled enjoyment of life, an unconscious but deep spiritual hunger is gradually making itself known.

To the degree that the modern plight is seen, to that degree is man's craving for an absolute bearing witness to two things. First, man's prime obligation is to seek for the "absolute Truth and Ultimate Reality" in which he was created; second, "he cannot produce it by his own efforts." If God has placed the eternal within man's heart, man can never create Ultimate Truth, but can be only its humble receiver. The problem is that this truth is not seen. Relativism remains the decisive reality in modern life, and where relativism is not dominant, man is threatened by flight from it through such self-made absolutes as Communism, Fascism, and National-Socialism. This contemporary situation is universal, the only difference being that in the West the crisis is the result of an inner development, while in the East the primary cause is the penetration of West into East.

The Christian Church is also in a state of crisis. But since there should always be a tension between the Church's essential nature and its empirical condition in the world to which it belongs, its real crisis today is its blindness to its true critical nature. The representatives of religion, because of their diluted conception of religion, have contributed to the contemporary notion of God's irrelevance. There is hope, however, for the contemporary Church is beginning to sense the crisis caused by its capitulation to culture. Out of this awareness is growing a theological revolution that is driving the Church back to the basic Christian revelation. What has been lost and must be regained is "the vision of what God in Christ meant the Christian community to be—a fellowship of believers, rooted in God and His divine

redemptive order, and therefore committed to the service and the salvation of the world." The Church must live in opposition to evil by a fundamental identification with the sufferings and needs of the world.

This loss of the meaning of the unique Christian revelation has led to a wholesale confusion concerning the missionary enterprise, so that now there is a cry for reorientation and clarification. The Christian mission has represented either escapism, on the one hand, or, as is more often the case, a reflection of modern society "with all its respectabilities, entrenched interests, prejudices and hypocrisies. . . ." Because of this identification of Christianity with Western civilization, much of the rejection of Christianity has been political.

With the breakdown of Western culture, however, is coming the awareness that the missionary movement must work by purely religious and moral persuasion. Ironically, crisis is drawing the Church away from the cultural atmosphere of its history back to its true nature and calling. Secondary arguments for missions, such as social or political enlightenment, often usurped the primary motive; now the primary motive alone can remain, for the "spell of the erroneous identification of Christianity and the progressive West is broken, and, still deadlier, the prestige of Western culture has decreased enormously." To promise that Christianity will cure economic and social problems is to court disillusionment, for these are caused and cured by many factors outside the Church's mission. The real motive and purpose of the Christian mission is founded not on anything that men ask for, but exclusively upon "the divine commission to proclaim the

Lordship of Christ over all life," whether there are "results" or not.

No matter how important the task of translating Christian faith to modern man, the fundamental task, as Kraemer sees it, is to recapture the original Christian faith whose only source is the Bible. Christianity is utterly unique; its origins are irreducible. Christianity offers no moral or religious philosophy, no theology or world-view. The whole content of the Bible is the living, eternally active God, revealed redemptively in the crucified and risen Lord. Christ is the crisis of all religions and philosophies, for all others evade *the* problem: how sinful man can walk with the holy God. There is only one answer: "Jesus Christ and the forgiveness of sins are the divine elements; repentance is the human element. . . ." The joy which is at the heart of the Christian mission is rooted in the miraculous forgiveness coming from God's free and sovereign grace in Jesus Christ, creating a new life in the Spirit. On this basis alone can the Christian "stand in the world, the object of God's saving and renewing activity, as His co-worker in service and love."

Kraemer understands Christian ethics in like manner. All other ethics are forms of eudaemonism, the search for the highest value. The goal of the Christian ethic, however, is "the fulfilment of God's will from which various values derive as fruits and results." This will is intensely concrete and eternally changing according to the situation, yet absolute, for it is *God's* will. One must love another, not because the other is of value, but because God wills every man as His creature. Consequently, we can love only because God first loved us in Jesus Christ. From this base, no political or social programs can

be derived, for the Kingdom of God is beyond human realization. Instead, the Christian must work as *"a ferment and an explosive"* in every relative human sphere. Only openness to God's holy will in loving freedom brings moral sensitivity to the utmost intensity where the depths of the relative may be plumbed for absolute direction, without falling into nihilism.

The Christian atttiude toward non-Christian religions is governed by two poles of the revelation in Christ: a knowledge of God that upsets all other conceptions of the divine, and a knowledge of man that is revolutionary in comparison with all other views. The issue here is not one of pragmatic value, but of truth. The Christian must insist that "God has revealed *the* Way and *the* Life and *the* Truth in Jesus Christ and wills this to be known through all the world." This is a matter of faith, never of rational argument. Yet there is no room here for arrogance or the feeling of superiority, for the Christian stands always as a forgiven *sinner*.

There is a universal religious consciousness among men of all ages, but man's sin corrupts all his religious creations and achievements. The same is true of all attempts at natural theology, for "to reject the God of revelation inevitably means to erect man in some form as god." Nor is there such a thing as general revelation, for, by nature, revelation is special. "The real Christian contention is not: 'We have the revelation and not you,' but pointing gratefully and humbly to Christ: 'It has pleased God to reveal Himself fully and decisively in Christ; repent, believe and adore.' " God shines through man's yearning for truth, beauty, goodness, and holiness, but in a broken and troubled way. The highest and loftiest religious and moral achievements in the non-Christian religions, Kraemer insists, need Christian regeneration.

The point of contact for the Christian message is the perverted human quest for God. Consequently, such a point is not the agent that makes possible missionary results. "The sole *agent* of real faith in Christ is the Holy Spirit." In the end, the only real point of contact is the genuine and continuous interest of the missionary in the total life of the people.

Kraemer's book divides non-Christian religions into naturalist religions of self-realization (primitive, Hinduism, Buddhism, Confucianism, Taoism) and the prophetic religions of revelation (Christianity, Judaism, Islam), attempting to show by a general summary of these religions how each stands in fundamental contrast to Christianity. The difference is not one of grade or richness of religious experience; it is a difference of kind in regard to the understanding of God and man.

It follows, for Kraemer, that the Christian mission cannot be understood as the attempt to permeate other religions and cultures with Christian ideas and ideals. Under the influence of Christianity, Gandhi became not an "unbaptized Christian" but an "invigorated Hindu." What is necessary is a *decision* for Christ; this means not a sympathetic attitude toward Jesus, but a break with one's religious past. The Christian Church must stand firm against the present aversion to evangelizing, proselytizing, and conversion. For the Christian understanding, the primary need of man is conversion. Adaptation and social service, although a necessary part of the Christian witness, must find their basic motivation in evangelism.

So understood, adaptation becomes not assimilation but vital involvement for the sake of exposing the intrinsic inadequacy of man's religious efforts. This dare not mean that the missionary's own theological approach and forms of ecclesiastical life and worship are normative for African or Asiatic Christians. Christian adaptation emerges as the challenge to express the religion of revelation in vigorous indigenous forms in such a way that it is true to its real character. To do this is to expose the relevance of Christianity to all concrete social situations. This is not a matter of relating Christianity to the thought of a society, but a matter of expressing Christianity through this thought. Understood in this fashion, social and cultural activities are not accessories to the Church's witness, but are expressions of it.

Kraemer attempts in the latter portions of his work to suggest how regenerative work can be done in the concrete situations of key missionary fields today. His underlying understanding of such work is that the main aspects of Christianity are worship, witness, and ministry, in integral relation. If any of these elements is given priority, if service, for example, is favored over against evangelism, the meaning of Christianity is lost. To understand these ingredients in their interrelatedness is to grasp the meaning of the Church. Missions in the past have made the mistake of being either evangelical-minded, cultural-minded, or church-minded, according to the dominant interests of their supporters. Each of these attempts has made significant contributions, but today the weakness of each is becoming manifest. That goal toward which these weaknesses point as corrective is the indigenous Church. Such a goal, Kraemer believes, both calls for and results from radical rethinking concerning missions. Such rethinking emerges in the call to take seriously the Church as a radically theocentric community, united in common faith, common love, common worship, and common witness, brought into being by the divine miracle which is the forgiveness of sins.

Such considerations, Kraemer insists, are not a matter of theory, but a matter of the life or death of the Christian Church. Missions are not an optional matter; the introverted Church is without a future. In the end, Kraemer's prophetic call is not for a lessening of Christian permeation; it is a call for even greater scope and influence by a purifying of motive and spirit through a return to the unique foundation of Christianity.

THE IDEA OF A CHRISTIAN SOCIETY

Author: T(homas) S(tearns) Eliot (1888-   )
Type of work: Christian social philosophy
First published: 1939

Principal Ideas Advanced

Because of its concern that every man achieve both his natural and his supernatural end, the Church must interest itself in the problems of society.

But reforms which do not alter fundamental social attitudes fall short of what Christianity demands.

Since the neutral society which characterizes the Western democracies does not favor the true ends of man, Christians must work to replace it with a society based on Christian principles.

Moreover, since a neutral society will be unable to hold its own in competition with the new pagan states, a Christian society is the only plausible alternative to the totalitarian degradation of man.

In *The Idea of a Christian Society*, T. S. Eliot presents a thesis which, although familiar from the writings of Roman Catholics such as Christopher Dawson and Jacques Maritain, is bolder than we are accustomed to hear defended by Protestants; namely, that Christians ought not content themselves with a neutral society in which the practice of religion is merely permitted, but ought rather to work for a

society worthy to be called Christian. For Eliot, who became a Christian and joined the Anglican Church after having given classic expression to the despair of the "lost generation" in the 1920's, it is not enough that Christians work with non-Christians in seeking to remedy the injustices of the present order; they must seek a new social order "in which the natural end of man— virtue and well-being in community—

is acknowledged for all, and the supernatural end—beatitude—for those who have the eyes to see it."

Eliot defends the thesis, further elaborated in *Notes towards the Definition of Culture* (1949), that religion is fundamental for the formation and preservation of any culture. Without religion, he says, there is nothing to give meaning to life, nothing to protect the masses from boredom and despair, and nothing to direct the artist and the philosopher or to counteract the ambition of entrepreneurs and politicians. Eliot nevertheless rejects the pragmatic contention that the truth or falsity of a religion consists in the benefits which it confers upon a people. "To justify Christianity because it provides a foundation of morality, instead of showing the necessity of Christian morality from the truth of Christianity is," Eliot writes, "a very dangerous inversion."

Christian teaching, Eliot reminds us, is that man has an eternal destiny, that his proper goal is the knowledge and love of God, and that what really matters in our earthly life is whether, when one leaves this earth, he enters fully into God's presence or is excluded from it. The world in which the Church finds itself is constantly changing, but the Christian faith does not change; thus, the task of Christianity in every age is to evangelize the world. This task, Eliot argues, has no bounds. A philosophy of co-existence with the world is contrary to the whole spirit of the Gospel, which wants everybody to be saved and to make the greatest possible progress in things of the spirit. The Church does not exist merely for those who are temperamentally suited to attend its services while the rest of mankind goes on its way.

Indeed, says, Eliot, it is folly to think that pious exercises on Sunday are in any way sufficient for the spiritual development even of those who want to be Christians while devoting their lives to a society in which industry, politics, and education are dominated by a secular scheme of values. The Church has no choice but to interest itself in social problems; it "must struggle for a condition of society which will give the maximum of opportunity for us to lead wholly Christian lives, and the maximum of opportunity for others to become Christians." One might suppose that because the Christian holds man's temporal welfare to be merely a means to an eternal goal, he will have less concern than worldly philosophers for the betterment of social conditions. The contrary is the case, says Eliot; precisely because "they are means and not an end in themselves, Christians are more deeply committed to realizing these ideals than are those who regard them as ends in themselves."

For these and similar reasons, Eliot argues that Christians are not doing their full duty when they team up with secular reformers in an effort to remedy particular injustices. Such reforms are worthwhile insofar as they bring about changes which make it possible for persons to live a more fully Christian life, but in most cases the possible benefit of any reform is lost because our culture does not favor Christian pursuits. Nothing will do, Eliot insists, but to alter our whole social enterprise so that, instead of impeding the life of devotion, society will foster it.

Eliot's idea of a Christian society is by no means utopian. A Christian, he says, will not make the mistake of the secular reformer who thinks that he can convert society without being himself converted. Christians believe that the Kingdom of God, although it is continually being realized, can never be consummated in history. Aware that a society will be no more just or humane than are its members, Christians are resigned to the fact that in any society which they can hope to achieve, immorality and hypocrisy will still appear in high places and in low, and that the majority of people will continue to devote most of their attention to their work, their families, and their recreations. Nonetheless, it would be a marked gain if the average man, no matter what his personal interests, were to be grounded in the teachings of the Church and to acknowledge the rightness of its precepts; however slight his own inclination toward things of the spirit, he ought to respect the religious vocation in others.

Such a society, Eliot maintains, can be the foundation for a Christian state; that is to say, for a state of which the laws and policies are based on Christian principles. There is no need for the rulers of a Christian state to be saints; they need not even be professing Christians. But they should be men of statesmanlike vision, and they must be masters in the art of government. As such, they will be ruled by the ethos of the people and compelled to temper their policies to Christian teachings. Even when they perform un-Christian acts, they will have to defend them on Christian grounds.

Because religion remains for most people a matter of habit, we must distinguish within the Christian Community, which comprises all believers, that part which Eliot calls the "Community of Christians." The latter consists of "consciously and thoughtfully practicing Christians, especially those of intellectual and spiritual superiority." They will not form a separate social class. Some of them will choose to live in cloisters; but others will lead an active life as teachers, artists, scholars, and priests. This is not to say that all who are engaged in intellectual callings or ministering to men's souls will belong to the "Community of Christians." But there will be a sufficient number of these keener Christian spirits, and they will have enough identity of belief and purpose, of background and culture, to "enable them to influence and be influenced by each other, and collectively to form the conscious mind and the conscience of the nation."

Eliot is writing chiefly with the old Christian countries of Europe in mind, which have the tradition of an established Church. (In America and other countries where variety of races and religion has long prevailed, the problem of a Christian society is, says Eliot, vastly more complicated.) In Eliot's opinion, the principle of establishment must be reinforced. Churches must come together again into one body, under a hierarchy standing in official relation to the state, and with a parish system reaching down to the smallest units of society. The "Community of Christians," forming a kind of "Church within the Church," will help to keep the Church spiritually alert and make it effective in matters of public policy and in the daily lives of the people. The Church must be Catholic both in the sense that it is the guardian of the high Christian culture of former ages, and in the sense that it is part of a world-wide Christian communion. Thus, it will serve as a counterpoise to hasty opportunism and to narrow nationalism wherever these appear in society. Eliot does not suppose that dissident sects will cease to exist; in fact, he is quite sure that besides sectarians there will be outright skeptics and unbelievers; but, in a society such as he has imagined, the positive culture will derive from the establishment, and the contributions of others will remain marginal—though not necessarily unimportant.

Eliot knows as well as anyone how unpopular his proposal must be, not merely with secularists but also with modern Christians, who have come to take for granted the freedom of a neutral society and are suspicious of any kind of social discipline or restraint. But the author of *The Waste Land* (1922) and *The Hollow Men* (1925) finds little to commend in the present order. He argues that the little that is positive in it, such as its feeling for social justice, is rooted in Christian faith, and that the more Christianity loses its effectiveness, the farther the Western democracies will sink into apathy and despair, "without faith, and therefore without faith in themselves; without a philosophy of life, either Christian or pagan; and without art." A second possibility, which Eliot regards as more likely, is that, spurred to compete with the new pagan civilizations (Fascism and Communism), the Western nations will unintentionally transform themselves into totalitarian states: "a state of affairs in which we shall have regimentation and conformity, without respect for the needs of the individual soul; the puritanism of a hygienic morality in the interest of efficiency; uniformity of opinion through propaganda, and art only encouraged when it flatters the official doctrines of the time."

Most people, Eliot complains, do not have enough imagination to believe that the world will ever be any different from the way it is at the present time; and almost no one would be able to feel at home in any future age, no matter how it turns out. But the harsh realities are that the world is changing at a rapid pace, and that powerful new economic and spiritual forces are at work which, if Christians do not stand up to them, seem destined to organize society along pagan, that is, idolatrous, lines. Even non-Christians, Eliot thinks, when faced with the bankruptcy of liberalism and the alternative of aggressive paganism, will not hesitate to throw their energies into the recovery of a Christian society. It will not be a paradise; it will involve "discipline, inconvenience and discomfort"; it will, in a word, be purgatory; but this, says Eliot, is the only alternative to hell on earth.

Paganism has sometimes been identified with the life of nature and thus has been thought to contrast favorably with Christianity. Eliot is sympathetic with the sentiments which give rise to this view. The attempt of D. H. Lawrence (1885-1930), for example, to recover the sense of man's relation to nature and to God, seems to Eliot important, even though it was ill-conceived. But truly understood, says Eliot, Christianity recovers the natural life more fully than primitive paganism ever did, and today it is the only force in the world which refuses to bow down to the idol of unregulated industrialism. The "deformation of humanity" and the "exhaustion of natural resources" are part of the ritual of the neo-paganism of our times. What we can learn from the pagan civilizations of the past, says Eliot, is that in order for human powers to flourish, art, religion, and society must function together. The error of modern Western civilization has been to suppose that man can enjoy the advantages of new material knowledge and power without raising himself to a higher plane of spiritual knowledge and power. The error must be corrected by Christianity if technological society is not to destroy itself.

A PHILOSOPHY OF RELIGION

Author: Edgar Sheffield Brightman (1884-1953)
Type of work: Philosophy of religion
First published: 1940

PRINCIPAL IDEAS ADVANCED

Religion descriptively defined is an attitude of devotion to the source and sustainer of the highest values; religion normatively defined is co-operation among human persons and the Divine Person for the realization of individual and social values.

The conception of God as a conscious and creative person immanent both in nature and in values provides the most coherent interpretation of all the facts of experience taken synoptically.

The problem of good-and-evil requires a revision of the traditional theistic conception; the power of God is limited by given, nonrational conditions, which God's will neither created nor approves; hence, God is viewed as the finite-infinite controller of the Given.

During the second quarter of this century Edgar Sheffield Brightman was the leading proponent of personalism (or personalistic idealism) in America. Brightman had studied at Boston University under Borden Parker Bowne (1847-1910), the first philosopher in America to develop the personalistic position. Brightman occupied the chair of Borden Parker Bowne Professor of Philosophy at Boston University from 1925 to his death in 1953. Under his leadership a flourishing graduate department of philosophy grew up.

A Philosophy of Religion contains Brightman's mature, systematic, and controversial formulation of the distinctive conception of God for which he has become widely known. Two earlier books, *The Problem of God* (1930) and *The Finding of God* (1931) had prepared the ground for his approach and argument in the 1940 book. A crisp statement of his position was also given in Brightman's presidential address, "An Empirical Approach to God," to the Eastern Division of the American Philosophical Association in December, 1936.

The personalistic perspective, according to Brightman, provides the strongest philosophical foundations for theism. In *A Philosophy of Religion*, Brightman starts by advocating a radically empirical method; that is, a method which considers the whole field of experience, "all that is at any time present in consciousness," including value experience as well as sense experience. He, therefore, rejects three other methods; namely, (1) the method which grounds the truths of faith on *a priori* principles which are independent of experience; (2) the method of logical positivism which restricts the meaning of experience to sense experience, thus eliminating statements about religion (non-sense) as meaningless discourse; and (3) the method associated with the theology of the Swiss Karl Barth, a theology which identifies vertical revelation, uncontaminated by human reason or experience, as the source of salvation.

On the basis of a consideration of "Religion as a Fact" (in a lengthy but illuminating chapter presenting the basic results of the various sciences of religion), Brightman offers the following descriptive definition: "Religion is concern about experiences which are regarded as of supreme value; devotion toward a power or powers believed to originate, increase, and conserve these values; and some suitable expression of this concern and devotion, whether through symbolic rites or through other individual and social conduct." Philosophy of religion is a *"rational interpretation of religion"* which seeks to determine *"the truth of religious beliefs and the value of religious attitudes and practices."* Since religion is rooted in value experience, Brightman devotes the third chapter to analyzing religious values, emphasizing both their uniqueness and their coalescence with other values. Since religious values are re-

lated to other dimensions of life, the problem of relating ideal values to existence, and of reconciling conflicting religious value-claims and beliefs, is a problem which calls for a philosophy of religion.

Brightman accepts empirical coherence as the criterion of religious truth. A principle of verification by coherence does not claim to provide theoretical certainty for religious belief, but it does give a basis for commitment (risk-taking action), and it keeps one open to new truth. Coherence is a better way of gaining knowledge of—that is, of understanding—the nature of God than immediate experience of God (mystical intuition), revelation, faith, *a priori* principles (rationalism), or action (pragmatism).

Having established his descriptive foundations and his methodological principles, Brightman turns to the substantive questions, the most important of which is the problem of God.

The generic *religious* meaning of the idea of God is "objective source and conserver of values." "Only the source of value is God," Brightman writes. The question is not whether there is a source of value (that is, whether God exists), but rather, how are we to *conceive* the source of value? As a background for answering this question, in the fifth chapter Brightman canvasses the major alternative available conceptions. He defines and analyzes polytheism, henotheism, monotheism, pantheism, agnostic realism, humanism, deistic supernaturalism, impersonal idealism, religious naturalism, and theism. In the seventh chapter Brightman evaluates these conceptions and develops his case for the superior adequacy of theism, the belief that God is "a conscious mind (spirit or person), immanent both in physical nature and in value experiences."

It is misleading to think of this case for personalistic theism as an "argument" for God. Brightman does not cast his argument in the form of traditional proofs. Indeed, he makes only the most cursory mention of the ontological, cosmological, teleological, and moral arguments. The basic thesis is essentially this: the hypothesis of a personal God provides the most coherent interpretation of all the available evidence; it gives the most adequate account of all the facts of experience taken synoptically. Consequently, the "argument" consists in presenting the following supporting evidence: (1) conscious experiences constitute all of the actual first-order data; (2) all physical entities are known only to the extent that they produce and affect conscious experience; (3) evidence of law and order suggests, though it does not logically entail, a cosmic ordering mind; (4) evidences of purpose, whether psychological, biological, or in evolution, point to a personal God; (5) the evidence supplied by history of religion, psychology of religion, and sociology of religion is best explained "by the hypothesis that one supreme personal God is at work in all religious experience"; (6) the entire range of value experience is most adequately grounded by this same hypothesis. Brightman concludes that the superiority of personalistic theism to impersonalistic naturalism is shown by its "more inclusive coherence."

In another connection, Brightman develops a theme which can be viewed as an argument for a personal God. This theme is what is called "the dialectic of desire." Dialectic is "the mind's search for completeness and co-

herence," and desire is the most universal psychological fact. The progression of the dialectic of desire leads, in a way that can only be barely outlined here, from the desire for pleasure (enjoying), to the desire for physical things (having), to the desire for activity (doing), to the desire for other persons (sharing), to the desire for ideals (planning), which leads to desire for the Supreme Person as a resolution of "the antinomy of the ideal."

The core of Brightman's case for a personal God becomes clear, however, only in his grappling with the problem of evil. It is really, Brightman maintains, the problem of good-and-evil. Naturalism can give no satisfactory explanation of value, nor can traditional theism account adequately for evil. The seriousness with which Brightman confronts the problem (in Chapter 7) may be indicated in two ways: (1) He makes a careful analysis of value and disvalue, intrinsic and instrumental, moral and nonmoral; there is a realistic recognition of the factuality of evil which is epitomized in his view of surd evil, "a type of evil which is inherently and irreducibly evil and contains within itself no principle of development or improvement"; (2) Brightman takes an inventory of ten possible and prevalently proposed solutions of the problem of evil and finds them singly and collectively not worth further consideration.

Brightman's constructive proposal for dealing with the problem of evil involves significant modifications in the theistic conception of God. His distinctive analysis of the nature of a personal God is elaborated first by a critique of traditional theism (or as Brightman calls it, "theistic absolutism"). Theistic absolutism is defined as "the view that the will of God faces no conditions within the divine experience which that will did not create (or at least approve)." The chief objections to it are that (1) it appeals to ignorance; (2) it ascribes surd evils to the divine will; (3) it tends to make good and evil indistinguishable; (4) it cuts the nerve of moral endeavor; and (5) it is unempirical.

The position which Brightman accepts and advocates is theistic finitism, the view that "the will of God does face conditions within divine experience which that will neither created nor approves." It is easy to misunderstand what Brightman means by speaking of God as finite. Brightman does not mean (1) that God is dependent on anything other than His being, or (2) that God, though personal, is human. God, according to Brightman's conception, is in legitimate and prevalent senses *infinite* (uncreated and unending), *eternal* (everlasting), *absolute* (ultimate reality, unconditioned by any external environment), *omnipotent* (having all the power there is except that which He delegates to created beings), and *perfect* in His complete and continuous commitment to the highest values.

What differentiates theistic finitism from theistic absolutism is the insistence of the former that the divine nature includes a nonrational aspect. This aspect Brightman calls the "Nonrational Given"; it refers to refractory data, brute fact, such as sensation. A second aspect of God's nature Brightman calls the "Rational Given"; it corresponds very closely to the traditional notion of the divine reason. The third aspect of the divine being is the divine will. God's will does not, according to Brightman, create either the Nonra-

tional Given (brute fact) or the Rational Given (rational norms). God's will does, however, control the Nonrational Given according to His rational principles, giving significant form to what is otherwise meaningless content. Although God is never absolutely in control, He never loses control and is always at work overcoming obstacles. New values are continually being created through heroic struggle and sacrificial love. God is thus, in Brightman's terms, the "Finite-Infinite Controller of the Given."

The basis for this characterization of God is Brightman's analysis of the structure of experience. All persons are complex unities of experience consisting of rational form, activity (purpose), and nonrational content, inextricably interwoven. (The problem of human personality is dealt with separately in Chapters 10 and 11.) If God is personal, it is more intelligible to think of Him in this fashion. Furthermore, such a conception would be more consistent with the facts of evolution and surd evil. Brightman denies that the traditional notion of God's absolute power is a presupposition of the religious consciousness.

The last major issue which Brightman treats is that of personal immortality. Weak arguments both against and for immortality are considered and rejected. The crucial argument against immortality is physiological psychology. The answer to this consists in a critique of the naturalistic assumptions of the argument. The crucial argument for immortality is the goodness of God. The case for immortality is thus seen to depend on the general theistic position which Brightman has developed.

The last two chapters of the book seem more like appendices, but they are most interesting. One (Chapter 15) deals with internal criticisms of religion; that is, with religion's self-criticism. The other considers external criticisms of religion; for example, the criticism that religion is a device in the class struggle.

For Brightman, religion normatively conceived is "cooperation with God and man for the realization of individual and of shared values."

Personalistic theism represents an effort to go between traditional supernaturalism and current naturalism. Brightman would claim that personalism is more adequately empirical than positivism and more genuinely person-centered than existentialism.

CHRISTIAN DOCTRINE

Author: J. S. Whale (1896-   )
Type of work: Systematic theology
First published: 1941

PRINCIPAL IDEAS ADVANCED

All Christian doctrines are the doctrine of God.

The doctrine of creation affirms a divine purpose for man, and the doctrine of the Fall expresses the conflict between man's will and the divine purpose.

Belief in the Resurrection is the Christian faith.

Since the Church belongs to Christ, it is more than an earthly society; it is the visible institution that gives expression to the Word of God.

Christian Doctrine includes the eight lectures which J. S. Whale, president of Cheshunt College, presented to the faculties of the University of Cambridge during the Michaelmas Term of 1940. The lectures provide an analytic exposition of the central features of Christian doctrine, and they have been well received as offering a clear modern statement of Christian ideas as developed from a Protestant viewpoint.

Whale considers, in the order named, the following Christian doctrines: the Christian doctrine of Creation, of the Fall, of history, of the atonement, of the Trinity and the Incarnation, of the Church, of the Word and the Sacraments, and of Last Things.

Whale's presupposition, which is an expression of his faith, is that all Christian doctrines are concerned with the reality and nature of God. No doctrine can be made clear unless reference is made to God by whom, or by reference to whom, all problems are resolved. "Christian doctrines," he writes, "presuppose and illustrate the fundamental doctrine that God is, and that man's chief end is to know him."

The claim that all doctrines reduce to the fundamental doctrine of God's reality is illustrated by reference to six common Christian ideas. The Christian conception of man, for example, is the conception of that being made in the image of God; thus, man cannot be understood unless God is known. The idea of sin involves the idea of moral evil relative to God's will. Redemption cannot be conceived except by reference to God's grace. Jesus is the Savior only if He is regarded as divine. The Church is nothing more than a moral society if it is not an expression of God's will. Finally, the Christian doctrine of history is without content unless God is considered to be the beginning and the end of all things.

Thus, God's reality is central to Christian doctrine. But how is God to be known? Whale points out that there have been three types of answers to that question: God is known through the authority of the Church; God is known through reference to the Bible; and God is known through mystical experience. Many persons have had the tendency to emphasize one source of knowledge at the expense of the others, but Whale argues that the three sources of knowledge about God interlock and are not mutually exclusive.

The author considers the place of reason in the effort to appreciate the reality of God, and he maintains that the proofs of God's existence are important as providing testimony of God's presence; only through revelation, however, is it possible to know *"who* God is. . . ."* To pass from rational argument to the "living awareness of God" entails being ready to know God "experimentally" and with the heart. Christian doctrines, such as that of the Creation, are best understood not as cosmological theories but as expressions of faith in a transcendent God.

Having described the Christian doctrine of Creation as an expression of man's trust in the primacy of God, Whale turns to the doctrine of the Fall. He first of all rejects two views of human nature which are not compatible with the Christian faith; namely, naïve optimism and cynical pessimism. The former view is unrealistic, even sentimental, in regarding man as marked for continued progress and happiness; the fact is, Whale asserts, that the tragic view of human nature, a view which regards man as liable to sin, is closer to the truth than is the bland philosophy of naive optimism. Cynical pessimism, however, is equally mistaken in its extreme portrait of the human condition; to suppose that man is utterly abandoned and that his sin is without any hopeful issue is unchristian. The Christian view of man's Fall, a view customarily described as "Christian anthropology," is that man is God's creature; man sins by denying God and rebelling against Him; he is alienated and incurs the wrath of God; and each man is guilty with his fellowmen: no man stands alone in his sin. The doctrine of the Fall, like the doctrine of Creation, is important as symbolism; just as the doctrine of Creation calls attention to God's existence and the primacy of His being, so the doctrine of the Fall calls attention to man's "recalcitrant will" and to man's tendency to misdirect his life by turning himself from the divine.

A Christian doctrine of history is necessary if there is to be any satisfactory understanding of the relation of man in time to an eternal God who is "above history." The Greek and Hebrew attempts to resolve the problem of history failed, claims Whale; only the Christian answer succeeds. Christian doctrine presents God as infinite and eternal, ineffable and *"totum simul"*; at the same time, God makes finite man's worship possible by bridging the gap between the eternal and the temporal; the miraculous resolution of paradox was accomplished when "The Word was made flesh, and dwelt among us." Christian doctrine, then, regards history as a divine instrument; God has taken certain events out of history and has made time a part of eternity. It may be supposed by some persons that every event in time is equally significant, but in opposition to this claim Whale calls attention to the central fact in all history: the "redeeming activity of God." But the Redeemer cannot logically be considered apart from the fact of the Resurrection. "Belief in the Resurrection is not an appendage to the Christian faith," writes Whale; "it is the Christian faith." The Resurrection "explains the Gospels," Whale insists, and he adds that the Resurrection, which is "the mightiest of the mighty acts of God" provides the foundation of the Christian doctrine of history.

Whale describes atonement as "the creation of the conditions whereby God and man come together." Man needs to be reconciled to God because through his sin man has destroyed the harmony between himself and the source of all being. The Christian doctrine of the atonement, as Whale analyzes it, is the doctrine that the divine sacrifice is a revelation of God's love, a revelation which calls for a human response which will make reconciliation possible. There are theological problems which arise from the doctrine of the atonement—in particular, the problem of explaining the triune being of God and the motivation for the sacrifice of Christ—but it is clear, asserts Whale, that the atonement was that decisive act by which man, despite his weakness, was allowed to draw close to God.

The problem of explaining the Trinity and the Incarnation arises because the intellect demands a philosophical resolution of such a paradox as that God, although one, is three. But Whale begins his exposition of the Christian doctrine of the Trinity and the Incarnation by calling attention to the historic evidence which the Gospels provide, evidence which establishes both the humanity and the divinity of Jesus Christ. In a striking pair of sentences Whale explains the distinctive power of the idea of Christ: "He is what God means by 'Man.' He is what man means by 'God.'" Liturgical testimony also implies that Jesus is to be identified with God. Finally, theological dogma includes the Christian doctrine that Christ is unique; if no problem arose because of His uniqueness, the claim of His uniqueness would not survive.

Whale insists that man must serve God not only with the heart but also with the mind, but he concedes that to describe that which is finally unique is to end in paradox. The effort which theologians have put into the attempt to clarify the idea of the Trinity is worth while as a "monument" to what must remain a mystery to the intellect, but like the doctrine of the Incarnation the idea of the Trinity expresses the faith in God's unity and love, together with the belief that God came into— not out of—history in order that man might once again be in harmony with God.

Whale begins his consideration of the Christian doctrine of the Church by agreeing with those who maintain that religion is a personal matter. But religion cannot be a private matter, he adds, for "redemption must mean the restoration of that community of sons which God wills eternally." The Christian life is "necessarily corporate," Whale insists; the Church is the Body of Christ. It is true that the Church is divided and that the pure Church is with God, but the pure Church is one in spirit; it is more than an earthly society; it is the visible expression— through the Scriptures, the sacraments, the rites, the offices, the buildings—of the Word of God. Thus, the Church as an institution makes a new life possible through its corporate life. The Church provides finite man with the opportunity to attend now to the infinite and the eternal; through the Church man looks beyond the limited and beyond death to those final spiritual matters that ultimately concern his most personal being.

The Church provides two elements which are commonly called "the means of Grace": "the preaching and the hearing of the Word" and "the Sacrament of the Eucharist." These two elements are not two in spirit, for the Word which is spoken is the very Word which is shown in the Eucharist, the breaking of the "Bread."

The sacraments perpetuate the natural symbols which Christ made meaningful through His acts. Whale insists that the symbols which the Church uti-

lizes were not chosen arbitrarily, for they call attention to the means of grace which Christ Himself employed; and when the sacraments are taken seriously, they continue to serve as means of grace. Thus, they are not merely symbolic acts; the sacraments are "signs of God acting."

It is important to be clear about death, Whale claims in his concluding chapter, because to understand life one must consider its end, and to consider the end of life is to consider death and the purpose of death. Death is certain, tragic (in that man alone knows that he is mortal), universal, and inescapably compelling (in that it forces man to choose between despair and faith). To choose faith is to make life meaningful; the end of life is not the dissolution of the body but the realization of eternal life. Thus, the Christian eschatology calls attention to the end already realized in Christ, but at the same time Christian eschatology reminds man of his mortality and of the possibility of his refusing to accept the eternal. Although God is gracious, man is responsible for making the effort to realize the end for which he was created.

THE MEANING OF REVELATION

Author: H. Richard Niebuhr (1894-1962)
Type of work: Confessional theology
First published: 1941

PRINCIPAL IDEAS ADVANCED

All human knowledge and action, revelation included, is radically conditioned by historical relativism.

Since to act is to decide in the face of objective uncertainty, faith is necessary at every stage; to become a self is to have a "god" as the orienting value which makes existence meaningful.

Man has dual perspectives regarding all things: objective appraisal in terms of "external history," subjective appropriation in terms of "internal history."

Since "internal history," the realm of revelation, is known only through participation, there can be no defense of one revelation against another; the only viable theology is confessional, a recital of one's inner history for the sake of sharing.

The year 1781 serves well to divide modern Protestant theology from its orthodox foundation, for in that year Immanuel Kant published his *Critique of Pure Reason*. From this point on, the awareness that emerged to unify the efforts of Protestant theologians was that, for perhaps the first time in the history of Christianity, the theologian no longer knew what revelation was.

The Reformers, such as Martin Luther (1483-1546), not only rejected the excesses of Roman Catholic ecclesiastical practices, but also found in both the Pauline view of human sinfulness and in the nominalist insistence on the finitude of reason a firm basis for challenging the ambitious attempts by Scholastic philosophy to reach the divine by human effort.

Although the Reformers distinguished between the revelatory Word grasped through Scripture by faith and the actual words of Scripture, irrational subjective interpretation of the Bible in the post-Reformation period forced theologians to make an unqualified identification of Scripture with revelation. "Protestant scholasticism" substituted an infallible Scripture for an infallible Church. Under the further influence of rationalism, the personal, experiential aspects of revelation were minimized in favor of propositional belief, thereby shifting reliance to natural, philosophical knowledge of God in order to defend, supplement, and often to interpret Scripture.

During the generations that followed, Biblical literalism was subject to the impact of literary criticism extended to Scripture, and to the challenge of natural science in regard to miracles and the Biblical account of creation. Studies in the history of religions showed similarities between supposedly "unique" religions. With the publication of Kant's *Critique of Pure Reason*, the questioning of revelation was complete, for the claim that reason can support revelation by framing proofs for God's existence was critically weakened.

For over a century, liberal Protestant theology attempted to answer the question of revelation, developing answers along lines established by the three Kantian *Critiques*. Friedrich Schleiermacher (1768-1834) developed religious knowledge in terms of feeling (*Gefühl*), a unique but universal "faculty" of man. Albrecht Ritschl (1822-1889) interpreted revelation in terms of moral consciousness. G. W. F. Hegel (1770-1831) understood revelation in terms of rationalism, within the confines of Absolute Idealism.

With the beginning of the twentieth century, it became clear to many scholars that in interpreting and judging revelation from the perspective of finite categories, liberal theologians had reduced the uniqueness of Christianity to a series of "universal truths."

It is within this context that twentieth century Protestant theology must be understood. While such neo-orthodox theologians as Karl Barth have returned through Kant to a radical Reformation understanding of revelation, H. Richard Niebuhr stands as one of the leading "mediating" theologians of the present. He is concerned in *The Meaning of Revelation* not only with the uniqueness of Christian revelation, but also with both the finality of the Kantian critique of human reason and the effect of revelation on all human knowledge and action. Revelation must be true to its uniqueness, but this uniqueness, if it is to be relevant, can be understood only in terms of the situation of *modern* man. Niebuhr's answer is the development of a "confessional" theological methodology.

Niebuhr's underlying problem is this: "We are aware today that all our philosophical ideas, religious dogmas and moral imperatives are historically conditioned and this awareness tempts us to a new agnosticism." There can be no denying the Kantian dictum that there is no universal knowledge of things in themselves; *all* knowledge is conditioned by the standpoint of the knower, whether the subject is ethics, political theory, or revelation. Knowledge emerges through experience, and experience is limited by space and time; that is, by the historical. Even language, the communicator of experience, bears radically the marks of the flux permeating all things finite.

It is the burden of Niebuhr's work to show that it is not the case that "the man who is forced to confess that his view of things is conditioned by the standpoint he occupies must doubt the reality of what he sees." In the midst of universal relativity man must still act. Action is thus always in the face of objective uncertainty; it is a faith risk. Yet the object of action is truth, for its justification is in its fruits.

The case is similar in regard to revelation. Religious faith is circular in the sense that statements about God can be made only from the point of view of faith in Him, but such circularity the Christian holds in common with every man. Theology, then, because of the nature of the human situation, must be resolutely confessional. Its function is to confess "what has happened to us in our community, how we came to believe, how we reason about things and what we see from our point of view." Anything less than confession robs religion of its distinctive personal involvement; anything more than confession is the idolatry of substituting human categories, conceptions, and institutions for the living God to whom one is confessing.

It is confessional theology that is loyal to the human situation, for it has as its task the determination of "what revelation means for Christians rather than what it ought to mean for all men, everywhere and at all times." Such an inquirer realizes that what he sees is from a limited point of view, yet his faith is an orienting acceptance of that truth as true for him *in that situation.*

This understanding, Niebuhr insists, is not a retreat for a Christianity threatened with extinction, but a rediscovery of the original Biblical witness. The early Christians neither argued for the existence of God, nor attempted any defense of absolute moral norms. The proclamation of the Christian was no more, *but no less,* than a "recital of the great events connected with the historical appearance of Jesus Christ and a confession of what had happened to the community of disciples."

The motive for Christian declaration must be that underlying the early disciples' recital of their lives; there must be an inner compulsion to share that which is possessed only in sharing. Thus revelation is history, and its communication is historical. To understand Christian revelation is to look out at the world of history and nature through the eyes of the believer and from his particular perspective. The Scriptures are revelation only when read from the perspective of the community of which the Scriptures are a record.

What becomes clear is that Niebuhr's analysis is based on the Kantian distinction between pure and practical reason, between objective and subjective necessity. According to Niebuhr, all things, even history itself, can be interpreted from two perspectives. The first is the mode of objectivity, of externality, accounting for events environmentally, concerned with pure, uninterpreted facts. It is this perspective when made exclusive that leads to skeptical relativism.

But such pure objectivity is existentially impossible, for in the process of acting, one necessarily imbues facts with meaning. In so doing, history is discriminately appropriated as "inner history." Thus history has two dimensions, established by the dual types of human relation. There is "history as contemplated" and "history as lived." Niebuhr illustrates this distinction brilliantly by comparing the events of July 4, 1776, from the "objective" perspective of spectatorship characterizing the *Cambridge Modern History* and the "subjective" perspective of involvement reflected in Abraham Lincoln's Gettysburg Address. These are two different orders. For one the subject is "Congress," and for the other it is the reality known as "Our Fathers." For one it is a matter to be described; for the other it is an idea to be defended to the death. All events can be so appraised from without or from within. Every individual and every community lives in the midst of two histories so drawn.

This difference in perspective is in no way a distinction between true and false. It must remain a matter of perspective, and a dual perspective is unavoidable, for no man nor group nor society can escape the search for a normative knowledge that transcends the purely descriptive, for value beyond pure fact, for meaning beyond mere information. One must study history not only with scientists, but with poets; that is, in terms of persons, purposes, and destinies.

It is Niebuhr's insistence that man has no option but to engage in this faith-dimension. At the most basic level, man is a creature of faith, for external reality is life lived in trust of repeated experiences. Likewise, on a higher level, either man must believe in something that makes life worth living or he cannot exist. Man as a practical, living being never exists without a god or gods. To be a self is to have a god; to have a god is to have history. To have one god is to have one history. Thus, belief in a god is a necessity founded in man's nature. The only question left to man is to ascertain which God is loyal in everyday existence. This can be known only by appropriating external history internally.

The traditional distinction between nature and supernature, then, must be seen as pertaining not to the type of thing perceived, but to the perspective employed. "We can speak of revelation only in connection with our own history without affirming or denying its reality in the history of other communities into whose inner life we cannot penetrate without abandoning ourselves and our community." Only a leap of faith can lead from observed to lived history. In no way can objective inquiry create faith, for no event is ever known as it really is. God alone knows in one act what something is from within and without. One must think *with* Isaiah and Paul rather than *about* them in order to verify their visions; so to participate in thought is to share their history. For man, there is no metaphysical solution to historical dualism. The solution is a practical one.

Yet, external history is important, for it is the medium in which internal history rests and comes to life. The alternation which is life is the dialogue of internal and external history. Internal history rests upon Pascal's "reasons of the heart," but rather than conflicting with the "head," such revelation becomes the base by which reason detects the meaning of all history through the spectacles of illuminating pattern, of image.

For the Christian, this image is Jesus Christ, for through Him history as a "tale told by an idiot, full of sound and fury, signifying nothing" becomes a grand epic. Even more, inner history makes past and present a living whole, exposing in our presence both those who are corrupted for thirty pieces of silver, and those whose bodies this moment are being broken for our sake.

Thus, by nature, revelation is dynamic; as the starting point for the interpretation of past, present, and future history, revelation is subject to progressive validation. For the Christian, the God revealed in history continues to reveal Himself through history in all times and places.

Jesus Christ is not the only divine self-disclosure that the Christian knows, for there is the echo of conscience, the numinous in nature, the craving of reason for a beginning and end. Yet, through Christ, all is radically transvalued, for what is revealed is not what was expected, and our expectations are put to shame. "We sought a good to love and were found by a good that loved us." It is the value and meaning of the world, grasped through an inner history, molded by him who makes all things new, that provides the existential answer to the problem of revelation in a world of relativities, and the answer is a confession. Niebuhr concludes his account of the meaning of revelation with the following comment: "Whatever other men may say we can only confess . . . that through our history a compulsion has been placed upon us and a new beginning offered us which we cannot evade."

THE NATURE AND DESTINY OF MAN

Author: Reinhold Niebuhr (1892-   )
Type of work: Philosophical theology
First published: Volume I, 1941; Volume II, 1945

PRINCIPAL IDEAS ADVANCED

Man is the created conjunction of spirit and nature.

Sin consists in man's self-centered refusal to recognize his creaturely limits.

In contrast to two other perspectives, namely, the Greek view of man as a rational animal, and the modern view of man as ever-progressing, the Christian or Biblical view defines man as image of God, creature, and sinner.

In contrast to views which reduce history to nature and also to those in which history is swallowed up in eternity or supernature, the Christian view of man is indefeasibly historical; the Christian view of historical destiny may be characterized as a drama which begins at Creation, rises to climax at the coming of Christ, and moves on to conclusion at Judgment Day.

The Nature and Destiny of Man is the most definitive and comprehensive statement of Reinhold Niebuhr's theology. It consists of his Gifford Lectures delivered at the University of Edinburgh in 1939, and historically it marks the clear and forceful emergence in American religious thought of the new theological viewpoint which originated in Germany with Barth's The Epistle to the Romans in 1919. Niebuhr's formulation of this theology consists of a study of man in what the subtitle of the present work terms "a Christian interpretation." Throughout both volumes runs a comparison of the Christian interpretation of man with alternative schemes of interpretation, Greek classical views in the ancient world, and naturalism and idealism in the modern world. The viewpoint of Christian faith upon human nature and destiny is also frequently contrasted with that of Marxism and of secular liberalism which are its contemporary alternatives. Niebuhr's enterprise is apologetic in the classical sense of offering an *apologia*, though not an apology, for the Christian view. Believing that this view is more adequate to all the facts of human existence than alternative views, Niebuhr proposes and undertakes a comparative study. Yet it is a study which appeals to facts and avoids defensiveness and special pleading. Indeed, Niebuhr is sharply critical of forms of Christian thought which exhibit these latter traits.

Niebuhr's viewpoint may be characterized as Christian existentialism, in that it centers upon the question of man and seeks a Biblical or Christian answer to this question. While he has much to say of God and other basic religious matters, they enter discussion as answers to the question raised by human nature and destiny. Among other existentialist features of Niebuhr's thought are his emphasis upon man's actual being, prior to any rational theory concerning the human essence, and also his emphasis upon the self-alienation of man in sin. In contrast to many other types of existentialism, Niebuhr emphasizes man's social being as well as his solitude.

The Christian character of Niebuhr's thought is based upon the Protestant Reformers, the Church Fathers, particularly Augustine, and most of all upon the Bible. It may thus be said to have a pronounced Protestant character. Niebuhr's thought as illustrated by *The Nature and Destiny of Man* has both influenced and been influenced by the current revival of Biblical studies.

Among current forms of Neo-Protestant theology, Niebuhr's shows both similarities to and differences from other formulations. Along with Karl Barth and Emil Brunner, Niebuhr emphasizes the radically transcendent character of the God of Biblical and Christian tradition, and the consequent creatureliness and sin of man. The influence of Brunner's *Man in Revolt*, a work which was published in 1939, on *The Nature and Destiny of Man* is particularly apparent. Yet the differences from the work by Barth, Brunner, and other contemporary theologians appear in Niebuhr's freer and more critical approach to traditional theology as well as in his lifelong concern with the issues of a responsible and functioning social ethic.

The two volumes of *The Nature and Destiny of Man,* entitled respectively *Human Nature* and *Human Destiny*, are so closely interrelated that neither can be considered apart from the other without serious distortion of the author's purpose. Human nature defines for Niebuhr the structures of created freedom, sin, judgment, and redemption which find application in the historical process. Conversely, human destiny is the drama of history in which man's nature is acted out.

The argument begins with man as a problem to himself. According to the author, all the various views of man, ancient and modern, may be observed to raise radical problems for themselves. If we seek to define man in terms of mind, rationality, or spirit, we are immediately confronted with his involvement in nature. If, on the other hand, we define man as an aspect of nature or natural process, the question arises of how we shall understand his self-conscious and self-transcendent freedom.

Greek philosophical views in Plato and Aristotle tend to define man in terms of his rationality, though Niebuhr notes in passing a sharply contrasting view of man in Greek tragedy. Distinctively modern views of man, while moving between philosophic idealism and naturalism, have in common an optimism regarding human good and evil which generates the characteristically modern view of progress with its confidence in human autonomy, reason, and virtue.

In sharpest contrast to both ancient and modern alternatives, Niebuhr's Christian view of man finds the source and also the key to man's fulfillment in his relation to God. This view emphasizes in Biblical fashion the integral unity of body and spirit, and of freedom and creatureliness, in human nature. Thus, according to the author, the Christian view combines the truths and avoids the failures and errors of the alternative views of man. This thesis concerning the Christian view is maintained throughout the work.

Chapter 2 of the first volume analyzes the elements of form and vitality in non-Christian views of man, ranging from the classical rationalism of Plato to the apotheosis of vitality in modern romanticism. Again the argument is that the Christian view is best able to hold together these contrasting aspects of man's nature. The third chapter devotes similar arguments to the idea of individuality in modern culture. While individuality has a basis in physical and biological nature, it finds expression in various cultural forms. The modern West exhibits forms of individualism ranging from the economic individualism of liberal democracy to the romantic individualism of a Goethe or an Emerson. Yet by a curious dialectical process, this trait so proudly and so characteristically asserted by modern thought is asserted by Niebuhr to be "lost" in conclusions which subordinate the individual person completely or totally to the state or to society. Idealist social philosophies like that of Hegel are offered as illustrations. Modern totalitarianism is cited as a practical manifestation of this loss of the individual in a modern culture originally dedicated to individualism. In contrast to the extremes of individualism and collectivism in practice, the Christian view of man is asserted to maintain a viable balance between individuality and community.

If there is a single pervasive trait of the modern mind which embraces all the many conflicting varieties of modern thought and life, it is, according to Niebuhr in the words of the title to Chapter IV, "The Easy Conscience of Modern Man." From Pico to Dewey, and from Helvetius to Hegel, modern man has thought well of himself and has refused to take seriously the traditional Christian doctrine of original sin. Indeed, one of the primary motivations of modern thought has been a criticism of the Christian idea, and a contrary or opposite assertion that man has in his own nature sufficient virtue and intelligence to solve his problems and master his fate. This modern viewpoint has tended to diagnose existent human evil as inertia or ignorance which may be conquered by improved education and social reform. Such characteristically modern ideas of good and evil give birth to the idea of human progress and also to the utopian strain of thought from Thomas More to Condorcet, Comte, H. G. Wells, and the Marxists. From Niebuhr's viewpoint, all such views represent a radical misreading of the nature and extent of evil in man. History wreaks its vengeance upon such inadequate ideas.

The Biblical view of man is asserted to be rooted in the idea of the God who reveals Himself to man, and in whose presence alone man sees himself as he truly is. Niebuhr argues for a general revelation or disclosure of God in the structure of creation. Thus, in the ordered and determinate structure of the world and in the freedom and conscience of man are to be found significant intimations of the same God who speaks through the Bible.

Niebuhr's view of man comes to explicit formulation in the exposition of the idea of man as the image of God and as the self-venerating sinner. What is the image of God in man, and where is it located? Speaking historically, many of the early Church Fathers who were under the influence of Greek philosophy sought to identify the image of God with human reason. Niebuhr disagrees. Following Augustine, he sees the image of God as the self-conscious and self-transcendent character of the human mind and self. It is this trait of man's nature which drives him to push beyond every fixed context or structure, forcing the distinctively human questions: Who am I?, Why am I alive? It is this trait which constitutes man as a self-conscious and centered self with the capacity of self-determination. Yet this freedom of self-transcendence is inextricably and integrally related to man's finite, mortal nature as a part of God's creation.

Man, who is both image of God and creature, is also, according to Niebuhr, a sinner. By sin is meant the human tendency to egotism or self-centeredness. It is, in Niebuhr's phrase, man's attempt "to play God"; that is, to make himself the center of all things. Such arrogant self-deification is the content of the traditional Christian vice, pride. The Genesis story of the Fall of man resulting in original sin is regarded by Niebuhr as a mythical statement of this aspect of man's observable behavior. There is no absolute necessity for a human self to be self-centered, for he is still free to find his proper center in God, yet the combination of man's freedom and creatureliness constitutes a situation of temptation which makes self-centeredness overwhelmingly probable. In the vertical relation of man to God, egotism manifests itself as self-deification, while in the horizontal relation of man to man, its consequence is injustice.

One of the most trenchant and original features of Niebuhr's thought is his fresh development of the social implications of such traditional theological ideas as sin. Thus, Chapter 8, entitled "Collective Egotism," is for the author completely in character.

He argues that egotism is an even more pronounced and significant feature of social than of individual behavior. All human groups, whether states, nations, races, classes, or churches, exhibit an inevitable tendency toward self-centeredness which is then rationalized by an identification of group interest with that of civilization, humanity, God, or whatever is taken as ultimate. Such efforts "to put God on our side" are by no means limited to traditional religious groups; Marxist parties and nations exhibit a similar belief in the absolute rightness of their cause, rationalized by science and Marxist dialectics. Such a belief, wherever it occurs or however rationalized, constitutes a kind of final expression of pride.

Similar tendencies are exhibited in the higher life of man's mind and spirit. Righteousness, perverted by pride, becomes self-righteousness. Human reason is degraded—and becomes intellectual pride or arrogance. Man's vision of God can similarly become pride of religion, amounting to individual or collective self-deification.

By these lines of thought Niebuhr is led to a reassertion of a Pauline or Augustinian view of human nature which attempts to deal realistically with the extent and nature of evil in man. Final chapters in the first volume seek to relate sin to guilt, and both sin and guilt to human responsibility and to the doctrine of *justitia originalis*, which asserts the originally good character of man.

The second volume, dealing as it does with the problem of human destiny, begins with a basic distinction between historical and nonhistorical views of man. The latter include views which, like ancient or modern naturalism, subsume history to nature, and at the opposite pole, those faiths and philosophies in which history is swallowed up in eternity, as is the case in Neoplatonism and in philosophic Hinduism.

A clear characteristic of the historical type of faith is held to be the expectation of a Messiah, a figure in whom the meaning of history is fulfilled or realized. While various types of national messianism are mentioned, Niebuhr devotes most of his analysis to the development of Biblical or Hebrew messianism from the prophetic period to the first century, A.D. Against this background he proceeds to analyze the Messianic claims and significance of Jesus, arguing that, while in some respects Jesus fulfills Hebrew messianism, in others, such as in His rejection of Jewish legalism and particularism, He rejects or radically reforms it.

The figure of Christ is interpreted by Niebuhr in the Pauline phrase, the wisdom and power of God. That is to say, Christ is to be understood as God's decisive word to man concerning the nature of human life; Christ is God's power at work reconciling man to Himself. The human figure in whom this wisdom and power are manifested is a man utterly dedicated to sacrificial love, of which the Cross is the climactic expression.

The figure of the crucified Christ also defines the limits and possibilities of history. For love is a human possibility, yet no man or group does in any total or realistic sense live by the sacrificial love of the Cross. To this extent historical existence is involved in sin and must be saved by the divine grace revealed in Christ's sacrifice.

God's grace is understood by Nie-

buhr as the divine love toward man which is able to fulfill and perfect man's fragmentary and corrupted life. He compares and contrasts the two main theological interpretations of grace, the Catholic idea of grace *in nobis* (in us) and the Protestant idea of grace *pro nobis* (for us), coming to strongly Protestant conclusions. Against the Catholic view of infused grace, Niebuhr points to the continuance of sinful, egotistical behavior on the part of presumably regenerate men.

The Reformation is understood by Niebuhr as a powerful assertion of the Protestant view against the problems and perversions of the late medieval church. Yet the Reformation took place at a historical time when, due to the Renaissance and its new and optimistic estimate of man, it was being widely suggested that man does not really need divine grace at all. To summarize Niebuhr's conclusions, it may be said that the Renaissance, with its views of the goodness and self-sufficiency of man, won a victory over the Reformation in the battle for men's allegiance. So it is that modern thought has in this respect followed the Renaissance rather than the Reformation.

Yet, in another sense, the debate between these two views of the nature and destiny of man has continued throughout modern history. The Renaissance viewpoint assumes the virtue and self-sufficiency of man and affirms the infinite possibilities of progress that lie ahead, whereas the Reformation viewpoint asserts the finitude and corruption of man and concludes that man's only hope lies in God's grace. Niebuhr proposes a synthesis of these two viewpoints in which man's life in the course of history will be seen to stand before ever new possibilities of both good and evil.

Two aspects of this resultant synthesis are developed in detail; namely, the idea of tolerance, in Chapter 8, entitled significantly "Having and Not Having the Truth," and the idea of justice expounded in Chapter 9, "The Kingdom of God and the Struggle for Justice." The former chapter turns upon the paradoxical problem of holding a truth in genuine conviction, yet without the arrogant finality or absoluteness which generates intolerance. The test of tolerance comes not in ideas to which there is no real attachment, but rather in those believed with deep and genuine conviction. The solution in the view that man has truth and not final Truth. Absolute Truth must be affirmed as an aspect of God rather than as a human achievement. Historically, the origin of religious toleration may be seen to lie in the leftwing sects of the Protestant Reformation.

The Kingdom of God remains Niebuhr's statement of ideal society to which he relates the various structures and achievements of human law and justice. All such structures must ac-

cordingly be placed "under" the Kingdom of God. This means that their validity derives from their capacity to point toward the Kingdom. But it also means in full realism that all actual human structures and achievements fall short of the perfection of the Kingdom of God. They do so because man is both creaturely and sinful.

These considerations place limits on man's historical actions to achieve justice, but they have the more affirmative significance of freeing man from static absolutism for free historical action in the service of God. Niebuhr is critical both of Christian social conservatism from Paul and Augustine to Luther, and of the utopian illusions of much radical thought. Between the two lies Christian realism.

A final character develops the significance of the doctrine of Judgment Day as the end of history. Here, as elsewhere, Niebuhr's viewpoint is that one must take the Bible seriously but not literally. Hence, Judgment Day is to be taken no more literally than is Creation. Rather, it must be taken seriously as the final fulfillment of history's meaning.

PRAYER

Author: George Arthur Buttrick (1892-   )
Type of work: Devotional philosophy
First published: 1942

Principal Ideas Advanced

The chief theoretical obstacle to prayer is an unexamined conception of natural law which leaves no place for God's action in the created order; the chief practical obstacle is a sense of sufficiency that presumes no need of His help.

Without prayer morality becomes hollow, knowledge reaches an impasse, science turns to destructive use, and religion grows flat and lifeless.

Our truest knowledge of prayer comes from the example and teaching of Jesus.

The path to success in prayer is a discipline that combines form with freedom.

Prayer by George Arthur Buttrick is a carefully written discussion of the obstacles to prayer, of its nature and practice, and of the fruits that come from its faithful performance. The approach of the book ranges from weighty argument against philosophical and psychological criticisms of prayer to simple and practical advice concerning the cultivation of the prayer life. The book repeatedly contends that prayer is the central feature of a deep religious life and that if prayer falls before the assaults of objections to it, all religion is lost. These modern objections are both theoretical and practical in character, involving both scientific agnosticism and temperamental nihilism. Written with urgency and vigor, the argument sets allegiance to prayer in the sharpest possible contrast to the contemporary rejections of prayer, especially to the unexamined conception of natural law which leaves no place for God to act in His creation. In prescribing the practice of prayer, however, the tone of the book is melioristic and its suggestions varied. Throughout his book Buttrick emphasizes the creativeness of prayer.

Beginning with a brief discussion of the absence of prayer in modern life and the corrosive consequences, the book turns to the contribution made toward our understanding of prayer by the teachings and example of Jesus. Jesus' teaching about prayer is scanty, yet ultimate. It is terse yet demanding. Prayer may be lonely and hard; it is to be humble and done in secret; it must be pursued with untiring persistence.

Calvary teaches us that prayer must not expect to issue in selfish gain; it must be undertaken at great risk. But the spirit of Jesus also shows us the genuine possibility of radiance as the issue of prayer, even amidst trial. Above all else, according to Buttrick, from Jesus we learn that prayer is the path by which we find God and become related to Him in surrender and in trust.

The world has many criticisms to make of prayer. The criticisms can be refuted by argument but practice alone is the confirmation for prayer itself. The world accuses prayer of originating in fear, but origins alone do not condemn a current reality which has enlarged and grown since its inception. The world considers prayer a form of auto-suggestion or wishful thinking, but the same judgment is not applied to the criticism itself. The scientific world-view does not enlarge its borders to take in prayer, but confines its discussions to the external, fractional, and analytical sides of life. With its vision thus limited, it has no right to consider the reality of prayer.

No discussion of prayer is possible, according to the author's thesis, without presuming both human freedom and divine providence. The first is crucial because prayer involves the consent of will acknowledged in doctrines of human freedom, while the second is necessary because a God enmeshed in a mechanistic order could never qualify as Friend and Father. The freedom of man is experienced in life, not defended with logic. Even the logical arguments made against human freedom are cited by Buttrick as proof of this fact, for the men who make such arguments act as though others are free to accept them as true. In assuming, but never arguing, the existence of God, the man who prays acts as though God is faithful as well as flexible. The dependable quality of the universe witnesses to God's faithfulness. The flexibility of God presupposes that the same universe is subject to His controlling activity.

The activity of God is a mystery. He cannot do everything, but the limits to His power, like the limits to the scope of prayer, are difficult to define with precision. The sharpest issues concerning the relationship of prayer to the lawful order seen in creation arise with respect to petitionary prayer. Its religious validity is not in doubt since it is right and proper to ask God in candor to meet human needs. But its consequences are less easy to consider, for we must acknowledge God does not always give men what they ask for. Intercessory prayer, less prone to selfish yearning, is also religiously valid. Its fulfillment depends upon God and therefore defies prediction. Any telepathic theory of intercessory prayer would put too much control in human hands, hands not properly trusted with such power.

In a section on "Prayer and Personality" Buttrick explores the psychological and behavioral implications of prayer. In his constructive argument he builds a case largely independent of technical matters, but he does take pains to refute what he regards as false conclusions drawn from contemporary theories of personality. Where psychology is critical of prayer Buttrick is critical of psychology and accuses it of be-

ing recent, fractional, dogmatic, and limited in understanding. Where conscience is attributed to mere conditioning, Buttrick takes pains to explore its larger meaning of "knowing with" God. But the criticisms are not all aimed at the aberrations found in secular points of view. The description of faith as mere assent to propositions or as unfounded credulity must give way to a conception of faith as the axiom of the spirit which engenders expectancy and bestows a quiet confidence in self, in neighbors, and in Creation itself. To those who argue that prayer must be considered a matter of pure spirit, Buttrick retorts that form and body are essential to experience and to the practice of prayer. In contrast with the plea for unfettered freedom in the spiritual life Buttrick suggests that habit has a place in our devotions. To those who would regard prayer as a purely individual matter Buttrick has much to say about its corporate and communal possibilities.

The functions of prayer in relationship to personality seem twofold in the author's mind, though many variations of each function are explored in the several chapters. The chapters deal with the roles of instinct, memory, imagination, and conscience, among other topics. On the one hand Buttrick holds that prayer directs attention to proper objects of loyalty and into constructive moods of life; on the other hand prayer cleanses and purges human attitudes of the poisons which plague the spirit.

The directing and releasing functions of prayer are many and varied. Prayer creates a fundamental honesty in man, which enables man to put his inner house in order. True prayer and hypocrisy are incompatible. Prayer focuses the conscious mind upon God and provides a proper focus for man's attention. The focus carries over to the subconscious. The new orientation thus given to man makes him ready to receive events and to meet them with poise. It gives a standard against which to measure alternatives and thus it guides decision. It gives man power to act after a decision has been properly reached. Prayer enables the spirit to break out in spontaneous joy as it acknowledges the providence of God. Prayer turns the attention of the self toward others. Prayer trains the conscience. It prepares men to meet crises.

The cleansing function of prayer is equally important and complex. Confessional prayer enables the soul to purge itself of guilt. It lances the infected wound of the inner life so that healing can take place. Buttrick is appreciative of the concern of the Roman Catholic church to provide such a cleansing process through its confessional, and he pleads that each man must have some means of experiencing the release which such a practice intends. Confessional prayer must not become excessive, however, since men then become morbid and self-centered in a negative way. Prayer cleanses and purifies the motives of men; it purges, redeems, and trains the memory; it provides, through intercession for others, an outflow from the stagnant pool of our own thinking.

The concluding several chapters of the book are a pleasant and surprising contrast to the main argument. They discuss in very practical terms the ways and means of prayer. Consistent with Buttrick's strong contention that prayer must have body and form, the book surveys the actual forms that prayer can take. Buttrick admits that forms are subject to both use and misuse and

deems them "inevitable, dangerous, and precious." Thus the suggestions he offers are intended as guides and not as prescriptions and they draw upon many sources from both private diaries of prayer and the liturgies of the Church.

Buttrick argues that the Church has been remiss in its failure to provide men with specific instruction in the way of private prayer. Seeking to set right the scales Buttrick proffers specific advice about the life of personal prayer. He suggests that such prayer should be undertaken in a quiet and a private place which becomes an accustomed place as a result of regular use. Evening seems to Buttrick the best time for regular prayer, though ejaculatory utterance throughout the day is commended to the reader. The merits of silent and uttered prayer are weighed, but there is no preference expressed for one to the exclusion of the other.

In the discussion of corporate prayer Buttrick provides a brief yet helpful discussion of public worship. Prayer is the central feature of such worship, as he sees it, and much is said in criticism of traditions in which the prayer is relegated to a secondary place, either in position or in preparation. Worship is related to the realms of work and education, to which its moods and resources should be carried. The family altar, the weekly prayer meeting, and other forms of group worship are urged in revived and recreated forms.

The final chapter recapitulates without summarizing. It restates the case without merely rehearsing the arguments. A short paragraph from near the end of the work will introduce the reader better than extended commentary to both the gist of the argument and the flavor of its presentation: Speaking of the loneliness of man in a vast cosmos, Buttrick writes:

"Always that loneliness, to which the new astronomy has added a dismay. But in other ages the yearning was endurable; for then men by faith and prayer caught glimpses of a homeland, and were sure that at death they would live at home. Their paradox of loneliness and at-homeness had a certain smart of tension which gave tang to life. But now mankind no longer accepts orthodoxy—which the church has often made angular and narrow—and can find no hope or nourishment in the nihilism of natural law. Behind our wars is the loss of ultimate Sanction: the wars will not end until the Sanction is recovered. Behind our weariness, which is not disproved but only underscored by our insistence that we are 'having such a good time,' is the loss of Horizons; the play will be boring until there is some background of mountains and sky. Behind our restlessness and nervous breakdown is a fear we dare not face—the fear that there is no Home, and that we are only driven fugitives of time and dust: the fear will vex us until we find God!"

THE SCREWTAPE LETTERS

Author: C(live) S(taples) Lewis (1898-   )
Type of work: Christian ethics
First published: 1942

PRINCIPAL IDEAS ADVANCED

Modern man is confronted by serious obstacles in the effort to become and to remain a Christian; the chief obstacle is man's failure to utilize his reason in the acquisition of the virtues of faith, hope, charity, justice, temperance, and courage.

The young convert to Christianity is beset by temptations of the body and mind, by the enticement to illicit sexual activity, by fear, anxiety, pride, and flippancy; in his struggle to lead the Christian life, the young convert receives little assistance from the Church or society.

The faithfulness, love, and mercy of God are, however, sufficient to overcome the wiles of the Devil and to bring the Christian safely to his eternal home.

The Screwtape Letters is a profound analysis of the pitfalls that confront a Christian living in the twentieth century. The book is an application of such virtues as justice, courage, temperance, faith, hope, and love to the life of the Christian. The literary form of the work is an imaginary correspondence between Screwtape and Wormwood. The former, a devil in Hell, is entrusted with the task of instructing the latter, a devil on earth, in the art of successfully luring a particular human being from the path of virtue into the pseudo-pleasures of vice. The activity of the devils is hampered by their "enemy," God, who loves the human creatures.

The work of the devils has been made easier because many human beings either have come to disbelieve in their existence or to take an excessive and unhealthy interest in Satan. Both attitudes are beneficial to Wormwood's success.

Screwtape's instruction to Wormwood may be divided into two parts; the first is designed to prevent the "patient," the human being entrusted to Wormwood's care, from becoming a Christian; the second is designed to destroy the faith of the patient if he has accepted Christianity.

A few centuries ago, Screwtape points out, argumentation might have been used to keep an intelligent human being out of the Christian fold, for in the past people knew when a proposition was proven and when it was not, and if it was proven, they accepted it. Thinking was connected with doing, and a chain of reasoning could lead to the altering of a way of life. Today, however, modern man is more sophisticated. He can entertain a dozen incompatible philosophies. Doctrines are no longer thought of as true or false, but as conventional or ruthless, contemporary or outworn, academic or practical. Therefore, it is jargon, not argument, that can best keep a man from becoming a Christian. Argumentation is dangerous because reason is on the side of Christianity. It is not necessary to argue that materialism is true; it is sufficient to create the attitude that materialism is the philosophy of the future, that it is strong, courageous, and somehow connected with real life. Attitudes are created by practical propaganda, by attending to the stream of immediate sense experi-

ences, by the ordinariness of things. The real sciences in no way support a defense against Christianity, for they encourage reflection upon what cannot be seen or touched. The belief to be encouraged is that whatever ideas the patient has casually picked up are the findings of scientific investigation. In this way materialism is accepted unchallenged and without proof. But in spite of the merit of the advice given by Screwtape, Wormwood's initial efforts to prevent his patient from becoming a Christian were unsuccessful.

The second course of instruction, as Screwtape presents it, makes it clear that not all is lost. For hundreds of converts have been reclaimed after a brief stay in the Enemy's camp. The mental and physical habits of the patient are not readily overcome. In fact the visible Church is one of Satan's greatest assets. The liturgy used in worship is unintelligible, the lyrics are poorly composed, and many Church members are hypocrites. The patient is encouraged to look around for the church that suits him. He may then join a faction and become a critic when he should be a pupil. He may find a minister who has watered down the faith and has deserted the liturgy. Or he may find a minister who preaches only what is calculated to shock, grieve, puzzle, or humiliate.

The prayer life of the patient must also be rendered innocuous. This can be accomplished by making his prayers so spiritual that they are far removed from his daily problems. They should be made spontaneous, inward, informal, and unregularized, aimed at producing a devotional mood, without real concentration of will and intelligence. His gaze should be turned away from God towards himself. His efforts should be directed towards the manufacturing of feelings. Instead of asking God for charity, he should be encouraged to arouse charitable feelings; instead of praying for forgiveness, he should feel forgiven. The value of each prayer should be measured by the success in attaining the desired feeling.

The outbreak of a war may be of use in the destruction of the Christian faith, but it is not necessarily Satan's ally. Whether the patient is a pacifist or an ardent patriot can be put to good use by Wormwood. Wars can create anxiety and hatred, but there is also the danger of the growth of benevolence. What is most important for the Devil's purpose is that the patient adopt an extreme position. Every extreme, except devotion to God, is to be encouraged. Our age is unbalanced and prone to faction. Any small group which is bound together by an unpopular interest tends to make its members proud and hateful of outsiders. Whether the patient is a conscientious objector or patriot is unimportant as long as he can be made to make his pacifism or patriotism a part of his religion, for then he can be led to make it the most important part, until finally it becomes the whole of his belief.

The spiritual life of the young Christian can be expected to hit a series of troughs and peaks: periods of emotional richness will alternate with periods of numbness and poverty. The periods of depression provide ample opportunity for temptation. The patient must never be permitted to know that ups and downs are normal. Rather he should be made to feel that the first ardors of his conversion should have

lasted forever. He may then be led to despair, or he may be made to feel content with a low-ebb religion which is as good as no religion at all. In such periods of despondency his faith is open to direct assault. From the feeling that he is losing interest, he may be led to the conclusion that his faith is false, merely an adolescent phase in his development.

The young Christian can further be distracted from the path of righteousness by being brought into the company of rich, smart, superficial intellectuals who are skeptical about everything. Such people can appeal to his social, sexual, and intellectual vanity, and with encouragement they can destroy temperance, chastity, and sobriety and arouse cynicism, skepticism, and self-satisfaction.

The patient is to be encouraged in mistaking flippancy for humor and joy. The Devil would have him discover that he can do almost anything with approval, if it can be treated as a joke. To make a real joke is difficult, but to be flippant about virtue and to treat it as if it were a joke is quite easy. Flippant people always assume that the joke has been made, without anyone actually making it. Every serious subject can then be discussed as if a ridiculous side to it had already been found. Genuine joy, fun, and laughter which arise from a sudden perception of incongruity are of no aid to Satan, for such delight can actually promote charity, courage, and contentment.

The patient must be kept from the genuine enjoyments of the Christian life. It is quite proper if he keeps the habits of a Christian externally, as long as he gradually becomes inattentive to their real meaning. He need not commit spectacular sins; little sins will do. Positive pleasures, doing what he really likes, ought never to be allowed. Above all, the young Christian ought never to be allowed to hope for the daily and hourly grace to meet the daily and hourly temptations. Let him expect grace for life; let him hope for perpetual virtue. Should he become humble, the Devil's purpose is best served by implanting the awareness of his own humility, so that humility will then be transformed into pride; pride at his own humility will appear. The true end of humility, namely, self-forgetfulness, must be concealed from the young Christian. The latter must not be allowed to turn his attention away from himself to God, and to his neighbors; he must be made to be concerned only with himself, and to have contempt of himself so that he can then have contempt for others. He will become gloomy, cynical, and cruel. He must be made to feel that humility consists in trying to believe that his talents are of no value. This will breed dishonesty and will prevent him from loving himself in such a way that he can love his neighbor.

The young Christian is to be encouraged in intemperance, not only in the sphere of sex, but also in regard to food. Gluttony of excess is, however, of no more value than gluttony of delicacy, where no large quantities are involved. By enslaving the young Christian's life to this form of sensuality, the gluttonous appetite for food can be used to produce querulousness, impatience, uncharitableness, and self-concern.

In the area of sex, the Christian is enjoined by his faith to complete abstinence or unmitigated monogamy. The foundation of the latter is undermined by inculcating the notion that the usually short-lived experience of "being in love" is the only respectable basis for marriage. A marriage that does not render this excitement permanent is, therefore, no longer binding. Loyalty to a partnership for mutual help, for the preservation of chastity, and for the transmission of life must be made to be regarded as something less worthy than a storm of emotion.

When sexuality cannot be transformed into brutal cynicism or unchastity, a marriage can be used to serve the Devil's purposes equally well. The desires of men can be carefully directed so that husbands will desire what is not attainable. If a man should happen to marry a real Christian, it is still possible to use her family and friends for Satanic purposes. A proper Christian atmosphere, a Christian family, and Christian friends may even be used to awaken in the young Christian a feeling of spiritual pride. It may be used to arouse the feeling that the outsiders who do not share his new-found belief are stupid and ridiculous.

The new Christian is to be encouraged to add something to his Christianity. Mere Christianity threatens the Devil's purposes, but if it be coupled with something else, such as Christianity and social crises, or Christianity and the new psychology, then Christianity can be made to be a means to something else. The Devil wants men to treat Christianity as a means—preferably as a means to their own advancement, but if necessary even as a means to social justice. If social justice is valued as something God wants most of all, it is then easy to value Christianity because it produces social justice.

The young Christian is to be encouraged further to despise the same old thing, to look for novelty. Novelty produces heresies in religion, folly in counsel, infidelity in marriage, and inconstancy in friendship. It diminishes pleasure and increases desire, and it distracts attention from real danger.

It matters not whether the patient is in physical danger; the Devil's concern is with his spiritual state. Courage can be turned into pride, and cowardice can be turned into hatred. What is to be encouraged is the feeling that man has something other than God to fall back on. Man's fears and fatigue can be turned into anger, malice, and impatience, but they can also lead to trust in God, to kindness, and courage. Physical death by no means serves Satan; it can in fact spell defeat. For it is the spiritual state of the believer at the time of his death that is important. The soul of the Christian who dies in a state of grace passes into the presence of his Savior, and the Devil is defeated. The soul of the believer escapes the torments of Hell and passes on to its eternal reward.

CHRIST AND TIME

Author: Oscar Cullmann (1902-   )
Type of work: Christology
First published: 1946

Principal Ideas Advanced

Because of the Biblical understanding of time, Christian theology ought to be, fundamentally, a recital of Biblical history, all speculation being based upon and controlled by it.

History is an ascending time-line, moving forward purposefully to its predestined completion in a new creation.

Christ is the center of history, the absolute revelation of God in terms of which all of history and nature are to be understood: everything was created to be subjected to the Lordship of Christ, and to be reconciled to God through Christ.

To understand time as meaningless and eternity as opposed to time is to substitute an alien philosophy for the New Testament faith which sees time as the locus of God's actions and eternity as continuous with time.

Oscar Cullmann, author of *Christ and Time* and a leading Protestant New Testament scholar, is one of a group of theologians who have been given the name "Biblical theologians." This group, in its two-fold battle against fundamentalism (insistence upon the infallibility of Scripture in every detail) and modernism (the replacing of Christian faith by modern philosophy), has as its defining characteristic an effort to be Biblical without being bound, to derive controlling insights from the Biblical view of God and history without at the same time accepting the whole Bible as eternally binding.

Cullmann has attempted in *Christ and Time* to determine "what is central in the Christian proclamation." Attention must be given to both halves of this statement, for he tries both to isolate what is central and to find it within and because of the Christian past. Thus, one of his major adversaries has been the author Rudolf Bultmann, the controversial Continental theologian, who, according to Cullmann, has used the method of modern existentialist philosophy and has reduced all theological statements to symbols about the meaning of human existence. Bultmann, recognizing with Cullmann that the Biblical proclamation centers upon the activity of God, nevertheless has rejected the time-structure of the Bible as being important for modern Christianity.

An example of proper theologizing, according to Cullmann, is provided by Karl Barth, the most forceful and eminent of the "neo-orthodox" theologians, who has attempted to base his theology upon the Bible historically considered and to present a Christ-centered theology which incorporates the basic elements of the Biblical view of God, history, and nature. Cullmann's only criticism is that Barth's work has been marred by an un-Biblical view of eternity, a view which Barth derived from Greek philosophy. *Christ and Time* is the result of an attempt to carry Barth's views to their correct conclusion by developing the Biblical understanding of eternity as continued time.

Christ and Time embodies the results of Cullmann's exploration of the basic presupposition of New Testament theology; namely, its conception of time and history. In opposition to philosophies which have *cyclical* views of history and which devaluate time as meaningless or evil and therefore as something to be escaped by means of a salvation which lifts one "above" history, Biblical man believed that history and nature are the deliberate creation of a God who intended to manifest His revelation and salvation in history. History is not meaningless but meaningful; history is not a circle but a straight line. God rules over history and acts in history, creating all things to be subjected to the Lordship of Christ, bringing to pass the crucial events leading up to the first manifestation of that Lordship, and manifesting that Lordship fully through a new creation which, for us, is still to come. Thus the ages of pre-creation, creation, and new creation are segments of an ascending time-line, each age being higher in value than the preceding one.

History is, then, the locus of the revelation and redemptive activity of God. The time-line is a redemption line, and the meaning of that line is to be found in the moment when redemption takes place. Jesus of Nazareth is the decisive point in the time-line, His death and resurrection is the manifestation of that Lordship for which creation was intended and is the *"absolute divine revelation* to men." Both creation, as the creation of that over which this Lordship is to be manifested, and new creation, as the age of the full manifestation of that Lordship, are thus to be understood only in terms of this absolute divine revelation. The whole time-line takes its meaning from its midpoint, the revelation of God in Christ. History is thus decisively Christ-centered, as our modern system of reckoning time counting forward and backward from the date of Christ's birth can be used to symbolize.

Judaism shares with Christianity the view that the ascending time-line has three ages, pre-creation, creation, and new creation. The difference is that Judaism still looks forward to an event to come, whereas Christianity looks back upon an event which has already taken place. According to the early Church, the decisive battle in the new creation has already been won. Although mankind still remains in the age of creation and will continue to remain there for an undisclosed period of time, the crucial event for salvation has taken place in the death and resurrection of Christ, which accomplished His victory over the evil powers and the manifestation of His Lordship over the whole of creation. It was because the early Christians knew that the decisive event *had* happened that they were not dismayed when the end of the age did not come as quickly as they had originally anticipated.

The "scandal" of Christianity is this, that it proclaims that in a particular moment of time salvation was affected for the whole temporal order. The act of faith that was demanded of the early Christians was thus enormous, for they were called upon to accept as fact that a man who dressed and spoke as they did had, just a few days before, won salvation for all mankind. They were confronted by the necessity of believing that a man with whom they had been acquainted was God's appointed means for redeeming the world.

That this belief has been perennially difficult is shown by the fact that the first great heresy, still quite active, was Docetism (from the word *doceo*, "to seem"; thus, the teaching that Christ only *seemed* to have a body and only *seemed* to die). Cullmann uses this name broadly to denote all those who deny that redemption takes place in history and who therefore look for salvation apart from history. Docetism understands salvation spatially, in terms of the removal of man from the temporal realm of being to a nontemporal realm of eternity which lies alongside this realm, whereas Christianity understands salvation temporally, finding salvation in the death and resurrection of an actual historical being and finding it to involve continued temporal activity. For Christianity, salvation is measured in terms of then and now, not here and there.

The most controversial feature of *Christ and Time* is its insistence that eternity and time are continuous with each other. Eternity must be taken in neither the Platonic nor the modern philosophical sense, but, rather, as merely endless time. "Thus in the New Testament field," Cullmann writes, "it is not time and eternity that stand opposed, but limited time and unlimited, endless time. . . . This latter time is not different from the former. The difference consists only in the fact that it is not limited." The future age, the age of the new creation which is yet to come, is also temporal in character, not timeless. Biblical expressions such as "the first and the last," "the beginning and the end," ought to be interpreted as they actually read; namely, as temporal concepts rather than as symbols for some nontemporal eternity.

The New Testament, as Cullmann shows through abundant citation, does contain an understanding of past, present, and future in terms of Christ. Christ is presented as the creative Word, the Mediator foreordained from before the foundation of the earth. He is the one toward whom the whole creation and all of past history has pointed, the one for whom the whole earth has longed. The Old Testament portrays redemptive history, a history which points forward to His coming, and is to be understood "as preparation for the incarnation and the cross." The various events portrayed in this revelation are part of redemptive history, but they are not complete in themselves; they require Christ for their completion.

Present time is also understood in terms of Christ. The Apostles knew themselves to be persons commissioned to carry on the redemptive work of Christ by proclaiming the fact of salvation to the Gentiles. That which was promised to Israel had come; the decisive manifestation of God's power and purpose had taken place, and the Gentiles had been included. The Church was created in order to preach to the rest of the world that Jesus Christ is actually Lord. It is Cullmann's claim that the New Testament Church believed that the Lordship of Christ has actually been manifested over the Gentiles, the supernatural powers, the state, the whole of creation. All things have actually been subjected to Christ, but since they do not know it, it is necessary to proclaim what has taken place.

The future time, the age of the new creation, is also understood in terms of Christ. Christ will come again, bringing to a close the present segment of the time-line, manifesting his authority absolutely over the whole of creation, and every tongue will then confess that Jesus Christ is Lord. The Lordship of Christ which was accomplished in His death and resurrection, but which is now largely unrecognized by those who are really his subjects, will become fully obvious when He comes again.

Thus the meaning of all of history and nature is to be understood by reference to Christ. Cullmann writes: "In the three decisive stages of the Christ-line of salvation the general process is drawn into the redemptive process. It is so in Creation: everything is created through Christ. It is so in Christ's death and resurrection: everything is reconciled through him. It is so in the eschatological completion: everything is subjected to God, who is all in all." Time is an ascending line, with creation, reconciliation, and the subjection of the whole of creation to God, as its segments, and all points of this redemptive line are related to "one historical fact" at the mid-point, a fact which . . . is decisive for salvation."

This book is primarily descriptive, being an inquiry into the meaning of New Testament texts in an effort to discover what is central in them, but it is also obviously prescriptive. Cullmann intends to suggest that the New Testament view of time be normative for Christianity; he does not (some critics maintain) consider concepts of time which can be found in the Bible but which differ from his own. Rejecting not only modern attempts to base theology upon non-Biblical concepts of time and eternity, but also classical Christian deviations from Biblical doctrine, Cullmann criticizes some of the Church Fathers for their neglect of history and their preoccupation with nontemporal views of eternity. Because his conception of Christ and time stands at variance with the classical Christian tradition at so many points, Cullmann's thesis has been severely criticized as overstated. From the standpoint of the classical tradition his view is a radical one, for he defends the claim that the Bible had no sense whatsoever of a nontemporal eternity, that, as a matter of fact, Biblical man thought *only* in terms of a temporal eternity continuous with present temporal process. The oft-encountered "paradox" of time and eternity results, in Cullmann's view, from the illegitimate union of the Biblical idea of time with an idea of eternity drawn from an alien philosophy. There is a scandal connected with Christianity, the scandal that in a particular segment of time the meaning of the whole temporal process is revealed, but this has nothing to do with the "paradox" of the eternal entering time.

In addition, some interpreters see in the views expressed in *Christ and Time* radical implications for traditional doctrines of divine impassibility (the doctrine that God is neither acted upon from without nor emotionally affected) and election (the doctrine that only some are elected to salvation), although Cullmann does not raise either of these questions for discussion. That God's time is also man's time seems to imply that God is not impassible, and the fact that Christ reconciles both history and nature suggests the possibility that *all* men are saved.

DOGMATICS

Author: Emil Brunner (1889-   )
Type of work: Systematic theology
First published: Volume I, 1946; Volume II, 1950; Volume III, 1960

Principal Ideas Advanced

The dogmatic task of the Church is to understand the contemporary relevance of the confession, "Thou art the Christ, the Son of the Living God."

Dogmatics is based upon the revelation of God in Christ: God, who by His nature cannot be known, makes Himself known in revelation.

Jesus Christ, as the final revelation of God, is the revelation of God as a person, "The Word became flesh."

God has not permitted any man to be without some knowledge of Himself; a knowledge of God forms part of the creaturely existence of every man.

The world as it has been created by God is the "proper" sphere of natural knowledge, although it too, must be understood "Christologically."

Three volumes of Emil Brunner's *Dogmatik* have appeared. Volume I is entitled *The Christian Doctrine of God (Die christliche Lehre von Gott);* Volume II, *The Christian Doctrine of* *Creation and Redemption (Die christliche Lehre von Schöpfung und Erlösung);* and Volume III, *The Christian Doctrine of the Church, Faith, and Fulfillment (Die christliche Lehre von der Kirche, vom Glauben und von der Vollendung).*

Brunner believes that the Christian Church stands or falls on the basis of the confession, "Jesus Christ, the same yesterday, today, and forever." The revelation of God in Jesus Christ is the central feature of any Christian dogmatic system. Brunner asserts that at all times in history, if faith is to be true and genuine, it must become "contemporary" with Jesus Christ, with His Cross and with His resurrection. The Church, however, can never make the claim that it is identical with revelation; nonetheless, it is a *form* of revelation. It is through this "form" that the Christian Gospel is propagated to the world.

The task of dogmatics is therefore an essential one for the Christian Church in the modern world. Dogmatics is, for Brunner, the fundamental "function" of the Church. The Church must at all times be clear about the content of her message. But dogmatics presupposes the life *within* the Church. Brunner writes, "Dogmatics is itself a function of the Church. Only one who is a genuine 'believer' and, as such, believes in the Church and its teaching, can render to the Church the service which is implied in the idea of dogmatics. The presupposition of dogmatics is not only the existence of the Church and its doctrine, but life *within* the Church, and *in* its doctrine. Dogmatic thinking is not only thinking *about* the Faith, it is *believing* thinking."

Dogmatics points beyond itself to a reality which it cannot contain. Christian dogma deals with God, and God by His very nature is far beyond all human doctrinal conceptions. A doctrine of God, Brunner maintains, cannot be taught, because God is not a "something"; He is not even a "concrete reality." God is, rather, Absolute Subject. Since man is competent to deal only with the world, God stands outside the area in which human knowledge and experience are relevant. How then, asks Brunner, can man come to a knowledge of God, which would be the proper subject matter for dogmatics? The answer is that the knowledge of God exists only in so far as there is a self-disclosure, a self-manifestation of God; that is, only in so far as there is revelation. Brunner writes, "There is a doctrine of God, in the legitimate sense of the words, only in so far as God Himself imparts it. The human doctrine of God—which is undoubtedly the doctrine of the Church—is thus only legitimate, and can only claim to be 'truth,' in so far as the divine revelation—that which God teaches about Himself—is validly expressed by it."

Christian dogma, therefore, is merely a pointer to something outside itself; that is, to the God who is beyond human conception, but who discloses something about Himself. Dogma (dogmatics) and revelation are, for Brunner, categories which are inextricably bound together.

In the New Testament the idea of *revelation* is clearly oriented to the historical event of Jesus Christ. "The Word became flesh" is the central affirmation of the original Christian witnesses in the New Testament period. It is obvious, however, says Brunner, that the "Word" or the "Word of God" has nothing to do with a human conception of a word. Jesus Christ is more than all of the words man can put together regarding Him, His person, or His works. Furthermore, the "Word of

God", the divine self-communication, is in the form of a person, a human being, a man in whom God Himself comes to us and "encounters" us. Revelation has therefore one meaning for the Christian: Emanuel, God with us. In Brunner's words, "It is the same Son of God who in Jesus Christ became man, whom the Prophets discerned dimly from afar; He is the same in whose image man has been created, and in whom lies both the meaning and the foundation of the Creation of the world. It is He who constitutes the secret or manifest centre of all the testimony of Scripture; He it is whom the Word of the Church has to proclaim and to teach, whom the Holy Spirit attests in the heart of the believer, and through whom the 'new man' is created. It is also for that complete revelation at the end of the age that the Church waits, in whom the 'faithful will see God face to face.'"

Revelation, therefore, becomes the key theological category for Brunner; revelation originates with Jesus Christ and only in the light of God's revelation in Christ is it possible for man to know God's creation, and subsequently to know himself as part of God's creation.

The Holy Scriptures testify to the revelation of God in Christ. The Old Testament testifies to this revelation as promise, the New Testament as fulfillment. The New Testament is called the New Covenant for a reason, says Brunner, for it is in the New Testament that God is "with us." When, in the Prologue to the Gospel of John, the author asserts that "The Word became Flesh," he means, argues Brunner, that "He who could only be foretold previously in human language through the speech of the Prophets, is

now present in His own Person." The message of the Prologue to John is that Jesus Christ, the Son of God, is the *principle of creation* to which the Old Testament could refer only in the form, "God spoke." The revelation of God in Christ, so Brunner claims, is no longer a provisional, indirect form of speech, a pointer, but the *form* of revelation itself. The word about God is now translated into God himself, who becomes part of the historical setting.

The revelation of God in Christ is never completed, writes Brunner, until it is made manifest in a human life; that is, until a human being knows Jesus to be the Christ. Revelation is objective in the Incarnation of the Son in history, but it is also subjective—in the inner witness of the Spirit to man. Brunner argues that it is important to localize the revelation within man. The divine Spirit confronts the human spirit, and the human spirit responds as it is illuminated by the divine Spirit. This confrontation, Brunner indicates, is a necessary factor in the New Testament conception of the knowledge of God.

Because the "Word became flesh," the story of Jesus had to be told. The New Testament witnesses performed this function, and their report is found in the Four Gospels. But, in addition to this intimate, personal account of the revelation, Brunner writes, there is further need for doctrinal testimony: "It is the task of the doctrinal testimony to make the subject of these deeds and words, of this suffering and victory, visible, which is invisible in the narrative as such. While this is only suggested in the narrative of the Gospels, it comes out clearly in the doctrinal testimony. Just as the narrative moves deliberately, in order to show who He is, and what is His secret, within the sphere of time and space, so the doctrine develops gradually, within the sphere of thought, in order to make the meaning of the mystery clear."

The original confession of faith, which Brunner calls the "Thou" form of faith, is widened into dogmatics where one speaks about God by the use of the term "He." Now, in the development of doctrine, reflective speech *about* God replaces the spontaneous, personal response, which is the most primitive and original witness to the revelation of God in Christ. Dogmatics is therefore concerned primarily with right thinking; as the logical function of the Church, it is concerned to define clearly the teaching of the Church. Dogmatics, however, is necessarily confessional (and Brunner very clearly labels his dogmatics as Reformed), but it must also be related to a truly ecumenical spirit, which believes that the knowledge of divine truth is present in many churches.

The concept of revelation occupies much of Brunner's concern in *Dogmatics*. It is clear for Brunner that God is known only "where He Himself makes Himself known." Apart from this self-manifestation, He is unknowable and therefore remote and inaccessible. God can never be discovered, says Brunner; He can only make Himself known; that is, He gives knowledge of Himself to man.

But even the man to whom God has not made Himself known is not without a certain knowledge of God, Brunner argues. A knowledge of God forms part of the creaturely existence of every man.

The world as it has been created by God can be the proper sphere of natural knowledge. This knowledge, Brunner insists, which is acquired through the senses and the intellect, is not something profane, but sacred knowledge. Brunner writes, "Through the Creator, the world, and the knowledge of the world, are destined for each other. Both are rooted in the Logos of Creation; from it they derive both the objective basis of existence and the subjective basis of knowledge. This Logos of Creation, however, is no other than He who in Jesus Christ became Man and thus revealed to us His secret."

Creation, therefore, for Brunner, is also to be understood "Christologically." All revelation in creation is derived from the Eternal Son (or the Logos). All of the "orders of creation" which became norms of action have been created through the Logos-Son, and are related to His plan and purpose for the world.

The capacity of man to know is an aspect of his being made in "the image of God." Man is distinguished from the rest of creation by the fact that he can "grasp" natural knowledge. This fact, too, gives man a particular dignity and a special destiny. Natural knowledge is, of course, never a final and complete truth, for this truth belongs to God alone, but natural knowledge is a real possibility for modern man. Indeed, Brunner claims, natural knowledge of God's creation is necessary for the achievements of modern civilization and technics.

Brunner does not believe that to affirm that there is natural knowledge in creation permits a natural theology to come into being. It is certain, he says, that the Creator leaves some signs of His Spirit upon His creation. However, one can never deny the reality of sin and its negative effect upon perception.

Sin not only perverts the will; it also "obscures" the power of perceiving truth of the knowledge of God. On the one hand, Brunner insists, the reality of the revelation in creation is to be admitted, but on the other hand, the possibility of a correct and valid natural knowledge of God is to be contested. (In this context, Brunner in his *Dogmatik* refers the reader back to his *Natur und Gnade* where he asserted (a) that the revelation in creation is a reality; (b) that natural theology, as a legitimate possibility, does not exist; (c) that the fact of natural theology as an empirical fact, as something which belongs to the nature of the natural man, is understood in its ambiguity.) Brunner feels that in this way he relates the question of the knowledge of God in creation to anthropology, or to

a doctrine of man. He refers to Paul and Romans 1:19ff., and to the fact that man has knowledge of God in creation. Man is, therefore, responsible for his sin and idolatry, even though man has a *distorted* vision of God in creation. Human responsibility is, nevertheless, based upon this general revelation. The quality that makes man "human" is derived from the revelation in creation; that is, from the relation which God established at the very outset between man and his Creator. Responsible existence, that is, the existence of man in contrast to that of every other creature, is his existence as *person*. No sinful man ceases to be a responsible person, for his responsibility as a person, which is grounded in creation, cannot be lost.

THE IDEA OF CHRIST IN THE GOSPELS

Author: George Santayana (1863-1952)
Type of work: Christology
First published: 1946

PRINCIPAL IDEAS ADVANCED

The Gospels are not historical records but are products of inspiration.

Behind the eschatological figure of the Christ a new and more complete image of man was revealed.

Uniting in His person the divine and the human, Christ marks out the tragic path which man must travel in order to achieve spiritual victory.

Although never an orthodox believer in Roman Catholicism, Santayana maintained all through his life that there is more wisdom in the creeds and precepts of the Roman Catholic Church than in most secular philosophies. His book *The Idea of Christ in*

the Gospels, written toward the end of his life, is a devout exposition of this viewpoint. As is indicated by the alternative title, *God in Man,* Santayana maintained that the Christ presented by the authors of the Gospels is first, last, and always, the incarnate Son of

God. The Christ of faith is no mere moralizing teacher; neither is He a god in human disguise. In one person He combines essential divinity with essential humanity; in so doing, He becomes the architect of man's redemption.

There is no point, according to Santayana, in trying to discover in the four Gospels the lineaments of the Jesus of history. The Christ in whom the early Christians trusted was the risen Lord, who dwelt in the hearts of believers by His spirit. Because He was the promised Messiah or Christ, the true meaning of His earthly career was to be found in the Old Testament. Because He lived and reigned at God's right hand, His mercies and ordinances were daily renewed in the experience of the Church. To have known Christ "after the flesh" was no special advantage to missionaries or evangelists who, like inspired preachers of every age, identified themselves so completely with their Master that they freely read their own experience of redemption into every report of Jesus' ministry and teaching that came down to them.

The writers of the four Gospels had no account of Christ to draw from other than that which lived in the faith of the Church, and two of them, at least, were themselves in the living Apostolic tradition. Mark's account is the most lifelike, so much so that it has misled modern critics into thinking that they could there recover the Jesus of history. On the contrary, Mark's portrait of Christ is a powerful image of the Son of God in the flesh, a man leading a "double life." As Mark represents him, Christ has human moods and a human memory and foresight; yet He knows that He is more than human, and the drama of the story arises from the way in which His divinity now conceals and now boldly reveals itself. John's account, on the other hand, emphasizes the inward life of the Son of God and the tensions and paradoxes which result from His dwelling amidst the conditions of sin and death. His humanity is genuine and unethereal, but it is recognizably an instrument for spiritual graces which Heaven seeks to bestow upon earth. The other two Gospels, according to Santayana, are somewhat removed from the living stream of Christian tradition. In the case of Matthew, a didactic purpose has taken the place of the initial impulse to confront men with the image of Christ; Luke seems to have regarded his task as a literary one. Still, the image which they preserve is in conformity with that of the community of believers.

Santayana attributes this common image of Christ to "inspiration," by which he means a perfectly normal activity of man's psyche. Our image of the world, according to Santayana, always includes a large mixture of fancy. But in moments of special inspiration, the psyche "remakes the image of the world, or unmakes it, according to the mood of the soul." External circumstances are sometimes especially propitious to inspiration, but they contribute merely "by stimulating the organism to fuse scattered impressions, to revive and transform forgotten images, to invent, as in dreams, scenes that justify ripening emotions, and to feel affinities or equivalence in apparently disparate things." In themselves, inspirations are neither true nor false, neither helpful nor harmful. They become such when they are adopted as clues for understanding the world, or as goals toward which we must aspire.

The Christian inspiration, according to Santayana, had its origin in the lively Jewish nationalism of the time. The ancient prophetic hope of a political kingdom, to be achieved through the prowess of some future son of David, had given place in the Hellenistic age to apocalyptic dreams of a heavenly Kingdom, which would bring a cataclysmic end to gentile world-rule and establish the rule of God on earth by the hand of a divine Messiah. Exoterically, according to Santayana, the Christian Gospel was simply the claim that, in a cryptic manner, the Messiah had been revealed and that the heavenly Kingdom had begun; the humiliation and death of the Anointed One was part of the terrible drama by which the powers of sin and death must be broken before the new heaven and earth could be manifest. But behind the myth of world-redemption subtler motifs were being worked out. The substitution of a crucified Messiah in the place of a Joshua-style deliverer betokened a fundamental conversion from physical to spiritual goods. At the heart of the Gospel, never entirely lost behind the eschatological symbols, was the conception of a new and higher humanity which, having died to sin, was raised to newness of life in fellowship with Christ. This esoteric strain, which brought consolation to saddened and disillusioned spirits throughout the Roman world, makes the image of Christ in the Gospels, in Santayana's opinion, the soundest ideal that has been offered to humankind. That ideal constitutes a revaluation of values, as Nietzsche said, but, according to Santayana, Nietzsche was wrong in thinking that the ideal subverted the essential human image. On the contrary, the idea of Christ expresses the judgment to which wise and mature men must ever and again return.

What impressed Santayana in the figure of Christ was the degree to which the natural and the spiritual sides of man's nature were rendered compatible within a single image. It was a standing complaint of Santayana against mysticism that it violates the legitimate aspirations of the human spirit; its ecstatic vision of the whole is an impoverished one which, although legitimate, has nothing to recommend it over many other partial ideals. On the other hand, Santayana objected to any ethics which, when worked out to its ultimate conclusions (as, for example, by Marcus Aurelius or Benedict Spinoza), sacrifices everything specifically human and personal to the inexorable laws of nature. Classic Christianity reaffirms the human good, so transfigured as to be both faithful to the Church and compatible with the conditions of man's existence. The Christian ideal is an ascetic ideal, and it enjoins man from much that is instinctive and habitual to the race, but it does this without violating human nature.

What is distinctive of human nature, according to Santayana, is the dualism introduced into animal life by the presence of consciousness. As a physical organism, man is continuous with the material world, but as consciousness, man transcends nature, including his own body, and new worlds of truth and value are opened to his view. The true philosophy must, therefore, embrace a diversity of principles, even at the sacrifice of unity and completeness. But an ultimate pluralism such as Santayana calls for is more congenial to poetry and myth than it is to speculative philosophy and systematic morality. Thus, in Santayana's view, the Hebrew conception of a monarchical deity squares better with the facts of moral life than does the rationalism of the Greeks.

The idea of Christ, combining as it does the divine and the human natures in one person, has, in Santayana's judgment, proved uniquely suggestive of true insights into nature and life. The divine in Christ is for the most part tempered to our understanding. As the Son of God, Christ opens the way for all men to call God "Father"; through His miracles and parables, He exhibits the presence in nature of a kindly, ministering presence; by the victory of His resurrection, He removes the last doubt concerning man's favored place in creation. Still, God is not made over in the human image; there remain hard sayings, arbitrary judgments, acts that from a human point of view are inappropriate and cruel. (For example, the parable of the laborers in the vineyard; the miracle of cursing the barren fig tree.) As revealed in Christ, God's ways remain higher than our ways, and His thoughts higher than our thoughts.

The human nature of Christ, according to Santayana, differed from that of mankind generally in that it was free from ordinary desire (*eros*) and was governed by divine love (*agape*). Christ sought nothing for Himself, but desired the good of every natural thing with the love which the Creator has for His creatures. Such an exten-

sion of the affections demanded, however, a profound renunciation of man's normal purposes, the tragic quality of which appears in Christ's agony in the Garden. Charity, when perfect, is the loving submission of man's will to the will of the Heavenly Father. Not merely for Christ, but for all who would be His disciples, divine love demands the way of self-denial and cross-bearing.

According to Santayana, the union in Christ of the divine and the human is a parable of the union of the spiritual and the physical in man. "The Incarnation is the palmary instance of God uniting himself with man at the human level. Yet the whole life and teaching of Christ, and especially his Passion and death, show that this descent was not accomplished for its own sake, as the creation was. It had an ulterior object: the salvation of man, his elevation from the human to the divine level. This demands a tragic transformation in man himself, who must sacrifice his animal will and a great part of his nature in order to assimilate his spirit to that of God. No wonder that mankind is recalcitrant: nor do I think we could blame them if *all* the sweets and *all* the virtues proper to our nature had to be renounced in honestly following Christ. But that is not the case. There is nothing more human or more satisfying than self-transcendence; and the liberation and light that comes of renouncing the will seem, when really attained, the fulfillment, not the surrender, of our inmost powers."

THE SOURCE OF HUMAN GOOD

Author: Henry Nelson Wieman (1884-   )
Type of work: Naturalistic theology
First published: 1946

PRINCIPAL IDEAS ADVANCED

The ultimate reality is a creative event which transforms persons so as to enrich the qualitative meanings of their appreciable world.

The creative event is immediately and fully accessible to man through perception and is open to observation and experiment.

The central creative event is God, and a naturalistic theism can best interpret and make available the resources of the Christian faith.

Henry Nelson Wieman's "naturalistic theism" is one of the most provocative successors to the liberal period in American theology. Wieman's major critical thrusts have been directed against a liberalism which, emphasizing the moral values in Jesus' teaching, tended toward humanism, and also against a Neo-Protestantism which abandoned liberalism on the grounds of divine-human discontinuity and stressed the ambiguous and paradoxical nature of the human situation.

The Source of Human Good contains Wieman's fullest statement. It furnishes the outline of the theological system that has emerged in his other writings. The touchstone of the work is an analysis of value experiences in terms of a "newer naturalism" which takes the basic reality accessible to men as "events, their qualities and relations (structure)." This contextualistic definition is deemed to be the best definition of value as well as the only one sufficient for discussion of matters pertaining to philosophy of religion. Wieman also contends that such an analysis of value is more consonant with the Jewish Christian stress upon divine creativity in history as opposed

to the Greek Christian emphasis of transcendental form.

Rejecting interpretations of value as goods, as satisfaction, as quality, or as human control, Wieman focuses on "qualitative meaning," defined as "that connection between events whereby present happenings enable me to feel not only the quality intrinsic to the events now occurring but also the qualities of many other events that are related to them." This is "created good," and it depends upon a prior "creative good."

The "creative event," Wieman's process-synonym for creative good, may be analyzed empirically into four classes of subevents (also processes): (1) the "emergings" of the awareness of qualitative meaning communicated from another organism; (2) the "integratings" with previous meanings, usually done in solitude; (3) the "expandings" of qualities and possibilities of the appreciable world; and (4) the "deepenings" of community based upon previous subevents.

Creative good, thus defined, may be distinguished from both instrumental and intrinsic good, although it contains elements of both. The most significant element for Wieman is the dialectic between creative and created good. Whenever the latter has emerged there is the danger that men will hold it to be final. When this is done, it becomes "demonic," blocking and excluding further creativity. In similar fashion, qualitative meaning can erroneously be preferred to its source in the creative event.

For new goods to emerge, continual transformations of the organism are required. The danger in religion is that it tries to conserve previous structures of transformation at the price of precluding future ones. Our contemporary situation, dominated by science and technology, is releasing vast new human powers. These will destroy us unless they can be guided to increase the growth of creative good. Wieman argues that current religious attacks on "reason" move in precisely the opposite direction, one "fatal to man in the days of his power."

Were any religious revelation to transcend reason, as is often asserted, it would be indistinguishable from its opposite. A similar problem arises from religious appeals to an "eternal" reality, in that we are thrust back into the temporal realm helpless to find creativity there.

The proper source of human devotion is the creative event, working in history and accessible to empirical analysis. Such was the originating event of Christian faith. The fellowship around Jesus of Nazareth experienced transformations characteristic of the creative event. Jesus' death ended the possibility of interpreting these transformations in traditional Jewish terms. Subsequent experiences of continuing transformation led the disciples to speak of "resurrection," but,

Wieman writes, "what rose from the dead was not the man Jesus; it was creative power."

"Faith" is therefore an act rather than a belief. It presupposes fellowship with men of faith, and dissatisfaction with present purposes. It is characterized by the giving of the self to that which will creatively transform the self. The only "authority" of any religious teaching is the evidence, produced by inquiry, that the teaching can sustain creative changes.

The creative event, which operates in history, is also operative at the subhuman level, Wieman claims. Evolution depends upon increasing sensitivity and diversified responsiveness. The price of specialized protective mechanisms has been degeneration.

Of even greater importance is the supra-human quality of the creative event which "cannot be caused by human intention and effort, because it can be produced only by a transformation of human intention and effort." Previous mythologies, for this reason, have often described the creative event as "supernatural." Since it is not beyond all our appreciation, however, the creative event is best treated as a part of the "temporal, spatial, material world."

Creative good may be regarded as "absolute good" in that it is not relative to human desire; its demands are unlimited; its value is infinite; it is unqualified by any perspective; and it is "entirely trustworthy." It must not, however, be termed all-powerful.

Events which negate created good are characterized by Wieman as "destructive" evils, while opposition to creative good is termed "obstructive" evil. This second form is absolute in that it is universal, unqualified, ultimate, and unconfined. Neo-orthodoxy is criticized at this point for its historical pessimism (which overlooks the increase of qualitative meaning in the evolution of life) and for its ultimate romanticism (based on the "overbelief" in an ultimately all-powerful goodness).

Pain and suffering are to be distinguished in that suffering is a meaningful, communicable event. It is inevitably related to increases in qualitative meaning. Emotional maturity is precisely the willingness to incur suffering in order that creative good may emerge. The mature man does not seek suffering, but he recognizes it as the concomitant of transformation.

Certain evils are rooted in the nature of things. One is "inertia," which Wieman describes as "insensitivity and resistance to creativity." The most serious modern form is that "tolerance" which has characterized much of secular and religious liberalism. A person's ultimate commitments are arbitrary and trivial if they are simply determined by birth; that is, by class or national or religious origin. There is a sovereign, absolute goodness, which may be demonstrated "rationally and empirically." Unless this is done, our increasing control over nature simply aggravates our sense of futility.

A second class of natural evils is composed of the "protective hierarchies" of sensitivity, prestige, control, and intimidation. These are necessary, but subject to change. "Progress" in history may be measured by the widening of the upper levels of the hierarchies accompanied by increased communication, apprehension, and integration.

A third class of evils is more specifically human. "Sin," for instance, Wieman writes, is "any resistance to creativity for which man is responsible." Like creativity, it is always social. It is not always the result of pride; sometimes it grows from a prideless frivolity.

The second half of the book illustrates the general thesis by examining specific values. "Beauty" is similar to qualitative meaning, but it operates within a sharply delimited whole. Aesthetic form stresses the quality of events. It cannot, and does not, point "beyond existence," although the richness of qualities is often such as to evoke this claim. Folklore and myth convey these qualities which are determinant of history.

Our difficulty lies in the maladjustment of our two cultural structures. The traditional matrix which in medieval times could sustain rich communication through aesthetic and other noncognitive forms is increasingly unable to sustain intercommunication within the supertechnological matrix. An effective "proletarian art" is needed to guide industrial workers toward the good inherent in the new technology and to enable them to avert its evils.

Tragedy is the contrast between the actual and the possible, a contrast from which creativity may spring. Art can mediate this to us symbolically in many cases where a direct encounter would be more than we could survive. The Cross of Christ is such a symbol.

Art also supplements our quest for truth by reminding us of the qualitative richness of events that is always sacrificed in our drives toward clarity and precision.

Truth cannot be the goal of life since life rests on value. Wieman defines truth as "any specifiable structure pertaining to events and their possibilities." Truth is infinite since the totality of all structures is infinite. "Knowledge" is "structures specified." Our knowledge of truth rests initially upon our "noncognitive feeling-reactions." Western thought has impoverished itself, Wieman claims, when it has tried to depart from its feeling-matrix. Our intellects move more comfortably among "linguistic events" rather than "heavy events," but both must be preserved. Prophetic Judaism emphasized those rich structures which give value to our lives. Much of our religion, however, has reflected the partiality of the Greeks toward clarity of form.

"Heavy events," so often depicted mythologically, remain only possibilities until "observation and experiment" have rendered them actualities. A proper analysis of the perceptual event furnishes us with all the necessary metaphysical categories. "Mind" is meanings as "generated, communicated, and received by an organism." "Intuition" is simply a dramatic instance. "Mystical experience" is simply a form of intuition.

Knowledge is related by Wieman to human cultural development and to linguistic structures. But since certain basic meaning-structures characterize the world of the human organism, his epistemology is not a complete relativism. Both "mind" and "world" are ultimately determined by the creative event. The knowledge of the sciences supplements rather than supplants common sense, and "religious knowledge" is a branch of philosophical knowledge. The teachings of Jesus, for instance, do not represent any special knowledge. Instead, Wieman writes, "the total impact of events gives power

to the teachings." All knowledge is certified by the same tests: observation, agreement between observers, and coherence.

Morality is conduct guided by principles which facilitate creative interchange. This is "obligatory," Wieman insists, in that "we cannot continue to be human if we do not act morally." Modern men cannot hope to eliminate all barriers to communication between cultures and specialists. We can, however, all discuss the creative event since it concerns each of us.

Sexuality functions pre-eminently in rendering us capable of indefinite transformations by the creative event. Recognizing this, an adequate sexual morality will be constructive and point us toward creativity.

"Christian love," which embraces that which is hostile, is possible only for the unselfish person. It retains a certain mutuality, however, in that it expands the appreciable world of the lover.

A society is "just," Wieman writes, when each member may seek and find "what he most needs for the creativity of life." Love increases the dynamic toward such a society. Our need for restoration and our despair over the limits and failures of our own righteousness point us toward religion.

Western man has no effective alternative to the Judaeo-Christian religion, Wieman believes. The "Christian myth" in the past has functioned to turn men away from lesser, created goods, and toward the source of good. Myth "known to be myth," however, loses its power unless its representations can be established as actualities. Wieman reinterprets the metaphysically transcendent Christian level in functionally transcendent terms as the creative event. Only psychologically may this God be understood as "personal." Theologically, Christianity has proffered a "revelation of God, forgiveness of sin, and the salvation of man—these all by way of Jesus Christ." Interpreting nature from the standpoint of the creative event, we may discern its three "triumphs" to date: the living cell, man, the living Christ. Subsequent transformations are anticipated in eschatological mythology.

To worship is to practice ritual which, Wieman says, "loosens the coercive grip of fears and desires" obstructing the creative event. The main duty of the Church is to demand those human relations which release this power.

The major influences upon Wieman's thinking have been Henri Bergson (1859-1941), John Dewey (1859-1952), and Alfred North Whitehead (1861-1947). He sees naturalism as affording the best method for interpreting the central realities of Christianity to a modern world. Wieman's ideas are theistic in the sense that he believes that the creative event is a determinant of man rather than that it is determined by man, and that in this sense man is incapable of foreseeing the structures of the future. God, so described, is the proper name for that creativity which is the dynamic part of reality.

THE DIVINE RELATIVITY

Author: Charles Hartshorne (1897-   )
Type of work: Metaphysics, theology
First published: 1948

PRINCIPAL IDEAS ADVANCED

Classical theology affirmed that although God is absolute, He causes, knows, and loves His creation; such a doctrine is obviously self-contradictory since to know or to love is to be related and thus not to be absolute.

Contradiction can be avoided by distinguishing between those aspects of God which are relative and those aspects which are absolute.

A God who is relative is required by both metaphysics and religion, whereas a God who is absolute in every respect is compatible with neither.

A relation between two things can be internal to one and external to the other; hence such a relation relativizes the first and leaves the second absolute.

Charles Hartshorne, author of *The Divine Relativity,* stands firmly within the classical metaphysical tradition at least in one sense. He is one of the few contemporary philosophers who still find compelling cosmological and ontological arguments for the existence of God. He holds that the existence of God can be rationally demonstrated either by proceeding from the nature of the world to a necessary Creator or by proceeding from the definition of what it is to be God.

In another sense, however, Hartshorne is not within the classical tradition; his metaphysical ideas follow closely those of Alfred North Whitehead (1861-1947) and not those of past Western metaphysicians. Hartshorne, following Whitehead and others, conceives of reality as social (not individual) and in terms of process (not static substance). So-called "individual" entities are not simple, independent substances; they are processes which are intimately interrelated with other processes. Stated simply, all that anyone meets or has met is really part of him. He is a spatio-temporal process, made up of all of the relations which he has with other things including his own past. He is an ever-changing personal process, ever growing by the addition of new experiences and relationships which literally alter his being so that it constantly becomes something new.

All reality is social process, undergoing constant change and growth; hence, God, who is the all-inclusive reality, is also a growing social process. God, then, cannot be described in an unqualified way as immutable, simple, or absolute, for, in Hartshorne's terms, God is supreme *yet indebted to all*, absolute *yet related to all*. In short, God is divinely relative. The major claim in this book, originally presented in the form of lectures delivered at Yale University as the twenty-fourth series of Terry Lectures, is that it is both possible and necessary to describe God as *divine* (that is, as absolute and supreme), but also as *related* (involved in relativity).

Classical metaphysics and theology mistakenly maintained that God is purely absolute, nonrelative in every respect. God was said to be timeless, changeless, related only to His own self and therefore not really related to His creatures, and gaining nothing from His creatures. However, it was also claimed, inconsistently, that God is Creator, and that He knows and loves the creatures that He has made. Theology certainly affirmed this, and so did metaphysics inasmuch as metaphysics used as its basic argument for the existence of God the argument that God is first cause.

Hartshorne observes that it is an intolerable contradiction to assert both that God is related and that He is absolute and hence not related in any respect. If it is said that God creates, then it must be admitted that God is related; if it is said that God loves, then it must be admitted that God is related to and receives from the objects of His love; if God really knows, then God is really related; and a God who is really related cannot be absolute in every respect. Hartshorne analyzes some of the ways in which the classical tradition attempted to evade this dilemma and he concludes that the attempt failed.

It is Hartshorne's contention that the doctrine of God can be stated in such a way as to avoid this self-contradiction by distinguishing those aspects of God by which He is absolute from those aspects by which He is relative. There is no contradiction in holding that God is both absolute and relative, provided that these contraries are applied to different aspects of God. As to the relation which holds between these aspects, "the main thesis . . . is that the 'relative' or changeable, that which depends upon and varies with varying relationships, includes within itself and in value exceeds the non-relative, immutable, independent, or 'absolute,' *as the concrete includes and exceeds the abstract.* From this doctrine . . . it follows that God, as supremely excellent and concrete, must be conceived not as wholly absolute or immutable, but rather as supremely-relative, 'surrelative,' although, or because of this superior relativity, containing an abstract character or essence in respect to which, but only in respect to which, he is indeed strictly absolute and immutable."

Chapter 1 develops the notion of God as relative, presenting the case, both metaphysical and religious, for a God who is all-inclusive, supremely relative, indebted to and enriched by all. Chapter 2 shows that a related God is also absolute and shows what the relation between relativity and absoluteness in God is. Chapter 3 discusses the attributes of God, particularly the attributes of omniscience, omnipotence, and goodness, showing exactly in what way both relativity and absoluteness must be specified with respect to each of these, and concludes with an account of the beneficial consequences which would flow from a notion of divine relativity.

A conception of God as both absolute and relative is both logically sound and metaphysically necessary according to Hartshorne. In three earlier works, *Beyond Humanism* (1937), *Man's Vision of God* (1941), and *Reality as Social Process* (1953)—the latter composed of articles most of which were written before 1948—Hartshorne presents his full metaphysical argument, and much of this groundwork is presupposed in *The Divine Relativity.* In all these books

Hartshorne tries to show that modern metaphysical theory requires the existence of God, the sort of God who is Himself the supreme exemplification of the categories of metaphysics, and who Himself, while involved in process, exists necessarily and persists eternally in time. Many arguments are presented, including forms of the cosmological and ontological arguments, which take into account developments in modern metaphysics and which prove the existence of a God who is Himself a being in process rather than the timeless absolute being of classical metaphysics.

But more than metaphysics is at stake, Hartshorne argues, for the moral and religious needs of mankind can be satisfied only by a God who is related and who includes within Himself all value. Morality and religion both demand an ultimate value which is unrestrictedly worthy of worship, and thus a value which contains all value and which is unrestrictedly good in its own actions, always working for good. Such a God, because He literally includes all actual values, is enriched as new values and combinations of value are added to His experience; hence He is a God who is really served by man. Classical theology, however, Hartshorne observes, could not allow that God be served. To allow this would be to admit that God profits from something outside Himself and, hence, is not in all respects absolute. But if creation added nothing to God, added nothing to the fullness of His value, it could not be said that creation was a good. Only if creation *adds* to value can it be a good. God must profit from creation and from everything which takes place within it. Such a God can be served by men and can satisfy their moral and religious longings.

God is perfection, but He is self-surpassing or growing perfection; God is the greatest conceivable being, but He is able to surpass His present states as He grows into richer, fuller states. God is the greatest conceivable being because only God includes all value, but God can surpass His own present state by creating and including more values, by bringing novel values and richer relationships among values into existence and including them in future states of His being. As men create richer social orders, as artists create and share new art works and forms, as human sensitivities are increased, new values come into existence and the state of God which includes those values surpasses the state of God before those values were actual.

What does it mean, after all, to say that something is good, or what does it mean to say that something is better than something else? Hartshorne argues that higher levels of existence, such as the level of human existence, are said to be higher levels because such beings as men are more related, more sensitive to other things, more dependent upon other things, than are lower forms of existence. A stone is "impassible," but a person receives richly from other things. God as highest or best or supreme being is, then, the maximal case of dependence. Classical theology made the word "best" mean the absolutely independent and unrelated, but it is not at all clear that the independent is what is really best. Rather, that which is maximally related, related to and considerate of all values, is best.

Hartshorne's central claim is supported by typical analogies used in religion. To speak of God as "father" is to use a social analogy to describe the nature of God, an analogy which suggests that just as a human father is related to his children, so God is related to His, the difference being that God is a perfect Father and His relationships to all creation are much more intimate and rich. It would be an equivocation, not an analogy, to say God is a father *but* one who is absolutely independent of His children, one who neither knows nor loves His children. To be a father is to love, to enjoy, and to share. Classical theology equivocates in affirming that God is Father but denying that He is related to His children.

One must begin first with the notion of God as social being, as love, intimately related to all, and only then ask about the ways in which such a being can be absolute. An "immutable" *person* is a person who is not subject to death or degeneration and who is not vacillating because of fear or weakness; he is not unchanging in every respect. A *person* who exists necessarily is a being who persists endlessly in time and cannot not exist, yet as a person he may change in some respects and hence in those respects be contingent, not necessary. A being that is absolute in all respects cannot be related, but a being who is related can still be absolute.

The idea that God is supreme, yet indebted to all, and that God is Absolute, yet related to all, is in marked contrast to the ideas of classical theology and humanism. Classical theology drew the conclusion that God is the Absolute Being who is related to and indebted to none. Humanism has maintained that because all being is related to and indebted to other things there is no absolute. Both are wrong, for a being can be related to all yet be in some respects absolute.

The classical view, in its way of conceiving of the eminence of God, the perfection of God, was one-sided. It affirmed perfection of only one of equally legitimate opposites. Similarly, modern views as a rule are one-sided, affirming only the alternative one of each pair of opposites. Hartshorne affirms both in each case. Classical thought conceived God as eminently absolute; Hartshorne adds eminent relativity; to eminent permanence he adds eminent change; to eminent simplicity he adds eminent complexity; to eminent activity he adds eminent passivity (God is not merely cause; He is also effect). In each pair it is the term which emphasizes relativity which must be stressed as the more significant, for what is relative is the fullness of God, while what is absolute is merely His abstract essence.

A basic distinction, Hartshorne claims, can save the doctrine of God from internal self-contradiction. In *essence,* in terms of His kind of being, God is absolute; in *actuality,* in terms of His concrete actual being, God is relative. For example, all instances of knowing share an abstract essence, but this abstract essence is not itself an instance of knowing, just as twoness is not itself a pair. The abstract characteristic by means of which one defines instances of knowing is absolute and independent, even though every concrete being which embodies this characteristic is relative and dependent. Similarly, then, it can be said that God in essence is abstract and independent, whereas in concrete being, as an instance of Godness, He is relative.

In a knowing relation, such as a subject-object relation, the object is absolute, the subject relative. God as object of all subjects is absolute; God as subject of all objects is maximally relative.

Similar observations hold with respect to the cause-effect relationship. A cause is absolute and independent, whereas its effect is relative and dependent. God as first cause, then, is absolute; God as effect, God as including all that is, is maximally relative.

In His completeness, God is the divine relativity, for the relative includes the absolute as a mere aspect of the relative, just as an actual entity includes its essence, as a knower includes the known, as the concrete includes the abstract, as a whole includes its parts, and as an effect includes its cause. In each of these cases a relation is specified which is internal to (that is, relativizes) the first, but external to (that is, leaves absolute) the second. Such a solution of the problem of God, then, is intimately related to the problem of relations and occupies a great deal of Hartshorne's discussion. He argues that since relations can be external to one term and internal to the other, this solution to the problem of God is possible, for externality is absoluteness, and internality is relativity.

God exists necessarily, Hartshorne claims; He knows all and does all that is possible to do consistent with His nature; He loves all things literally and knows all things fully, whereas men neither love nor do anything fully. God is above the battle, independent in the sense that nothing that happens can threaten His being, for He necessarily exists. Because God includes and harmonizes all value, past and present, nothing can take place which would destroy the divine blessedness. God experiences tragedy (as He must if He really loves and enters into the experience of his creatures), but tragedy cannot overwhelm Him. In all these respects God is metaphysically differ-ent from all other beings. God *is Supreme, yet indebted to all; Absolute, yet related to all.* By means of a logical distinction and a conception of reality as social process Hartshorne is able to provide a God who is both metaphysically necessary and religiously satisfactory.

GOD WAS IN CHRIST

Author: Donald M. Baillie (1887-1954)
Type of work: Christology
First published: 1948

Principal Ideas Advanced

Traditional understandings of Christ tend to undercut the humanity of Jesus; modern Christological thinkers, while recognizing His humanity, tend to make it irrelevant.

The dogma of the God-man is a confession based on Christian experience; consequently, the clue to the meaning of this paradox is the experience of the paradox of grace.

Jesus is the Incarnation of God, for in every moment His self-consciousness was sacrificed to the will of God and was dependent always on divine grace.

The doctrine of the Trinity is the confession that the union of Jesus with God is available after Jesus' death through the Divine Spirit: the doctrine of the atonement is the declaration that forgiveness is costly for God, occurring within the divine life itself.

Three basic creeds which were forged during the formative days of Christianity have served almost every major strand of Christianity as theological guidelines. These are the Apostles' Creed (developed from c.160 to c.650), the Nicene Creed (325), and the Chalcedonian Creed (451). These creeds have been of central importance not because of the depth of their theological penetration into major doctrines of faith, but because of their utility as channel markers for theologi-cal reflection concerning the essence of Christianity.

Despite its usefulness, the Chalcedonian Creed in particular has been the cause of perennial dissatisfaction. Few theologians will question the worthy intent of its formulators in insisting upon Jesus Christ as "fully God and fully man." Yet, in trying to give meaning to this confession of faith, the resulting creed bristles with many statements which are either contradictory or meaningless for faith.

Most difficult of all is the declaration that Christ was "made known in two natures, inconfusedly, immutably, indivisibly, inseparably, the differences of the natures by no means annulled through the union, but rather the peculiarity of each nature being preserved and concurring into one person and one substantial individual, not divided or separated into two persons, but one self-same and only Son. . . ." The difficulty here is not simply linguistic; it goes far deeper, for such a statement rests heavily on a Greek metaphysical understanding that is little accepted or understood today.

In nineteenth century liberal Protestant theology there were many attempts to make the person of Christ understandable, but almost always in a manner that sacrificed Christ's uniqueness for his "perfect humanity." Donald M. Baillie's *God Was In Christ* is thus perhaps one of the most important works in contemporary Christology, for in a manner both original and suggestive Baillie attempts to give meaning to the orthodox Chalcedonian understanding. His approach is an attempt to mediate the truths of liberalism and neo-orthodoxy.

For Baillie, the attempt by nineteenth century theologians to recover the historical Jesus helpfully countered the tendency from the beginning of Christian thought toward Doceticism; that is, the view that Jesus is fully divine, although He appears to be human. There can be no denying the humanity of Jesus. The Bible clearly witnesses to the fact that since Jesus was human, His knowledge was limited; His miracles were possibly only through the power of God, a power available to every man; He had temptations that were real struggles;

He prayed to God as would any other religious human being.

Contemporary theologians have accepted the unqualified humanity of Jesus without question, certain theologians even declaring that, historically regarded, Jesus was not even a remarkable man. Such an awareness of the humanity of Jesus is regarded by Baillie as a real gain, but many theologians render Christ's humanity irrelevant by contending that Jesus is the Christ, not through His humanity, but in spite of it. The "Jesus of history" thus takes second place to the "Christ of faith." Thus the Resurrection becomes the revelation of the divinity of Christ. Protestant theologian Karl Barth, for example, insists that we know no more about God through Christ than was known through the Old Testament; we know through Him only that the promise of God has been fulfilled. Baillie's task, consequently, becomes that of showing how, *in* and *through* His humanity, Jesus was "the very life of God Himself." If God's nature is not revealed in Jesus, there is no meaning to the affirmation that God became man.

Much of the loss of interest in the historical Jesus stems from the position fostered by form criticism, which holds that the historical Jesus cannot be known because Scripture is the creation of the faith of the early Church rather than an objective account of the historical Jesus. The mistake such thinkers make, according to Baillie, is the mistake of forgetting that "the story may have been handed on simply or primarily *because it was true,* because the incident had actually taken place in the ministry of Jesus. . . ." The quest for the historical Jesus becomes impossible only for those who radically prejudge Scripture from their own perspectives. Such persons refuse to admit that the Biblical writers were probably interested in reporting everything Jesus said and did; Scriptural interpretation may very well be more the effect of selection than of imagination.

Yet Baillie is fighting not only against those "who wish to sacrifice the Jesus of history to a high Christology," but also against "those who wish to sacrifice Christology to the Jesus of history." It is not sufficient to say with the liberals that Jesus is the climax of man's search for God, nor even that He is "the living Way, through whom alone we can surely come to the Father." The neo-orthodox have rightly seen that the God "discovered" by Jesus is the God who acts, who seeks His creatures before they seek Him. If we are to believe what Jesus tells us of God, "we must pass beyond words like 'discovery' and even 'revelation' to words like 'incarnation.'" The idea of the Incarnation is the only idea by which the Christian understanding of God becomes either credible or expressible. The center of Baillie's insistence is that "a true Christology will tell us not simply that God is *like* Christ, but that God was *in* Christ. Thus it will tell us not only about the *nature* of God, but about His *activity*. . . ." Theology, as Baillie insists, must be Christology, for the New Testament writers regarded every act that Jesus did as an act of God.

Quite clearly, the Incarnation is a paradox, but it becomes a contradiction unless restated in the language of each generation. The creeds are only signposts against heresy; the meaning of their affirmations must be thought out in every age. There are three lines of Christological thinking in modern theology. The anhypostasia understanding maintains that Christ is a divine Person who assumed human nature without assuming human personality. The kenotic theory holds that the Second Person of the Trinity laid aside His distinctively divine attributes and lived on earth within the limits of humanity. Both of these explanations Baillie finds unacceptable, for in each case the humanity of Jesus is undermined. Finally, Karl Heim's highly original understanding of Christ in terms of the political category of "Leader" (Führer) is rejected by Baillie as avoiding the Christological question altogether.

Baillie's attempt at a new approach to the problem begins with the assertion that the only justification for and reconciliation of paradox is experience. The experience which is the heart of Christian life is thus the illuminating clue to the Incarnation. This clue is the experience of grace. (Here Baillie shows the influence of Augustinian thought.) The Christian experiences all good things to be the product of God, and yet human action is never more truly personal, responsible, and free than when the divine foundation of all is affirmed. The key paradox of Christian experience is the lived truth stated by St. Paul: "I laboured more abundantly than you all; yet not I, but the grace of God which was with me."

There is no boundary that can be drawn between God's work and our own; both sides of the paradox of grace must be affirmed. Nor can the boundary be drawn in Jesus' case; He claimed nothing for Himself. "I, . . . yet not I, but the Father." Jesus' sinlessness consisted in denouncing all claim to ethical heroism, in throwing

Himself totally on God's grace. He attempted to bring others into His own close union with God, into a life in which self-consciousness is swallowed up in God-consciousness. The Fourth Gospel states boldly that all Christ's people should achieve the same kind of unity with God as did Jesus. Jesus' choices were human choices, but like all human choices they were dependent upon God's grace. It was because what Jesus did was always pleasing to God that this prevenience of grace "was nothing short of Incarnation. . . ."

Is this simply to say that any perfect man would be God Incarnate? For Baillie, to ask such a question is to take a far too optimistic view of human nature; it is not to take divine prevenience seriously. "When we really accept the paradox of grace, when we really believe that every good thing in a man is wrought by God . . . and have taken that divine priority in earnest, the question loses its meaning, and . . . fades away into the paradox of the Incarnation."

Such a view of Incarnation, Baillie insists, sheds light on the related doctrine of the Trinity. In Jesus Christ human selfhood came fully to its own because it was wholly yielded to God. Thus Jesus' life *was* the life of God; the initiative was always God's. After His death, Christ's divine presence returned. It was "independent of His actual presence in the flesh, though not independent of His *having* lived on earth in the flesh." Christ now drew believers into His union with God, even those who had not known Him in the flesh. This experience was interpreted as the "era of the Holy Spirit"; it provides the experiential basis for the doctrine of the Trinity.

Throughout history, God was continually pressing through into human life. But He became incarnate only when at last a man was perfectly receptive. The Father's love for the Son was conditional on Jesus' fulfilling His vocation as "Son." When the Christian speaks of the "pre-existent Son," Baillie declares, he does not refer to Jesus of Nazareth but to the divine priority in the total life of Jesus.

Likewise, the meaning of the ascension must be taken radically. "If we believe in the Incarnation, we cannot possibly say that Jesus ceased to be human when He departed from this world." This means that the divine presence that came into the world in Jesus continues through the Holy Spirit to dwell in us. Our knowledge of God is not like Christ's knowledge, but it is dependent on that knowledge.

Baillie's understanding of the atonement is developed by the same method as that which led to an understanding of the Incarnation. Through an analysis of human experience, Baillie attempts to show that moral failure, disobedience of conscience, is at the heart of psychic disorder and is something concerning which the individual himself is powerless. Sin is self-centeredness, the refusal of divine and human community; it is an absorption in oneself which kills true individuality and destroys the soul. Such a self cannot change itself, for the more it tries, the more its concentration is focused on the self. Divine forgiveness is the only possible instrument for fulfilled existence.

Yet divine forgiveness is impossible without atonement, for there is a great difference between "a good-natured indulgence and a costly reconciliation." Neither God nor man can be moral and still take sin lightly. Since sin is disloyalty to God, such "ultimate betrayal" can be rectified only by divine action. The atonement is God's act, and its meaning is that forgiveness takes place "in the very heart and life of God. . . ." Divine forgiveness involves Divine suffering. Such Divine forgiveness is not the result of the Crucifixion; the Crucifixion occurred because God loved the world. The love which led Jesus to the cross is the love of God Himself coming to man in Christ.

Yet divine sin-bearing is not confined to the moment of Crucifixion, for God "has a direct 'vertical' relation to each moment. . . ." The Cross "is actually a part (the incarnate part) of the eternal divine sin-bearing." There has never been an age when God was not carrying the sins of His people and thus making atonement and offering forgiveness.

THEOLOGY OF THE NEW TESTAMENT

Author: Rudolf Bultmann (1884-   )
Type of work: Exegesis of the New Testament
First published: 1948-1953 (3 fascicles)

PRINCIPAL IDEAS ADVANCED

Faith is man's response to the Word of God that encounters him in the Church's kerygma, which proclaims the crucified and risen Christ to be God's eschatological act of salvation.

Theology is the unfolding of the thoughts of faith; it is necessarily existential in character, since the Christian's new understanding of God, the world, and man involves inseparably a new understanding of himself in his concrete existence.

New Testament theology is the scientific endeavor to set forth the thoughts of faith found in the New Testament writings.

The message of Jesus is a presupposition for, rather than a part of, the theology of the New Testament.

The theologies of Paul and John form the center and apex of theological interpretation in the New Testament; within the framework of Hellenistic Christianity they historicize the Jewish apocalyptic eschatology of the earliest Church, so that the eschatological occurrence of salvation is interpreted in existential-human categories rather than natural-cosmic categories; in the later development toward the ancient Church the eschatological tension is relaxed, and the Church more and more conceives of itself as a sacramental institution of salvation.

The publication in Germany of *Theologie des Neuen Testaments* marked the crowning achievement of one of the truly creative and challenging theologians of the twentieth century. The author was Rudolf Bultmann, Professor of New Testament Studies at the University of Marburg from 1921 to 1951. His work combines rigorous historico-critical analysis with a passionate desire to interpret Christian faith in a way meaningful for modern man. Bultmann is firmly grounded in the research into early Christianity conducted by the "history-of-religious school," and he became one of the first New Testament scholars to apply the historical method of "form criticism" to the material of the Synoptic Gospels. Moreover, Bultmann joined Karl Barth in repudiating the anthropological basis of "liberal theology" in favor of a "dialectical theology" that recognized what Søren Kierkegaard (1813-1855) had called "the infinite qualitative distinction between time and eternity." Fruitful study of the philosophy of the early Martin Heidegger, which is strongly oriented on Kierkegaard, led Bultmann to call for an existentialistic interpretation of the New Testament texts; finally, he instituted his controversial program of demythologizing the proclamation of the New Testament. In his work, mythological concepts are interpreted according to the self-understanding which is operative in them. In this way Bultmann intends to carry through the Pauline-Lutheran doctrine of justification in the realm of knowledge.

In his *Theology of the New Testament* the author attempts to set forth the theological thoughts of the New Testament writings, not in a systematically ordered unity but in their variety, by indicating the locus of each in the historical development of the early Church. In opposition to orthodoxy's method of collecting Biblical quotations to confirm dogmatic propositions,

as well as to rationalism's method of formulating concepts of doctrine in accordance with rational truth, Bultmann explicates theological thoughts in their connection with the "act of living"; that is, he regards theological ideas as expressions of faith's self-understanding in response to the kerygma (proclamation) as God's personal word spoken to man in his concrete situation. Because of this inevitable involvement of the believer's self-understanding, the theological task of unfolding the understanding of God, the world, and man, a task which arises from faith, can never be accomplished once and for all, but requires ever-repeated solutions.

Bultmann has divided his work into three parts: (1) "Presuppositions and Motifs of New Testament Theology," (2) "The Theologies of Paul and John," and (3) "The Development toward the Ancient Church." The second part is the central and most detailed part of the book, and it is considered to contain the most profound understanding of Christian faith available in the New Testament. Parts One and Three present, respectively, a progression toward and a regression from the outstanding theological achievements of Paul and John.

In sharp contrast to "liberal" interpretations, Bultmann boldly affirms that "the message of Jesus is a presupposition for the theology of the New Testament rather than a part of that theology itself." If theology is an unfolding of the thoughts of faith, and if faith is response to the Christian kerygma, and if the kerygma proclaims the crucified and risen Christ to be God's eschatological act of salvation, then Bultmann's affirmation is a logical conclusion. Jesus' eschatological message of the imminent inbreaking of the reign of God, and His call for decision between God and "the world" sets the stage, as it were, for God's saving act; but faith affirms Jesus and His coming. His crucifixion and resurrection are to be the saving event. He who was *bearer* of a message became the essential *content* of the message of the early Church.

The earliest Church, however, conceived Jesus as the *coming* Messiah, the "Son of Man" whose impending advent would bring an end to world history and inaugurate the perfect reign of God. The "end of days" was near, and the Church believed itself to be the "eschatological congregation" which would finally be saved. The Easter faith declared the crucified Jesus of Nazareth to be the Messiah who will come, and in this sense there is attributed to Him a power to determine the present. All of this, of course, remains within the context of Jewish eschatological expectation, with its apocalyptic picture of the future.

The Jewish Christianity represented by the earliest Church in Palestine presupposed an understanding of the history of salvation embodied in the Old Testament-Judaic tradition, with its emphasis on the centrality of the Law for the People of God. When Christianity, under the impetus of the missionary movement, moved into the Hellenistic (Greek) world, it inevitably met with difficulties that forced the transformation of the form of its proclamation. First, there was the difficulty that arose from Hellenistic Christianity's acknowledgment of the authority of the Old Testament, while at the same time denying the validity of the Old Testament

Law for Christians. Thus, Christians were brought into conflict with the Jews of the Hellenistic synagogues. A second difficulty emerged in the problem of communicating the kerygma in the Hellenistic cultural and religious milieu, with its popular Greek philosophies, its mystery religions, and its Gnostic myths of salvation.

Bultmann contends that pre-Pauline Christianity is by no means a unity, so that there were various solutions to the above-named difficulties. Christian preaching in the Gentile world could not have been simply Christological; it had to begin with the proclamation of the one God, who is both Creator and Judge of a world which has fallen into the sin of idolatry. However, beside God, or even in His place, Jesus Christ appears as God's plenipotent representative who will judge the world and save those who belong to the Congregation of the faithful. This eschatological Judge and Savior is none other than the *crucified* Jesus of Nazareth whom God raised from the dead and exalted to his eschatological role at the time when the dead shall be raised for judgment. Indeed, Bultmann declares that first in Hellenistic Christianity is Jesus Christ (now a proper name) given the title "Lord" and decreed worthy of cultic worship. In addition, the title "Son of God," which for the earliest Church denoted the Messianic king, came to mean in Hellenistic Christianity the divinity of Christ, by virtue of which He is differentiated from the human sphere. Christ is now the pre-existent Son of God who became man, the "Logos" or "Word" who was also the agent of creation. The terminology of the mystery religions, with their dying and rising "divinities," and that of Gnosticism, with its mythological figure of the "Redeemer," is now employed to interpret Christian faith, and this represented at once a danger and an opportunity. The critical question, emphasizes Bultmann, is whether the newly interpreted eschatological event of salvation inaugurated by the history of Jesus Christ will be conceived as natural process or as genuinely historical, that is, as existential, happening.

It is the remarkable service of Paul and John, contends the author, that they, standing in their different ways _within_ Hellenistic Christianity and using its terminology, were able to demythologize the Gnostic cosmological-dualistic conceptuality and to present the eschatological occurrence of salvation as taking place in the present. The salvation-event is not a cosmic-natural occurrence, but is present solely "in the proclaiming, accosting, demanding, and promising word of preaching." Judgment and salvation are no longer considered to be in the indefinite future, but to be present now in the response of men to the kerygmatic word of Jesus.

Bultmann considers Paul to be the real founder of Christian theology. Unlike a Greek philosopher or a modern theologian, Paul did not theoretically and systematically develop his thoughts in an independent scientific treatise, but he lifted the knowledge inherent in faith into the clarity of conscious knowing. His theology, then, is not speculative; he does not deal with "God in Himself" nor with "man in himself," but with them only in their relation to each other. Thus, "every assertion about God is simultaneously an assertion about man and vice versa," and it is in this sense that

Paul's theology is, at the same time, anthropology. In like manner, Paul is not concerned with the metaphysical essence or the "natures" of Christ, but with Him as the one through whom God is working for the salvation of the world and man. Thus, Paul's Christology is simultaneously soteriology.

Pauline theology is dealt with under two main headings: "Man Prior to the Revelation of Faith" and "Man Under Faith." Bultmann thereby indicates his intention to present Biblical theology as an anthropology, by means of an existentialist interpretation. Man's existence prior to faith is an existence "according to the flesh," in which he sinfully tries to live out of his own resources and consequently falls into the power of death. The man of faith, however, surrenders his self to God and receives the gift of salvation which God has wrought in the crucifixion and the resurrection of Jesus Christ. He now lives "according to the Spirit," made righteous by God's act of grace and set free from sin, death, and the tyranny of the Law. In faith, which comes from hearing the word of preaching and which primarily involves obedience, God's eschatological salvation-event becomes a present reality but never a possession, so that the decision of faith must be made again and again. The life of faith, then, is understood as a dialectic between "no longer" and "not yet," between the indicative and the imperative.

The historicizing of eschatology that begins in Paul, who, nevertheless, still retained terminology relating to the Old Testament-Judaic conception of the history of salvation, is carried through in radical fashion by John, in whom the history-of-salvation perspective is missing altogether. The central topic for discussion for John is not, as for Paul, the way to salvation, but, rather, salvation itself. Jesus Christ is understood as the Revelation of God, the Son or Word of God whose very coming brings salvation to the fallen world. In the Son's own person man is given life and truth as the reality out of which he can exist, and faith means transition into eschatological existence, which, at the same time, involves a turning away from the world, desecularization. The believer is in the world, but not of the world. All this is made possible, of course, by the word of preaching, in which the saving event of the "Word made flesh" becomes present reality through the activity of the Spirit.

Bultmann sees in the development toward the ancient Church a gradual transformation of the Church's understanding of itself. The eschatological tension relaxes, and the Church begins to organize itself as a new religion. The constituting element of the Church changes from the activity of proclaiming the Word to the congregational office and the sacrament. The Church conceives itself as an institution of salvation; thus, the Church is able to mediate transcendent powers in the present through its sacramental cultus and priestly office. The Lord's Supper becomes the "medicine of immortality." Right doctrine, rather than faith, comes to distinguish Christians from Jews and heathen. An ideal of moralistic piety begins to replace the eschatological consciousness and the consciousness of being endowed with spiritual gifts. The keeping of commandments becomes the condition for salvation, and a radical understanding of sin gives way to a conception that differentiates between "light" and "grave" sins. Baptism is thought to secure forgiveness only for those sins committed prior to its administration, so that post-baptismal sins become a problem. The genuine understanding of "grace" is lost, and the Church moves ineluctably toward the legalism of the Catholic penitential system.

ETHICS

Author: Dietrich Bonhoeffer (1906-1945)
Type of work: Christian ethics
First published: 1949

PRINCIPAL IDEAS ADVANCED

To meet the opposition of anti-Christian forces, Western man must recover a totally Christian world view.

Taking the revelation of God in Christ as central, Christianity has the task of "conforming" the world to Christ.

In this undertaking, it must avoid the extremes of compromising with the world and of radically denying the world.

While respecting natural law and rationality, the Christian is not guided by abstract principles but is directly responsible to Christ.

The Christian's responsibility is not confined to "religious" concerns but embraces labor, marriage, and government.

During the first three years of the second World War, before he was imprisoned, Dietrich Bonhoeffer spent whatever time he could find while engaged in underground activities against the Nazis in writing what he intended to be a full-length theological work concerning Christian ethics. Bonhoeffer was executed by the S. S. Black Guards, in the concentration camp at Flossenburg, on April 9, 1945. The present work comprises those parts of his projected book which have been recovered from the places where they were hidden. Some parts are in nearly finished form; others are little more than sketches. For the most part, the editors have been able to follow Bonhoeffer's outline, so that the work reads consecutively.

The task which Bonhoeffer sets for himself in *Ethics* is to recover the foundation and the structure of a totally Christian way of life. As Western man has moved away from the foundations of his faith, his life has become increasingly meaningless. The Church is to blame, because it has failed in its responsibility to make the reality of God visible everywhere. There is only one recourse, to take Christ as the absolute revelation of God's will toward men, and to bring every aspect of life under that revelation.

Thus, Bonhoeffer's *Ethics* is Christ-centered. But, unlike the liberal gospel (see Adolf Harnack's *What is Christianity?*, 1900), it does not find its basis in the teachings of Jesus. Rather, like the Gospel of Paul, it sees in the incarnation, death, and resur-

rection of Christ, God's purpose to form man according to His eternal will. For Bonhoeffer, Christian ethics is "formation." It is the concrete, historical working out of divine redemption in the whole length and breadth of creation, beginning with the Church, but embracing labor, marriage, and government as well. The Christian's duty is to implement the will of God, and in every situation God's will is that the world may be "conformed" to Christ.

Bonhoeffer contends that in and of itself the world of time and change is meaningless. Only as time and change are seen in relation to divine reality do they become significant. The one place where time and eternity meet is in Christ Jesus. Hence, it is to Christ that we must look if our lives are to be redeemed from futility and death. By the Incarnation, God took upon Himself the nature of man, raised that nature from the level of brute creation, and established its dignity. By the Crucifixion, He bore our guilt, making it possible for us to accept ourselves and to live with our past. By the Resurrection, He broke the chains of death and evil and proclaimed that Christ is Lord over all the world. The wisdom of life, says Bonhoeffer, is all present here; the simplest man, by submitting his life to Christ, finds all that he needs for performing God's will. The Church exists to confront persons with Christ. Its members, when conformable to Christ, become the agents of God to bring society into conformity with Him.

Bonhoeffer intended his theology to be free from the errors of what he called compromise and radicalism. The problem is, What shall be the attitude of the Church to the wisdom of the non-Christian world? The compromisers, symbolized by Dostoevski's Grand Inquisitor, destroy the ultimacy of Christianity by subordinating its demands to things as they are. The radicals, symbolized by Ibsen's Brand, make an exclusive commitment to the ultimate the basis for denying their responsibility toward the world. Each of these positions, says Bonhoeffer, contains elements of truth as well as of falsity. The truth is that *ultimately* it is only in Christ that the will of God is manifest, even though *penultimately* God's will is manifest in the world and in society. In other words, God's redemptive purpose finds its realization only in conforming the world to Christ; however, as means to that final condition, subordinate realms have been established by God and have been given relative validity. Nature, the state, reason, and natural law thus exist as means; they must not be taken as ultimate, but neither may they be ignored. The state, for example, must respect the rights with which the Creator has invested every living thing. Specifically, the rights of individual men and women must not be contravened in the name of communal rights. On the other hand, the state as an instrument of order is ordained of God and must be obeyed except when, as Bonhoeffer believed true of Hitler, the ruler openly repudiates the state's legitimate function.

Christian ethics, then, does not go against nature and reason but vindicates them even as it surpasses them. For, according to Bonhoeffer, ordinary morality, with its distinction between what is and what should be, shows man at odds with God and with himself. Like the Mosaic law, a rigid morality is likely to lead to Pharisaism. But the ethics of civilized man is on the way to Christ. Good, honest, honorable men are working toward Christianity. The Church should raise no barrier against such men but should take them in, in the hopes of bringing them the rest of the way.

The Christian, having received the forgiveness and renewal which God offers to sinful man in Christ, no longer judges his duty in terms of abstract right and wrong. Although he respects the penultimate order, he is free from complete obedience to its requirements because he is directly responsible to Christ.

The concept of responsibility was to have been an important one in Bonhoeffer's system. Responsibility depends on the tension between obligation and freedom, a tension which, in Bonhoeffer's experience, constituted the life of Christian discipleship. On the one hand, following Christ means the negation of our "apostate life," the life which as children of the world we seek to live apart from the will of God. On the other hand, it means affirming the new life which God has constituted everywhere—not just in believers—through the incarnation, death, and resurrection of Christ. "This concept of responsibility," says Bonhoeffer, "is intended as referring to the concentrated totality and unity of the response to reality which is given to us in Jesus Christ, as distinct from the partial responses which might arise, for example, from a consideration of utility or from particular principles."

Christian ethics, according to Bonhoeffer, has no need for rules or principles. As abstractions, principles are not adequate to disclose God's will for particular situations. On the contrary, they are apt to frustrate God's purpose, as Bonhoeffer declares was actually the case with conscientious but rule-venerating Christians under Hitler. To the Christian, it is the revelation of God in Christ which gives any situation its meaning. This is not to imply that the Christian relies on intuition. Bonhoeffer uses Paul's words; the Christian must "prove the different situations." Bonhoeffer writes, "The heart, the understanding, observation and experience must all collaborate in the task." But the crucial condition for knowing one's duty is the change in one's being which comes from "conformation with the form of the new man Christ." Intelligence pervaded by prayer beholds each new situation through the eyes of Christ. In thus seeing what is, the Christian sees what is to be done.

Bonhoeffer was particularly concerned to bridge the chasm, which has widened in recent decades, between the Church and secular society. As against the view, prevalent in Lutheran circles, that the Church and the world are exclusive spheres, he maintains that through Christ's work the world is already redeemed; the Church is even now confronting the world with its Redeemer. Bonhoeffer did not favor the "activist" approach to "worldly problems"; the world's problems, posed in terms of the penultimate order, are incapable of solution. His view is, rather, that those who make up the "body of Christ," or the Church, will carry out Christ's mandates in every sphere of human activity.

In a penetrating analysis of our times, Bonhoeffer maintains that the void which threatens to swallow Western civilization is "a specifically Western void, a rebellious and outrageous void, and one which is the enemy of both God and man." Nations and civilizations have declined before without leaving men's souls in such desperation. But because Western civilization owes its special character to Christ, its loss of faith has assumed a peculiarly virulent quality. "It is not the theoretical denial of the existence of a God. It is itself a religion, a religion of hostility to God." Ostensibly the West proclaims the deification of man, his natural goodness, his new-found freedom; in fact it proclaims nihilism, an unrestrained vitalism, and a negation of order and law which can lead only to self-destruction. For the West, in particular, Christianity is healing and reconciliation. The West can recover its historical and political form only in returning to justice, order, and peace, but it can scarcely hope to regain these virtues unless the form of Christ is renewed in its midst, through a revival of faith in the Body of the Church.

FAITH AND HISTORY

Author: Reinhold Niebuhr (1892-   )
Type of work: Christian apologetics
First published: 1949

Principal Ideas Advanced

The Christian interpretation of history makes the claim for an eternal Gospel which has universal application amidst the changes and relativities of the historical process.

The Christian view is contrasted with the classical Greek view, which seeks a meaning for history by seeking within a changeless realm of ideas; the Christian view is also contrasted with the modern view which sees both time and history as self-explanatory.

The Christian view, based on a Biblical interpretation, begins with the sovereignty of God as this sovereignty expresses itself in creation, judgment, and redemption.

The sovereignty of God finds its most decisive revelation in Jesus as the Christ, who is the center of historical meaning, who discloses the divine love which transfigures historical justice, and who reconciles the antinomies and ambiguities of human existence.

In *Faith and History* Reinhold Niebuhr formulates a Christian theology of history and develops its unique contrast with rival views. The basic presupposition of the Christian view is that the Gospel of Christ is true for all men and is thus relevant to the historical process in all ages. The peculiar relevance of the Christian Gospel to history is discussed in detail and the idiosyncracies which distinguish the Christian view from classical and modern conceptions are delineated. The method of argumentation is that of apologetics, tacit if not explicit. Although it is clearly stated by the author that there is no simple Christian "philosophy of history," the validity of which can be rationally demonstrated as it is set over against the classical and modern conceptions, nonetheless it is argued that an indirect defense is possible by showing that the alternative views do not account for nor give meaning to the complexities of historical experience. "The Christian philosophy of history is rational, therefore, only in the sense that it is possible

to prove that alternatives to it fail to do justice to all aspects of human existence; and that the basic presuppositions of the Chrisitan faith, though transcending reason, make it possible to give an account of life and history in which all facts and antinomies are comprehended."

The classical conception, informed primarily by the philosophies of Plato and Aristotle, advances a consistent rationalism in which it is affirmed that life and history have a rational intelligibility by virtue of their relation to a world of changeless and eternal ideas. Since the world of temporal and historical becoming was understood as merely a corruption of the eternal world, it was ultimately devalued and negated. The basic presupposition of the Greek view is that of an otherworldliness which negates the vitalities and possibilities of history itself. Correspondingly, historical time is regarded as an extension of natural time. The temporal world is a cycle of natural-historical recurrences ever coming to be and passing away. Meaning is attained only in a liberation from this cycle through a participation in the eternal ideas.

The modern view rejects the other-worldliness stressed in the Greek conception and also the equation of historical time with natural time. Proponents of the modern view agree with the Greeks that there is a rational intelligibility which explains the historical process, but unlike the Greeks the moderns argue that this rational intelligibility is within the historical process itself rather than localized in a supra-temporal world. The growth of reason in the historical process is affirmed to be limitless, and history becomes the story of man's ever increasing rationality, power, and freedom. Unlike the Greek conception, the modern conception advances a linear rather than a cyclical view. History is a process of linear development, ever moving onward and upward. The religious expression of such a view is that God is made wholly immanent and becomes a symbol for history itself, which in the last analysis is self-derived and self-explanatory; and redemption is equated with the progressive realization of freedom. The modern view thus emancipates history from its dependence upon nature and recognizes the unique significance of historical development.

In granting history its autonomy and intrinsic "laws" the modern view, according to Niebuhr, is subject to a most grievous illusion in affirming that history is self-explanatory and self-redemptive. This illusion itself rests upon two miscalculations: (1) an exaggerated estimate of the quality and growth of human freedom and power, and (2) the easy identification of freedom and virtue. In its extravagant estimate of historical freedom the modern conception loses sight of the irreducible finitude of man which imposes multitudinous restrictions upon his freedom. Man is subject to biological limitations, surveys the world from a particular perspective, is restricted by the particularity of his speech, conditioned by his social institutions, and unequivocally limited by his death. In its identification of freedom and virtue the modern view conceals the inevitable moral ambiguities which arise from the actualization of freedom. It fails to recognize that human freedom and power contain destructive as well as creative possibilities and thus it fails to do justice to the tragic antinomies and discontinuities which recur throughout the historical development.

The Christian interpretation, although in some respects similar to both the Greek and modern conceptions, differs from these two views both in its general presuppositions and in details of doctrine. It rejects the criterion of rational intelligibility as the final court of appeal. History is rationally intelligible neither by virtue of its participation in eternal ideas nor by virtue of its intrinsic laws of development. It derives its meaning through the revelation of Biblical faith which centers around the rationally offensive "scandal of particularity." It is a scandal for all rationalistically oriented interpretations of history that the final meaning of the historical process should be rooted in a particular and concrete historical event, whether it be the event of a covenantal bond between God and Israel or the event of a man who is received and acclaimed as the Christ. More specifically, the Christian view rejects the non-historical classical approach with its equation of history and nature and its otherworldliness through which historical events are deprived of existential significance. It rejects the modern view because of its abortive effort to localize redemption within the historical process itself, inviting an unwarranted optimism as to the possibilities of human reason and human freedom.

Founded on a Biblical faith, the Christian approach affirms the sovereignty of God over man's individual and collective historical destiny. God as Creator, Judge, and Redeemer is the Lord of history, providing history with the only universalism which can give it meaning. History is conceived as a meaningful unity because all historical destinies are under the governance of a single divine sovereignty. Although the idea of a divine creation of the temporal world is not a uniquely Biblical concept, it does distinguish Christian thought both from classical thought with its idea of the temporal world as a corruption of the eternal world and from modern thought with its idea of a self-explanatory time and history. Divine judgment plays a peculiarly important role in Christian thought in that it displaces the locus of historical meaning as an extension of relative and finite goods, such as national purposes and human reason. These relative and finite goods are constantly subject to divine judgment. All moral, political, and cultural claims are seen as relative and contingent, partial and parochial; and every attempt to confer absolute and final significance upon these claims is condemned to historical disappointment as an abortive defiant rebellion of the creature against the Creator. It is thus that the divine judgment entails a con-

tinuing protest against any and all false absolutes which intermittently arise in history. The author is aware of the tragic tendency in Christian civilizations to fall into the error of worshiping such false absolutes. It is for this reason that Christian interpretations of life and history must be constantly re-examined in light of the truth of divine judgment.

The sovereignty of God finds its most decisive revelation in the Biblical faith of redemption, as this faith proclaims the foolishness of the Cross in its denial of the "wisdom of the world." Reason is scandalized by the claim that a particular event in history can be the locus of the final revelation of God's redeeming activity. This events unites within itself two decisive movements—Crucifixion and Resurrection. These movements not only climax the whole series of previous revelations but also disclose the unique relationship which obtains between man and God. The Crucifixion and Resurrection incomparably express the decisive obligation of dying to sin with Christ and arising with him to newness of Life. The Crucifixion and Resurrection elucidate the drama of sin and redemption as these unfold in historical experience. The Christian interpretation alone takes sin and guilt seriously; thus, the Christian view is able to take full account of the moral ambiguities, tragic cross-purposes and abuses of power which emerge throughout man's actualization of his freedom. But the Biblical faith does not rest with these tragic implications of human sin. It receives its final expression in the conviction that man's fragmentary historical existence is completed by a power not his own, and that the ambiguities of his moral existence are forgiven by a love which purges and heals the effects of his sinful pride.

Eschatology plays a dominant role in the Christian interpretation of history. History has an end in the sense of *Telos*. There is a point of reference which marks history's moral and spiritual culmination and confers upon the historical process its final meaning. This point of reference, symbolized by the final judgment and general resurrection, is not localized within history itself. *Die Weltgeschichte* is not *das Weltgericht*. There is no possibility of a final judgment within history, only at the end of it. But this *Telos*, prefigured in the Resurrection, must not be confused with a quantitative spatio-temporal point in chronological time. It indicates a qualitative judgment which is imminent every moment. This is why the New Testament introduced a note of urgency and emphasized that "the time is short" (I Corinthians 7:29). The eschatology of which the Christian Gospel speaks teaches an existential urgency in which one experiences the impingement of divine judgment in each moment of time as this moment becomes the locus for historical decision. Although judgment and redemption are not contained within nor derived from history, they are at every moment relevant to it. The symbol of the Last Judgment paradoxically expresses the tension between the historical and the trans-historical both by claiming a point of reference beyond history and by affirming the existential relevance of divine judgment as it becomes effectual in the historical process itself. It thus rejects both the utopian dreams of the optimistic modern interpretation of history and the Platonic flight from the historical process into a realm of eternal forms. Although the eschatological symbols point to that which transcends time and history, they also indicate the eternal dimensions within man's historic existence.

GOD'S GRACE AND MAN'S HOPE

Author: Daniel Day Williams (1910-   )
Type of work: Christian ethics
First published: 1949

PRINCIPAL IDEAS ADVANCED

A better world can be made by men who are devoted to God, for God is present and working in human history.

The thought categories of process philosophy are better able to indicate the nature of God than are the thought categories of static being.

Protestant theological liberalism has been overly optimistic about the human contribution to historical change, and Neo-orthodoxy has been too pessimistic. Therefore, neither has adequately understood the redemptive activity of God.

Man's hope is rooted in the realization and affirmation of the divine activity; such hope cannot be based upon what man can do for himself or upon what God will do without man.

God's Grace and Man's Hope was first delivered as the Rauschenbusch Lectures at Colgate-Rochester Divinity School in the spring of 1947. It is widely appreciated as a thoughtful attempt to find a meaningful synthesis between Protestant liberalism and Protestant Neo-orthodoxy, both of which were prevalent schools of thought at the time of its delivery. In the book, Williams argues that a better world can be made since God is present and working in human history. According to its author, the book's chief problems can be described as follows: ". . . the nature of God's working and our knowledge of Him; the conflict between Christian love and power politics; the mystery of time and its relation to the idea of human progress; the meaning of the Christian's 'calling' in the making of moral choices; the question whether there is a Christian ideal for society, and how such an ideal is to be stated; and finally the query which searches the human heart, whether and how it is possible for a man to love his neighbor as himself."

Throughout most of the book a contrast is drawn between theological liberalism and Neo-orthodoxy. Seeking to incorporate and preserve valid insights from each, the author threads his way to a position sometimes between and often beyond each of these dominant theological outlooks. These two theological perspectives agree in claiming that history is the place where God is working out the redemption of the world, though they have contrasting ways of interpreting how God works in the world. Liberalism sees the work of God evidenced in man's progress toward the coming of the Kingdom of God on earth. This Kingdom is under-stood in terms of universal brotherhood and peace and is advanced when men respond to God with reasonableness and moral earnestness. Neo-orthodoxy places its reliance upon the justifying love of God for sinful men and it re-places the progressive view of history with a tragic view. In this tragic view the Kingdom of God is understood as coming suddenly and in the indefinite future whereas in the liberal view it is described as possible only by means of a gradual shift from evil to goodness brought about as a consequence of human endeavor. According to Williams, neither formulation makes a sufficient place for the fact of God's redeeming activity, since liberalism sees no need for it and Neo-orthodoxy postpones it to the "end." What is needed is a vision of the goodness of creation coupled to an acknowledgement that evil has invaded that goodness and over-arched with a realization that God is redemptively at work to restore the goodness.

In making his case for the redemptive activity of God, Williams relies upon the categories of process philosophy. God is said to be at work in the world, encountering the sinner with His mercy. The activity of God may be experienced in human life just as much as real objects are experienced, though in different ways. To be sure, God is above all, and hence we speak of His transcendence, but He is known in Christ and in other manifest evidences of His love for man. Evil is real, but it is met and finally overcome by the redemptive activity of God, who ". . . does transform rebellious and self-sufficient men into persons who can begin to love their fellows." This process is described by the traditional term "grace."

Love is central to the idea of grace and is the symbol of God's unity. This love expresses itself in the continual divine process of urging men to live in universal, free, and genuine community. Love must be conceived in terms of a viable relation to the actualities of human history. Williams chides those commentators who define love in terms so absolute as to remove it from possible contact with the everyday realities of human life. Selfless love is not full love, since the Kingdom of God does not exclude any good, even the good of the individual self.

Williams discusses the social as well as the personal expression of love. He acknowledges that it is initially more difficult to reconcile the harsh facts of power conflict with the idea of love than to see the evidence of love in personal relations. Again, he criticizes liberalism for oversimplifying the role of love and Neo-orthodoxy for seeming to deny the place of love within the impersonal structure of human life. He affirms that God's redemptive work in human history will express itself through both the personal and the social instrumentalities of life, never finding complete expression, yet always present in a profound and important degree.

This central thesis is explored in relationship to the idea of time. Time itself does not heal, nor is it redemptive apart from God's power. Time itself is a threat as well as a potential aid to the achievement of value, and there is a deep and persistent rent in human history. Neo-orthodoxy, following the thought of Søren Kierkegaard (1813-1855), stresses time as being both an individual and existential source of meaning, and the view loses sight of historical time. In order to avoid the errors inherent in the idea of progress, Neo-orthodoxy makes the movement toward God alien to any common human experience. Even though subsequent interpreters have been less extreme than Kierkegaard, they have sometimes lost sight of the fact that life is process and that our present history proceeds under the reign of Christ. Because Christ reigns, and only because He reigns, can we serve one another in love. In the light of this reign the author feels it is wrong to imply that the love of God cannot overcome the obstacles that beset the expression of love in history even though we must not expect the love of God to find a quick and easy expression.

Two-thirds of the way through his argument Williams changes both his problem and his categories. The new problem is the problem of law and grace, a problem to be illuminated by a consideration of the Catholic and Protestant understandings of the moral imperative. Williams claims that the problem of knowing the good, difficult as it is, is secondary to the great need of man for power to do the good. Even so, the problem of knowing the good is difficult and contains many perplexing dilemmas. Williams is dissatisfied with Catholic sources of ethical guidance since they falsely absolutize a human institution and prevent the individual from speaking a prophetic word against the Church. The Reformation doctrine of vocation, on the other hand, has been stunted by its identification with the ethos of success and worldliness. The Christian will not be totally transformed nor will he totally transform the life of the world when he responds to the vocation of God, but this does not mean that he is to acquiesce in the given sinfulness of the world. He is to do whatever is possible to effect a positive good, reckoning all the time with the grim necessities that seem to hinder the achievement. Williams says, "The divine call to us men, and our response to it, means that we are responsible for doing here and now in the situation in which we stand whatever will serve the work of God who is seeking to bring all life to fulfillment in that universal community of love which is the real good of every creature."

Perfectionistic withdrawal and unbothered subservience to the *status quo* are contrasting mistakes which must be avoided by the Christian who would adequately serve God in the realities of the world. In serving God the specific injunctions of moral law are to be taken as guides to responsible action and cannot be dispensed with even though the Gospel appears to supersede all law. Williams does not embrace antinomianism in order to escape legalism. Moreover, the faithful Christian can be reinforced in his vocation by the community of faith and the life of prayer.

The concluding portion of the book addresses itself to the grounds of Christian hope. Rightly understood utopian impulses are given a place in the Christian life because they contribute great social dynamism even when they fail to achieve their objectives. They spring from the thirst for a better life, a thirst which is one of the continuing signs of God's image in man, and they keep alive the trust that society can be transformed through God's active involvement in history. Christians are to hope for a good society and to focus their attention on the pragmatic possibilities of improving the conditions of existence for all men, keeping the exchange of work and ideas between men free and orderly, preserving the right of voluntary groups to make their contribution to social good and the healing of broken lives, and insisting that men have a voice in the making of those decisions that affect their own lives and destiny. There is no place in Christian thinking for a kind of fatalism that destroys the zest for new and more fruitful achievements of social betterment.

Williams is especially critical of those thinkers who insist that Christian love must be defined in perfectionistic and selfless terms. No man possesses perfect or completely selfless love, but all men can grow in grace. The proximate achievements of men who are faithful to God, even when that faith itself is imperfect and the achievements are limited or ambiguous in character, can be both genuine and fruitful. But Williams also guards against every easy identification of particular achievements with the divine fullness. He asserts that every stage of new life is open to the possibility of new temptation, particularly if men forget their dependence upon the divine mercy or let pride creep into their lives. When men grow in grace they grow in response to the action of God made known in Christ and learn to serve Him fruitfully without presuming to regard the human achievements made in such service as the basis of hope. The source of man's hope lies in the divine power and grace, yet the two are kept in living and dynamic relationship with each other.

Williams states, "The God we serve is the giver of this life with its obligations and possibilities. There is no situation in which the Christian cannot find meaning and hope. There is no social wrong which need remain unattacked, unmitigated, unreformed. There is no private desperate struggle with anxiety and bitterness and failure which cannot yield new hope when we discover that God does not leave us forsaken. But those who know this, while they are released to spend themselves in doing what needs to be done, live with a certain divine carelessness concerning earthly fortunes. Their hope sees beyond the years and they live in this demanding present under the everlasting assurance of God's love."

THE LIVING WORD

Author: Gustaf Wingren (1910-   )
Type of work: Homiletics
First published: 1949

PRINCIPAL IDEAS ADVANCED

Preaching is proclamation of the Biblical message of the death and resurrection of Jesus Christ by which life and freedom are offered to men who are in bondage to sin and death.

Through faith man is called to share Christ's death and resurrection, dying in his earthly calling and ultimately completing the resurrection of Christ's Body, the Church.

Until Christ's final victory over Satan and death, man cannot separate the law which kills from the Gospel which gives life.

The *Living Word* by Gustaf Wingren, professor of systematic theology at the University of Lund, Sweden, is a study of preaching viewed from the vantage point of systematic theology. The purpose of preaching, according to Wingren, is to create an encounter between man and the word of God. This word is a message centering about the death and resurrection of Jesus Christ through which the hearer is summoned also to die and rise, in order thereby to be created and to live.

Since, according to Wingren, the congregation is already present in the text, the preacher's problem is not that of making a subjective application to an objective message. Since, furthermore, man is a prisoner of Satan, the primary opposition with which preaching must reckon is not between God and man, but between God and Satan. Deliverance for man through Jesus Christ is to be proclaimed, which deliverance takes place in the context of the congregation, as man recovers the humanity God intended he should have.

The Bible, which provides the texts the preacher uses, is a book about the acts of God. These acts continue in preaching as the history the Bible records, namely God's victory over Satan, continues. In this way the Bible through being preached receives a unity it would not otherwise have.

Christ is the Lord of the Scriptures. The Old Testament looks forward to Him, while the New Testament interprets His death and resurrection as the defeat of man's enemy, the Devil. The decisive victory over Satan has been won, but the struggle continues in the hearts of men. Christ's victory is heard but not seen. As the word which proclaims this victory is heard again and again man is created.

Man is created by God's word, Wingren writes, but God works against opposition. Prior to being reached by this creative word man is subject to sin, death, and guilt. Only in the final resurrection will he be completely free from these enemies.

Though man has been conquered by Satan he belongs to God. Therefore Christ in the Incarnation did not come to an alien world, but to creatures who had been alienated. The central theme of the Bible is not, accordingly, that God meets man in the Incarnation (at this point Wingren is criticizing Karl Barth, the eminent Swiss theologian), but that there is victory over death in the Resurrection. Barth regards it natural for man not to believe and interprets faith as a paradox. Martin Luther (1483-1546), on the other hand, held that unbelief was demonic. When God is said to be life, this means that man receives authentic existence from God. When Satan is said to be death, this means that man loses his humanity under Satan's dominion, for Satan is a murderer.

Through the creative word mediated through preaching, which is the link between Christ's resurrection and our own, Satan is forced to let go his grip on us. Those who are ministers of the word are sent into the camp of the enemy, as "sheep among wolves." Man is to be delivered from sin through forgiveness and from death through resurrection.

Since the Bible presupposes unity between the messenger and the sender of the message, he who hears preaching hears Christ. In sending the Apostles Jesus appears as Lord of the whole world, making claims on all peoples. Through the ascension Jesus achieves the divine attribute of omnipresence. Thus the basis for preaching is the ascension and the outpouring of the Spirit which follows. Through the ministry Christ, the Word, moves among men till the end of the world. To insist upon a particular kind of ecclesiastical succession implies doubt as to the reality of the living Christ, and is similar to the doctrine of the verbal inspiration of the Bible. It is to hold that God once lived and acted, but does so no longer.

The authority of the ministry rests upon the fact that the meaning of the message is clear. Those who insist it is unclear then need authorities to interpret it, who in turn become judges of the Scriptures. But the lordship of the word must be affirmed. The ministry receives its validity from the word; the word does not derive its validity from the ministry.

The ministry of the word belongs to the interim of struggle between Easter and the return of Christ, and will end when Satan is destroyed. Christ will eventually reign visibly, though now His lordship is preached. Christ's resurrection is being completed as His Body, the Church, rises through the mediation of word and sacrament.

The New Testament presupposes a conflict between God and Satan in which man is necessarily involved. The only alternatives are faith or unbelief, both of which imply activity. Unbelief is not natural, but demonic. Faith is freedom from that which destroys, fellowship with the source of life, the Creator. In this relationship one can, accordingly, speak unreservedly of both human and divine activity.

According to Wingren, faith and the word belong together. God creates through the word. To believe is to receive the life God gives. Faith belongs to the present, as one awaits the time that Christ's victory will be fully visible. This time of faith is the time of conflict with sin, but thereby creation also takes place. By faith authentic man frees himself from all alien controls. Faith is our death and resurrection by which the word is given freedom to accomplish its destroying and life-giving work.

The question of the truth of what is preached must now be considered. Wingren states two theses: The only valid ground for preaching is the factual death and resurrection of Jesus Christ, for faith is not valid apart from the fact which it believes. But the fact which faith believes does not remain the same fact if faith is absent.

Although the necessary foundation for preaching is the resurrection of Christ, this cannot be treated as simply a matter of scientific truth. We must approach this question as men who are in bondage. If Christ is not risen, we are still in our sins, but if He is risen, we are freed from sin and thus also from death. Our own resurrection is therefore involved. Christ's body arose from the grave, but Christ's Body is the Church, ourselves. This is not to say that the resurrection of the body of Jesus that was laid in the grave need not be affirmed. Faith in creation is absent when one can leave the body outside of Jesus' resurrection.

Wingren points out that in the sixteenth century it was hard to understand that God could forgive. Now the difficulty is accepting the fact that He can create life. The guilty conscience finds it hard to believe in forgiveness, while the intellectual conscience finds it hard to believe in resurrection. To reaffirm Christ's resurrection as an external event is, however, to strengthen both the faith in God's creation of the external world and our eschatological hope.

The message of death and resurrection has implications for an understanding of the relation between law and Gospel. The law does not represent a message which is in addition to the Gospel. There is but one message, the message of death and resurrection. The law serves this message, exercising its function together with the Gospel so that man can die and rise. The law is God's defense against sin, and it was already functioning in the world to which Jesus came. Through Christ's death and resurrection the law began to come to an end. This process continues in the death of the "old man" in each Christian; it will culminate in the final fall of Satan in the last times. Until this consummation is complete, however, law and Gospel belong together.

Thus the Christian conscience is free from the law, Wingren declares, and the conscience may be said to be in Heaven, but the Christian as a sinner in this bodily existence lives under the discipline of the law, his body having not as yet risen. Through the law God creates life by demanding that duties be performed. It is the law that calls man's attention to his neighbor and directs him to labor for his neighbor's welfare. This process of sanctification, in which the old man is crucified and the new man is born, is not to be regarded as peculiarly religious, as though there were a special law for Christians. Life even for Christians in this world is to be left as it is, hard and honorable labor, a journey through death's valley listening to the word, with the forgiveness of sins as our only piety and the resurrection at the last day as our only ultimate hope.

The message of death and resurrection is also proclaimed in the sacraments. These sacraments are rooted in the history of Israel. Israel received its "baptism" in the Red Sea and thus became a people. But Israel was chosen to die. Only in the role of the Suffering Servant does Israel become a light to the nations. This is anticipated in the Old Testament, but is fulfilled only in the death and resurrection of Jesus Christ, which in turn is identified as Jesus' "baptism" (Luke 12:50). This is also a baptism which Jesus' disciples may share (Mark 10:38). To pass through baptism, then, is to die and rise again.

If Jesus was baptized in order to fulfill the role of the Suffering Servant, becoming in this way identified with sinners, the Christian in being baptized is identified with Christ, sharing His death and resurrection. The Christian's baptism is fulfilled in his earthly calling and ultimately in bodily death, when the true life of the resurrection is finally gained. So also Jesus' resurrection is not complete until His Body, the Church, has died and risen again. Thus in each baptism

the power of the Resurrection enters into this world and the dawning of the last day becomes nearer.

In the Lord's Supper the fulfillment of Israel's calling through death and resurrection is also central. The food of this sacrament is sustenance as the Church wanders through the present wilderness toward the eschatological consummation. Now Christ's real presence is heard; then it will be seen. This interim of listening to the word in preaching and sacrament is the Church's place in the history of redemption.

Just as the sacraments rest upon events that have occurred, writes Wingren, so also they point to events which are to occur. The resurrected body to which they point, however, is not supernatural; the resurrected body is a liberated and purified body. Thus also the sacramental elements are not supernatural substances, but are water, bread, and wine, with the power of the word to expel unbelief and create anew human life.

Baptism like birth occurs only once, but the Lord's Supper, which gives food for the journey, is repeated. If the imagery of conflict is used, baptism is deliverance from the land of darkness, while the Lord's Supper provides strength for continued conflict with sin. That the sacraments point to the eschatological consummation is another way of saying that through them man receives a life which begins here and now, but is fulfilled in the final resurrection.

Satan has been defeated and he will be defeated. Victory has begun, but its final completion has not yet taken place. This means, Wingren claims, that man now has the forgiveness of sins and that he awaits the resurrection of the dead. Death and sin are both enemies of God, but sin is attacked first and is overcome by means of death, for to kill the "old man" is really to produce life. But death also will finally be destroyed. Then Satan's whole tyranny will be broken, and man will be completely free.

Until this consummation takes place man lives in the Church. Yet Christians are also to remain in their earthly callings, where sanctification is to take place. The Church is to be bound to word and sacrament, but it is to be open to the world, losing its life in its ministry to all men. The Church does not so much draw men to itself, as it sends them out with the forgiveness of sins into the world. Just now it is not important to determine who belongs and who does not belong to the Church. This division will take place at the Last Judgment. The Church's present task is to go out into the world with the word it has received.

This word is heard, a bit at a time, by men who are on a journey, and who are thus led on their way towards life. The Christian life was originally lived in terms of the week, in which both the Cross and the Resurrection were celebrated. In a similar way the Christian year developed, with Easter as the feast about which the others were grouped. The addition of many martyrs' days did not in principle change this emphasis of the Christian year, Wingren suggests, for these days pointed to the mystery that life in the Body of Christ rises out of death. In the Middle Ages, however, many more saints' days were added and the concept of merit changed the structure of theology. Thus Luther's re-

form of the Christian year was needed to restore its earlier character.

The Christian year indicates that the history of salvation continues. The emphasis on the order of salvation in pietism, however, suggested that the work of salvation was finished, the only problem being man's appropriation of it. Thus the individual rather than Christ and the congregation became the center of reference. If one is to speak of an order of salvation, writes Wingren, one must say that the Christian year is the order of salvation in which we live, move, and have our being, just as the local congregation is the place in which we find our calling.

The concept of an order of salvation has been related to attempts to structure preaching so as to adapt it to different groups of people, such as the unconverted, the awakened, and the converted. Wingren states that it is the word rather than the congregation that is to be divided, and that the word is to be divided into law and Gospel. But this division cannot really be made either by the preacher or the hearer. The text is to be preached and the Holy Spirit then divides the word in such a way that it is adapted in each particular situation, either as law to put to death the "old man," or as Gospel to bring to birth the "new man."

This problem of the division of law and Gospel is related to the Lutheran doctrine of "the sharing of the attributes" (*communicatio idiomatum*), a doctrine which affirms that in Jesus Christ human and divine attributes are shared in such a way that God suffers and dies, while man is raised to Heaven. Wingren states that those who criticize this doctrine presuppose a fundamental cleavage between God and man. Luther, however, knew God only in Jesus Christ. Therefore he saw God's glory revealed in the humiliation of the Cross, and the man Jesus exalted in the Resurrection.

Just as law and Gospel are intermingled in the word, so the attributes of death and resurrection jointly characterize the present existence of the Christian, and we are unable to separate them. Thus one arrives at the two rules of preaching: Christ who is both God and man must be preached, and the plain sense of the text must determine what is said. The doctrine of the sharing of the attributes points to our incapacity to speculate at this point and our need simply to accept the word and proclaim it, believing that the word is God and is even now becoming flesh. Such a nonspeculative approach, Wingren finally affirms, is needed not only in preaching but also in systematic theology.

BASIC CHRISTIAN ETHICS

Author: Paul Ramsey (1913-)
Type of work: Christian ethics
First published: 1950

PRINCIPAL IDEAS ADVANCED

Christian morality is an expression of religious and theological commitments and cannot be understood apart from knowledge about the nature and righteousness of God.

Christian ethical obligation is best described by reference to "obedient love"; obligation based on love transcends the rules of code morality without diminishing the rigor of morality itself.

God is the only legitimate object of unqualified allegiance; He alone creates and sustains virtue in the individual and in the community.

Christian ethical considerations are rooted in the nature and activity of God as portrayed in Biblical material and elaborated by the great thinkers of the Church. Starting from this conviction, Paul Ramsey opens his discussion of *Basic Christian Ethics* with a study of the righteous nature of a loving God and the presence of God's righteousness in His Rule, or Kingdom. According to Ramsey, the righteousness of God is expressed both in His judgment and in His faithfulness to the convenantal bond. Hence, it includes elements of steadfast mercy and even of sure love. Moreover, the righteousness of God is normative for the justice of man. The God who shows mercy to His people, even to the widow, the outcast, and the resident alien, expects His people to show similar mercy to their neighbors. Justice, righteousness, and mercy are interrelated in the activity of God; hence, God requires of men a special bias toward the needy and the outcast and not mere equality before the law of abstract fairness. The moral duty of men must be expressed in active concern for those who stand in greatest need of such concern. In the teachings of Jesus the obligation to meet human need is rooted in response to God's loving work, and hence both the old and the new covenants put primary emphasis upon a concerned and outpouring righteousness and mercy.

The reign of God in His Kingdom is the crucial focus of Christian morality and explains both the eschatological thrust and the radical demands upon the believer which are found in the teachings of Jesus. The terms of this teaching are so strenuous that some commentators, such as Albert Schweitzer, have come to regard them as valid only for a limited interim while other thinkers, such as Martin Dibelius (1883-1947), regard them as intended for an eventful future situation. Ramsey suggests that the teachings of Jesus are intended as an absolute portrayal of the nonpreferential and uncalculating love ultimately demanded of the Christian. Such a nonpreferential element means that the Christian must treat as neighbor the immediately encountered fellow man. Moreover, it effectively removes self-regarding motives from the ground floor of Christian love since love is required even when no return is assured.

While Ramsey understands the source of Christian morality to be rooted in the righteousness of God, he suggests that the nature of Christian morality combines binding and strenuous obligation with freedom and liberty of action. Code morality, illustrated by Ramsey with several colorful examples from the Pharisaical legal system at the time of Jesus as well as from much subsequent moralism in the Christian movement itself, endlessly expands the law by minute descriptions of specifically required or forbidden acts until the major intention of a moral ideal is buried under a mountain of detailed prescriptions. The life and teachings of Jesus are interpreted as a significant break with legalism. Partly by His overt disregard for the provisions of the law and primarily because He taught that allegiance to God transcends all the codification devised to describe it in detail, Jesus provided "an ethic of perfection which transcends any possible legal formulation." St. Paul is primarily responsible for showing in his letters what the Christian does without a code. Paul nullified laws that even Jesus did not question, but in doing so he remained true to the intentions of his Lord and elaborated a moral understanding basically the same as that which Jesus Himself displayed. According to the Apostle Paul, freedom from the law sets men in bondage to the whole need of the neighbor.

With these basic understandings set forth as the foundation of discussion, Ramsey devotes the remainder of his work to a discussion of Christian morality in relationship to religious and philosophical systems both outside and inside the Church of later centuries as well as to the social problems of the contemporary scene. The first part of this discussion revolves around issues raised by philosophical ethics, particularly those concerning the place of self-regard in the ethical life. The Christian, says Ramsey, embraces love that is uncalculating and disinterested, nonresisting and nonpreferential. Such love is poured forth before it is merited, expressed before being sought. "No more disastrous mistake can be made than to admit self-love onto the ground floor of Christian obligation, however much concern for self-improvement, for example, may later come to be a secondary, though entirely essential, aspect of Christian vocation." The higher virtues sought by philosophical morality are entirely compatible with Christian ethics when they are sought for the good of the neighbor. "Whose good?" is prior in the Christian ethic to the question "What is the good?" Even the love of God must be understood, not as the aspiration of the soul for union with the supernatural, but as the love shed by God into the heart of the believer, turning the believer's heart toward the need of the neighbor. Salvation must not be the motivation for doing good works, as in many religious patterns of the Middle Ages, since good works thus motivated are means for achieving selfish ends rather than for serving other men.

When Christian duty becomes involved with the service of the neighbor, problems of conflicting claims arise which can be solved only in terms of Christian vocation. Christian duty to others may involve duties to the self. Concern about the self is permissible to the extent that it results in such prudence as to render a contribution to the neighbor more profound and adequate. The self may, for example, protect itself if by such protection a contribution to the neighbor is preserved or enhanced. Moreover, the Christian may need to employ physical resistance to evil and is even required to do so in forceful defense of the neighbor if such means are available to him. Nonviolent resistance is not

preferable to violent resistance nor can it be defended merely because it employs different, and supposedly "spiritual," techniques in the exercise of its function. The Christian, however, will guard against a rationalization by which he justifies duties to the self as a service to the neighbor when in reality he is largely pleasing his own fancies. The Christian becomes virtuous only when he bends all his energies to the service of the neighbor's needs.

Elaborating upon his doctrine of Christian virtue, Ramsey draws heavily upon historical example. Augustine is credited with one facet of a complex truth because he insisted that virtue is elicited when love bends the personal will to the service of the neighbor; Aquinas is also commended for his view that grace, operating primarily but not exclusively in the sacraments, infuses virtue; while the Aristotelian view that virtue should be cultivated and developed is credited with yet another partial contribution. The Reformation view of Christian virtue as the grace which flows from God in the relationship of justification is considered by Ramsey to be the most adequate view of the matter, despite the fact that Protestant morality has not always made a place for some of the partial truths noted in Augustine, Aquinas, and the view that virtue is to be cultivated. The Protestant view of virtue precludes any autonomy in the virtues themselves, but insists that only in relationship to God can the Christian come to his fullness. Unlike virtues sought for their own sakes, which must be held in moderation, Christian virtues may embrace the dimensions of intemperance when the service of God is enhanced by abandoning a philosophical ideal of the mean in favor of an unconditional commitment.

The relationship of Christian love to the social philosophies of the nineteenth century is treated as a problem in the creating and sustaining of human community and in the valuing of human personality. Ramsey shows that the philosophical consideration of values does not function well to create community because the pressing issue of *whose* value overshadows the question of *what* value. The Christian may need to treat similar cases differently rather than similarly, since the needs of the neighbor and the particularities of each situation defy the generalizations created by abstract rules and by philosophical efforts to define the general good. It is Christian love which prompts men to regard the value of one another. Therefore, Christian love should be honored as the source rather than as the derivative of regard for human personality.

In this chapter on the nature of man Ramsey begins by considering how the doctrine of God's image in man should be understood. He first considers those philosophies which have found the divine spark in reason. He is more sympathetic with personal idealism and its view that the moral will represents the divine element in man. But he rejects both theories in favor of the contention that it is the relationship between man and God rather than some capacity innate to man which most adequately symbolizes the idea of the image. Naturalism as a theory of man's relationship to reality is examined and found wanting, even though its pragmatic elements are considered valuable. While Ramsey is more inclined to make common cause

with an idealistic metaphysic, he never compromises his basic insistence that only insofar as man is related to God may he be considered important and valuable.

Christian moral theory must face the problem of sin. Sin involves willful decision and causes disruption in the relationship between man and God. It occurs as idolatry, or self-love, even when that self-love is unconscious and takes the form of loyalty to false goals which really serve the self while supposedly serving others. The will remains the source, or origin, of sin. Anxiety is the occasion, since the self is prompted to sin when it is in dread concerning its own status. In the discussion of these matters Ramsey draws upon contemporary theological and literary writings, thus remaining faithful to the covertly historical framework of his discussion.

Contemporary issues occupy the final part of the book, but as theological considerations and not in terms of practical suggestions for action. The role of love in restraining sin is considered in relationship to the place of statutory law and the role of the state. Statutory law cannot embody all that love requires, but love must employ for its purposes the instrumentalities of justice which such law represents. Love remains to prompt and criticize all social ideals and policies and must never subordinate itself in order to cooperate with them. It is to remain dutiful, yet free; co-operating, yet independent of all vitalities with which it makes common cause for the rendering of its service to God.

The fundamental orientation of the book is theological in the best sense of the term. It explores the nature of the covenantal relationship between God and man which forms the basis of all Christian behavior and action. It therefore furnishes the perspective out of which all Christian moral decision must spring, and it leaves to the reader the making of such decisions in the many complex and practical issues of life.

CHRIST AND CULTURE

Author: H. Richard Niebuhr (1894-1962)
Type of work: Christian social ethics
First published: 1951

PRINCIPAL IDEAS ADVANCED

The relationship between Christ and culture is an enduring one which finds different expression under varying historical circumstances.

The relevance of Christ to the human world of time and history may be understood in terms of five major types of relationship between Christ and culture.

The two polar positions are "Christ against culture" and "the Christ of culture."

The three median positions are "Christ above culture," "Christ and culture in paradox," and "Christ transforming culture."

Although each position contains validity and there can be no one "Christian answer," each Christian makes an individual answer in the dialogue he carries on between Christ and culture in his own life.

Christ and Culture by H. Richard Niebuhr is frequently cited as the best single volume in the field of Christian social ethics. It deals with the all-important theme of the interaction between faith and culture. The study of the relationships between religion and society has become the concern of the theologian and the social scientist as well as of the thoughtful Christian layman.

H. Richard Niebuhr considers a pivotal and perennial question of Christian life and thought. Every Christian carries on a dialogue in his own life between Christ and culture. Each person's conception of "Christ" influences his participation in culture, and his involvement in culture shapes his understanding of faith in Christ.

Niebuhr's incisive study of the problem is the product of nearly a lifetime of reflection and teaching of the subject to many grateful generations of seminary students at the Divinity School of Yale University. Not one to rush rapidly into print, the author has written three earlier books, each of which stands as a seminal contribution to literature in the field of religion: *The Social Sources of Denominationalism* (1929), *The Kingdom of God in America* (1937), and *The Meaning of Revelation* (1941). In *Christ and Culture*, he contributes a polished and precise essay that is at once a work of art and a reflection of mature scholarship.

One of the influential scholars at the turn of the present century to whom Niebuhr is most indebted is Ernst Troeltsch (1865-1923), author of the monumental two volume work, *The Social Teaching of the Christian Churches.* Niebuhr acknowledges that his *Christ and Culture* seeks "to do no more than to supplement and in part to correct" Troeltsch's great work. It is a correction in the sense that Niebuhr is more explicitly theological and theocentric than Troeltsch in dealing with the relativities of history. Niebuhr's account supplements Troeltsch's analysis in that Niebuhr discerns five main types of relationship between Church and world in contrast to Troeltsch's three: Church, sect, and mysticism.

Before he sets forth the five types, Niebuhr defines what he means by "Christ" and by "culture." There are different views of Christ, but they are all based on the historic Jesus with His several virtues. Often one of these virtues is extolled at the expense of the others—*love* by the liberals, *humility* by the monastics, and *obedience* by contemporary Christian existentialists —but the real key to understanding Christ is His Sonship to God. The Christian virtues can be understood only as they are related to God, and Christ is the intermediary between man and God. Niebuhr uses the term "Christ" as a kind of theological shorthand by which one may refer to one's faith in the entire Christian tradition.

"Culture" is "that total process of human activity and that total result of such activity to which now the name *culture,* now the name *civilization,* is applied in common speech. Cul-

ture is the 'artificial, secondary environment,' which man superimposes on the natural." Culture is the social heritage which is received and transmitted through either written or oral tradition. Culture is a purposive human achievement, aimed toward the preservation of values. Culture is also pluralistic in that it sustains many values.

The five major theological positions or "ideal types" which Niebuhr delineates are as follows:

(1) *Christ Against Culture.* The first theological position gives all authority to Christ and rejects culture's claims to authority. *God* and the *world* are opposed and the Christian can love only the former. Corruption and sin are equated with civilization. This position is epitomized by the sectarian viewpoint, the monastic movement, and is found in men like Amos, Tertullian, and Tolstoy. Tolstoy sees Christ as the giver of laws which are to be literally interpreted and which force us to reject the institutions of the world, such as property, church, and state.

Niebuhr considers the "Christ against culture" view as necessary for its own witness and as a balance to other positions, but he finds serious fault with it. Primarily, persons adopting this first position are mistaken in thinking they can depend solely on Christ and thus can reject culture, for a man's very habits, language, and reason are culturally derived. Even when a "perfect society" is set up it is governed by cultural rules. The problem here is that this group relates itself only to Christ and not to God the Creator and hence, in effect, rejects the creation as evil and unnecessary. Moreover, there is a tendency to legalism and an unawareness of sin as a vital force in all human nature.

(2) *The Christ of Culture.* The second solution stands at the opposite pole from the first. It identifies Jesus with what is best in one's particular culture and sees Him as the one who fulfills and perfects that culture's best. Though there is selection in both realms of Christ and culture, what is enduring in each is in agreement (and what does not agree is therefore not enduring). Thus there is no tension felt between the demands of the two. The "Christ of culture" position characterizes those who feel no conflict between Church and world. The Christian Gnostics interpreted Christ solely in the terms of their own culture. In the era of liberalism the emergence of "culture-Protestantism" moved in this direction and Albert Ritschl is a prime example of one who holds the "Christ of culture" view. Ritschl saw man's problem as the conflict with nature and he found Christ to be man's ally in this struggle.

"The Christ of Culture" answer does help any culture to accept and to understand Christ, and it does show that Christ is relevant to cultural concerns, but it has serious faults. It accommodates Christ to culture only by distorting the historic Jesus. Moreover, while its advocates wish to rely on reason to the exclusion of revelation, they are dependent on the historic but nonrational fact of Jesus. Furthermore, unlike the first approach, the second view does not involve the realization that all culture is pervaded by sin. Finally, while it relates well to the Immanent God, the idea fails to apply to the God who is Lord and Creator.

(3) *Christ Above Culture* (Synthesist). To argue that Christ is above culture is to adopt the median answer of synthesis. The final three approaches agree on demanding *both* Christ *and* culture. They see the way in which Christ's demands run counter to culture and yet they see culture as a good, arising from God the Creator and thus containing objects of loyalty and laws which must be obeyed. These three viewpoints, seeing the universality of sin and the values of culture, cannot easily oppose Christ and culture, but rather must center on the opposition between God and man.

The "Christ Above Culture" position combines the opposing elements in a single system so that a synthesis between Christ and culture is possible in which both are affirmed. Clement of Alexandria realized that a man must be good in the cultural sense before he can go on to the Christian graces. Thomas Aquinas saw such a hierarchy in all areas. Reason is necessary as far as it goes; then revelation appears. Natural law exists but only with the divine law above it. The goods of culture have their place as do the divine goods.

The major objection to this position is that there is no recognition in it of the pervasion of the natural world and its value by sin. Also, when Thomas Aquinas examines natural law, he fails to see that he cannot escape his culture and that he therefore sanctifies a particular cultural system.

(4) *Christ and Culture in Paradox* (Dualist). This position involves a radical dualism. The dualist sees sin in all of man's works. Before the holiness of God there is no distinction between what we call good and evil. The dualist attacks all culture, yet he realizes that he is a sinful part of it and must

live in it. He sees the radical demands of God but knows his inability to obey. St. Paul viewed the institutions of culture as of negative value only in restraining sin. Luther's dualism is quite clear. God's forgiveness affects the inner man but social life cannot be redeemed.

This position represents a more realistic view, but since it merely describes our situation, it gives us no viable solution. Moreover, it tends toward antinomianism or at least toward cultural conservatism.

(5) *Christ the Transformer of Culture* (Conversionist). The final position, like the dualist one, takes sin seriously but places greater emphasis on the Incarnation and on the present creative work of God. The emphasis is not merely on restraining sin, but on overcoming it. Creation and the Fall tend to be confused by the dualist but not here, for the Fall is a corruption of creation. Creation may be redeemed and all things are possible for God in history. Eschatology is, at least in part, already realized. F. D. Maurice is important here for emphasizing

both Christ the King and sin, and for regarding the conversion of men and society as a universal possibility. Culture is under the governance of God, and Christians must be socially responsible in obedience to God. Their duty is to make Christ the Lord of culture.

These five major types of relationship between Christ and culture are found manifested in different periods of history. In a concluding chapter ("Concluding Unscientific Postscript"), Niebuhr refuses to choose one or another of the types as representing *the* Christian answer. While some scholars have praised this relativistic and objective approach, many have criticized the author for not making his personal point of view explicit. Niebuhr maintains that knowing the five alternatives and knowing our own limited perspective, we must make a particular choice in the existential moment of decision. But to do this is not to be relative or individualistic or independent, for we rely at all times on the Christian community, on history, and, by faith, on God.

THE CHRISTIAN UNDERSTANDING OF GOD

Author: Nels F. S. Ferré (1908-   )
Type of work: Philosophical theology
First published: 1951

PRINCIPAL IDEAS ADVANCED

God is best understood as personal spirit who is sovereign love.

This uniquely Christian concept, if taken seriously enough for thought, can provide both a more coherent explanation of philosophic problems arising for Christians and a more adequate interpretation of the true claims of Christianity than can traditional approaches premised on alien notions of God.

God as sovereign love eternally creates for the sake of fellowship. Through His loving providence and self-revelation, God ultimately wins all His children to free acceptance of never-ending joy and growth in love.

The Christian Understanding of God represents the first thoroughgoing attempt to derive consistently the substance of Christian doctrine from Christianity's central affirmation, "God is love." The author, Nels F. S. Ferré, was impressed by the systematic consistency and coherence of his professors in philosophy, Edgar S. Brightman (1884-1953) and Alfred North Whitehead (1861-1947), but he remained unconvinced of the adequacy of the central concepts around which their thoughts were structured. Later Ferré found his professors in theology at Lund University in his native Sweden correct in pointing to *agape* (other-centered love) as the dominant and fully adequate motif of Christianity, but he was dissatisfied at the incompleteness with which implications of this motif were made normative for Christian thought by nonphilosophical Lundensian theologians like Anders Nygren, author of the classic *Agape and Eros.*

Consequently, in a series of books importantly typified by *The Christian Understanding of God,* Ferré has engaged in the formidable task of joining the theoretical strength of philosophical rigor to the saving adequacy of Christian content. This proposed marriage is not, however, to commit Christianity to accepting into its household philosophy's ancient Greek dowry. Theology's own insights are not to be dominated or diluted by alien presuppositions—however familiar—about the nature of the ultimate.

With this motive, Ferré turns in *The Christian Understanding of God* to consider the explanatory potential of sovereign love when it, rather than being, is rigorously taken as the key concept for ultimate reality. Beginning from the master motif of cosmic *agape,* Ferré finds that the traditional philosophic puzzles of being and becoming dissolve within his analysis. Being, first, is itself to be understood in terms of the intrinsic stability of love, that concrete total concern which is supremely self-sustaining and self-directed; love is only mistakenly conceived under the rubric of the abstract category, "being." Thus correctly defined, being is discovered to be intimately related to—not, as is usually supposed, in radical opposition to—nonbeing; creative love, even as being, requires nonbeing as the bottomless abyss of potentiality thanks to which it may endlessly increase its self-sharing through new creation. Another traditional difficulty, understanding how ultimate reality, or the Absolute, can remain absolute and yet have relations to beings other than itself, disappears once the notion of absolute being is viewed in the light of cosmic love. Relations are not alien to, but are required by, love; it is a a false conception of the Absolute which would force it logically into an abstraction from all relatedness.

Although being is best understood in terms of love, love is not comprehended in being. Of equal or greater importance is the illumination that love throws on the nature of becoming, inasmuch as love is that which can *be* what it most truly is only by *becoming*. Standard philosophical problems in relating being to becoming are thus transcended: "Only by becoming can being become what it is." Change, in terms of growth and fulfillment, is as intrinsic to love as is stability; the form of love's stability, indeed, is found precisely in such controlled and constructive change. The concept of becoming thus subordinates that of being, while at the same time presupposing it, when both are seen in terms of the primacy of love. "Start with being as ultimate, and arrive at no adequate doctrine of becoming; start with becoming as ultimate, and find no real interpretation of being. Start with love as ultimate, and being and becoming are both inherent within His nature; being and becoming are then abstractions from the fullness of reality."

A long step toward concreteness from the abstractions of beings and becoming is represented by the concept of personality. It is only in the personal, not in sheer being-in-becoming, that we find love. Taking love seriously as our starting point, therefore, strongly suggests the legitimacy of considering God as personal. Besides including concretely both being and becoming, the concept of the personal indicates the complex truth about God: that He is being-in-becoming who is characterized by self-transcendence (relating to others), self-consciousness, self-direction, self-perpetuation, and creative purpose. The concept of the personal, further, may aid us in conceiving of those elements in His nature analogous to the bodies through which all persons we know express their capacities for overt manipulation of the impersonal, for communication with other persons, and for objectifying the past in memory.

God, for Ferré, is not basically to be described even in such terms, however, despite their essential place in our understanding of sovereign love. The personal cannot be the ultimate form of love, first, because love may work (analogously to bodily functions) in impersonal ways and, second, because personalities—however intimate —never "interpenetrate" one another in that spiritual harmony which is the essence of completely realized fellowship and the goal of creative love. *Agape,* then, no less than "spirit," is the principle (as Ferré defines it) of union or cohesiveness. This concept of spirit, including but transcending the concepts of personality, becoming, being, and nonbeing, is alone adequate to the master motif of sovereign love.

The understanding of God as personal spirit who is creative love brings a solution to the traditional philosophic problem of "the One and the many." How can God, if infinite, exist together with a world of change and multiplicity that is somehow not Himself? If He is really infinite, is it not a contradiction to suppose that there exists anything *besides* the infinite? Does this not make of God merely one being alongside other beings—beings which must inevitably limit His infinitude simply by existing as other than Himself? Supposing God to be infinite, then, would seem to entail holding "the many" to be mere illusion; while taking "the many" of our experience as real would seem to require believing "the One" to be finite, merely one being among others, and without unique status. Ferré's answer to this dilemma is to point out that once again a needless puzzle has been generated by the false adoption of the abstract notion of being as the essence of God. Infinite being *qua being* cannot permit the coexistence of rival beings, but infinite being *qua love* has no such difficulty. God's unique identity is established by His uncreated status as infinite creative love and by the constancy of love's purposes and activities. The situation of "the One and the many" is not a contradiction, therefore, but a consequence of the distinctively Christian concept of the ultimate who creates and enters into relations with His world.

The relational character of the Christian God not only fails to pose a problem for consistent thought on Christian premises but also undergirds the otherwise vexing doctrine of the Trinity. Love is not relational by accident; God's very essence is social. The fellowship of the Persons of the Godhead is the model and ground for all created fellowship. Considered thus, instead of in terms of alien substance-philosophy, the Christian understanding of Trinity makes irrelevant many of the problems that have so often obscured it.

If social relations and the mutual interplay and successive experiences of personal love are present within God Himself, then the otherwise thorny metaphysical concept of time and its relation to eternity is illuminated by Ferré's account. God's successive experience is what we mean by eternity, "God's time." The specific nature of such time we are unable to imagine; but we may know of its character in principle through our own experience of time, the function of which is essentially the same for us and for God: to make fellowship possible. Time is the means and medium for learning,

for growth, for coming to love. Time itself, Ferré shows us, is best interpreted through the primacy of *agape*.

In like manner, space serves love. Just as time is the condition for becoming in fellowship, so space is most basically the condition for "simultaneous otherness" without which fellowship would be inconceivable. Space-time, therefore, is in its broadest sense not accidental in the structure of things but an eternal element in a universe created by and sustained for *agape*.

If time is real, even for God, can God know the future? Ferré's answer requires us to make a distinction between "knowing the future" in the general sense of knowing confidently the outcome of all God's ultimate purposes and "knowing the future" in the specific sense of knowing precisely the details of that which is not yet real. In the former sense God knows the future, for He knows that He is sovereign and competently in control of all times; in the latter sense God does not know the future, since He permits His children, for the sake of free fellowship in love, to have genuine power to determine the specific future. Knowledge of what is not yet determinate would be false knowledge. God's omniscience is complete inasmuch as He knows all there is to know; His knowledge is not limited by His not knowing what is not yet real.

Does God's sharing of power with His children for the sake of their freedom limit His nature? Not in the slightest, answers Ferré. Power is not the essence of God; power is properly defined in terms of "the capacity of love to effect its end." If the end of love is the free fellowship of responsible persons, it is not a limitation but an expression of God's nature to provide power enough to His children for freedom and learning in love. God must remain in ultimate control, of course, if His sovereign love is to be responsible. His creatures' powers are never infinite, as the world with its blend of predictability and precariousness constantly reminds us. The rebellious creature may call such a world "evil" and formulate a "problem of evil" with regard to the pedagogical precariousness of the world; but God's love remains responsible, and His benevolence remains great enough even to cause us pain for a time to remind us that ultimate fulfillment is not to be found in our own power—real and responsible though it is.

Even this stern holiness of God is no contradiction to His essence as love. Holiness, above all, is "the infinite purity of love or internal self-consistency of its nature." *Agape* is far from sentimentality. The demands of holy love may, Ferré thinks, cause God to suffer; but even if this is so (and it is by no means certain), the sufferings of the Sovereign can never have the quality of despair that would make His suffering incompatible with supreme joy in present fellowship and the certainty of future joy in still wider fellowship.

With this developed concept of the nature of God, Ferré turns to an examination of the work of God in creation and redemption. God as love is inevitably creator, not out of blind necessity but as a free expression of cosmic *agape* itself. Creation, then, is as much an expression of God's love as is redemption. The nature of His creations, too, reflect God's sovereign concern. He has made, in our particular "cosmic epoch" (and it would be unthinkably parochial to suppose that our own universe, however vast, is God's only creation), an "open" universe, open to His providential purposes as well as to our lesser purposes. Even general providence, God's permissive way of allowing things to happen as they normally do for the sake of our growth in freedom, is best understood through reference to love. All providence, whether general or "special" (in which God takes a more personally active part in events through suggesting ideas to His children or influencing directly chains of causation), remains "the patient guidance by God of all His creation toward the best possible end for it."

Redemption involves revelation. As love, God wants to be known, but as personal spirit, God must reveal Himself (as must any person) if He is to be known by others. Ferré discusses God's self-revelation in nature, or the possibility of a natural theology, and finds that while some general revelation must be present even in nature, God cannot be found in His full character of *agape* in nature or in history. Only through His working in the Holy Spirit is God present with us as personal spirit who is love; hence, Christian thought should focus not on natural theology but on a theology grounded in study of the Church and Incarnation, where, and nowhere else, God is to be found as He most reliably is.

God's work in Incarnation is thoroughly and supremely redemptive. Jesus, whose much controverted "virgin birth" has no essential bearing on biological fact, was the Christ through the unprecedented initiative of the love of God. To this dependence on an extraordinary act of God the doctrine of "virgin birth" symbolically attests, whatever the historical facts (now unascertainable one way or the other) surrounding Mary's impregnation. The doctrine of atonement must, Ferré holds, also be seen consistently in the light of love; God was working through the whole atoning life of Jesus (not just through His death) to bring men back into fellowship with Himself, a fellowship without which there is no fulfillment for man. Resurrection, on the other hand, illustrates the sovereignty of eternal love. In the doctrine of the resurrection of Jesus is symbolized, Ferré believes, God's inevitable victory over the forces of evil, destruction, and despair. The resurrection may well be more than a symbol; it may be—Ferré thinks it probable—a historic fact, a foretaste of God's triumph over all lovelessness and self-defeating rebellion.

A theology based on sovereign love will, Ferré insists, uncompromisingly stand for universal salvation. Anything less would be inconsistent with God's sovereignty and would impugn God's love. Such a universalistic position presupposes an afterlife, of course; and Ferré does indeed strongly maintain that life after our physical death is an absolutely essential tenet of Christian faith. Without providing further opportunity for the expression of His pedagogical concern beyond the present life, God would have to be supposed either not to care enough about His children to pursue their welfare after the grave or not to be sufficiently in control of events to carry out His aims. Neither supposition is compatible with the distinctive motif of Christianity. Also clearly incompatible with sovereign love is the vicious doctrine of eternal Hell. It may be that "hell" exists as a post-mortem condition of unrepentant self-separation from loving fellowship with the holy God, but the "gates of hell" must always be hinged so as to open outward at the touch of the penitent child. Only so can there be joy in Heaven. "Heaven, to those who truly love all, can be heaven only when it has emptied hell." Even Judgment and Hell, therefore, and the consequent preaching of fear or of life's seriousness, need definition in terms of love's aim. Life is earnest and sin has consequences; purgatory, Ferré believes, may exist as a state in which the repentant and forgiven sinner works willingly toward repairing the destructive effects of his sin on himself and others. God is too good a Father to spoil His children but God is the one Father who "has no permanent problem children." He never coerces, but infinite love is the one reality strong enough and patient enough to be sure of winning all, not despite our freedom but through our freedom.

Thus Ferré's final vision is of God, love constantly beyond limit, as He surges from victory to greater victory in sharing Himself with the countless myriads of creatures for each of whom He has unlimited individual concern. Before this cosmic vision Ferré stands —and asks us to stand—in amazement and adoration toward Him who offers us out of sheer love the prospect and the certainty of unceasing adventure from joy to joy, fulfillment beyond creative fulfillment, worlds without end.

Ferré's vision and his entire enterprise of rethinking theology (and much of philosophy) demand time for assimilation; and although the contemporary theological and philosophical communities in general have not yet fully felt the radical impact of *The Christian Understanding of God*, it may with justice be supposed that a work of this kind, whose influence is already noteworthy, has been ad-dressed not merely to our own decades but to generations still to come.

INTRODUCTION TO THE PHILOSOPHY OF RELIGION

Author: Peter Anthony Bertocci (1910-   )
Type of work: Philosophy of religion
First published: 1951

Principal Ideas Advanced

The core of religion is the personal belief that one's most important values are sponsored by the enduring structure of the universe.

Neither strict logical consistency nor immediate religious experience is an adequate foundation for religious knowledge; reason as a method of gaining coherence in our total experience can lead to reasonable faith.

The wider teleological argument supports the hypothesis of a Personal Source of Value as the most comprehensive and coherent explanation of the interconnectedness of physical nature, life, and human experience, and of man's intellectual, moral, aesthetic, and religious values.

Excess evil is due to a recalcitrant aspect of God's own nature; God nevertheless creates and preserves values through never-ending heroic struggle and sacrificial love.

Since mid-century, Bertocci's *Introduction to the Philosophy of Religion* has become the best-known philosophical treatment of religion from the point of view of personalism (or personalistic idealism). In America personalism was first elaborated by Borden Parker Bowne (1847-1910). Bertocci has been Borden Parker Bowne Professor of Philosophy at Boston University since 1953. Two thinkers have had a notable influence on Bertocci's philosophic position. One was Edgar Sheffield Brightman (1884-1953), the leading proponent of personalism during the second quarter of the century, and Bertocci's predecessor at Boston University. The other major influence on Bertocci's thought has come from F. R. Tennant (1866-1957), British philosopher and author of the two volume work, *Philosophical Theology* (1930).

In general, Bertocci develops what may be called a broadly empirical philosophy of religion in the tradition of personalistic idealism. He proceeds on the assumption that religious beliefs must be examined and understood in "the light of the believer's total experience." The essence of religion, Bertocci maintains, is "the personal belief that one's most important values are sponsored by, or in harmony with, the enduring structure of the universe," even if they are not supported by society. After exploring briefly some of the factors that affect religious belief, Bertocci raises the question: Can reason justify or repudiate religious beliefs? That is, is reason competent to judge among religious beliefs in the complex of human experience? To answer this question, Bertocci finds it necessary to distinguish between two conceptions of reason. He argues that reason as *logical consistency among premises* is indispensable to the life of thought, but it is not sufficient to interpret the concrete concerns of religion; while reason as *empirical coherence* (the finding of connections among the experienced facts) may not provide logical certainty, but it can provide growing though probable truth when applied to religion.

A major alternative to this approach is the view that faith has unilateral access to indubitable religious truth, that religious experience contains its own warrant for the absolute knowledge it reveals. Bertocci takes sharp exception to this position. He seeks to show that religious experience is not cognitive, that no immediate experience can give indubitable guarantee to religious belief. He emphatically denies "the *independent* validity of religious experience as a source of knowledge." Bertocci's criticism is based on the general epistemological argument that all immediate experience requires interpretation before it will yield knowledge, and on the "instability" and "vagueness" of the nonsensory qualitative content of religious experience. Bertocci criticizes William James (1842-1910), Rudolph Otto (1869-1937), and Henri Bergson (1859-1941) for maintaining in different ways that religious experience is directly cognitive. Religious experience,

Bertocci concludes, makes whatever contribution it does only within the total context of life.

Reason as a method of gaining coherence in experience can lead to reasonable faith. Reasonable faith, according to Bertocci, has a close affinity to scientific method. Religion and science are, therefore, not incompatible; they both involve the conception of reason as empirical coherence. But what about the conflict between the religious and scientific perspectives? Bertocci holds that this clash reflects the tension between two contrasting but not irreconcilable intellectual motives. The first is expressed in the desire to know the "how" of things. In the developed scientific perspective this motive takes the form of mechanical explanation; that is, understanding the causal sequences of the parts or elements in the natural world. The second motive is expressed in the desire to know the "why" of things. In the developed religious perspective this motive takes the form of teleological explanation; that is, understanding the purposes and plans which give order to the whole. According to Bertocci, the conflict between these two modes of explanation becomes a problem only when either is taken as final, exclusive of the other.

Consistent with the contextual approach characterized above and preparatory to the synoptic outlook of his argument for God, Bertocci devotes a section of five chapters (6-10) to scientific questions (facts and issues) about the physical, biological, psychological, and moral orders. The most distinctive feature of these chapters is found in Bertocci's discussion of the moral dimension and particularly in his treatment of the problem of free will.

Bertocci draws a distinction between "will-agency" and "will-power." Will-agency is an innate, not acquired, property of a person in virtue of which he chooses among alternatives. But will-agency is not an autonomous faculty; will-power refers to the "actual efficacy . . . of the willing to reach a chosen objective." The capacity to choose (will-agency) is affected by other facets of the personality and by environmental factors. The concept of will-power is thus used to acknowledge limits on free-will but without jeopardizing the reality of choice.

Bertocci's treatment of the standard arguments for God in the Western tradition is appreciative, yet critical. The ontological argument, given its classic formulation by St. Anselm of Canterbury (c.1033-1109), maintains that the idea of perfection, possessed by every human being, implies the existence of a perfect being. Unfortunately, the existence of God cannot be deduced from the idea of God. Nevertheless, the emphasis on perfection is a distilled though perhaps vague intellectual transcription of the central religious affirmation; namely, the relevance of the highest values (perfection) to reality (God).

The cosmological argument, associated classically with Aristotle (384-322 B.C.) and St. Thomas Aquinas (c.1225-1274), maintains that the changing world requires an unchanging First Cause. Dissatisfaction with the infinite regress of finite causes shows a commendable interest in the metaphysical ultimacy and unity "behind" the order of change. Ambiguity as to the meaning of "cause" seriously vitiates the argument. Is the First Cause an uncaused cause wholly other than the series of causes it initiates, or is the First Cause "a productive power initiating change" and "the basic continuant in all change"? Furthermore, what is it that allows us to identify the First Cause with the God of faith?

The classic teleological argument infers the existence of a providential God from evidences of design, from "the *adaptive* order of the world." This argument is implicated in the issues raised regarding the cosmological argument. In addition, it suffers from a static pre-Darwinian formulation and from the tendency of its advocates to overlook the purposeless and disharmonious in nature.

The moral argument for God is based on the contention that the existence of God is a presupposition of man's moral consciousness and of an objective realm of ideal values to which this consciousness gives access. Since moral values figure prominently in Bertocci's argument for God, no further comment is needed here.

The difficulties in the traditional arguments are underlined by Bertocci's analysis of the attributes traditionally ascribed to a personal God. Bertocci raises the issues that arise when God is conceived as a supremely good creator who is immutable and eternal, transcendent and/or immanent, omnipotent, and omniscient. For example, is God's omniscience consistent with human freedom?

The residue of truth in each of the traditional arguments needs to be reformulated and coordinated. This Bertocci attempts to do in what he calls "the wider teleological argument for a personal God," an argument influenced by Tennant's work. The wider teleological argument differs from the traditional arguments in that it does not claim to be definitive or demonstrative; rather, it offers a tentative and probable hypothesis. Thus the wider teleological argument is less rationalistic and more empirical than the traditional arguments. It rests its case on a comprehensive and cumulative interpretation. It appeals to a wide range of evidence, insisting "on the interconnectedness of physical nature, life, and human experience" and blending intellectual, moral, aesthetic, and religious values into the texture of the hypothesis. The wider teleological argument is metaphysical in maintaining that the theistic hypothesis (that is, the "hypothesis of a Personal Source of Value") provides the most intelligible and coherent explanation of all the contextual interrelations adduced. This hypothesis, Bertocci argues, gives the most adequate account of both the continuity and the development in the total process.

In detail, the wider teleological argument consists of seven links. Link One stresses "the purposive interrelation of matter and life." Life is dependent on but cannot be reduced to matter. That a cosmic creative Intelligence is at work in the natural order is, Bertocci holds, the best explanation of the collocation of matter and life. Link Two draws attention to "the relevance of thought to reality." Knowledge depends on reliable interaction between man and nature. Mind is thus relevant to its world. Indeed, reality seems to put a premium on the development of moral disciplines.

Link Three discusses "the interrelation of the moral effort and the order of nature." "Unless man is free, there is no real point to moral effort," *but* un-

less there is also a dependable natural order, there is no significant moral effort. Link Four broadens the scope to emphasize "the interrelation between value and nature." This theme, in conjunction with Link Five, which interprets "this world as good for man," constitutes the heart of the wider teleogical argument. Here Bertocci seeks to weld the positive features of the cosmological and moral arguments. Human values are not merely man-made but are a joint product of man and his world. Human values disclose "what nature can be." For Bertocci, "that human beings should be co-creating values in his universe is *the* value attending all other values." Thus, "the value of values is character." The fact that the universe promotes and sustains moral growth is best explained by a conscious cosmic sponsor of value. This fact is also the basis for believ-ing in the goodness of God. "The world in which man lives can best be understood as a moral order in which God purposes creative love as the source of all goodness and happiness."

Link Six adds "the significance of aesthetic experience" to the argument. The aesthetic dimension reflects another creative interaction between man and the universe. Link Seven is now able to treat "religious experience as confirmatory." Although religious experience taken independently is an insufficient basis for belief in a personal God, it reinforces and is reinforced by other aspects of our experience.

Bertocci now turns to the problem of evil. The traditional explanations of evil are not convincing. To say that evil is the result of man's abuse of his freedom overlooks the superfluous sufferings that human existence so often brings. To say that evil is ultimately part of the divine plan overlooks the evidence "that God is not omnipotent." Bertocci concludes that the weight of moral guilt and natural evil cannot be squared with the traditional theodicy.

How, then, is excess evil to be explained? Is it due to divine ill-will or neglect? No, Bertocci answers, there is too much positive evidence (already adduced in support of the wider teleological argument) of ultimate goodness. Then there must be some limitation on God's power, some impediment to God's good purposes. Bertocci expounds three conceptions of the nature of an impediment which partially frustrates God's plan and leads to excess evil.

First is Plato's view that God is a cosmic artist who shapes a raw material he did not create. In other words, the impediment (to use Plato's term) is the "receptacle of becoming," an environment external to God, unshaped and obdurate, but subject to control. The second conception of the impediment which Bertocci considers is that of the American philosopher, W. P. Montague (1873-1953). Montague holds that the impediment is within God, an internal environment which is the world. That is, the world is part of God's being but is external to His infinite mind.

The third explanation of excess evil which Bertocci examines is that of his teacher and predecessor, E. S. Brightman. Bertocci holds that Brightman corrects weaknesses in Plato's and Montague's conceptions of the impediment. Bertocci therefore adopts Brightman's position. In *A Philosophy of Religion* (1940), Brightman argues forcefully that excess evil is due to "a recalcitrant aspect of God's own nature." This aspect Brightman calls the "Nonrational Given"; it refers to refractory data, brute fact such as sensation. A second aspect of God's nature Brightman calls the "Rational Given"; it corresponds very closely to the traditional notion of the divine reason. The third aspect of the divine being is the divine will. God's will does not, for Brightman, create either the Nonrational Given (brute fact) or the Rational Given (rational norms). God's will does, however, control the Nonrational Given according to His rational principles, giving new significant form to what is otherwise meaningless content. Although God is never absolutely in control, He never loses control and is always at work overcoming obstacles. New values are continually being created through heroic struggle and sacrificial love. God is thus the "Finite-Infinite Controller of the Given," in Brightman's terms. Bertocci believes that Brightman's view preserves more adequately the integral unity and rich complexity of a supreme personal God than does that of either Plato or Montague. It is also, Bertocci maintains, a firmer basis for the religious consciousness than the traditional theodicy.

Bertocci now concludes: "Religion is the faith that God is the ultimate Personal Creator and Sustainer of all values, and that human beings realize the utmost in value when they join him, conscientiously and joyously, in the creation of value." It follows from this that prayer occupies a central place in the religious life. For prayer is "the conscious attempt of the individual to commune with God for the purpose of fellowship." Furthermore, the urgency of establishing an open and growing world community is rooted in such a faith. Finally, Bertocci's moving justification of personal immortality (in the concluding chapter) draws the consequences for man's destiny of the religious hypothesis which the book develops.

Whether Bertocci's personalistic philosophy of religion will continue to be a viable alternative to the competing contemporary perspectives of naturalistic humanism and theological existentialism only time can determine.

SYSTEMATIC THEOLOGY

Author: Paul Tillich (1886-   )
Type of work: Philosophical theology
First published: Volume I, 1951; Volume II, 1957

PRINCIPAL IDEAS ADVANCED

Theology is a systematic and disciplined investigation of that which concerns man ultimately; the method of theology is the "method of correlation," correlating man's basic questions about himself and his world with the symbols of the Christian message which provide the answers to these questions.

Revelation provides the answer to the questions implied in the existential conflicts of reason; revelation does not destroy reason, but is continuous with the depth of reason.

The symbol of God provides the answer to the question implied in human finitude; the question of human finitude arises in the awareness of the possible disruption of the essential structures of finite being—the shock of possible nonbeing; the answer to this question is God, who is Being-itself, living, creating, and related.

The symbol of the Christ provides the answer to the question implied in man's existential estrangement and self-destruction; the reality element of this symbol is the New Being disclosed in the unique event of Jesus as the Christ who conquers estrangement through His power of salvation.

Systematic Theology comprises Paul Tillich's effort to formulate a theological system which is at the same time universal and peculiarly relevant to contemporary man. The projected system consists of five parts: I. Reason and Revelation, II. Being and God, III. Existence and the Christ, IV. Life and the Spirit, and V. History and the Kingdom of God. In all of the five parts the method of correlation provides the guiding methodological motif. Revelation comes as an answer to the conflicts of reason; God is the answer to the question of the finitude of being; Christ is the answer to the question of human finitude under the conditions of estrangement; Spirit provides the answer to the ambiguity of life; and the Kingdom of God constitutes the answer to the question of the meaning of history. Only the first three parts of Tillich's system are contained in Volumes I and II, discussed here.

Tillich has appropriately characterized his theology as an "answering theology," thus indicating both the method and content of his theological system. In its general form the problem is presented in terms of the relation between philosophy and theology; in one of its specific forms the focus is upon the relation between reason and revelation. On the one hand, philosophy and theology diverge; on the other hand, they converge; in the last analysis they are understood as being mutually dependent. They diverge in their respective cognitive attitudes. The attitude of philosophy towards its subject is theoretical; the attitude of theology towards its subject is existential. In the theoretical attitude the distance between the knower and the known is decisive; in the existential attitude the unity of the knower and the known is decisive. Yet the convergence of the two must be acknowledged insofar as philosophy always arises in a concrete situation and therefore has existential presuppositions, and theology in dealing with the logos of being has theoretical implications. The two thus become mutually dependent. Insofar as it has existential presuppositions philosophy is dependent on theology; insofar as it has theoretical implications theology is dependent on philosophy.

The problem of the relation between reason and revelation arises as an instance in the wider relation which obtains between philosophy and theology generally. Reason and revelation are distinct but not discontinuous. Tillich finds it necessary to distinguish between an ontological and technical concept of reason. The former, expressed predominantly in Greek rationalism and German classical idealism, indicates a structure in which

mind is related to the reality which it grasps and transforms. The latter, expressed predominantly in British empiricism, has to do with methodological tools and logical procedures which determine the means in a given means-end relationship. Although Tillich sees ontological and technical reason as companions, the relation of reason and revelation arises only on the level of ontological reason. This does not mean that ontological reason and revelation are to be identified (the mistake of idealistic philosophy). Such an identity is present only in the realm of essential perfection. Ontological reason as actualized appears under the conditions of finitude, existential estrangement, and the ambiguities of life and history. Actual reason moves in and through finite categories and self-destructive conflicts. Nonetheless, in spite of its finitude and estrangement, reason is aware of its infinite depth, and the quest for revelation proceeds by virtue of this relatedness of reason to the infinite; and the quest culminates in the reintegration of the existential conflicts and historical ambiguities of reason. It is thus that revelation constitutes an answer to the questions which arise in the actualization and conflicts of reason.

The fundamental theological issue has to do with the idea and reality of God. God is the answer to the question implied in the finitude of being. The question of finitude is most decisively posed in the experience of "metaphysical shock"—the shock of possible nonbeing. To be finite is to be limited by nonbeing. Nonbeing makes its appearance as the "not yet" of being and the "no more" of being and indicates an irreducible dialectical constituent of finitude. The question initiated by the metaphysical shock leads to an interest in the structures of being. These structures are discussed by the author on four levels of ontological analysis: the self-world correlation as the basic ontological structure; the polar elements of individualization and participation, dynamics and form, and freedom and destiny as the constituents of the ontological structure; the duality of essential and existential being; and the categories of time, space, causality, and substance as the basic forms of thought and being. In the finitude of being these structures, elements, and forms are threatened with disruption and self-destruction. This threat gives rise to ontological anxiety on various levels. There is the anxiety of the possible loss of self and world. There is an anxiety of not being what one essentially is as one confronts the possible disruption of the polar elements of individualization and participation, dynamics and form, freedom and destiny. There is the anxiety of nonbeing arising from the possible dissolution of the categories or forms of thought and being. Expressed specifically, the anxiety of nonbeing is the anxiety of transitoriness because of one's having to die, the anxiety of insecurity because of the loss of one's space, the anxiety of formless change and becoming because of the loss of one's substance, and the anxiety of contingency because of the dissolution of causality. In these threats of disruption and self-distruction the duality of essence and existence is of paramount importance. Being is not essentially in a state of disruption. The breaking of the polarities, as an implication of freedom and destiny, occurs only in the transition to existential actualization. Finitude must thus be understood in terms both of its essen-

tial being (as potential perfection) and of its existential actualization. Religiously speaking this distinction is that which holds between the created and the actual world.

God is the answer to the question implied in the finitude of being as this being is threatened with nonbeing in the possible disruption of its structures, giving rise to ontological anxiety. The reality of God is described by the author as Being-itself, living, creating, and related. Only God thus understood can provide the answer to the question of finite being. *God is Being-itself.* This is the only statement about God which is non-symbolic. God is neither *a* being nor the totality of beings. He transcends the basic ontological structure which underlies every definition of finite being. Although both self and world are rooted in God as Being-itself, they are in no sense constitutive of God nor can they provide symbolic material for the understanding of the being of God. Being-itself infinitely transcends every finite being.

God as Being-itself is also *living.* Life, however, as applied to God must be understood in its symbolic sense, and this can be done through the symbolic use of the elements which constitute the basic ontological structure —individualization and participation, dynamics and form, freedom and destiny. These elements can become symbols because they do not speak of kinds of being (self and world) but rather of qualities of being which can be applied universally to all beings and symbolically to being-itself. God is symbolically the "absolute individual" and the "absolute participant." The divine life is the ground of everything individual and personal as well as the principle of participation in everything that is. The polarity of dynamics and form also applies symbolically to God. A living God is one in whom these two elements remain in tension.

According to Tillich, the classical definition of God as *actus purus* is misleading, for it involves a neglect of the dynamic side of God. God is symbolically structured by both form and dynamism. The polarity of freedom and destiny likewise can be symbolically applied to the divine life. Freedom points to the aseity of God; there is nothing given in God which is not at the same time affirmed by His freedom. Destiny as attributed to God means that God is His own destiny. His freedom is not limited by a destiny imposed from the outside; in God freedom and destiny are one.

The third general description of the reality of God is *creativity*. The doctrine of creation constitutes the answer to the question implied in man's experience of his creatureliness. This divine creativity is expressed in an originating creativity, sustaining creativity, and directing creativity (purpose and providence).

Finally, God as *related* comprises the symbols of holiness, power and love. God as Being-itself is the ground of every relation. The holiness of God describes His unapproachable character—His majesty and glory. The divine power of God describes his ultimacy by virtue of which He can properly be understood as the "object" of man's ultimate concern. The courage through which man is able to conquer the anxiety of finitude is founded upon participation in God as the ultimate power of being. Divine love (*agape*) describes God's acceptance of the creature in spite of his resistance

and is thus the final answer to man's finitude.

In Part III of his system Tillich examines man's existential estrangement and the reality of Jesus as the Christ as an answer to the questions implied in this estrangement. Already in part II of the system we have been made aware that there are two sides to the finite being of man—the essential and the existential. Man's essential being is his created being, mythologically expressed in the Biblical story of man in Paradise. Man's existential being is his being as subject to estrangement and self-destruction, mythologically expressed in the Biblical story of the Fall of man. Demythologized, the story of the Fall of Adam expresses the truth of man's transition from his essential unity with God to his condition of existential estrangement. This is the meaning of sin (*suendo*)—a cutting off or estrangement from God. This estrangement from God comes about through man's actualization of himself as finite freedom, which is always in a polar relationship with destiny. Insofar as sin is an expression of freedom it becomes a matter of personal responsibility; insofar as it is an implication of destiny it is a matter of tragic universality.

The marks of estrangement, as implications of the Fall, are fundamental and pervasive. They are unbelief, *hubris,* and concupiscence. Unbelief is the movement whereby man removes his center from the divine center. *Hubris* is the movement of self-elevation whereby man seeks to establish himself as the center of creation. Concupiscence indicates the unlimited desire of man to draw the whole of reality into himself. These three movements of estrangement lead to existential self-destruction, which manifests itself in the various forms of existential anxiety—the anxiety of fate and death, guilt and condemnation, spiritual loneliness, doubt and meaninglessness, and despair. Despair is the final index of the human predicament. It constitutes man's final boundary situation; it is that limit beyond which men cannot go, for in despair all of his possibilities are obliterated. Man in despair exists "without hope." This experience of despair is indicated in the symbol of the "wrath of God."

It is the awareness of man's existential estrangement and self-destruction which motivates the quest for the New Being and for the meaning of the Christ. The New Being in Jesus as the Christ provides the answer to the questions implied in human existence, just as, in Part II of the work, God provided the answer to the questions implied in human finitude. The formulation of the symbol for the conquest of estrangement, *Jesus as the Christ,* is not accidental. Both sides of the symbol, the humanity of Jesus and the divinity of Christ, must be maintained. Jesus as the Christ is both a historical fact and a subject of believing reception. To conquer estrangement the New Being must become historical and be subjected to the anxieties of finitude and existence, but also He must retain an unbroken unity with God for only thus does He have the power to conquer estrangement. Jesus as the Christ is subject to all the consequences of existential estrangement. He has to die and to experience the anxiety of death. He must experience the anxiety of physical and social displacement, the anxiety of uncertainty and doubt ("My God why has thou forsaken me?"), and the anxiety of guilt. But through His courageous faith, His perfect obedience, and His unbroken unity with God, He is able to conquer the estrangement of existence and thus to fulfill His Messianic vocation.

This picture of the New Being in Jesus as the Christ becomes the basis for the Church's doctrine of salvation. Salvation means healing, and healing means the reuniting of that which is estranged. The doctrine of the atonement is the description of the effect of the New Being in Jesus as the Christ on those who are grasped by Him in their state of estrangement and thus experience His healing power. Through His atoning work the split between man and God is healed and man receives the power to face courageously the tragic implications of his existence. The anxieties of death, loneliness, guilt, doubt, and meaninglessness are not removed, but man in the state of salvation has the power to accept them and to affirm himself creatively in spite of them.

TIME AND ETERNITY

Author: Walter T. Stace (1886-   )
Type of work: Religious metaphysics
First published: 1952

PRINCIPAL IDEAS ADVANCED

All religious and theological language is symbolic.
God is nothing to the conceptual intellect.
Religious symbolism becomes meaningful when the symbol is related by mystic intuition to God.
God is utterly other; His mystery is absolute; all ideas of relations between God and the world are metaphorical ideas.

In September 1947 Professor Walter T. Stace of Princeton University published an article in the *Atlantic Monthly* entitled "Man Against Darkness." The article was a defense of philosophic naturalism and a call for courage and creative action in the face of the unconcerned void which naturalism presents as the true picture of reality. The article provoked a considerable amount of controversy, and Professor Stace was accused of being atheistic. Less than five years later *Time and Eternity* appeared, and the critics were surprised to discover that Stace had made what appeared to be a definitive about-face, for *Time and Eternity* is certainly a defense of theism, of supernaturalism, of mysticism, of religion and theology, and of the evocative effect of religious discourse. But Stace himself regards his book as making complete a description that told only half the story. One must of course recognize time and the particular, he writes, and naturalism can handle the assignment of making conceptual sense out of the finite and temporal world; but there is also eternity and the divine, and naturalism is unable even to make sense of these aspects of reality. *Time and Eternity* is a philosopher's attempt to argue that both naturalism and religion are on the track of the truth; the conceptual intellect, Stace maintains, orders the world for limited, practical purposes, but only the mystic consciousness, through union with the divine, transcends the intellect and acquires knowledge of God and eternity.

Stace argues that all religious discourse and thought is symbolic. To take religious discourse literally is to try to conceptualize what is beyond all distinction. Paul Tillich, Friedrich Schleiermacher (1768-1834), and St. Thomas Aquinas (c.1225-1274) are mentioned as prominent theologians who, from different ages and perspectives, came to much the same conclusion. The author also acknowledges an indebtedness to Immanuel Kant (1724-1804) and to Rudolf Otto (1869-1937); the latter's *Idea of the Holy* and Sri Aurobindo's *The Life Divine* (1914) are mentioned as having had, after Kant, considerable influence on Stace's thought.

Religion is described by Professor Stace as "the hunger for the non-being which yet is." Religion is the attempt to get beyond the ordinary world of experience and thought to the ultimate Being which is Non-Being, or nothing, from a nonmystical point of view. The fact that over the centuries men of great intelligence and sensitivity have supposed that such an effort should be made suggests to Stace that the experience of the divine is a common, although often unappreciated, feature of ordinary life.

Stace agrees with Dean William Ralph Inge (1860-1954), who argues that it is an error to take the negative divine as the whole truth. To think of God as nothing but emptiness and the void is to give priority to the conceptual and to eliminate the possibility of appreciating the positive divine.

Although no conceptual understanding of God is possible, it is possible, Stace maintains, to use certain terms which more than others which might have been chosen prepare the mind for an intuitive recognition of God. He mentions such positive terms as "spirit," "mind," "person," "love," "power," and "bliss."

Not only is it not possible to conceive of God intellectually, but also any attempt to understand the divine by reference to relations is bound to fail. God transcends all relations; He is not simply an additional term to be related to other terms which the mind can isolate. Since all relations attributed to God are attributed to Him metaphorically, and since even the idea of relation is metaphorical, any attempt to conceive of God in relation to time, even when He is identified with the eternal, cannot bring man closer to the truth. Only in a moment of mystical illumination is it possible to understand that time and eternity are somehow united in the divine.

Nonreligious symbols can be translated into literal symbols, Stace writes, but religious symbols do not permit such reformulation. An even more important distinction between nonreligious and religious symbols is that the former "mean" what they symbolize, while religious symbols "evoke" their significance through intuitive experience. An utterance in religious language evokes an experience by which a nonconceptual understanding of the divine is made possible.

Stace refers with approval to Rudolph Otto's description of the experience of the divine as "numinous," that is, as having to do with the ineffable and nonnatural. But Stace objects to Otto's analysis of the mode of symbolism exhibited by religious language. It is an error, Stace maintains, to suppose that similarities constitute the basis of religious discourse. Such terms as "awful" (awe-full) and "fascinating," used to describe the numen, are effective not because it is possible to draw analogies between the natural and the divine, but because in the mystic moment there is an "intersection of the natural order by the divine order. . . ." The relation between the religious symbol and what it symbolizes "is not that of resemblance," Stace writes, "but that of greater or less *nearness* to the full self-realization of God." There are degrees of adequacy in the use of religious symbolism: "Thus it is truer to say that God is a mind or a person than that He is a force." It is Stace's contention that predicates taken from language about persons and minds tend to be more adequate in evoking mystic awareness than are predicates used to describe physical forces and lower forms of life.

Although a distinction may be drawn between ethically neutral predicates—such as "mind," "person," and "power"—and value predicates—such as "love," "pity," and "mercy"—and although one may discern both an order of being (within which the first set of predicates applies) and an order of values (which calls for the predicates of the second set), one must realize, Stace writes, "that what is lower in the one scale is also lower in the other scale, and that what is higher in the one is also higher in the other." Only the mystic is able to discover the scale of values within the order of being which points to the divine.

The belief that there are higher and lower pleasures and that the higher pleasures are those of the mind or spirit is a belief based on an almost universal intuitive discovery that results from the intersection of the natural and the divine. Stace fills out his natural-supernatural theory of values by maintaining that values are both absolute and relative: "There is an absolute scale of values, but it does not belong to the natural order. It is revealed only in the supreme moment of mystical illumination. . . . But if we look at these value revelations from the outside, from that standpoint in which they appear as successive moments of time, they are then relative, temporal, and subjective."

Stace describes God as "the Truth" and as "the Supreme Reality," but he points out that God cannot be true in the sense in which propositions, or sentences, are true. The term "Truth" is a value term; to say that God is the Good, the True, and the Beautiful is to emphasize His status as the supreme value. God is Truth in the sense that "He is the content of revelation."

Naturalism insists that the divine is illusory and that discourse about God is meaningless. Stace suggests that the naturalistic view is true—given the naturalistic method of experiencing and conceiving the world. But the claim that ultimate reality is divine is also true—from the mystical point of view. Confusion results when the conceptual language of the naturalist is used in the interpretation of the symbolic language of the mystic.

Naturalistic critics cannot be satisfied with a view like the one presented by Professor Stace. The naturalist wants to be given a method for determining the difference between the divine and the natural; if there is no observable difference, says the naturalist, there is no distinction in meaning. But Stace rejects a theory of meaning which cannot encompass the world which is "other" than the natural world. He argues that the religious consciousness "lies in a region which is forever beyond all proof or disproof."

All attempts to prove the existence of God must fail, Stace maintains, because there is no logical passage from the natural order to the eternal order. However, the divine order, like the natural order, is self-contained, and it is possible to find arguments for the divine within the divine order itself. By seeking within himself, by using his intuitive powers, a person may learn of the divine.

To the objection that intuitions are variable, Stace responds by arguing that it is the rational element, which is introduced in the act of interpretation, which is responsible for differences— not of intuition, but of opinion. He compares disagreement in intuitive matters to disagreement in the aesthetic sphere. Despite differences in reports based on intuitive experiences, there is considerable agreement among those mystics who claim to have known the divine immediately. Finally, Stace asserts, there is no conflict between faith and intuition; the two are "one and the same thing."

Stace concludes his book by examining the relations between mysticism and logic. Logic cannot be applied to mystic truths, he argues, for logic is the instrument of the conceptual mind. Intuitive experience is not analyzable, and it does not afford man with any basis for logically consistent descriptions of the divine. If logic is used to express intuition, the result is contradiction. Stace concludes by reasserting his claim that "God is utterly other" and that "the mystery and incomprehensibility of God are absolute and irremovable. . . ."

Time and Eternity is a cogent and responsible defense of the intuitive method of grasping religious truth. Unfortunately—perhaps by the very nature of the case—no analysis of intuition as a method is offered by Professor Stace. It would not be possible, by reading this book, to discover what intuition is. Thus the naturalist who does not admit the divine side of reality cannot possibly be converted to Stace's view.

NATURAL RELIGION AND CHRISTIAN THEOLOGY

Author: Charles E. Raven (1885-   )
Type of work: Natural theology
First published: 1953

Principal Ideas Advanced

Contemporary science is moving toward a unified vision of the universe and man which makes a natural theology possible even as current neo-orthodox theology rejects the possibility.

The organismic, evolutionary universe now presented to us can be adequately interpreted only in terms of its present highest emergent—human personality.

The historical understanding of Jesus shows Him to be the best exemplar of human emergence, and such an understanding renders a liberal Christian theology again relevant.

In the 1951-52 Gifford Lectures, *Natural Religion and Christian Theology,* Charles Raven, a distinguished theologian, scientist, and educator, calls for a "New Reformation" which will place "natural theology" in the center of Christian thinking. The contemporary nature of the sciences makes this feasible. The first series of lectures, "Science and Religion," reviews the scientific scene; and the second, "Experience and Interpretation," is devoted to a reassessment of Christian

doctrine in scientific terms, by the use of which, Raven contends, the central affirmations of orthodoxy can be maintained.

Raven criticizes historians of science as having created a "papal succession" from Copernicus to Newton. Such a view took present successes (in physics, for example) as normative, and it stressed only those thinkers and trends which led to success as being significant. Science has thus been seen as quantitative and mathematical. Raven claims that this historiography resembles the treatment of Christian doctrine, which took the fourth century Nicene formulation as orthodoxy and judged earlier tendencies which did not support it as heretical.

Classical Greek and Jewish thought were in fact coming together in their treatment of nature, and the New Testament reflects this "intimate and fruitful union." Jesus typically used illustrations from nature; and Paul, too, emphasized the evidences of divine plan in the creation. Raven sees both Jesus and Paul as less dualistic than Augustine, Luther, or Calvin.

In the early Church, the Logos-theology developed at Alexandria emphasized the immanence of God; consequently, science and philosophy were held in high regard as sources of Christian truth and as evidences to be used in controversy. Later theologians, especially in the West, rejected this position. In place of a real concern for nature and history, they turned to allegorization and hagiography. The imagery of ancient fable and bestiary was deemed an adequate source of natural knowledge.

In the medieval period, Franciscans like Robert Grosseteste (c.1175-1253) and Roger Bacon (c.1214-1292) moved toward a more positive view of nature, but the dualism of Dominicans like Albertus Magnus (c.1200-1280) and Thomas Aquinas (c.1225-1274) prevailed. The natural world, uncritically viewed, yielded a minimal natural theology, but the central doctrines of Christianity rested upon a "supernatural" revelation. The final medieval chapter was the skepticism of Johannes Duns Scotus (c.1264-1308) and William of Ockham (c.1300-c.1349).

The first thinker to suspend the tradition and to publish detailed field investigations of natural history (fish, birds, Alpine flora) was Konrad von Gesner (1516-1565). "Before Copernicus had been appreciated enough to be condemned," biological studies, through Gesner's efforts, had reached a high level, Raven claims. In fact, he writes, "the modern scientific movement began" in biology.

The role of the British Royal Society in spreading the New Philosophy of the seventeenth century is well known, as is Francis Bacon's utilitarian emphasis upon the power created by knowledge. What is often overlooked is Bacon's equal insistence upon the correlation of knowledge, which would provide a surer foundation for living than religion. The Cambridge Platonists sensed this and initially felt greater affinity with Descartes. The position they ultimately achieved, however, was of great significance in tempering Cartesian dualism and mechanism. Benjamin Whichcote (1609-1683) spoke of two books, Creation and Scripture, as showing forth the same God. Ralph Cudworth (1617-1688) went on to describe a "plastic nature" that was clearly organic and nonmechanistic. John Ray (1627-1705) endorsed Cudworth's thesis, illustrated it, and asserted the existence of intelligence on the animal level. His rejection of "spontaneous creation," in spite of Scripture and the classics, was a major step toward a uniform conception of nature.

From the seventeenth century until quite recent times, Raven claims, the mainstream of scientific development flowed necessarily, but unfortunately, through narrowing, mechanistic channels. Newtonian physics had no place for human values, and its very success revived theological dualism and a wide range of romantic protests. Biological science was similarly diverted by the influence of Linnaean classifications which were theoretically trivial, thus leaving conceptual formulations to the chemists, physicists, and astronomers.

Mechanism was, thus, a real challenge to the traditional religious interpretation of man and his world. One of the ironies of the nineteenth century was that the battle of science and religion took place in biology and geology. The Bridgewater Treatises of 1829 reflect the bewilderment of eight eminent British scientists commissioned to defend Christianity. Yet they also reflect the consensus among Christians and nonbelievers as to the orderliness of nature.

It was this teleology that received Darwin's bombshell. Did the universe evolve by chance or by design? Charles Darwin (1809-1882) confessed himself in "an utterly hopeless muddle," but many of his followers, especially after the results of work by Gregor Mendel (1822-1884) were confirmed, took natural selection and heredity to be the ultimate proofs of the mechanistic hypothesis.

Under such circumstances, an uneasy truce prevailed between science and religion in Britain. Elsewhere the battle lines were sharply drawn. Everywhere the dilemma seemed to be: "an agnostic humanism or an authoritarian supernaturalism." With the advent of relativity and quantum, however, a "new situation" emerged. The determinate, closed, predictable universe passed into limbo. Variability, the keystone of biological theory, was in some measure also found in suborganic realms.

Finally it was psychology and psychiatry that climaxed the new understanding of the scientific enterprise. The inadequacy of simple, reductive analysis became apparent; and the stress upon objective, general, ponderable facts, already suspect in physics, was ended. This larger view outmoded previous distinctions between science, on the one hand, and history and theology on the other. The universe was one, and it included persons. Organismic thought appeared in writers like Alfred Whitehead (1861-1947), Samuel Alexander (1859-1938) and Lloyd Morgan (1852-1936). Religious thinkers such as William Temple (1881-1944) and John Oman (1860-1939) developed a similar yet more specifically Christian interpretation.

By the middle 1930's, however, dualism came to be reasserted in religious circles. Just as the scientists were reaching for new syntheses that would include man and his values, the theologians retreated to what Raven calls "their ivory towers, cells and catacombs."

Raven calls for a "new Reformation" which will reverse this trend in theological circles and make full use of the new scientific situation. This theology would be clearly in the "liberal" tradition, which in Britain sprang more from the Cambridge Platonists than from the Enlightenment. British liberals have been characterized, Raven says, by "an insistence upon a reasonable faith, a regard for scientific studies and an emphasis upon history." Liberalism is a tradition which correlates well with the new scientific attitude that a problem is answered only "as it is related to the whole body of knowledge." Scientists and theologians alike should now agree, Raven argues, that "the whole story of our universe is a serial and that the volume dealing with the evolution and character of life on this planet begins (perhaps) with the amoeba and ends (at present) with the saint." Both the general and the particular, order and uniqueness, atoms and history, fall within the scope of the new kind of inquiry. The creative process in history embodies continuity and novelty. Adequate explanation must start from the end. Our universe "cannot be explained in lower than personal categories," Raven insists. The new liberal theology will therefore make no claims of a special preserve of knowledge, but will culminate and integrate the whole.

Raven's theological construction begins with an analysis of "experience," which always precedes "interpretation." Our encounters with the universe as a whole are the raw material of religion, and they display an inescapable polarity of self-consciousness and contemplation. Interpretation of the primal experience as "dread" or "shame" overlooks the companion aspect of "wonder." Historical religions have sought to integrate these modes in two ways. The negative way of most mystics proceeds by "subtraction," a concentrating and narrowing of attention. Some success may be achieved this way, but it seldom yields much energy or inspiration. A more positive approach is by "sublimation," the disciplining and training of attention. The positive approach is preferable, Raven says, because it leads to "world-acceptance" and "world-redemption," whereas the negative approach typically results in "world-rejection." No symbolism is sufficient to describe the sublimation process—it can be "shown" but not "said."

As we pass from the unitary experi-ence of the ineffable to its interpretation, we become aware of attractions and repulsions, the ground of our value experiences. By selection and examination, we scrutinize our attitudes, thereby introducing a certain limitation on adequacy. Our interpretations are expressed in emotive, cognitive, and conative activities. In religion, these are epitomized by cult, creed, and morality.

It will not do, however, Raven argues, to insist on the simple subjectivity of all resulting interpretations. The commonality of categories is too great. The Johannine "Light, Love, Life" could, for instance, subsume Christian and Buddhist interpretations. It is then but "a short step" to agreement on the "perfect Son of Man."

Raven reviews the records of Jesus of Nazareth, rejecting both the miraculous affirmations of the conservatives and the historical skepticism of the neo-orthodox. What we can learn shows that Jesus was "one of ourselves" and yet is able "to awaken and quicken our sensitiveness" as no other man has done. This conclusion, Raven notes, agrees with that of traditional orthodoxy.

The fact of agreement does not mean, however, that the traditional interpretations will be valid for us today. The period in which the creeds emerged was permeated by a conditioning social despair that makes the traditional formula "unreal and to many of us a stumbling-block." We moderns would do better to turn from controversial doctrines of Incarnation, which are often dualistic and speak of a divine intruder, to a fresh statement of atonement. Each previous epoch has worked this out in terms of its deepest needs. Our need, and here we resemble the third-century Alexandrians, is for a comprehensive image of the personal culmination of the creative process in the universe.

Our problem is to understand man —the creature emerging in a universe of infinite size, possibly doomed by entropy, surrounded by a measure of natural ruthlessness, enmeshed in sin, suffering, beauty, and freedom. We must not say, with Emil Brunner and Neo-orthodoxy, that this creature is a "sinner." Man is both "sinful and redeemable," Raven writes. Evil has a reality, and much of it is created by us. Unless men are to be automata, however, evil is the price a loving God must pay for human freedom. Progress in eliminating evil is possible, though neither inevitable nor automatic. God is involved, Raven says, "not as spectator or judge but as partner and guide."

How does such a world come into being? By evolution, in the broadest sense. Raven rejects the idea that mutation alone can account for variation and he notes that botanists never accepted the doctrine of an isolated germ plasm, a doctrine advanced by August Weissmann (1834-1914). Organism and environment are related more intimately than such a doctrine allows. Although our theories are still imperfect, we can affirm, Raven suggests, that "the world is so ordered that life and life more abundant prevails in it." If we reject the Cartesian mind-body dualism which generated the debates of mechanists and vitalists, we can outline an immanental teleology. There is a Nisus, a Model, and a Being that we encounter in our "fullest experience." This interpretation corresponds rather closely to that involved in the Nicene faith.

The key doctrine in the new ref-ormation will be the indwelling Holy Spirit (the most neglected aspect of traditional theology). This doctrine can preserve Christianity from gnostic dualism and make it possible to see deity reflected in each stage of an evolutionary process whose goal, Raven says, is "the attainment by mankind of its true status and significance." In psychological terms, the doctrine of the Holy Spirit will remind us that sensitivity precedes perception.

The Spirit is seen in the operation of true communities where an "integrative loyalty" appears. The primitive Church is a prime example. While we can affirm a "divine initiative," this is always present and must be "voluntarily conditioned" by man's response. The Church should be such a community, Raven insists; in our day it can exist only by creating full social reform. The nature of nuclear warfare makes it impossible to retreat from the world's problems.

Raven's natural theology thus leads him to a kind of panpsychism, in which to all intents and purposes he identifies the Spirit and the Logos, although traditional theology has separated them.

No theology can ignore the persistent human desire for immortality. The eschatological expectancy of early Christianity has, however, been overemphasized. Raven rejects any idea of an "immortal soul," and he interprets the "eternal life" taught by Paul and the Fourth Gospel as a way of facing and mastering death. We are, Raven writes, "to behave in this work-a-day world as if the Kingdom of Heaven was already here, as in some sense indeed it is." Man is what he loves, and "we abide so far as we love what is real and abiding."

CHRISTIAN THEOLOGY: AN ECUMENICAL APPROACH

Author: Walter Marshall Horton (1895-   )
Type of work: Ecumenical theology
First published: 1955

PRINCIPAL IDEAS ADVANCED

An ecumenical approach to the central problems of Christian theology is most likely to lead to satisfactory resolutions.

There is a consensus of Christian opinion concerning the following claims: God is known through the specific revelation in Christ; God is both Creator and Redeemer; He is holy, good, and powerful; the world is dependent on its Creator and is adapted to God's purposes; man is a sinner who is regenerated by God's redemptive grace; Jesus is the divine-human Savior of the world; the Church is the Body of Christ; the Christian hope is in the coming of the Kingdom of God.

Walter Marshall Horton, professor of theology at Oberlin College, argues in his *Christian Theology: An Ecumenical Approach* that "a sectarian theology is something just as absurd as the 'Baptist astronomy' which a devout Baptist trustee of the University of Chicago wanted to have taught there in the early days." Horton's conviction that if God is one, theology should also be one, led him to pursue his theological studies at Union Theological Seminary, where the ecumenical approach is endorsed and practiced. Subsequent experience as a teacher and as a student of theological reform through ecumenical conferences strengthened his faith in the value of the ecumenical approach.

Horton describes his book as an exercise in systematic theology, and he uses the ecumenical approach to seven areas of theological concern: (1) The knowledge of God, (2) the nature of God, (3) God and the world, (4) God and man, (5) Christ the Savior, (6) The Church and the means of grace, and (7) the Christian hope (God's Kingdom).

He asks, in regard to each of the seven topics, "What is the universal ('ecumenical') human problem which underlies this topic in theology? . . . What is the universal ('ecumenical') Christian answer to this problem, so far as the Christian churches and schools of thought are now agreed? . . . What are the principal disagreements and conflicts which obscure the clarity of the Christian answer to this particular problem?" He warns that the ecumenical approach is not likely to resolve the problems once and for all; in fact, he argues, a "flat uniformity" would make progress in theology through honest dissent impossible. But the ecumenical approach is valuable in that it centers attention upon the central issues and illuminates the areas of agreement.

Before proceeding to the specific discussion of the seven problems with which the body of the book is concerned, Horton attempts to resolve the ambiguity of the term "ecumenical" by asking, "Does 'ecumenical' imply a literally world-wide perspective on the theological thought currents of our age?" and "Does 'ecumenical' imply a literally universal perspective on all denominations claiming to be Christian?" His answer to the first question is that the present ecumenical effort must center on the theological views being developed in Continental Europe, the British Commonwealth, and the United States. But the ideal ecumenical effort, an ideal which suggests lines of development for the future, would be one which encompassed Christian theology wherever in the world it is developing. The answer to the second question is that since Roman Catholics, Unitarians, and Jehovah's Witnesses do not participate in the World Council of Churches, they cannot participate in the parliamentary effort to achieve ecumenicity. But, once again, although there are practical limitations to a universal effort, the ideal would be to devise a theology which would achieve, among other objectives, "a vital union between the Catholic sacramental principle and the Protestant prophetic principle"—an ideal suggested by Paul Tillich.

According to Horton, the human needs which religion must satisfy are the need for an object of trust, the need for a final goal of hope, and the need for divine salvation as a means to the satisfaction of both trust and hope. The historic religions have incorporated these three elements of trust, hope, and salvation. Religion is needed as a unifying activity by which material means are adapted to moral or spiritual ends and controlled by a concept of man in relation to God. Christianity attempts to satisfy the needs of man by acting on the truth claim that through the reconciling love of Christ man can achieve the salvation which vitally connects his trust and his hope. Horton summarizes the ecumenical definition of essential Christianity by stating that Christianity "presents the God and Father of Jesus Christ as the Ground of trust, his everlasting Kingdom as the Goal of hope, and Christ himself as 'the Way, the Truth and the Life.'"

Systematic theology cannot be considered in a linear fashion, Horton claims. Although consideration of God, the world, man, Christ, the Church, and the Kingdom are necessary, that consideration cannot proceed by beginning with some basic matter and then developing, in a logical way, the remaining topics. Horton insists that "each topic presupposes what follows, as well as what precedes it. . . ." Systematic theology, then, must be circular in the sense that it cannot consider the discussion of any one topic adequate which has not received correction from the discussion of the remaining topics.

The first topic which Horton discussed ecumenically is the problem of religious knowledge: How can God be known? The Christian answer is that a purely rational approach is not adequate; revelation is necessary. Revelation is achieved through historical events and personages. The central figure in the historical revelation of divine purposes is Jesus the Christ, who is not merely the Messiah, Israel's answer, the fulfillment of Hebraic prophecy, but also God's Son, the Word made flesh. The problem for the Christian Church, Horton writes, is to interpret and to apply God's central revelation in Christ.

But although Christians are agreed in claiming that the revelation in Christ is central, there remain questions concerning the relation between the revelation in Christ and the general revelation in nature, history, and other religions; and there is disagreement, also, concerning the value of tradition as a source of revelatory knowledge. Horton considers with careful attention the Catholic positions (Roman and non-Roman), the Protestant positions (Conservative, Liberal, Radical, and Neo-Orthodox), and the Anglican positions, on these questions concerning revelation; he comes to the conclusion that some specific, concrete revelation is needed if general experience is to serve as a source of illumination concerning religious matters.

An ecumenical approach to the problem of God's nature yields, first of all, the conclusion that God must possess the attributes of holiness, goodness, and greatness. The universal necessity to men of faith in a deity, "an Object of ultimate trust and devotion," involves attributing holiness to God, for without holiness He would not be able to draw men to Him in wonder and awe; and without goodness and greatness, He could not adequately respond to men's trust and hope. The Christian answer to the question concerning God's nature is that He is the God of Israel, the Creator and Judge; He walked with men in the person of Jesus the Christ; He abides as Holy Spirit in the community of believers, the Church. Power, judgment, and love are the divine attributes by which God's holiness manifests itself. God is both Creator and Redeemer.

The central unresolved issue concerning the nature of God is whether the Absolute Being of Greek metaphysics can be reconciled with the conception of God as Father and Creator. Another issue concerns the sense in which God is personal. Horton discusses the various views, philosophical

and theological, which center about these issues.

What is the relation between God and the world? Horton argues that the Christian answer, insofar as there is a consensus of opinion, is that the world has real existence; it is dependent on its Creator; and it is adapted to God's purposes. (This particular formula, involving reference to the reality, dependence, and adaptation of the world, is derived by Horton from William Adams Brown's *Christian Theology in Outline*, which appeared in 1906.)

For theologians there is still the problem of reconciling the Biblical conception of the world with the modern scientific conception. And the problem of evil continues to provoke conflicting resolutions. Horton's discussion of these controversial problems is both cogent and provocative.

The next question which is considered is the relation of man to God. Horton suggests as the consensus of Christian opinion the view that man, who is made for fellowship with God, must honor God by loving his neighbor; man is a sinner who opposes the divine will; man is regenerated by God's redemptive grace through Christ. In other words, man is created by God, judged by God, and redeemed by God.

Unresolved issues having to do with the relation between God and man center about the doctrines of the Fall and Original Sin. The Augustinian view of the Fall as making all men sinners has always provoked opposition, and the controversy continues. Horton reviews Pelagian and Arminian views, and he turns his attention to the contemporary opinions of such outstanding theologians as Reinhold Niebuhr and Paul Tillich. It is Horton's hope that the assertion of human freedom can be balanced with the Augustinian view.

Christology arises in response to the problem of mediation. How can God be ultimate and yet concretely in touch with human needs? The Christian consensus of opinion is that Jesus is "the divine-human Savior of the world, the Man in and through whom God turned the course of history and reconciled a rebellious world to himself."

The two contemporary issues concerning Christ as Savior are raised by those who question the doctrine of the Trinity and the doctrine of the Virgin Birth. The Unitarians are the most forceful exponents of the view that Christ was not God, while Protestants are often among those who challenge the belief, to which the Roman Catholics hold firmly, that Christ was born of the Virgin Mary. As Horton points out, even "neo-orthodox Christians like Brunner and Aulén express the most ardent and unwavering faith in the Incarnation, while remaining skeptical or unconcerned about the Virgin Birth." If Christians who believe in the Trinity would insist upon the unity of God, while nevertheless regarding Christ as "the Word made flesh" and the Holy Spirit as God's activity in the world, the tensions between the Unitarians and the trinitarians might be reduced, even if differences of opinion remained. The conflict between the Protestants and the Roman Catholics concerning the Virgin Birth is even more serious, but again there is some possibility of a reduction in the tension of disagreement, Horton suggests, if Catholics admit the danger of idolatry in the veneration of the Virgin and if Protestants admit the danger of losing the sense of "God with us" if they reject mediators other than Christ.

There are various Christian churches or sects, Horton points out, precisely because there is disagreement concerning the Church and the means of grace. Yet there is agreement centering about the claim that the Church is the community of those chosen by God; it is the Body of Christ; and it is the community of the Holy Spirit. Christians are also agreed that the Church is "positively related to the Kingdom of God," but they disagree as to the precise nature of that relationship.

Unresolved issues concerning the Church are considered by Horton by reference to three questions suggested by C. T. Craig in his book *The One Church* (1951): "(1) What are the limits of this one Church which alone can exist? (2) Is there a prescribed form for the Church? (3) How is continuity to be maintained within this Church?" Only "ecumenical conversation" among the conflicting churches can make possible the realization of a Church which men can recognize as the Body of Christ.

Horton concludes his ecumenical examination of issues central to Christianity by examining the Christian hope. Earlier in his book he had analyzed "the logic of monotheism" as involving man's hope, man's trust, and man's salvation through a vital relation to God. The problem of hope is the problem of finding an object of hope that will be trustworthy and will actually fulfill man's highest desires.

The Christian answer is that man's hope is in the Kingdom of God. Many Christians have answered that man's hope is in Christ, but since Christ may be understood to have come to establish God's Kingdom, there need be no difference of opinion, other than verbal, concerning the answer to man's hope. The Kingdom of God is not yet realized in every respect; although a Christian becomes a son of God through Christian love, he has not yet received that spiritual fulfillment which will come when Christ brings the redeemed together, and all men will be "like him" (I John 3:2).

Unresolved issues concerning the Christian hope include, according to Horton, the question of the Second Coming, the question of eternal punishment, and the question of progress: Will Jesus literally come again to establish the Kingdom of God on earth? Will some men receive eternal punishment, or will all men be saved? Is it any longer sensible to speak of human progress? Once again, rather than at-

tempt to force definitive answers to issues best resolved through "ecumenical conversation," Horton discusses the various positions involved, and he suggests the strengths and weaknesses of the alternatives.

As a systematic and clearly expressed account of issues of first importance within Christian theology, as a source of information concerning areas of Christian consensus and disagreement, and as a persuasive but reasonable plea for an ecumenical approach to the central issues, Walter Marshall Horton's *Christian Theology* has won a modest but useful place within the company of books which illuminate the Christian faith.

THE DIVINE MILIEU

Author: Pierre Teilhard de Chardin (1881-1955)
Type of work: Devotional theology
First published: 1957

PRINCIPAL IDEAS ADVANCED

Organic theories of the universe find their complement in the doctrine of the Mystical Body of Christ.

Because the Incarnation has as its goal the perfection of the human race, Christians are bound to exercise their capacities in active human undertakings.

The growth of Christ's Body in the world has only begun, and it will continue until this earth has been changed into a paradise; afterwards, Christ will return and will translate His Body from time to eternity.

Teilhard de Chardin was both a priest of the Jesuit order and a paleontologist, best known for his part in the discovery of Peking man. In a book called *The Phenomenon of Man,* written in 1940, Father Teilhard viewed the whole scheme of cosmic evolution

in the light of the Christian doctrines of Creation, Incarnation, and Resurrection. In *The Divine Milieu,* written in 1927, he dealt more intimately with the life of Christian obedience. The two books supplement each other in that, according to Teilhard, to live as a

Christian is to participate in the divine work of creation, to be co-creator with God, and to die as a Christian is to be united with the Mystical Body of Christ, which is the Omega-point, the goal toward which the whole creation moves.

The Divine Milieu is a deeply meditated work of the sort that rewards careful and repeated reading. It is the record of Father Teilhard's own struggles with the Christian faith, of his intimate discussions with believers and unbelievers, and of certain mystical experiences which came to him. With a nod to his scientific background, Teilhard introduces the book as "a simple *description* of a *psychological* evolution observed *over a specified interval.*" He says that all he has tried to do is note down "a possible series of inward perspectives gradually revealed to the mind in the course of a humble yet 'illuminating' spiritual ascent." But in spite of the calculated objectivity of presentation, it is impossible to doubt that the experiences here recorded are the author's own. Consequently, the book is for the advanced Christian who has himself struggled with his faith.

Teilhard says that there is nothing in his writings that is not in accord with the "eternal lesson of the Church," and that he has sought merely to reinterpret Christianity in a modern idiom. "Is the Christ of the Gospels, imagined and loved within the dimensions of a Mediterranean world, capable of still embracing and still forming the centre of our prodigiously expanded universe?" Teilhard asks. For his answer, he draws copiously from the more mystical and eschatological parts of the New Testament, particularly from the writings of Paul and of John; but he interprets these Biblical teachings in terms of a hierarchical world-view, patterned upon that of Aristotle, but including also the fundamental assumptions of modern developmentalism.

Teilhard views the evolution of the cosmos as the gradual gain in complexity and individuality of its multiple components. "Organization" and "organism" are notions fundamental to his understanding of development within the cosmos, but these ideas are no less fundamental to his understanding of the cosmos as a whole. Holding that the distinction between matter and spirit is only relative, Teilhard argues that man, in virtue of his reflective powers, is the terminus of physical evolution; that each human being, as the center of an independent perspective, recapitulates and sums up the whole world in a unique and incommunicable way. But the ultimate end of creation is not a multiplicity of separate minds, each forming an independent milieu; it is, rather, "a unitive transformation" by means of which the monads are brought together into eternal harmony with the mind of the Creator. By the Incarnation, God introduces into the world the ultimate organizing principle, in terms of which the universe becomes truly one. "What," Teilhard asks, "is the supreme and complex reality for which the divine operation moulds us? It is revealed to us by St. Paul and St. John. It is the quantitative repletion and the qualitative consummation of all things: it is the mysterious Pleroma, in which the substantial *One* and the created *many* fuse without confusion in a *whole* which, without adding anything essential to God, will nevertheless be a sort of triumph and generalisation of being." The efficacy of this higher principle of organization is what Teilhard means by "the divine milieu."

The reader who is interested in Teilhard's speculation must turn to *The Phenomenon of Man*. The present work is chiefly devoted to the practical problem of following the Christian way of perfection. Teilhard identifies two main objections which modern unbelievers bring against the Christian ideal. The first is that it introduces a duality into a man's soul, setting the claims of God over against the claims of the world. The second is that, instead of teaching men to resist evil, it teaches submission to the will of God. Teilhard admits that these objections are all too valid against the greater part of the Church's traditional teaching. Christians ought, he maintains, to be more concerned than secular humanists with the tasks of increasing the sum of knowledge about the world and of improving the conditions for human living; but, too often, because they have failed to keep in view the scope of Christ's dominion, Christians have allowed these tasks to pass by default into the hands of unbelievers.

Teilhard finds it helpful to distinguish between man's "activities" and his "passivities," and to explore the significance of the Christian's commitment with respect to each of these.

Applying his conception of creative evolution to man's *active* life, Teilhard seeks to recover a true sense of the spiritual significance of work. In theory, he says, there has never been any doubt but that a believer is serving God when he tills the soil, or builds a house, or writes a book; but, in practice, nine out of ten devout Christians think of their work as a "spiritual encumbrance." Teilhard calls, therefore, for a rethinking of the distinction between the sacred and the profane. "Everything," he says, "is sacred to those capable of distinguishing that portion of chosen being which is subject to the attraction of Christ in the process of consummation. Try, with God's help, to perceive the connection—even physical and natural—which binds your labour with the building of the Kingdom of Heaven; . . . then, as you leave church for the noisy streets, you will remain with only one feeling, that of continuing to immerse yourself in God."

Teilhard is mindful, however, that in most of the relations which go to make up our lives, we are not active but *passive*. Our current energies are almost entirely beyond our control, and we had nothing at all to do with the chain of events which gave us being in the first place. We can form all sorts of projects in the mind, but we have little to say about whether they will come to pass. Teilhard finds the situation frightening to contemplate. He is reminded of the Patriarch Jacob who wrestled with the angel of the Lord; and, like Jacob, he too ends by adoring that against which he struggled.

On the one hand, says Teilhard, there are the "passivities of growth," those salutary circumstances which silently minister to our health and our development. These "blessed passivities," as Teilhard calls them, ("the will to be, the wish to be thus and thus, and the opportunity to realize myself according to my desire") are all manifestations of God's organizing energy, to be received by the Christian with gratitude and humility. We must never trifle them away; but, confiding in God's universal Providence, we must make the most of every opportunity to realize our several beings.

More perplexing are the other kind of passivities, those which stand in the way of our growth and rob us of our happiness. Teilhard calls them "the passivities of diminishment." Often, because they have too static a concept of God's omnipotence and perfection, Christians are inclined to accept these passivities with an air of resignation. In a world that is progressing from imperfection toward perfection, there must necessarily be these "shocks and diminishments," says Teilhard; but by his power and wisdom, God is able to turn every defect to some advantage and to make "all things work together for good to them that love him."

Teilhard suggests that it will help the Christian determine his practical attitude towards evil if he distinguishes two phases or periods in dealing with it. In the first phase, he must struggle to overcome all circumstances which threaten to diminish his being. He may say confidently, "God wants to free me from this diminishment." He has a right to see the working of Providence in the arts and sciences, and he has the duty to avail himself of every means presently known to man for removing his ill. But he has no assurance that his struggles will succeed; therefore, in the event of failure, he must be prepared for the second phase, that of defeat and its transfiguration. Now, he may ask God to convert his evil into good, and he may rest in the confidence that God never fails to do this, even in the most difficult case of all, that of death. For, says Teilhard, every diminishment can be used by God to spiritualize desires and ambitions, and thus to unite our lives more closely to Christ. "God must, in some way or other, make room for Himself, hollowing us out and emptying us, if He is finally to penetrate into us. And in order to assimilate us in Him, He must break the molecules of our being so as to re-cast and re-model us. The function of death is to provide the necessary entrance into our inmost selves."

The Christian, says Teilhard, is both the most "attached" and the most "detached" of men. He is as interested in this world as it is possible for anyone to be, and he finds the fullest development of his own being in engaging in the work of the world. But his interest in *things* derives from their absolute dependence on God, and the goal of his striving does not lie in his own personal advantage but in the fulfillment of the Creator's purpose. Teilhard finds in the Cross of Christ the proper symbol of this tension between the active and the passive elements of the Christian's life. The disciple must achieve something with his life; otherwise, he has nothing to bring to Christ in the way of an offering.

So far, we have spoken only of the individual believer and of the divinization or supernaturalization of his milieu; for, according to Teilhard, "there are as many partial divine milieux as there are Christian souls." A few words remain to be said about the way in which these individual milieux are integrated into a single, comprehensive milieu; how, in the words of the Fourth Gospel, many mansions are joined together to form the Father's house.

Like certain existentialist philosophers, Teilhard holds that every man naturally tends to regard every other man as a threat to his own being. "Would I," he asks, "be sincere if I did not confess that my instinctive reaction [to the 'other'] is to rebuff him? and that the mere thought of entering into spiritual communication with him disgusts me?" Through the influence of Christ, however, the envelope in which each one tends to isolate himself is broken. In proportion as men's lives are centered in Christ, they converge in a community; their "partial rays" merge into "the principal radiance of Christ."

Teilhard believes, of course, that the Mystical Body of Christ, in which Christians are linked together by the bond of charity, is an actuality in the present state of things. But, accustomed as he was to think in geological epochs, Teilhard describes the unification and divinization of the human race as having but just begun. In time to come, he writes, the greater portion of the race will be united to Christ, and, having at its disposal resources of knowledge and skill as yet undreamed of, mankind will make of this world the holy paradise envisaged by the Hebrew prophets. One day, however, man will have exhausted his possibilities on this planet; then, says Teilhard, will take place the great consummation of the universe, the *Parousia,* when Christ will suddenly be revealed, and humanity be translated to its eternal habitation.

Teilhard has some difficulty with the doctrine of Hell. A prospect of universal salvation might seem to accord better with his thesis that the world is progressing toward the unity of a perfect whole. Nevertheless, he accepts the existence of Hell on the authority of Scripture, and prays for strength of mind to see how it fits into the structure of the universe. That conscious elements or souls possess the freedom to set themselves in opposition to the beneficent forces of creation and to separate themselves eternally from the Mystical Body does, he ventures, add "an accent, a gravity, a contrast, a depth" to the historical process.

When *The Divine Milieu* was written, evolutionary philosophies were more common than they are today. Teilhard's outlook, however, remained unchanged through the remainder of his life, probably because it owed less to philosophical fashions than to the eschatological outlook of the New Testament. In the year of his death, he wrote: "Today, after forty years of constant reflection, it is still exactly the same fundamental vision which I feel the need to set forth and to share." It is the vision of humanity united, master of its potentialities, and reflecting in its consciousness the perfection of the Creator.

FAITH AND KNOWLEDGE

Author: John Hick (1922-   )
Type of work: Apologetics; philosophy of religion
First published: 1957

Principal Ideas Advanced

The traditional association of "knowledge" with objective infallibility is logically mistaken; human knowledge can in principle aspire to no more than subjective rational certainty.

Although volition, moral experience, and general epistemological principles are relevant to a correct understanding of religious faith, the latter is not to be interpreted merely as a voluntary "will to believe," or merely as a theoretical implication of moral experience, or merely as parallel to ordinary judgments of fact.

In an ambiguous universe where all cognition requires interpretation, faith's true epistemological status is the free interpretative apprehension of all experience as religiously significant.

In *Faith and Knowledge* John Hick attempts to bring to bear on theistic religion in general and on Christian faith in particular the methods and epistemological findings of contemporary analytical philosophy. Born and educated in Britain, the homeland of analytical philosophy, Hick is well situated to provide what he calls a "bridging operation" between current movements in philosophy and theology.

If such a bridge is to be built, the general character of "knowledge" first requires Hick's philosophic scrutiny. Traditionally, and even within much contemporary analytical theory, the concept of knowledge is inseparably joined to the notion of infallibility. If one *knows* (so the standard argument runs) one cannot—logically cannot —be wrong. The propositions one "knows" *must* be true, or they do not constitute genuine knowledge. It simply fails to make good sense ("It is a misuse of language," say many analytical philosophers) to assert that one *knows* something but that one might be mistaken about it. In this respect "knowledge" differs from mere "belief," which entails nothing with respect to the truth or falsity of the propositions believed. Such an account of "knowledge" Hick firmly rejects.

First, the "infallibilist" theory maintains that when one "knows" one must also "know that he knows." Knowledge unaware of itself as knowledge is a contradiction. In this requirement, however, Hick finds a fatal flaw. It all too frequently happens that what we claim to know turns out to be false; evidently there exists no mark within cognitive experience itself that infallibly indicates when one is "truly knowing" and when one is only "seeming to know." Without such a mark, however, one can never—even in principle—*know* that he knows, and the entire theory falls to the ground.

Second, every supposed item of "infallible knowledge" that is actually put forward as such either fails to achieve perfect *certainty* or is unable to provide real *information,* the hallmark of genuine knowledge. Sense experience is notoriously uncertain; the immediate awareness of one's sense field or of one's bodily states offers no information about the world; and, similarly, analytic truths of logic or mathematics purchase their icy certainty at the cost of informational content. The class of infallible truths turns out to be empty, to the discomfiture of those who hold to the infallibilist theory.

Given, then, that "knowledge" as defined by infallibilism is an unattainable ideal, it becomes Hick's task to show what it is that constitutes knowledge in actual cognitive practice. There is no cause for despair, as though the forced abandonment of infallibilism destroyed all hope for genuine knowledge; on the contrary, a way is now opened to bring our understanding of the term into greater contact with the real situation of the human knower. This situation has always been such that those beliefs are claimed as "knowledge" of which men are most certain. Certainty, though inevitably subjective, need not, however, be arbitrary; and Hick maintains that knowledge as *rational* certainty will involve a degree (a degree which in principle defies specification) of critical examination. For the rational man, then, knowledge will consist in the psychological "sense of intellectual satisfaction, of security, or immoveableness, achievement, finality" which follows inquiry. If his inquiry has taken all relevant evidence into account and has not violated the rules of correct reasoning, the rational man is entitled to assume confidently that any other person in his position would agree that his certainty is well grounded; Hick finds that such certainty provides an objective element even when knowledge is defined subjectively.

The subjective definition of knowledge accords well, Hick believes, with the general analysis of cognition which recent philosophical debate has helped to clarify. Belief, as the genus of which knowledge is a specific mode, involves a fourfold subjective movement: ". . . the entertainment of a proposition in thought; assent to this proposition, or the adoption or embracing of it as true; a resulting disposition to act, both in thought and in overt deed, upon the adopted proposition; and a disposition to feel an emotion of conviction toward the proposition whenever its truth is challenged." Knowledge is distinguished from other beliefs only by the certainty with which the proposition believed is "em-

braced" as true, as we have seen; and with respect to the other elements of the cognitive situation, items of knowledge no less than other propositions believed to be true have an intimate bearing on action and emotion. Among the claims to knowledge most profoundly relevant to feelings and behavior are religious beliefs, and it is to an analysis of this domain of cognition that Hick next turns his attention.

Adopting as his acknowledged starting point the nearly universal rejection of the standard theistic arguments, Hick proceeds to examine the cognitive status left to a religious faith shorn of its proofs. Can an adequate analysis of this status be given in terms of volition alone? Is it possible adequately to understand faith as a "will to believe," a deliberate gamble, in the absence of coercive theoretical arguments for or against theism? Hick doubts that such an analysis can succeed in revealing the epistemological structure of faith: first, because an appeal to pure volition licenses too much, any number of mutually exclusive religious options being open to "cognitive justification" on such a theory, and, second, because a volitional analysis (modeled after a game of chance) is unable to account for the sense of immediate personal acquaintance with numinous reality—an attitude quite different from the gambler's—actually reported by religious persons.

A second theory, allegedly better suited to the recognition of the believer's sense of experiential involvement with the object of his belief, attempts to analyze the cognitive status of faith in terms of moral experience. On the basis of one's sense of obligation one can know that a moral order exists and, consequently, a moral orderer or lawgiver, God. Hick, however, is unconvinced by this theory, at least as long as God remains for it a mere unapprehended postulate of the moral life (once again religious experience is unaccounted for) or of ethics (a logically coercive argument from ethics to religion has yet to be advanced). If moral experience is taken as a channel for the direct apprehension of God, there may be value in the moral theory, but no claims of logical "proof" or "demonstration" from ethics are allowable.

Finally, a theory may be advanced to account for religious cognition by appeal to the existence of data so plentiful and pervasive as to defy clear and exhaustive articulation. Religious knowledge may be compared with other common beliefs of which we are justly certain without absolute or indisputable evidence. We rightly accept as knowledge many propositions concerning which doubt, though far-fetched, would be logically possible: our knowledge, for example, that the earth is approximately a sphere. The justification for such cognitive practice is found in the infinitely complex concatenation of bits and pieces of evidence the drift of which points to the same conclusion and undergirds our informal inference, even though we may not be able to express this inference formally in such a way as to overcome the doubts of an obstinate skeptic. Religious faith, on this theory, shares such a logic of informal inference. Hick, though accepting the justice of this analysis within many departments of ordinary knowledge and agreeing that the religious believer is able to *know* what he cannot formally

prove, remains unable to accept the theory's applicability in questions of religious belief. The assumption of this theory is that judgments of religious faith are of the same logical type as judgments referring to limited and particular facts of the empirical world. This assumption, however, is false. Religious belief is logically far more complex than this theory is equipped to recognize.

In what, then, does the logical complexity of religious faith consist? Hick reminds us that all cognition rests ultimately on interpretation; religious faith, in a hierarchy of interpenetrating interpretive schemes, functions as man's ultimate interpretation of the significance of reality as a whole.

Defending this theory, Hick shows that even on the level of our cognition of *nature* knowledge is not free from the need for interpretative decision for which there can be no logically coercive justification. It requires an act of interpretation, he points out, to hold that one's sense experience is of a world existing independent of oneself. Solipsism, the position that nothing but one's self exists and that the apparent world is no more than a figment constructed by one's own experiences, is logically irrefutable. The fact that nearly all men make the same free act of interpretation, rejecting solipsism and finding in experience a significance that goes beyond the self, should not blind us to the fact that interpretation is actually present. That such an interpretation is cognitively meaningful despite positivist doubts is shown by the fact that solipsism has a different "cash value" in experience from that of our normal interpretation; sense experiences would have a different quality if they were apprehended as self-manufactured illusions; one's behavior toward other persons would differ if he "saw" them as mere appearances reducible to fictional products of his own psyche instead of as independently real centers of consciousness and value.

Mention of *value* brings us to another level of apprehension on which agreement about the significance of our world is far less uniform and on which interpretation is consequently more often noticed *as* interpretation. We may, or we may not, apprehend scenes in the world as beautiful; we may, or we may not, apprehend events in the world as laying moral obligations upon us. Just as all men seem to have an innate tendency to interpret experience as signifying an objectively existing world, so all men seem to have a tendency to interpret their world in value terms, aesthetic and moral. The parallel, however, is not exact. The former interpretation is a precondition for the latter, since for a solipsist there could be neither beautiful *objects* nor moral obligations toward other *persons*, but value interpretations are not a requirement for an interpretation of nature as an independently existing world. As such, apprehending values is more clearly voluntary than is apprehending the world as objectively real—an interpretation on which survival may depend! Still, seeing the world as aesthetically and morally significant in general, despite specific differences of interpretation, is a normal part of human life.

Another normal characteristic of human existence is the apprehension of the totality of things as *religiously* significant. As an interpretation, once again, religious faith is no more open to coercive proof than is the apprehen-

sion of the world *as* a world or *as* aesthetically or morally significant. Just as the logic of a determined solipsist or amoralist may be impeccable, so may an atheist's reasoning be formally valid. For the religious believer, however, such considerations are quite literally beside the point, since he has seen nature, beauty, and morality as mediating for him an apprehension of reality that puts all earlier levels of significance into an ultimate context of meaning and truth. The theist puts his trust in no argument that will lead him securely from facts of nature or of value to certainty about the existence of God. Instead, he finds all experience freshly illuminated by his certainty; and this kind of certainty, as we have seen, equals knowledge. The theist genuinely knows, therefore, what he cannot prove, just as the informal inference theory of religious cognition maintained; he finds that moral experience as a dimension of interpretation is deeply relevant to his faith, as the moral theory insisted; and he discovers that his faith is a matter not of theoretical necessity but of responsible decision in an ambiguous world, as the voluntarist theory (stripped of its abstract "wagering" overtones) correctly taught.

Hick now needs to meet two possible objections to his theory of religious knowledge. First, what in experiential terms does theism *mean*? Any allegedly cognitive assertion that means anything specific at all must somehow inform us that, if it is true, we may expect to have certain experiences (the assertions "cash value") and expect *not* to have other specifiable experiences. If an alleged assertion is compatible with *every* conceivable experience, it is uninformative, but we have seen that a hallmark of knowledge is that it must be informative; therefore, religious belief must be incompatible with *some* expectation of experience before it can qualify as a candidate for belief or knowledge. Hick's theory, however (so the objection continues), maintains that theistic faith is a total interpretation of *all* experience as religiously significant. If we take this seriously, then any experience whatever will be "apprehended" as compatible with theistic belief, but this consequence entails that theism is uninformative; hence, religion is ruled out as a cognitive enterprise. Hick acknowledges the force of the requirement that genuine cognition entail determinate experiential expectations, but he rejects the assumption that theism offers no specifiable expectations of its own. On the contrary, theism maintains that after death certain experiences will be available which, if theism is correct, should verify adequately for rational certainty the truth of the religious assertions made in this life. Thus theism's eschatological dimension, together with the experiences of new qualities of life and power in this world, provides quite enough promise of significant experience to establish the total theistic interpretation as cognitive.

A second objection might hold that the religious interpretation of experience is altogether too much a matter of personal choice to be compatible with the actual existence of a supposedly all-powerful God eager to make Himself known to men. Why, if God exists, does He make it so easy for men to decide against their (supposed) natural inclination to apprehend Him? Hick's answer is that a loving God should be expected, if He exists, to permit cognitive freedom to His children. If men are to be genuinely free rather than automata, if they are to turn to God in responsible fellowship rather than in coerced slavery, a gracious God must veil Himself from their immediate vision so that they may come to Him of themselves, not as overawed sycophants, but as grateful children.

Such a concept of God is not without its historical origins, of course, and it is to the religious total-interpretation of Christianity that Hick alludes in concluding *Faith and Knowledge*. In the person of Jesus is seen a *man* who at the same time is apprehended by Christians as the revelation of *God*. Faith in Christ is a seeing of divine significance in His loving life and teaching, through which faith apprehends the world afresh under the God known in Jesus. Is this an interpretation which defies proof? Yes, Christian faith never becomes less than a matter of responsible choice; but from that choice springs an apprehension of a significance in all experience of nature, beauty, and morality, a significance which confirms and reconfirms the Christian's certainty that in his faith he has found unparalleled knowledge.

THE FORM OF THE PERSONAL

Author: John Macmurray (1891-   )
Type of work: Philosophic reconstruction; philosophy of religion
First published: Volume I (*The Self as Agent*), 1957; Volume II (*Persons in Relation*), 1961

PRINCIPAL IDEAS ADVANCED

Modern philosophy is in a state of crisis due to two initial errors: first, the error of considering man as primarily thinker rather than agent, and, second, the error of considering man in solitude rather than in social relation.

Questions insoluble by traditional philosophy are freshly illuminated by considering the self as agent.

The nature of morality, politics, and religion may be clarified through an approach which makes central the concrete situation of rational agents in personal relation.

The two volumes which constitute the published version of John Macmurray's 1953-1954 Gifford Lectures, entitled *The Form of the Personal,* are pioneering ventures aimed at redirecting current thought toward greater philosophic adequacy and consequently towards greater appreciation of the nature, importance, and truth of religious belief. Since the time of René Descartes (1596-1650), the "father of modern philosophy," the direction of philosophic thinking has been toward atheism, Macmurray holds; but that this should be so is *prima facie* odd in view of the overwhelming tendency of men at all times and of all conditions to find religious expression a natural and enormously significant element in life. Religious belief, on the evidence, is no aberration. If, then, modern philosophy, on its premises, can find no theoretically valid place for religion, may it not be that the theories and premises of modern philosophy are themselves aberrant and in need of re-examination?

Macmurray in *The Self as Agent*

(1957) finds that he is not alone in raising radical questions as to the foundations of traditional philosophy in a revolutionary age. Contemporary analytical philosophy, with its accent on new and rigorous techniques, has thrown in doubt the propriety of many of the problems which are traditionally considered the stock in trade of philosophy. Existentialism, on the other hand, has with equally radical impact tended to put in question the traditional methods of philosophy for the sake of heightened emphasis on basic human problems. Both radical movements, however, are for Macmurray unsatisfying because one-sided. Analysis dismisses the problems for the sake of technique; existentialism scorns technique for the sake of the problems: both recognize the urgent need for re-evaluation of traditional thought, but neither in itself offers constructive adequacy, and neither identifies the nature of our current crisis with sufficient clarity to go to its root.

The crisis of our age, Macmurray

insists, is the crisis of the *personal*. Existentialism is aware of the threat to personality, but it lacks the techniques needed to meet this threat with philosophic rigor. Analysis, by the very rigor of its techniques, exposes the depth of the threat through its inability to deal constructively with such deeply personal questions as morality, metaphysics, and religion. In practical terms, likewise, the crisis of the personal is represented by the growth of the state and the consequent decline in personal responsibility in favor of the collectivism of fascism and communism. The same crisis is further manifested in the widely noticed decline both in the power of religion and in the general level of sensitivity to human values within a world of massive industry and inconceivably destructive warfare.

Although the overwhelming problem of our age is the crisis of the personal, traditional philosophy is ill-equipped even to form an adequate concept of the person. What is the self? Macmurray points out that this question defies answer for those who approach it with the usual categories of thought fashioned for dealing with impersonal forms of being. The British empiricist philosopher David Hume (1711-1776), for example, showed the impossibility of constructing a concept of self out of substantial categories relevant to the "form of the material." On the other hand, Søren Kierkegaard (1813-1855), "father of existentialism," showed the inadequacy of the attempt by the idealist philosopher G. W. F. Hegel (1770-1831) to describe the self in terms of the "form of the organic," concepts drawn from living things on the subpersonal level. Only by developing concepts adequate to the subject matter, only by constructing and applying a new form— the "form of the personal"—will the crisis in philosophy, and in our culture, be resolved.

The difficulties which have prevented modern philosophy from creating an adequate form of the personal begin at the birth of modern philosophy itself, with Descartes's *Cogito ergo sum*. His "I think, therefore I am" has involved its philosophic heirs in two egregious mistakes: first, in the false supposition that the self may be conceived as being in isolation from other selves; and, second, in the mistaken identification of the self as primarily a thinking thing. Neither of these assumptions can withstand examination: the first leads to the absurdities of solipsism and the second leads to the irrelevancies of subjectivism and thus to abstraction from real life and experience.

Turning first, in *The Self as Agent*, to the second assumption, that the self is essentially a thinking thing, Macmurray first acknowledges the obvious —that the self is capable of thought and is in this sense a subject. Such acknowledgment is not, however, tantamount to accepting thought as the essential constitutive characteristic of the self. On the contrary, pure thought is seen, if we examine our experience, to be negative, a remainder left when we deliberately abstract ourselves from our full existence as thinking *agents*. We are rational agents first; we are inactive thinkers only derivatively. Pure thought, the self as subject, is over against the world. Only as agent does the self have existence in the world. For the "I think" of traditional philosophy Macmurray substitutes the "I do." If we take such a substitution seriously, what light may we expect to find shed on traditional problems in philosophy? The problem of perception, first, is shown to be misconceived if put (as it too often is) in terms of a theory of vision. Vision is far from an appropriate standard for perception if the self is correctly understood as primarily agent. Touch, rather, is the agent's paradigm for perception; touch is the one sense which is not merely contemplative but does something to— acts against—the object perceived. The other senses then may be interpreted in terms of touch. Vision, for example, can be understood as a form of symbolism in which present experience (the sight of an object) signifies a possible future tactual experience in which the object will be given immediately to the perceiver rather than mediately through the fallible images of sight.

The nature of space and time, second, are illuminated by Macmurray's proposed shift. Space, for an agent, is best understood as the possibility of movement. Logically prior even to space is time, the very presupposition for action, and thus for space. Reference to our own most concrete experience shows that these great sources of metaphysical puzzlement become, for agents, direct implicates of action.

Other major problems for philosophy have been posed by the interpretation of "cause" and the status of the "world." From Macmurray's starting point, however, the concept of cause can be seen to be reducible to an abstraction from the agent's personal experience. If cause is best described in terms of a recurrent pattern of change, the experience of *habit*—that domain of activity from which the element of thought has been abstracted—can best ground our understanding of causality. Similarly, the physical world, as the realm of causes, can best be interpreted as an abstraction from personal experience of activity.

Science, as the deliberately abstract study of the physical world, is shown from Macmurray's perspective to be the mode of reflection in which the causal regularities of the world are objects of reflection in order that agents may discover what is to be counted on toward furthering action. As such, science is interested in the world as means; it deliberately limits its attention to the general and ignores the unique. Art, on the other hand, is that form of reflection which, from the point of view of the self as agent, is primarily interested in the intrinsically valuable, the unique which may be worthy of the agent's valuation in its own right. Art, therefore, is considered by Macmurray to be a higher form of reflection than science; from attention to the unique one may be able to recognize general features of things, but from exclusive concentration on the general one is never able to appreciate the unique.

History, finally, is interpreted by Macmurray as neither art nor science. In terms of the philosophy of the "I do," history's role is illuminated as reflection on action itself. History is interested both in the particular and unique (thus resembling art) and in the general and lawful (thus resembling science), but its primary task is the provision of a social memory. This social memory, interested in all action, exhibits the form of the personal as a whole; and, in so doing, it finds a continuity within all past actions, revealing the world as an intentional unity of personal activity.

At this point, however, the focus of Macmurray's attention has begun to move from the isolated self to the broader subject of selves in society. For the most part *The Self as Agent,* while shifting the concept of self from a thinking thing to an actor, has left unchallenged the solipsistic assumption implicit in Descartes's *Cogito ergo sum.* It has therefore remained incapable of interpreting essentially social phenomena like morality, political theory, and religion. To this cluster of subjects Macmurray next turns in his second volume, *Persons in Relation* (1961).

The first necessity is to establish fundamental categories through a formal examination of the fully personal in its simplest manifestation, which Macmurray finds in the initial condition and development of the human infant. A baby, the author points out, finds himself from birth within the field of the personal; the infant's original situation is within an environment dominated by personal intention; his one naturally given adaptive capacity is for communication of feelings of comfort and discomfort to agents who deliberately care for his needs; his first knowledge is of the personal Other. It is only when the developing child learns to discriminate within the Other that he is forced—as an agent—to acknowledge the nonpersonal, "that in the Other which does not respond to my call." The form of the personal, consequently, is originally and irremediably social. The "It" comes second, temporally and logically. The baby is constituted as a person by the Other, the You, with whom he communicates.

In the simple case of the infant, the motive consciousness which directs his communication exhibits a fundamental polarity, as we have seen, between discomfort (the "negative" phase) and comfort (the "positive" phase). Developing his thesis, Macmurray finds the positive and negative poles—love and fear, broadly understood—basic to the personal at all levels of development. If the child is to grow, his mother must deliberately disappoint his well-grounded expectations and at some point refuse to do for him what he must learn for himself. This experience of the withdrawal of the personal Other cannot fail to arouse fear, the negative phase, which by its essential egocentric character may smother the positive and heterocentric pole of love, without which real personal relation is impossible. The goal of the mother is to reinstate the dominance of the positive phase, without sacrificing the increasing capacities of the child to do for himself, by convincing him of her love despite all appearances. If she succeeds, love is more and more richly possible through the cycle of withdrawal and return; if she fails, the child's personal consciousness may more and more be dominated by the negative pole, which may express itself in either of two basic forms: aggressiveness (overcoming fear by forcing the Other to conform to one's will) or fantasy (overcoming fear by escape to an ideal world of imagination where there is no conflict between the Other and one's will).

Equipped with the model provided by this description, Macmurray turns to the philosophical task of giving an account of morality, political philosophy, and religion in terms of the person.

Morality, first, falls into three modes corresponding to the one positive and two negative personal responses outlined above. Each of the three moves the person in whom it may be dominant to select differently what he shall notice about the Other and himself. These three modes of apperception are the communal (positive pole), the pragmatic (negative-aggressive pole), and the contemplative (negative-escapist pole). Each mode of apperception leads to a mode of morality. The goal of morality for philosophy based on the form of the personal is given as realizing personal relation; but though morality is to "intend" community, community may be differently intended depending on one's mode of apperception. One may intend community pragmatically, taking ends for granted and finding the primary moral problems in aggressively developing means for achieving the good in actual life; one may, on the other hand, intend community contemplatively, finding the moral good in fantasies of an ideal realm and considering spiritual life as the only *real* life; or, Macmurray hopes, one may intend community communally, taking the Other as the center of loving concern and finding the primary moral problem in the overcoming of egocentricity and fear.

Political philosophy, too, is believed to be more adequately illuminated by the form of the personal than by means of other conceptual models. Once again Macmurray finds the two ambivalent negative possibilities standing over against the one positive pole of the personal. The views of the philosopher Thomas Hobbes (1588-1679) on the state, for example, reflect the negative-aggressive mode of apperception; the theories of the French philosopher Jean Jacques Rousseau (1712-1778), on the other hand, illustrate in this field the negative-escapist mode. But neither can find true *community*, which goes beyond mere *society* in being founded on the positive heterocentric mode of apperception and intention.

True community is the concern of religion. Religion, interpreted through the form of the personal, is a reflective activity engaged, on the one hand, in symbolically celebrating the achievement of community in so far as community is actual and, on the other hand, in strengthening the will to community by helping to overcome the negative pole in the personal, substituting the motive of love for the motive of fear in social relations. These two complementary functions require, Macmurray believes, the symbol of a personal Other who (1) stands in personal relation to each member of the community (this symbol, God, focuses joyful attention on the achieved community and helps withstand fear of losing this community through eventual relapse into mere society) and who (2) is the Agent for whom nature stands as his action (this symbol helps to overcome not only the fear of losing community but also the fear of the impersonal Other). Religion, as the reflective activity of community itself, can be recognized as the primary form of reflection from which art and science are derived. Art, reflection on what is worthy for its own sake, and science, reflection on how to attain given ends within the (abstract) impersonal Other, are both specialized limitations drawn from religion's fully concrete concern for both ends and means.

Persons in Relation ends with a defense of the intellectual right of the religious person to represent the universe in personal terms. We not only *may* conceive of the Other in its totality as personal, we *must* do so if our conception is to be adequate. Alternative conceptions of the universe are logically possible, of course, but a philosophy based on the form of the personal will expose them all as abstractions—legitimate, perhaps, within the context of their own subordinate (personal) intentions, but culpably partial when taken as the model for our conception of all things. The form of the Personal, the only model of the cosmos which can strengthen our full capacity to act as what we most surely know ourselves to be—persons—is the one which alone has the capacity to include ourselves in the universe, which alone makes possible an understanding of personal activity, and which alone reflects our original and most incorrigible knowledge.

In these volumes Macmurray, it is evident, has offered a major challenge to modern philosophy and has demonstrated a creativity of thought and breadth of conception for which he is widely respected. It will be both surprising and unfortunate if his ideas—both critical and constructive—are not widely debated in the years to come.

THE REALITY OF FAITH

Author: Friedrich Gogarten (1887-   )
Type of work: Existential theology
First published: 1957

PRINCIPAL IDEAS ADVANCED

Implicit within Christian faith—understood as creaturely existence-in-relation made possible by the reception of the creative Word of God—is a two-fold freedom: for God and toward the world.

This freedom born of faith, which was discovered by Paul in his understanding of the believer's release from the soteriological claim of the Jewish law and the Hellenistic cosmic powers, and rediscovered by Luther as justification by faith, guarantees the secularity of the world which it turns over to man, the stewardson, for examination and responsible mastery.

Subjectivism, the historical source of modern man's freedom toward the world at a time when freedom was denied him by the Church, proves inadequate to provide meaning and unity to a technologically fragmented world.

In Christian faith this unity is made available, not as a metaphysical world view but as an existential reality in freedom for God and toward the world.

The *Reality of Faith* is one of several works emerging out of Friedrich Gogarten's later period. In this book he seeks to come to grips with contemporary technologically oriented secularism from the standpoint of Christian faith. Far from being antithetical to faith, secularism is implicit in the Biblical understanding of man's relationship to God and the world, claims Gogarten. As the "image" and the "son," man is that creature entrusted with a peculiar responsibility for the world. He is steward over a world which, according to the Biblical writers, has been purged of the numinous power and soteriological value which the world has for religions generally. The "principalities and powers" have been defeated by God through His victory in Jesus Christ, writes the Apostle Paul. Whereas previously man was victimized by worldly powers claiming divine authority, he now participates through faith in the victory of God as freeing him to live in a world depopulated of controlling spirits and demons, a secularized world. Genuine faith guarantees the preservation of this secularity, for in faith man receives his meaningful existence as a son from the Father. Since the world provides him with no ultimate meaning, it can make no ultimate claim upon him. The world remains properly secular.

This understanding of man's relationship to the world was not and could not have been adequately preserved in the medieval Church, Gogarten writes, because the understanding by faith which would have made it possible was obscured. Rather than a quality of being created in the relationship with the Father, faith became trust in and assent to a certain kind of world, the world of the Church. Divine reality was merged with ecclesiastical reality, and the fear and reverence which medieval man felt in the presence of natural and cosmic forces was redirected toward this Church-world. Admirable though the unity achieved by the medieval world may

have been, it was doomed to be broken by two developments which sought to restore to man the freedom which is his according to the Christian Gospel: the Reformation, with its emphasis on justifying faith, and the Renaissance and Enlightenment, with their emphasis on reason.

Understanding faith not as assent to doctrines or as adherence to a world view of the Church but as a trusting response to the Word grasped as the intention of God directed toward man, Luther reintroduced the Biblical view of the relationship between man and God as dependent upon the event of revelation. Wherever revelatory communication takes place, in which God gives himself to man as man's God, the creature is freed from the necessity of releasing himself from the world and is freed for a responsible interaction with the Creator. Unfortunately this freedom for God was soon obscured even within the Reformation churches themselves as they fell back into medieval scholasticism, thereby transforming Christian faith once again from direct responsibility to a living God into adherence to certain doctrines; that is, into conformity to a certain kind of world view which was supposed to assure salvation. The implications of Luther's position as freeing man for independent and responsible investigation of the world as unencumbered by doctrinal limitations—as seen for instance in Luther's own relationship to his colleague on the Wittenberg faculty, Rhaeticus, who championed the views of Copernicus—never had a chance to develop, for the Reformation churches soon reaffirmed the medieval tradition of the Bible as the canon of the natural sciences. It remained for forces outside the Church to bring about the revolution which would make available to man the freedom toward the world which is rightly his in genuine Christian faith.

With the high valuation placed upon reason by the Renaissance and Enlightenment, man was given a principle by which he could stand over against his world and examine it in a way hitherto impossible—dispassionately and without religious anxiety. The assumed correspondence of reason within man to reason without gave man a position of pre-eminence as that being "who gives all being its measure and applies the plumb line," as Martin Heidegger has written. This development provided man with a degree of control over his world which steadily has been enlarged through the growth of the empirical sciences, until today man's control over his world is simply taken for granted—if not as a present attainment, at least as a future certainty. Not with cosmic spiritual powers and demons does the responsibility of the maintenance of the world lie, but with man.

The orientation which has accomplished this revolution is the "subjectivism" with which Gogarten wishes to enter into dialogue, as he indicates in the subtitle of the book, "The Problem of Subjectivism in Theology." The designation of this development as "subjectivism" may seem strange, especially since the concern of so much of the movement is for objective reality. Yet Gogarten sees, from the standpoint of the whole history of thought, the dominant motif as subjectivistic; that is, as that way of thinking which regards the thinking subject as the center of that which is thought, as the one who holds the plumb line to all reality. Contemporary scientific relativism only intensifies this orientation. Subjectivism succeeded where the Church did not in freeing man from religious worship of his world and in turning him toward the scientific control of it. Thus the initial point of contact between theology and subjectivism lies in the fact that subjectivism has brought to realization the second part of the two-fold freedom (freedom toward the world) which is available in the Christian faith. In order to draw the parallel and contrast between subjectivism and theology as sharply as possible, however, Gogarten proceeds to describe Christian faith in such a way as to make it appear closely akin to subjectivism, calling faith a "fully reflected self-consciousness," and quoting Luther to the effect that man's faith is the presupposition (*Voraussetzung*) of the reality of God's revelation. Man's faith "creates deity," as Martin Luther (1483-1546) wrote. What does this mean?

The first thing which must be said is that the faith here described is not the product of man but of God. Indeed, Gogarten interprets Luther's whole discussion of "the bondage of the will" as an attempt to make plain the fact that faith is the result of God's activity. And apart from this activity God cannot be known. But if this be the case, how can one say that man's faith is the presupposition of God's revelation? Precisely because God is known in his "creative power and deity" only when He is known as one's own Creator; that is, only as one receives one's very being, one's meaningful historical existence out of the encounter with Him. God is not God as a metaphysical hypothesis but only as one's own Lord in an actual faith relationship. It follows that one cannot speak meaningfully—that is, in a way which corresponds to an existing reality—of God without speaking of this kind of involvement with Him, for to speak without involvement is at best to use an unknown cipher and, at worst, a word, "God," which becomes a hoax, a subterfuge for a human longing or desire which has no external referent. The being which the believing man is given in the creative encounter with God, on the other hand, is the presupposition of everything he knows, not only concerning God but his world and himself as well; his being is fundamentally conditioned by this encounter, and therefore his knowledge reflects this same conditioning and is inseparable from it. Thus it can be said that Christian faith is "fully reflected self-consciousness" in the sense that the self-consciousness (*Selbstbewusstsein*) of the man in faith is the product of the encounter with God in which the being with which man entered into the encounter is reflected back as a new image "conformed to the image of His Son" (Romans 8:29), conditioned fundamentally by the revelation of God in Jesus Christ. Therefore faith is the presupposition of God in the only sense in which it is appropriate to speak of God at all, in speech which is the product of historical involvement and relativity. Thus Christian faith, analyzing itself, can see certain similarities to subjectivism's understanding of the nature of knowledge and reality.

Having come—to borrow a phrase from John Wesley—"within a hairsbreadth" of subjectivism, Gogarten now turns to point out the basic difference between Christian faith and the subjectivism of the modern era. Modern subjectivism began as the result of the discovery within man of an autonomous principle which provided direct access to the world and made the supernaturally given medieval metaphysical view of the world quite irrelevant (including the theology constructed thereupon). The locus of subjectivism's initial strength is the source of its eventual bankruptcy, however, for the ever present temptation to which the human reason again and again succumbs is the temptation to pull the world together into some kind of unity and wholeness which seems to be necessary to sustain meaning, a unity and wholeness lost with the dissolution of the heteronomous unity of the medieval world. Yet the technological mastery of the world can proceed only by breaking down one by one these unifying constructs of the human mind, with the ironic result that the successive failure of these attempts at meaning has insured the continuing success of man's ever expanding technological control and responsibility, making it appear ever more necessary to have an overall system, a universal scheme of things, to bring order and integration to a technologically fragmented life. The quest for unity is doomed to frustration, however, as long as it continues to go back to that source which is already known to be relative, man's mind, while seeking to find something absolute. World views do not become more absolute as they become more pretentious and grandiose. They cannot complete man's world but can only curve it in upon itself, thus rounding off the sphere of meaning within its own source. What is the alternative to this built-in frustration in subjectivism?

The Christian faith, claims Gogarten, does not seek to complete the world in terms of a scheme of the world, a metaphysic, to which the world must conform. Instead, the two-fold freedom given in faith not only turns the world over to man's reason for examination independently of metaphysical limitations, apart from the sheer givenness of the world itself, but it demands that the secularity of the world be maintained. This secularity is of course qualitatively different from the secularism of subjectivism. It not only rids the world of gods but refuses to allow other gods to be put in their places. It is secularity born of faith in the one God, not as a meta-physical theory but as the one source of existence in freedom. Delivered from "the horrible delusion" that the world will have meaning only if he can give it one, man is freed to examine the world as his rightful object as "son" and steward. Nor is it necessary, Go-garten concludes, for man to squeeze ultimate meaning out of the world, for he has his being and meaning from the Father.

CHRISTIANITY AND PARADOX

Author: Ronald W. Hepburn (1927-   )
Type of work: Critique of theological methods
First published: 1958

PRINCIPAL IDEAS ADVANCED

Philosophical analysis shows that certain essential Christian claims about God and our knowledge of God embody conceptual confusion rather than legitimate paradox.

Attempts by contemporary theologians to base assertions about God on immediate acquaintance through "encounter" experiences or knowledge of Jesus Christ are doomed to failure.

Equally futile as justifications for theological claims are appeals to history, morality, or the world as a whole.

Despite the conceptual weakness of their theology, Christians need not fear that the only alternative to Christian faith is life without ethical or religious meaning.

Ronald W. Hepburn's *Christianity and Paradox* throws down a challenge to theology—a challenge offered by a contemporary analytical philosopher who characterizes himself as a critic with a "naturally religious mind." To what extent, Hepburn asks, are the long-recognized peculiarities of Chris-tian language legitimate paradoxes, justifiable by the unique subject mat-ter of theology, and to what extent are these oddities attributable to logical confusion? Can the sympathetic phi-losopher find satisfaction, without violating his rigorous critical stand-ards, in the answers given by modern theologians? If not, must intellectual integrity be paid for at the cost of personal meaningfulness?

A possible objection, that philosophy has no business meddling with questions of faith, is quickly turned aside by Hepburn. The moment a theologian engages himself in scrutiny of his own concepts, terming them "symbols" or "analogies" or the like, he is engaged in philosophic endeavor. There can be no bar, therefore, against an acknowledged philosopher's examining the theologian's philosophical theories or offering theories of his own. In like manner, a theologian who ventures to judge any viewpoint incompatible with Christian faith, any morality at variance with Christian ethics, has thereby entered the philosophical arena and cannot object when his ideas attract the professional attentions of his colleagues. Even if the theologian refrains (as he usually does not) from the foregoing activities, his assertions are fair grist for the philosopher's mill to the extent that theological utterances are supposed to carry meaning and truth. There is no side-tracking the enterprise of *Christianity and Paradox* by demanding that the philosopher mind his own business; any claim to meaning or truth *is* the philosopher's business.

How can meaning or truth be expressed by language which characteristically takes the form of apparent contradictions, as in the statement cited by Hepburn from *De trinitate,* in which Augustine writes that God is "good without quality, great without quantity, a creator though he lacks nothing, ruling but from no position, eternal yet not in time"? How can it be maintained that God is both three and one, that God acts in the world but is in neither time nor space? How can such paradoxical claims be defended as anything other than confused or meaningless utterances?

One popular defense proposed by contemporary theologians is to claim that the language of Christian faith is abnormal because of the abnormality of its subject matter, and that the resulting verbal difficulties are resolved in immediate experience of Him to whom they refer. Given such experience, the apparent contradictions of Christian language should be no more philosophically troublesome than are the apparent contradictions in the physicist's talk about light, with respect to which he speaks as though his subject matter were at the same time a wave and a particle. We do not doubt the existence of light or the propriety of physical theory, despite this logical oddness, because light can be given an "ostensive definition" (it can be pointed to in experience); similarly, if God can be defined ostensively, we must not cavil at the inevitable peculiarities of speech about Him. Hepburn agrees that *if* an ostensive definition can be provided for the word "God," the theologian is standing on firm ground, but is such a definition actually possible with respect to Him who is beyond the reach of our senses? The philosopher's duty is to examine the theories of theologians who answer affirmatively.

One theological school of thought, much influenced by the Jewish philosopher-theologian Martin Buber (*I and Thou*), claims that the required ostensive definition of "God" is available in experiences of encounter with a personal *"Thou"* who transcends the sense-bound "impurities" inherent in personal relations with human beings.

Hepburn is unable to agree. The basis of this theological position is the assumption—plausible at first—that personal encounters are in principle independent of any objective test or check-up procedure. Is it not the case that there is a spectrum of personal encounter ranging from radically "impure" meetings in which the other person is reduced to an observable thing to be studied, manipulated, or used, to the comparatively "pure" personal encounters in which objective factors, those features of one's friend which are open to observation, are of much diminished importance? Hepburn agrees, but he points out that such a spectrum does not in the least entitle the theologian to maintain that somewhere *off* the spectrum exists the possibility of a personal encounter with *no* observational or objective characteristics. Quite the opposite, the relative unimportance of objective characteristics when a profoundly personal relation is achieved itself depends on the objective features being so well known, so intimately understood, their significance so often confirmed by experience, as to be taken for granted. The fleeting gesture, the unconscious twitch of a muscle, even the pregnant silence—all contribute to the sense of encounter. What, however, of the radically different theological claim that personal encounter can be experienced without any gestures, without any breaking of silence to discover that both persons have been following similar trains of thought, without any indication at any time that there even exists a *Thou* brooding behind the objectively unbroken stillness? "Personal encounter" of this sort has torn itself free from the essential moorings of our universal experience of genuine "encounter," and in so doing it has been emptied of any meaning which might be of use to theologians in offering an ostensive definition of the divine *Thou*. In an age made aware by Freudian psychology of the tricks constantly being played on our minds by unconscious factors, the theologian cannot hope to rest his case on a peculiar sense of personal presence that shares none of the objective characteristics of real meetings between persons. If he wishes to found the peculiarities of his speech on the nature of an ostensively definable reality, he must look elsewhere.

A second school of Christian thought relies for its answer not on feelings of personal communion but exclusively on Jesus Christ. The doctrine of Incarnation, it is claimed, licenses the Christian to point to the God-man as the ostensive definition of God. Hepburn, however, doubts the logical strength of this move, at least when taken by itself. Certainly statements about Jesus cannot be made logically equivalent to statements about God without heretical departure from Christian faith. According to orthodox belief Jesus died, Jesus was limited in knowledge, Jesus was bounded by time and space; but God cannot be considered finite or mortal. Even a Christocentric theology must remain within certain bounds. Jesus fails to provide "God" with an adequate ostensive definition, nor is it possible to evade this verdict by insisting that it is to the Christ, to the Second Person of the Trinity, that reference is given by such a theory: such a move simply pushes the problem back one step to the notorious difficulty of describing intelligibly the relation between Jesus, the man of Galilee, and the eternal Christ.

No escape is offered by this route, and the enterprise of offering ostensive definitions for God seems fruitless.

Another way of justifying problematic language, however, is to show that for all its peculiarities such language is required to explain certain features of experience. Can theological statements be defended on the basis of their explanatory power?

Hepburn turns first to claims that the events of history are best interpreted in terms of God's activity. He detects an unfortunate logical conflict, however, between the contemporary theologian's assertion that "history matters" and the insistence of many theologians that Christian faith does not stand or fall on any events open to the probing of the historian. If Christianity is to claim historical roots and explanatory value, it must take the risks of falsification by growing historical knowledge, but theologians who demand a faith imperturbable by fact undermine the very basis of their explanatory claim.

A second area of alleged explanatory power is found by some theologians in the domain of morality. Apart from Christian faith, they contend, the fullness of moral experience can neither be illuminated by thought nor achieved by life. Hepburn agrees that secular ethical thought may be arid and shallow, but he challenges the claim that this *must* be the case when ethics is separated from theology. A "man-centered" ethic need not be equivalent to egotistic meanness; Christian doctrine is not the only avenue to the recognition of human corruption or human possibility; and, most significantly of all, Christian faith cannot in any event obviate the need for making a human moral judgment—that God's will is good and that it is right to obey His commands—which judgment must inevitably precede the adoption of any theological ethic. Theology is neither a necessary nor a sufficient explanation for morality.

At last it may be urged by the theologian that the world as a whole requires explanation in terms of God. Why should there be anything rather than nothing? Surely the cosmos demands a ground beyond itself, a causal source and sustainer, who is God. For Hepburn such an argument has an appeal, reflecting both a sense of wonder at the cosmos as a whole and a sense of "ontological anxiety" at the recognition of our own precarious place in existence, but as a rational proof for the existence of God and thus for the legitimacy of theological language it has serious shortcomings. The argument presupposes that every event must have a cause, including the world, the totality of all observable events. The "certainty" of the argument depends, however, (1) on its proponents shifting illicitly from making an uninformative statement (true by definition) about the mere meaning of "cause" and "effect," and (2) on the dubious supposiiton that the world as a whole can meaningfully be talked about in language applicable primarily to things *in* the world. Even granting that the statement "Everything must have a cause" is informative and true, the causal argument defeats itself, since on this premise God must also have His cause; and even granting that the world as a whole can meaningfully be spoken of, it is not clear that causal language is ever applicable to the universe itself. That it is so applicable must be shown, not merely assumed.

Hepburn offers an alternative both to traditional Christianity and to blank frustration of the religious impulse. The alternative is a recognition of the importance of parable and of imaginative construction within a life sensitive both to the values of religious experience and to the seriousness of the moral pilgrimage. Within profoundly evocative parable may be found the basis for an imaginative response to one's fellows and one's world that will furnish the religiously sensitive skeptic with support in his moral endeavors and integration for his life—but without violating his intellectual integrity. Even religious experience, for such a person, can be valued for its high worth independent of such dogmatic interpretations as, offending the mind, too often have been allowed to stultify the experience.

CHRISTIANS AND THE STATE

Author: John Coleman Bennett (1904-   )
Type of work: Christian ethics
First published: 1958

PRINCIPAL IDEAS ADVANCED

The Christian faith places the state under the providence, judgment, and redeeming love of God.

The government of the United States is neither secular nor neutral regarding religion; it officially recognizes theism.

The negative religious freedom of the minority ought not to outweigh the positive religious freedom of the majority.

The Christian ethic stands in an objective moral order broader than the Judeo-Christian tradition.

Absolute judgments regarding the state are inappropriate for the Christian whose proper relationship to it is compounded of judgment and responsibility.

The Christian Church ought not to be identified with any particular social or political order.

In *Christians and the State*, John C. Bennett develops his views of the theological basis of the state, the nature of the state and its functions, and the problems of political ethics. The work is important for three reasons: its themes are perennial perplexing issues of vital significance, its author is qualified to speak authoritatively for much of mainline Protestantism in the mid-twentieth century, and it is written so clearly that it demonstrates that a work of responsible scholarship can be made available to the general reader.

Dealing with the Christian faith in a religiously pluralistic society, Bennett presents in Part One the very basic questions to which his work is addressed: (a) How should Christians in such a society express their faith that both nation and state stand under the providence, judgment, and redeeming love of God? (b) How should they co-operate with those of other faiths or with those who reject traditional religion? and (c) How should they conceive of the relationship of their own faith and its ethic to the more general moral convictions present in the culture?

Restricting his discussion to the United States, Bennett notes that its heritage is vitally Christian but is not committed to any one faith. Though the state is friendly toward organized religion, American Christians cannot participate in the "advantages and illusions" of a formal Church-state relationship. Yet, Bennett argues, the state is not in principle secular, nor is it even neutral as between religion and the rejection of it. There is an officially recognized theism in the United States as evidenced in various of our state documents, the Constitution, official prayers, and the like. The criticisms leveled against the vagueness of this national theism are important, but they are only part of the truth, as is illustrated so well by Abraham Lincoln's genuine worship of God without the use of divisive Christian symbols. Bennett advocates a clear understanding that while the state is neutral as between faiths, it is not secular or indifferent to religion. It does not profess a common-denominator religion, nor act as a teacher of religion. The state uses symbols and provides for acts of religious recognition which "refer to the Reality which the churches and other religious bodies alone are competent to interpret."

Naturalistic humanists, atheists, and agnostics who reject traditional religious symbols advocate an absolutistic version of separation of Church and state. Bennett feels that while their protest against obscurantism and clericalism is important, one has to weigh the negative religious freedom of this small minority with the positive religious freedom of the majority. Restraint and consideration are needed on both majority and minority sides.

Especially noteworthy in the light of the theological environment with which Bennett is familiar is his explicit repudiation of that rejection of a natural theology which leads to rejection of general revelation. He thinks of the religious responses to God that are broader than distinctively Christian when he observes that "the rejection of general revelation represents a theological austerity that denies deep human realities." The Christian who believes that Christ fulfills and transforms the ideas of the Deity cannot deny that there is much in the broad religious response of mankind to be fulfilled and transformed.

The distinctively Christian ethic needs to be set in the context of moral convictions whose base is broader than the Judeo-Christian tradition. Such moral convictions may be defended as true apart from Christian revelation, Bennett claims. There is an objective moral order which includes both Christians and non-Christians. The objectivity of the ethical notion of love is demonstrated by the suicidal effects of hatred as shown internationally in war and individually in the mental illness of the person who is driven by hate. The real unity of the human race, the common fate of humanity, the concern for justice, freedom, honesty, integrity, and personal discipline —all have more than narrowly Christian dimensions, Bennett insists. Dedication to the goals of the common morality are often present outside the Christian community, but it is within the Christian understanding that one finds the most adequate context for such goals.

Considering characteristic Roman Catholic and Protestant views in the light of New Testament warnings against anarchy and the absolute state, Bennett expounds his own constructive position in which the state's coercive power is viewed as a necessary factor in but not the definition of the state's role. The power of evil is greater than either Roman Catholic or Protestant Liberal thought has understood. The Fall of Adam is best understood in a dynamic way which removes the emphasis from the condition of Adam before the Fall as contrasting with the condition of humanity since and places it rather on the experience of sinfulness in every man. Sin rooted in spiritual pride reaches to all areas of human life, and it is in this sense that the traditional notion of total depravity is to be understood. Toward human sin the state has the complex relationship of simultaneously restraining it, embodying it, and being limited by it. Theological realism of the type which Reinhold Niebuhr represents has shown the limitations of moral idealism which is so often preoccupied with inapplicable solutions and is frequently used as the basis for rationalizations of tyranny.

In view of the presence of both the negative and positive aspects of the state, what can the Christian position be regarding resistance to the state? Absolutistic judgments are not appropriate, but when, as in a democracy, the government provides for its own correction, the Christian has the responsibility of respect for the government. The Christian must insist that the state be seen as a limited instrument of society and not as the all-encompassing social reality itself. There is a high degree of agreement between Protestant and Catholic on this point.

Though the characteristic movement in the modern period has been the loosening of the relationship between the law of the state and the law of God, the government of the United States was set in the context of belief in a higher or divine law. The influence of this higher law remains in American constitutional law. Natural law, of which God is the Author and which is known to reason and confirmed by revelation, is accepted as the criterion of all positive law for Roman Catholic thought. Protestants have tended to have reservations about natural law in view of man's fallen state, for fallen man is not able to know or properly to apply such law. The rise of the totalitarian state has provoked renewed concern for the criteria of justice above the law and the state. Consistently Bennett counsels moderation and restraint in situations in which the state and individual conscience collide. He argues that absolutes are inappropriate in the area of Church and state discussions.

Cautioning repeatedly against the danger which the state poses to freedom, Bennett sees the role of the state as essential in certain spheres such as the economic. Only the state has sufficient scope to deal effectively with national problems, and there is nothing morally or socially wrong in the state's participating in economic affairs. It is, in fact, the state which often stands as the one effective guarantee of freedom for much of the population. Discussions associated with the ecumenical movement have featured a helpful scrutiny of economic ideologies which has resulted in rejection of rigid thinking regarding either capitalism or socialism. Capitalism as unfettered free enterprise has received especially serious scrutiny. Bennett makes it clear that insofar as capitalism presents many centers of power and initiative in society and regulates large segments of the economy by the market, and takes seriously the problem of incentive, Americans can well preserve it and recommend it to other nations. Yet only the great changes in capitalism in the past decades have made it morally tolerable. The Christian must avoid identifying his Christianity with any economic system, be it capitalist or socialist. The same is true with identifying Christianity with any form of government, though Bennett shows the affinity of Christianity with the responsible democratic society whose government is based upon the consent and participation of all elements in the population and which has constitutional safeguards for freedom of expression and minority rights.

Central to the final third of Bennett's work are his presuppositions regarding the nature of the Church. He stresses the Church as a human institution whose purpose is to relate man to the redeeming acts of God. Community itself is an essential part of the Gospel. The Church is a universal community having responsibility for the total society. Its authority rests not in itself but in the Word of God. It ought not to be confused with any particular social order. In his discussion of the meaning of separation of Church and state, the author recalls that the word "separation" never appears in the Constitution, and that the First Amendment was a compromise which ought not be subjected to too rigid an interpretation. The state and local communities ought to be given the benefit of the doubt when they are experimenting with solutions of the very difficult problems involved when the positive and the negative forms of religious liberty are brought into heightened tension. Genuine misunderstanding often exists when those whose faith is secularism take an extreme view of separation as it involves the system of public education. They see their position as a valuable concern for fairness and freedom. It may be such for the minority but not for the majority whose rights must also be considered. Bennett approves the government's going out of its way to encourage voluntary associations, such as churches, which are important for the general welfare of the community.

In the perplexing and frequently rancorous area in which Church and state meet in concern for education, Bennett succeeds in presenting a balanced view of various interests. He advocates the encouragement of experiments rather than unyielding rigidity of movement within narrow limits. The only generalization he permits is that all proposed solutions create difficulties and none apply universally. Teaching the "common-core" of the Judeo-Christian tradition has value, but such instruction easily becomes sectarian and encourages a public school "doctrine." Teaching about religion has merit but is often less than many want in the way of direct religious education. Released time has been tried and found wanting by many Protestant leaders, though it still offers a significant area for experimentation. Noting that the idea of parochial schools is hardly un-Protestant, Bennett cites the almost universal Protestant opposition to direct government aid to such schools. He accepts the view that public financial encouragement of parochial schools would be destructive not only of public schools but of the level of education generally. Bennett is less rigid than many, however, and he advocates experimentation in this area. The welfare of the pupils and the harmony of the community receive strong emphasis in his thinking.

Bennett's presentation of the Protestant view of Roman Catholic power in America is distinguished not so much by the thoroughness of its rehearsal of the fears of Roman Catholic dogmatic intolerance and its frequent companion, civil intolerance, as in its insistence that it is an error to project such fears indiscriminately into an indefinite future. No attempt is made to deny that Protestants fear a powerful Church which suffers or tolerates a pluralistic democracy only as an expediency on the way to its goal of a Church-dominated confessional state. There is real tension between an authoritarian, centralized hierarchical Church and the spirit of an open, pluralistic, democratic society. Yet Protestants need to be aware that some of their fears stand in need of scrutiny.

The Roman Catholic Church is not without variation among the various nations and cultures where it is found. "The difference between French Catholicism and Spanish Catholicism almost belongs to the study of comparative religion," Bennett writes. The Roman Catholic aggressiveness in the United States which offends so many Protestants has its roots in the cultural situation which was alien to it. Further, Roman Catholicism is far more divided on matters of principle than is generally understood so far as the proper view of religious liberty and social policy are concerned. Bennett hopes that exaggerated fear may be allayed, that Protestants will stress their own positive teaching more, and that both religious groups will exhibit greater understanding and share more in striving for common goals.

Most churches have spoken out regularly on public issues. When the cry is heard that the Church ought to stay out of politics, the objection is more likely to be against what the Church is saying rather than that it is speaking forth. Self-restraint is advisable in technical and strategic issues lying outside the specific competence of Christian wisdom, but the Church's nature is such that its interests are inclusive. What must be guarded against is making the ethos of one part of the community the basis of the law of the whole community. Protestants and Roman Catholics alike have need to exercise great care here as the experience with Prohibition and with birth-control legislation suggests. Bennett advocates that the Church should affect the state through emphasis upon the spiritual values of the society and its individual members, by being true to itself, by refusing to yield to forces of political manipulation, and by teaching its members about the relevance of Christian faith for the great public issues. Indirect forms of action are more important than the direct. Any direct action needs to be most thoroughly scrutinized and should represent an overflow from the indirect action. Christians may be expected to differ on political matters, and Christian political parties and movements generally misrepresent Christianity as implying a particular political program. The area of politics is one of moral ambiguity because real alternatives are so limited that compromise must be achieved. Compromise and corruption ought not be identified, for compromise can be a legitimate expression of Christian concern.

It is not difficult to understand why John Bennett's book received an excellent reception, for it is marked by comprehensiveness and clarity, and its critical passages are presented with an irenic concern for balanced positive solutions.

COMMENTARY ON GALATIANS

Author: Ragnar Bring (1895-   )
Type of work: Exegetical theology
First published: 1958

PRINCIPAL IDEAS ADVANCED

The law, according to Paul, must be recognized as a part of the redemptive history of the Old Testament, and interpreted in the light of the fulfillment of this redemptive history in Jesus Christ.

Christ fulfilled the law by accepting its curse on the cross, thus revealing the law's true function of revealing man's sin, but also freeing all men from condemnation by the law.

The Christian's freedom from the law expresses itself as faith active in love: thus, the righteousness that the law could not create is realized.

Commentary on Galatians by Ragnar Bring, professor of systematic theology at the University of Lund, Sweden, is intended to be neither philological nor popular and devotional; it is, rather, an attempt to present the content of thought and the context of ideas to be found in Paul's Letter to the Galatians.

According to Bring, Paul's letter shows how the early Church differentiated itself from Judaism, though this differentiation did not mean emancipation from the Old Testament and the law. The letter was occasioned by a controversy in congregations established by Paul. Some congregations were insisting that Christians, in addition to responding in faith to the Gospel of salvation through Christ as preached by Paul, were also obligated to keep the Old Testament law. Paul answered these critics, establishing his Apostolic authority and defining the proper understanding of the Old Testament, and more particularly its first part, the Pentateuch or the law, in the light of the revelation in Christ.

The Gospel for Paul was not a human doctrine but a divine revelation, a renewal of the prophetic interpretation of the Scriptures. Thus the message was the same whoever proclaimed it. There was not complete clarity in the Church, however, as to the implications of the Gospel message for the Gentile mission, especially in so far as the law was concerned. Included in the Old Testament law were required observances by which the Jew separated himself from the Gentile. According to Paul, since the law had been fulfilled in Christ these observances were no longer necessary, and it was now possible to see that the real function of the law was to reveal man's sin. In the old age prior to Christ's coming the demands of the law had been misunderstood to mean that man through keeping them could achieve righteousness. But with Christ a new righteousness had been revealed, and the condemning function of the law could now be freely recognized.

The Jews claimed to be Abraham's children, but Paul insisted that Christians are the true children of Abraham. The concept of election as Paul interpreted it excluded any emphasis on human qualities as providing the basis for the divine blessing. Instead election pointed forward to the fulfillment of the promise made to Abraham, which fulfillment had now come. Thus for Gentiles to be circumcised in order to separate themselves from other Gentiles involved a denial of the covenant with Abraham, for Abraham had not received the promise on the basis of his circumcision. Nor was God's election to be limited by such efforts to separate men from one another.

Whereas Jews drew a line from Abraham to Sinai, Paul drew a line from Abraham to Christ, in whom the law was fulfilled and brought to an end. According to Paul the law is holy and good, but it condemns man. The law is fulfilled only in the righteousness revealed in Christ. Until Christ came the purpose of the law was to put man under a curse, to demand of man what man was unable to perform.

In order to explain Paul's understanding of the fulfillment of the law in Christ, Professor Bring paraphrases a crucial passage, Galatians 3:11-12: "Righteousness is connected with faith. It does not say in Scripture that righteousness comes through observance of the law. It says rather, he who does what is written in the book of the law shall thereby receive eternal life." The law is to be fulfilled. This fulfillment is not contrasted with faith, but comes with the Messiah. Christ fulfilled the law in that He submitted to God's will to the extent of going the way of the cross. To gain life through the law is therefore to gain it through the fulfillment of the law wrought by Christ. The right relation to the law is to submit in faith to its judgment and to believe in Christ. Thus "the just by faith" and "he who does the law" are not opposites, but mean the same thing, since for Paul even the commandments of the Old Testament witness to Christ. In the light of the Gospel, Paul sees a deeper meaning in the Old Testament references in Leviticus 18:5 and Deuteronomy 30:11-20 which speak of life coming through fulfilling the law, for these passages, according to Paul, may now be interpreted as referring to Christ.

The law came because of transgressions and was a judgment on sin, not a guide to a righteous life. Thus true obedience to the law was to submit to its judgment, while to try to make oneself righteous through the law was to disobey it. Christ, on the other hand, identifying Himself with sinful humanity, accepted death on the cross, thereby showing himself to be righteous, and fulfilling the law. This judgment could be accepted only by one who was Himself personally free from judgment. The judgment was actually the curse of God, but Christ's encounter with this condemnation had cosmic dimensions. Blessing could now come to all, for all who were in any way bound by the curse of the law were now freed by Christ. The self-righteousness of the Jews, on the other hand, reached its ultimate expression in their rejection of Christ. Yet the result of this act was that Israel was itself freed from the curse of the law, and the Gospel could also now be proclaimed to Gentiles. If the Gentiles, however, were to accept the necessity of circumcision and other law observances, this would be to identify themselves with the concept of law that had led to the rejection of Christ.

Paul held that if the promise to Abraham was correctly understood, there could be no ultimate opposition between the law and the promise. To think that righteousness according to the law was a condition for sharing in the fulfillment of the promise in Christ was to fail to see salvation in Christ as the fulfillment of the promise. Paul did not criticize the Jews for valuing the law too highly, but for making it something God had not intended it to be. Instead of the law being a part of God's redemptive history, it had become an idol worshiped by the Jews in the interest of their own self-righteousness. But to idolize the law, Paul insisted, was to dishonor the law.

Since the law was given because of trespasses, it was not present prior to the creation, nor was it a complete expression of God's nature. The law could demand righteousness, but the law could not create righteousness. While the law therefore had a place in God's pedagogy, the law was not the goal divine. When the law, furthermore, led to legalistic righteousness, the law could no longer reveal sin. The depth and meaning of sin thereby became hidden. The law increased sin and thus drove people from faith in the one God which the law proclaimed. The Galatians accordingly were led away from Christ to Moses, though Moses was to lead to Christ.

Paul saw that through Christ God was to be the one God of all people, as all men became one, with no distinctions whereby some among them could claim more merit than others. Thus belief in Christ, according to Paul, was no threat to monotheism. On the contrary, through faith in Christ faith in the one God was fully realized.

Christ through the Spirit was now at work in the believer, and thus the goal of creation was being achieved, for Christ was the origin and goal of creation. Through baptism all shared in Christ's death and resurrection, becoming united with Christ and with other Christians. No distinctions between men were here insignificant. Since at the most basic point all Christians were alike, other differences between them could not be degrading. Some of these differences were even to disappear, while others were to be gratefully acknowledged as making possible the many and varied ministries which the welfare of the Christian fellowship required.

Bring points out that in this letter

Paul is not primarily concerned to tell people to change their ways of thinking. He is more interested in proclaiming an objective fact which has changed the human situation and has made possible a new religious orientation. That Christ came with life and righteousness, which can come only from God, manifests His divinity. Since the law had divine validity, freedom from the law could not be achieved through teaching. The law could be set aside only if God, who gave the law, now allowed it to be fulfilled.

Paul strongly emphasized that those who had been made free must not return to bondage. The powers to which one was subservient in legalistic righteousness had been made powerless by God in Christ, but apart from Christ they were real powers. Yet to worship temporal powers was fraudulent, for in the deepest sense they lacked real existence. Paul writes to the Galatians as if he were a mother who in travail had given them birth. Now new labor was necessary that Christ be formed again with them. Paul wishes that he could present the Gospel so clearly that the Galatians would at last be firmly rooted in it. The allegory of Sarah and Hagar may represent such an attempt.

Sarah and Hagar represent two covenants, one which is to terminate, the other which is to continue. In their emphasis on physical descent from Abraham, the Jews were like Ishmael, the son of Hagar and Abraham, who had physical descent but no promise. So also Hagar had prided herself over Sarah, just as the Jews did over the Gentiles. Hagar thought her son would be the only heir, and the Jews had similar opinions of their privileged status. The promise to Abraham that

he would have many descendants in terms of redemptive history looked forward to the coming time when righteousness would be realized through the Messiah. This is the understanding of Scripture that Paul presupposes. Bring suggests that though Paul's interpretation of the story of Sarah and Hagar appears allegorical, it might better be called typological, for it is this understanding of the Scriptures in terms of redemptive history which determines the meanings Paul finds in the story. Bring also points out that Paul may during his stay in Arabia have heard of Arab legends about Ishmael. Thus he could say that Israel's claims to descend from Abraham were like the claims of the Arabs. What distinguished Isaac was the promise, now fulfilled in Christ, but the Jews rejected the promise. Thus the Jews through their use of the law had become like those outside the covenant of promise.

The Christian's freedom from the law according to Paul, however, is to be a freedom in the spirit expressing itself as faith active in love, and not a freedom in the flesh. Fleshly freedom would simply be a new form of bondage. Love for Paul is not egoistic desire and its satisfaction, but a willingness to serve. The freedom of which he speaks is not the freedom of fulfilling one's own desires and asserting one's own interests against others, but a freedom which naturally realizes itself in a selfless love. Yet this new behavior is possible only through the Spirit given through Christ. Thus Paul's ethical exhortations are implications of his doctrinal exposition.

In the eagerness of the Galatians to add various law observances to faith, they had ceased to love one another.

The opposite of love is that men destroy one another. Christ revealed the truth that men are created to love and to serve one another.

Paul does not teach sinlessness, Bring concludes, for although sin is a power overcome in Christ, as long as man lives on earth he continues to feel the power of sin. Man is, however, not wholly passive in this struggle. He can turn away from the flesh and toward that which belongs to the life of faith.

Christians are not to judge one another, but to share one another's burdens. To live by sharing is to live in accord with the love of Christ. At the same time one is to see one's own faults and thus to be spared from the self-righteousness that comes from comparing oneself to others. This carrying of one's own burdens will in turn make one more willing to carry those of others.

THE NATURE OF FAITH

Author: Gerhard Ebeling (1912-   )
Type of work: Systematic theology
First published: 1959

PRINCIPAL IDEAS ADVANCED

The Christian Church can no longer proclaim its faith by means of the traditional language of Bible and creed, nor can it rely on contemporary language.

Christian faith is not religious allegiance to creeds and doctrines or intellectual assent to the conclusions of historical research, but a mode of existence through the witness of faith in the words and actions of Jesus.

Christian faith is a summons and a gift that comes to man out of history and places the individual in a new relationship to the world (the sphere of faith), endowing the present with the power of reconciling love, and filling the future with hope.

Das Wesen des christlichen Glaubens, by the Protestant theologian Gerhard Ebeling, contains a course of lectures given in the winter of 1958-59 at the University of Zürich for students of all faculties. It was not the author's intention "to present complete dogmatics, but to give an introduction to the understanding of Christian faith." Thus the work is clear in its structure, avoids technical language as much as possible, and does not

involve discussion with alternate points of view through extended footnotes.

Gerhard Ebeling began his academic career at Tübingen as a Church historian. In 1942 he published a study of Luther's hermeneutics, a study entitled *Evangelische Evangelienauslegung: Eine Untersuchung zu Luthers Hermeneutik.* His studies in the problem of hermeneutics (which is the problem of the character of historical knowledge and, in particular, the problem of understanding historical documents delivered by tradition) led him into the field of systematic theology. In 1956 Ebeling joined the faculty of Zürich as professor of dogmatics. In 1959 *Das Wesen des christlichen Glaubens* was published, and in 1960 a volume of collected essays appeared under the title *Wort und Glaube*. Since 1950 he has been the editor of one of the leading German theological periodicals, *Zeitschrift für Theologie und Kirche*.

The free English translation of the title *Das Wesen des christlichen Glaubens* as *The Nature of Faith* is misleading. In this work Ebeling is not concerned with either a psychological analysis of religious experience (as was William James) or with a phenomenological and ontological analysis of the dynamics of faith (as Paul Tillich has been); Ebeling is concerned, rather, with the "essence" (*Wesen*) of Christian faith; that is, with the peculiar nature of Christian religious experience as an exercise of faith which involves one's total existence, and with the relevance of such a conception of faith to man's existence in the contemporary scene. With the Marburg theologian Rudolf Bultmann (*Theology of the New Testament*) and Karl Heim (*Jesus the Lord*), Ebeling shares an acute awareness of the irrelevance of formalized Christian faith to most churchmen. He writes as follows: "Christians have become accustomed to existence in two spheres, the sphere of the church and the sphere of the world. We have become accustomed to the co-existence of two languages, Christian language with the venerable patina of two thousand years, and the language of real life round about us. Certainly, it may happen that the

spark of understanding leaps across the gap. But there are no comprehensive rules for translating from the one language to the other. . . . It is not a matter of understanding single words, but of understanding the word itself, not a matter of new means of speech, but of a new coming to speech."

It is the problem of a "new coming to speech," of "understanding the word itself," that is, the word of "faith" that concerns Ebeling. He is fully aware, with Bultmann, that the cosmology of the first century and the language appropriate to it are foreign to twentieth century man and that the distinction of "kerygma" (the Gospel which the Church proclaims) and "myth" (the historically relative language and forms of expression employed in proclaiming the Gospel) must be made. But this distinction, the product of literary and historical criticism of the Biblical text, must not be translated into a distinction between "faith" and "history."

It is central to Ebeling's theological program that "faith comes to us out of history, and takes us into its history." Faith is "event," "movement," "happening." Faith comes to a man in his existential situation, informing and transforming it. Faith comes to him in and through the witness of others (the historical tradition) as they, like the figure of the evangelist in the Grünewald altar painting of the Crucifixion, point to *the* witness and ground of faith, Jesus Christ.

Given this initial definition of the essence of Christian faith, Ebeling proceeds to examine the traditional themes of theological discourse: Jesus Christ, God, the Word of God, the Holy Spirit, man, justification, love, the Church, the world, temptation, and hope; and he seeks to rediscover and to disclose the significance of these theological themes in delineating the nature of faith.

Prior to pursuing the major theological themes Ebeling treats briefly the historical sources of faith: "tradition," which he calls "the history of faith," and "Scripture," "the record of faith." Faith is not an idea or a mode of existence that an individual can create for himself. Faith is received, constantly received. Faith "comes into being as the consequence of the witness of faith. And it depends for its nourishment on the constantly renewed witness, the Word of faith. That is to say, faith comes into being, and continues in being, when it is handed on, in tradition." By "tradition" Ebeling is not referring to the deposit of creeds and doctrines found in theological libraries. "Tradition," understood as "the history of faith," refers to the preaching of the Church through the ages. It was this ancient and continuous witness to the Word of faith that Martin Luther received and to which he appealed in his attacks upon a static and foreign conception of Christian faith in the sixteenth century. Tradition therefore is the ongoing, changing, and cumulative witness of the Church throughout the ages. It is the history of faith and thus reflects the changes that the proclamation has undergone as the Church witnesses in diverse places and eras. What, then, is the constant, the norm for judging the history of faith? Like Luther, Ebeling refers to Scripture, "the record of faith," for it is Scripture that "bears witness, in its witness to Christ, primarily to that on which faith lives, namely the creative power which summons faith out of unbelief. . . ." The Bible is not

a document of law, but a document of preaching; it does not provide answers to the questions how or what one is to believe or what once was believed. The Bible is a document of preaching, and as such it suffers all the limitations and inadequacies of human creation. But the decisive thing about the Bible is its witness to Christ, to that which Christian faith must cling to, and its peculiar, original relation to the historical person and event Jesus Christ.

It is at this point that Ebeling's departure from Rudolf Bultmann, and especially from Fritz Buri, is most evident. In Chapter 4, "The Witness of Faith," Ebeling asserts that to speak of Christian faith is to speak of faith in Jesus Christ, and this is to have to do with a historical figure. Ebeling accepts fully the task of historical criticism, but he rejects the use of it that seeks to make Jesus the awkward object of faith by establishing certain "facts" concerning Jesus as objects of faith; as, for example, the fundamentalist beliefs in the Virgin Birth and the miracles. Ebeling also rejects the claims of those who assert that few, if any, historical facts are ascertainable and that the Biblical kerygma is concerned not with a historical Jesus, but primarily with a self-understanding that requires a personal decision. Ebeling has persisted in his support of what James M. Robinson has called "a new quest of the historical Jesus." There is, Ebeling believes, "a historically reliable general impression of Jesus," an impression which is preserved in the Synoptic Gospels. There is the essential structure of the narrative of events concerning Jesus' ministry and death. More importantly, there is the message of Jesus, which "cannot be separated from his Person." It is clear that Ebeling shares with Gunther Bornkamm (author of *Jesus von Nazareth,* 1956) and Ernst Fuchs (author of *Zur Frage nach dem historischen Jesus,* 1960) the conviction that the secret of Jesus' being is enclosed in His words and that being and speaking cannot be completely separated. Thus the historical Jesus may be approached most significantly through the message of Jesus. The historical Jesus to which Ebeling is referring is, therefore, not a figure whose deeds and words become objects of faith. On the contrary, what is known of the deeds and words of Jesus refer beyond themselves. Jesus is "the witness of faith." His message, proclaimed in deed and word, is "the nearness of the rule of God, the clarity of his will, and the simplicity of discipleship, with joy, freedom, and lack of anxiety." In this proclamation Jesus is the witness of faith. He is faith, which calls to faith and shares faith with him who hears. As He is heard and known, He becomes the historical ground or "the basis of faith." This, in fact, is the Easter witness of the early Church; it is knowing Jesus as the basis of faith, as the author and originating power of faith, as the one who discloses God's will for men. The Resurrection is not an object or article of faith among others to be believed. "Rather," according to Ebeling, "faith in the Resurrected One simply expresses faith in Jesus."

James M. Robinson notes that in his formulation of the relationship of the Jesus of history and the Christ of faith Ebeling has returned to Wilhelm Herrmann's "distinction between the historical Jesus as the ground of faith (upon which it falls back in moments of trial) and Christology . . . as the content of faith (in terms of which faith expresses itself)." However, while it is true that Ebeling is indebted to both Wilhelm Herrmann (author of *Der Verkehr des Christen mit Gott,* 1886) and Adolf von Harnack (author of *Das Wesen des Christentums,* 1900), it is important to observe that Ebeling does not separate the words of Jesus from the mystery of His being and thereby efface the character of Jesus as Christ either by a psychological concern with Jesus' "inner life" or by making Jesus primarily a teacher. The point of shared conviction of Ebeling and the nineteenth century theologians is that Christ is correctly preached not where something is said about Him, but only where He Himself becomes the proclaimer.

What is known in and through Jesus Christ, the witness and basis of faith, is "the truth of faith"; namely, God. What the word "God" means apart from Jesus Christ can be expressed only as a question, "as a pointer to the radical questionableness which touches everyman." This questionableness is portrayed most fully in the Crucifixion, for it would appear that for man death is his sole destiny. It would appear that man is without a future and, hence, without an answer to the problem of guilt, which is the "sting of death" (I Corinthians 15:55). But the Biblical question: "Adam, where art thou?" (Genesis 3:9), which raises the question of man's nature and destiny, receives its answer in Jesus Christ. In the witness of faith one encounters God as the provider of man's future and the redeemer of his present. It is Jesus Christ who is "the communication of faith," the Word of God to man. In His life, death, message, and the Church's experience of His resurrection Jesus Christ makes clear what is essential about human existence: that man is created for community with God and with other men.

It is the act of making man's nature and destiny clear that is expressed in the term "God's Word." The communication of faith does not refer to knowledge about faith. It refers to knowing as "an event in the event of speech." Communication takes place where the content of the word and the fulfilling of the word, its reaching its goal, are identical. Faith, the experience of grace and love, the firm hope of a future free from what Kierkegaard called "a sickness unto death," is the fulfilling of the Word of God, the receiving of God's promises in and through the words and actions of Jesus Christ. When men respond in faith to the words of one who witnesses to the truth of faith, there is the Word of God. God himself is communicated. Such is the humanity of God.

As God is the truth of faith (Father) who addresses man in and with His Word (Son), so it is the same God who awakens the heart of man and upholds him with "the courage of faith" (Holy Spirit). The happening, the realizing, the knowledge of God's presence in His Word, the courage to hear and respond to God's Word is the work of God as Holy Spirit. While the primacy of the Christological theme is preserved by Ebeling, the doctrine of the Holy Spirit is not given an auxiliary role as in Reformation thought. In the tradition of Friedrich Schleiermacher and Wilhelm Herrmann, and later of Karl Heim (author of *Jesus der Herr*, 1935), Ebeling's thought has a polar character. It

is at once both theocentric and Christocentric. For Schleiermacher and Herrmann, God is the culmination of religious experience and Christ is the means to the culmination. So too for Heim and Ebeling. But whereas the nineteenth century theologians could speak in a rather positive way of man's "God-consciousness" or "pious self-awareness," which is enlivened or informed and brought to completion in Christ, and which reflects the "primary relationship" between the Spirit of God and the spirit of man, Heim and Ebeling speak of the presence of God to man as the awakener of man's conscience to an awareness of man's *Gottesferne* ("distance or estrangement from God"). Man does not possess a prior knowledge of God which is then "completed" by the revelation in Christ. Man is estranged from God. But in the midst of and in spite of his estrangement God stands present to man as the One who encourages faith and bestows the courage of faith.

To speak of faith is not only to speak of God, but also to speak of man, the believing subject, "the I of faith." For as the true knowledge of God is of God who is for us and with us, so the true knowledge of man is of man in his relation to God. Ebeling affirms the priority of God's grace, for faith has the character of being a gift. It is the gift of freedom. In his *Gottesferne* man is caught up in the concern about himself—his guilt and death. His whole life is thus spent in clinging to himself in resolute despair or concealed self-loathing. The gift of grace is freedom from the bondage of such concern. It is not something added to man's being, but a transformation of his mode of existence; from existence projected to death (slavery) to existence projected to life (history or purposeful existence). Faith, as God's gift, discloses a new view of reality in which the future is opened and is seen as belonging to God. The knowledge of the future as salvation, as belonging to God, is the knowledge of justification, which is "the reality of faith."

To speak of the reality of faith is to speak of its power. Apart from God, man's situation is one of powerlessness. He is limited and determined physically and intellectually. He is powerless over the past which contains his guilt and helpless in his guilt before the relations and decisions facing him in the future. The gift of a transformed existence, of the reality of faith, is the gift of "the power of faith."

So concerned is Ebeling to preserve the antecedent reality of God throughout his theological exposition of Christian faith that rather than speak of the Church in such traditional terms as people, community, fellowship, or congregation, he employs the phrase "the summons of faith." For Ebeling the Church is not understood in terms of its place, structure, or the extent of its representation of peoples. These are secular bases of definition. What constitutes the reality of the Church is the summons of God. The Church exists solely in virtue of God's call to men to be his people in faith through Jesus Christ. The life of the Church therefore is service in the summons of faith; service to God in worship and to man in witness.

The "sphere of faith," writes Ebeling, is the world. Christian faith is not life removed from the world in ascetic withdrawal, mystic flight, or speculative thought in quest of the perfection of being. Faith is lived in the immediate temporal order with all its ambiguities and disteleological features. The language of "beyond" so often employed regarding the sphere of faith is appropriate only in so far as it witnesses to the fact that faith and the community of faith do not have their origin, their power of being, from the world. Nonetheless the Church is summoned to be in the world and for the world and to affirm it in word and action as the creation of God. But since the world is fallen creation, living in the world is living perilously in the confrontation of temptation with only "the steadfastness of faith."

According to Ebeling, eschatology is not an appendix to faith. Faith and the future belong together. Faith means letting the future approach. It surrenders the future to God, acknowledging that He alone can and shall have the last word.

OUR EXPERIENCE OF GOD

Author: H. D. Lewis (1910-   )
Type of work: Christian epistemology
First published: 1959

Principal Ideas Advanced

Unless religion is supported by conviction as to the truth of certain religious statements, it cannot be taken seriously.

Intellectual arguments for the existence of God attempt to demonstrate by a series of logical steps what is basically a single insight.

God is the incomprehensible, unconditioned, and transcendent source of all reality.

Religious experience is the response, in the course of ordinary experience, to the presence of the transcendent "Other."

In moral action, finite experience is transmuted into the disclosure of the transcendent.

Professor H. D. Lewis of King's College in the University of London, who has held chairs in philosophy and in the history and philosophy of religion, concerns himself in *Our Experience of God* with answering the question, "How are particular religious assertions justified?" The author expresses his conviction that this question is urgent because of the spread of religious indifference and the fear that it is not possible to be religious without suffering a loss of intellectual integrity.

Lewis begins with a point which the pragmatic interest in religion has obscured; namely, that unless a religion is supported by a conviction as to the truth of certain central beliefs, it cannot be taken seriously as religion. The question, then, as to how religious beliefs are to be justified, becomes a crucial one. It is not enough for the religious devotee to believe that he possesses the truth in regard to religious matters; he would also like to know how he can defend his beliefs against criticism. If it be maintained that religion must be true in the sense that it must be faithful in answering the needs of the devotee, Lewis responds by insisting that religious beliefs must be true in the ordinary sense in which

statements are said to be "true," as distinguished from "false" or "meaningless": "A religion must stand the test of truth and falsity in the normal sense . . . there must be at the core of a religion something significant to which the distinction of true and false in the normal or literal sense applies. . . ."

Lewis insists that true belief is essential in religion not only because a religion without belief would be, at the most, an emotively motivated moral effort, but also because religious beliefs are "of the most momentous nature, and if sound and acceptable . . . could hardly fail to make an overwhelming difference to our outlook." The belief in the survival of bodily death, for example, has implications concerning the present behavior of man.

Lewis refers to recent empiricist and linguistic trends in philosophy. He agrees that a great deal of religious language has been so used that what the religious believer tries to say is either meaningless or confusing. But Lewis cannot accept the generalized conclusion that all religious discourse is meaningless or emotive, and he resists with religious fervor the claim made by Professor R. B. Braithwaite, who has argued that "religion is no more than a moral policy and that whatever there seems to be over and above this are mere stories."

The author agrees with the linguistic philosophers insofar as they maintain that a critical examination of language is almost always helpful in the process of clarifying ideas. He thinks that religious apologists are mistaken who attempt to defend religious claims by arguing exclusively for their "peculiarity" or by calling attention to the open texture of language and to the various types of discourse. Lewis's own predilection is to attempt to make a positive defense in support of certain notions the empiricist objects to: for example, the idea of an abiding self, or the belief in moral principles which are independent of human sentiments. The problem of clarifying religious discourse and of supplying evidence in support of religious claims is a difficult one, Lewis asserts, because religion, by its very nature, is concerned with matters that are beyond the scope of ordinary intelligence. The problem of justifying religious claims is best handled, Lewis concludes in his initial statement, not by giving way to unreason, but by making reasonable the claim that our examination of nature leads us to believe that "the world cannot be an ultimately random one" and that there is something incomprehensible, a positive mystery, which must somehow be posited as "accounting for" the world of our experience.

Lewis's criticism of the intellectual arguments for the existence of God is that the arguments attempt to demonstrate by a series of logical steps what is basically a single insight. A study of the traditional arguments has value, however, in calling attention to the basic conviction that some single unconditioned Being is somehow the source of the conditioned and incomplete reality which men encounter in ordinary experience.

The problem which positing God as the incomprehensible and unconditioned source of reality presents is that if religion rests on mystery, it would seem inevitable that religion be without content. The problem is not to be solved, writes Lewis, simply by talking in the existentialist manner about "encountering" God, as if it were possible to encounter a being about whom one had no knowledge. The only hopeful line of development involves making sense out of the claim that religion concerns both what is beyond man and what is altogether within. Although there is a sense in which one cannot know God by an appeal to evidence, there is, nevertheless, an experience of God which provides abundant evidence "of what God is like and what He does."

Lewis makes it clear that he does not intend to prove the existence of God by an appeal to religious experience; nor does Lewis argue that religious experience consists in a literal union of God and man; finally, he denies that reflection on what has been called "the human situation" is sufficient to the kind of knowledge he seeks.

The word "religion" is notoriously ambiguous, Lewis points out; he suggests that the term be reserved to mean an activity or attitude which involves some awareness of a transcendent being, and by a "transcendent" being, Lewis means a being "beyond" or "other than" man in that He is perfect and absolutely complete. A consideration of primitive religions shows, Lewis claims, that the religious experience of those who have lived close to nature bears striking affinities to the religious experience of modern and civilized man; in fact, a consideration of primitive experience may very well serve to emphasize and bring out the experience of the "beyond" in one who, because of the cultural complexity of his life, has forgotten or tended to ignore his own religious experience.

Idolatry begins, Lewis explains in a particularly striking passage, when men are overwhelmed by the consciousness of the transcendent and, sensing the demands that God makes upon them and the inescapable power of His reality, attempt "to resist God, to be in conflict with Him or try to escape Him, *just because He is God*. But they will not do this in the first instance by merely forgetting or disregarding God. For they are also drawn to Him and need Him. They will thus try to limit or restrict their own consciousness of God by containing it within the media and symbols which are needed for its articulation. This seems to me the essence and beginning of idolatry."

(In a note on Ronald Hepburn's *Christianity and Paradox* (1958), Lewis rejects Hepburn's suggestion that religion can provide the myths for a life pilgrimage, and Lewis also objects to Hepburn's claim that the experience of the numinous is not necessarily a religious experience.)

As Lewis continues his examination of religious experience, it becomes more and more certain that he means to limit religious experience to the sense of the presence of the God. The religious experience is not simply an awareness of power and mystery in nature; such a feeling might very well be a function of human ignorance and frailty; the religious experience is, rather, an undeniable sense of wonder which accompanies the conviction that an absolute and unconditioned being is the source of all reality. Although the religious experience is a response to the transcendent and mysterious "Other," it is an experience which is vitally related to other experiences in life.

Religious imagery may play a significant role in religious experience, but unlike the basic sense of the presence of the transcendent—an experience mediated by what Lewis calls "first-order symbols"—the experience which depends on imagery is not a direct experience of the divine. Nor is the historian able to report on the influence of religious ideas if he is not finally grounded in the religious experience itself.

Dogma has a place in the religious life, says Lewis, only to the extent that it makes possible "the constant renewal of personal experience of God and the sense of His presence." Ritual acts and the material objects which figure in them form another class of religious symbols, other than first-order symbols, by which the religious experience can be provoked and enriched. It is possible, Lewis suggests, that certain physical disciplines, or the use of certain drugs, may initiate physical conditions which make first-hand religious experience possible, but he reminds the reader that not all kinds of physical excitation, for example, sexual stimulation, are conducive to religious experience. There is always the danger that an absorption in physical practices or the uses of the instruments of worship may lead to the degenerate practice of magic and an idolatry which is incompatible with true religion. Symbolism and tradition may become sentimentalized, and the strenuous moral demands of Christianity may be forgotten; when joy is expressed because of Christ's triumph over the Cross, it is possible that the symbol of the Cross loses its element of horror and thus fails to remind the Christian of the strenuous kind of struggle which Christianity demands.

Preternatural experiences, particularly abnormal experiences such as those the mystics report, or those which accompany the exercise of such powers as levitation, precognition, and clairvoyance, are not necessarily religiously significant, Lewis warns. Going beyond ordinary experience is not enough; to be religious, an experience must provide a sense of the presence of the absolute and unconditioned Being who lies at the center of all reality.

Lewis devotes two chapters to a consideration of the problems which arise in connection with petitionary prayers. He argues that a belief in the efficacy of petitionary prayers is compatible with the belief in the presence of a concerned God. But the independence of the divine will must be insured, and it may be that the most illuminating answer to any petitionary prayer is an enlivened sense of the presence of God.

According to Lewis, morality supplies "the sphere *par excellence* where finite experience is transmuted into the disclosures and operations of the transcendent within the world we know." It is on the moral or ethical level that the personal character of the relation of man to God is completed. In his freedom and dignity man prepares himself, in his moral moments, for the most significant of his encounters with God.

Lewis concludes his work by emphasizing once again the point that God is a transcendent being and that a finite being cannot hope to resolve the mystery of the divine being by enjoying any momentary contact or unity with God. It is through responsible and devoted response to the challenges which arise in the ordinary course of social and cultural experience that man comes to experience God and to acquire the inspiration which strengthens him in his religious life. The vision of Jesus is possible, Lewis insists, "if we diligently seek it where God ordained that it should be found, in the live and continuing witness to what Jesus was and did."

CATEGORY INDEX

Allegory: 259, 530
Aphorisms: 663
Apologetics: 9, 19, 26, 29, 32, 39, 48, 51, 66, 71, 79, 145, 232, 367, 418, 432, 526,
    534, 573, 637, 641, 743, 766, 816, 832, 844, 890, 969, 1104, 1156
Autobiography: 128, 392, 506, 546, 581, 594, 612, 654, 743

Biblical commentary: 3, 61, 672, 679, 832, 847, 894, 1097

Casuistry: 445
Christian Science, principles of: 775
Christology: 83, 156, 162, 861, 1072, 1080, 1093
Church history: 87, 153, 181, 388, 409, 557, 823
Church practice: 1, 23, 54, 64, 117, 458, 728
Church theory and doctrine (See *Ecclesiology*)
Counseling, pastoral: 7, 17, 176, 485, 501, 844

Deistic theology (See *Theology, deistic*)
Devotional guide: 280, 291, 316, 441, 473, 481, 543, 566, 938, 1064, 1152
Diaries (See *Journals*)
Direction, spiritual (See *Instruction, spiritual*)
Doctrine, Christian: 153, 159, 381, 692, 950
Dogmatics (See *Theology, dogmatic*)

Ecclesiology: 73, 304, 367, 396, 414
Education, philosophy of Christian: 489, 736
Epistemology, Christian: 684, 1189
Epistles (See *Letters*)
Eschatology: 224
Ethics, Christian: 23, 121, 212, 321, 422, 445, 497, 590, 786, 790, 819, 873, 886,
    921, 942, 946, 954, 960, 977, 981, 986, 1028, 1068, 1101, 1108, 1117, 1121,
    1175
Evolution theory, Christian: 793, 805
Existential theology (See *Theology, existential*)

Hagiography: 95, 137, 264, 392
Heresiology: 111
History, Church (See *Church history*)
History, philosophy of (See *Philosophy of history*)
History, theology of (See *Theology of history*)

AUTHOR INDEX

I

II

III

IV

V